SRA

Core Lesson Connections

Enhanced instruction and digital tools to help teachers meet Common Core State Standards!

COMMON CORE
CCSS
ALIGNMENT
STATE STANDARDS

McGraw Hill

Grade 1

Nancy E. Marchand-Martella, Ph.D.
Ronald C. Martella, Ph.D.
Angela M. Przychodzin, M.Ed.
Susan Hornor, M.Ed.
Lisa Warner, M.Ed.

McGraw Hill **Education**

Bothell, WA • Chicago, IL • Columbus, OH • New York, NY

MHEonline.com

McGraw Hill Education

Send all inquiries to:
McGraw-Hill Education
8787 Orion Place
Columbus, OH 43240

ISBN: 978-0-02-128248-7
MHID: 0-02-128248-X

Printed in the United States of America.

1 2 3 4 5 6 7 8 9 RMN 17 16 15 14 13 12

Table of Contents

Table of Contents (cont.)

SRA
Reading Mastery
Signature Edition

Your Master Plan for
Core Comprehensive Reading

The comprehensive program that helps at-risk students succeed

- Validated by extensive and exhaustive research
- Proven to work in a wide range of classrooms, schools, and districts
- Systematic, explicit instruction for heightened academic achievement

SRA

A Core Comprehension Solution

Welcome to **Reading Mastery Signature Edition**! It's a comprehensive solution that is flexible enough to serve as your intervention program, in addition to your core program, or combine all strands to work together as a complete program. **Reading Mastery Signature Edition** is research-based and field-tested, and it meets rigorous Common Core State Standards.

How Reading, Language Arts, and Literature work together

Three strands address Reading, Oral Language/Language Arts, and Literature

- Activities within each strand reflect clearly stated goals and objectives

- Skills and processes are clearly linked within, as well as across, each strand

- Each strand can be targeted for use as an intervention program, in addition to the core program, or combined for use as a comprehensive stand-alone reading program

Reading Strand

- Addresses all five essential components of reading as identified by Reading First: phonemic awareness, phonics and word analysis, fluency, vocabulary, and comprehension

- Provides spelling instruction to enable students to make the connection between decoding and spelling patterns

- Develops student decoding and word recognition skills that transfer to other subject areas

Oral Language/Language Arts Strand

- Teaches the oral language skills necessary to understand what is spoken, written, and read in the classroom

- Helps students to communicate ideas and information effectively

- Develops the ability to use writing strategies and writing processes successfully

Literature Strand

- Supports the reading strand with a wide variety of literary forms and text structures

- Provides multiple opportunities for students to work with useful and important words

- Gives ample opportunity for each student to read at his or her independent level

SRA

What makes *Reading Mastery Signature Edition* unique is how:

- Information is presented
- Assignments are structured
- Understanding is tested

Strategy-based instruction allows students to learn new information in a more efficient way:

- Complex tasks are analyzed and broken into component parts
- Each part is taught in a logical progression
- The amount of new information is controlled and connected to prior learning
- Ample practice opportunities ensure mastery

Intensive, explicit, systematic instruction helps students use skills and processes with a high rate of success, because:

- Whatever is presented is **taught**, clearly and directly
- Whatever is taught is actively **practiced**, multiple times
- Whatever is practiced is **linked and applied** to new learning

Fully aligned materials help you guide students through the learning cycle and promote independent learning through:

- Highly detailed lessons
- Consistent teacher-friendly instructional routines
- Frequent teacher-student interactions
- Deliberate and carefully scaffolded teaching
- Specific correction techniques
- Cumulative review and application of skills

Continuous informal tests and curriculum-based assessments help:

- Monitor and report student, class, and district progress.
- Determine areas that need attention
- Guide placement and movement through the program

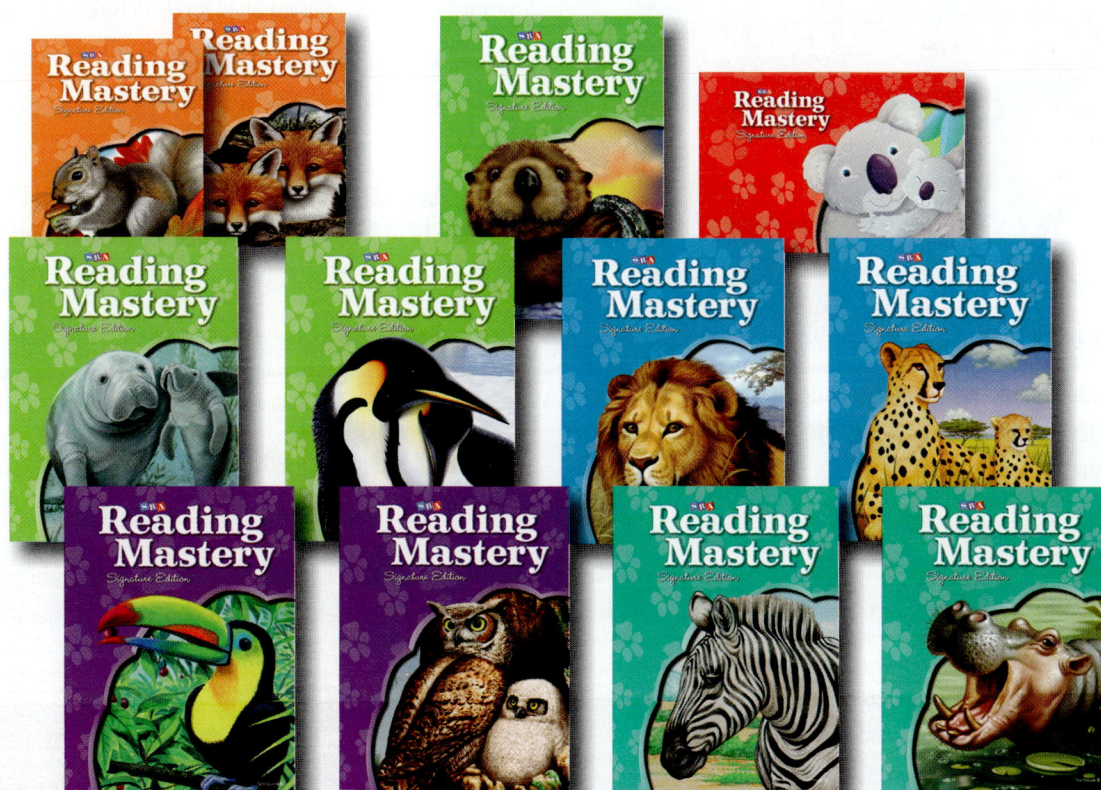

Reading Strand

Give students the keys to success

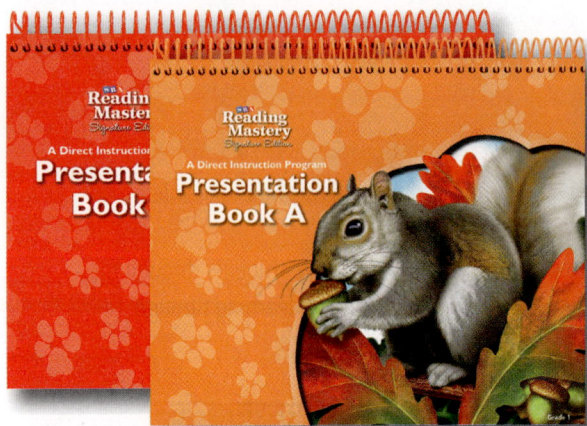

Grades K and 1

Designed to teach students skills needed to become **accurate and fluent readers**:

- Decoding is taught explicitly and systematically
- There are numerous opportunities for building fluency, allowing students to focus on the meaning of the text
- Comprehension instruction begins early to teach students how to infer, predict, and conclude

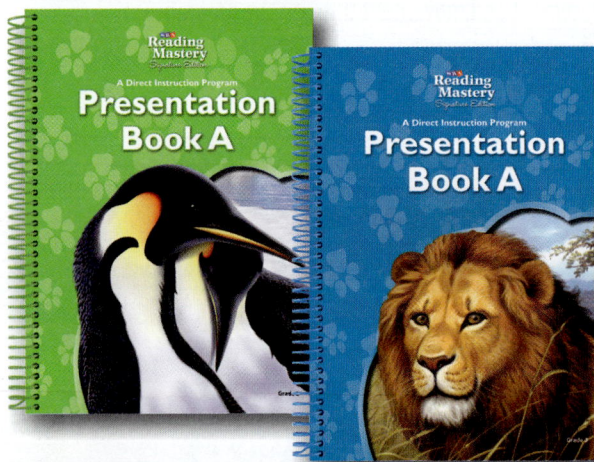

Grades 2 and 3

Continue to emphasize accurate and fluent decoding. The primary focus of these levels is to teach students how to **"read to learn."** Students are taught:

- The skills necessary to read, comprehend, and learn from informational text
- Background information needed for content area reading through information passages
- The background information that becomes the basis from which students make inferences as they read

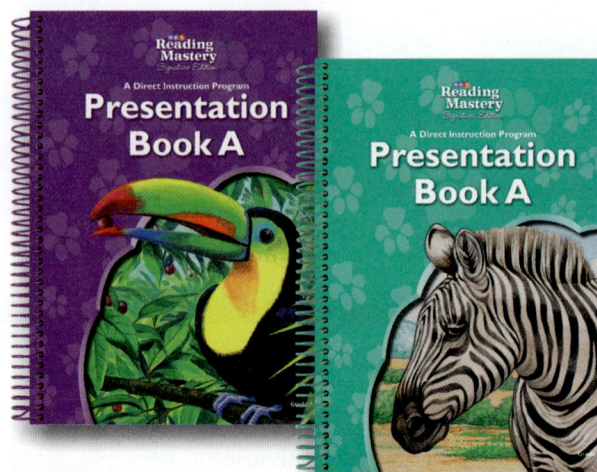

Grades 4 and 5

The focus is **literature**:

- Students are taught to analyze and interpret literature
- Students read classic and contemporary novels, short stories, poems, myths, folktales, biographies, and factual articles
- They learn new comprehension skills for interpreting all these different types of literature
- The reading selections are reinforced with literary analysis, reasoning strategies, and extended daily writing

Grades K–5

Spelling is explicitly taught at all levels to (Grades K–5):

- Engage beginning readers in activities at the phoneme and morphemic level
- Help older students identify known word parts
- Reduce confusion about words that are pronounced the same and provide a basis for using the appropriate word in context

A **Curriculum-Based Assessment and Fluency Handbook** combines with in-program mastery tests to provide a complete system for guiding student instruction. Use it to:

- Ensure students are properly placed in the program
- Measure student achievement within the program
- Identify skills students have mastered
- Present remedial exercises to students who are experiencing difficulty

Reading Mastery Signature Edition Core Components (Reading Strand)	K	1	2	3	4	5
Student Materials						
Storybook(s)	√	√				
Textbooks			√	√	√	√
Workbooks	√	√	√	√	√	√
Test Books	√	√	√	√	√	√
Teacher Materials						
Presentation Books	√	√	√	√	√	√
Teacher's Guide	√	√	√	√	√	√
Teacher's Takehome Book or Answer Key	√	√	√	√	√	√
Spelling Book	√	√	√	√	√	√
Curriculum-Based Assessment Handbook	√	√	√	√	√	√
Skills Profile Folder	√	√				
Audio CD	√					

Reading Mastery Signature Edition Tools to Differentiate Instruction (Reading Strand)	K	1	2	3	4	5
Library of Independent Readers	√	√				
Seatwork	√	√				
Activities Across the Curriculum			√	√	√	√
Practice and Review Activities	√	√	√	√	√	√

Language Arts Strand

Oral language skills are an essential part of learning to read. The early grades of **Reading Mastery Signature Edition** teach oral language skills necessary to understand what is spoken, written, and read in the classroom.

Starting at **Grade K**, students learn the important background information, vocabulary, and thinking skills they need to achieve high levels of comprehension. Students:

- Learn vocabulary words commonly used in school
- Engage in talking and answering questions
- Use different sentence forms and structures
- Acquire important information and concepts

As they progress into **Grade 1**, specific activities are added to integrate language arts with other important reading skills including:

- Continued vocabulary development
- Instruction that focuses on elements of story grammar
- Sentence construction
- Cooperative story writing

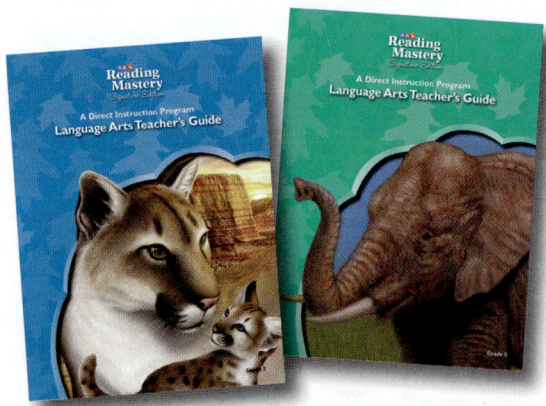

Grades 2–5 provide the structure and challenging materials that allow students to communicate effectively in writing and critique the writing of others. Students learn to:

- Write stories with a clear beginning, middle, and end
- Maintain focus on a single idea and develop supporting details
- Edit for standard conventions of grammar, usage, and mechanics
- Analyze persuasive text for misleading claims, faulty or inadequate arguments, and contradictory statements
- Develop skills related to real-world tasks—recall and summarize information presented orally, write directions, and take notes

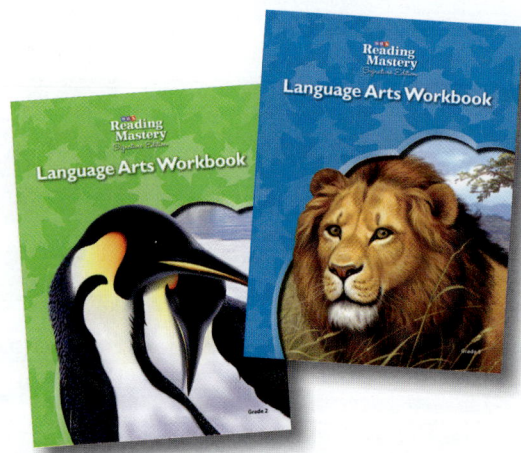

Core Components (Language Strand)	K	1	2	3	4	5
Student Materials						
Textbooks			√	√	√	√
Workbooks	√	√	√	√		
Teacher Materials						
Presentation Books	√	√	√	√	√	√
Teacher's Guide	√	√	√	√	√	√
Teacher's Take-Home Book or Answer Key	√	√	√	√	√	√
Skills Profile Folder	√					

SRA

Learning to read opens new doors for students

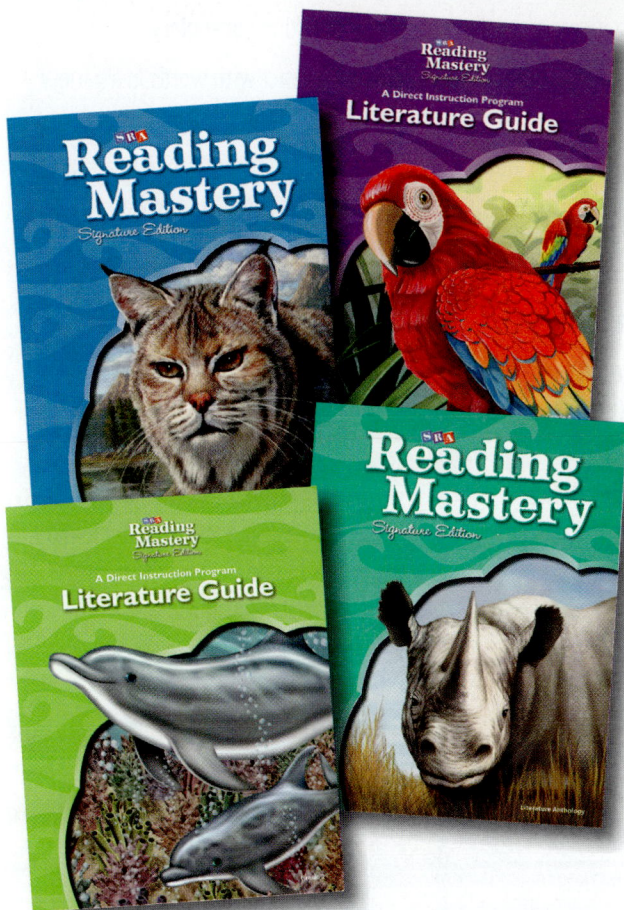

Literature Collection and Guide (Grades K and 1) expand on skills students are learning in **Reading Mastery Signature Edition**. The program:

- Develops their ability to listen attentively and demonstrate understanding
- Sharpens their understanding of story grammar and structure

Anthology and Guide (Grades 2–5) enrich students' experience with novels, poetry, and plays that complement the content and themes of the **Reading Mastery Signature Edition** Textbooks by featuring:

- Classics such as *The Bracelet; Thank You, Ma'am; The Velveteen Rabbit; Stone Soup;* and *The Story of Daedalus and Icarus*
- Insight into elements of story structure and literary strategies so students can discuss and write about the meanings of these selections

Literature Strand						
	K	**1**	**2**	**3**	**4**	**5**
Literature Guide	√	√	√	√	√	√
Collection	√	√				
Anthology			√	√	√	√

Literature

Robust vocabulary instruction tied closely to comprehension

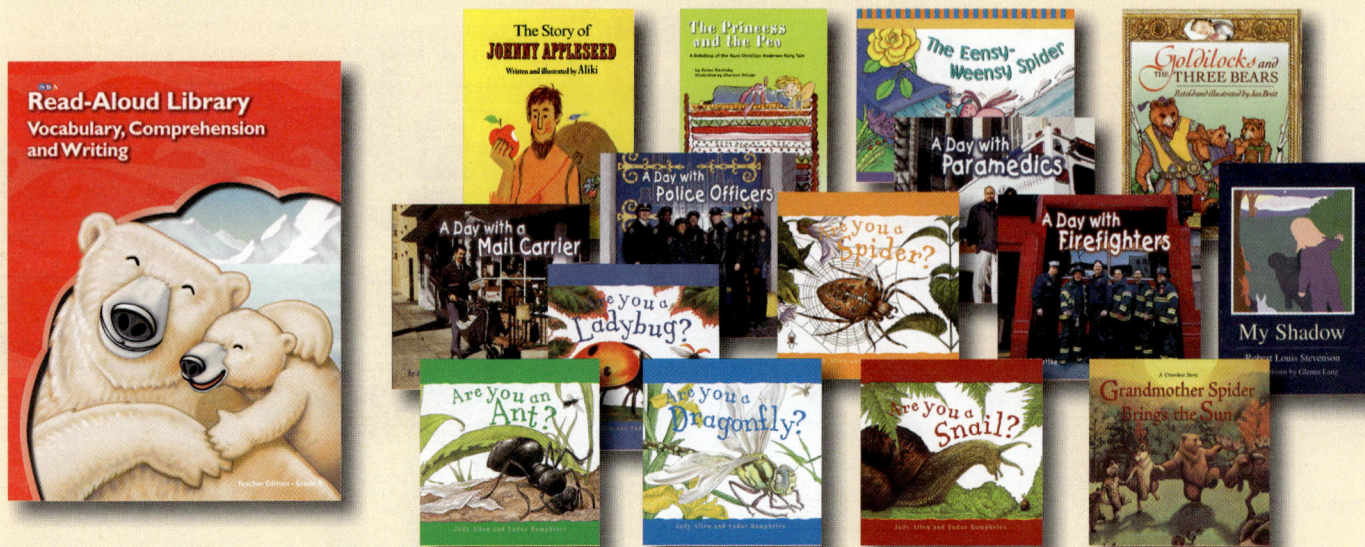

For **Grades K and 1**, daily reading with an emphasis on word meaning expands students' vocabulary into the world of mature speakers and provides:

• Lessons that offer direct teaching of Tier 2 words, enabling students to become more precise and descriptive with their language

• Numerous encounters with target words over time helps students to incorporate them into their speaking vocabulary

• Varied activities for students to interact with words in a variety of situations to deepen understanding

• Thirty high-quality books at each level including: folk tales, fairy tales, legends, poetry, as well as social studies and science expository works

From the introduction of new vocabulary to the informal assessment of understanding, the lesson plans expand oral language by encouraging conversation about the book.

Day 1: Students are introduced to the book and learn the key elements of a book such as title, author, and illustrator.

• They make predictions about what will happen in the story and share those predictions with their classmates.

• They formulate questions they may have about the story or the book.

• The story is read aloud to students with minimal interruptions.

• Target vocabulary words and their meanings are introduced within the context of how they are used in the story.

Day 2: The lesson begins with the story being read aloud by the teacher and discussed.

• Students become actively involved in responding to the story and constructing meaning.

• They are prompted to use target words throughout the discussion.

• Target vocabulary is reviewed.

Day 3: Students participate in varied activities using the new vocabulary words in and beyond the context of the story. Activities include:

• Retelling the story

• Playing word games

• Completing an activity sheet

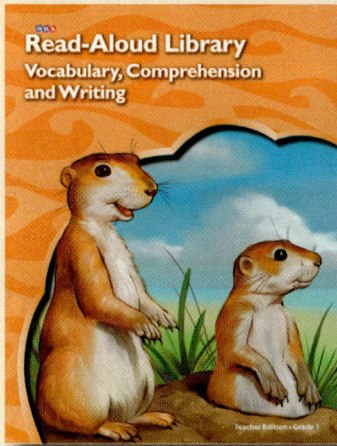

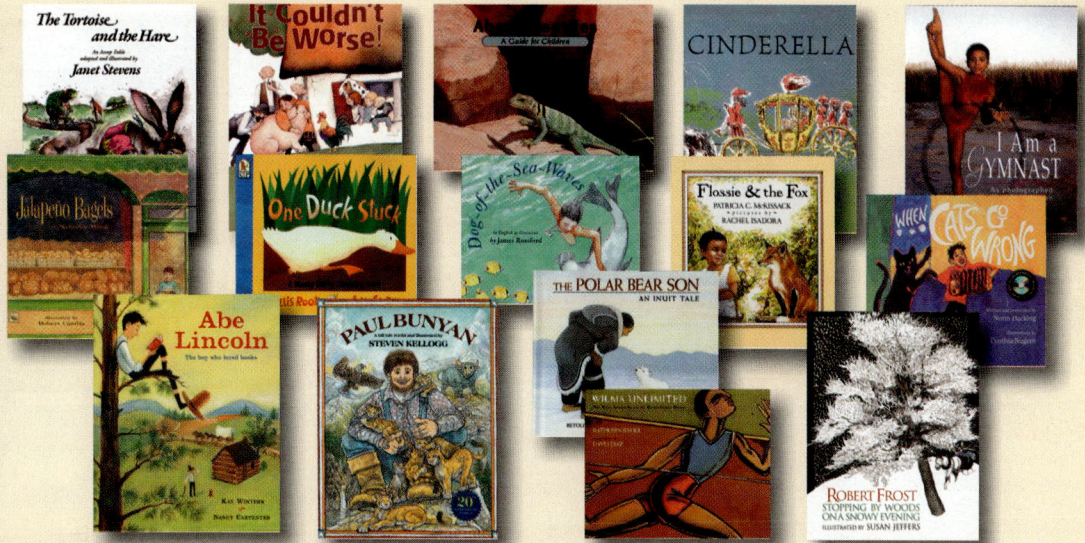

Day 4: Literary analysis and cumulative review are provided in the fourth day of instruction.

• Students play a verbal game that uses all of the new words in addition to words that have been taught in earlier lessons.

• Students also learn songs that help them recall the literary elements and patterns.

Day 5: On the last day students retell the story to a partner.

• An assessment is administered to measure students' mastery of the new vocabulary as well as review items.

• Students are allowed to choose a book they would like the teacher to read to them as a reward.

• Students are taught the routine for the learning center they will work in the following week. Students can practice new and previously learned vocabulary in the Super Words Center.

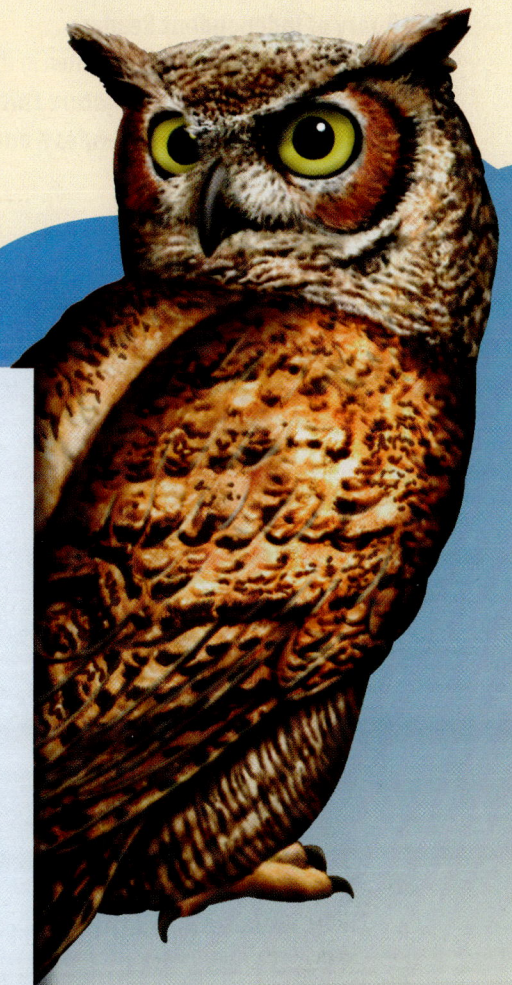

Reading Strand

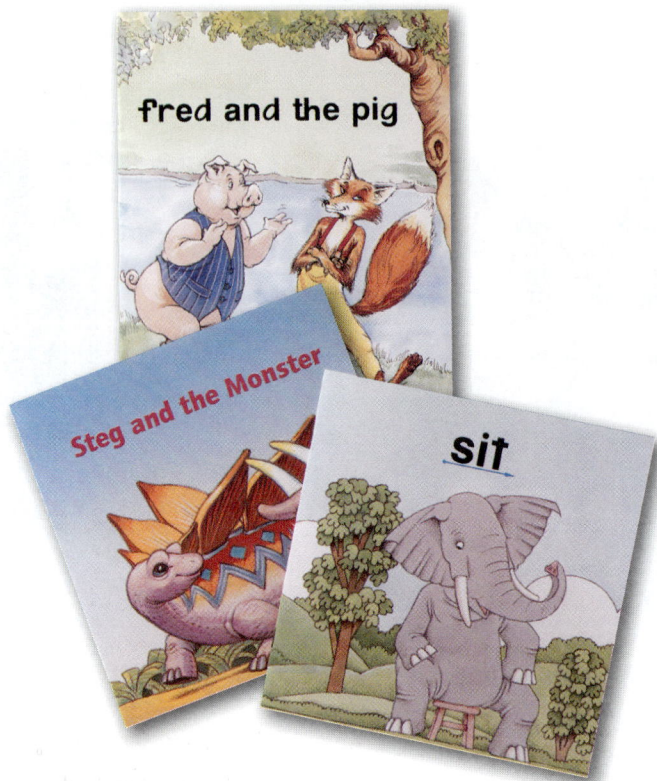

Library of Independent Readers
Entertaining, trade-style books written in the special *Reading Mastery Signature Edition* alphabet, one library each for **Grades K and 1**.

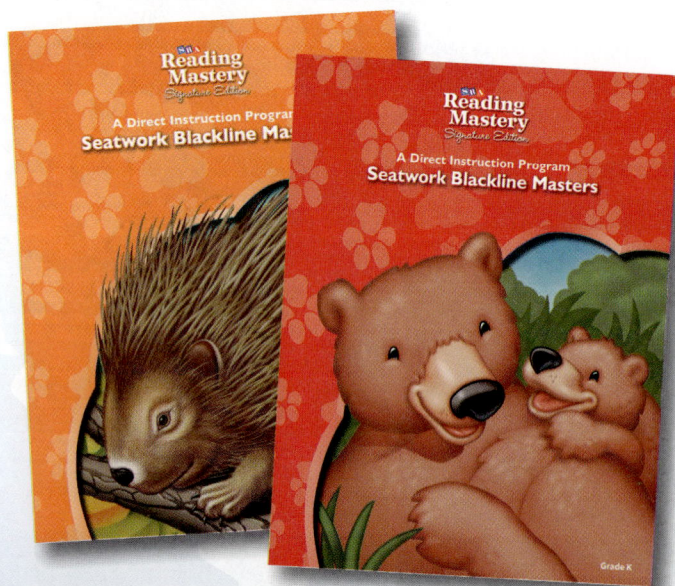

Activities Across the Curriculum
Encourage students in **Grades 2–5** to use reading, reference, and writing skills through activities that support science, social studies, math, and language arts.

Seatwork
Provide fun and rewarding reinforcement for students in **Grades K and 1**, that is closely correlated with lessons in *Reading Mastery Signature Edition*.

Practicing Standardized Test Formats help students understand test formats and learn test-taking skills by providing:

- Concepts to address important test content as well as instructional standards

- Short, daily activities familiarize students with questions and formats they will encounter on the most recent forms

- Help for students so they perform at their optimal levels and obtain scores that more accurately reflect the student's achievement

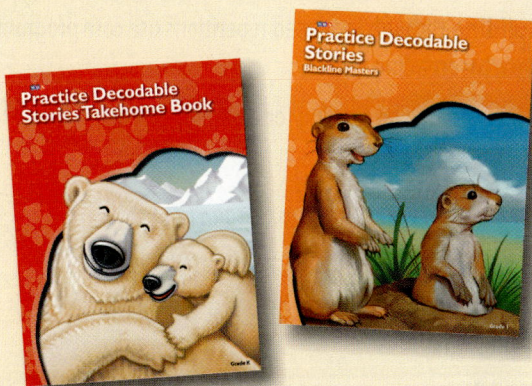

Research Assistant CD-ROM Packages
Grades 2–5

Presents a systematic process for the collection, processing, and presentation of information. Helps students:

- Generate ideas for a search

- Use appropriate resources to obtain information

- Present informational reports that include main ideas and relevant details with visual supports

Practice Decodable Takehome Books
Grades K and 1

Offers short, decodable stories for students to read independently:

- Provides additional opportunities for students to apply the skills and vocabulary they've learned

- Are available as Blackline Masters or 4-color pages to fold and staple into books each student can keep and read

- Can be taken home and shared with families

Interactive Student Review

Practice and Review Activities
Grades K–5

Practice Software offers engaging, interactive review to help students master key skills through:

- Brief, frequent practice activities and games

- Direct links to daily lessons

- Monitoring of student progress and performance

Proven lesson instruction

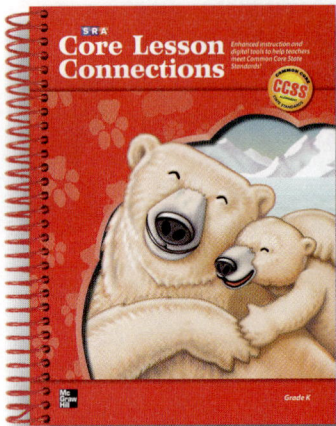

**Core Lesson Connections
Grades K–5**

Strategic, targeted instruction that supports and enhances the core reading program, including:

- Brief, 20-minute activities aligned to specific program lessons
- Explicit instruction with modeling, guided practice, and independent practice to develop word-learning and comprehension strategies
- An instructional model designed to be presented in conjunction with each program lesson

What you'll find:

**Phonological and phonemic awareness
Grades K and 1**

Develops through a wide variety of activities including:

- Word segmentation
- Rhyme recognition and production
- Syllable blending, segmentation, and deletion
- Onset-rime segmentation and blending
- Phoneme isolation (initial, medial, and final)
- Phoneme identification, segmentation, and blending

Vocabulary Instruction boosts the acquisition of word-learning strategies and contextual practice through:

- Daily instruction of specific words found in the core program
- Opportunities for students to develop, use, and apply word knowledge
- Word awareness through vocabulary journaling and practice activities
- Vocabulary notebook with word practice and study strategies

Comprehension Strategies are applied across lessons so students understand their usefulness while learning:

- Before-, during-, and after-reading strategies
- Bloom's Taxonomy level questions
- Narrative and expository text strategies
- Story grammar and story retell
- Graphic organizers
- Main idea and summarizing
- Comprehension monitoring
- Deep processing of text

Fluency Building through increased repetitions use core program stories and partner reading for:

- Emphasis on prosody and reading for meaning
- Effective partner reading
- Charting and decision making for maximum benefit

In addition, the following resources help you enhance learning for all students by providing:

- A **Scope and Sequence** chart to assist you in planning, conducting, and assessing instruction
- **Differentiated Instruction** with suggestions to boost the academic success for approaching mastery, at mastery, and ELL students
- **Professional Development** discusses how you can help students select appropriate material to read for personal pleasure and supplies tips/strategies to help students who struggle with reading fluency
- **Correlation** to the Common Core State Standards to help you keep students on target for meeting standards.

New tools help you promote student engagement and extend learning

Dynamic Digital Resources
Powered by **McGraw-Hill ConnectED**

Interactive Whiteboard Activities
Deliver key concepts and skills with academic vocabulary practice, graphic organizers, critical writing, and more

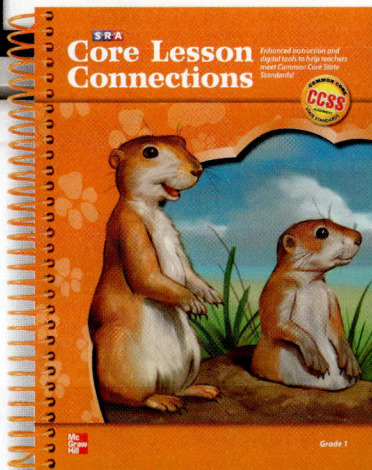

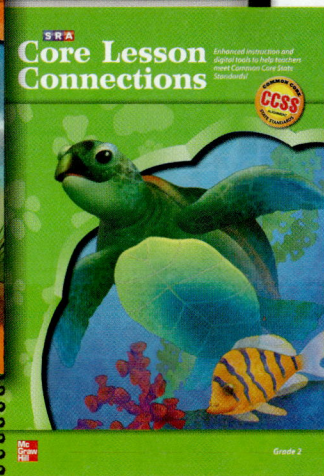

Online Progress Monitoring
Collect data, monitor performance, and administer reports to inform instruction

eInquiry
Helps students solve problems through writing, presenting, preparing reflection tasks, and completing assessments

Research Projects
Allow students to collaborate on common topics and systematically collect, process, and present information

Online Professional Development via the Teaching Tutor
Access on-demand routine formats for topics such as optimal pacing, classroom arrangement, daily lesson characteristics, error corrections, and achieving mastery

Professional Development Videos

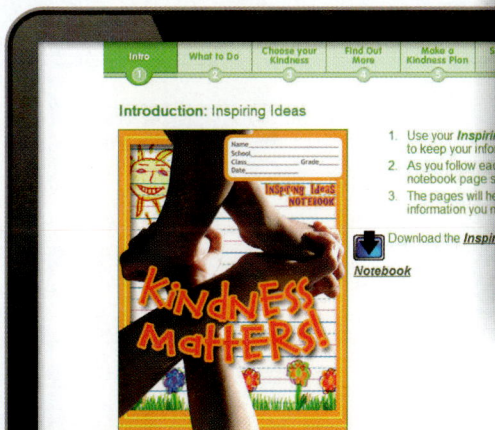

eInquiry

Online Progress Monitoring

SRA

SRA Reading Mastery

Signature Edition

Three strands
work together to form a
core comprehensive program

- Reading, Language Arts, and Literature integrated into a coherent instructional design
- Content focused on the five essential components of reading and aligned with Common Core State Standards
- Explicit instructional strategies for efficient, effective learning
- Student materials that support what you are teaching in daily lessons
- Frequent assessments that track student progress

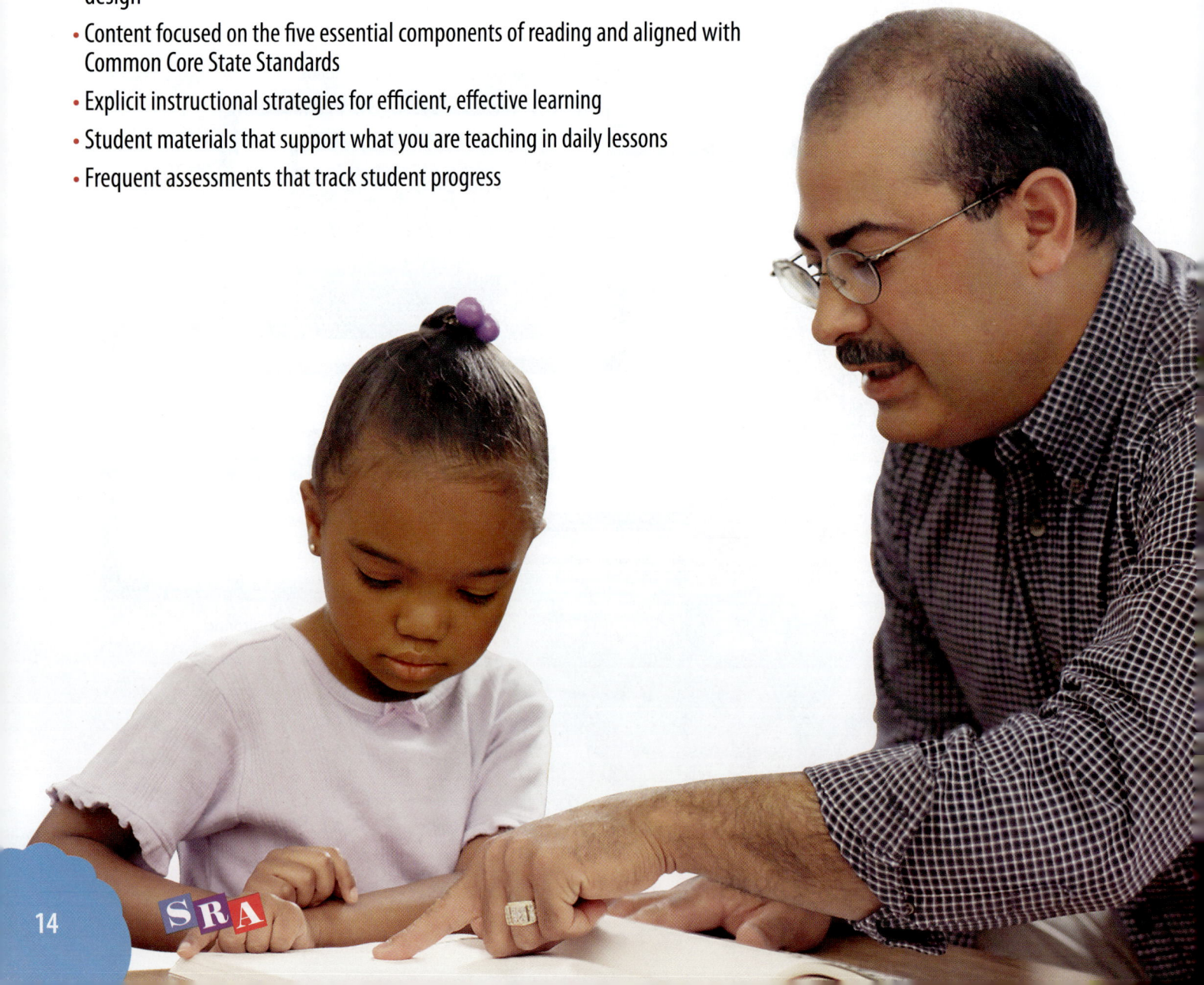

SRA

Introduction

What is SRA Core Lesson Connections?

SRA Core Lesson Connections provides targeted instruction that is related to the skills and information presented in the Reading Strand of the **Reading Mastery Signature Edition** program. Used in conjunction with **Reading Mastery Signature Edition,** *Core Lesson Connections* offers strategic support to master the Common Core State Standards for English Language Arts. Each lesson links with the core daily lesson. Explicit instruction through modeling, guided practice, and independent practice helps students meet the rigorous vocabulary, writing, and comprehension strands of the Common Core State Standards.

Core Lesson Connections uses the same teacher-script conventions that appear in **Reading Mastery Signature Edition.** These conventions include what the teacher says, what the teacher does, and what the correct students' responses should be. As with **Reading Mastery,** the teacher calls for group responses, uses clear signals, and employs specific correction procedures. Additionally, teachers deliver key concepts and skills with academic vocabulary practice, graphic organizers, critical writing, and more through interactive whiteboard activities.

How do you use Core Lesson Connections?

There are 160 lessons in Grade 1 *Core Lesson Connections,* aligned with Grade 1 of **Reading Mastery.** Each lesson requires approximately 20 minutes.

The **Reading Mastery Signature Edition** lesson should always take priority when scheduling instruction. The *Core Lesson Connections* activities are designed to enhance and extend the learning of the **Reading Mastery** lesson. Each lesson corresponds with the **Reading Mastery Signature Edition** lesson—for example, Lesson 11 of *Core Lesson Connections* corresponds with Lesson 11 of **Reading Mastery Signature Edition**— Reading Strand.

Some activities are important to conduct **before, during,** or **after** the **Reading Mastery Signature Edition** program lesson. These activities are specifically identified in the *Core Lesson Connections.* The following suggestions are noted:

- Provide a reading center to display books being read so that students can enjoy them again during free time.
- Choose narrative and informational texts that are appropriate for students in your class. You may want to refer to Appendix B of the Common Core State Standards for a list of exemplar texts for read-aloud selections for specific grade levels. Otherwise, you may choose from your own classroom or school library.

Core Lesson Connections lessons are divided into major parts or strands. For example, Comprehension Strategies is an important part of the *Core Lesson Connections* for Level 1 and appears as Part B (Lessons 1-80) or Part C (Lessons 81-160). Each part includes:

- Suggested instructional minutes (top left-hand column),
- Instructional materials for the teacher and student (left-hand column),
- What the teacher does (black type, right-hand column),
- What the teacher says (blue type, right-hand column), and
- What the students say/do (black italic type, right-hand column).

Here's an example from Lesson 111.

<table>
<tr><td colspan="2">

Part B: Comprehension Strategies

</td></tr>
<tr>
<td>

12 minutes

IWB

Teacher Materials:
Storybook 2

My Prediction Chart

Student Materials:
Storybook 2

</td>
<td>

Activity 1 Confirm Predictions—An After-Reading Strategy

Refer to Story 110, pages 75–77.

Guide discussion based on recorded predictions made in Lesson 110. **Elicit** responses to questions. **Guide** as needed.

In the last lesson, you made some predictions about what would happen in the Boo story. You made the predictions before you read the story.

Why do you make predictions? (Idea: *Making predictions helps you understand the story better.*)

Now that you've read the story, let's check to see if your predictions were in the story. That's called confirming predictions.

What are you doing when you check to see if your predictions are correct? *Confirming predictions.*

</td>
</tr>
</table>

Lessons correspond to and enhance instruction found in the **Reading Mastery Signature Edition** program. The lesson example shown above and found in Lesson 111 of the *Core Lesson Connections* aligns with the Boo the Ghost story located in Lesson 110 of the **Reading Mastery Signature Edition** Teacher Presentation Book for Level 1. *Core Lesson Connections* enhances rather than supplants the **Reading Mastery** program.

What Major Parts Compose Core Lesson Connections?

There are four major parts of *Core Lesson Connections* for Level 1. These include: **phonemic awareness, vocabulary instruction, comprehension strategies, and fluency building.** Explicit instruction for each of these major parts is based on best practices in reading research (see recommendations provided by Armbruster, Lehr, & Osborn, 2003; Carnine, Silbert, Kame'enui, & Tarver, 2010; National Institute of Child Health & Human Development [NICHD], 2000; Snow, Burns, & Griffin, 1998; and Vaughn & Linan-Thompson, 2004). Skills taught and examples for each part follow.

<table>
<tr><td>

Phonemic Awareness

</td></tr>
<tr><td>

Overview

</td></tr>
<tr><td>

- Daily phonemic awareness instruction
- Explicit instruction with modeling, guided practice, and independent practice
- Phonemic segmentation and blending focus

</td></tr>
<tr><td>

Skills Taught

</td></tr>
<tr><td>

- Phoneme blending
- Phoneme segmentation

</td></tr>
</table>

Vocabulary Instruction

Overview

- Daily instruction of specific words found in basic program
- Explicit instruction with modeling, guided practice, and independent practice
- Opportunities for students to develop, use, and apply word knowledge over time, within context, and in different contexts
- Word awareness through the use of word learning strategies, vocabulary journaling, and practice activities that are engaging, encourage deep processing, and connect word meaning to prior knowledge
- Vocabulary notebook with word practice and study strategies

Skills Taught

- Specific word meaning with contextual practice
- Vocabulary notebook use
- Acquisition and use of vocabulary including shades of meaning

Comprehension Strategies

Overview

- Daily focus on comprehension strategies applied across lessons so students understand their usefulness
- Explicit instruction with modeling, guided practice, and independent practice
- Stories/passages linked to basic program
- Reading for understanding and constructing meaning from text
- Inclusion of readers' theatre with dialogue linked to basic program
- Independent strategic learning, engagement, and deep processing of text

Skills Taught

- Reading with prosody
- Narrative and informational text strategies
- Before-, during-, and after-reading strategies
- Bloom's Taxonomy level questions
- Making connections
- Story grammar
- Predictions
- Story retell
- Graphic organizers
- Activating background knowledge
- Strategy generation
- KWL
- Summarizing
- Comprehension monitoring
- Connections through writing

Fluency Building
Overview
• Daily focus on oral reading fluency • Increased repetitions using basic program stories and partner reading • Emphasis on prosody and reading for meaning • Charting and decision making for maximum benefit
Skills Taught
• Reading with prosody • Reading with improved fluency • Effective partner reading

What Other Components Compose Core Lesson Connections?

Core Lesson Connections includes eight other important sections.

First, a **summary of skills** and **scope and sequence chart** are provided. These charts provide an overview of the skills taught in the program by major part. In a quick glance, teachers can see what skills are taught for each lesson of the program as well as the span of lessons that cover a specific skill.

Second, **graphic organizers** are used to carefully scaffold instruction for comprehension, writing, and phonemic awareness. These organizers also appear as interactive whiteboard activities online via McGraw-Hill's *ConnectED*. Teachers can write on, save, and print the organizers. Interactive whiteboard activities increase student engagement and improve understanding.

Third, **differentiated instruction** appears in *Core Lesson Connections* to help teachers enhance learning for **all** students. Instructional tips provide teachers and parents (called "home connection") with important suggestions to enhance academic success for approaching mastery, at mastery, and ELL students. Teacher and parent tips align with assessments found in the ***Reading Mastery*** program.

Here is an example from Appendix B.

Test	Tips for Teachers	Home Connections
Assessment (after Lesson 20	• See "Remedial Exercises and Retesting the Students" guidelines on pages 54 and 55 in *Curriculum-Based Assessment and Fluency Teacher Handbook.*	• Provide word flash cards for children to take home for additional practice. • Encourage children to share their take-home sheets with their families. • Encourage adult at home to conduct "see-say-write" activity for each difficult word.
Approaching Mastery	• Partner with "at mastery" student and review various activities. • Reteach difficult words using "good-bye" list.	
At Mastery	• Have student "be the teacher": Partner with "approaching mastery" or ELL student and review various activities.	
ELL	• See "Tips for Teachers" for "approaching mastery" and "at mastery" students. • Describe and model mouth formations for difficult sounds and words, then guide student while practicing with mirror.	• See "Home Connections" for "approaching mastery" and "at mastery" students. • Provide recording for use with word flash cards and sentence strips to take home for additional practice; encourage children to practice with a mirror at home, as needed.

Fourth, teachers can access tips to help ensure maximum access for students with intellectual disabilities. These suggestions are linked to the **Reading Mastery** content and provide guidance for three **levels of support** to allow all students the opportunity to access learning with the program materials.

Fifth, teachers can increase their knowledge about fluency building and reading level determination through a **professional development** section. This section provides the latest research on fluency and how to include fluency building through effective instructional activities. Strategies for students who struggle with fluency are also provided.

Sixth, explicit instructional activities for **fluency/paired reading** give teachers the necessary scaffolding to incorporate fluency into the daily lesson. These guidelines incorporate modeling, guided practice, and independent practice so that students read text quickly, accurately, and with expression.

Seventh, a **five-day lesson planning chart** is provided. This chart shows a "week at a glance," illustrating all major parts of the program and specific skills taught within these parts in groups of five lessons. This chart assists teachers in planning, conducting, and assessing instruction.

Finally, a **correlation to the Common Core State Standards** for English Language Arts is presented. The correlation notes the standards for the specified grade level with detailed notations of how the content of **Reading Mastery Signature Edition** supports the standard.

References

Armbruster, B., Lehr, F., & Osborn, J. (2003). *Put reading first: The research building blocks of reading instruction: Grades K-3* (2nd ed.). Washington, DC: Center for the Improvement of Early Reading Achievement, National Institute for Literacy, U.S. Department of Education.

Carnine, D. W., Silbert, J., Kame'enui, E. J., & Tarver, S. G. (2010). *Direct Instruction reading* (5th ed.). Upper Saddle River, NJ: Pearson Education.

National Institute of Child Health and Human Development [NICHD]. (2000). *Report of the National Reading Panel. Teaching children to read: An evidence-based assessment of the scientific research literature on reading and its implications for reading instruction: Reports of the subgroups* (NIH Publication NO. 00-4754). Washington, DC: U.S. Government Printing Office.

Snow, C., Burns, M., & Griffin, P.(eds.). (1998). *Preventing reading difficulties in young children*. Washington, DC: National Academy Press.

Vaughn, S., & Linan-Thompson, S. (2004). *Research-based methods of reading instruction: Grades K-3*. Alexandria, VA: ASCD.

A. Phonemic Awareness (1-80)

1. Blending (1-70)
2. Segmentation (11-80)

B. Vocabulary Instruction

1. Explicit Instruction (1-160)
2. Review/Knowledge Check (2-160)
3. Vocabulary Notebook (81-160)
4. Acquisition and Use (5, 10, 15, 20, 25, 30, 35, 40, 45, 50, 55, 60, 65, 70, 75, 80, 85, 90, 95, 100, 105, 110, 115, 120, 125, 130, 135, 140, 145, 150, 155, 160

C. Comprehension Strategies

1. Explicit Instruction (1–160)
2. Narrative Text (1-20, 21-70, 71-74, 76-80, 81, 83-92, 94-103, 105-113, 116-128, 131-144, 147- 153, 157-160)
3. Before Reading Strategies (1-7, 9-12, 14, 17, 19, 20, 21, 31- 33, 38-40, 46-48, 50, 60-62, 68, 72, 74, 75, 80, 82, 85, 87, 91, 93, 94, 96, 97, 100, 101, 104, 105, 108-111, 113-115, 118, 120, 121, 123, 125, 127, 129, 130, 134- 136, 140, 141, 143, 145-147, 149, 154, 155, 157, 160)
4. Read with prosody (1-3, 5-11, 13, 14, 16, 19, 20, 23, 24, 27, 30, 31, 33, 35, 37, 40, 50, 51, 56, 63, 65, 66, 69-71, 73, 79-81, 89, 102, 109, 120, 124, 136, 137, 151, 158, 160)
5. Purpose for Reading (1, 3-5, 9-11, 14, 19, 33, 40, 72, 80, 83, 85, 91, 94, 96, 97, 100, 105, 108, 113, 115, 118, 120, 121, 123, 125-127, 130, 134-136, 140, 141, 143, 146, 147, 149, 155, 157, 160)
6. Story Grammar (2-13, 15-19, 21, 28, 33, 34, 36, 39, 41, 43-47, 49, 52, 53, 58, 59, 61, 62, 65-69, 71, 76, 79, 83, 85, 91, 95, 97-99, 102, 103, 106, 112, 117, 127, 134, 138, 139, 142-144, 149, 150, 159, 160)
7. After Reading Strategies (2-13, 15, 16, 18-23, 27-29, 33, 34, 36, 39-50, 52, 53, 55, 57, 59, 61, 62, 65-67, 69, 71, 72, 74-77, 79, 80, 83-85, 88, 90, 91, 93-100, 102, 103, 105, 106, 108, 111, 115, 117-120, 123, 125-128, 130, 132-136, 138-144, 146, 148-150, 153, 155, 156, 159, 160)
8. Graphic Organizers (2-10, 12-16, 18, 22, 23, 28, 29, 33, 34, 39, 47, 48, 67, 68, 75-77, 82, 83, 85, 91, 93-95, 97-99, 104, 105, 114, 115, 126-130, 132-134, 138, 139, 143-146, 149, 150, 154-156)
9. Story Retell (2-10, 12, 13, 16, 18, 22, 28, 34, 39, 40, 41, 43- 45, 48, 49, 68, 71, 77, 80, 95, 96, 98, 100, 106, 108, 109, 111, 112, 117, 118, 120, 123, 135, 136, 138, 141, 159, 160)
10. During Reading Strategies (2, 3, 6-8, 11-16, 19-21, 23-26, 30-38, 40-44, 49-52, 54, 56, 58, 60, 63-66, 68, 70, 73, 78-81, 83, 84, 86, 89, 90, 92, 107, 109, 112, 116, 120-122, 124, 131, 136, 137, 147, 151, 152, 158, 160)
11. Activate background knowledge (2, 6, 7, 14, 19, 33, 48, 50, 60, 68, 79, 80, 113, 120, 136, 141, 157, 160)

12. Comprehension monitoring/fix ups (14, 26, 41-43, 49, 52, 54, 60, 64, 66, 80, 84, 90, 109, 119-121, 136, 141, 147, 158, 160)
13. Predictions (17, 20, 21, 31, 32, 38-40, 46, 47, 61, 62, 80, 87, 88, 110, 111, 113, 117, 120, 157, 159, 160)
14. Make Connections (20-23, 27, 29, 40, 42, 48, 50, 58, 59, 60, 72, 79, 80, 88, 103, 113, 117, 119, 120, 128, 132, 133, 139, 141, 142, 148, 153, 159, 160)
15. Compare/Contrast (22, 23, 29, 59, 99, 126, 128, 132, 133, 139, 140, 142)
16. Generate Questions (24-26, 32, 34-38, 40, 44, 55, 57, 78, 80, 86, 92, 107, 116, 120, 122, 131, 144, 150, 152, 160)
17. Strategy Generation (40, 80, 109, 113, 117, 120, 136, 158, 159, 160)
18. Summarizing (71, 77, 80, 84, 90, 96, 100, 102, 108, 109, 111, 117, 118, 120, 123, 135, 136, 141, 158, 159, 160)
19. Expository Text (74, 75, 82, 83, 93, 94, 104, 105, 114, 115, 117, 120, 125, 126, 129, 130, 145, 146, 154-156, 160)
20. KWL (74, 75, 82, 83, 93, 94, 104, 105, 114, 115, 117, 120, 129, 130, 145, 146, 154-156, 160)
21. Develop Opinions (10, 20, 30, 40, 50, 60, 70, 80, 90, 100, 110, 120, 130, 140, 150, 160)

D. Fluency Building (81–160)

E. Writing/Language Arts

1. Write and Use Parts of Speech and Conventions (15, 25, 35, 45, 55, 65, 75, 85, 95, 105, 115, 125, 135, 145, 155

Scope and Sequence
of SRA Core Lesson Connections

Scope and Sequence (1-80)

Skills	1 – 5	6-10	11-15	16-20	21-25	26-30
PHONEMIC AWARENESS						
Blending	√	√	√	√	√	√
Segmentation			√	√	√	√
VOCABULARY INSTRUCTION						
Explicit Instruction	•	•	•	•	•	•
Review/Knowledge Check	•	•	•	•	•	•
Vocabulary Notebook						
Acquisition and Use	•	•	•	•	•	•
COMPREHENSION STRATEGIES						
Purpose for Reading/Test Type	•	•	•	•		
Story Retell	•	√	•	•	•	
Story Elements	•	•	•	•		•
Read with Prosody	•	•	•	•	•	•
Activate Background Knowledge	•	•	•			
Comprehension Monitoring			•			
Make Predictions				•		
Make Connections				•	•	•
Confirm Prediction					•	
Generate Questions					•	•
Compare/Contrast						•
Strategy Generation						
Mental Imaging						
Sequencing						
Reader's Theatre						
Summarizing						
KWL						
Develop Opinions		•		•		•
FLUENCY BUILDING	√	√	√	√	√	√
WRITING/LANGUAGE ARTS						
Write and Use Parts of Speech and Conventions			•		•	

Key
√ = skill in every lesson
• = skill in some of the lessons

31-35	36-40	41-45	46-50	51-55	56-60	61-65	66-70	71-75	76-80
√	√	√	√	√	√	√	√		
√	√	√	√	√	√	√	√	√	√
•	•	•	•	•	•	•	•	•	•
•	•	•	•	•	•	•	•	•	•
•	•	•	•	•	•	•	•	•	•
•								•	
•	•	•	•				•	•	•
•	•	•	•			•	•	•	•
•	•		•	•	•	•	•	•	
			•		•		•		•
				•			•		
•	•	•				•			
		•			•			•	
•	•	•	•			•			
•	•	•		•	•				•
	•								•
		•	•	•	•	•			
		•	•	•	•		•		
		•							
								•	•
								•	
	•		•		•		•		•
√	√	√	√	√	√	√	√	√	√
•		•		•		•		•	•

Scope and Sequence (81-160)

Skills	81 – 85	86-90	91-95	96-100	101-105	106-110
PHONEMIC AND PHONOLOGICAL AWARENESS						
VOCABULARY INSTRUCTION						
Explicit Instruction	•	•	•	•	•	•
Review/Knowledge Check	•	•	•	•	•	•
Vocabulary Notebook	√	√	√	√	√	√
Acquisition and Use	•	•	•	•	•	•
COMPREHENSION STRATEGIES						
Purpose for Reading/Test Type	•		•	•	•	•
Story Retell			•	•	•	•
Story Elements	•		•	•		
Read with Prosody		•				
Activate Background Knowledge						
Comprehension Monitoring						•
Make Predictions		•				•
Make Connections		•			•	
Confirm Prediction		•				
Generate Questions		•	•			•
Compare/Contrast				•		
Strategy Generation						•
Mental Imaging	•	•				
Sequencing						
Reader's Theatre			•			•
Summarizing	•	•		•		•
KWL	•		•		•	
Develop Opinions		•		•		•
FLUENCY BUILDING	√	√	√	√	√	√
WRITING/LANGUAGE ARTS						
Write and Use Parts of Speech and Conventions	•		•		•	

Key
√ = skill in every lesson
• = skill in some of the lessons

111-115	116-120	121-125	126-130	131-135	136-140	141-145	146-150	151-155	156-160
•	•	•	•	•	•	•	•	•	•
•	•	•	•	•	•	•	•	•	•
√	√	√	√	√	√	√	√	√	√
•	•	•	•	•	•	•	•	•	•
•	•	•	•	•	•	•	•	•	•
•	•					•			
			•		•	•	•		
		•			•			•	
						•			
			•	•	•	•	•		
	•							•	
•									
	•	•		•				•	
		•	•	•	•	•			•
•	•				•				
	•	•					•		
•									
•	•	•			•		•		
•			•			•	•	•	•
	•		•		•		•		•
√	√	√	√	√	√	√	√	√	√
•		•		•		•		•	

Lessons

Lesson 1

Materials

Teacher: Trade book narrative text of choice

Student: *Storybook 1*

Part A: Phonemic and Phonological Awareness

3 minutes

Activity 1 Phoneme Blending for One-Syllable Words

Elicit responses. **Guide** as needed.
We have a new activity today that is going to help you to become very good readers. I'm going to say a word very slowly so you can hear each sound. You need to listen carefully so you can put the sounds together and say the word. Let me show you how it works.

Model holding each continuous sound for 2 to 3 seconds without stopping between sounds.
My turn. Listen. **/mmm/ /ēēē/.** Listen again. **/mmm/ /ēēē/.** I can put it together. **Me.**
Your turn. Listen. **/mmm/ /ēēē/.** Listen again. **/mmm/ /ēēē/.** Put it together. *Me.*

(Continue the activity with the following examples:
knee [nnn-ēēē], see [sss-ēēē], we [www-ēēē].)

Part B: Vocabulary Development

5 minutes

Activity 1 Learn New Vocabulary Word

Elicit responses to questions. **Guide** as needed.
Today you'll start learning important skills to help you understand what you read. The first skill you'll work on is learning vocabulary words. Vocabulary words are all the words that make up our language. Learning vocabulary words will help you unlock the meaning of what you read. New vocabulary words will also help you in speaking and writing.

Today you'll learn a new vocabulary word. **Applaud. Applaud** means **clap.** What does **applaud** mean? *Clap.*

Another word for **clap** is **applaud.** What's another word for **clap?** *Applaud.*

You **clap** at the end of a show if you like the show. You **applaud** at the end of a show you like. Show me how you **applaud** at the end of a show you like.
Observe students. **Guide** as needed.
Discuss examples of when students would applaud.

What's another word for **clap?** *Applaud.*

12 minutes

Teacher Materials:
Trade book narrative
text of choice

Activity 1 Overview—Importance of Comprehension

Discuss why reading is important. **Discuss** what kinds of reading students enjoy doing. When we read it's important to understand what we read. If you read something and do not understand it, it's not really reading. We read for lots of reasons. We read for fun. We read to learn. We read to find out new information. We read to follow directions.

Sometimes when you read, it is easy to just say the words but not think about what you are reading. When you just read the words and you don't think, you are not really reading. This year, you will practice ways to think when you read. When you learn to read and think, you will be a very smart reader.

Activity 2 Establish a Purpose for Reading—A Before-Reading Strategy

Elicit responses to questions. **Guide** as needed.
One type of text is called narrative text. Narrative text tells a story. We read narrative text for fun. Today we will read narrative text. Remember: narrative text tells a story. What does narrative text tell us? *A story.*

I'm going to read a narrative text to you today. We're going to have fun.

Read trade book narrative text of choice. **Model** prosody during read-aloud.
Ask questions to engage students as you read (e.g., who, what, when, where, why).

Discuss why it was fun to read the story.

Provide a reading center to display books being read so that students can enjoy them again during free time.

Part D: Fluency Building

5 minutes

(See Appendix E for Fluency/Paired Reading Guidelines.)

Conduct after the lesson, using story of the day.

Model partner reading. **Direct** students to assigned partners. **Monitor** student reading.

Lesson 2

Part A: Phonemic and Phonological Awareness

3 minutes

Activity 1 Phoneme Blending for One-Syllable Words

Elicit responses. **Guide** as needed.
Let's put some sounds together to make words. I'm going to say a word very slowly so you can hear each sound. You need to listen carefully so you can put the sounds together and say the word. Let me show you how it works.

Model holding each continuous sound for 2 to 3 seconds without stopping between sounds.
My turn. Listen. **/nnn/ /ōōō/.** Listen again. **/nnn/ /ōōō/.** I can put it together. **No.**
Your turn. Listen. **/nnn/ /ōōō/.** Listen again. **/nnn/ /ōōō/.** Put it together. *No.*

(Continue the activity with the following examples:
so [sss-ōōō], row [rrr-ōōō], mow [mmm-ōōō].)

Part B: Vocabulary Development

5 minutes

Student Materials:
Storybook 1

Activity 1 Learn New Vocabulary Word

Elicit responses to questions. **Guide** as needed.
Today you'll learn a new vocabulary word. **Hoist. Hoist** means **lift.**
What does **hoist** mean? *Lift.*

Another word for **lift** is **hoist.** What's another word for **lift?** *Hoist.*

When you **lift** something heavy, you **hoist** it. Show me how you **hoist** your backpack.
Observe students. **Guide** as needed.
Discuss examples of students might hoist something.

What's another word for **lift?** *Hoist.*

Activity 2 Review Vocabulary Word

Elicit responses to questions. **Observe** students. **Guide** as needed.
What does **applaud** mean? *Clap.* Show how you'd **applaud** when a show is over.

Review vocabulary words in appropriate context in *Storybook 1.*

12 minutes

IWB

Teacher Materials:
Storybook 1

Narrative Story Map

Student Materials:
Storybook 1

Copy of Narrative
Story Map

Activity 1 **Read With Prosody—A During-Reading Strategy**

Today I'll read the narrative story "The Cow and the Road." If you pause at the end of each sentence, you can understand what you read better. Listen to me stop at the end of each sentence and take a small breath.

Read title and first three paragraphs of Story 1, page 1, of *Storybook 1* with prosody, attending to the punctuation.

Elicit responses to questions as you read. **Guide** as needed.

Who went down the road? *Men.* What was on the road? *A cow.*

Now I'll read the story without stopping at the periods. See if you can tell the difference. See if it's easier or harder to understand the story.

Read last two paragraphs and ending of Story 1 without prosody, running sentences together in a monotone voice.

Which way sounds better—when you stop at periods or when you don't stop at periods? *When you stop at the periods.*

Which way helps you understand the story better—when you stop at periods or when you don't stop at periods? *When you stop at the periods.*
Discuss how your last reading sounded and if you could understand the story well.

Remember that when you read, you'll understand the story better if you take a small breath at each period.

Reread last two paragraphs and ending with prosody, attending to punctuation.
Elicit responses to questions. **Guide** as needed.

Activity 2 **Parts of a Narrative—An After-Reading Strategy**

Show Narrative Story Map.
Things happen in narrative text. These things help tell a story. They are called events. What are things that happen in a story called? *Events.*

Draw simple sketches on Narrative Story Map to show beginning, middle, and end of story.

Beginning: Men in car
Middle: Cow in road
End: Cow in car

Events include things that happen during the beginning, the middle, and the end of the story. So stories have a beginning, middle, and end. What do stories have? *A beginning, a middle, and an end.*

Stories have three parts—a beginning, a middle, and an end. When you listen to a story, you can remember the story better if you try to remember the events of the story—the beginning, the middle, and the end. Watch as I draw pictures to help me remember the story events.

Model retelling story, using Narrative Story Map.

Activity 3 Activate Background Knowledge—A Before-Reading Strategy

Elicit responses to questions. **Guide** as needed.
The title of today's story is "Paint That Nose." What's the title of today's story? *Paint That Nose.*

If I think about things that I know about painting noses, it will help me understand the story better.

Model think-aloud of when you might paint your nose (with sunscreen, if you are a clown, etc.). **Discuss** examples of when students might paint their nose.

Part D: Fluency Building

5 minutes

Student Materials:
Storybook 1

(See Appendix E for Fluency/Paired Reading Guidelines.)

Conduct after the lesson, using story of the day.

Model partner reading. **Direct** students to assigned partners. **Monitor** student reading.

Lesson 3

Materials

Teacher: 1-Narrative Story Map; trade book narrative text of choice, *Storybook 1*

Student: Copy of 1-Narrative Story Map, *Storybook 1*

Part A: Phonemic and Phonological Awareness

3 minutes

Activity 1 Phoneme Blending for One-Syllable Words

Elicit responses. **Guide** as needed.

Let's put some sounds together to make words. I'm going to say a word very slowly so you can hear each sound. You need to listen carefully, put the sounds together, and say the word. Let me show you how it works.

Model holding each continuous sound for 2 to 3 seconds without stopping between sounds.

My turn. Listen. **/mmm/ /īīī/.** Listen again. **/mmm/ /īīī/.** I can put it together. **My.**

turn. Listen. **/mmm/ /īīī/.** Listen again. **/mmm/ /īīī/.** Put it together. *My.*

(Continue the activity with the following examples: why [www-īīī], lie [lll-īīī], shy [shshsh-īīī].)

Part B: Vocabulary Development

5 minutes

Student Materials:
Storybook 1

Activity 1 Learn New Vocabulary Word

Elicit responses to questions. **Guide** as needed.

Today you'll learn a new vocabulary word. **Angry. Angry** means **mad.** What does **angry** mean? *Mad.*

Another word for **mad** is **angry.** What's another word for **mad?** *Angry.*

When someone takes your ball at recess, you feel **mad.** You're **angry** when someone takes your ball at recess. Show me how you look when you're **angry.**

Observe students. **Guide** as needed.

Discuss examples of when students have felt angry.

What's another word for **mad?** *Angry.*

Elicit responses to questions. **Observe** students. **Guide** as needed.
What does **hoist** mean? *Lift.*
Show how you'd **hoist** your book.

Review vocabulary words in appropriate context in *Storybook 1*.

Part C: Comprehension Strategies

12 minutes

IWB

Teacher Materials:
Storybook 1

Narrative Story Map

Trade book narrative
text of choice

Student Materials:
Storybook 1

Narrative Story Map

Activity 1 Set Purpose for Reading—A Before-Reading Strategy

Before you read, you think about what you're going to read to help you understand the story.

Today I'll read a narrative story. Remember: narrative stories are for fun. So the purpose of reading today's story is to have fun.

Activity 2 Read with Prosody—A During-Reading Strategy

Today I'll read the first part of the story "Paint That Nose." Listen to me stop and take a small breath after each sentence. When you pause after each sentence, it's easier to understand what you read.

Read title and first three paragraphs of Story 2, page 3, of *Storybook 1* with prosody.

Elicit responses to questions as you read. **Guide** as needed.

Who had a red nose? *Both dogs.* Who did not like having a red nose? *The little dog.*

Read last two paragraphs of Story 2 without prosody, running sentences together in a monotone voice. **Elicit** responses to questions. **Guide** as needed.

How did the reading sound different? (Idea: *You didn't take a breath at periods.*)

Was it easier to understand the story? *No.*

Reread last two paragraphs and ending with prosody, attending to punctuation.

Now is it easier to understand the story? *Yes.*

What happened at the end of the story? (Idea: *The little dog kissed the fat dog.*)

Remember to stop at each period before starting the next sentence to help you understand the story.

Activity 3 Beginning, Middle, End—An After-Reading Strategy

Show Narrative Story Map.

A narrative story has three parts—a beginning, a middle, and an end. What parts does a narrative story have? *A beginning, a middle, and an end.*

When you fill out a Narrative Story Map, it helps you remember what happened in the story. Then you can retell the story.

Watch as I draw pictures on my Narrative Story Map to help me remember the story. Then I can tell the story again.

Draw simple sketches on Narrative Story Map to show beginning, middle, and end of story.

Beginning: Two dogs with red noses
Middle: Can of black paint
End: One dog with red nose, one dog with black nose

Model retelling story, using Narrative Story Map.

Part D: Fluency Building

5 minutes

Student Materials:
Storybook 1

(See Appendix E for Fluency/Paired Reading Guidelines.)

Conduct after the lesson, using story of the day.

Model partner reading. **Direct** students to assigned partners. **Monitor** student reading.

Lesson 4

Materials

Teacher: 1-Narrative Story Map; trade book narrative text of choice; *Storybook 1*
Student: Copy of 1-Narrative Story Map; *Storybook 1*

---

3 minutes

Part A: Phonemic and Phonological Awareness

Activity 1 Phoneme Blending for One-Syllable Words

Elicit responses. **Guide** as needed.
Let's put some sounds together to make words. I'm going to say a word very slowly so you can hear each sound. Listen carefully, put the sounds together, and say the word. Let me show you how it works.

Model holding each continuous sound for 2 to 3 seconds without stopping between sounds.
My turn. Listen. **/sss/ /āāā/.** Listen again. **/sss/ /āāā/.** I can put it together. **Say.**
Your turn. Listen. **/sss/ /āāā/.** Listen again. **/sss/ /āāā/.** Put it together. *Say.*

(Continue the activity with the following examples:
may [mmm-āāā], way [www-āāā], ray [rrr-āāā].)

---

5 minutes

Student Materials:
Storybook 1

Part B: Vocabulary Development

Activity 1 Learn New Vocabulary Word

Elicit responses to questions. **Guide** as needed.
Today you'll learn about shortened words. Shortened words are called contractions. When two words are put together, they can be shortened.

Write <u>did not</u> and <u>do not</u> on board. **Model** taking out <u>o</u> and adding apostrophe to each word.
You can shorten **did not** to **didn't** by taking out the **o** in **not** and **adding** an **apostrophe.**

Didn't means **did not.** What does **didn't** mean? *Did not.*

Another word for **did not** is **didn't.**

What's another word for **did not?** *Didn't.*
Didn't is a contraction.

Activity 2 Review Vocabulary Word

Elicit response to questions. **Observe** students. **Guide** as needed.
What does **angry** mean? *Mad.*
Show how you'd look when you're **angry.**

Review vocabulary words in appropriate context in *Storybook 1*.

12 minutes

IWB

Teacher Materials:
Narrative Story Map

Trade book narrative text of choice

Student Materials:
Narrative Story Map

Activity 1 Set Purpose for Reading—A Before-Reading Strategy

Elicit responses to questions. **Guide** as needed.
Before you read, you think about **what** you're going to read to help you **understand** the story. Today I'm going to read a narrative story. Remember: you read narrative stories to have fun. So what's the purpose of reading today's narrative story? *To have fun.*

Narrative stories have a beginning, a middle, and an end. What parts do narrative stories have? *A beginning, a middle, and an end.*

Listen to the story, and see if you can figure out the three parts of the story.

Read trade book narrative text of choice, noting events at the beginning, the middle, and the end. **Ask** questions to engage students as you read (e.g., who, what, when, where, why).

Activity 2 Beginning, Middle, End—An After-Reading Strategy

Show Narrative Story Map. **Give** Narrative Story Map to each student.
Remember: a narrative story has three parts—a beginning, a middle, and an end. Making a Narrative Story Map helps you remember the story. When you retell a story, you can use the map to help you tell what happened in the beginning, the middle, and the end of the story.

Draw a simple picture in the first box of your Narrative Story Map to show only the **beginning** of the story.

Draw a simple sketch on Narrative Story Map to show the beginning. **Guide** students as they draw a sketch for the beginning part of the Narrative Story Map.

Tell your neighbor the beginning of the story, using your Narrative Story Map to help you remember.

Draw simple sketches on Narrative Story Map to show middle and end. **Model** retelling story using Narrative Story Map. **Guide** as needed. **Collect** papers to use in Lesson 5.

Part D: Fluency Building

5 minutes

Student Materials:
Storybook 1

(See Appendix E for Fluency/Paired Reading Guidelines.)

Conduct after the lesson, using the story of the day.

Direct students to assigned partners. **Monitor** partner reading.

Lesson 5

Materials

Teacher: 1-Narrative Story Map previously completed in Lesson 4; same trade book narrative text of choice used in Lesson 4; *Storybook,* 2-Vocabulary Acquisition and Use

Student: Copy of 1-Narrative Story Map previously completed in Lesson 4; *Storybook 1,* Copy of 2-Vocabulary Acquisition and Use

---

Part A: Phonemic and Phonological Awareness

3 minutes

Activity 1 Phoneme Blending for One-Syllable Words

Elicit responses. **Guide** as needed.
Let's put some sounds together to make words. I'm going to say a word very slowly so you can hear each sound. Listen carefully, put the sounds together, and say the word.

Model holding each continuous sound for 2 to 3 seconds without stopping between sounds.
Your turn. Listen. **/ēēē/ /t/.** Listen again. **/ēēē/ /t/.** Put it together. *Eat.*

(Continue the activity with the following examples:
at [aaa-t], off [ooo-fff], if [iii-fff].)

Part B: Vocabulary Development

5 minutes

IWB

Teacher Materials:
Vocabulary Acquisition and Use

Student Materials:
Storybook 1

Vocabulary Acquisition and Use

Activity 1 Cumulative Vocabulary Review

Elicit responses to questions. **Guide** as needed.
Directions: Listen and tell me the correct vocabulary word for each question.

What's another word for **lift?** *Hoist.*
What's another word for **did not?** *Didn't.*
What's another word for **mad?** *Angry.*
What's another word for **clap?** *Applaud.*
Repeat difficult words as needed.

Review vocabulary words in appropriate context in *Storybook 1.*

Activity 2 Vocabulary Acquisition and Use

Display Vocabulary Acquisition and Use. **Have** students work with a neighbor to complete Vocabulary Acquisition and Use.
Today's vocabulary words are _____ and _____ [and _____ and _____].
Vocabulary words: **applaud** and **clap; hoist** and **lift**
Write the words on the lines provided. Then write the words in the boxes based on whether you think each word is less/smaller or more/larger than the

other word. Below the boxes, write why you think word 1 is less/smaller and word 2 is more/larger than word 1.

Repeat for words 3 and 4. **Have** students share what they wrote. **Discuss** examples of how these words might be used.

Part C: Comprehension Strategies

12 minutes

IWB

Teacher Materials:
Narrative Story Map previously completed in Lesson 4

Same trade book narrative text of choice used in Lesson 4

Student Materials:
Narrative Story Map previously completed in Lesson 4

Activity 1 Set Purpose for Reading—A Before-Reading Strategy

Call on student to provide title of story. **Elicit** responses to questions. **Guide** as needed. What kind of story is this? *Narrative.*

Why do we read narrative stories? *To have fun.*

The parts of a narrative story include a beginning, a middle, and _____? *End.*

Read the trade book narrative text from Lesson 4 with prosody, modeling how to pause at the end of each sentence.

Ask questions to engage students as you read (e.g., who, what, when, where, why).

Activity 2 Beginning, Middle, End—An After-Reading Strategy

Give Narrative Story Map from Lesson 4 to each student. **Show** previously completed Narrative Story Map done in Lesson 4 to show beginning and middle.
Remember: a narrative story has three parts—a beginning, a middle, and an end. When you retell a story, you tell what happened in the beginning, then you tell what happened in the middle, and then you tell what happened in the end.

Draw a simple picture in the middle box of your map.

Guide students as they draw a sketch for the middle part of Narrative Story Map.

Now it's time to tell the beginning and middle of today's story to a partner, using the pictures you made.

Model retelling the beginning and middle parts of the story. **Guide** as needed.

Collect papers to complete in Lesson 6.

Part D: Fluency Building

5 minutes

Student Materials:
Storybook 1

(See Appendix E for Fluency/Paired Reading Guidelines.)

Conduct after the lesson, using the story of the day.

Direct students to assigned partners. **Monitor** partner reading.

Lesson 6

Part A: Phonemic and Phonological Awareness

3 minutes

Activity 1 Phoneme Blending for One-Syllable Words

Elicit responses. **Guide** as needed.

Today we're going to put two sounds together and make words. This time you're going to help me say the sounds before we make the word. I'm going to say a word very slowly so you can hear each sound. You need to listen carefully and say the sounds. When you say the sounds, it will sound almost like you're singing them. Then we'll put the sounds together and say the word.

Hold up one finger for each phoneme in word, back of hand to students.

My turn. Listen. **/mmm/ /ēēē/.**

Say those sounds with me. */mmm/ /ēēē/.*

Now say the sounds by yourself. */mmm/ /ēēē/.*

Your turn again, say the sounds. */mmm/ /ēēē/.*

Now let's put it together. What word? *Me.*

Let's try some more. My turn. Listen. **/sss/ /ēēē/.**

Say those sounds with me. */sss/ /ēēē/.*

Now say the sounds by yourself. */sss/ /ēēē/.*

Your turn again. Say the sounds. */sss/ /ēēē/.*

Now let's put it together. What word? *See.*

(Continue the activity with the following words:
no [nnn-ōōō], so [sss-ōōō].)

Part B: Vocabulary Development

5 minutes

Student Materials:
Storybook 1

Activity 1 Learn New Vocabulary Word

Elicit responses to questions. **Guide** as needed.

Today you'll learn a new vocabulary word. **Fond.** To be **fond** of something means **liking something very much.**

What does it mean to be **fond of something**? *Liking something very much.*

Discuss things students are fond of and why they're fond of these things.

Another way to say **liking something very much** is to say being **fond** of it. What's another way to say **liking something very much?** *To be fond of it.*

I **like** teddy bears. I am **fond** of teddy bears.

What's another way to say **liking something very much?** *Being fond of it.*

Activity 2 Review Vocabulary Word

Elicit responses to questions. **Guide** as needed.
What's another way to say **did not?** *Didn't.*
What's another way to say **didn't?** *Did not.*

Review vocabulary words in appropriate context in *Storybook 1.*

Part C: Comprehension Strategies

12 minutes

IWB

Teacher Materials:
Narrative Story Map used in Lessons 4 and 5

Storybook 1

Student Materials:
Narrative Story Map used in Lessons 4 and 5

Storybook 1

Activity 1 Beginning, Middle, End—An After-Reading Strategy

Call on student to provide story title. **Elicit** responses to questions. **Guide** as needed.

What kind of story did we read? *Narrative.*
Why do we read narrative stories? *To have fun.*
What are the three parts of a narrative story? *Beginning, middle, and end.*

Show Narrative Story Map completed in Lesson 4.
It's time to finish your Narrative Story Map by drawing a picture in the end box.

Reread or **retell** the trade book narrative story from Lesson 5, referencing the pictures drawn on the Narrative Story Map. **Ask** questions to engage students as you read (e.g., who, what, when, where, why) if you reread book. **Guide** as needed.

Now it's time to retell the story in your own words to a partner. Use your map to help you remember the parts.
Direct students to retell the story to a partner from their Narrative Story Map. **Guide** as needed.

Activity 2 Read with Prosody—A During-Reading Strategy

Today I'll read the first part of the story "The Talking Cat." Watch me stop and take a small breath after each sentence. When I pause after each sentence, it's easier to understand what I read.

Read the title and first three paragraphs of Story 5, page 7, of *Storybook 1,* modeling prosody.
Elicit responses to questions as you read. **Guide** as needed.

Who did the girl meet on her walk? *A cat.*

What did the cat say to the girl? (Idea: *I can talk but I do not talk to girls.*)

Did the girl like the cat? *No.*

Read last four paragraphs and ending of Story 2 without prosody, running sentences together in a monotone voice. **Elicit** responses about how this reading sounded and if they could understand the story well.
How did this reading sound different? (Idea: *Reader didn't take a breath at periods.*)

Was it easier to understand the story? *No.*

Reread last four paragraphs and ending with prosody, attending to punctuation.
Now is it easier to understand the story? *Yes.*
What happened at the end of the story? (Idea: *The girl and the cat ate fish cake together.*)

Remember to take a small breath after each period, before starting the next sentence, to help you understand the story.

Activity 3 Activate Background Knowledge—A Before-Reading Strategy

Today we are going to read a story about a dog and a cop. If I think about things that I know about dogs and cops, it will help me understand the story better.

Discuss who has a dog, what dogs like to do, who knows a cop, what cops do, etc.

Provide a reading center to display books being read so that students can enjoy them again during free time.

Part D: Fluency Building

5 minutes

Student Materials:
Storybook 1

(See Appendix E for Fluency/Paired Reading Guidelines.)

Conduct after the lesson, using story of the day.

Direct students to assigned partners. **Monitor** partner reading.

Lesson 7

Part A: Phonemic and Phonological Awareness

3 minutes

Activity 1 Phoneme Blending for One-Syllable Words

Elicit responses. **Guide** as needed.

Today we're going to put two sounds together and make words. This time you're going to help me say the sounds before we make the word. I'm going to say a word very slowly so you can hear each sound. You need to listen carefully and say the sounds. When you say the sounds, it will sound almost like you're singing them. Then we'll put the sounds together and say the word.

Hold up one finger for each phoneme in word, back of hand to students.

My turn. Listen. **/mmm/ /īīī/.**
Say those sounds with me. */mmm/ /īīī/*.
Now say the sounds by yourself. */mmm/ /īīī/*.
Your turn again. Say the sounds. */mmm/ /īīī/*.
Now let's put it together. What word? *My.*

Let's try some more. My turn. Listen. **/shshsh/ /īīī/.**
Say those sounds with me. */shshsh/ /īīī/*.
Now say the sounds by yourself. */shshsh/ /īīī/*.
Your turn again. Say the sounds. */shshsh/ /īīī/*.
Now let's put it together. What word? *Shy.*

(Continue the activity with the following words:
say [sss-āāā], may [mmm-āāā].)

Part B: Vocabulary Development

5 minutes

Student Materials:
Storybook 1

Activity 1 Learn New Vocabulary Word

Elicit responses to questions. **Guide** as needed.

Today you'll learn a new vocabulary word. **Cop. Cop** means **police officer.** What does **cop** mean? *Police officer.*

Another name for **police officer** is **cop.** What's another name for **police officer?** *Cop.*

Discuss what police officers do, how they help people, etc.

If I'm lost and need help, I'd ask a **police officer.** I'd ask a **cop** if I was lost and needed help.

What's another name for **police officer?** *Cop.*

Activity 2 **Review Vocabulary Word**

Activity 2 **Review Vocabulary Word**

Elicit responses to questions. **Guide** as needed.
What does it mean to be **fond** of something? *Liking something very much.*
What does liking something very much mean? *Being fond of something.*

Review vocabulary words in appropriate context in *Storybook 1.*

Part C: Comprehension Strategies

12 minutes

IWB

Teacher Materials:
Narrative Story Map

Storybook 1

Student Materials:
Narrative Story Map

Storybook 1

Activity 1 Read with Prosody—A During-Reading Strategy

Today I will read the beginning of "Digging in the Yard" on page 9. I will stop at the end of each sentence and take a little breath. If I do that, I will understand the story better.

Model reading first paragraph of Story 6, page 9, with prosody.

Now you will read the first paragraph with me, and we'll take a little breath after each sentence. Watch for the periods.
Guide students as needed.

Your turn to read the rest of the story to your partner. Be careful to take a small breath after each sentence. Remember: the periods and the question marks tell you where to take a small breath.
Monitor student reading.

Activity 2 Beginning, Middle, End—An After-Reading Strategy

Elicit answers to questions. **Guide** as needed.
The story we just read is a narrative story. It is fun to read. How do you know it is a narrative story? *It is fun to read.*

What are the three parts of a narrative story? *Beginning, middle, end.*

Think about the story we just read. What happened at the beginning of the story? (Idea: *A dog was digging in the yard.*)

What happened in the middle? (Idea: *A cop came and said to stop digging.*)

What happened at the end? (Idea: *The dog became a cop dog.*)

Think about the beginning, the middle, and the end of the story. Draw a very quick picture on your Narrative Story Map of the beginning, the middle, and the end.

Monitor students as they draw a picture for each part of the Narrative Story Map.

Beginning: dog digging, man is mad
Middle: cop comes
End: dog goes with cop

Guide students as they retell the story in their own words, if time allows.

Activity 3 Activate Background Knowledge—A Before-Reading Strategy

In today's lesson you are going to read a story about an old car. If you think about things that you know about old cars, it will help you understand the story better.

Discuss what students know about old cars.

Part D: Fluency Building

5 minutes

Student Materials:
Storybook 1

(See Appendix E for Fluency/Paired Reading Guidelines.)

Conduct after the lesson, using story of the day.

Direct students to assigned partners. **Monitor** partner reading.

Lesson 8

Materials

Teacher: 1-Narrative Story Map; *Storybook 1*

Student: Copy of 1-Narrative Story Map; *Storybook 1*

Part A: Phonemic and Phonological Awareness

3 minutes

Activity 1 Phoneme Blending for One-Syllable words

Elicit responses. **Guide** as needed.

Today we're going to put two sounds together and make words. This time you're going to help me say the sounds before we make the word. I'm going to say a word very slowly so you can hear each sound. You need to listen carefully and say the sounds. When you say the sounds, it will sound almost like you're singing them. Then we'll put the sounds together and say the word.

Hold up one finger for each phoneme in word, back of hand to students.

Listen. **/ēēē/ /t/.**

Say those sounds with me. /ēēē/ /t/.

Now say the sounds by yourself. /ēēē/ /t/.

Your turn again. Say the sounds. /ēēē/ /t/.

Now let's put it together. What word? *Eat.*

Let's try some more. My turn. Listen. **/aaa/ /t/.**

Say those sounds with me. /aaa/ /t/.

Now say the sounds by yourself. /aaa/ /t/.

Your turn again. Say the sounds. /aaa/ /t/.

Now let's put it together. What word? *At.*

(Continue the activity with the following words: off [ooo-fff], if [iii-fff].)

Part B: Vocabulary Development

5 minutes

Teacher Materials:
Storybook 1

Student Materials:
Storybook 1

Activity 1 Learn New Vocabulary Word

Elicit responses to questions. **Guide** as needed.

Today you'll learn a new vocabulary word. **Reward. Reward** means **prize.** What does **reward** mean? *Prize.*

Another word for **prize** is **reward.** What's another word for **prize?** *Reward.*

Discuss examples of rewards and when students might get them.

When you do your chores, you might get a **prize.** You might get a **reward** when you do your chores.

What's another word for **prize?** *Reward.*

Activity 2 Review Vocabulary Word

Elicit responses to questions. **Guide** as needed.
What's another name for **police officer?** *Cop.*
What does **cop** mean? *Police officer.*

Review vocabulary words in appropriate context in *Storybook 1*.

Part C: Comprehension Strategies

12 minutes

IWB

Teacher Materials:
Narrative Story Map

Storybook 1

Student Materials:
Narrative Story Map

Storybook 1

Activity 1 Read with Prosody—A During-Reading Strategy

Model how to read a sentence with a question mark.
Today I will read the beginning of "Will the Old Car Start?" The title of this story asks a question, so it ends with a question mark. When I read a sentence that ends with a question mark, I make my voice go up a little to show that I am asking a question.

Say the title with me. Be sure to make your voice go up a little at the end. "*Will the Old Car Start?*"

Model reading title and first paragraph of Story 7, page 11, with prosody.

Now you will read the title and first paragraph with me, and we'll take a little breath after each sentence. Watch out for the periods or question marks.
Guide students as needed.

Now read the first paragraph to your partner. Be careful to take a small breath after each sentence and make your voice go up when you read a question. Remember: the periods and question marks tell you where to take a small breath.
Monitor individual students. **Reverse** student roles.

Activity 2 Beginning, Middle, End—An After-Reading Strategy

Elicit answers to questions. **Guide** as needed.
The story we just read is a narrative story. How do you know it is a narrative story? *It is fun to read.*

What are the three parts of a narrative story? *Beginning, middle, end.*

Think about the story we just read. What happened at the beginning of the story? (Idea: *The old car did not start.*)

What happened in the middle of the story? (Idea: *A big man got in the car.*)

What happened at the end of the story? (Idea: *The car started.*)

Think about the beginning, the middle and the end of the story. Draw a very quick picture on your Narrative Story Map of the beginning, middle, and end.

Direct students to fill out Narrative Story Map.

Beginning: an old car
Middle: a big man in a car
End: the car starts

Guide students to retell the story in their own words if time allows.

Part D: Comprehension Strategies

5 minutes

Student Materials:
Storybook 1

(See Appendix E for Fluency/Paired Reading Guidelines.)

Conduct after the lesson, using story of the day.

Direct students to assigned partners. **Monitor** partner reading.

Lesson 9

Part A: Phonemic and Phonological Awareness

3 minutes

Activity 1 Phoneme Blending for One-Syllable Words

Elicit responses. **Guide** as needed.
Let's put some sounds together and make words. I'm going to say a word very slowly so you can hear each sound. You need to listen carefully and say the sounds. When you say the sounds, it will sound almost like you're singing them. Then we'll put the sounds together and say the word.

Hold up one finger for each phoneme in word, back of hand to students.
My turn. Listen. **/shshsh/ /ōōō/.**
Say those sounds with me. */shshsh/ /ōōō/.*
Now say the sounds by yourself. */shshsh/ /ōōō/.*
Your turn again. Say the sounds. */shshsh/ /ōōō/.*
Now let's put it together. What word? *Show.*

Let's try some more. My turn. Listen. **/lll/ /ōōō/.**
Say those sounds with me. */lll/ /ōōō/.*
Now say the sounds by yourself. */lll/ /ōōō/.*
Your turn again. Say the sounds. */lll/ /ōōō/.*
Now let's put it together. What word? *Low.*

(Continue the activity with the following words:
moo [mmm-oooooo], zoo [zzz-oooooo].)

Part B: Vocabulary Development

5 minutes

Student Materials:
Storybook 1

Activity 1 New Vocabulary Word

Elicit responses to questions. **Guide** as needed.
Today you'll learn a new vocabulary word. **Road.** Another word for **road** is **street.** What's another word for **road?** *Street.*

Another word for **street** is **road.** What's another word for **street?** *Road.*

You ride your bike down the **street.** You ride your bike down the **road.**

You spell this type of **road r-o-a-d.** Spell **road.** *R-o-a-d.*
Discuss examples of roads students know, what they are made of, and what vehicles use roads.

What's another word for **street?** *Road.*

Activity 2 Review Vocabulary Word

Elicit responses to questions. **Guide** as needed.
What word means **reward?** *Prize.*
What does **prize** mean? *Reward.*

Review vocabulary words in appropriate context in *Storybook 1.*

Part C: Comprehension Strategies

12 minutes

IWB

Teacher Materials:
Narrative Story Map

Trade book narrative
text of choice

Student Materials:
Narrative Story Map

Activity 1 Set Purpose for Reading—A Before-Reading Strategy

Elicit responses to questions. **Guide** as needed.
Before we read, we think about what we are going to read to help us understand the text we read. Today I'm going to read a narrative story. Remember: we read narrative stories for fun.

What parts does a narrative have? *Beginning, middle, and end.*

Listen to the story, and see if you can figure out the three parts of the story.

Read trade book narrative text of choice, with prosody. Pause briefly after sentences, and take note of how to read sentences with a question mark.

Ask questions to engage students as you read (e.g., who, what, when, where, why).

Activity 2 Beginning, Middle, End—An After-Reading Strategy

Elicit oral responses to questions.
Today I want you to think about the story we just read. What happened at the beginning of the story? What happened in the middle of the story? What happened at the end of the story? Think about these important parts of a narrative story. Draw a very quick sketch of the beginning, the middle, and the end of the story on your Narrative Story Map.

Direct students to fill out Narrative Story Map for trade book narrative text of choice.
Guide students as they retell the story in their own words if time allows.

Part D: Fluency Building

5 minutes

Student Materials:
Storybook 1

(See Appendix E for Fluency/Paired Reading Guidelines.)

Conduct after the lesson, using the story of the day.

Direct students to assigned partners. **Monitor** partner reading.

Lesson 10

Materials

Teacher: Trade book narrative text of choice; 1-Narrative Story Map; *Storybook 1*, 2-Vocabulary Acquisition and Use, 3-My Book Review

Student: Copies of 1-Narrative Story Map, 2-Vocabulary Acquisition and Use, and 3-My Book Review; *Storybook 1*

Part A: Phonemic and Phonological Awareness

3 minutes

Activity 1 Phoneme Blending for One-Syllable Words

Elicit responses. **Guide** as needed.
Let's put some sounds together and make words. I'm going to say a word very slowly so you can hear each sound. You need to listen carefully and say the sounds. When you say the sounds, it will sound almost like you're singing them. Then we'll put the sounds together and say the word.

Hold up one finger for each phoneme in word, back of hand to students.
Listen. **/www/ /ēēē/.**
Say those sounds with me. */www/ /ēēē/.*
Now say the sounds by yourself. */www/ /ēēē/.*
Your turn again. Say the sounds. */www/ /ēēē/.*
Now let's put it together. What word? *We.*

Let's try some more. My turn. Listen. **/shshsh/ /ēēē/.**
Say those sounds with me. */shshsh/ /ēēē/.*
Now say the sounds by yourself. */shshsh/ /ēēē/.*
Your turn again. Say the sounds. */shshsh/ /ēēē/.*
Now let's put it together. What word? *She.*

(Continue the activity with the following words:
ear [ēēē-rrr], each [ēēē-ch].)

Part B: Vocabulary Development

5 minutes

IWB

Teacher Materials:
Vocabulary Acquisition and Use

Student Materials:
Storybook 1

Vocabulary Acquisition and Use

Activity 1 Cumulative Vocabulary Review

Elicit responses to questions. **Guide** as needed.
Directions: Listen and tell me the correct vocabulary word for each question.

What's another word for **lift?** *Hoist.*
What's another word for **like?** *Fond.*
What's another word for **did not?** *Didn't.*
What's another word for **mad?** *Angry.*
What's another word for **prize?** *Reward.*
What's another word for **clap?** *Applaud.*
What's another word for **street?** *Road.* Spell **road.** *R-o-a-d.*
What's another word for **police officer?** *Cop.*

24 *Lesson 10*

Repeat difficult words as needed.

Review vocabulary words in appropriate context in *Storybook 1*.

Activity 2 Vocabulary Acquisition and Use

Display Vocabulary Acquisition and Use. **Have** students work with a neighbor to complete Vocabulary Acquisition and Use.
Today's vocabulary words are _____ and _____ [and _____ and _____].
Vocabulary words: **angry** and **mad; fond** and **liking**
Write the words on the lines provided. Then write the words in the boxes based on whether you think each word is less/smaller or more/larger than the other word. Below the boxes, write why you think word 1 is less/smaller and word 2 is more/larger than word 1.
Repeat for words 3 and 4. **Have** students share what they wrote. **Discuss** examples of how these words might be used.

Part C: Comprehension Strategies

12 minutes

IWB

Teacher Materials:
Trade book narrative text of choice

Narrative Story Map

My Book Review

Student Materials:
Narrative Story Map

My Book Review

Activity 1 Set Purpose for Reading—A Before-Reading Strategy

Elicit responses to questions. **Guide** as needed.
Before we read, we think about **what** we are going to read to help us **understand** the text we read. Today I'm going to read a narrative story. Remember: we read narrative stories for fun. What's the purpose of reading a narrative story today? *To have fun.*

What parts does a narrative have? *Beginning, middle, and end.*

Listen to the story, and see if you can figure out the three parts of the story.

Read trade book narrative of choice with prosody. **Pause** briefly after sentences, and take note of how to read sentences with a question mark. **Ask** questions to engage students as you read (e.g., who, what, when, where, why).

Activity 2 Beginning, Middle, End—An After-Reading Strategy

Today I want you to think about the story we just read. What happened at the beginning of the story? What happened in the middle of the story? What happened at the end of the story? Think about these important parts of a narrative story. Draw a very quick sketch of the beginning, middle, and end of the story on your Narrative Story Map.

Direct students to fill out Narrative Story Map for trade book narrative text of choice. **Guide** students as they retell the story in their own words if time allows.

Activity 3 Develop Opinions—An After-Reading Strategy

Today we'll found out your opinion or how you feel about the stories you read. You will choose a book to read and then complete the My Book Review form. You'll need to tell if you like or don't like the book and why. You must give a reason for why you like or don't like the book. Finally, you can tell if you would recommend the book to others.

Have students read a narrative or expository trade book of their choice. **Have** students complete My Book Review form when they are finished reading their book. **Model** how to complete the My Book Review form. **Guide** students as needed. **Have** students share their book reviews with the class as time permits.

Part D: Fluency Building

5 minutes

Student Materials:
Storybook 1

Conduct after the lesson, using story of the day.

Activity 1 Partner Reading

It's time for partner reading.

Direct students to the story of the day. **Assign** student partners as Partner 1 and Partner 2. **Monitor** partner reading. **Guide** as needed.

Lesson 11

Materials

Teacher: *Storybook 1*

Student: *Storybook 1;* drawing paper

3 minutes

Part A: Phonemic Awareness

Activity 1 Phoneme Blending for One-Syllable Words

Elicit responses. **Guide** as needed.

Let's put some sounds together and make words. I'm going to say a word very slowly so you can hear each sound. You need to listen carefully and say the sounds. When you say the sounds, it will sound almost like you're singing them. Then we'll put the sounds together and say the word.

Model holding each continuous sound for 2 to 3 seconds without stopping between sounds. **Hold** up one finger for each phoneme in word, back of hand to students.
My turn. Listen. **/aaa/ /t/.**
Say those sounds with me. */aaa/ /t/.*
Now say the sounds by yourself. */aaa/ /t/.*
Your turn again. Say the sounds. */aaa/ /t/.*
Now let's put it together. What word? *At.*

Let's make a bigger word. My turn. Listen. **/mmm/ /aaa/ /t/.**
Say those sounds with me. */mmm/ /aaa/ /t/.*
Now say the sounds by yourself. */mmm/ /aaa/ /t/.*
Your turn again. Say the sounds. */mmm/ /aaa/ /t/.*
Now let's put it together. What word? *Mat.*

(Continue the activity with the following words:
sat [sss-aaa-t], rat [rrr-aaa-t], fat [fff-aaa-t].)

Activity 2 Phoneme Segmentation

Elicit responses. **Guide** as needed.

You have learned to blend sounds together to make words. Now we're going to try something a little harder. We're going to break words apart by each sound. I'm going to tell you a word. You'll need to listen closely and tell me the different sounds you hear in the word. I'll show you how to do the first one.

Pause briefly between each sound so students can hear each phoneme as an individual sound. **Model** holding each continuous sound for 2 to 3 seconds. **Say** stop sounds quickly. **Hold** up one finger for each phoneme in word, back of hand to students.
My turn. The word is **me.** I can say the sounds in **me.** **/mmm/ /ēēē/.** Those are the sounds in the word **me.**

Try it with me. The word is **me.** Tell me the sounds you hear in **me.** */mmm/ /ēēē/.*
Your turn by yourself. The word is **me.** Tell me the sounds you hear in **me.** */mmm/ /ēēē/.*
Yes. You said the sounds in the word **me.**

(Continue the activity with the following words:
see [sss-ēēē], we [www-ēēē].)

Part B: Vocabulary Development

5 minutes

Student Materials:
Storybook 1

Activity 1 Learn New Vocabulary Word

Elicit responses to questions. **Guide** as needed.
Today you'll learn a new vocabulary word. **Amusing. Amusing** means **funny.**
What does **amusing** mean? *Funny.*

Another word for **funny** is **amusing.** What's another word for **funny?**
Amusing.

You think the clown at the circus is **funny.** The clown at the circus is
amusing. Show me how you'd look when something is **amusing.**
Observe students. **Guide** as needed.

Discuss examples of when you would find something amusing.

What's another word for **funny?** *Amusing.*

Activity 2 Review Vocabulary Word

Elicit responses to questions. **Guide** as needed.
What's another word for **road?** *Street.*
What's another word for **street?** *Road.*

Review vocabulary words in appropriate context in *Storybook 1.*

Part C: Comprehension Strategies

12 minutes

Teacher Materials:
Storybook 1

Student Materials:
Storybook 1

Drawing paper

Activity 1 Set Purpose for Reading and Parts of a Narrative—A Before-Reading Strategy

Elicit responses to questions. **Guide** as needed.
You've learned that narratives have a beginning, a middle, and an end. You've
also learned why you read narrative stories. What's the purpose of reading
today's narrative story? *To have fun.*

Narratives also have characters. Characters are the people or animals in a
story. What do you call the people or animals in the story? *Characters.*

Activity 2 Determine Main Character—A During-Reading Strategy

Elicit responses to questions.
Today I'll read a narrative story. As I read, I'll stop and write the characters on the board. Remember: characters are the people or animals in the story. What are characters? *The people or animals in the story.*

Read "The Dog and the Bath," Story 10, page 15, from *Storybook 1* with prosody.

List characters on board (Sal, two girls).

Activity 3 Identify Main Character—An After-Reading Strategy

Elicit responses to questions. **Guide** as needed.
The main character is the person or animal the story is mostly about. What is the main character? *The person or animal the story is mostly about.*

If a story is mostly about Sally, a girl who loves to ride horses, the main character is Sally. If a story is mostly about Juan, a boy who moves to a new neighborhood, and his dog, Skyler, there would be two main characters—Juan and Skyler. The story is mostly about a boy and his dog. Let's say you read a story about how Jason spent his summer vacation. Who do you think the main character would be? *Jason.*

Provide drawing paper to each student.
Choose the main character from the story "The Dog and the Bath," and draw that character on your paper. After you have made the picture, look in your storybook, and find the name of that character. Copy the name of the character on your drawing. Remember to put your name on your drawing also.

Part D: Fluency Building

5 minutes

Student Materials:
Storybook 1

Conduct after the lesson, using story of the day.

Activity 1: Partner Reading

It's time for partner reading.
Direct students to the story of the day. **Assign** student partners as Partner 1 and Partner 2. **Monitor** partner reading. **Guide** as needed.

Lesson 12

Part A: Phonemic Awareness

3 minutes

Activity 1 Phoneme Blending for One-Syllable Words

Elicit responses. **Guide** as needed.

Let's put some sounds together and make words. I'm going to say a word very slowly so you can hear each sound. You need to listen carefully and say the sounds. When you say the sounds, it will sound almost like you're singing them. Then we'll put the sounds together and say the word.

Model holding each continuous sound for 2 to 3 seconds without stopping between sounds; say stop sounds quickly. **Hold** up one finger for each phoneme in word, back of hand to students.

My turn. Listen. **/aaa/ /nnn/.**

Say the sounds. */aaa/ /nnn/.*

Again, say the sounds. */aaa/ /nnn/.*

Now let's put it together. What word? *An.*

Let's make a bigger word. My turn. Listen. **/mmm/ /aaa/ /nnn/.**

Say the sounds. */mmm/ /aaa/ /nnn/.*

Again, say the sounds. */mmm/ /aaa/ /nnn/.*

Now let's put it together. What word? *Man.*

(Continue the activity with the following words:
ran [rrr-aaa-nnn], fan [fff-aaa-nnn], than [ththth-aaa-nnn].)

Activity 2 Phoneme Segmentation

Elicit responses. **Guide** as needed.

Let's work on our new activity. We're going to break words apart by each sound. I'm going to say a word. You'll need to listen closely and tell me the different sounds you hear in the word. I'll show you how to do the first one.

Pause briefly between each sound so students can hear each phoneme as an individual sound. **Model** holding each continuous sound for 2 to 3 seconds. **Say** stop sounds quickly. **Hold** up one finger for each phoneme in word, back of hand to students.

My turn. The word is **may.** I can say the sounds in **may. /mmm/ /āāā/.** Those are the sounds in the word **may.**

Try it with me. The word is **may.** Tell me the sounds you hear in **may.** */mmm/ /āāā/.*

Your turn by yourself. The word is **may.** Tell me the sounds you hear in **may.** /mmm/ /āāā/.
Yes. You said the sounds in the word **may.**

(Continue the activity with the following words:
say [sss-āāā], way [www-āāā].)

Part B: Vocabulary Development

5 minutes

Student Materials:
Storybook 1

Activity 1 Learn New Vocabulary Word

Elicit responses to questions. **Guide** as needed.
Today you'll learn a new vocabulary word. **Brave. Brave** means **not afraid to do something dangerous.** What does **brave** mean? *Not afraid to do something dangerous.*

Another word for **not afraid to do something dangerous** is **brave.** What's another word for **not afraid to do something dangerous?** *Brave.*

The firefighter was **not afraid to do something dangerous.** He saved a baby from a burning building. The firefighter was **brave.**

What's another word for **not afraid to do something dangerous?** *Brave.*

Discuss examples of when someone is brave.

Activity 2 Review Vocabulary Word

Elicit responses to questions. **Observe** students. **Guide** as needed.
What does **amusing** mean? *Funny.*
Show me how you look if something is **amusing.**

Review vocabulary words in appropriate context in *Storybook 1.*

Part C: Comprehension Strategies

12 minutes

IWB

Teacher Materials:
Storybook 1

Narrative Story Map

Student Materials:
Storybook 1

Activity 1 Parts of a Narrative—A Before-Reading Strategy

Elicit responses to questions. **Guide** as needed.
In the last lesson you learned about characters in a narrative story. Characters are the people or animals in the story. What are characters? *The people or animals in the story.*

You also learned about the main character. The main character is the person or animal the story is mostly about. What is the main character? *The person or animal the story is mostly about.*

We're going to figure out who the characters are in today's story. We will also figure out the main character. As I read the story, think about who the characters are. Think about who the main character is.

Activity 2 Determine Characters—A During-Reading Strategy

Elicit responses to questions. **Guide** as needed.

Today as I read the story, I'll read to find the characters. I'll stop and write the name of each character on the board. What are characters? *People or animals in the story.*

What is the main character? *Person or animal the story is mostly about.*

Read Story 11, page 17, of *Storybook 1*.

List characters on board as they are located in text. **Identify** main character.

Activity 3 Narrative Story Map—An After-Reading Strategy

Elicit responses to questions. **Guide** as needed.

After reading a story, it helps you remember the story if you use a Narrative Story Map. Today our Narrative Story Map will change. Now our Narrative Story Map has a place to make a picture of the main character in the story.

Who were the characters in the story? (Idea: *Arf, the other sharks, and the big fish.*)

Who was the main character in the story? *Arf.*

How do you know that Arf was the main character in the story? (Idea: *The story was mostly about Arf.*)

Watch me as I draw the main character in the new Narrative Story Map. **Model** filling in Character section of Narrative Story Map.

Now you can help me fill in the beginning and the middle of the story. We can't fill in the end of the story until we read the next chapter.

Elicit ideas from students for what to draw in the Beginning and Middle sections of Narrative Story Map.

Remember: filling out a Narrative Story Map with all the parts of a narrative helps us remember the story, so we can retell the story in our own words. **Retell** the beginning and middle of the story by referencing pictures.

Part D: Fluency Building

5 minutes

Student Materials:
Storybook 1

Conduct after the lesson, using story of the day.

Activity 1 Partner Reading

It's time for partner reading.
Direct students to the story of the day. **Assign** student partners as Partner 1 and Partner 2. **Monitor** partner reading. **Guide** as needed.

Lesson 13

Materials

Teacher: 1-Narrative Story Map from Lesson 12; 4-Semantic Web; *Storybook 1*

Student: *Storybook 1*; copy of Narrative Story Map from Lesson 12

3 minutes

Part A: Phonemic and Phonological Awareness

Activity 1   Phoneme Blending for One-Syllable Words

Elicit responses. **Guide** as needed.

Let's put some sounds together and make words. I'm going to say a word very slowly so you can hear each sound. You need to listen carefully and say the sounds. When you say the sounds, it will sound almost like you're singing them. Then we'll put the sounds together and say the word.

Model holding each continuous sound for 2 to 3 seconds without stopping between sounds; say stop sounds quickly. **Hold** up one finger for each phoneme in word, back of hand to students.

My turn. Listen. **/iii/ /t/.** Say the sounds. /iii/ /t/.
Again, say the sounds. /iii/ /t/.
Now let's put it together. What word? *It.*

Let's make a bigger word. My turn. Listen. **/mmm/ /iii/ /t/.** Say the sounds. /mmm/ /iii/ /t/.
Again, say the sounds. /mmm/ /iii/ /t/.
Now let's put it together. What word? *Mit.*

(Continue the activity with the following words:
sit [sss-iii-t], fit [fff-iii-t], knit [nnn-iii-t].)

Activity 2   Phoneme Segmentation

Elicit responses. **Guide** as needed.

Let's work on our new activity. We're going to break words apart by each sound. I'm going to say a word. You'll need to listen closely and tell me the different sounds you hear in the word. I'll show you how to do the first one.

Pause briefly between each sound so students can hear each phoneme as an individual sound. **Model** holding each continuous sound for 2 to 3 seconds. **Say** stop sounds quickly. **Hold** up one finger for each phoneme in word, back of hand to students.
My turn. The word is **my.** I can say the sounds in **my. /mmm/ /īīī/.** Those are the sounds in the word **my.**
Try it with me. The word is **my.** Tell me the sounds you hear in **my.** /mmm/ /īīī/.
Your turn by yourself. The word is **my.** Tell me the sounds you hear in **my.**
/mmm/ /īīī/.

Yes. You said the sounds in the word **my.**

(Continue the activity with the following words:
shy [shshsh-īīī], lie [lll-īīī].)

Part B: Vocabulary Development

5 minutes

IWB

Teacher Materials:
Semantic Web

Student Materials:
Storybook 1

Activity 1 Learn New Vocabulary Word and Develop Semantic Web

Elicit responses to questions. **Guide** as needed.
Today you'll learn about the word **where. Where** means **in what place.** What does **where** mean? *In what place.*

Another word for **in what place** is **where.** What's another word for **in what place?** *Where.*

Some words tell us **in what place.** They tell us about **where.** The lake tells us **where.** A school tells us **where.** The park tells us **where.** The stream tells us **where.**

What's another word for **in what place?** *Where.*
Discuss other words that tell where.
Show Semantic Web. **Record** words on Semantic Web.

Activity 2 Review Vocabulary Word

Elicit responses to questions. **Guide** as needed.
What does brave mean? *Not afraid to do something dangerous.*
What word means **not afraid to do something dangerous?** *Brave.*

Review vocabulary words in appropriate context in *Storybook 1.*

Part C: Comprehension Strategies

12 minutes

IWB

Teacher Materials:
Storybook 1

Narrative Story Map
from Lesson 12

Student Materials:
Storybook 1

Narrative Story Map
from Lesson 12

Activity 1 Read with Prosody—A During-Reading Strategy

Elicit responses to questions. **Guide** as needed.
Today I'll read both chapters of the Arf story. I'll read the story the right way some of the time by stopping and taking a small breath after each sentence. When I pause after each sentence, it's easier to understand what I read.

But, I'll try to trick you sometimes by reading the wrong way. When I read the wrong way, say "STOP."

Why do we stop and take a small breath after the periods and question marks? (Idea: *So it is easier to understand.*)

Read Stories 11 and 12, pages 17–20, with prosody and then read in monotone voice and disregard punctuation. **Guide** students to say "stop" when story is read the wrong way.

Remember: it helps you understand what you read if you read the text the right way.

Activity 2 Narrative Story Map—An After-Reading Strategy

Show Narrative Story Map from Lesson 12. **Elicit** responses to questions. **Guide** as needed.

After reading a story, it helps you remember the story if you fill in a Narrative Story Map. Today we can finish the Narrative Story Map that we started yesterday because now we know the end of the story. Who were the characters in the story? (Idea: *Arf, the other sharks, and the big fish.*)

Draw quick sketch on Narrative Story Map to finish what was begun in Lesson 12. Who was the main character of the story? *Arf.*

What happened at the beginning of the story? (Idea: *Arf did not have friends because of his bark.*)

What happened in the middle of the story? (Idea: *A big fish began to chase sharks.*)

Now what shall we draw for the end of the story? (Idea: *Arf barks and scares the big fish away.*)

Is Arf brave? *Yes.* Why? (Idea: *Arf scared the big fish away.*)

Now you can tell the Arf story to a partner. Use our Narrative Story Map to help you remember the story. Be sure to tell about the characters as well as the beginning, middle, and end.

Guide students as they use Narrative Story Map to retell Arf story to a partner, remembering to include characters, beginning, middle, and end.

Part D: Fluency Building

5 minutes

Teacher Materials:
Storybook 1

Conduct after the lesson, using story of the day

Activity 1 Partner Reading

It's time for partner reading.
Direct students to the story of the day. **Assign** student partners as Partner 1 and Partner 2. **Monitor** partner reading. **Guide** as needed.

Lesson 14

Part A: Phonemic and Phonological Awareness

3 minutes

Activity 1 — Phoneme Blending for One-Syllable Words

Elicit responses. **Guide** as needed.
Let's put some sounds together and make words. I'm going to say a word very slowly so you can hear each sound. You need to listen carefully and say the sounds. When you say the sounds, it will sound almost like you're singing them. Then we'll put the sounds together and say the word.

Model holding each continuous sound for 2 to 3 seconds without stopping between sounds; say stop sounds quickly. **Hold** up one finger for each phoneme in word, back of hand to students.

My turn. Listen. **/ēēē/ /t/.** Say the sounds. /ēēē/ /t/.
Again, say the sounds. /ēēē/ /t/.
Now let's put it together. What word? *Eat.*

Let's make a bigger word. My turn. Listen. **/mmm/ /ēēē/ /t/.**
Say the sounds. /mmm/ /ēēē/ /t/.
Again/say the sounds. /mmm/ /ēēē/ /t/.
Now let's put it together. What word. *Meat.*

(Continue the activity with the following words:
seat [sss-ēēē-t], feet [fff-ēēē-t], sheet [shshsh-ēēē-t].)

Activity 2 — Phoneme Segmentation

Elicit responses. **Guide** as needed.
Let's work on breaking words apart by each sound. I'm going to say a word. You'll need to listen closely and tell me the different sounds you hear in the word. I'll show you how to do the first one.

Pause briefly between each sound so students can hear each phoneme as an individual sound. **Model** holding each continuous sound for 2 to 3 seconds. **Say** stop sounds quickly. **Hold** up one finger for each phoneme in word, back of hand to students.
My turn. The word is **so.** I can say the sounds in **so. /sss/ /ōōō/.** Those are the sounds in the word **so.**
Try it with me. The word is **so.** Tell me the sounds you hear in **so.** /sss/ /ōōō/.
Your turn by yourself. The word is **so.** Tell me the sounds you hear in **so.** /sss//ōōō/.

Yes. You said the sounds in the word **so.**

(Continue the activity with the following words:
no [nnn-ōōō], show [shshsh-ōōō].)

Part B: Vocabulary Development

5 minutes

Student Materials:
Storybook 1

Activity 1 Learn New Vocabulary Word

Elicit responses to questions. **Guide** as needed.
Today you'll learn **two** new vocabulary words. These two words mean the same thing. The first word is **creek. Creek** means **small river.** What does **creek** mean? *Small river.*

Another word for **small river** is **creek.** What's another word for **small river?** *Creek.*

The second word is **stream. Stream** also means **small river.** What does **stream** mean? *Small river.*

Another word for **small river** is **stream.** What's another word for **small river?** *Stream.*

Creek and **stream** mean the same thing. They both mean **small river.** You go fishing in a **small river.** You go fishing in a **creek** or **stream.**

What's another word for **small river?** *Creek or stream.*

Discuss where students can find a creek or stream and what they might find there.

Activity 2 Review Vocabulary Word

Elicit responses to questions. **Guide** as needed.
What's another word for **in what place?** *Where.*
Words like **by the barn, in the yard,** and **on the porch** tell **in what place.** What do they tell us? *Where.*

Review vocabulary words in appropriate context in *Storybook 1.*

Part C: Comprehension Strategies

12 minutes

Teacher Materials:
Trade book narrative
text of choice

Activity 1 Set a Purpose for Reading—A Before-Reading Strategy

Provide title of story to students. **Elicit** responses to questions. **Guide** as needed.
Today I'll read a story for fun. What type of story will I read? *Narrative story.*

How do you know it is a narrative story? (Idea: *Because we will read it for fun.*)

What kinds of things will we hear in this narrative story? (Idea: *Characters; beginning, middle, and end.*)

Activity 2 Reread: A Fix-Up—A During-Reading Strategy

When I'm reading this story, I'll show you what I do when I get confused about what I'm reading. I stop and reread the section to make sure that I understand the story. Listen!

Read trade book narrative text of choice to students, modeling prosody. As story is read, model rereading to ensure understanding. **Ask** questions to engage students (e.g., who, what, when, where, why).

Wow! When I reread a sentence or a section that is confusing, I can usually understand the story better.

Activity 3 Activate Background Knowledge—A Before-Reading Strategy

Before you read a new story, it's a good idea to think about what you're going to read and why you're reading it. You might understand the story better if you think about what you already know.

Guide discussion of student background knowledge about cowboys, and help link background knowledge to story.
The next story in the storybook is about cowboys. What do you know about cowboys? (Idea: *They work on ranches. They ride horses. They take care of cows.*)

Do you think any of these facts will be in the cowboy story that we are going to read today? (Student responses.)

When you think about what you already know, it helps you better understand the story you're reading.

Part D: Fluency Building

5 minutes

Student Materials:
Storybook 1

Conduct after the lesson, using story of the day.

Activity 1 Partner Reading

It's time for partner reading.
Direct students to the story of the day. **Assign** student partners as Partner 1 and Partner 2. **Monitor** partner reading. **Guide** as needed.

Lesson 15

Materials

Teacher: *Storybook 1;* 1-Narrative Story Map, 2-Vocabulary Acquisition and Use, Writing Prompts, 5-My Writing Checklist

Student: Copy of 1-Narrative Story Map, 2- Vocabulary Acquisition and Use, and 3-My Writing Checklist; *Storybook 1*, Lined Paper

Part A: Phonemic and Phonological Awareness

3 minutes

Activity 1 Phoneme Blending for One-Syllable Words

Elicit responses. **Guide** as needed.

Let's put some sounds together and make words. I'm going to say a word very slowly so you can hear each sound. You need to listen carefully and say the sounds. When you say the sounds, it will sound almost like you're singing them. Then we'll put the sounds together and say the word.

Model holding each continuous sound for 2 to 3 seconds without stopping between sounds; say stop sounds quickly. **Hold** up one finger for each phoneme in word, back of hand to students.

My turn. Listen. **/iii/ /nnn/.** Say the sounds. */iii/ /nnn/.*
Again, say the sounds. */iii/ /nnn/.*
Now let's put it together. What word? *In.*

Let's make a bigger word. My turn. Listen. **/fff/ /iii/ /nnn/.**
Say the sounds. */fff/ /iii/ /nnn/.*
Again, say the sounds. */fff/ /iii/ /nnn/.*
Now let's put it together. What word. *Fin.*

Continue the activity with the following words:
shin [shshsh-iii-nnn], win [www-iii-nnn], thin [ththth-iii-nnn].)

Activity 2 Phoneme Segmentation

Elicit responses. **Guide** as needed.

Let's work on breaking words apart by each sound. I'm going to say a word. You'll need to listen closely and tell me the different sounds you hear in the word. I'll show you how to do the first one.

Pause briefly between each sound so students can hear each phoneme as an individual sound. **Model** holding each continuous sound for 2 to 3 seconds. **Say** stop sounds quickly. **Hold** up one finger for each phoneme in word, back of hand to students.

My turn. The word is **shoe.** I can say the sounds in **shoe. /shshsh/ /uuu/.** Those are the sounds in the word **shoe.**

Your turn by yourself. The word is **shoe.** Tell me the sounds you hear in **shoe.** /shshsh/ /uuu/.

Yes. You said the sounds in the word **shoe.**

(Continue the activity with the following words: zoo [zzz-uuu], moo [mmm-uuu].)

Part B: Vocabulary Development

5 minutes

IWB

Teacher Materials:
Vocabulary Acquisition and Use

Student Materials:
Storybook 1

Vocabulary Acquisition and Use

Activity 1 Cumulative Vocabulary Review

Elicit responses to questions. **Guide** as needed.
Directions: Listen and tell me the correct vocabulary word for each question.

What's another word for **funny?** *Amusing.*
What's another word for **small river?** (Idea: *Creek or stream.*)
What's another word for **not afraid to do something dangerous?** *Brave.*
What's another word for **in what place?** *Where.*

Repeat difficult words as needed.

Review vocabulary words in appropriate context in *Storybook 1.*

Activity 2 Vocabulary Acquisition and Use

Display Vocabulary Acquisition and Use. **Have** students work with a neighbor to complete Vocabulary Acquisition and Use.
Today's vocabulary words are _____ and _____ [and _____ and _____].
Vocabulary words: **amusing** and **funny; brave** and **unafraid**
Write the words on the lines provided. Then write the words in the boxes based on whether you think each word is less/smaller or more/larger than the other word. Below the boxes, write why you think word 1 is less/smaller and word 2 is more/larger than word 1.
Repeat for words 3 and 4. **Have** students share what they wrote. **Discuss** examples of how these words might be used.

IWB

Teacher Materials:
Storybook 1

Narrative Story Map

Student Materials:
Storybook 1

Narrative Story Map

Activity 1 Determining Characters—A During-Reading Strategy

Direct students to Story 14, pages 22–24.

Today you're going to reread "The Cowboy and the Cow." This is the first chapter of the cowboy story. So, this chapter tells the beginning of the story. You'll read the story with your partner. When you're finished, talk with your partner about who the main character is. Then we will check on what you decided. We'll decide what happened at the beginning of this story. When you're finished, we'll fill out the first two parts of our Narrative Story Map together.

Monitor students as they read Story 14.

Activity 2 Story Map—An After-Reading Strategy

Model drawing information on Narrative Story Map.

Who do you think are the main characters? (Idea: *The cowboy and the cow.*)

What event happened at the beginning? (Idea: *The cowboy got a cow to ride.*)

I'd like you to fill out two sections of your Narrative Story Map with your partner. When you work with a partner, you have to take turns. Decide who is going to do which part before you begin. Then draw the main characters in the Characters box and a picture of the beginning event in the Beginning box.

Monitor as students fill out maps cooperatively. **Save** Narrative Story Maps for Lesson 16.

Part D: Fluency Building

Conduct after the lesson, using story of the day.

Activity 1 Partner Reading

It's time for partner reading.
Direct students to the story of the day. **Assign** student partners as Partner 1 and Partner 2. **Monitor** partner reading. **Guide** as needed.

10 minutes

IWB

Teacher Materials:
Writing Prompts

My Writing Checklist

Student Materials:
Lined Paper

My Writing Checklist

Activity 1 Write and Use Parts of Speech and Conventions

Time to write using a writing prompt based on the stories we've been reading.

Assign student partners. **Distribute** lined paper to students. **Display** writing prompts and have students choose one to write about or assign a writing prompt of your choice. **Review** parts of speech and punctuation as well as the writing checklist with students. **Tell** students to write one paragraph (minimum of four sentences per paragraph) on their own to answer the writing prompt. **Tell** them to use their writing checklist (first column labeled "Did I use them?") to ensure they include important parts of speech or punctuation in their writing. **Tell** students which parts of speech or punctuation to focus on, if you wish. **Model** what it means to answer a writing prompt and to use the writing checklist during and after the writing process, as needed. **Monitor** and guide students as needed. **Model** what it means to have a neighbor look over his or her neighbor's writing and to complete the writing checklist (second column labeled "Did my neighbor use them?"), as needed. **Have** students share what they wrote as time permits.

Writing Prompt 1	Writing Prompt 2	Writing Prompt 3
What would you do if you found a cow sitting on the road?	What would you do if you went to feed your friend's cat and it began to talk to you?	If you were a dog, would you enjoy taking a bath? Why or why not?

Lesson 16

Materials

Teacher: 1-Narrative Story Map from Lesson 15; *Storybook 1*

Student: Copy of Narrative Story Map from Lesson 15; *Storybook 1*

3 minutes

Part A: Phonemic and Phonological Awareness

Activity 1 Phoneme Blending for One-Syllable Words

Elicit responses. **Guide** as needed.

Let's put some sounds together and make words. I'm going to say a word very slowly so you can hear each sound. You need to listen carefully and say the sounds. When you say the sounds, it will sound almost like you're singing them. Then we'll put the sounds together and say the word.

Model holding each continuous sound for 2 to 3 seconds without stopping between sounds; say stop sounds quickly. **Hold** up one finger for each phoneme in word, back of hand to students.

My turn. Listen. **/ooo/ /p/.** Say the sounds. */ooo/ /p/.*

Again, say the sounds. */ooo/ /p/.*

Now let's put it together. *op.*

Let's make a bigger word. My turn. Listen. **/mmm/ /ooo/ /p/.** Say the sounds. */mmm/ /ooo/ /p/.*

Again, say the sounds. */mmm/ /ooo/ /p/.*

Now let's put it together. What word. *Mop.*

(Continue the activity with the following words:
shop [shshsh-ooo-p], ut [uuu-t], nut [nnn-uuu-t], shut [shshsh-uuu-t].)

Activity 2 Phoneme Segmentation

Pause briefly between each sound. **Elicit** responses. **Guide** as needed.

Let's work on breaking words apart by each sound. I'm going to tell you a word. You'll need to listen closely and tell me the different sounds you hear in the word.

Listen. The word is **she.** What word? *She.*

Your turn. Tell me the sounds you hear in **she.** */shshsh/ /ēēē/.*

Yes, you said the sounds in the word **she.**

(Continue the activity with the following words:
knee [nnn-ēēē], fee [fff-ēēē]. If children need more practice, continue with **me, see,** and **we.**)

5 minutes

Student Materials:
Storybook 1

Activity 1 Learn New Vocabulary Word

Elicit responses to questions. **Guide** as needed.
Today you'll learn a new vocabulary word. **Bank. Bank** means **land beside a small river or lake.** What does **bank** mean? *Land beside a small river or lake.*

Another word for **land beside a small river or lake** is **bank.** What's another word for **land beside a small river or lake?** *Bank.*

If you stand on the **land beside a small river or lake,** you stand on the **bank.**

What's another word for **land beside a small river or lake?** *Bank.*

Discuss if students have ever stood on a bank and what they might do there.

Activity 2 Review Vocabulary Word

Elicit responses to questions.
Stream and **creek** mean the same thing. What do **stream** and **creek** mean? *Small river.*
What's another word for a **small river?** (Idea: *Creek or stream.*)
What's the other word for a **small river?** (Idea: *Creek or stream.*)

Review vocabulary words in appropriate context in *Storybook 1.*

Part C: Comprehension Strategies

12 minutes

Teacher Materials:
Narrative Story Map
from Lesson 15

Storybook 1

Student Materials:
Narrative Story Map
from Lesson 15

Storybook 1

Activity 1 Read with Prosody—A During-Reading Strategy

Elicit response to questions. **Guide** as needed.
Today I'll read the first two chapters of the cowboy story. I'll read the story the right way some of the time by stopping and taking a small breath after each sentence. When I pause after each sentence, it's easier to understand what I read.

But I'll try to trick you sometimes by reading the wrong way. When I read the wrong way, say "STOP." What will you say when I read the story without taking a small breath at the end of each sentence? *Stop.*
Why do we stop and take a small breath after the periods and question marks? *So it is easier to understand.*

Also as I read, you can also think about what happens in the middle of the story so you and your partner can fill in the next part of your Narrative Story Map.

Read Story 14 & 15, pages 22–26, from *Storybook 1*. **Read** sentences with prosody, and then read in monotone voice and disregard punctuation. **Guide** students to say "stop" when story is read the wrong way. **Reread** any section that was read incorrectly.

Remember: it helps you **understand** what you read if you read the text the right way.

Activity 2 Beginning, Middle, End—An After-Reading Strategy

Elicit responses to questions. **Guide** as needed.
The Characters and Beginning sections of our map are already done. We did those yesterday. Now we are going to figure out an event to put in the box for the Middle section.

What is an event that we could put in the middle? (Idea: *The cowboys went to the creek to have a contest.*)

I will draw a creek and some cowboys and horses for the Middle section.

Please fill out the next section of your Narrative Story Map with your partner. When you work with a partner, you have to take turns. Decide who is going to do which part before you begin. Then fill out the Middle section of the Narrative Story Map.

Monitor as students fill out maps cooperatively.

Tell your partner about the characters, beginning, and middle of the story. Use your Narrative Story Map to remind you of the parts.

Guide student to use the Narrative Story Map to help prompt retelling of the story. **Save** Narrative Story Map to finish in Lesson 18.

Part D: Fluency Building

5 minutes

Student Materials:
Storybook 1

Conduct after the lesson, using story of the day.

Activity 1 Partner Reading

It's time for partner reading.
Direct students to the story of the day. **Assign** student partners as Partner 1 and Partner 2. **Monitor** partner reading. **Guide** as needed.

Lesson 17

Materials

Teacher: *Storybook 1,* 6-My Prediction Chart

Student: *Storybook 1,*

3 minutes

Part A: Phonemic and Phonological Awareness

Activity 1 Phoneme Blending for One-Syllable Words

Elicit responses. **Guide** as needed.

Let's put some sounds together and make words. I'm going to say a word very slowly so you can hear each sound. You need to listen carefully and say the sounds. When you say the sounds, it will sound almost like you're singing them. Then we'll put the sounds together and say the word.

Model holding each continuous sound for 2 to 3 seconds without stopping between sounds; say stop sounds quickly. **Hold** up one finger for each phoneme in word, back of hand to students.

My turn. Listen. **/aaa/ /d/.** Say the sounds. */aaa/ /d/.*
Again, say the sounds. */aaa/ /d/.*
Now let's put it together. *Ad.*

Let's make a bigger word. My turn. Listen. **/mmm/ /aaa/ /d/.**
Say the sounds. */mmm/ /aaa/ /d/.*
Again, say the sounds. */mmm/ /aaa/ /d/.*
Now let's put it together. What word. *Mad.*

(Continue the activity with the following words:
sad [sss-aaa-d], ear [ēēē-r], near [nnn-ēēē-r], fear [fff-ēēē-r].)

Activity 2 Phoneme Segmentation

Pause briefly between each sound. **Elicit** responses. **Guide** as needed.
Let's work on breaking words apart by each sound. I'm going to tell you a word. You'll need to listen closely and tell me the different sounds you hear in the word.

Listen. The word is **ray.** What word? *Ray.*
Your turn. Tell me the sounds you hear in **ray.** */rrr/ /āāā/.*
Yes. You said the sounds in the word **ray.**

(Continue the activity with the following words:
they [ththth-āāā], lay [lll-āāā]. If children need more practice, continue with may, say, and way.)

Part B: Vocabulary Development

Activity 1 Learn New Vocabulary Word

Elicit responses to questions. **Guide** as needed.
Today you'll learn a new vocabulary word. **Contest.** A **contest** is a **test to find a winner.** What's a **contest?** *Test to find a winner.*

Another word for a **test to find a winner** is **contest.** What's another word for a **test to find a winner?** *Contest.*

At the fair, James won an eating **test to find a winner.** James won an eating **contest** at the fair.

What's another word for **test to find a winner?** *Contest.*

Discuss examples of contests and what they have in common.

Activity 2 Review Vocabulary Word

Elicit response to questions. **Guide** as needed.
What does **bank** mean? *Land beside a small river or lake.*
What do you call the **land beside a small river or lake?** *Bank.*

Review vocabulary words in appropriate context in *Storybook 1.*

12 minutes

IWB

Teacher Materials:
Storybook 1

My Prediction Chart

Student Materials:
Storybook 1

Part C: Comprehension Strategies

Activity 1 Review of the Story—A Before-Reading Strategy

Elicit responses to questions. **Guide** as needed.
When you get ready to read a new story, it's a good idea to remember everything you know about the story so that the next part makes sense. Let's think about what you know so far about the story.

Tell me the title of yesterday's story. *"The Cowboys Try."*

What kind of story is it? *Narrative story.*

Why do you read narratives? *For fun.*

Who are the main characters in the story? (Idea: *Cowboy and the cow.*)

Who are other characters in the story? (Idea: *Cowboys, horses.*)

What happened in chapter one? (Idea: *The cowboy had to ride a cow because he had no horse.*)

What happened in chapter two? (Idea: *The cowboys had a contest to see if horses or a cow can jump farther.*)

What happened in chapter three? (Idea: *The horses fell in the creek. A cowboy fell in the creek. The cowboy on the cow started to jump.*)

Now you're ready to read the end of the story because you have thought of everything that has happened so far.

Activity 2 Prediction—A Before-Reading Strategy

Guide students to look at title and picture for Story 17, pages 31–33, in *Storybook 1*.

Show My Prediction Chart

Now you'll read the last chapter of the cowboy story to find out the ending. When you read, it might help you understand the story better if you **predict** what might happen in the story. When you make a prediction, you make a good guess about what will happen next. You make a guess from clues in the story. The title or the picture can give you some clues for a guess.

The title of the last chapter of the cowboy story is "The Happy Jumping Cow." Think about the title. Check the picture in the book.

Record the title on My Prediction Chart.

I'll show you what prediction I'd make.

Model think-aloud for making a prediction about outcome of story. **Record** the prediction on My Prediction Chart to discuss in Lesson 18.

Sample Wording for Think-Aloud

The title makes me think that because the cow is happy, the cow wins the contest. The picture shows the cow jumping over the stream, so I am pretty sure my prediction is correct. Do you agree? Do you have a different idea? Why?

Remember that making a prediction about the story you're going to read may help you understand the story better.

Part D: Fluency Building

5 minutes

Student Materials:
Storybook 1

Conduct after the lesson, using story of the day.

Activity 1 Partner Reading

It's time for partner reading.

Direct students to the story of the day. **Assign** student partners as Partner 1 and Partner 2. **Monitor** partner reading. **Guide** as needed.

Lesson 18

Materials

Teacher: 4-Semantic Web; *Storybook 1;* 1-Narrative Story Map from Lessons 15 and 16

Student: Copy of Narrative Story Map from Lessons 15 and 16; *Storybook 1*

3 minutes

Part A: Phonemic and Phonological Awareness

Activity 1 Phoneme Blending for One-Syllable words

Elicit responses. **Guide** as needed.

Let's put some sounds together and make words. I'm going to say a word very slowly so you can hear each sound. You need to listen carefully and say the sounds. When you say the sounds, it will sound almost like you're singing them. Then we'll put the sounds together and say the word.

Model holding each continuous sound for 2 to 3 seconds without stopping between sounds; say stop sounds quickly. **Hold** up one finger for each phoneme in word, back of hand to students.

My turn. Listen. **/iii/ /k/.** Say the sounds. */iii/ /k/.*

Again, say the sounds. */iii/ /k/.*

Now let's put it together. *Ick.*

Let's make a bigger word. My turn. Listen. **/sss/ /iii/ /k/.** Say the sounds. */sss/ /iii/ /k/.*

Again, say the sounds. */sss/ /iii/ /k/.*

Now let's put it together. What word? *Sick.*

(Continue the activity with the following words:
lick [lll-iii-k], et [eee-t], net [nnn-eee-t], vet [vvv-eee-t].)

Activity 2 Phoneme Segmentation

Pause briefly between each sound. **Elicit** responses. **Guide** as needed.

Let's work on breaking words apart by each sound. I'm going to tell you a word. You'll need to listen closely and tell me the different sounds you hear in the word.

Listen. The word is **mow.** What word? *Mow.*

Your turn. Tell me the sounds you hear in **mow.** */mmm/ /ōōō/.*

Yes. You said the sounds in the word **mow.**

(Continue the activity with the following words:
low [lll-ōōō], row rrr-ōōō]. If children need more practice, continue with **so, no,** and **show.**)

5 minutes

IWB

Teacher Materials:
Storybook 1

Semantic Web

Student Materials:
Storybook 1

Activity 1 Learn New Vocabulary Word and Develop Semantic Web

Elicit responses to questions. **Guide** as needed.
Today you'll learn about the word **when. When** means **at what time something happened.** What does **when** mean? *At what time something happened.*

Another word for **at what time something happened** is **when.** What's another word for **at what time something happened?** *When.*

Some words tell us **at what time something happened.** They tell **when. Yesterday** tells **when. 2:00 pm** tells **when. Monday** tells **when. Next week** tells **when.**

What's another word for **at what time something happened?** *When.*

Discuss other words that tell when. **Have** students look for other words that mean <u>when</u> in Story 18. **Show** Semantic Web. **Record** words on Semantic Web.

Activity 2 Review Vocabulary Word

Elicit responses to questions.
What does **contest** mean? *A test to find a winner.*
What word means **a test to find a winner**? *A contest.*

Review vocabulary words in appropriate context in *Storybook 1.*

Part C: Comprehension Strategies

12 minutes

IWB

Teacher Materials:
Storybook 1

Narrative Story Map
from Lessons 15 and 16

Student Materials:
Storybook 1

Narrative Story Map
from Lessons 15 and 16

Activity 1 Review of the Story—An After-Reading Strategy

Elicit responses to questions. **Guide** as needed.
When you have finished a story, it's a good idea to review everything you know about the story to make sure that you can remember it. Let's think about what you know about the story.

Who can tell me the title of yesterday's story? *"The Happy Jumping Cow."*

What kind of story is it? *Narrative.*

Why do you read narratives? (Idea: *For fun.*)

Who are the main characters in the story? (Idea: *Cowboy and the cow.*)

Who are other characters in the story? (Idea: *Cowboys, horses.*)

Tell me what happened at the beginning of the story? (Idea: *The cowboy had no horse so he had to ride a cow.*)

Tell me some events that happened in the middle of the story? (Idea: *The cowboys made fun of the cowboy. They had a jumping contest at the creek. The cowboy on the cow won.*)

What happened at the end of the story? (Idea: *The cow won the contest and was happy. The cowboy was happy. The cowboy kept the cow for many years.*)

Activity 2 Story Map—An After-Reading Strategy

Elicit responses to questions. **Guide** as needed.
It is time to finish the Story Maps we worked on in the last lesson. The only section left to fill out is the End. What happened at the end of the story? (Idea: *The cow won the contest and was happy. The cowboy was happy. The cowboy kept the cow for many years.*)

I will fill out the End section with a picture of the cow winning the contest. I will make smiles on the cow and the cowboy to show they are both happy.

Model drawing the ending of the story in the appropriate box.

It is your turn to draw a picture in the box for the end of the story. Be sure to talk to your partner about what you will each draw before you do it. Then tell your partner the story using the Narrative Story Map to remind you of the parts. Your partner gets to tell you the story when you are finished.

Guide students to finish Narrative Story Map started in Lesson 15. **Guide** students if there is time to retell the story from their copies of Narrative Story Map, which should be complete.

Part D: Fluency Building

5 minutes

Student Materials:
Storybook 1

Conduct after the lesson, using story of the day.

Activity 1 Partner Reading

It's time for partner reading.
Direct students to the story of the day. **Assign** student partners as Partner 1 and Partner 2. **Monitor** partner reading. **Guide** as needed.

Lesson 19

Materials

Teacher: Trade book narrative of teacher choice; *Storybook 1*
Student: *Storybook 1*

3 minutes

Part A: Phonemic and Phonological Awareness

Activity 1 Phoneme Blending for One-Syllable Words

Elicit responses. **Guide** as needed.
Let's put some sounds together and make words. I'm going to say a word very slowly so you can hear each sound. You need to listen carefully and say the sounds. When you say the sounds, it will sound almost like you're singing them. Then we'll put the sounds together and say the word.

Model holding each continuous sound for 2 to 3 seconds without stopping between sounds; say stop sounds quickly. **Hold** up one finger for each phoneme in word, back of hand to students.

My turn. Listen. **/āāā/ /k/.** Say the sounds. */āāā/ /k/.*
Again, say the sounds. */āāā/ /k/.*
Now let's put it together. *Ache.*

Let's make a bigger word. My turn. Listen. **/mmm/ /āāā/ /k/.** Say the sounds. */mmm/ /āāā/ /k/.*
Again, say the sounds. */mmm/ /āāā/ /k/.*
Now let's put it together. What word. *Make.*

(Continue the activity with the following words:
rake [rrr-āāā-k], shake [shshsh-āāā-k], ice [īīī-sss], nice [nnn-īīī-sss], mice [mmm-īīī-sss], rice [rrr-īīī-sss].)

Activity 2 Phoneme Segmentation

Pause briefly between each sound. **Elicit** responses. **Guide** as needed.
Let's work on breaking words apart by each sound. I'm going to say a word. You'll need to listen closely and tell me the different sounds you hear in the word.

Listen. The word is **eat.** What word? *Eat.*
Your turn. Tell me the sounds you hear in **eat.** */ēēē/ /t/.*
Yes. You said the sounds in the word **eat.**

(Continue the activity with the following words:
ear [ēēē-rrr], each ēēē-ch].)

Part B: Vocabulary Development

Activity 1 Learn New Vocabulary Word

Elicit responses to questions. **Guide** as needed.
Today you'll learn a new vocabulary word. **Attempt. Attempt** means **try.**
What does **attempt** mean? *Try.*

Another word for **try** is **attempt.** What's another word for **try?** *Attempt.*

I **try** to run very fast in races. In races I **attempt** to run as fast as I can.

What's another word for **try?** *Attempt.*

Discuss what it means to attempt to do something.

Activity 2 Review Vocabulary Word

What does **when** mean? *Time something happened.*
Words like **Today, last week, 7:00 a.m.,** and **next month** tell **at what time something happened.** What is another way to say **at what time something happened?** *When.*

Review vocabulary words in appropriate context in *Storybook 1.*

Part C: Comprehension Strategies

Activity 1 Set Purpose for Reading—A Before-Reading Strategy

Elicit responses to questions. **Guide** as needed.
Before I read, I think about **what** I'm going to read to help me understand the text I read.

Today I'm going to read a narrative text. What is the title? (Student response.)

What will the story have? *Beginning, middle, end.*

What else will it have? *Characters.*

Why am I reading this narrative? *For fun.*

What do you think the story will be about?
Activate background knowledge by asking questions about what students know about book topic.

Activity 2 Determine Story Elements—A During-Reading Strategy

While I read the story, listen to the story and see if you can figure out the characters, the beginning, the middle, and the end of the story. I'll ask you questions after I read to see if you could figure out all those things.

Read trade book narrative text of choice with prosody. **Encourage** students to listen for story elements while you read.

Activity 3 Identify Story Elements—An After-Reading Strategy

Elicit responses to questions. **Guide** as needed.
Let's see if you can tell me all the parts of the narrative I just read to you.

Who is the main character(s) in the story? (Student response.)

Who are some other characters in the story? (Student response.)

What happened at the beginning of the story? (Student response.)

What happened in the middle of the story? (Student response.)

How did the story end? (Student response.)

Part D: Fluency Building

5 minutes

Student Materials:
Storybook 1

Conduct after the lesson, using story of the day.

Activity 1 Partner Reading

It's time for partner reading.
Direct students to the story of the day. **Assign** student partners as Partner 1 and Partner 2. **Monitor** partner reading. **Guide** as needed.

Lesson 20

Materials

Teacher: *Storybook 1,* 2-Vocabulary Acquisition and Use, 3-My Book Review, 6-My Prediction Chart

Student: *Storybook 1,* Copy of 2-Vocabulary Acquisition and Use and 3-My Book Review

3 minutes

Part A: Phonemic and Phonological Awareness

Activity 1 Phoneme Blending for One-Syllable Words

Elicit responses. **Guide** as needed.

Let's put some sounds together and make words. I'm going to say a word very slowly so you can hear each sound. You need to listen carefully and say the sounds. When you say the sounds, it will sound almost like you're singing them. Then we'll put the sounds together and say the word.

Model holding each continuous sound for 2 to 3 seconds without stopping between sounds; say stop sounds quickly. **Hold** up one finger for each phoneme in word, back of hand to students.

My turn. Listen. **/īīī/ /d/.** Say the sounds. /īī/ /d/.

Again, say the sounds. /īī/ /d/.

Now let's put it together. *ide.*

Let's make a bigger word. My turn. Listen. **/sss/ /īīī/ /d/.** Say the sounds. /sss/ /īī/ /d/.

Again, say the sounds. /sss/ /īī/ /d/.

Now let's put it together. What word. *Side.*

(Continue the activity with the following words:
ride [rrr-īīī-d], wide [www-īīī-d], ine [īīī-nnn], shine [shshsh-īīī-nnn], line [lll-īīī-nnn], fine [fff-īīī-nnn].)

Activity 2 Phoneme Segmentation

Pause briefly between each sound. **Elicit** responses. **Guide** as needed.

Let's work on breaking words apart by each sound. I'm going to say a word. You'll need to listen closely and tell me the different sounds you hear in -the word.

Listen. The word is **ate.** What word? *Ate.*

Your turn. Tell me the sounds you hear in **ate.** /āāā/ /t/.

Yes. You said the sounds in the word **ate.**

(Continue the activity with the following words:
age [āāā-j], ape [āāā-p].)

5 minutes

IWB

Teacher Materials:
Vocabulary Acquisition
and Use

Student Materials:
Storybook 1

Vocabulary Acquisition
and Use

Activity 1 Cumulative Vocabulary Review

Elicit responses to questions. **Guide** as needed.
What's another word for **funny?** *Amusing.*
What's another word for **not afraid to do something dangerous?** *Brave.*
What's another word for **in what place?** *Where.*
What's another word for a **small river?** (Idea: *Creek or stream.*)
What's another word for **land beside a small river or lake?** *Bank.*
What's another word for a **test to find a winner?** *Contest.*
What's another word for **at what time something happened?** *When.*
What's another word for **try?** *Attempt.*

Repeat difficult words as needed.

Review vocabulary words in appropriate context in *Storybook 1*.

Activity 2 Vocabulary Acquisition and Use

Display Vocabulary Acquisition and Use. **Have** students work with a neighbor to complete Vocabulary Acquisition and Use.
Today's vocabulary words are _____ and _____ [and _____ and _____].
Vocabulary words: **attempt** and **try; jump** and **leap**
Write the words on the lines provided. Then write the words in the boxes based on whether you think each word is less/smaller or more/larger than the other word. Below the boxes, write why you think word 1 is less/smaller and word 2 is more/larger than word 1.
Repeat for words 3 and 4. **Have** students share what they wrote. **Discuss** examples of how these words might be used.

12 minutes

IWB

Teacher Materials:
Storybook 1

My Prediction Chart

My Book Review

Student Materials:
Storybook 1

My Book Review

Activity 1 Text-to-Self Connections—A During-Reading Strategy

When you read narratives, it helps you understand the text you're reading better if you connect what you are reading to something you already know about. You make text-to-self connections when you think of an experience you have had that is like the story. I will read "Jill and Her Sister" to you and show you what I mean.

Read Story 19, pages 36–37, with prosody.

Model think-aloud for making text-to-self connections. Make a connection to an actual experience you had.

Remembering an experience you have had might help you understand the story you are reading better.

Activity 2 Text-to-Self Connection—An After-Reading Strategy

Elicit responses to questions. **Discuss** response.
Have you ever tried to do or learn something new? (Student response.)

How is it the same as Jill? (Student response.)
Did she keep trying? (Student response.)

Who gave up? (Student response.)

Do you understand the Jill story better if you think about a time when you tried something new? (Student response.)

Activity 3 Making Predictions—A Before-Reading Strategy

Show My Prediction Chart
When you read stories, it's a good strategy to make predictions about what you're going to read to help you understand the story better. I'm going to show you what I mean.

I'll predict what will happen in the next story by looking at the title, "Jill Tried and Tried." I'll also look at the story and the picture to predict what Jill will do and what her sister will do.

Model think-aloud for prediction from the title and picture.

Record predictions on My Prediction Chart for further discussion in Lesson 21.

Activity 4 Develop Opinions—An After-Reading Strategy

Today we'll found out your opinion or how you feel about the stories you read. You will choose a book to read and then complete the My Book Review form. You'll need to tell if you like or don't like the book and why. You must give a reason for why you like or don't like the book. Finally, you can tell if you would recommend the book to others.

Have students read a narrative or expository trade book of their choice. **Have** students complete My Book Review form when they are finished reading their book. **Model** how to complete the My Book Review form. **Guide** students as needed. **Have** students share their book reviews with the class as time permits.

Part D: Fluency Building

5 minutes

Student Materials:
Storybook 1

Conduct after the lesson, using story of the day.

Activity 1 Partner Reading

It's time for partner reading.

Direct students to the story of the day. **Assign** student partners as Partner 1 and Partner 2. **Monitor** partner reading. **Guide** as needed.

Lesson 21

Materials

Teacher: A version of the story "The Little Red Hen"; 6-My Prediction Chart from Lesson 20; *Storybook 1*

Student: *Storybook 1*

3 minutes

Part A: Phonemic and Phonological Awareness

Activity 1 Phoneme Blending for One-Syllable Words

Elicit responses. **Guide** as needed.
Let's put some sounds together and make words. I'm going to say a word very slowly so you can hear each sound. You'll need to listen carefully and say the sounds. When you say the sounds, it will sound almost like you're singing them. Then we'll put the sounds together and say the word.

Model a short pause between first and second phonemes. **Guide** students to hold continuous sounds for 2 to 3 seconds without stopping between sounds. **Hold** up a finger for each phoneme in word, back of hand to students.
My turn. Listen. **/aaa/ /t/.** Say the sounds. */aaa/ /t/.*
Again, say the sounds. */aaa/ /t/.*
Now let's put it together. What word? *At.*

Let's make a bigger word. My turn. Listen. **/mmm/ /aaa/ /t/.** Say the sounds. */mmm/ /aaa/ /t/.*
Again, say the sounds. */mmm/ /aaa/ /t/.*
Now let's put it together. What word? *Mat.*

Now we're going to make a bigger word that has a quick sound at the beginning. Listen closely. My turn. Listen. **/k/ /aaa/ /t/.** Say the sounds. */k/ /aaa/ /t/.*
Again, say the sounds. */k/ /aaa/ /t/.*
Now let's put it together. What word? *Cat.*

(Continue the activity with the following words:
sat [sss-aaa-t], hat [h-aaa-t], bat [b-aaa-t], pat [p-aaa-t].)

Activity 2 Phoneme Segmentation

Pause briefly between each sound. **Elicit** responses. **Guide** as needed.
Let's work on breaking words apart by each sound. I'm going to tell you a word. You'll need to listen closely and tell me the different sounds you hear in the word.

Listen. The word is **it.** What word? *It.*
Your turn. Tell me the sounds you hear in **it.** */iii/ /t/.*
Yes, you said the sounds in the word **it.**

Listen. My turn. The word is **sit.** What word? *Sit.*
I'll say the sounds in **sit. /sss/ /iii/ /t/.** Your turn. Tell me the sounds you hear in **st.** */sss/ /iii/ /t/.*
Yes, you said the sounds in the word **sit.**

(Continue the activity with the following words:
mit [mmm-iii-t], fit [fff-iii-t], knit [nnn-iii-t].)

Part B: Vocabulary Development

5 minutes

Student Materials:
Storybook 1

Activity 1 Learn New Vocabulary Word

Elicit responses to questions. **Guide** as needed.
Today you'll learn a new vocabulary word. **Moral. Moral** means **lesson learned from a story.** What's a **moral?** *Lesson learned from a story.*

Another word for **lesson learned from a story** is **moral.** What's another word for **lesson learned from a story?** *Moral.*

After we read a story that teaches a lesson on helping others, we say, "The **moral** of the story is to help others."

What's another word for **lesson learned from a story?** *Moral.*

Discuss stories or fables that have a moral. **Read** a fable to illustrate what a moral is.

Activity 2 Review Vocabulary Word

Elicit responses to questions. **Guide** as needed.
What does **when** mean? *At what time something happened.*
Words like **today, last week, January,** and **next month** tell **at what time something happened.** What do they tell? *When.*

Review vocabulary words in appropriate context in *Storybook 1.*

Part C: Comprehension Strategies

8 minutes

IWB

Teacher Materials:
A version of "The Little Red Hen"

My Prediction Chart
Lesson 20

Storybook 1

Student Materials:
Storybook 1

Activity 1 Confirm Predictions—An After-Reading Strategy

Reference Story 20, pages 39–41.

Elicit responses to questions. **Guide** as needed.
In the last lesson, we made some predictions about what Jill and her sister would do. We made the predictions before we read the story. Making predictions helps you understand the story better. Now that you've read the story, let's check and see if the predictions were correct or incorrect.

Show My Prediction Chart

You **confirm predictions** when you check to see if they were correct. What do you do when you check to see if your predictions were correct? *Confirm predictions.*

What was the first prediction? What did Jill do? (Idea: *She tried until she learned to read.*)

Is that what you predicted? (Student response.)

Was your prediction correct? (Student response.)

What was the next prediction? What did her sister do? (Idea: *She learned to cry because that is what she practiced.*)

Is that what you predicted? (Student response.)

Was your prediction correct? (Student response.)

Complete the section on "Was My Prediction Correct?".

Sometimes, we do not predict correctly. That's okay. Just trying to make a prediction will help you understand what you read better.

Activity 2 Prepare for a Text-to-Text Connection—An After-Reading Strategy

Today I will read a story called "The Little Red Hen." Listen carefully to the story, and look at the pictures. I want you to be able to tell me the parts of this narrative after I have read the story.

Read a version of "The Little Red Hen." **Discuss** story as you read. **Ask** questions to engage students during reading (e.g., who, what, when, where, why).

Elicit responses to questions after reading story. **Guide** as needed.

Who is the main character in this story? (Idea: *The red hen.*)

Who are the other characters in this story? (Idea: *Other animals.*) (Depending on the version of the story read.)

What events happened first in the story? (Ideas: *The red hen found some wheat and wanted help to plant the seeds. No one would help.*)

What events happened in the middle of the story? (Ideas: *The red hen harvested the wheat, ground the wheat, and baked the bread. No one would help.*)

How did the story end? (Ideas: *All the animals wanted to eat the bread when it was baked. The little red hen ate the bread herself because no one helped her do the work.*)

Remember this story, because we will talk about it again in the next lesson.

Provide a reading center to display books being read so that students can enjoy them again during free time.

Part D: Fluency Building

5 minutes

Student Materials:
Storybook 1

Conduct after the lesson, using story of the day.

Activity 1 Partner Reading

It's time for partner reading.

Direct students to the story of the day. **Assign** student partners as Partner 1 and Partner 2. **Monitor** partner reading. **Guide** as needed.

Lesson 22

Materials

Teacher: 7-Compare-Contrast Venn Diagram; *Storybook 1*

Student: *Storybook 1*

Part A: Phonemic and Phonological Awareness

3 minutes

Activity 1 Phoneme Blending for One-Syllable Words

Elicit responses. **Guide** as needed.

Let's put some sounds together and make words. I'm going to say a word very slowly so you can hear each sound. You need to listen carefully and say the sounds. When you say the sounds, it will sound almost like you're singing them. Then we'll put the sounds together and say the word.

Model a short pause between first and second phonemes. **Guide** students to hold continuous sounds for 2 to 3 seconds without stopping between sounds. **Hold** up a finger for each phoneme in word, back of hand to students.

My turn. Listen. **/ēēē/ /t/.** Say the sounds. /ēēē/ /t/.

Again, say the sounds. /ēēē/ / /t/.

Now let's put it together. What word? *Eat.*

Let's make a bigger word. My turn. Listen. **/sss/ /ēēē/ /t/.** Say the sounds. /sss/ /ēēē/ /t/.

Again, say the sounds. /sss/ /ēēē/ /t/.

Now let's put it together. What word? *Seat.*

Now we're going to make a bigger word that has a quick sound at the beginning. Listen closely. My turn. Listen. **/b/ /ēēē/ /t/.** Say the sounds. /b/ /ēēē/ /t/.

Again, say the sounds. /b/ /ēēē/ /t/.

Now let's put it together. What word? *Beat.*

(Continue the activity with the following words:
meat [mmm-ēēē-t], heat [h-ēēē-t], cheat [ch-ēēē-t].)

Activity 2 Phoneme Segmentation

Pause briefly between each sound. **Elicit** responses. **Guide** as needed.

Let's work on breaking words apart by each sound. I'm going to say a word. You'll need to listen closely and tell me the different sounds you hear in the word.

Hold up a finger for each phoneme in word, back of hand to students.

Listen. The word is **an.** What word? *An.*

Your turn. Tell me the sounds you hear in **an.** /aaa/ /nnn/.

Yes, you said the sounds in the word **an.**

Listen. My turn. The word is **ran.** What word? *Ran.*
I'll say the sounds in **ran. /rrr/ /aaa/ /nnn/.** Your turn. Tell me the sounds you hear in **ran.** */rrr/ /aaa/ /nnn/.*
Yes, you said the sounds in the word **ran.**

(Continue the activity with the following words:
man [mmm-aaa-nnn], fan [fff-aaa-nnn], than [thththth-aaa-nnn].

Part B: Vocabulary Development

5 minutes

Student Materials:
Storybook 1

Activity 1 Learn New Vocabulary Word

Elicit responses to questions. **Guide** as needed.
Today you'll learn a new vocabulary word. **Dime. Dime** means **a coin worth ten cents.** What does **dime** mean? *A coin worth ten cents.*

Another word for **a coin worth ten cents** is **dime.** What's another word for **a coin worth ten cents?** *Dime.*

When we count **coins worth ten cents,** we count **dimes.** We count by **tens.** Count by tens to 100.

Remember a **dim**e is a **coin worth ten cents.**

What's another word for **a coin worth ten cents?** *Dime.*

Discuss things that might cost a dime.

Activity 2 Review Vocabulary Word

Elicit responses to questions. **Guide** as needed.
What does **moral** mean? *Lesson learned from a story.*
What do you call a **lesson learned from a story?** *Moral.*

Review vocabulary words in appropriate context in *Storybook 1.*

Part C: Comprehension Strategies

12 minutes

IWB

Teacher Materials:
Compare-Contrast Venn Diagram

Storybook 1

Student Materials:
Storybook 1

Activity 1 Text-to-Text Connections—An After-Reading Strategy

Sometimes stories you read remind you of other stories you have read. When you think about other stories you know, you make text-to-text connections. We read "The Little Red Hen" in the last lesson so that we can make a text-to-text connection today.

Retell "The Little Red Hen" and "Jon Bakes a Fish Cake" briefly. **Refer** to Story 21, pages 42 and 43, if needed for "Jon" story.

To make a text-to-text connection, we think about how the stories are the same and how they are different. How do we make text-to-text connections? (Idea: *We think about how stories are the same and how they are different.*)

Today I'll show you how I think the stories "Jon Bakes a Fish Cake" and "The Little Red Hen" are the same.

Show Compare-Contrast Venn Diagram. **Model** think-aloud about what elements of stories are the same. **List** elements that are the same on Compare-Contrast Venn Diagram. **Discuss** other possibilities with students.

Sample Wording for Think-Aloud

Jon wanted to make a fish cake and Little Red Hen wanted to make bread, so both main characters wanted to do a job. Jon asked for help from his mother, sister, and brother, and Little Red Hen asked for help from other animals. So they both asked for help from characters in the story.

No one would help Jon, and no one would help the Little Red Hen, so neither main character got any help from anyone in the story.

Text-to-text connections are great ways to help us understand stories.

Part D: Fluency Building

5 minutes

Student Materials:
Storybook 1

Conduct after the lesson, using story of the day.

Activity 1 Partner Reading

It's time for partner reading.
Direct students to the story of the day. **Assign** student partners as Partner 1 and Partner 2. **Monitor** partner reading. **Guide** as needed.

Lesson 23

Materials

Teacher: 7-Compare-Contrast Venn Diagram from Lesson 22; *Storybook 1*
Student: *Storybook 1*

⏱ **3 minutes**

Part A: Phonemic and Phonological Awareness

Activity 1 Phoneme Blending for One-Syllable words

Elicit responses. **Guide** as needed.
Let's put some sounds together and make words. I'm going to say a word very slowly so you can hear each sound. You need to listen carefully and say the sounds. When you say the sounds, it will sound almost like you're singing them. Then we'll put the sounds together and say the word.

Guide students to hold continuous sounds for 2 to 3 seconds without stopping between sounds. **Model** stop sounds by saying sounds quickly. **Hold** up a finger for each phoneme in word, back of hand to students.
My turn. Listen. **/iii/ /t/.** Say the sounds. /iii/ /t/.
Again, say the sounds. /iii/ /t/.
Now let's put it together. What word? *It.*

Let's make a bigger word. My turn. Listen. **/sss/ /iii/ /t/.** Say the sounds. /sss/ iii// /t/.
Again, say the sounds. /sss/ /iii/ /t/.
Now let's put it together. What word. *Sit.*

Now we're going to make a bigger word that has a quick sound at the beginning. Listen closely. My turn. Listen. **/b/ /iii/ /t/.** Say the sounds. /b/ /iii/ /t/.
Again, say the sounds. /b/ /iii/ /t/.
Now let's put it together. What word? *Bit.*

(Continue the activity with the following words:
hit [h-iii-t], pit [p-iii-t], mitt [mmm-iii-t].)

Activity 2 Phoneme Segmentation

Pause briefly between each sound. **Elicit** responses. **Guide** as needed.
Let's work on breaking words apart by each sound. I'm going to say a word. You'll need to listen closely and tell me the different sounds you hear in the word.

Listen. The word is **eat.** What word? *Eat.*
Your turn. Tell me the sounds you hear in **eat.** /ēēē/ /t/.
Yes, you said the sounds in the word **eat.**

Listen. My turn. The word is **meat.** What word? *Meat.*
I'll say the sounds in **meat. /mmm/ /ēēē/ /t/.** Your turn. Tell me the sounds you hear in **meat.** */mmm/ /ēēē/ /t/.*
Yes. You said the sounds in the word **meat.**

(Continue the activity with the following words:
seat [sss-ēēē-t], feet [fff-ēēē-t], sheet [shshsh-ēēē-t].)

Part B: Vocabulary Development

5 minutes

Student Materials:
Storybook 1

Activity 1 Learn New Vocabulary Word

Elicit responses to questions. **Guide** as needed.
Today you'll learn a new vocabulary word. **Deaf. Deaf** means **not able to hear.** What does **deaf** mean? *Not able to hear.*

Another word for **not able to hear** is **deaf.** What's another word for **not able to hear?** *Deaf.*

Spot the dog is **not able to hear.** He is **deaf.**

What's another word for **not able to hear?** *Deaf.*

Discuss what it means to be deaf and how sign language may be used.

Activity 2 Review Vocabulary Word

Elicit responses to questions. **Guide** as needed.
What's a **dime?** *A coin worth ten cents.*
What's a **coin worth ten cents?** *A dime.*
Count by tens to fifty.

Review vocabulary words in appropriate context in *Storybook 1.*

Part C: Comprehension Strategies

12 minutes

Teacher Materials:
Compare-Contrast Venn Diagram from Lesson 22

Storybook 1

Student Materials:
Storybook 1

Activity 1 Read with Prosody—A During-Reading Strategy

Elicit responses to questions. **Guide** as needed.
Today I'll read the two chapters of the Jon story. I'll read the story the right way some of the time by stopping and taking a small breath after each sentence. When I pause after each sentence, it's easier to understand what I read. But, I'll try to trick you sometimes by reading the wrong way. When I read the wrong way, say "STOP." Why do we take a small breath after the periods and question marks? *So it is easier to understand.*

Remember to read carefully, paying attention to the periods and question marks to help you understand what you read.

Read Stories 21 and 22, page 42–47 from *Storybook 1*.

Read parts with prosody, and then read parts in a monotone voice and disregard the punctuation. **Guide** students to say "stop" when story is read the wrong way. **Reread** parts that were read incorrectly the right way.

Activity 2 Text-to-Text Connections—An After-Reading Strategy

Show Compare-Contrast Venn Diagram started in Lesson 22. **Elicit** responses to questions. **Guide** as needed.

In the last lesson, you learned about making text-to-text connections. What's the name of the stories we were talking about? (Idea: *"The Little Red Hen"* and *"Jon Bakes a Fish Cake."*)

When you make text-to-text connections, you tell how the stories are the same and how they are different. In the last lesson, we made a list of how the stories are the same. Let's go over the list we made.

Review list created in Lesson 22.

Today we will work on how the stories are different. I will show you how I think about each story and what I do to show how the stories are different.

Model think-aloud for how the stories are different. **Write** ideas on Compare-Contrast Venn Diagram. **Discuss** other possibilities with students.

Sample Wording for Think-Aloud

Jon baked a fish cake, **but** the Little Red Hen baked bread. So I will put these ideas on my chart. Jon baked something he did not like, **but** the Little Red Hen baked something she liked. I will put these ideas on my chart.

Remember: when you talk about how two stories are the same and different, you are making text-to-text connections. Making text-to-text connections is important because it helps you understand stories better.

Part D: Fluency Building

5 minutes

Student Materials:
Storybook 1

Conduct after the lesson, using story of the day.

Activity 1 Partner Reading

It's time for partner reading.
Direct students to the story of the day. **Assign** student partners as Partner 1 and Partner 2. **Monitor** partner reading. **Guide** as needed.

Lesson 24

Materials

Teacher: *Storybook 1*

Student: *Storybook 1*

3 minutes

Part A: Phonemic and Phonological Awareness

Activity 1 Phoneme Blending for One-Syllable words

Elicit responses. **Guide** as needed.

Let's put some sounds together and make words. I'm going to say a word very slowly so you can hear each sound. You need to listen carefully and say the sounds. When you say the sounds, it will sound almost like you're singing them. Then we'll put the sounds together and say the word.

Guide students to hold continuous sounds for 2 to 3 seconds without stopping between sounds. **Model** stop sounds by saying sounds quickly. **Hold** up a finger for each phoneme in word, back of hand to students.

My turn. Listen. **/ooo/ /t/.** Say the sounds. */ooo/ /t/.*

Again, say the sounds. */ooo/ /t/.*

Now let's put it together. What word? *ot.*

Let's make a bigger word. My turn. Listen. **/nnn/ /ooo/ /t/.** Say the sounds. */nnn/ /ooo/ /t/.*

Again, say the sounds. */nnn/ /ooo/ /t/.*

Now let's put it together. What word. *Not.*

Now we're going to make a bigger word that has a quick sound at the beginning. Listen closely. My turn. Listen. **/h/ /ooo/ /t/.** Say the sounds. */h/ ooo// /t/.*

Again, say the sounds. */h/ /ooo/ /t/.*

Now let's put it together. What word? *Hot.*

(Continue the activity with the following words:
cot [c-ooo-t], pot [p-ooo-t], lot [lll-ooo-t].)

Activity 2 Phoneme Segmentation

Pause briefly between each sound. **Elicit** responses. **Guide** as needed.

Let's work on breaking words apart by each sound. I'm going to say a word. You'll need to listen closely and tell me the different sounds you hear in the word.

Listen. The word is **at.** What word? *At.*

Your turn. Tell me the sounds you hear in **at.** */aaa/ /t/.*

Yes, you said the sounds in the word **at.**

Listen. My turn. The word is **mat.** What word? *Mat.*

Your turn. Tell me the sounds you hear in **mat.** */mmm/ /aaa/ /t/.*
Yes, you said the sounds in the word **mat.**

(Continue the activity with the following words:
rat [rrr-aaa-t], fat [fff-aaa-t], sat [sss-aaa-t].)

Part B: Vocabulary Development

5 minutes

Student Materials:
Storybook 1

Activity 1 Learn New Vocabulary Word

Elicit responses to questions. **Guide** as needed.
Today you'll learn a new vocabulary word. **Pay. Pay** means **give money.**
What does **pay** mean? *Give money.*

Another word for **give money** is **pay.** What's another word for **give money?**
Pay.

When Ms. Sanchez goes to the store, she will **give money** for oranges. Ms.
Sanchez has to **pay** for the oranges she is buying.

Discuss how much oranges cost.

What's another word for **give money?** *Pay.*

Activity 2 Review Vocabulary Word

Elicit responses to questions. **Guide** as needed.
What does **deaf** mean? *Not able to hear.*
What's another word for **not able to hear?** *Deaf.*

Review vocabulary words in appropriate context in *Storybook 1.*

Part C: Comprehension Strategies

12 minutes

Teacher Materials:
Storybook 1

Student Materials:
Storybook 1

Activity 1 Read with Prosody—A During-Reading Strategy

Direct students to Story 23, pages 48 and 49.

Elicit responses to questions. **Guide** as needed.
In the last lesson, you played the stop game. Today we'll read together the
first part of the "Spot" story. I'll read, and you can read with me. We will
remember to take a breath after each period or question mark. If we make a
mistake, we will reread the sentence.

Monitor students as they read with prosody with you, attending to punctuation marks.
Guide as needed.

When we get to the next page, I will stop reading with you, and you can all read together. If there is a mistake, I will say "Stop," and we will reread the sentence. Reading stories the right way helps us understand the story better.

Monitor students as they read the text without you. **Guide** as needed.

Why is it important to pause between sentences? *To understand the text better.*

Activity 2 Generate Questions—A During-Reading Strategy

Refer to Story 23, pages 48–50.

Elicit responses to questions. **Guide** as needed.
I noticed something interesting in the story about Spot. Right in the middle of the story is this sentence: "Tell Spot what the man said." When you come to that part, you have to stop in the middle of the story and tell the answer.

This is a smart way to help you remember and understand what you read. When you stop in the middle of a story and think about what has happened in the story so far, it helps you understand the story.

Sometimes you have a question. Sometimes you know the answer. Sometimes you have to keep reading to find the answer. Answering questions in the middle of the story is very smart if you want to remember the story. If you want to remember a story, what is a smart thing to do in the middle of the story? (Idea: *Answer a question.*)

Listen to me read the Spot story to you. I will show you how I stop and think and answer when I read the questions in the middle of the story.

Model think-aloud, reading questions in story, and answering.

Why is it important to stop and ask questions or think while I am reading a story? (Idea: *To help understand the story better.*)

Part D: Fluency Building

5 minutes

Student Materials:
Storybook 1

Conduct after the lesson, using story of the day.

Activity 1 Partner Reading

It's time for partner reading.
Direct students to the story of the day. **Assign** student partners as Partner 1 and Partner 2. **Monitor** partner reading. **Guide** as needed.

Lesson 25

Materials

Teacher: *Storybook 1,* 2-Vocabulary Acquisition and Use, Writing Prompts, 5-My Writing Checklist

Student: *Storybook 1,* Copy of 2-Vocabulary Acquisition and Use and 5-My Writing Checklist; Lined Paper

3 minutes

Part A: Phonemic and Phonological Awareness

Activity 1 Phoneme Blending for One-Syllable words

Elicit responses. **Guide** as needed.

Let's put some sounds together and make words. I'm going to say a word very slowly so you can hear each sound. You need to listen carefully and say the sounds. When you say the sounds, it will sound almost like you're singing them. Then we'll put the sounds together and say the word.

Guide students to hold continuous sounds for 2 to 3 seconds without stopping between sounds. **Model** stop sounds by saying sounds quickly. **Hold** up a finger for each phoneme in word, back of hand to students.

My turn. Listen. **/aaa/ /k/.** Say the sounds. */aaa/ /k/.*
Again, say the sounds. */aaa/ /k/.*
Now let's put it together. *ack.*

Let's make a bigger word. My turn. Listen. **/sss/ /aaa/ /k/.** Say the sounds. */sss/ /aaa/ /k/.*
Again, say the sounds. */sss/ /aaa/ /k/.*
Now let's put it together. What word. *Sack.*

Now we're going to make a bigger word that has a quick sound at the beginning. Listen closely. My turn. Listen. **/b/ /aaa/ /k/.** Say the sounds. */b/ aaa/ /k/.*
Again, say the sounds. */b/ /aaa/ /k/.*
Now let's put it together. What word? *Back.*

(Continue the activity with the following words:
tack [t-aaa-k], pack [p-aaa-k], rack [rrr-aaa-k].)

Activity 2 Phoneme Segmentation

Pause briefly between each sound. **Elicit** responses. **Guide** as needed.
Let's work on breaking words apart by each sound. I'm going to say a word. You'll need to listen closely and tell me the different sounds you hear in the word.

Listen. The word is **in.** What word? *In*
Your turn. Tell me the sounds you hear in **in.** */iii/ /nnn/.*
Yes, you said the sounds in the word **in.**

Listen. My turn. The word is **shin.** What word? *Shin*
Your turn. Tell me the sounds you hear in **shin.** */shshsh/ /iii/ /nnn/.*
Yes, you said the sounds in the word **shin.**

(Continue the activity with the following words:
fin [fff-iii-nnn], win [www-iii-nnn], thin [ththth-iii-nnn].)

Part B: Vocabulary Development

5 minutes

IWB

Teacher Materials:
Vocabulary Acquisition and Use

Student Materials:
Storybook 1

Vocabulary Acquisition and Use

Activity 1 Cumulative Vocabulary Review

Elicit responses to questions. **Guide** as needed.
Directions: Listen and tell me the correct vocabulary word for each question.

What's another word for **dime?** *A coin worth ten cents.*
What's another word for **pay?** *Give money.*
What's another word for **deaf?** *Not able to hear.*
What's another word for **moral?** *Lesson learned from a story.*

Repeat difficult words as needed.

Review vocabulary words in appropriate context in *Storybook 1.*

Activity 2 Vocabulary Acquisition and Use

Display Vocabulary Acquisition and Use. **Have** students work with a neighbor to complete Vocabulary Acquisition and Use.
Today's vocabulary words are ____ and ____ [and ____ and ____].
Vocabulary words: **pay** and **give; help** and **assist**
Write the words on the lines provided. Then write the words in the boxes based on whether you think each word is less/smaller or more/larger than the other word. Below the boxes, write why you think word 1 is less/smaller and word 2 is more/larger than word 1.
Repeat for words 3 and 4. **Have** students share what they wrote. **Discuss** examples of how these words might be used.

12 minutes

Teacher Materials:
Storybook 1

Student Materials:
Storybook 1

Activity 1 **Generate Questions—A During-Reading Strategy**

Refer to Story 24, pages 51–53. **Elicit** responses to questions.

Today I noticed that there are questions right in the middle of the story again. Listen to some of the questions. "Did Spot hear well?" "What did she say?" When you come to those parts, you have to stop in the middle of the story and tell the answer. Why do you answer questions in the middle of the story? (Idea: *You think about what happens in the story.*)

This is a smart way to help you remember and understand what you read. When you stop in the middle of a story and think about what has happened in the story so far, it helps you understand the story. Sometimes you have a question. Sometimes you know the answer. Sometimes you have to keep reading to find the answer. Asking and answering questions in the middle of the story is very smart if you want to remember the story. If you want to remember a story, what is a smart thing to do in the middle of the story? (Idea: *Ask and answer questions.*)

Listen to me read "Spot and the Cop" to you and show you how I stop and think and ask questions in the middle of the story.

Model think-aloud, generating questions while reading text. **Model** telling the answers, or reading further to find answer.

Sample Wording for Think-Aloud

"One day Spot went for a walk to the other side of town." I will stop and think and ask a question. I wonder why Spot is going to the other side of town. I will read some more to see if I can find out. "When she got there, she said, 'I can not find my way back home.'" That sentence did not tell me why, so I still do not know why she went across town. But I know she got lost. Now I have a new question. I wonder if she will find her way home. (Read the rest of the story to answer question.) I found out that the cop helped Spot get back home. I found out the answer to my question. To understand narrative text better, it is a smart strategy to stop, think, and ask questions to help me understand what I am reading.

Part D: Fluency Building

Conduct after the lesson, using story of the day.

Activity 1 Partner Reading

It's time for partner reading.

Direct students to the story of the day. **Assign** student partners as Partner 1 and Partner 2. **Monitor** partner reading. **Guide** as needed.

Part E: Writing/Language Arts

IWB

Teacher Materials:
Writing Prompts

My Writing Checklist

Student Materials:
Lined Paper

My Writing Checklist

Activity 1 Write and Use Parts of Speech and Conventions

Time to write using a writing prompt based on the stories we've been reading.

Assign student partners. **Distribute** lined paper to students. **Display** writing prompts and have students choose one to write about or assign a writing prompt of your choice. **Review** parts of speech and punctuation as well as the writing checklist with students. **Tell** students to write one paragraph (minimum of four sentences per paragraph) on their own to answer the writing prompt. **Tell** them to use their writing checklist (first column labeled "Did I use them?") to ensure they include important parts of speech or punctuation in their writing. **Tell** students which parts of speech or punctuation to focus on, if you wish. **Model** what it means to answer a writing prompt and to use the writing checklist during and after the writing process, as needed. **Monitor** and guide students as needed. **Model** what it means to have a neighbor look over his or her neighbor's writing and to complete the writing checklist (second column labeled "Did my neighbor use them?"), as needed. **Have** students share what they wrote as time permits.

Writing Prompt 1	Writing Prompt 2	Writing Prompt 3
If you were a cowboy, what would you rather ride—a cow or a horse? Why?	What would you do if your friend did not want to try something new that you thought was fun?	What is your favorite kind of cake or dessert? Why?

Lesson 26

Materials

Teacher: *Storybook 1*

Student: *Storybook 1*

3 minutes

Part A: Phonemic and Phonological Awareness

Activity 1 Phoneme Blending for One-Syllable Words

Elicit responses. **Guide** as needed.

Let's put some sounds together and make words. I'm going to say a word very slowly so you can hear each sound. You need to listen carefully and say the sounds. When you say the sounds, it will sound almost like you're singing them. Then we'll put the sounds together and say the word.

Guide students to hold continuous sounds for 2 to 3 seconds without stopping between sounds. **Model** stop sounds by saying sounds quickly. **Hold** up a finger for each phoneme in word, back of hand to students.

My turn. Listen. **/ōōō/ /nnn/.** Say the sounds. */ōōō/ /nnn/.*
Again say the sounds. */ōōō/ /nnn/.*
Now let's put it together. *Own.*

Let's make a bigger word. My turn. Listen. **/fff/ /ōōō/ /nnn/.** Say the sounds. */fff/ /ōōō/ /nnn/.*
Again, say the sounds. */fff/ /ōōō/ /nnn/.*
Now let's put it together. What word? *Phone.*

Now we're going to make a bigger word that has a quick sound at the beginning. Listen closely. My turn. Listen. **/b/ /ōōō/ /nnn/.** Say the sounds. */b/ /ōōō/ /nnn/.*
Again, say the sounds. */b/ /ōōō/ /nnn/.*
Now let's put it together. What word? *Bone.*

(Continue the activity with the following word:
cone [c-ōōō-nnn].

Then blend the following:
eep [ēēē-p], sheep [shshsh-ēēē-p], deep [d-ēēē-p], peep [p-ēēē-p].)

Activity 2 Phoneme Segmentation

Pause briefly between each sound. **Elicit** responses. **Guide** as needed.

Let's work on breaking words apart by each sound. I'm going to tell you a word. You'll need to listen closely and tell me the different sounds you hear in the word.

Listen. The word is **add.** What word? *Add.*
Your turn. Tell me the sounds you hear in **add.** */aaa/ /d/.*
Yes, you said the sounds in the word **add.**

Listen. The word is **mad.** What word? *Mad.*
Your turn. Tell me the sounds you hear in **mad.** */mmm/ /aaa/ /d/.*
Yes, you said the sounds in the word **mad.**

(Continue the activity with the following words:
sad [sss-aaa-d], fad [fff-aaa-d], lad [lll-aaa-d].)

Part B: Vocabulary Development

5 minutes

Student Materials:
Storybook 1

Activity 1 Learn New Vocabulary Word

Elicit responses to questions. **Guide** as needed.
Today you'll learn a new vocabulary word. **Curious. Curious** means **want to
know more.** What's **curious** mean? *Want to know more.*

Another way to say **want to know more** is **curious.** What's another way to
say **want to know more?** *Curious.*

If you read every book you can find about sharks, you **want to know more**
about sharks. You are **curious** about sharks.

What's another word for **want to know more?** *Curious.*

Discuss things students are curious about.

Activity 2 Review Vocabulary Word

Elicit responses to questions. **Guide** as needed.
What does **pay** mean? *To give money.*
What does **give money** mean? *Pay.*

Review vocabulary words in appropriate context in *Storybook 1.*

Part C: Comprehension Strategies

12 minutes

Teacher Materials:
Storybook 1

Student Materials:
Storybook 1

Activity 1 Generate Questions—A During-Reading Strategy

Refer to Story 25, pages 54–56.

Elicit responses to questions. **Guide** as needed.

Today I noticed that there are questions right in the middle of the story again. You learned that asking questions when you read is a smart thing to do. Listen to some of the questions. "What did she say?" "What did his brother say?" "What did the boy say?" When you come to those parts, you have to stop in the middle of the story and tell the answer. That helps you understand the story better.

Sometimes you have a question. If you have a question, you should stop, think, reread, and see if you can figure out the answer. What should you do if you have a question while reading? (Idea: *Stop, think, reread and try to figure out the answer.*)

Sometimes you have to keep reading to find the answer. You might have a question that the story has not answered yet. Then you keep on reading to try and find the answer.

Asking and answering questions in the middle of the story is very smart. If you want to remember a story, what is a smart thing to do in the middle of the story? *Ask and answer questions.*

Listen to me read "The Boy Asked Why" to you and show you how I stop and think and ask questions in the middle of the story.

Model think-aloud emphasizing questions in the text and answering them before reading further.

Sample Wording for Think-Aloud

"A boy named Don liked to ask why." I wonder why he likes to ask why. Oh, I bet he is curious. I will read on to find out. "His mother told him to stay in the yard." That part did not tell me if he is curious. I will read on to find out. "He asked 'Why?'" That sentence says he wants to know why. Curious people always want to ask why. So I think he is curious.

To understand narrative text better, it is smart to stop, think, and ask and answer questions so I make sure I understand what I am reading.

Provide a reading center to display books being read so that students can enjoy them again during free time.

Part D: Fluency Building

5 minutes

Student Materials:
Storybook 1

Conduct after the lesson, using story of the day.

Activity 1 Partner Reading

It's time for partner reading.
Direct students to the story of the day. **Assign** student partners as Partner 1 and Partner 2. **Monitor** partner reading. **Guide** as needed.

Lesson 27

Materials

Teacher: *Storybook 1*

Student: *Storybook 1*

3 minutes

Part A: Phonemic and Phonological Awareness

Activity 1 Phoneme Blending for One-Syllable Words

Elicit responses. **Guide** as needed.

Let's put some sounds together and make words. I'm going to say a word very slowly so you can hear each sound. You'll need to listen carefully and say the sounds. Then we'll put the sounds together and say the word.

Guide students to hold continuous sounds for 2 to 3 seconds without stopping between sounds. **Model** stop sounds by saying sounds quickly. **Hold** up a finger for each phoneme in word, back of hand to students.

My turn. Listen. **/uuu/ /nnn/.** Say the sounds. */uuu/ /nnn/.*

Again, say the sounds. */uuu/ /nnn/.*

Now let's put it together. *un.*

Let's make a bigger word. My turn. Listen. **/sss/ /uuu/ /nnn/.** Say the sounds. */sss/ /uuu/ /nnn/.*

Again, say the sounds. */sss/ /uuu/ /nnn/.*

Now let's put it together. What word. *Sun.*

(Continue the activity with the following words:
bun [b-uuu-nnn], ton [t-uuu-nnn].

Then blend the following:
ig [iii-g], wig [www-iii-g], pig [p-iii-g], jig [j-iii-g].)

Activity 2 Phoneme Segmentation

Pause briefly between each sound. **Elicit** responses. **Guide** as needed.

Let's work on breaking words apart by each sound. I'm going say a word. Listen closely, and tell me the different sounds you hear in the word.

Listen. Say **ip.** *ip.*

Your turn. Tell me the sounds you hear in **ip.** */iii/ /p/.*

Yes, you said the sounds in **ip.**

Listen. The word is **sip.** What word? *Sip.*

Your turn. Tell me the sounds you hear in **sip.** */sss/ /iii/ /p/.*

Yes, you said the sounds in the word **sip.**

(Continue the activity with the following words:
lip [lll-iii-p], zip [zzz-iii-p], ship [shshsh-iii-p].)

Student Materials:
Storybook 1

Part B: Vocabulary Development

Activity 1 New Vocabulary Word

Elicit responses to questions. **Guide** as needed.
Today you'll learn a new vocabulary word. **Mope. Mope** means **act sad.**
What does **mope** mean? *Act sad.*

Another way to say **act sad** is **mope.** What's another way to say **act sad?**
Mope.

When Jennifer hangs her head and **acts sad,** her mom says, "Don't **mope.**"
Show me how you would look if you **mope.**

Observe students. **Guide** as needed.

What's another word for **act sad?** *Mope.*

Discuss times when students might mope.

Activity 2 Review Vocabulary Word

Elicit responses to questions. **Guide** as needed.
What does **curious** mean? *Want to know more.*
What's another word for **want to know more?** *Curious.*

Review vocabulary words in appropriate context in *Storybook 1.*

Part C: Comprehension Strategies

12 minutes

Teacher Materials:
Storybook 1

Student Materials:
Storybook 1

Activity 1 Text-to-Self Connections—An After-Reading Strategy

Refer to Stories 25 and 26, pages 54–59.

When you read narratives, it helps you understand the text you're reading better if you connect what you are reading to something you already know. I will read the Don story and then show you how I connect that story to my own experience.

Read both stories quickly, with prosody, to review the story with the students.

Model think-aloud for making text-to-self connections.

Sample Wording for Think-Aloud

When I read the story of Don, it reminded me of when I painted my bedroom. It was fun to paint because it made my room pretty. But I remember that I got paint all over the place and it was not easy to clean it up. I had to wash my hands and elbows. I had to scrub places where I spilled. After reading the Don story, I think he had fun at first while he painted his bike. But then he started to paint things he should not paint. I think he will have a big mess to clean up and it will not be easy. Does the Don story make you think of any experience you have had? Have you ever gotten your brother or sister in trouble? Have you ever been in trouble with your mom?

Remember: when you connect something that has happened to you to something that happens in the story, you are making text-to-self connections. It is a good way to help you understand what you read.

Part D: Fluency Building

5 minutes

Student Materials:
Storybook 1

Conduct after the lesson, using story of the day.

Activity 1 Partner Reading

It's time for partner reading.

Direct students to the story of the day. **Assign** student partners as Partner 1 and Partner 2. **Monitor** partner reading. **Guide** as needed.

Materials

Teacher: 1-Narrative Story Map; *Storybook 1*

Student: Copy of 1-Narrative Story Map; *Storybook 1*

---

3 minutes

Part A: Phonemic and Phonological Awareness

Activity 1 Phoneme Blending for One-Syllable words

Elicit responses. **Guide** as needed.

I'm going to say a word very slowly so you can hear each sound. You need to listen carefully and say the sounds. Then we'll put the sounds together and say the word.

Guide students to hold continuous sounds for 2 to 3 seconds without stopping between sounds. **Model** stop sounds by saying sounds quickly. **Hold** up a finger for each phoneme in word, back of hand to students.

My turn. Listen. **/uuu/ /g/.** Say the sounds. */uuu/ /g/.*

Again, say the sounds. */uuu/ /g/.*

Now let's put it together. *ug.*

Let's make a bigger word. My turn. Listen. **/b/ /uuu/ /g/.** Say the sounds. */b/ /uuu/ /g/.*

Again, say the sounds. */b/ /uuu/ /g/.*

Now let's put it together. What word? *Bug.*

(Continue the activity with the following words:
rug [rrr-uuu-g], hug [h-uuu-g].

Then blend the following:
op [ooo-p], chop [ch-ooo-p], mop [mmm- ooo-p], hop [h-ooo-p].)

Activity 2 Phoneme Segmentation

Pause briefly between each sound. **Elicit** responses. **Guide** as needed.

Let's work on breaking words apart by each sound. I'm going to say a word. Listen closely, and tell me the different sounds you hear in the word.

Listen. Say **ine.** *ine.*

Your turn. Tell me the sounds you hear in **ine.** */īī/ /nnn/.*

Yes, you said the sounds in **ine.**

Listen. The word is **line.** What word? *Line.*

Your turn. Tell me the sounds you hear in **line.** */lll/ /īī/ /nnn/.*

Yes, you said the sounds in the word **line.**

(Continue the activity with the following words:
shine [shshsh-īīī-nnn], vine [vvv-īīī-nnn], mine [mmm-īīī-nnn].)

Part B: Vocabulary Development

Activity 1 Learn New Vocabulary Word

Elicit responses to questions. **Guide** as needed.
Today you'll learn a new vocabulary word. **Collect. Collect** means **save things that are special.** What does **collect** mean? *Save things that are special.*

Another word for **save things that are special** is **collect.** What's another word for **save things that are special?** *Collect.*

Some kids like to **save things that are special** such as baseball cards. They **collect** baseball cards.

What's another word for save things does **collect** mean? *Save things that are special.*

Discuss examples of things students like to collect.

Activity 2 Review Vocabulary Word

Elicit responses to questions.
What does **mope** mean? *Act sad.*
What's another word for **act sad?** *Mope.*

Review vocabulary words in appropriate context in *Storybook 1.*

12 minutes

IWB

Teacher Materials:
Narrative Story Map

Storybook 1

Student Materials:
Narrative Story Map

Storybook 1

Part C: Comprehension Strategies

Activity 1 Story Map—An After-Reading Strategy

Refer to Story 24, pages 51–53.

Show visual of Narrative Story Map. **Elicit** responses to questions. **Guide** as needed.
You have read "Spot Helps the Cop." Now it is time to fill in a Narrative Story Map with the boxes for Characters, Beginning, Middle, and End.

Who is the main character in this story? *Spot.*

Who are the other characters in this story? (Idea: *The cop and the robbers.*)

Draw quick sketches as questions are answered.
I will draw a picture on my Narrative Story Map of Spot because she is the main character.

What events happened at the beginning? (Idea: *Robbers were taking money from a store.*)

I will draw that in the box for the beginning.

What events happened in the middle? (Idea: *The cop came but could not stop them because they had a loud horn that made his ears hurt.*)

I will draw that in the box for the middle.

What events happened at the end? (Idea: *Spot bit the robbers so the cop could catch them.*)

I will draw that in the box for the end.

Now it's your turn to draw. Work with a partner today to make a story map of "Spot Helps the Cop," pages 60–62. Draw quick sketches in each box to help you remember how to retell the story. Decide with your partner who will draw which part. Then work quickly to finish.

Monitor students as they complete Narrative Story Map. **Assist** students as needed. **Guide** students to retell the story, referencing Narrative Story Map, if there is time.

Part D: Fluency Building

5 minutes

Student Materials:
Storybook 1

Conduct after the lesson, using story of the day.

Activity 1 Partner Reading

It's time for partner reading.
Direct students to the story of the day. **Assign** student partners as Partner 1 and Partner 2. **Monitor** partner reading. **Guide** as needed.

Lesson 29

Materials

Teacher: *Storybook 1;* 7-Compare-Contrast Venn Diagram
Student: *Storybook 1*

---

3 minutes

Part A: Phonemic and Phonological Awareness

Activity 1 Phoneme Blending for One-Syllable Words

Elicit responses. **Guide** as needed.

Let's put some sounds together and make words. I'm going to say a word very slowly so you can hear each sound. You need to listen carefully and say the sounds. Then we'll put the sounds together and say the word.

Guide students to hold continuous sounds for 2 to 3 seconds without stopping between sounds. **Model** stop sounds by saying sounds quickly. **Hold** up a finger for each phoneme in word, back of hand to students.

Listen. **/āāā/ /nnn/.** Say the sounds. */āāā/ /nnn/.*
Again, say the sounds. */āāā/ /nnn/.*
Now let's put it together. *ain.*

Let's make a bigger word. My turn. Listen. **/rrr/ /āāā/ /nnn/.** Say the sounds. */rrr/ /āāā/ /nnn/.*
Again, say the sounds. */rrr/ /āāā/ /nnn/.*
Now let's put it together. What word? *Rain.*

(Continue the activity with the following words:
pain [p-āāā-nnn], cane [c-āāā-nnn].

Then blend the following:
ive [īīī-vvv], dive [d-īīī-vvv], hive [h- īīī-vvv], five [fff-īīī-vvv].)

Activity 2 Phoneme Segmentation

Pause briefly between each sound. **Elicit** responses. **Guide** as needed.

Let's work on breaking words apart by each sound. I'm going to say a word. You'll need to listen closely and tell me the different sounds you hear in the word.

Listen. Say **ock.** *ock.*
Your turn. Tell me the sounds you hear in **ock.** */ooo/ /k/.*
Yes, you said the sounds in **ock.**

Listen. The word is **sock.** What word? *Sock.* Your turn. Tell me the sounds you hear in **sock.** */sss/ /ooo/ /k/.*
Yes, you said the sounds in the word **sock.**

(Continue the activity with the following words:
lock [lll-ooo-k], rock [rrr-ooo-k], shock [shshsh-ooo-k].)

Part B: Vocabulary Development

Activity 1 Learn New Vocabulary Word

Elicit responses to questions. **Guide** as needed.
Today you'll learn a new vocabulary word. **Purchase. Purchase** means **buy.**
What does **purchase** mean? *Buy.*

Another word for **buy** is **purchase.** What's another word for **buy?** *Purchase.*

I want to **buy** a new car. I want to **purchase** a new car.

What's another word for **buy?** *Purchase.*

Discuss examples of things students like to purchase.

Activity 2 Review Vocabulary Word

Elicit responses to questions.
What does **collect** mean? *Save things that are special.*
What's another word for **save things that are special?** *Collect.*

Review vocabulary words in appropriate context in *Storybook 1.*

Part C: Comprehension Strategies

12 minutes

IWB

Teacher Materials:
Storybook 1

Compare-Contrast Venn
Diagram

Student Materials:
Storybook 1

Activity 1 Text-to-Text Connection—An After-Reading Strategy

Make a text-to-text connection with the Jill stories in Lessons 19 and 20, pages 36–41.

Elicit responses to questions. **Guide** as needed.
Sometimes stories you read remind you of other stories you have read. When you think about other stories you know, you make text-to-text connections. Making text-to-text connections can help you understand a story better.
Story 28 reminds me of another story in your *Storybook 1.*
Can anyone think of a story you have read that reminds you of "Flying is Fun" on page 63? (Idea: *The Jill stories.*)

To make a text-to-text connection, you think about how the stories are the same and how they are different. How do you make text-to-text connections? (Idea: *You think about how stories are the same and different.*)

Show Compare-Contrast Venn Diagram.
Let's see if we can make a text-to-text connection between "Jill and Her Sister" and "Flying is Fun."

Model think-aloud for how stories are the same and different. **Record** responses on Compare-Contrast Venn Diagram. **Elicit** responses to questions. **Guide** as needed.

Sample Wording for Think-Aloud

First let's think of ways the stories are the same.
Jill's sister will not try to do anything, and the little bird will not try to fly.
Jill's sister always cries, and the little bird cries. Jill tries to get her sister to do things, and the little bird's sisters try to get him to fly. Jill was happy she learned to read, and the little bird was happy he learned to fly.

Now let's try to think of ways the stories are different.
Jill's sister never learns to do anything, **but** the little bird does stop crying and he learns to fly. Jill has one sister, **but** the bird has six sisters. Jill learned to do lots of things, **but** the little bird learned only one thing. That is how I think about how the two stories are the same and different.

When you tell how stories are the same and different, you are making text-to-text connections.

Why do we make text-to-text connections? *To understand stories better.*

Part D: Fluency Building

5 minutes

Student Materials:
Storybook 1

Conduct after the lesson, using story of the day.

Activity 1   Partner Reading

It's time for partner reading.
Direct students to the story of the day. **Assign** student partners as Partner 1 and Partner 2. **Monitor** partner reading. **Guide** as needed.

Materials

Teacher: *Storybook 1,* 2-Vocabulary Acquisition and Use, 3-My Book Review,

Student: *Storybook 1,* Copy of 2-Vocabulary Acquisition and Use and 3-My Book Review

⏱ **3 minutes**

Part A: Phonemic and Phonological Awareness

Activity 1 Phoneme Blending for One-Syllable Words

Elicit responses. **Guide** as needed.

Let's put some sounds together and make words. I'm going to say a word very slowly so you can hear each sound. You need to listen carefully and say the sounds. Then we'll put the sounds together and say the word.

Guide students to hold continuous sounds for 2 to 3 seconds without stopping between sounds. **Model** stop sounds by saying sounds quickly. **Hold** up a finger for each phoneme in word, back of hand to students.

My turn. Listen. **/ōōō/ /zzz/.** Say the sounds. */ōōō/ /zzz/.*

Again, say the sounds. */ōōō/ /zzz/.*

Now let's put it together. *ose.*

Let's make a bigger word. My turn. Listen. **/h/ /ōōō/ /zzz/.** Say the sounds. */h/ /ōōō/ /zzz/.*

Again, say the sounds. */h/ /ōōō /zzz/.*

Now let's put it together. What word? *Hose.*

(Continue the activity with the following words:
rose [rrr-ōōō-zzz], those [thththā-ōōō-zzz].

Then blend the following:
ed [eee-d], bed [b-eee-d], red [rrr-eee-d], shed [shshsh-eee-d].)

Activity 2 Phoneme Segmentation

Pause briefly between each sound. **Elicit** responses. **Guide** as needed.

Let's work on breaking words apart by each sound. I'm going to say a word. You'll need to listen closely and tell me the different sounds you hear in the word.

Listen. Say **ight.** *ight.*

Your turn. Tell me the sounds you hear in **ight.** */īīī/ /t/.*

Yes, you said the sounds in **ight.**

Listen. The word is **right.** What word? *Right.*

Your turn. Tell me the sounds you hear in **right.** */rrr/ /īīī /t/.*

Yes, you said the sounds in the word **right.**

(Continue the activity with the following words:
night [nnn-īīī-t], light [lll-īīī-t], fight [fff-īīī-t].)

Part B: Vocabulary Development

IWB

Teacher Materials:
Vocabulary Acquisition
and Use

Student Materials:
Storybook 1

Vocabulary Acquisition
and Use

Activity 1 Cumulative Vocabulary Review

Elicit responses to questions. **Guide** as needed.
Directions: Listen and tell me the correct vocabulary word for each question.

What's another word for **act sad?** *Mope.*
What's another word for **want to know more?** *Curious.*
What's another word for **did not?** *Didn't.*
What's another word for **buy?** *Purchase.*
What's another word for **a coin worth ten cents?** *Dime.*
What's another word for **give money?** *Pay.*
What's another word for **not able to hear?** *Deaf.*
What's another word for **lesson learned from a story?** *Moral.*

Repeat difficult words as needed.

Review vocabulary words in appropriate context in *Storybook 1.*

Activity 2 Vocabulary Acquisition and Use

Display Vocabulary Acquisition and Use. **Have** students work with a neighbor to complete Vocabulary Acquisition and Use.
Today's vocabulary words are _____ and _____ [and _____ and _____].
Vocabulary words: **mope** and **pout; purchase** and **buy**
Write the words on the lines provided. Then write the words in the boxes based on whether you think each word is less/smaller or more/larger than the other word. Below the boxes, write why you think word 1 is less/smaller and word 2 is more/larger than word 1.
Repeat for words 3 and 4. **Have** students share what they wrote. **Discuss** examples of how these words might be used.

Part C: Comprehension Strategies

12 minutes

Teacher Materials:
Storybook 1

My Book Review

Student Materials:
Storybook 1

My Book Review

Activity 1 Read with Prosody—A During-Reading Strategy.

Direct student to Story 29 in *Storybook 1.*

Today you will read "the Farmer and His Buttons." Story 29, pages 66 and 67, with a partner. Your partner will listen to you read. Your partner will say "STOP" when you forget to take a small breath at the periods and question marks. Then you can go back and fix it.

Then you will trade places, and you will say "STOP" to your partner if he or she forgets to take a breath. Remind each other to fix up your reading when you forget to take a breath between sentences.

Monitor students as they read with prosody, attending to punctuation marks. **Elicit** responses to questions. **Guide** as needed.

Why is it important to pause between sentences? *To understand the text better.*

Activity 2 Develop Opinions—An After-Reading Strategy

Today we'll found out your opinion or how you feel about the stories you read. You will choose a book to read and then complete the My Book Review form. You'll need to tell if you like or don't like the book and why. You must give a reason for why you like or don't like the book. Finally, you can tell if you would recommend the book to others.

Have students read a narrative or expository trade book of their choice. **Have** students complete My Book Review form when they are finished reading their book. **Model** how to complete the My Book Review form. **Guide** students as needed. **Have** students share their book reviews with the class as time permits.

Part D: Fluency Building

5 minutes

Student Materials:
Storybook 1

Conduct after the lesson, using story of the day.

Activity 1 Partner Reading

It's time for partner reading.

Direct students to the story of the day. **Assign** student partners as Partner 1 and Partner 2. **Monitor** partner reading. **Guide** as needed.

Lesson 31

Materials

Teacher: *Storybook 1;* 8-Phonemic Awareness; 3 manipulatives such as blocks, discs, chips, counters (if not using IWB), 6-My Prediction Chart

Student: *Storybook 1;* copy of 8-Phonemic Awareness ; 3 manipulatives such as blocks, discs, chips, counters

Part A: Phonemic and Phonological Awareness

3 minutes

IWB

Teacher Materials:
Phonemic Awareness

3 manipulatives such as blocks, discs, chips, counters

Student Materials:
Phonemic Awareness

3 manipulatives such as blocks, discs, chips, counters

Activity 1 Phoneme Blending for One-Syllable Words

Elicit responses. **Guide** as needed.
Let's put some sounds together and make words. I'm going to say a word very slowly so you can hear each sound. You'll need to listen carefully and say the sounds. Then we'll put the sounds together and say the word.

My turn. Listen. **/mmm/ /āāā/ /k/.**
Say the sounds. */mmm/ /āāā/ /k/.*
Again, say the sounds. */mmm/ /āāā/ /k/.*
Let's put it together. What word? *Make.*

My turn. Listen. **/mmm/ /aaa/ /p/.**
Say the sounds. */mmm/ /aaa/ /p/.*
Again, say the sounds. */mmm/ /aaa/ /p/.*
Let's put it together. What word? *Map.*

(Continue the activity with the following words:
meal [mmm-ēēē-lll], met [mmm-eee-t], mice [mmm-īīī-sss], mitt [mmm-iii-t], moon [mmm-oooooo-nnn], mop [mmm-ooo-p], moth [mmm-ooo-ththth], mud [mmm-uuu-d].)

Activity 2 Phoneme Segmentation

Show 8-Phonemic Awareness. **Elicit** responses. **Guide** as needed.
You've done such a great job breaking words apart by each sound. Today we're going to use chips to show how many sounds there are in a word. For each sound in a word, we'll push one chip up to the arrow on the page. I'll show you how to do the first one.

Model use of the chips by moving the chips to the arrow for each word and then back to the bottom when finished.
Listen. I can say a word and move a chip for each sound in the word. **At. /aaa/ /t/. At.** Say the sounds in **at** with me, and move a chip for each sound. */aaa/ /t/.*

Now bring your finger back to the dot of the arrow. Let's slide our fingers under the chips and say the word. *At.* Let's move our chips back to the bottom so you can try it by yourselves. Say the sounds you hear in **at,** and move a chip for each sound. */aaa/ /t/.*

Move your finger back to the dot. What word? *At.*
Great job. Move your chips back and let's try another one.

(Continue the activity with the following words:
mat, sat.)

Part B: Vocabulary Development

5 minutes

Student Materials:
Storybook 1

Activity 1 Learn New Vocabulary Word

Elicit responses to questions. **Guide** as needed.
Today you'll learn a new vocabulary word. **Wish. Wish** means **want.** What does **wish** mean? *Want.*

Another word for **want** is **wish.** What's another word for **want?** *Wish.*

When you see a cool toy at the store, you might **want** the toy. You **wish for** the toy.

What's another word for **want?** *Wish.*

Discuss things that students want.

Activity 2 Review Vocabulary Word

Elicit responses to questions. **Guide** as needed.
What does **collect** mean? *Save things that are special.*

What's another word for **save things that are special?** *Collect.*

Review vocabulary words in appropriate context in *Storybook 1.*

Part C: Comprehension Strategies

12 minutes

IWB

Teacher Materials:
My Prediction Chart

Storybook 1

Student Materials:
Storybook 1

Activity 1 Read With Prosody (Questions)—A During-Reading Strategy

Elicit responses to questions. **Guide** as needed.
It is important to read text the right way so that you can understand what you are reading. Let's review the right way to read questions. When you read questions, your voice goes up a little at the end of the sentence. Listen to me read a question from the story. "What did the farmer like?" Say it with me. "What did the farmer like?"

What does your voice do when you read a question? *Go up.*

Your turn to read some questions the right way. Look at Story 30, page 69, and read the first three questions the right way to your partner. Then your partner will read the questions to you. Remember to stop and reread the question if you forget to make your voice go up.

Monitor students as they practice reading three questions from *Storybook 1*, Story 30, page 69.

Activity 2 Prediction—A Before-Reading Strategy

Direct students to Story 31, pages 72–74.

Show My Prediction Chart. **Elicit** responses to questions. **Guide** as needed.

Today you're going to read a story called "Spot Takes a Trip." When you read stories, you can understand the story better if you think before you read about what you are going to read. When you make a good guess about what you'll read in the story, it's called making a prediction. You make predictions based on clues. You get the clues from the title and from the pictures. Let's look at the story you're going to read and make some predictions about what will happen in the story.

Do you predict that this story might be a narrative? *Yes.*

Why do you think so? (Idea: *It looks like it might be fun to read.*)

What will the story be about? (Idea: *Spot will take a trip.*)

What clue gave you that idea? (Idea: *The title.*)

What do you think might happen in the story? (Idea: *A lady will tell Spot how to get somewhere.*)

What clue made you think that? (Idea: *The picture shows a lady pointing down the road and Spot in the car.*)

Do you have any more predictions? (Student response.)

What clue made you think that? (Student response.)

Remember: making predictions helps us better understand the text we read.

Record some of the predictions that students make for follow-up discussion in Lesson 32.

Provide a reading center to display books being read so that students can enjoy them again during free time.

Part D: Fluency Building

5 minutes

Student Materials:
Storybook 1

Conduct after the lesson, using story of the day.

Activity 1 Partner Reading

It's time for partner reading.
Direct students to the story of the day. **Assign** student partners as Partner 1 and Partner 2. **Monitor** partner reading. **Guide** as needed.

Lesson 32

Materials

Teacher: *Storybook 1*; 2-My Prediction Chart from Lesson 31; 8-Phonemic Awareness; 3 manipulatives such as blocks, discs, chips, counters (if not using IWB)

Student: *Storybook 1*; copy of 8-Phonemic Awareness; 3 manipulatives such as blocks, discs, chips, counters

---

Part A: Phonemic and Phonological Awareness

3 minutes

IWB

Teacher Materials:
Phonemic Awareness

3 manipulatives such as blocks, discs, chips, counters

Student Materials:
Phonemic Awareness

3 manipulatives such as blocks, discs, chips, counters

Activity 1 Phoneme Blending for One-Syllable Words

Elicit responses. **Guide** as needed.
Let's put some sounds together and make words. I'm going to say a word very slowly so you can hear each sound. You need to listen carefully and say the sounds. Then we'll put the sounds together and say the word.

My turn. Listen. **/sss/ /āāā/ /fff/.**
Say the sounds. */sss/ /āāā/ /fff/.*
Again, say the sounds. */sss/ /āāā/ /fff/.*
Let's put it together. What word? *Safe.*

My turn. Listen. **/sss/ /aaa/ /t/.**
Say the sounds. */sss/ /aaa/ /t/.*
Again, say the sounds. */sss/ /aaa/ /t/.*
Let's put it together. What word? *Sat.*

(Continue the activity with the following words:
seed [sss-ēēē-d], set [sss-eee-t], side [sss-īīī-d], sick [sss-iii-k], soon [sss-üüü-nnn], soap [sss-ōōō-p], sod [sss-ooo-d], sun [sss-uuu-nnn].)

Activity 2 Phoneme Segmentation

Show 8-Phonemic Awareness. **Elicit** responses. **Guide** as needed.
You've done such a great job breaking words apart by each sound. Today we're going to use chips to show how many sounds there are in a word. For each sound in a word, we'll push one chip up to the arrow on the page. I'll show you how to do the first one.

Model use of the chips by moving the chips to the arrow for each word and then back to the bottom when finished.
Listen. I can say a word and move a chip for each sound in the word. **At.** **/aaa/ /t/. At.** Say the sounds in **at** with me, and move a chip for each sound. */aaa/ /t/.*

Now bring your finger back to the dot of the arrow. Let's slide our fingers under the chips and say the word. *At.* Let's move our chips back to the bottom so you can try it by yourselves. Say the sounds you hear in **at,** and move a chip for each sound. */aaa/ /t/.*

Move your finger back to the dot. What word? *At.*
Great job. Now move your chips back to the bottom, and let's try another one.

(Continue the activity with the following words: rat, fat.)

Part B: Vocabulary Development

5 minutes

Student Materials:
Storybook 1

Activity 1 Learn New Vocabulary Word

Elicit responses to questions. **Guide** as needed.
Today you'll learn a new vocabulary word. **Mole.** A **mole** is **an animal that lives underground.** What's a **mole?** *An animal that lives underground.*

Another word for **an animal that lives underground** is **mole.** What's another word for **an animal that lives underground?** *Mole.*

An animal that lives underground, digs tunnels, and pops up in your yard is a **mole.**

What's another word for **an animal that lives underground?** *Mole.*

Discuss moles and other animals that live underground.

Activity 2 Review Vocabulary Word

Elicit responses to questions. **Guide** as needed.
What does **wish** mean? *Want.*
What's another word for **want?** *Wish.*

Review vocabulary words in appropriate context in *Storybook 1.*

Part C: Comprehension Strategies

12 minutes

IWB

Teacher Materials:
Storybook 1

My Prediction Chart

Student Materials:
Storybook 1

Activity 1 Confirm Predictions—A During-Reading Strategy

Elicit responses to questions. **Guide** as needed.
In the last lesson, you made some predictions about what Spot would do in the story. You made the predictions before you read the story. Making predictions helps you understand the story better. You confirm predictions if you check to see if your predictions were correct. What do you do when you check and see if your predictions were right? *Confirm predictions.*

Guide discussion on what predictions were made in Lesson 21, based on recorded predictions.
Now that you've read the story, let's check to see if your predictions were correct or incorrect. What did Spot do? (Idea: *She asked for directions on her trip.*)

Is that what you predicted? (Student response.)

Elicit comments on whether predictions were correct or incorrect.
Was your prediction correct? (Student response.)

Check whether or not the prediction was correct. **Assure** students that it does not matter if the prediction was correct. What is important is to think about making the prediction.
Sometimes, we don't predict correctly. That's okay. Just trying to make a prediction will help you understand what you read better.

Activity 2 Generate Questions—A During-Reading Strategy

Refer to Story 31, page 72–74.

Asking questions is a smart thing to do when you are reading stories. It is also a hard thing to do. When you have learned how to ask questions while you are reading, you will be smart at understanding what you read. Today we are going to make up some questions.

Model think-aloud for asking a question from information.

Here's something that happened in the story. Spot went on a trip. I can make up a question. "Where did Spot go?" Say the question with me. *"Where did Spot go?"*

Here is another part of the story. She got in her car. I can turn that into a question. "What did Spot get into?" Say the question with me. *"What did Spot get into?"*

Guide students to complete question, not give the answer to the question.
Here is another part of the story. Spot went to Best Street for gas. Help me make up a question. You finish the question after I start it. "Where did Spot go to get _____?" *Gas.*

Yes. "Where did Spot go to get gas?" Very good job making a question instead of giving the answer to the question.

What is the answer to the question "Where did Spot go to get gas?"
Best Street.

Part D: Fluency Building

5 minutes

Student Materials:
Storybook 1

Conduct after the lesson, using story of the day.

Activity 1 Partner Reading

It's time for partner reading.
Direct students to the story of the day. **Assign** student partners as Partner 1 and Partner 2. **Monitor** partner reading. **Guide** as needed.

Lesson 33

Materials

Teacher: Trade book narrative text of choice that has characters and events for the beginning, middle, end; 1-Narrative Story Map; 8-Phonemic Awareness; 3 manipulatives such as blocks, discs, chips, counters (if not using IWB)

Student: Copy of 1-Narrative Story Map; copy of 8-Phonemic Awareness; 3 manipulatives such as blocks, discs, chips, counters

3 minutes

Part A: Phonemic and Phonological Awareness

IWB

Teacher Materials:
Phonemic Awareness

3 manipulatives such as blocks, discs, chips, counters

Student Materials:
Phonemic Awareness

3 manipulatives such as blocks, discs, chips, counters

Activity 1 Phoneme Blending for One-Syllable Words

Elicit responses. **Guide** as needed.
Let's put some sounds together and make words. I'm going to say a word very slowly so you can hear each sound. You'll need to listen carefully and say the sounds. Then we'll put the sounds together and say the word.

My turn. Listen. **/rrr/ /āāā/ /s/.** Say the sounds. /rrr/ /āāā /s/.
Again, say the sounds. /rrr/ /āāā /s/.
Let's put it together. What word? *Race.*

My turn. Listen. **/rrr/ /aaa/ /t/.** Say the sounds. /rrr/ /āāā/.
Again, say the sounds. /rrr/ /āāā/.
Let's put it together. What word? *Ray.*

(Continue the activity with the following words:
read [rrr-ēēē-d], red [rrr-eee-d], ride [rrr-īīī-d], rib [rrr-iii-b], road [rrr-ōōō-d], rock [rrr-ooo-k], row [rrr-ōōō], rug [rrr-uuu-g].)

Activity 2 Phoneme Segmentation

Show 8-Phonemic Awareness. **Elicit** responses. **Guide** as needed.
You've done such a great job breaking words apart by each sound. Today we're going to use chips to show how many sounds there are in a word. For each sound in a word, we'll push one chip up to the arrow on the page. I'll show you how to do the first one.

Model use of the chips by moving the chips to the arrow for each word and then back to the bottom when finished.
Listen. I can say a word and move a chip for each sound in the word. **It. /iii/ /t/. It.** Say the sounds in **it** with me, and move a chip for each sound. /iii/ /t/.

Now bring your finger back to the dot of the arrow. Let's slide our fingers under the chips and say the word. *It.* Let's move our chips back to the bottom so you can try it by yourselves. Say the sounds you hear in **it,** and move a chip for each sound. /iii/ /t/.

Move your finger back to the dot. What word? *It.*
Great job. Now move your chips back and let's try another one.

(Continue the activity with the following words: mit, sit.)

Part B: Vocabulary Development

Student Materials:
Storybook 1

Activity 1 Learn New Vocabulary Word

Elicit responses to questions. **Guide** as needed.
Today you'll learn a new vocabulary word. **Speak. Speak** means **talk.** What does **speak** mean? *Talk.*

Another word for **talk** is **speak.** What's another word for **talk?** *Speak.*

Sometimes it's okay to **talk.** That means it's okay to **speak.**

Discuss when it's an appropriate time for students to speak or not to speak.

What's another word for **talk?** *Speak.*

Activity 2 Review Vocabulary Word

Elicit responses to questions. **Guide** as needed.
What's a **mole?** *An animal that lives underground.*
What's another word for **an animal that lives underground?** *A mole.*

Review vocabulary words in appropriate context in *Storybook 1.*

Part C: Comprehension Strategies

IWB

Teacher Materials:
Trade book narrative text of choice that has characters and events for the beginning, middle, end

Narrative Story Map

Student Materials:
Narrative Story Map

Activity 1 Set Purpose for Reading—A Before-Reading Strategy

Read title of story. **Elicit** individual responses to questions. **Guide** as needed.
Before I read, I think about what I'm going to read to help me understand the text I read.

Today I'm going to read a narrative text. What will the story have? (Idea: *Beginning, middle, end.*)

What else will it have? (Idea: *Characters.*)

Why am I reading this narrative? *For fun.*

Activate background knowledge by asking questions about what students know about book topic.
What do you think the story will be about? (Student response.)

Activity 2 Determine Story Elements—A During-Reading Strategy

While I read the story, listen to the story, and see if you can figure out the characters and events that happen in the beginning, middle, and end of the story. I'll ask you questions after I read to see if you could figure all those things out.

Read trade book narrative of choice with prosody. **Ask** questions to engage students during reading (e.g., who, what, when, where, why). **Encourage** students to listen for story elements while you read.

Activity 3 Identify Story Elements—An After-Reading Strategy

Show Narrative Story Map. **Elicit** responses to questions. **Guide** as needed.
Let's see if you can tell me all the parts of the narrative that I just read to you.

Touch the Narrative Story Map as you ask questions referencing each box.
What is the title of the story? (Student response.)

Who is the main character in the story? (Student response.)

Are there any other characters in the story? (Student response.)

What events happened at the beginning of the story? (Student response.)

What events happened in the middle of the story? (Student response.)

What events happened at the end of the story? (Student response.)

Elicit information from students to draw in Narrative Story Map for Character and Beginning.
Let's work together to fill out the boxes of the Narrative Story Map for Characters and the Beginning.

Your turn to make the pictures on your own Narrative Story Map for the Characters box and the Beginning box. We will finish the map in the next lesson.

Save Narrative Story Maps for Lesson 34.

Part D: Fluency Building

5 minutes

Student Materials:
Storybook 1

Conduct after the lesson, using story of the day.

Activity 1 Partner Reading

It's time for partner reading.
Direct students to the story of the day. **Assign** student partners as Partner 1 and Partner 2. **Monitor** partner reading. **Guide** as needed.

Materials

Teacher: *Storybook 1*; trade book used in Lesson 33; 1-Narrative Story Map from Lesson 33; 8-Phonemic Awareness; 3 manipulatives such as blocks, discs, chips, counters (if not using IWB)

Student: *Storybook 1*; copy of 1-Narrative Story Map from Lesson 33; copy of 8-Phonemic Awareness; 3 manipulatives such as blocks, discs, chips, counters

Part A: Phonemic and Phonological Awareness

3 minutes

IWB

Teacher Materials:
Phonemic Awareness

3 manipulatives such as blocks, discs, chips, counters

Student Materials:
Phonemic Awareness

3 manipulatives such as blocks, discs, chips, counters

Activity 1 Phoneme Blending for One-Syllable Words

Elicit responses. **Guide** as needed.
Let's put some sounds together and make words. I'm going to say a word very slowly so you can hear each sound. You'll need to listen carefully and say the sounds. Then we'll put the sounds together and say the word.

My turn. Listen. **/d/ /āāā/ /t/.** Say the sounds. */d/ /āāā/ /t/.*
Again, say the sounds. */d/ /āāā/ /t/.*
Let's put it together. What word? *Date.*

My turn. Listen. **/d/ /aaa/ /shshsh/.** Say the sounds. */d/ /aaa/ /shshsh/.*
Again, say the sounds. */d/ /aaa/ /shshsh/.*
Let's put it together. What word? *Dash.*

(Continue the activity with the following words:
deep [d-ēēē-p], deck [d-eee-k], dime [d-īīī-mmm], ditch [d-iii-ch], dove [d-ooo-vvv], doll [d-ooo-lll], dough [d-ōōō], duck [d-uuu-k].)

Activity 2 Phoneme Segmentation

Show 8-Phonemic Awareness. **Elicit** responses. **Guide** as needed.
You've done such a great job breaking words apart by each sound. Today we're going to use chips to show how many sounds there are in a word. For each sound in a word, we'll push one chip up to the arrow on the page. I'll show you how to do the first one.

Model use of the chips by moving the chips to the arrow for each word and then back to the bottom when finished.
Listen. I can say a word and move a chip for each sound in the word. **In.**
/iii/ /nnn/. In. Say the sounds in **in** with me, and move a chip for each sound. */iii/ /nnn/.*

Now bring your finger back to the dot of the arrow. Let's slide our fingers under the chips and say the word. *In.* Let's move our chips back to the bottom so you can try it by yourselves. Say the sounds you hear in **in,** and move a chip for each sound. */iii/ /nnn/.*

Move your finger back to the dot. What word? *In.*
Great job. Now move your chips back and let's try another one.

(Continue the activity with the following words: win, fin.)

5 minutes

Activity 1 — Learn New Vocabulary Word

Elicit responses to questions. **Guide** as needed.
Today you'll learn a new vocabulary word. **Stall. A stall** is **a room in a barn for animals.** What's a **stall?** *A room in a barn for animals.*

Another word for **a room in a barn for animals** is **stall.** What's another word for **a room in a barn for animals?** *Stall.*

A horse has a **room in a barn.** A horse has a **stall.**

What's another word for **a room in a barn for animals?** *Stall.*

Discuss other animals that could live in a stall.

Activity 2 — Review Vocabulary Word

Elicit responses to questions. **Guide** as needed.
What does **speak** mean? *Talk.*
What does **talk** mean? *Speak.*

Review vocabulary words in appropriate context in *Storybook 1.*

12 minutes

IWB

Teacher Materials:
Storybook 1

Trade book used in Lesson 33

Narrative Story Map from Lesson 33

Student Materials:
Storybook 1

Narrative Story Map from Lesson 33

Activity 1 — Identify Story Elements (Review)—An After-Reading Strategy

Reread or **retell** same trade book narrative text of choice as in Lesson 33. **Elicit** responses to questions. **Guide** as needed.
Let's see if you can tell me all the parts of the narrative that I read to you yesterday.

Show Narrative Story Map. **Touch** appropriate section as you ask question referencing each box.
What is the title of the story? (Student response.)

Who is the main character in the story? (Student response.)

Are there other characters in the story? (Student response.)

What events happened at the beginning of the story? (Student response.)

What events happened in the middle of the story? (Student response.)

What events happened at the end of the story? (Student response.)

Elicit information from students to draw in Narrative Story Map sections.
Let's fill out last parts of the Narrative Story Map. Draw pictures for the Middle and End boxes on your maps.

Guide students to retell the story by referencing their Narrative Story Maps, if there is time.

Activity 2 Generate Questions—A During-Reading Strategy

Refer to Story 33, page 77–79.

Asking questions is a smart thing to do when you are reading stories. It is also a hard thing to do. When you've learned how to ask questions while you're reading, you'll be smart at understanding what you read. Today we are going to make up some questions.

Model asking a question from information. **Elicit** responses to questions. **Guide** as needed.
Here is a part of the story. The tall man had a dog that liked to talk. I can make up a question. "What did the dog like to do?" Say the question with me. *"What did the dog like to do?"*

Here is another part of the story. The dog was reading a book. I can turn that into a question. "What did the dog read?"

Say the question with me. *"What did the dog read?"*

Guide students to complete question, not give the answer to the question.
Here is another part of the story. The man went into the room for his coat. Help me make up a question. You finish the question after I start it. "What did the man get from _____?" *The room.*

Yes. "What did the man get from the room?" Very good job making a question instead of giving the answer to the question.

What is the answer to the question "What did the man get from the room?" *His coat.* Great job making up questions.

Part D: Fluency Building

5 minutes

Student Materials:
Storybook 1

Conduct after the lesson, using story of the day.

Activity 1 Partner Reading

It's time for partner reading.
Direct students to the story of the day. **Assign** student partners as Partner 1 and Partner 2. **Monitor** partner reading. **Guide** as needed.

Lesson 35

Materials

Teacher: *Storybook 1;* 8-Phonemic Awareness; 3 manipulatives such as blocks, discs, chips, counters (if not using IWB), 2-Vocabulary Acquisition and Use, Writing Prompts, 5-My Writing Checklist

Student: *Storybook 1;* copy of 8-Phonemic Awareness; 3 manipulatives such as blocks, discs, chips, counters, Copy of 2- Vocabulary Acquisition and Use and 3-My Writing Checklist; Lined Paper

Part A: Phonemic and Phonological Awareness

3 minutes

IWB

Teacher Materials:
Phonemic Awareness

3 manipulatives such as blocks, discs, chips, counters

Student Materials:
Phonemic Awareness

3 manipulatives such as blocks, discs, chips, counters

Activity 1 Phoneme Blending for One-Syllable Words

Elicit responses. **Guide** as needed.
Let's put some sounds together and make words. I'm going to say a word very slowly so you can hear each sound. You'll need to listen carefully and say the sounds. Then we'll put the sounds together and say the word.

My turn. Listen. **/fff/ /āāā/ /s/.** Say the sounds. */fff/ /āāā/ /sss/.*
Again, say the sounds. */fff/ /āāā/ /sss/.*
Let's put it together. What word? *Face.*

My turn. Listen. **/fff/ /aaa/ /t/.** Say the sounds. */fff/ /aaa/ /t/.*
Again, say the sounds. */fff/ /aaa/ /t/.*
Let's put it together. What word? *Fat.*

(Continue the activity with the following words:
feet [fff-ēēē-t], fed [fff-eee-d], fight [fff-īīī-t], fill [fff-iii-lll], foam [fff-ōōō-mmm], fog [fff-ooo-g], food [fff-oooooo-d], fun [fff-uuu-nnn].)

Activity 2 Phoneme Segmentation

Show 8-Phonemic Awareness. **Elicit** responses. **Guide** as needed.
Let's use our chips to show how many sounds there are in a word. For each sound in the word, we'll push one chip up to the arrow on the page. When we finish, we'll read the whole word.

Listen. I can say a word and move a chip for each sound in the word. **An.**
/aaa/ /nnn/. An. Your turn. Say the sounds you hear in **an,** and move a chip for each sound. */aaa/ /nnn/.*

Move your finger back to the dot. What word? *An.*
How many chips did you move for the word **an?** *Two.*
Yes, you moved two chips, so there are two sounds in the word **an.**
Great job.

(Continue the activity with the following words: man, fan.)

Part B: Vocabulary Development

5 minutes

IWB

Teacher Materials:
Vocabulary Acquisition
and Use

Student Materials:
Storybook 1

Vocabulary Acquisition
and Use

Activity 1 Cumulative Vocabulary Review

Elicit responses to questions. **Guide** as needed.
Directions: Listen and tell me the correct vocabulary word for each question.

What's another word for **an animal that lives underground?** *Mole.*
What's another word for **talk?** *Speak.*
What's another word for **want?** *Wish.*
What's another word for **a room in a barn for animals?** *Stall.*
Repeat difficult words as needed.

Review vocabulary words in appropriate context in *Storybook 1*.

Activity 2 Vocabulary Acquisition and Use

Display Vocabulary Acquisition and Use. **Have** students work with a neighbor to complete Vocabulary Acquisition and Use.
Today's vocabulary words are _____ and _____ [and _____ and _____].
Vocabulary words: **wish** and **want; speak** and **talk**
Write the words on the lines provided. Then write the words in the boxes based on whether you think each word is less/smaller or more/larger than the other word. Below the boxes, write why you think word 1 is less/smaller and word 2 is more/larger than word 1.
Repeat for words 3 and 4. **Have** students share what they wrote. **Discuss** examples of how these words might be used.

Part C: Comprehension Strategies

12 minutes

Teacher Materials:
Storybook 1

Student Materials:
Storybook 1

Activity 1 Generate Questions—A During-Reading Strategy

Refer to Story 34, page 80–82.

Elicit answers to questions. **Guide** as needed.
Remember: asking questions is a smart thing to do when you are reading stories. It is also a hard thing to do. Why do you ask questions when you are reading a story? (Idea: *To understand the story better.*)

Model asking a question from information.
Here is something that happened in the story. The bug went to live in a tree. I can make up a question. "Where did he go to live?" Say the question with me. *"Where did he go live?"*

Here is another part of the story. He lived in a hole. I can turn that into a question. "Where did the bug live?" Say the question with me. *"Where did the bug live?"*

Guide students to complete question, not give the answer to the question.

Here is another part of the story. Then he lived in a stall on a farm. Help me make up a question. You finish the question after I start it. "Where did the bug _____?" *Live.*

Yes! "Where did the bug live?" Very good job making a question instead of giving the answer to the question.

What is the answer to the question "Where did the bug live?" *In a stall on the farm.*

Way to do a hard skill!

Activity 2 Read with Prosody—A During-Reading Strategy

Direct student to Story 34 in *Storybook 1.*

Elicit response to question. **Guide** as needed.
Today you'll read "The Small Bug Went to Live in a Ball," Story 34, page 80–82, with a partner. Your partner will listen to you read. Your partner will say "STOP" when you forget to take a small breath at the periods. Then you can go back and fix it.

Then you will trade places, and you will say "STOP" to your partner if he or she forgets to take a breath. Remind each other to fix up your reading when you forget to take a breath between sentences.

Why is it important to pause between sentences? (Idea: *To understand the text better.*)

Monitor students as they read with prosody, attending to punctuation marks.

Part D: Fluency Building

5 minutes

Student Materials:
Storybook 1

Conduct after the lesson, using story of the day.

Activity 1 Partner Reading

It's time for partner reading.
Direct students to the story of the day. **Assign** student partners as Partner 1 and Partner 2. **Monitor** partner reading. **Guide** as needed.

10 minutes

IWB

Teacher Materials:
Writing Prompts

My Writing Checklist

Student Materials:
Lined Paper

My Writing Checklist

Activity 1 Write and Use Parts of Speech and Conventions

Time to write using a writing prompt based on the stories we've been reading.

Assign student partners. **Distribute** lined paper to students. **Display** writing prompts and have students choose one to write about or assign a writing prompt of your choice. **Review** parts of speech and punctuation as well as the writing checklist with students. **Tell** students to write one paragraph (minimum of four sentences per paragraph) on their own to answer the writing prompt. **Tell** them to use their writing checklist (first column labeled "Did I use them?") to ensure they include important parts of speech or punctuation in their writing. **Tell** students which parts of speech or punctuation to focus on, if you wish. **Model** what it means to answer a writing prompt and to use the writing checklist during and after the writing process, as needed. **Monitor** and guide students as needed. **Model** what it means to have a neighbor look over his or her neighbor's writing and to complete the writing checklist (second column labeled "Did my neighbor use them?"), as needed. **Have** students share what they wrote as time permits.

Writing Prompt 1	Writing Prompt 2	Writing Prompt 3
If you could paint anything you wanted, what would you paint? Why?	Where would you go if you could fly like a bird? Why?	If you could go on a trip, where would you go? Why?

Lesson 36

Materials

Teacher: *Storybook 1;* 8-Phonemic Awareness; 3 manipulatives such as blocks, discs, chips, counters (if not using IWB)

Student: *Storybook 1;* lined paper; copy of 8-Phonemic Awareness; 3 manipulatives such as blocks, discs, chips, counters

Part A: Phonemic and Phonological Awareness

3 minutes

IWB

Teacher Materials:
Phonemic Awareness

3 manipulatives such as blocks, discs, chips, counters

Student Materials:
Phonemic Awareness

3 manipulatives such as blocks, discs, chips, counters

Activity 1 Phoneme Blending for One-Syllable Words

Elicit responses. **Guide** as needed.
Let's put some sounds together and make words. I'm going to say a word very slowly so you can hear each sound. You'll need to listen carefully and say the sounds. Then we'll put the sounds together and say the word. Listen for some longer words today.

My turn. Listen. **/t/ /āāā/ /sss/ /t/.** Say the sounds. */t/ /āāā/ sss/ /t/.*
Again, say the sounds. */t/ /āāā /sss/ /t/.*
Let's put it together. What word? *Taste.*

My turn. Listen. **/t/ /aaa/ /p/.** Say the sounds. */t/ /aaa/ /p/.*
Again, say the sounds. */t/ /aaa/ /p/.*
Let's put it together. What word? *Tap.*

(Continue the activity with the following words:
team [t-ēēē-mmm], ten [t-eee-nnn], tiny [t-īīī-nnn-ēēē], tip [t-iii-p], toad [t-ōōō-d], top [t-ooo-p], town [t-ow-nnn], tug [t-uuu-g].)

Activity 2 Phoneme Segmentation

Show 8-Phonemic Awareness. **Elicit** responses. **Guide** as needed.
Let's use our chips to show how many sounds there are in a word. For each sound in a word, we'll push one chip up to the arrow on the page. When we finish, we'll read the whole word.

Listen. I can say a word and move a chip for each sound in the word. **Eat.**
/ēēē/ /t/. Eat. Your turn. Say the sounds in **eat,** and move a chip for each sound. */ēēē/ /t/.*

Move your finger back to the dot. What word? *Eat.*
How many chips did you move for the word **eat?** *Two.*
Yes, you moved two chips, so there are two sounds in the word **eat.**
Great job.

(Continue the activity with the following words:
feet, seat.)

5 minutes

Student Materials:
Storybook 1

Activity 1 Learn New Vocabulary Word

Elicit responses to questions. **Guide** as needed.
Today you'll learn a new vocabulary word. **Meet. Meet** means **come together.** What does **meet** mean? *Come together.*

Another word for **come together** is **meet.** What's another word for **come together?** *Meet.*

Carmen and Rachel went to the mall. They decided to **come together** at the candy store. They decided to **meet** at the candy store.

You spell this type of **meet m-e-e-t.** Spell **meet.** *M-e-e-t.*

What's another word for **come together?** *Meet.*

Discuss places students can meet.

Activity 2 Review Vocabulary Word

Elicit responses to questions. **Guide** as needed.
What does **stall** mean? *A room in a barn for animals.*
What's **a room in a barn for animals?** *A stall.*

Review vocabulary words in appropriate context in *Storybook 1.*

12 minutes

Teacher Materials:
Storybook 1

Student Materials:
Storybook 1

Lined paper

Activity 1 Generate Questions—A During-Reading Strategy

Refer to Story 35, page 83–85. **Elicit** responses to questions. **Guide** as needed.

Remember: asking questions is a smart thing to do when you are reading stories. It can also be a difficult thing to do. Why do you ask questions when you are reading a story? (Idea: *To understand the story better.*)

Model asking a question from information.
Here is a part of the story. The bug's home was in a ball. I can make up a question. "Where does the bug have a home?" Say the question with me. *"Where does the bug have a home?"*

Here is another part of the story. The bug was dreaming a nice dream. I can turn that into a question. "What was the bug doing?" Say the question with me. *"What was the bug doing?"*

Guide students to complete question, not give the answer to the question.

Here is another part of the story. The bug's ball hit the floor. Help me make up a question. You finish the question after I start it. "What did the ball _____?" *Hit.* Yes! "What did the ball hit?" Good for you. You asked a question instead of giving the answer.

What is the answer to the question "What did the ball hit?" *The floor.*

Activity 2 Identify Character—An After-Reading Strategy

Provide lined paper to students.

You are getting smart about telling the parts of a Narrative. Today I want you to find the characters in the story. Look at Story 35, "The Bug in the Ball Meets a Girl" on pages 83–85. Work with a partner to figure out who the main characters are in the story. Copy the names of the main characters on a piece of paper. Then we will check to see if you found all the names.

Monitor student partners as they find the characters in Story 35, page 83–85. **Guide** as needed. **Debrief** students when they are finished to identify main characters: bug and girl.

Provide a reading center to display books being read so that students can enjoy them again during free time.

Part D: Fluency Building

5 minutes

Student Materials:
Storybook 1

Conduct after the lesson, using story of the day.

Activity 1 Partner Reading

It's time for partner reading.

Direct students to the story of the day. **Assign** student partners as Partner 1 and Partner 2. **Monitor** partner reading. **Guide** as needed.

Materials

Teacher: *Storybook 1*; 8-Phonemic Awareness; 3 manipulatives such as blocks, discs, chips, counters (if not using IWB)

Student: *Storybook 1*; copy of 8-Phonemic Awareness; 3 manipulatives such as blocks, discs, chips, counters

Part A: Phonemic and Phonological Awareness

3 minutes

IWB

Teacher Materials:
Phonemic Awareness

3 manipulatives such as blocks, discs, chips, counters

Student Materials:
Phonemic Awareness

3 manipulatives such as blocks, discs, chips, counters

Activity 1 Phoneme Blending for One-Syllable Words

Elicit responses. **Guide** as needed.

Let's put some sounds together and make words. I'm going to say a word very slowly so you can hear each sound. You'll need to listen carefully and say the sounds. Then we'll put the sounds together and say the word. Listen for some longer words today.

My turn. Listen. **/nnn/ /āāā/ /mmm/.** Say the sounds. */nnn/ /āāā/ /mmm/.*
Again, say the sounds. */nnn/ /āāā/ /mmm/.*
Let's put it together. What word? *Name.*

My turn. Listen. **/nnn/ /aaa/ /p/.** Say the sounds. */nnn/ /aaa/ /p/.*
Again, say the sounds. */nnn/ /aaa/ /p/.*
Let's put it together. What word? *Nap.*

(Continue the activity with the following words:
needle [nnn-ēēē-d-lll], near [nnn-ēēē-rrr], nest [nnn-eee-sss-t], nice [nnn-īīī-sss], nibble [nnn-iii-b-lll], note [nnn-ōōō-t], nod [nnn-ooo-d], nut [nnn-uuu-t].)

Activity 2 Phoneme Segmentation

Show 8-Phonemic Awareness. **Elicit** responses. **Guide** as needed.

Let's use our chips to show how many sounds there are in a word. For each sound in a word, we'll push one chip up to the arrow on the page. When we finish, we'll read the whole word.

Listen. I can say a word and move a chip for each sound in the word.
Am. /aaa/ /mmm/. Am. Your turn. Say the sounds in **am,** and move a chip for each sound. */aaa/ /mmm/.*

Move your finger back to the dot. What word? *Am.*
How many chips did you move for the word **am?** *Two.*
Yes, you moved two chips, so there are two sounds in the word **am.**
Great job.

(Continue the activity with the following words:
ram, sam.)

Part B: Vocabulary Development

Activity 1 New Vocabulary Word

Elicit responses to questions. **Guide** as needed.

Today you'll learn a new vocabulary word. **Bet. Bet** means you **say you think something will or won't happen.** What does **bet** mean? *Say you think something will or won't happen.*

Another word for **say you think something will or won't happen** is **bet.** What's another word for **say you think something will or won't happen?** *Bet.*

If there are many dark clouds in the sky, you **say you think it will** rain. You make a **bet** that it will rain. However, if the sun is shining and no clouds are in the sky, you **say you think it won't** rain. You make a **bet** that it won't rain.

What's another word for **say you think it will or won't happen?** *Bet.*

Discuss times when students have made a bet.

Activity 2 Review Vocabulary Word

Elicit responses to questions. **Guide** as needed.
What does **meet** mean? *Come together.*
What's another word for **come together?** *Meet.* Spell **meet.** *M-e-e-t.*

Review vocabulary words in appropriate context in *Storybook 1*.

Part C: Comprehension Strategies

Activity 1 Generate Questions—A During-Reading Strategy

Refer to Story 36, page 86–88.

Elicit responses to questions. **Guide** as needed.
Asking questions is a strategy to use when you're reading stories. If you ask questions while you're reading, you're thinking about the story you're reading. Learning to ask questions is a hard skill. It takes lots of practice. Let's practice asking some more questions.

Model asking a question from information.
Here is a part of the story. The bug wanted to live in a ball. I can make up a question. "Where does the bug want to live?" Say the question with me. *"Where does the bug want to live?"*

Guide students to complete question, not give the answer to the question. **Elicit** responses to questions. **Guide** as needed.

Here's another part of the story. The bug began to cry. Help me make up a question from that sentence. "What did the bug _____?" *Do.* Yes! "What did the bug do?" It was smart to make a question instead of giving the answer to the question.

Say the question with me. *"What did the bug do?"*

What is the answer to the question "What did the bug do?" *Started to cry.*

Guide students to complete question, not give the answer to the question.

Here is another part of the story. The girl sat on the floor. Help me make up a question. You finish the question after I start it. "What did _____?" *The girl do.* Yes! "What did the girl do?" Great thinking. You asked a question instead of telling the answer.

What is the answer to the question "What did the girl do?" *Sat on the floor.*

You are getting good at this hard skill.

Activity 2 Read with Prosody—A During-Reading Strategy

Elicit responses to questions. **Guide** as needed.

We will play the "STOP" game today.

You will read "The Bug Wants to Stay in the Ball," Story 36, pages 86–88 with a partner. Your partner will listen to you read. Your partner will say "STOP" when you forget to take a small breath at the periods or make your voice go up at the question marks. Then you can go back and fix it.

Then you will trade places, and you will say "STOP" to your partner if he or she forgets to take a breath or read questions the right way. Remind each other to fix up your reading when you forget to pause between sentences.

Why is it important to pause between sentences? *To understand the text better.*

Monitor students as they read with prosody, attending to punctuation marks.

Part D: Fluency Building

5 minutes

Student Materials:
Storybook 1

Conduct after the lesson, using story of the day.

Activity 1 Partner Reading

It's time for partner reading.

Direct students to the story of the day. **Assign** student partners as Partner 1 and Partner 2. **Monitor** partner reading. **Guide** as needed.

Lesson 38

Materials

Teacher: *Storybook 1;* 8-Phonemic Awareness; 3 manipulatives such as blocks, discs, chips, counters (if not using IWB), 6-My Prediction Chart

Student: *Storybook 1;* copy of 8-Phonemic Awareness; 3 manipulatives such as blocks, discs, chips, counters

Part A: Phonemic and Phonological Awareness

3 minutes

IWB

Teacher Materials:
Phonemic Awareness

3 manipulatives such as blocks, discs, chips, counters

Student Materials:
Phonemic Awareness

Activity 1 · Phoneme Blending for One-Syllable Words

Elicit responses. **Guide** as needed.

Let's put some sounds together and make words. I'm going to say a word very slowly so you can hear each sound. You'll need to listen carefully and say the sounds. Then we'll put the sounds together and say the word. Listen for some longer words today.

My turn. Listen. **/k/ /āāā/ /g/.** Say the sounds. */k/ /āāā/ /g/.*
Again, say the sounds. */k/ /āāā/ /g/.*
Let's put it together. What word? *Cage.*

My turn. Listen. **/k/ /aaa/ /mmm/ /p/.** Say the sounds. */k/ /aaa/ /mmm/ /p/.*
Again, say the sounds. */k/ /aaa/ /mmm/ /p/.*
Let's put it together. What word? *Camp.*

(Continue the activity with the following words:
cattle [k-aaa-t-lll], coast [k-ōōō-sss-t], comb [k-ōōō-mmm], cow [k-ow], kiss [k-iii-sss], kind [k-īīī-nnn-d], key [k-ēēē], cozy [c-ōōō-zzz-ēēē].)

Activity 2 · Phoneme Segmentation

Show 8-Phonemic Awareness. **Elicit** responses. **Guide** as needed.

Let's use our chips to show how many sounds there are in a word. For each sound in a word, we'll push one chip up to the arrow on the page. When we finish, we'll read the whole word.

Listen. I can say a word and move a chip for each sound in the word. **Ice. /īīī/ /sss/. Ice.** Your turn. Say the sounds in **ice,** and move a chip for each sound. */īīī/ /sss/.*

Move your finger back to the dot. What word? *Ice.*
How many chips did you move for the word **ice?** *Two.*
Yes, you moved two chips, so there are two sounds in the word **ice.**
Great job.

(Continue the activity with the following words: nice, mice.)

Part B: Vocabulary Development

Student Materials:
Storybook 1

Activity 1 Learn New Vocabulary Word

Elicit responses to questions. **Guide** as needed.
Today you'll learn a new vocabulary word. **Contact. Contact** means **touch.** What does **contact** mean? *Touch.*

Another word for **touch** is **contact.** What's another word for **touch?** *Contact.*

When you **touch** the table, you **contact** the table. When you **touch** your reading book, you **contact** your book.

What's another word for **touch?** *Contact.*

Discuss things students can contact.

Activity 2 Review Vocabulary Word

Elicit responses to questions. **Guide** as needed.
What does a **bet** mean? *To say you think something will or won't happen.* What's another way of saying **you think something will or won't happen?** *Bet.*

Review vocabulary words in appropriate context in *Storybook 1.*

Part C: Comprehension Strategies

IWB

Teacher Materials:
Storybook 1

My Prediction Chart

Student Materials:
Storybook 1

Activity 1 Generate Questions—A During-Reading Strategy

Refer to Story 37, pages 89–92.

Elicit responses to questions. **Guide** as needed.
Asking questions is a strategy to use when you are reading stories. Why do you ask questions when you are reading? (Idea: *To understand the story better.*)

Learning to ask questions is a hard skill. It takes lots of practice. Let's practice asking some more questions.

Guide students to complete question, not give the answer to the question.
Here is a part of the story. He said he would sing. Help me make up a question. "What did he say he _____?" *Would do.* Yes! "What did he say he would do?"

Say the whole question with me. *"What did he say he would do?"*

What is the answer to the question "What did he say he would do?" *Sing.*

Here is another part of the story. Her brother came in the room. Help me make up a question from that sentence. "Who came _____?" *In the room.* Yes! "Who came in the room?" It was smart to make a question instead of giving the answer to the question.

Say the whole question with me. *"Who came in the room?"*

What is the answer to the question "Who came in the room?" *Her brother.*

Here is another part of the story. He didn't see the bug in the ball. Who can make up a question on this information? (Ideas: *"Who did not see the bug?" "What was in the ball?" "What did the brother not see?"*)

What is the answer to the question? (Student response.)

You are getting good at asking questions.

Activity 2 Prediction—A Before-Reading Strategy

Refer to Story 38, pages 93–96.

Show My Prediction Chart. **Elicit** responses to questions. **Guide** as needed.
Today you're going to read the rest of the story about the bug and the ball. The story is called "The Tall Girl Wins the Bet." What are you doing if you make a guess about what you'll read from clues? (Idea: *Making predictions.*)

Record title on My Prediction Chart.

You get the clues from the title and from the pictures. Where do you get clues to make predictions? (Idea: *From the title and the pictures.*)

Let's look at the story you're going to read and make some predictions about what will happen in the story. Look at the title and the picture. See if there are clues to help you predict what might happen in this story.

Discuss predictions with students. **Record** predictions.
I'll record your predictions. Do you predict that this story might be a narrative? *Yes.*

Why do you think so? (Idea: *It looks like it might be fun to read.*)

What will the story be about? (Idea: *The girl winning the bet.*)

What clue gave you that idea? *The title.*

What do you think might happen in the story? (Idea: *The girl gets a lot of stuff and is happy. The bug is happy.*)

What clue made you think that? (Idea: *The picture shows the girl sitting on the floor. The girl is smiling. The bug is kissing the girl's hand.*)

Remember: Making predictions helps us understand better the text we read.

Save recorded predictions.

Part D: Fluency Building

5 minutes

Student Materials:
Storybook 1

Conduct after the lesson, using story of the day.

Activity 1 Partner Reading

It's time for partner reading.
Direct students to the story of the day. **Assign** student partners as Partner 1 and Partner 2. **Monitor** partner reading. **Guide** as needed.

Lesson 39

Materials

Teacher: *Storybook 1;* 1-Narrative Story Map; 8-Phonemic Awareness; 3 manipulatives such as blocks, discs, chips, counters (if not using IWB), 6-My Prediction Chart from Lesson 38

Student: *Storybook 1;* copy of 1-Narrative Story Map; copy of 8-Phonemic Awareness; 3 manipulatives such as blocks, discs, chips, counters

Part A: Phonemic and Phonological Awareness

3 minutes

IWB

Teacher Materials:
Phonemic Awareness

3 manipulatives such as blocks, discs, chips, counters

Student Materials:
Phonemic Awareness

3 manipulatives such as blocks, discs, chips, counters

Activity 1 Phoneme Blending for One-Syllable Words

Elicit responses. **Guide** as needed.
Let's put some sounds together and make words. I'm going to say a word very slowly so you can hear each sound. You'll need to listen carefully and say the sounds. Then we'll put the sounds together and say the word. Listen for some longer words today.

My turn. Listen. **/h/ /āāā/ /lll/.** Say the sounds. /h/ /āāā/ /lll/.
Again, say the sounds. /h/ /āāā/ /lll/.
Let's put it together. What word? *Hail.*

My turn. Listen. **/h/ /aaa/ /p/ /ēēē/.** Say the sounds. /h/ /aaa/ /p/ /ēēē/.
Again, say the sounds. /h/ /aaa/ /p/ /ēēē/.
Let's put it together. What word? *Happy.*

(Continue the activity with the following words:
he [h-ēēē], head [h-eee-d], hive [h-īīī-vvv], hits [h-iii-t-sss], hope [h-ōōō-p], holly [h-ooo-lll-ēēē], hug [h-uuu-g], howl [h-ow-lll].)

Activity 2 Phoneme Segmentation

Show 8-Phonemic Awareness. **Elicit** responses. **Guide** as needed.
Let's use our chips to show how many sounds there are in a word. For each sound in a word, we'll push one chip up to the arrow on the page. When we finish, we'll read the whole word.

Listen. I can say a word and move a chip for each sound in the word.
Ad. /aaa/ /d/. Ad. Your turn. Say the sounds in **ad,** and move a chip for each sound. /aaa/ /d/.

Move your finger back to the dot. What word? *Ad.*
How many chips did you move for the word **ad?** *Two.*
Yes, you moved two chips, so there are two sounds in the word **ad.**
Great job.

(Continue the activity with the following words: mad, sad.)

5 minutes

Student Materials:
Storybook 1

Activity 1 Learn New Vocabulary Word

Elicit responses to questions. **Guide** as needed.
Today you'll learn a new vocabulary word. **Tumble. Tumble** means **fall.** What does **tumble** mean? *Fall.*

Another word for **fall** is **tumble. What's** another word for **fall?** *Tumble.*

I might **fall** down the stairs if I am running. I might **tumble** down the stairs if I am running.

What's another word for **fall?** *Tumble.*

Discuss examples of when students might tumble.

Activity 2 Review Vocabulary Word

Elicit responses to questions. **Guide** as needed.
What does **contact** mean? *Touch.*
What's another word for **touch?** *Contact.*

Review vocabulary words in appropriate context in *Storybook 1*

Part C: Comprehension Strategies

12 minutes

IWB

Teacher Materials:
Storybook 1

Narrative Story Map

My Prediction Chart
from Lesson 38

Student Materials:
Storybook 1

Narrative Story Map

Activity 1 Confirm Predictions—An After-Reading Strategy

Show My Prediction Chart. **Check** predictions recorded in previous lesson. **Elicit** responses to questions. **Guide** as needed.
In the last lesson, you made some predictions about what would happen in the "Bug and the Ball" story. You made the predictions before you read the story. Making predictions helps you understand the story better. Now that you've read the story, let's check and see if your predictions were in the story. You confirm your predictions when you check to see if they are correct. What do you do when you check to see if your predictions are correct? *Confirm predictions.*

What part in the story helps you confirm your predictions? (Student response.)

Assure students that predictions do not have to be correct.
Do all your predictions need to be correct? *No.*

Discuss with students the value of making predictions.
Why not? (Idea: *Making predictions helps me understand the story, even if they are not correct, because I am thinking about confirming my predictions.*)

Activity 2 Identify Story Elements—An After-Reading Strategy

Refer to Stories 34–38, pages 80–96.

Show Narrative Story Map. **Elicit** responses to questions. **Guide** as needed.
Now that you have read all the stories about the bug and the ball, let's see if we can fill out a Narrative Story Map and figure out all the parts of the story.

Touch spot on story map as you ask question referencing each box.

Who are the main characters in the story? *The bug and the girl.*

Who is another character in the story? *The brother.*

What events happened at the beginning of the story? (Idea: *The bug could not find a home.*)

What events happened in the middle of the story? (Ideas: *The bug moved into the ball. The girl wanted the bug to leave. The bug helped the girl win the bet.*)

How events happened at the end of the story? (Ideas: *The girl won the bet, and the bug got to live in the ball.*)

Elicit information from students to draw in Narrative Story Map sections. **Guide** as needed.
Let's fill out the last parts of the Narrative Story Map together.

Model drawing pictures in each section, based on student responses.

Your turn to draw the pictures on your Narrative Story Maps.

Assist student in drawing pictures on the Narrative Story Map. **Guide** students to retell the story by referencing their Narrative Story Maps if there is time.

Part D: Fluency Building

5 minutes

Student Materials:
Storybook 1

Conduct after the lesson, using story of the day.

Activity 1 Partner Reading

It's time for partner reading.
Direct students to the story of the day. **Assign** student partners as Partner 1 and Partner 2. **Monitor** partner reading. **Guide** as needed.

Lesson 40

Materials

Teacher: 8-Phonemic Awareness; 3 manipulatives such as blocks, discs, chips, counters (if not using IWB), 2-Vocabulary Acquisition and Use, 3-My Book Review

Student: Copy of 8-Phonemic Awareness; 3 manipulatives such as blocks, discs, chips, counters, Copy of 2-Vocabulary Acquisition and Use and 3-My Book Review

Part A: Phonemic and Phonological Awareness

3 minutes

IWB

Teacher Materials:
Phonemic Awareness

3 manipulatives such as blocks, discs, chips, counters

Student Materials:
Phonemic Awareness

3 manipulatives such as blocks, discs, chips, counters

Activity 1 Phoneme Blending for One-Syllable Words

Elicit responses. **Guide** as needed.
I'm going to say a word very slowly so you can hear each sound. You'll need to listen carefully and say the sounds. Then we'll put the sounds together and say the word. Listen for some longer words today.

My turn. Listen. **/ththth/ /iii /k/.** Say the sounds. /ththth/ /iii/ /k/.
Again, say the sounds. /ththth/ /iii/ /k/.
Let's put it together. What word? *Thick.*

My turn. Listen. **/ththth/ /ir/ /sss/ /t/.** Say the sounds. /ththth/ /r/ /sss/ /t/.
Again, say the sounds. /ththth/ /ir/ /sss/ /t/.
Let's put it together. What word? *Thirst.*

(Continue the activity with the following words:
theme [ththth-ēēē-mmm], thief [ththth-ēēē-fff], thin [ththth-iii-nnn], thumb [ththth-uuu-mmm], thorn [ththth-or-nnn], thud [ththth-uuu-d], thump [ththth-uuu-mmm-p].)

Activity 2 Phoneme Segmentation

Show 8-Phonemic Awareness. **Elicit** responses. **Guide** as needed.
Let's use our chips to show how many sounds there are in a word. For each sound in a word, we'll push one chip up to the arrow on the page. When we finish, we'll read the whole word.

Listen. I can say a word and move a chip for each sound in the word. **Ate. /āāā/ /t/.** Ate. Your turn. Say the sounds in **ate**, and move a chip for each sound. /āāā/ /t/.

Move your finger back to the dot. What word? *Ate.*
How many chips did you move for the word **ate?** *Two.*
Yes, you moved two chips, so there are two sounds in the word **ate.**
Great job.

(Continue the activity with the following words:
late, wait.)

Part B: Vocabulary Development

Activity 1 Cumulative Vocabulary Review

IWB

Teacher Materials:
Vocabulary Acquisition
and Use

Student Materials:
Storybook 1

Vocabulary Acquisition
and Use

Elicit responses to questions. **Guide** as needed.
Directions: Listen and tell me the correct vocabulary word for each question.

What's another word for **come together?** *Meet.*
What's another word for **touch?** *Contact.*
What's another word for **fall?** *Tumble.*
What's another word for **say you think something will or won't happen?** *Bet.*
What's another word for **an animal that lives underground?** *Mole.*
What's another word for **talk?** *Speak.*
What's another word for **want?** *Wish.*
What's another word for **a room in a barn for animals?** *Stall.*

Repeat difficult words as needed.

Review vocabulary words in appropriate context in *Storybook 1.*

Activity 2 Vocabulary Acquisition and Use

Display Vocabulary Acquisition and Use. **Have** students work with a neighbor to complete Vocabulary Acquisition and Use.
Today's vocabulary words are _____ and _____ [and _____ and _____].
Vocabulary words: **tumble** and **fall; contact** and **touch**
Write the words on the lines provided. Then write the words in the boxes based on whether you think each word is less/smaller or more/larger than the other word. Below the boxes, write why you think word 1 is less/smaller and word 2 is more/larger than word 1.
Repeat for words 3 and 4. **Have** students share what they wrote. **Discuss** examples of how these words might be used.

Part C: Comprehension Strategies

IWB

Teacher Materials:
My Book Review

Student Materials:
My Book Review

Record comprehension strategies on a chart if appropriate. If chart is made, you can refer to it during later lessons to identify strategy being used. Chart can also be updated as lessons proceed.

Let's talk about things we do before we read to help us understand narrative text better.

Activity 1 Review—Before-Reading Strategies

Discuss strategies that students have been using before reading narratives.
Let's talk about things you do before you read to help you understand narrative text better. What are some things to do before you read a new story? (Ideas: *Make prediction—***Make Predictions—***or think about what I will try to learn or figure out in the story—***Set Purpose for Reading.***)

Activity 2 Review—During-Reading Strategies

Discuss strategies that students have been using during reading narratives.
Let's talk about things you do while you read to help you understand narrative text better. What are some things you can do while you are reading to help you understand what you are reading? (Idea: Ask *questions*—**Generate Questions**—*and read while paying attention to the ends of sentences*—**Read with Prosody.**)

Activity 3 Review—After-Reading Strategies

Discuss strategies that students have been using after reading narratives.
Let's talk about things we do after we read to help us understand narrative text better. What are some things you can do after you read a story to help you understand or remember the story?
(Ideas: *Fill out a story map*—**Identify Story Elements**—*see if predictions were correct*—**Confirming Predictions**—*make text-to-self connections, text-to-text connections, and retell the story.*)

Wow, you have learned a lot about things to do that help you understand the stories you read. When you understand what you've read, you have good comprehension. Understanding what you read is really important. It will help you be successful in life.

Activity 4 Develop Opinions—An After-Reading Strategy

Today we'll found out your opinion or how you feel about the stories you read. You will choose a book to read and then complete the My Book Review form. You'll need to tell if you like or don't like the book and why. You must give a reason for why you like or don't like the book. Finally, you can tell if you would recommend the book to others.

Have students read a narrative or expository trade book of their choice. **Have** students complete My Book Review form when they are finished reading their book. **Model** how to complete the My Book Review form. **Guide** students as needed. **Have** students share their book reviews with the class as time permits.

Part D: Fluency Building

5 minutes

Student Materials:
Storybook 1

Conduct after the lesson, using story of the day.

Activity 1 Partner Reading

It's time for partner reading.
Direct students to the story of the day. **Assign** student partners as Partner 1 and Partner 2. **Monitor** partner reading. **Guide** as needed.

Lesson 41

Materials

Teacher: *Storybook 1;* 8-Phonemic Awareness; 3 manipulatives such as blocks, discs, chips, counters (if not using IWB)

Student: *Storybook 1;* copy of 8-Phonemic Awareness; 3 manipulatives such as blocks, discs, chips, counters

Part A: Phonemic and Phonological Awareness

3 minutes

IWB

Teacher Materials:
Phonemic Awareness

3 manipulatives such as blocks, discs, chips, counters

Student Materials:
Phonemic Awareness

3 manipulatives such as blocks, discs, chips, counters

Activity 1 Phoneme Blending for One-Syllable Words

Elicit responses. **Guide** as needed.
Let's put some sounds together and make words. I'm going to say a word very slowly so you can hear each sound. You'll need to listen carefully and say the sounds. Then we'll put the sounds together and say the word.

My turn. Listen. **/g/ /āāā/ /mmm/.**
Say the sounds. */g/ /āāā/ /mmm/.*
Again, say the sounds. */g/ /āāā/ /mmm/.*
Let's put it together. What word? *Game.*

My turn. Listen. **/g/ /aaa/ /sss/.**
Say the sounds. */g/ /aaa/ /sss/.*
Again, say the sounds. */g/ /aaa/ /sss/.*
Let's put it together. What word? *Gas.*

(Continue the activity with the following words:
geese [g-ēēē-sss], get [g-eee-t], gift [g-iii-fff-t], go [g-ōōō], got [g-ooo-t],
gown [g-ow-nnn], guest [g-eee-sss-t], gum [g-uuu-mmm].)

Activity 2 Phoneme Segmentation

Show Phonemic Awareness. **Elicit** responses. **Guide** as needed.
Let's use our chips to show how many sounds there are in a word. For each sound in a word, we'll push one chip up to the arrow on the page. When we finish, we'll read the whole word.

Listen. I can say a word and move a chip for each sound in the word. **Sack. /sss/ /aaa/ /k/. Sack.** Your turn. Say the sounds in **sack,** and move a chip for each sound. */sss/ /aaa/ /k/.*

Move your finger back to the dot. What word? *Sack.*
How many chips did you move for the word **sack?** *Three.*
Yes, you moved three chips, so there are three sounds in the word **sack.**
Great job.

(Continue the activity with the following words:
back, pack, shack, tack.)

Part B: Vocabulary Development

Activity 1 Learn New Vocabulary Word

Elicit responses to questions. **Guide** as needed.
Today you'll learn a new vocabulary word. **Unhappy. Unhappy** means **sad.**
What does **unhappy** mean? *Sad.*

Another word for **sad** is **unhappy.** What's another word for **sad?** *Unhappy.*

Sometimes a preschooler is **sad** when his parents leave him with a sitter. The preschooler is **unhappy.**

What's another word for **sad?** *Unhappy.*

Discuss times when students are unhappy.

Activity 2 Review Vocabulary Word

Elicit responses to questions. **Guide** as needed.
What does **tumble** mean? *Fall.*
What's another word for **fall?** *Tumble.*

Review vocabulary words in appropriate context in *Storybook 1.*

Part C: Comprehension Strategies

Activity 1 Mental Images—A During-Reading Strategy

Refer to Story 40, pages 101–103.

One thing good readers do to understand what they are reading is make pictures in their minds as they read. Let me show you how I make pictures in my mind.

Model think-aloud for making mental images. **Substitute** your own mental image for idea presented, if you wish.

Sample Wording for Think-Aloud

(Read first sentence from story.) I get a picture in my mind of a tall, skinny man who looks like my dad. I picture a dog speaking to my dad. It is a silly picture because dogs can't talk. But that is the picture I get in my mind.

Elicit mental images students have for the sentence.

The next sentence says: (Read next sentence.) Get a picture in your mind of that sentence. What kind of dog do you see? (Student response.)

How tall is the table? (Student response.)

What kind of book do you see in your mind? (Student response.)

Making mental images when you read is a good way to help you understand what you read.

Activity 2 Sequencing—An After-Reading Strategy

We're going to play a game today. I'm going to tell you events that happen in the story. But, I think I might get mixed up. You help me get the events in order.

Read each sentence with a pause between sentences.
The dog kicked the ball down the hall.

The dog took the book from the table.

The man said, "I cannot see my book."

Reread sentences again in the same order.

Elicit responses to questions. **Guide** as needed.
Which event happened first? (Idea: *The dog took the book from the table.*)

Which event happened next? (Idea: *The man said, "I cannot see my book."*)

Which event happened last? (Idea: *The dog kicked the ball down the hall.*)

Good for you. You put the events in order. Remembering to put events in the right order helps you retell the story the right way.

Part D: Fluency Building

5 minutes

Student Materials:
Storybook 1

Conduct after the lesson, using story of the day.

Activity 1 Partner Reading

It's time for partner reading.
Direct students to the story of the day. **Assign** student partners as Partner 1 and Partner 2. **Monitor** student reading. **Guide** as needed.

Lesson 42

Materials

Teacher: *Storybook 1;* 8-Phonemic Awareness; 3 manipulatives such as blocks, discs, chips, counters (if not using IWB)

Student: *Storybook 1;* copy of 8-Phonemic Awareness; 3 manipulatives such as blocks, discs, chips, counters

Part A: Phonemic and Phonological Awareness

3 minutes

IWB

Teacher Materials:
Phonemic Awareness

3 manipulatives such as blocks, discs, chips, counters

Student Materials:
Phonemic Awareness

3 manipulatives such as blocks, discs, chips, counters

Activity 1 Phoneme Blending for One-Syllable Words

Elicit responses. **Guide** as needed.

Let's put some sounds together and make words. I'm going to say a word very slowly so you can hear each sound. You need to listen carefully and say the sounds. Then we'll put the sounds together and say the word.

My turn. Listen. **/lll/ /āāā/ /sss/.**
Say the sounds. /lll/ /āāā/ /sss/.
Again, say the sounds. /lll/ /āāā/ /sss/.
Let's put it together. What word? *Lace.*

My turn. Listen. **/lll/ /aaa/ /mmm/ /p/.**
Say the sounds. /lll/ /aaa/ /mmm/ /p/.
Again, say the sounds. /lll/ /aaa/ /mmm/ /p/.
Let's put it together. What word? *Lamp.*

(Continue the activity with the following words:
leaf [lll-ēēē-f], leg [lll-eee-g], life [lll-īīī-fff], lift [lll-iii-fff-t], lip [lll-iii-p],
lost [lll-ooo-sss-t], loop [lll-oooooo-p], luck [lll-uuu-k].)

Activity 2 Phoneme Segmentation

Show Phonemic Awareness. **Elicit** responses. **Guide** as needed.

Let's use our chips to show how many sounds there are in a word. For each sound in a word, we'll push one chip up to the arrow on the page. When we finish, we'll read the whole word.

Listen. I can say a word and move a chip for each sound in the word. **Meat.** **/mmm/ /ēēē/ /t/. Meat.** Your turn. Say the sounds in **meat,** and move a chip for each sound. /mmm/ /ēēē/ /t/.

Move your finger back to the dot. What word? *Meat.*
How many chips did you move for the word **meat?** *Three.*
Yes, you moved three chips, so there are three sounds in the word **meat.** Great job.

(Continue the activity with the following words:
beat, heat, sheet.)

Part B: Vocabulary Development

Activity 1 Learn New Vocabulary Word

Elicit responses to questions. **Guide** as needed.
Today you'll learn a new vocabulary word. **Cheer. Cheer** means **yell loudly.**
What does **cheer** mean? *Yell loudly.*

Another word for **yell loudly** is **cheer.** What's another word for **yell loudly?**
Cheer.

Walter and his friends **yell loudly** for the football team when the tall boy runs with the ball. They **cheer** when the tall boy runs with the ball.

What's another word for **yell loudly?** *Cheer.*

Discuss times when students cheer.

Activity 2 Review Vocabulary Word

Elicit responses to questions. **Guide** as needed.
What does **unhappy** mean? *Sad.*
What's another word for **sad?** *Unhappy.*

Review vocabulary words in appropriate context in *Storybook 1.*

Part C: Comprehension Strategies

Activity 1 Make Mental Images—A During-Reading Strategy

Refer to Story 41, pages 104–106.

Elicit responses to mental images. **Guide** as needed.
Remember that good readers make mental images to help them understand what they are reading. If you want to be a good reader, you need to practice making mental images when you read.

These sentences say: (Read first two sentences from story on page 104.) Get a picture in your mind of that sentence. What kind of boy do you see?

Where is he? (Student response.)

What is he wearing? (Student response.)

What does he have in his hands? (Student response.)

What happens when he plays football? (Student response.)

Making mental images when you read is a good method to help you understand what you read.

Activity 2   Text-to-Self Connection—An After-Reading Strategy

Discuss connections that students can make to story. **Elicit** responses to questions. **Guide** as needed.

One way to understand stories better is to make text-to-self connections. What do you do when you make text-to-self connections? (Idea: *Connect your own experiences with a story you read.*)

Does the Walter story make you think of any experience you have had? (Student response.)

Have you ever been bad at sports? (Student response.)

Have you ever played football? Have you ever gone to a football game? (Student response.)

Remember: When you connect something that has happened to you to something that happens in the story, you're making text-to-self connections. Thinking about your experiences when you read is a good way to help you understand what you read.

Part D: Fluency Building

5 minutes

Student Materials:
Storybook 1

Conduct after the lesson, using story of the day.

Activity 1   Partner Reading

It's time for partner reading.

Direct students to the story of the day. **Assign** student partners as Partner 1 and Partner 2. **Monitor** student reading. **Guide** as needed.

Lesson 43

Materials

Teacher: *Storybook 1;* 8-Phonemic Awareness; 3 manipulatives such as blocks, discs, chips, counters (if not using IWB)

Student: *Storybook 1;* copy of 8-Phonemic Awareness; 3 manipulatives such as blocks, discs, chips, counters

Part A: Phonemic and Phonological Awareness

3 minutes

IWB

Teacher Materials:
Phonemic Awareness

3 manipulatives such as blocks, discs, chips, counters

Student Materials:
Phonemic Awareness

3 manipulatives such as blocks, discs, chips, counters

Activity 1 Phoneme Blending for One-Syllable Words

Elicit responses. **Guide** as needed.
Let's put some sounds together and make words. I'm going to say a word very slowly so you can hear each sound. You'll need to listen carefully and say the sounds. Then we'll put the sounds together and say the word.

My turn. Listen. **/www/ /āāā/ /t/.**
Say the sounds. */www/ /āāā/ /t/.*
Again, say the sounds. */www/ /āāā/ /t/.*
Let's put it together. What word? *Wait.*

My turn. Listen. **/www/ /āāā/ /g/.**
Say the sounds. */www/ /āāā//g/.*
Again, say the sounds. */www/ /āāā/ /g/.*
Let's put it together. What word? *Wag.*

(Continue the activity with the following words:
week [www-ēēē-k], we [www-ēēē], west [www-eee-sss-t], went [www-eee-nnn-t], wish [www-iii-shshsh], will [www-iii-lll], wide [www- īīī -d], woke [www-ōōō-k].)

Activity 2 Phoneme Segmentation

Show Phonemic Awareness. **Elicit** responses. **Guide** as needed.
Let's use our chips to show how many sounds there are in a word. For each sound in a word, we'll push one chip up to the arrow on the page. When we finish, we'll read the whole word.

Your turn. Say the sounds you hear in **sick,** and move a chip for each sound. */sss/ /iii/ /k/.*

Move your finger back to the dot. What word? *Sick.*
How many sounds are in the word **sick?** *Three.*
Correct. Now move your chips back to the bottom, and let's try another one.

(Continue the activity with the following words:
kick, lick, chick, thick.)

Part B: Vocabulary Development

5 minutes

Student Materials:
Storybook 1

Activity 1 Learn New Vocabulary Word

Elicit responses to questions. **Guide** as needed.
Today you'll learn a new vocabulary word. **Observe. Observe** means **look carefully.** What does **observe** mean? *Look carefully.*

Another word for **look carefully** is **observe.** What's another word for **look carefully?** *Observe.*

Scientists need to **look carefully** at experiments. They **observe** what is happening in the experiments.

What's another word for **look carefully?** *Observe.*

Discuss times when students might observe something.

Activity 2 Review Vocabulary Word

Elicit responses to questions. **Guide** as needed.
What does **cheer** mean? *Yell loudly.*
What's another word for **yell loudly?** *Cheer.*

Review vocabulary words in appropriate context in *Storybook 1.*

Part C: Comprehension Strategies

12 minutes

Teacher Materials:
Storybook 1

Student Materials:
Storybook 1

Activity 1 Mental Images—A During-Reading Strategy

Refer to Story 42, pages 107–109.

Elicit responses to mental images students have for the sentence. **Guide** as needed.
Remember that good readers make mental images to help them understand what they are reading. If you want to be a good reader, you need to practice making mental images when you read.

This sentence says: (Read first sentence in third paragraph on page 107.) Get a picture in your mind of that sentence. Where will the game take place?

What does the lot look like in your mind? (Student response.)

Where are the boys and girls? (Student response.)

What is Walter doing in your mind? (Student response.)

Who is on the football lot? (Student response.)

Making mental images when you read is a good strategy to help you understand what you read.

Activity 2 Sequencing—An After-Reading Strategy

Refer to Story 42, pages 107–109.

We're going to play the Put Events in Order game today. I'm going to tell you events that happen in the story. But I think I might get mixed up. You help me get the events in order.

Read each sentence with a pause between sentences.
The game started.

Walter said, "I wish I could help my team."

Walter went down to the lot.

Reread sentences again in the same order.

Elicit responses to questions. **Guide** as needed.
Which event happened first? (Idea: *Walter went down to the lot.*)

Which event happened next? (Idea: *The game started.*)

Which event happened last? (Idea: *Walter said, "I wish I could help my team."*)

Good for you. You put the events in the right order. When you remember to put events in the right order, it helps you retell the story the right way.

Part D: Fluency Building

5 minutes

Student Materials:
Storybook 1

Conduct after the lesson, using story of the day.

Activity 1 Partner Reading

It's time for partner reading.
Direct students to the story of the day. **Assign** student partners as Partner 1 and Partner 2. **Monitor** student reading. **Guide** as needed.

Lesson 44

Materials

Teacher: *Storybook 1;* 8-Phonemic Awareness; 3 manipulatives such as blocks, discs, chips, counters (if not using IWB)

Student: *Storybook 1;* copy of 8-Phonemic Awareness; 3 manipulatives such as blocks, discs, chips, counters

Part A: Phonemic and Phonological Awareness

3 minutes

IWB

Teacher Materials:
Phonemic Awareness

3 manipulatives such as blocks, discs, chips, counters

Student Materials:
Phonemic Awareness

3 manipulatives such as blocks, discs, chips, counters

Activity 1 Phoneme Blending for One-Syllable Words

Elicit responses. **Guide** as needed.
Let's put some sounds together and make words. I'm going to say a word very slowly so you can hear each sound. You'll need to listen carefully and say the sounds. Then we'll put the sounds together and say the word.

My turn. Listen. **/shshsh/ /āāā/ /p/.**
Say the sounds. */shshsh/ /āāā/ /p/.*
Again, say the sounds. */shshsh/ /āāā/ /p/.*
Let's put it together. What word? *Shape.*

My turn. Listen. **/shshsh/ /aaa/ /d/ /ōōō/.**
Say the sounds. */shshsh/ /aaa/ /d/ /ōōō/.*
Again, say the sounds. */shshsh/ /aaa/ /d/ /ōōō/.*
Let's put it together. What word? *Shadow.*

(Continue the activity with the following words:
sheet [shshsh-ēēē-t], she [shshsh-ēēē], shell [shshsh-eee-lll], shin [shshsh-iii-nnn], shout [shshsh-ou-t], shut [shshsh-uuu-t], show [shshsh-ōōō], shy [shshsh-īīī].)

Activity 2 Phoneme Segmentation

Show Phonemic Awareness. **Elicit** responses. **Guide** as needed.
Let's use our chips to show how many sounds there are in a word. For each sound in the word, we'll push one chip up to the arrow on the page. When we finish, we'll read the whole word.

Your turn. Say the sounds you hear in **phone,** and move a chip for each sound. */fff/ /ōōō/ /nnn/.*

Move your finger back to the dot. What word? *Phone.*

How many sounds are in the word **phone?** *Three.*

Correct. Now move your chips back to the bottom, and let's try another one.

(Continue the activity with the following words:
bone, cone, tone, zone.)

Part B: Vocabulary Development

Activity 1   Learn New Vocabulary Word

Elicit responses to questions. **Guide** as needed.
Today you'll learn a new vocabulary word. **Confidence. Confidence** means **a belief in yourself.** What does **confidence** mean? *A belief in yourself.*

Another word for **a belief in yourself** is **confidence.** What's another word for **a belief in yourself?** *Confidence.*

You had a **belief in yourself** that you could kick the football and help the team. You had **confidence** that you could kick the football.

What's another word for **a belief in yourself?** *Confidence.*

Discuss times when students have confidence.

Activity 2   Review Vocabulary Word

Elicit responses to questions. **Guide** as needed.
What does **observe** mean? *Look carefully.*
What's another word for **look carefully?** *Observe.*

Review vocabulary words in appropriate context in *Storybook 1.*

Part C: Comprehension Strategies

Activity 1   Generate Questions—A During-Reading Strategy

Refer to Story 43, page 110–112.

Elicit responses to questions. **Guide** as needed.
Asking questions is a strategy to use when you are reading stories. Why do you ask questions when you are reading? *To understand the story better.*

Learning to ask questions is a hard skill. It takes lots of practice. Let's practice asking questions some more.

Guide students to complete questions, not give the answer to the questions.
Here is something that happened in the story. Walter's team didn't have any scores. Help me make up a question. "Did Walter's team _____ ?" *Have any scores.*

Yes! "Did Walter's team have any scores?"

Say the whole question with me. *"Did Walter's team have any scores?"*

What is the answer to the question, "Did Walter's team have any scores?" *No.*

Here is another part of the story. He ran toward his team. Who can make up a question from that sentence? (Ideas: *"Where did Walter run?" "How did Walter go to his team?" "Who ran to his team?"*)

It was smart to make a question instead of giving the answer to the question. What's the answer to the question you made up? (Student response.)

Here is another part of the story. The team needed two scores to win the game. Who can make up a question on this information?
(Ideas: *"How many scores did they need?" "How can they win?" "Who needs two more scores to win the game?"*)

What is the answer to the question? (Student response.)

You are getting good at asking questions.

Activity 2   Sequencing—An After-Reading Strategy

Refer to Story 43, pages 110–112.

We're going to play the Put Events in Order game today. I'm going to tell you events that happen in the story. But you know I will be mixed up. You help me get the events in order.

Read each sentence with a pause between sentences.
Walter ran to his team.

Walter's team was not doing well.

The best player cut his arm.

Reread sentences again in the same order.

Elicit responses to questions. **Guide** as needed.
Which event happened first? (Idea: *Walter's team was not doing well.*)

Which event happened next? (Idea: *The best player cut his arm.*)

Which event happened last? (Idea: *Walter ran to his team.*)

Good for you. You put the events in the right order. Remembering to put events in the right order helps you retell the story the right way.

Part D: Fluency Building

Conduct after the lesson, using story of the day.

Activity 1 Partner Reading

It's time for partner reading.

Direct students to the story of the day. **Assign** student partners as Partner 1 and Partner 2. **Monitor** student reading. **Guide** as needed.

Lesson 45

Materials

Teacher: *Storybook 1;* 8-Phonemic Awareness; 3 manipulatives such as blocks, discs, chips, counters (if not using IWB), 2-Vocabulary Acquisition and Use, Writing Prompts, 5-My Writing Checklist

Student: *Storybook 1;* copy of 8-Phonemic Awareness; 3 manipulatives such as blocks, discs, chips, counters, Copy of 2- Vocabulary Acquisition and Use and 3-My Writing Checklist; Lined Paper

Part A: Phonemic and Phonological Awareness

3 minutes

IWB

Teacher Materials:
Phonemic Awareness

3 manipulatives such as blocks, discs, chips, counters

Student Materials:
Phonemic Awareness

3 manipulatives such as blocks, discs, chips, counters

Activity 1 Phoneme Blending for One-Syllable Words

Elicit responses. **Guide** as needed.
Let's put some sounds together and make words. I'm going to say a word very slowly so you can hear each sound. You'll need to listen carefully and say the sounds. Then we'll put the sounds together and say the word.

My turn. Listen. **/vvv/ /āāā/ /sss/.**
Say the sounds. */vvv/ /āāā/ /sss/.*
Again, say the sounds. */vvv/ /āāā/ /sss/.*
Let's put it together. What word? *Vase.*

My turn. Listen. **/vvv/ /aaa/ /nnn/.**
Say the sounds. */vvv/ /aaa/ /nnn/.*
Again, say the sounds. */vvv/ /aaa/ /nnn/.*
Let's put it together. What word? *Van.*

(Continue the activity with the following words:
vein [vvv-āāā-nnn], vent [vvv-eee-nnn-t], vet [vvv-eee-t], vine [vvv-īīī-nnn], voice [vvv-oi-sss], vote [vvv-ōōō-t], valley [vvv-aaa-lll-ēēē], veil [vvv-āāā-lll].)

Activity 2 Phoneme Segmentation

Show Phonemic Awareness. **Elicit** responses. **Guide** as needed.
Let's use our chips to show how many sounds there are in a word. For each sound in the word, we'll push one chip up to the arrow on the page. When we finish, we'll read the whole word.

Your turn. Say the sounds you hear in **dog,** and move a chip for each sound. */d/ /ooo/ /g/.*

Move your finger back to the dot. What word? *Dog.*

How many sounds are in the word **dog?** *Three.*

Correct. Now move your chips back to the bottom, and let's try another one.

(Continue the activity with the following words:
fog, log, jog, hog.)

5 minutes

IWB

Teacher Materials:
Vocabulary Acquisition
and Use

Student Materials:
Storybook 1

Vocabulary Acquisition
and Use

Part B: Vocabulary Development

Activity 1 Cumulative Vocabulary Review

Elicit responses to questions. **Guide** as needed.
Directions: Listen and tell me the correct vocabulary word for each question.

What's another word for **sad?** *Unhappy.*
What's another word for **look carefully?** *Observe.*
What's another word for **a belief in yourself?** *Confidence.*
What's another word for **yell loudly?** *Cheer.*

Review difficult words as needed.

Review vocabulary words in appropriate context in *Storybook 1.*

Activity 2 Vocabulary Acquisition and Use

Display Vocabulary Acquisition and Use. **Have** students work with a neighbor to complete Vocabulary Acquisition and Use.
Today's vocabulary words are _____ and _____ [and _____ and _____].
Vocabulary words: **observe** and **look; unhappy** and **sad**
Write the words on the lines provided. Then write the words in the boxes based on whether you think each word is less/smaller or more/larger than the other word. Below the boxes, write why you think word 1 is less/smaller and word 2 is more/larger than word 1.
Repeat for words 3 and 4. **Have** students share what they wrote. **Discuss** examples of how these words might be used.

Part C: Comprehension Strategies

Activity 1 Act Out the Story—An After-Reading Strategy

Refer to Stories 41–44, pages 104–114.

Putting on a play is a great way to help you remember what you read. Today you can put on a play. But first we have to make some decisions.

Elicit responses to questions and **choose** students to play parts in the play.
Where does the Walter story take place? (Idea: *The football lot.*)

Where will the football lot be in our classroom? (Student responses.)

Who is the main character in the story? *Walter.*

Who will play the Walter part? (Student responses.)

Who are other characters in the story? (Idea: *Walter's team, the other team, boys and girls on the sides of the lot.*)

Who will play those parts? (Student responses.)

I will tell the story. Sometimes I will tell you to say a part. You can move around to act out the story as I tell the story. Here we go.

Position actors appropriately. **Side-coach** by **retelling** the story and **prompting** students to move or say dialogue as appropriate.

Sample Wording for Play

Walter's team did not want him to play anymore because he did not play well. (Prompt team to tell Walter to go home.) Walter was very unhappy, and he went home to think. (Prompt Walter to look very unhappy and walk away.) On the day of the game, Walter decided to go to the football lot and watch the game. (Prompt Walter to walk to football lot.) Some kids were cheering for Walter's team. (Prompt half the kids on the sidelines to cheer for Walter's team. Prompt the others to cheer for the other team.) The teams started to play. The other team scored two times. (Prompt the other team to act out making two scores and the kids supporting the other team to cheer.) Walter said, "I wish I could help my team." (Prompt Walter to say words.) Then Walter's team got a score. (Prompt Walter's team to act out getting a score and the kids to cheer.) Then the best player on Walter's team cut his arm. (Prompt one student to pretend that he cut his arm and have the student leave the game.) Then Walter's team called him to come in the game. (Prompt team to call Walter to go in the game.) Walter's team needs two scores to win the game. (Prompt team to tell Walter to play well.) The team decided to kick the ball. Walter said he would kick. (Prompt Walter to say he will kick and mime kicking the ball.) The end.

Remind actors to take a bow. **Remind** the audience to applaud (a previous vocabulary word)

Oh, my. We can't act out any more until we read the rest of the story.

Part D: Fluency Building

5 minutes

Student Materials:
Storybook 1

Conduct after the lesson, using story of the day.

Activity 1 Partner Reading

It's time for partner reading.
Direct students to the story of the day. **Assign** student partners as Partner 1 and Partner 2. **Monitor** student reading. **Guide** as needed.

10 minutes

IWB

Teacher Materials:
Writing Prompts

My Writing Checklist

Student Materials:
Lined Paper

My Writing Checklist

Activity 1 **Write and Use Parts of Speech and Conventions**

Time to write using a writing prompt based on the stories we've been reading.

Assign student partners. **Distribute** lined paper to students. **Display** writing prompts and have students choose one to write about or assign a writing prompt of your choice. **Review** parts of speech and punctuation as well as the writing checklist with students. **Tell** students to write one paragraph (minimum of four sentences per paragraph) on their own to answer the writing prompt. **Tell** them to use their writing checklist (first column labeled "Did I use them?") to ensure they include important parts of speech or punctuation in their writing. **Tell** students which parts of speech or punctuation to focus on, if you wish. **Model** what it means to answer a writing prompt and to use the writing checklist during and after the writing process, as needed. **Monitor** and guide students as needed. **Model** what it means to have a neighbor look over his or her neighbor's writing and to complete the writing checklist (second column labeled "Did my neighbor use them?"), as needed. **Have** students share what they wrote as time permits.

Writing Prompt 1	*Writing Prompt 2*	*Writing Prompt 3*
Would you want to live inside a ball if you were a small bug? Why or why?	Tell me about a bet that you won or lost.	Tell me about a favorite book that you read. Why was it so good?

Materials

Teacher: *Storybook 1;* 6-My Prediction Chart; 8-Phonemic Awareness; 3 manipulatives such as blocks, discs, chips, counters (if not using IWB)

Student: *Storybook 1;* copy of 8-Phonemic Awareness; 3 manipulatives such as blocks, discs, chips, counters

Part A: Phonemic and Phonological Awareness

3 minutes

IWB

Teacher Materials:
Phonemic Awareness

3 manipulatives such as blocks, discs, chips, counters

Student Materials:
Phonemic Awareness

3 manipulatives such as blocks, discs, chips, counters

Activity 1 Phoneme Blending for One-Syllable Words

Elicit responses. **Guide** as needed.
Let's put some sounds together and make words. I'm going to say a word very slowly so you can hear each sound. You'll need to listen carefully and say the sounds. Then we'll put the sounds together and say the word.

My turn. Listen. **/p/ /āāā/ /sss/ /t/.**
Say the sounds. /p/ /āāā/ sss/ /t/.
Again, say the sounds. /p/ /āāā/ /sss/ /t/.
Let's put it together. What word? *Paste.*

My turn. Listen. **/p/ /aaa/ /sss/.**
Say the sounds. /p/ /aaa/ /sss/.
Again, say the sounds. /p/ /aaa/ /sss/.
Let's put it together. What word? *Pass.*

(Continue the activity with the following words:
paint [p-āāā-nnn-t], peel [p-ēēē-lll], pet [p-eee-t], pie [p-īīī], pitch [p-iii-ch],
pool [p-oooooo-lll], punt [p-uuu-nnn-t], puffy [p-uuu-fff-ēēē].)

Activity 2 Phoneme Segmentation

Show Phonemic Awareness. **Elicit** responses. **Guide** as needed.
Let's use our chips to show how many sounds there are in a word. For each sound in a word, we'll push one chip up to the arrow on the page. When we finish, we'll read the whole word.

Your turn. Say the sounds you hear in **five,** and move a chip for each sound. /fff/ /īīī/ /vvv/.

Move your finger back to the dot. What word? *Five.*
How many sounds are in the word **five?** *Three.*
Correct. Now move your chips back to the bottom and let's try another one.

(Continue the activity with the following words:
five, live, hive, dive.)

Part B: Vocabulary Development

Activity 1   Learn New Vocabulary Phrase (Idiom)

Elicit responses to questions. **Guide** as needed.
Today you'll learn a new vocabulary phrase. **Off like a shot. Off like a shot** means **goes fast and straight.** What does **off like a shot** mean? *Goes fast and straight.*

Another way to say **goes fast and straight** is **off like a shot.** What's another way to say **goes fast and straight?** *Off like a shot.*

The runner gets ready to start the race. When he hears 'go," he **goes fast and straight.** He is **off like a shot** to win.

What's another way to say **goes fast and straight?** *Off like a shot.*

Discuss times when students might go off like a shot.

Activity 2   Review Vocabulary Word

Elicit responses to questions. **Guide** as needed.
What does **confidence** mean? *A belief in yourself.*
What's another word for **a belief in yourself?** *Confidence.*

Review vocabulary words in appropriate context in *Storybook 1.*

12 minutes

IWB

Teacher Materials:
Storybook 1

My Prediction Chart

Student Materials:
Storybook 1

Part C: Comprehension Strategies

Activity 1   Identify Story Elements—An After-Reading Strategy

Refer to Stories 41–45, pages 104–116.

Elicit responses to questions. **Guide** as needed.
You had fun acting out the Walter story in our last lesson. Now let's review some things you know.

What kind of story is the Walter story? *Narrative.*

How do you know the story is a narrative? (Idea: *It is fun to read.*)

Who is the main character? *Walter.*

Who are other characters in the story? (Idea: *Boys on Walter's team, boys on the other team, kids cheering on the side of the lot.*)

Where does the story mostly take place? *The football lot.*

Tell me some events that happened at the beginning of the story. (Idea: *Walter did not play well. The team kicked Walter off the team.*)

Tell me some events that happened in the middle of the story.
(Idea: *Walter went to see the game. The other team was winning. The best player got hurt. The team called Walter to play. Walter was going to kick the ball.*)

You will read the end of the story today. So you cannot tell the end yet. You remembered a lot about the Walter story. Good for you!

Activity 2 Prediction—A Before-Reading Strategy

Refer to Story 46, pages 117–118.

Elicit responses to questions. **Guide** as needed. **Show** My Prediction Chart.
You're going to read the rest of the story about Walter. The story is called "Walter's Team Wins." When you make predictions, you're guessing what will happen from clues in the story. You get the clues from the title and from the pictures. Where do you get clues to make predictions? *From the title and the pictures.*

Discuss predictions with students. **Record** title and predictions on chart.
Let's look at the story you are going to read and make some predictions about what will happen in the story. Look at the title and the pictures. See if there are clues to help you predict what might happen in this story.

I will record our predictions. Do you predict that this story might be a narrative? *Yes.*

Why do you think so? (Idea: *It looks like it might be fun to read.*)

What will the story be about? (Idea: *Walter's team winning.*)

What clue gives you that idea? *The title.*

What do you think might happen in the story? (Idea: *Walter is the star of the game.*)

What clue makes you think that? (Idea: *The picture shows Walter on the shoulders of his teammates.*)

Do you have any more predictions? (Student responses.)

What clue makes you think that? (Student responses.)

Remember: making predictions helps you understand the text you read better.

Save recorded predictions.

Provide a reading center to display books being read so that students can enjoy them again during free time.

5 minutes

Student Materials:
Storybook 1

Conduct after the lesson, using story of the day.

It's time for partner reading.

Direct students to the story of the day. **Assign** student partners as Partner 1 and Partner 2. **Monitor** student reading. **Guide** as needed.

Lesson 47

Materials

Teacher: *Storybook 1;* 1-Narrative Story Map; 6-My Prediction Chart (from Lesson 46); 8-Phonemic Awareness; 3 manipulatives such as blocks, discs, chips, counters (if not using IWB)

Student: *Storybook 1;* Copy of 1-Narrative Story Map; copy of 8-Phonemic Awareness; 3 manipulatives such as blocks, discs, chips, counters

---

3 minutes

IWB

Teacher Materials:
Phonemic Awareness

3 manipulatives such as blocks, discs, chips, counters

Student Materials:
Phonemic Awareness

3 manipulatives such as blocks, discs, chips, counters

Part A: Phonemic and Phonological Awareness

Activity 1 Phoneme Blending for One-Syllable Words

Elicit responses. **Guide** as needed.
Let's put some sounds together and make words. I'm going to say a word very slowly so you can hear each sound. You'll need to listen carefully and say the sounds. Then we'll put the sounds together and say the word.

My turn. Listen. **/ch/ /āāā/ /nnn/.**
Say the sounds. */ch/ /āāā/ /nnn/.*
Again, say the sounds. */ch/ /āāā/ /nnn/.*
Let's put it together. What word? *Chain.*

My turn. Listen. **/ch/ /aaa/ /mmm/ /p/.**
Say the sounds. */ch/ /aaa/ /mmm/ /p/.*
Again, say the sounds. */ch/ /aaa/ /mmm/ /p/.*
Let's put it together. What word? *Champ.*

(Continue the activity with the following words:
cheek [ch-ēēē-k], cheese [ch-ēēē-zzz], chest [ch-eee-sss-t], child [ch-īīī-lll-d], chilly [ch-iii-lll-ēēē], chips [ch-iii-p-sss], chose [ch-ōōō-zzz], chop [ch-ŏŏŏ-p].)

Activity 2 Phoneme Segmentation

Show Phonemic Awareness. **Elicit** responses. **Guide** as needed.
Let's use our chips to show how many sounds there are in a word. For each sound in a word, we'll push one chip up to the arrow on the page. When we finish, we'll read the whole word.

Your turn. Say the sounds you hear in **sell,** and move a chip for each sound. */sss/ /eee/ /lll/.*

Move your finger back to the dot. What word? *Sell.*
How many sounds are in the word **sell?** *Three.*
Correct. Now move your chips back to the bottom, and let's try another one.

(Continue the activity with the following words:
bell, well, fell, shell.)

Part B: Vocabulary Development

Activity 1 New Vocabulary Word

Elicit responses to questions. **Guide** as needed.
Today you'll learn a new vocabulary word. **Felt. Felt** means **was feeling.**
What does **felt** mean? *Was feeling.*

Another way to say **was feeling** is **felt.** What's another way to say **was feeling?** *Felt.*

Walt **was feeling** sad that his team wasn't winning the game. Walter **felt** sad.

What's another word for **was feeling?** *Felt.*

Discuss times when students felt happy, sad, angry, etc.

Activity 2 Review Vocabulary Word

What does **off like a shot** mean? *Goes fast and straight.*
What's another way to say **goes fast and straight?** *Off like a shot.*

Review vocabulary words in appropriate context in *Storybook 1.*

Part C: Comprehension Strategies

12 minutes

IWB

Teacher Materials:
Storybook 1

Narrative Story Map

My Prediction Chart

Student Materials:
Storybook 1

Narrative Story Map

Activity 1 Confirm Predictions—An After-Reading Strategy

Show My Prediction Chart. **Guide** discussion based on recorded predictions made in Lesson 46. **Elicit** responses to questions. **Guide** as needed.
Yesterday you made some predictions about what would happen in the Walter story. You made the predictions before you read the story. Making predictions helps you understand the story better. Now that you've read the story, let's check to see if your predictions were in the story. What are you doing when you check to see if your predictions are correct? *Confirming predictions.*

What part in the story helps you confirm your predictions? (Student response.)

Discuss value of making predictions with students.
Do all your predictions need to be correct? *No.*

Why not? (Idea: *Making predictions helps me understand the story even if they are not correct, because I am thinking about confirming my predictions.*)

Activity 2 Story Map—An After-Reading Strategy

Show Narrative Story Map.
Let's work together to fill in our Narrative Story Map about Walter.

These chapters had lots of titles, so we will just call the whole story "Walter and the Football Game."

Give students Narrative Story Map. **Touch** each section of map. **Elicit** responses to questions, and **allow** students to draw quick pictures to fill in boxes. **Guide** students as needed.
What will you draw for the main character? *Walter.* Draw that in the box for Characters.

What events will you draw for the beginning? (Idea: *Walter cannot play with his team.*)

What events will you draw for the middle? (Idea: *Walter's team did not play well. The best player got hurt. Walter had to go into the game.*)

What events will you draw at the end? (Idea: *Walter helped win the game by kicking the ball.*)

When you fill out a Narrative Story Map, you really show that you remember all about the story.

Save student copies of completed Narrative Story Map for Lesson 48.

Part D: Fluency Building

5 minutes

Student Materials:
Storybook 1

Conduct after the lesson, using story of the day.

Activity 1 Partner Reading

It's time for partner reading.
Direct students to the story of the day. **Assign** student partners as Partner 1 and Partner 2. **Monitor** student reading. **Guide** as needed.

Lesson 48

Materials

Teacher: *Storybook 1;* 1-Narrative Story Map (from Lesson 47); 8-Phonemic Awareness; 3 manipulatives such as blocks, discs, chips, counters (if not using IWB)

Student: *Storybook 1;* copy of 1-Narrative Story Map (from Lesson 47); copy of 8-Phonemic Awareness; 3 manipulatives such as blocks, discs, chips, counters

Part A: Phonemic and Phonological Awareness

3 minutes

IWB

Teacher Materials:
Phonemic Awareness

3 manipulatives such as blocks, discs, chips, counters

Student Materials:
Phonemic Awareness

3 manipulatives such as blocks, discs, chips, counters

Activity 1 Phoneme Blending for One-Syllable Words

Elicit responses. **Guide** as needed.
Let's put some sounds together and make words. I'm going to say a word very slowly so you can hear each sound. You'll need to listen carefully and say the sounds. Then we'll put the sounds together and say the word.

My turn. Listen. **/b/ /āāā/ /k/.**
Say the sounds. */b/ /āāā/ /k/.*
Again, say the sounds. */b/ /āāā/ /k/.*
Let's put it together. What word? *Bake.*

My turn. Listen. **/b/ /aaa/ /ththth.**
Say the sounds. */b/ /aaa/ /ththth/.*
Again, say the sounds. */b/ /aaa/ /ththth/.*
Let's put it together. What word? *Bath.*

(Continue the activity with the following words:
bee [b-ēēē], bead [b-ēēē-d], belt [b-eee-lll-t], bike [b-īīī-k], bone [b-ōōō-nnn], bottle [b-ooo-t-lll], bus [b-uuu-sss], buzz [b-uuu-zzz].)

Activity 2 Phoneme Segmentation

Show Phonemic Awareness. **Elicit** responses. **Guide** as needed.
Let's use our chips to show how many sounds there are in a word. For each sound in a word, we'll push one chip up to the arrow on the page. When we finish, we'll read the whole word.

Your turn. Say the sounds you hear in **beep,** and move a chip for each sound.
/b/ /ēēē/ /p/.
Move your finger back to the dot. What word? *Beep.*
How many sounds are in the word **beep?** *Three.*
Correct. Now move your chips back to the bottom, and let's try another one.

(Continue the activity with the following words:
jeep, keep, weep, sheep.)

5 minutes

Student Materials:
Storybook 1

Activity 1 Learn New Vocabulary Word

Elicit responses to questions. **Guide** as needed.
Today you'll learn a new vocabulary word. **Field trip.** A **field trip** is **somewhere you go to learn new things.** What's a **field trip?** *Somewhere you go to learn new things.*

Another way to say **somewhere you go to learn new things** is **field trip.** What's another way to say **somewhere you go to learn new things?** *Field trip.*

The class goes **somewhere you go to learn new things.** The class goes on a **field trip.**

What's another way to say **somewhere you go to learn new things?** *Field trip.*

Discuss places students could go on a field trip.

Activity 2 Review Vocabulary Word

Elicit responses to questions. **Guide** as needed.
What does **felt** mean? *Was feeling.*
What's another word for **was feeling?** *Felt.*

Review vocabulary words in appropriate context in *Storybook 1.*

Part C: Comprehension Strategies

12 minutes

IWB

Teacher Materials:
Storybook 1
Narrative Story Map

Student Materials:
Storybook 1
Narrative Story Map

Activity 1 Retell the Story—An After-Reading Strategy

Distribute Narrative Story Map completed in Lesson 47 to students.
You did a great job filling out your Narrative Story Maps in the last lesson. Today you'll use your Narrative Story Map to retell the Walter story. Start by telling the title. Then look at the picture clues in the different boxes of your map to help you retell the story. Tell the story to your partner. Then have your partner tell the story to you.

Monitor student partners as they retell the story from the Narrative Story Map.

Activity 2 Activate Background Knowledge—An After-Reading Strategy

Refer to Story 49, pages 123 and 124.

Elicit responses to questions. **Guide** as needed.

All the things you know in your brain are called **schema.** Everyone has schema. Each of us has different schema, because each person has different experiences. You build schema every time you learn new information. You also build schema from all the experiences you have in life. The longer you live, the more schema you build. You build lots of schema in school because you are learning so much. Before you read a new story, it is a good idea to figure out your schema on the topic of the story. It is like opening the files in your mind and figuring out what you already know.

What is **schema?** (Idea: *Everything you know in your brain.*)

You will understand a story better if you connect what you know to what you learn in the new story. This is called building schema. You add new information to the file in your brain about any subject.

Today we will read a story about a field trip to a cow farm. You will understand the story better if you look in your brain and find out what you know about farms, field trips, and cows.

Discuss background knowledge to build schema. **Guide** as needed.
What is your schema about farms? (Student responses.)

What is your schema about field trips? (Student responses.)

What is your schema about cows? (Student responses.)

Schema is everything you know in your brain. What is the word to tell about everything you know in your brain? *Schema.*

Part D: Fluency Building

5 minutes

Student Materials:
Storybook 1

Conduct after the lesson, using story of the day.

Activity 1 Partner Reading

It's time for partner reading.
Direct students to the story of the day. **Assign** student partners as Partner 1 and Partner 2. **Monitor** student reading. **Guide** as needed.

Lesson 49

Materials

Teacher: *Storybook 1;* 8-Phonemic Awareness; 3 manipulatives such as blocks, discs, chips, counters (if not using IWB)

Student: *Storybook 1;* copy of 8-Phonemic Awareness; 3 manipulatives such as blocks, discs, chips, counters

Part A: Phonemic and Phonological Awareness

3 minutes

IWB

Teacher Materials:
Phonemic Awareness

3 manipulatives such as blocks, discs, chips, counters

Student Materials:
Phonemic Awareness

3 manipulatives such as blocks, discs, chips, counters

Activity 1 Phoneme Blending for One-Syllable Words

Elicit responses. **Guide** as needed.
Let's put some sounds together and make words. I'm going to say a word very slowly so you can hear each sound. You'll need to listen carefully and say the sounds. Then we'll put the sounds together and say the word.

My turn. Listen. **/yyy/ /aaa/ /k/.**
Say the sounds. */yyy/ /aaa/ /k/.*
Again, say the sounds. */yyy/ /aaa/ /k/.*
Let's put it together. What word? *Yak.*

My turn. Listen. **/yyy/ /ēēē/ /rrr/.**
Say the sounds. */yyy/ /ēēē/ /rrr/.*
Again, say the sounds. */yyy/ /ēēē/ /rrr/.*
Let's put it together. What word? *Year.*

(Continue the activity with the following words:
yes [yyy-eee-sss], yell [yyy-eee-lll], yet [yyy-eee- t], yellow [yyy-eee-lll-ōōō], yoke [yyy-ōōō-k], yoyo [yyy-ōōō-yyy-ōōō], yummy [yyy-ŭŭŭ-mmm-ēēē], you [yyy-ūūū].)

Activity 2 Phoneme Segmentation

Show Phonemic Awareness. **Elicit** responses. **Guide** as needed.
Let's use our chips to show how many sounds there are in a word. For each sound in a word, we'll push one chip up to the arrow on the page. When we finish, we'll read the whole word.

Your turn. Say the sounds you hear in **cut,** and move a chip for each sound. /c/ /uuu/ /t/.

Move your finger back to the dot. What word? *Cut.*
How many sounds are in the word **cut?** *Three.*
Correct. Now move your chips back to the bottom, and let's try another one.

(Continue the activity with the following words:
hut, shut, rut, nut.)

Part B: Vocabulary Development

5 minutes

Student Materials:
Storybook 1

Activity 1 Learn New Vocabulary Word

Elicit responses to questions. **Guide** as needed.
Today you'll learn a new vocabulary word. **Loud. Loud** means **very noisy.**
What does **loud** mean? *Very noisy.*

Another word for **very noisy** is **loud.** What's another word for **very noisy?**
Loud.

It's **very noisy** in the cafeteria. The principal said, "It's **loud,** so please quiet down."

What's another word for **very noisy?** *Loud.*

Discuss times when things are loud.

Activity 2 Review Word

Elicit responses to questions. **Guide** as needed.
What's a **field trip?** *Somewhere you go to learn new things.*
What's another way to say **somewhere you go to learn new things?**
Field trip.

Review vocabulary words in appropriate context in *Storybook 1.*

Part C: Comprehension Strategies

12 minutes

Teacher Materials:
Storybook 1

Student Materials:
Storybook 1

Activity 1 Make Mental Images—A During-Reading Strategy

Refer to Story 48, pages 120–122.

Elicit responses to mental images. **Guide** as needed.
Remember that good readers make pictures in their brains while they read to help them understand what they are reading. If you want to be a good reader, you need to practice making pictures in your brain when you read.

This sentence says: (Read third sentence from story on page 120.) Get a picture in your mind of that sentence. What picture do you see in your brain when you read that sentence?

What does Carmen look like? (Student response.)

What are the children doing? (Student response.)

Where is Carmen? (Student response.)

When you make mental images as you read, you will be better at understanding what you read.

Activity 2 Sequencing—An After-Reading Strategy

Refer to Story 48, pages 120–122.

We are going to play the Put Events in Order game today. I am going to tell you events that happen in the story. But you know me. I get mixed up. You can help me get the events in order.

Read each sentence with a pause between sentences.
A girl fell in a deep, deep hole.

One day some children came to a farm.

The children petted the cows.

Reread sentences again in the same order.

Elicit responses from questions. **Guide** as needed.
Which event happened first? (Idea: *One day some children came to a farm.*)

What event happened next? (Idea: *The children petted cows.*)

What event happened last? (Idea: *A girl fell in a deep, deep hole.*)

Good for you. You put the events in the right order. Remembering to put events in the right order helps you retell the story the right way.

Part D: Fluency Building

5 minutes

Student Materials:
Storybook 1

Conduct after the lesson, using story of the day.

Activity 1 Partner Reading

It's time for partner reading.
Direct students to the story of the day. **Assign** student partners as Partner 1 and Partner 2. **Monitor** student reading. **Guide** as needed.

Lesson 50

Materials

Teacher: *Storybook 1;* 8-Phonemic Awareness; 3 manipulatives such as blocks, discs, chips, counters (if not using IWB), 2-Vocabulary Acquisition and Use, 3-My Book Review

Student: *Storybook 1;* copy of 8-Phonemic Awareness; 3 manipulatives such as blocks, discs, chips, counters, Copy of 2-Vocabulary Acquisition and Use and 3-My Book Review

Part A: Phonemic and Phonological Awareness

3 minutes

IWB

Teacher Materials:
Phonemic Awareness

3 manipulatives such as blocks, discs, chips, counters

Student Materials:
Phonemic Awareness

3 manipulatives such as blocks, discs, chips, counters

Activity 1 Phoneme Blending for One-Syllable Words

Elicit responses. **Guide** as needed.

Let's put some sounds together and make words. I'm going to say a word very slowly so you can hear each sound. You'll need to listen carefully and say the sounds. Then we'll put the sounds together and say the word.

My turn. Listen. **/j/ /aaa /mmm/.**
Say the sounds. */j/ /aaa/ /mmm/.*
Again, say the sounds. */j/ /aaa/ /mmm/.*
Let's put it together. What word? *Jam.*

My turn. Listen. **/j/ /āāā/.**
Say the sounds. */j/ /āāā/.*
Again, say the sounds. */j/ /āāā/.*
Let's put it together. What word? *Jay.*

(Continue the activity with the following words:
jeans [j-ēēē-nnn-zzz], jelly [j-eee-lll-ēēē], jet [j-eee- t], job [j-ooo-b],
joke [j-ōōō-k], jump [j-uuu-mmm-p], jug [j-uuu-g], just [j-uuu-sss-t].)

Activity 2 Phoneme Segmentation

Show Phonemic Awareness. **Elicit** responses. **Guide** as needed.

Let's use our chips to show how many sounds there are in a word. For each sound in a word, we'll push one chip up to the arrow on the page. When we finish, we'll read the whole word.

Your turn. Say the sounds you hear in **mail,** and move a chip for each sound. */mmm/ /āāā/ /lll/.*

Move your finger back to the dot. What word? *Mail.*
How many sounds are in the word **mail?** *Three.*
Correct. Now move your chips back to the bottom, and let's try another one.

(Continue the activity with the following words:
mail, sail, tail, pail, nail.)

5 minutes

IWB

Teacher Materials:
Vocabulary Acquisition
and Use

Student Materials:
Storybook 1

Vocabulary Acquisition
and Use

Activity 1 Cumulative Vocabulary Review

Elicit responses to questions. **Guide** as needed.
Directions: Listen and tell me the correct vocabulary word for each question.

What's another word for **very noisy?** *Loud.*
What's another word for **sad?** *Unhappy.*
What's another word for **look carefully?** *Observe.*
What's another way to say **somewhere you go to learn new things?**
Field trip.
What's another word for **was feeling?** *Felt.*
What's another word for **yell loudly?** *Cheer.*
What's another word for **a belief in yourself?** *Confidence.*
What's another way to say **goes fast and straight?** *Off like a shot.*

Repeat difficult words as needed.

Review vocabulary words in appropriate context in *Storybook 1.*

Activity 2 Vocabulary Acquisition and Use

Display Vocabulary Acquisition and Use. **Have** students work with a neighbor to complete Vocabulary Acquisition and Use.
Today's vocabulary words are _____ and _____ [and _____ and _____].
Vocabulary words: **loud** and **noisy; happy** and **excited**
Write the words on the lines provided. Then write the words in the boxes based on whether you think each word is less/smaller or more/larger than the other word. Below the boxes, write why you think word 1 is less/smaller and word 2 is more/larger than word 1.
Repeat for words 3 and 4. **Have** students share what they wrote. **Discuss** examples of how these words might be used.

12 minutes

IWB

Teacher Materials:
Storybook 1

My Book Review

Student Materials:
Storybook 1

My Book Review

Activity 1 Read with Prosody—A During-Reading Strategy

Direct students to Story 49, pages 123 and 124.

Model how quotation marks are used on the board.
Lots of narratives have dialogue. Dialogue is the words that characters say in a story. Dialogue is always marked with special talking marks called quotation marks. The words that characters say are called dialogue. What are the words characters say? *Dialogue.*

Model example and non-example of the way the teacher might sound on dialogue sentence.

You need to read dialogue the way that the character might really say the words. That makes your reading more interesting. In Story 49, page 123, in the paragraph after the questions, the teacher says, "That sounds like a call for help." If I read it so it really sounds like the teacher talking, it makes the story more interesting. See if you can find more dialogue in the story. How would you say those words? (Student responses.)

When you read words between quotation marks, you're reading dialogue, and you should try to make your voice really interesting so the story sounds fun.

Activity 2   Activate Background Knowledge—An After-Reading Strategy

Elicit responses to questions. **Guide** as needed.
We talked about schema. Schema is everything that you know in your brain. What do you call everything you know in your brain? *Schema.*

It is a good idea to think about what you know about a topic before you read a new story. Then you can connect what you know to the new information you learn when you read.

Discuss background knowledge. **Guide** as needed.
Today the story is about a girl who wants a pet mouse.

What is your schema for pets? (Student responses.)

What is your schema for a mouse? (Student responses.)

When you connect what you already know with the story you read today, you'll be building more schema in your brain and your brain will be smarter.

Activity 3   Develop Opinions—An After-Reading Strategy

Today we'll found out your opinion or how you feel about the stories you read. You will choose a book to read and then complete the My Book Review form. You'll need to tell if you like or don't like the book and why. You must give a reason for why you like or don't like the book. Finally, you can tell if you would recommend the book to others.

Have students read a narrative or expository trade book of their choice. **Have** students complete My Book Review form when they are finished reading their book. **Model** how to complete the My Book Review form. **Guide** students as needed. **Have** students share their book reviews with the class as time permits.

Part D: Fluency Building

5 minutes

Student Materials:
Storybook 1

Conduct after the lesson, using story of the day.

Activity 1 | Partner Reading

It's time for partner reading.

Direct students to the story of the day. **Assign** student partners as Partner 1 and Partner 2. **Monitor** student reading. **Guide** as needed.

Lesson 51

Materials

Teacher: *Storybook 1;* 8-Phonemic Awareness; 3 manipulatives such as blocks, discs, chips, counters (if not using IWB)

Student: *Storybook 1;* copy of 8-Phonemic Awareness; 3 manipulatives such as blocks, discs, chips, counters

---

3 minutes

IWB

Teacher Materials:
Phonemic Awareness

3 manipulatives such as blocks, discs, chips, counters

Student Materials:
Phonemic Awareness

3 manipulatives such as blocks, discs, chips, counters

Part A: Phonemic and Phonological Awareness

Activity 1 Phoneme Blending for One-Syllable Words

Let's put some sounds together and make words. I'm going to say a word very slowly so you can hear each sound. You'll need to listen carefully and say the sounds. Then we'll put the sounds together and say the word. Listen closely because the words are getting harder.

Model pronouncing each phoneme clearly. **Elicit** responses. **Guide** as needed.
My turn. Listen. **/sss/ /mmm /aaa/ /shshsh/.**
Say the sounds. */sss/ /mmm/ /aaa/ /shshsh/.*
Again, say the sounds. */sss/ /mmm/ /aaa/ /shshsh/.*
Let's put it together. What word? *Smash.*

My turn. Listen. **/sss/ /mmm/ /eee/ /lll/.**
Say the sounds. */sss/ /mmm/ /eee/ /lll/.*
Again, say the sounds. */sss/ /mmm/ /eee/ /lll/.*
Let's put it together. What word? *Smell.*

(Continue the activity with the following words:
smile [sss-mmm-ī ī-lll], smog [sss-mmm-ooo-g], smooth [sss-mmm-oooooo- ththth].)

Activity 2 Phoneme Segmentation

Show Phonemic Awareness. **Elicit** responses. **Guide** as needed.
Let's use our chips to show how many sounds there are in a word. For each sound in a word, we'll push one chip up to the arrow on the page. When we finish, we'll read the whole word.

Your turn. Say the sounds you hear in **map,** and move a chip for each sound. */mmm/ /aaa/ /p/.*

Move your finger back to the dot. What word? *Map.*
How many sounds are in the word **map?** *Three.*
Correct. Now move your chips back to the bottom, and let's try another one.

(Continue the activity with the following words:
rap, cap, tap, zap.)

Part B: Vocabulary Development

Activity 1 Learn New Vocabulary Word

Model gesture with arm to show a sharp angled slope for steep (up and down).
Elicit responses to questions. **Guide** as needed.

Today you'll learn a new vocabulary word. **Steep. Steep** means **almost straight up or down.** What does **steep** mean? *Almost straight up or down.*

Another word for **almost straight up or down** is **steep.** What's another word for **almost straight up or down?** *Steep.*

The mountain climber used a walking stick to climb **almost straight up or down.** Her climb was **steep.**

What's another word for **almost straight up and down?** *Steep.*

Discuss things that are steep.

Activity 2 Review Vocabulary Word

Elicit responses to questions. **Guide** as needed.
What does **loud** mean? *Very noisy.*
What's another word for **very noisy?** *Loud.*

Review vocabulary words in appropriate context in *Storybook 1.*

Part C: Comprehension Strategies

Activity 1 Read with Prosody—A During-Reading Strategy

Direct students to Story 50, pages 125–127.

Point out quotation marks in story.
Dialogue is what the characters say in a story. Narratives have lots of dialogue. Dialogue is marked in stories with quotations marks. Can you see any quotation marks on page 125?

This is the story "Jill's Mouse." The dialogue is marked with quotation marks. Each time a different character speaks, a new set of quotation marks begins. The parts with no quotation marks are for the narrator, or the one telling the story. Look at the story. Can you see where one character's dialogue ends and another character's begins?

Select proficient readers to read parts with you. **Model** reading Jill's dialogue, the mother's dialogue, and the narrator's part to the class with two students as your partners. **Model** reading the story with expression several times until students are firm. Listen to me read with two partners, taking turns on the dialogue. I'll read the words for the mother. _____ will read the words for Jill. _____ will read the words of the narrator. Remember: The narrator reads the parts without quotation marks. Let's read the words so they sound interesting.

Your turn to read the story the same way with two partners. Try to read with expression. Decide who will read which character's words and who will read the words of the narrator. Take turns, and try to make the dialogue interesting.

Group students into groups of three to read the story with expression, and **provide** guidance as needed.

Provide a reading center to display books being read so that students can enjoy them again during free time.

Part D: Fluency Building

5 minutes

Student Materials:
Storybook 1

Conduct after the lesson, using story of the day.

Activity 1 Partner Reading

It's time for partner reading.

Direct students to the story of the day. **Assign** student partners as Partner 1 and Partner 2. **Monitor** student reading. **Guide** as needed.

Lesson 52

Materials

Teacher: *Storybook 1;* 8-Phonemic Awareness; 3 manipulatives such as blocks, discs, chips, counters (if not using IWB)

Student: *Storybook 1;* copy of 8-Phonemic Awareness; 3 manipulatives such as blocks, discs, chips, counters

Part A: Phonemic and Phonological Awareness

3 minutes

IWB

Teacher Materials:
Phonemic Awareness

3 manipulatives such as blocks, discs, chips, counters

Student Materials:
Phonemic Awareness

3 manipulatives such as blocks, discs, chips, counters

Activity 1 — Phoneme Blending for One-Syllable Words

Let's put some sounds together and make words. I'm going to say a word very slowly so you can hear each sound. You need to listen carefully and say the sounds. Then we'll put the sounds together and say the word. Listen closely because the words are getting harder.

Model pronouncing each phoneme clearly. **Elicit** responses. **Guide** as needed.
My turn. Listen. **/sss/ /t/ /aaa/ /k/.**
Say the sounds. */sss/ /t/ /aaa/ /k/.*
Again, say the sounds. */sss/ /t/ /aaa/ /k/.*
Let's put it together. What word? *Stack.*

(Continue the activity with the following words:
stem [sss-t-eee-mmm], stick [sss-t-iii-k], stone [sss-t-ooo-nnn], stuck [sss-t-uuu-k].)

Activity 2 — Phoneme Segmentation

Show Phonemic Awareness. **Elicit** responses. **Guide** as needed.
Let's use our chips to show how many sounds there are in a word. For each sound in a word, we'll push one chip up to the arrow on the page. When we finish, we'll read the whole word.

Your turn. Say the sounds you hear in **side,** and move a chip for each sound.
/sss/ /īī/ /d/.

Move your finger back to the dot. What word? *Side.*
How many sounds are in the word **side?** *Three.*
Correct. Now move your chips back to the bottom, and let's try another one.

(Continue the activity with the following words:
ride, hide, wide, tide.)

5 minutes

Student Materials:
Storybook 1

Activity 1 | Learn New Vocabulary Word

Elicit responses to questions. **Guide** as needed.
Today you'll learn a new vocabulary word. **Fog. Fog** is **clouds close to the ground.** What is **fog?** *Clouds close to the ground.*

Another word for **clouds close to the ground** is **fog.** What's another word for **clouds close to the ground?** *Fog.*

The girl and the hound climbed the steep mountain. Soon they came to a part where it was very hard to see. They were walking through **clouds close to the ground.** They were walking through **fog.**

What's another word for **clouds close to the ground?** *Fog.*

Discuss times when students have seen fog.

Activity 2 | Review Vocabulary Word

Elicit responses to questions. **Guide** as needed.
What does **steep** mean? *Almost straight up or down.*
What's another word for **almost straight up or down?** *Steep.*

Review vocabulary words in appropriate context in *Storybook 1.*

Part C: Comprehension Strategies

12 minutes

Teacher Materials:
Storybook 1

Student Materials:
Storybook 1

Activity 1 | Identify Setting in Narratives—An After-Reading Strategy

Elicit responses to questions. **Guide** as needed.
Today you will learn how to find a new part in narratives. Another part of narratives is called the setting. To find out the setting, you have to figure out where the story happens and when the story happens. What is the setting? (Idea: *When and where a story happens.*)

Link where and when words to previous learning
When you want to find out where a story happens, you figure out the place the story happens. Settings have a **where.** What do you try to find out when you figure out where a story happens? *The place.*

When you want to find out when a story happens, you have to figure out the time of the story. Settings have a **when.** What do you try to find out when you figure out the when in a story? *The time.*

What is the part of a narrative called that tells when and where? *The setting.*

I'll read the first part of the story "The Magic Pouch." I'll show you how to find the setting.

Model think-aloud for finding setting in a narrative.

Sample Wording for Think-Aloud

(Read first sentence of the story on page 128.) That is the first sentence in the story, and it tells me where the story happens. The where in the story means in what place the story happens. So, the place in the story is near a tall mountain. (In the next paragraph, read the first sentence.) This sentence tells when. When tells at what time something happened. "One day" tells about the time the girl was looking at the mountain. So the when in this story is "one day."

When we talk about finding the Setting in a Narrative, we're looking for when and where the story happens. What's the setting for this story? (Idea: *Where is "near a mountain," and when is "one day."*)

Activity 2 Reread (A Fix-Up Strategy)—A During-Reading Strategy

Refer to Story 51, pages 128–130.

When I'm reading and it does not make sense, one of the first things I should do is stop and **reread** the sentence. When I'm reading, I should always be thinking in my mind, "Does this make sense." If it does not make sense, I should reread until it makes sense.

Let me show you how I do that.
Model think-aloud of rereading several sentences to ensure the sentence makes sense.

Sample Wording for Think-Aloud

That part did not make sense to me. I was not thinking when I read it. If I stop and reread it, I might understand it better.

Wow! When I reread a sentence or a section that is confusing, I can usually understand the story. A great way to fix it if I'm confused when I read is to reread.

Part D: Fluency Building

5 minutes

Student Materials:
Storybook 1

Conduct after the lesson, using story of the day.

Activity 1 Partner Reading

It's time for partner reading.
Direct students to the story of the day. **Assign** student partners as Partner 1 and Partner 2. **Monitor** student reading. **Guide** as needed.

Lesson 53

Materials

Teacher: *Storybook 1;* 8-Phonemic Awareness; 3 manipulatives such as blocks, discs, chips, counters (if not using IWB)

Student: *Storybook 1;* copy of 8-Phonemic Awareness; 3 manipulatives such as blocks, discs, chips, counters

Part A: Phonemic and Phonological Awareness

3 minutes

IWB

Teacher Materials:
Phonemic Awareness

3 manipulatives such as blocks, discs, chips, counters

Student Materials:
Phonemic Awareness

3 manipulatives such as blocks, discs, chips, counters

Activity 1 Phoneme Blending for One-Syllable Words

Model pronouncing each phoneme clearly. **Elicit** responses. **Guide** as needed.

Let's put some sounds together and make words. I'm going to say a word very slowly so you can hear each sound. You'll need to listen carefully and say the sounds. Then we'll put the sounds together and say the word.

My turn. Listen. **/sss/ /p/ /āāā/ /sss/.**
Say the sounds. */sss/ /p/ /āāā/ /sss/.*
Again, say the sounds. */sss/ /p/ /āāā/ /sss/.*
Let's put it together. What word? *Space.*

My turn. Listen. **/sss/ /p/ /ēēē/ /d/.**
Say the sounds. */sss/ /p/ /ēēē/ /d/.*
Again, say the sounds. */sss/ /p/ /ēēē/ /d/.*
Let's put it together. What word? *Speed.*

(Continue the activity with the following words:
spy [sss-p-īīī], spot [sss-p-ooo-t], spun [sss-p-uuu-nnn].)

Activity 2 Phoneme Segmentation

Show Phonemic Awareness. **Elicit** responses. **Guide** as needed.

Let's use our chips to show how many sounds there are in a word. For each sound in a word, we'll push one chip up to the arrow on the page. When we finish, we'll read the whole word.

Your turn. Say the sounds you hear in **met,** and move a chip for each sound. */mmm/ /eee/ /t/.*

Move your finger back to the dot. What word? *Met.*
How many sounds are in the word **met?** *Three.*
Correct. Now move your chips back to the bottom, and let's try another one.

(Continue the activity with the following words:
jet, vet, pet, wet.)

Part B: Vocabulary Development

Activity 1 Learn New Vocabulary Word

Elicit responses to questions. **Guide** as needed.
Today you'll learn a new vocabulary word. **Suddenly. Suddenly** means **all at once.** What does **suddenly** mean? *All at once.*

Another word for **all at once** is **suddenly.** What's another word for **all at once?** *Suddenly.*

The girl and the hound were surprised when **all at once** a sound came from the house. The sound came **suddenly.**

What's another word for **all at once?** *Suddenly.*

Discuss things that happen suddenly.

Activity 2 Review Vocabulary Word

Elicit responses to questions. **Guide** as needed.
What does **fog** mean? *Clouds close to the ground.*
What's another word for **clouds close to the ground?** *Fog.*

Review vocabulary words in appropriate context in *Storybook 1.*

Part C: Comprehension Strategies

Activity 1 Identify Setting in Narratives—An After-Reading Strategy

Refer to Story 52, pages 131–133.

Elicit responses to questions. **Guide** as needed.
To find out the setting, you have to figure out where the story happens and when the story happens. What is the setting? (Idea: *When and where a story happens.*)

Remind students of <u>where</u> and <u>when</u> (previous vocabulary words).
When you want to find out where a story happens, you figure out in what place the story happens. Settings have a where. What do you try to find out when you figure out where a story happens? *The place.*

When you want to find out when a story happens, you have to figure out at what time the story takes place. Settings have a when. What do you try to find out when you figure out the when in a story? *The time.*

What is the part of a narrative called that tells when and where? *The setting.*

I'll read the next story "The Magic Pouch 2." I'll show you how to find the setting. Sometimes, the story only gives hints about the setting. This story only gives hints about the setting. Listen to me think about the setting in this story.

Model think-aloud for finding setting in a narrative. **Elicit** responses to questions. **Guide** as needed.

Sample Wording for Think-Aloud

(Read first sentence from the story on page 131.) That is the first sentence in the story, and it gives me a clue about where the story happens. The where in the story means in what place the story happens. I know that the girl is climbing the mountain, and so she must be in the clouds on the mountain. So, the place in the story is in the clouds on the tall mountain. (In the next paragraph, read the fourth sentence.) This sentence gives hints about when. When tells at what time something happened. "In the sun" gives a hint about the time. So, the when in this story is "one day."

When we talk about finding the Setting in a Narrative, we're looking for when and where the story happens. What is the setting for this story? (Idea: *Where is "near a mountain" and when is "one day."*)

Activity 2 Sequencing—An After-Reading Strategy

Reference Story 52, pages 131–133.

We are going to play the Put Events in Order game today. I am going to tell you events that happen in the story. Since I get mixed up, I need you to help me put the events into the right order.

Read each sentence with a pause between sentences.

A loud sound came from the house.

The girl sat down to rest.

The girl went into the fog.

Reread sentences again in the same order.

Elicit responses to questions. **Guide** as needed.

Which event happened first? (Idea: *The girl went into the fog.*)

Which event happened next? (Idea: *The girl sat down to rest.*)

Which event happened last? (Idea: *A loud sound came from the house.*)

Good for you. You put the events in the right order.

Part D: Fluency Building

5 minutes

Student Materials:
Storybook 1

Conduct after the lesson, using story of the day.

Activity 1 Partner Reading

It's time for partner reading.

Direct students to the story of the day. **Assign** student partners as Partner 1 and Partner 2. **Monitor** student reading. **Guide** as needed.

Lesson 54

Materials

Teacher: *Storybook 1*; 8-Phonemic Awareness; 3 manipulatives such as blocks, discs, chips, counters (if not using IWB)

Student: *Storybook 1;* copy of 8-Phonemic Awareness; 3 manipulatives such as blocks, discs, chips, counters

Part A: Phonemic and Phonological Awareness

3 minutes

IWB

Teacher Materials:
Phonemic Awareness

3 manipulatives such as blocks, discs, chips, counters

Student Materials:
Phonemic Awareness

3 manipulatives such as blocks, discs, chips, counters

Activity 1 Phoneme Blending for One-Syllable Words

Let's put some sounds together and make words. I'm going to say a word very slowly so you can hear each sound. You'll need to listen carefully and say the sounds. Then we'll put the sounds together and say the word. Listen closely because the words are getting harder.

Model pronouncing each phoneme clearly. **Elicit** responses. **Guide** as needed.
My turn. Listen. **/sss/ /nnn/ /āāā/ /lll/.**
Say the sounds. */ssss/ /nnn /āāā/ /lll/.*
Again, say the sounds. */ssss/ /nnn/ /āāā/ /lll/.*
Let's put it together. What word? *Snail.*

(Continue the activity with the following words:
sneeze [sss-nnn-ēēē-zzz], sniff [sss-nnn-iii-fff], snow [sss-nnn-ōōō], snooze [sss-nnn-oooooo-zzz].)

Activity 2 Phoneme Segmentation

Show Phonemic Awareness. **Elicit** responses. **Guide** as needed.
Let's use our chips to show how many sounds there are in a word. For each sound in the word, we'll push one chip up to the arrow on the page. When we finish, we'll read the whole word.

Your turn. Say the sounds you hear in **nose,** and move a chip for each sound. */nnn/ /ōōō/ /sss/.*

Move your finger back to the dot. What word? *Nose.*
How many sounds are in the word **nose?** *Three.*
Correct. Now move your chips back to the bottom, and let's try another one.

(Continue the activity with the following words:
rose, those, hose, chose.)

5 minutes

Student Materials:
Storybook 1

Activity 1 Learn New Vocabulary Word

Elicit responses to questions. **Guide** as needed.
Today you'll learn a new vocabulary word. **Pouch. Pouch** means **bag.** What does **pouch** mean? *Bag.*

Another word for **bag** is **pouch.** What's another word for **bag?** *Pouch.*

The girl saw a funny **bag** hanging on the wall. She saw a funny **pouch** hanging on the wall.

What's another word for **bag?** *Pouch.*

Discuss things students might put in a pouch.

Activity 2 Review Vocabulary Word

Elicit responses to questions. **Guide** as needed.
What does **suddenly** mean? *All at once.*
What's another word for **all at once?** *Suddenly.*

Review vocabulary words in appropriate context in *Storybook 1.*

Part C: Comprehension Strategies

12 minutes

Teacher Materials:
Storybook 1

Student Materials:
Storybook 1

Activity 1 Mental Imaging—A During-Reading Strategy

Elicit answers to mental images students have for the sentence. **Guide** as needed.
What do good readers do when they make mental images? (Idea: *Make pictures in their brains*.)

If you want to be a good reader, you need to practice making pictures in your brain when you read.

This sentence says, "The girl looked inside the house, but she did not see anyone." Get a picture in your mind of that sentence. What picture do you see in your brain when you read that sentence? (Student response.)

What does the house look like? (Student response.)

What is inside the house? (Student response.)

When you make mental images as you read, you will be better at understanding what you read

Activity 2 Reread (A Fix-Up Strategy)—A During-Reading Strategy

Refer to Story 53, pages 134–136.

When I'm reading and it does not make sense, one of the first things I should do is stop and reread the sentence. When I'm reading, I should always be thinking in my mind, "Does this make sense?" If it does not make sense, I should reread until it makes sense.
Let me show you how I do that.
Model think-aloud of rereading several sentences.

Sample Wording for Think-Aloud

That part did not make sense to me. I was not thinking when I read it. If I stop and reread it, I might understand it better.

Wow! When I reread a sentence or a section that is confusing, I can usually understand the story. A great way to fix it up if I am confused when I am reading is to reread.

Part D: Fluency Building

5 minutes

Student Materials:
Storybook 1

Conduct after the lesson, using story of the day.

Activity 1 Partner Reading

It's time for partner reading.
Direct students to the story of the day. **Assign** student partners as Partner 1 and Partner 2. **Monitor** student reading. **Guide** as needed.

Materials

Teacher: *Storybook 1;* 8-Phonemic Awareness; 3 manipulatives such as blocks, discs, chips, counters (if not using IWB), 2-Vocabulary Acquisition and Use, Writing Prompts, 5-My Writing Checklist

Student: *Storybook 1;* copy of 8-Phonemic Awareness; 3 manipulatives such as blocks, discs, chips, counters, Copy of 2- Vocabulary Acquisition and Use and 3-My Writing Checklist; Lined Paper

Part A: Phonemic and Phonological Awareness

3 minutes

IWB

Teacher Materials:
Phonemic Awareness

3 manipulatives such as blocks, discs, chips, counters

Student Materials:
Phonemic Awareness

3 manipulatives such as blocks, discs, chips, counters

Activity 1 Phoneme Blending for One-Syllable Words

Elicit responses. **Guide** as needed.
Let's put some sounds together and make words. I'm going to say a word very slowly so you can hear each sound. You'll need to listen carefully and say the sounds. Then we'll put the sounds together and say the word. Listen closely because the words are getting harder.

My turn. Listen. **/sss/ /k/ /āāā/ /t/.**
Say the sounds. */sss/ /k/ /āāā/ /t/.*
Again, say the sounds. */sss/ /k/ /āāā/ /t/.*
Let's put it together. What word? *Skate.*

My turn. Listen. **/sss/ /k/ /iii/ /n/.**
Say the sounds. */sss/ /k/ /iii/ /nnn/.*
Again, say the sounds. */sss/ /k/ /iii/ /nnn/.*
Let's put it together. What word? *Skin.*

(Continue the activity with the following words:
sky [sss-k-īīī], scoop [sss-k-oooooo-p], skunk [sss-k-uuu-nnn-k].)

Activity 2 Phoneme Segmentation

Show Phonemic Awareness. **Elicit** responses. **Guide** as needed.
Let's use our chips to show how many sounds there are in a word. For each sound in the word, we'll push one chip up to the arrow on the page. When we finish, we'll read the whole word.

Your turn. Say the sounds you hear in **ship,** and move a chip for each sound.
/shshsh/ /iii/ /p/.

Move your finger back to the dot. What word? *Ship.*
How many sounds are in the word **ship?** *Three.*
Correct. Now move your chips back to the bottom, and let's try another one.

(Continue the activity with the following words:
hip, chip, sip, tip.)

Part B: Vocabulary Development

Activity 1 Cumulative Vocabulary Review

IWB

Teacher Materials:
Vocabulary Acquisition and Use

Student Materials:
Storybook 1

Vocabulary Acquisition and Use

Elicit responses to questions. **Guide** as needed.
Directions: Listen and tell me the correct vocabulary word for each question.

What's another word for **clouds close to the ground?** *Fog.*
What's another word for **bag?** *Pouch.*
What's another word for **almost straight up or down?** *Steep.*
What's another word for **all at once?** *Suddenly.*

Repeat difficult words as needed.

Review vocabulary words in appropriate context in *Storybook 1.*

Activity 2 Vocabulary Acquisition and Use

Display Vocabulary Acquisition and Use. **Have** students work with a neighbor to complete Vocabulary Acquisition and Use.
Today's vocabulary words are _____ and _____ [and _____ and _____].
Vocabulary words: **steep** and **high; little** and **tiny**
Write the words on the lines provided. Then write the words in the boxes based on whether you think each word is less/smaller or more/larger than the other word. Below the boxes, write why you think word 1 is less/smaller and word 2 is more/larger than word 1.
Repeat for words 3 and 4. **Have** students share what they wrote. **Discuss** examples of how these words might be used.

Part C: Comprehension Strategies

Activity 1 Generate Questions—An After-Reading Strategy

Refer to Story 54, pages 137 and 138.

Elicit responses to questions. **Guide** as needed.
Asking questions is a strategy to use when you are reading stories. Why do you ask questions when you are reading? *To understand the story better.*

Learning to ask questions is a hard skill. It takes lots of practice. Let's practice asking questions.

Here is a sentence from the story. (Read the first sentence from the story on page 137.) Help me make up a question. "Who walked over to the _____?" *Pouch.*

Yes! "Who walked over to the pouch?" Say the whole question with me. *"Who walked over to the pouch?"*

What is the answer to the question, "Who walked over to the pouch?" *The girl.*

Here is another sentence from the story. (Read the first sentence from the last paragraph on page 138.) Make up a question from that sentence. (Ideas: *"What did the girl touch?" "Who touched the pouch?"*)

It was smart to make a question instead of giving the answer to the question. What's the answer to the question you made up? (Student responses.)

Here is another sentence from the story. (Read the first sentence from the last paragraph on page 137.) Make up a question on this information. (Ideas: *"Who started to open the pouch?" "What did the girl start to open?" "What did the girl start to do?"*)

What is the answer to the question? (Student responses.)

You are getting good at asking questions.

Part D: Fluency Building

5 minutes

Student Materials:
Storybook 1

Conduct after the lesson, using story of the day.

Activity 1   Partner Reading

It's time for partner reading.
Direct students to the story of the day. **Assign** student partners as Partner 1 and Partner 2. **Monitor** student reading. **Guide** as needed.

10 minutes

IWB

Teacher Materials:
Writing Prompts

My Writing Checklist

Student Materials:
Lined Paper

My Writing Checklist

Activity 1 Write and Use Parts of Speech and Conventions

Time to write using a writing prompt based on the stories we've been reading.

Assign student partners. **Distribute** lined paper to students. **Display** writing prompts and have students choose one to write about or assign a writing prompt of your choice. **Review** parts of speech and punctuation as well as the writing checklist with students. **Tell** students to write one paragraph (minimum of four sentences per paragraph) on their own to answer the writing prompt. **Tell** them to use their writing checklist (first column labeled "Did I use them?") to ensure they include important parts of speech or punctuation in their writing. **Tell** students which parts of speech or punctuation to focus on, if you wish. **Model** what it means to answer a writing prompt and to use the writing checklist during and after the writing process, as needed. **Monitor** and guide students as needed. **Model** what it means to have a neighbor look over his or her neighbor's writing and to complete the writing checklist (second column labeled "Did my neighbor use them?"), as needed. **Have** students share what they wrote as time permits.

Writing Prompt 1	Writing Prompt 2	Writing Prompt 3
Tell me about a time you tried to do something that you didn't think you could do that turned out to be fun.	Tell me when having a loud moo might come in handy for a cow.	If you had a mouse, would you want it to live in the house? Why or why not?

Lesson 56

Materials

Teacher: *Storybook 1;* 8-Phonemic Awareness; 3 manipulatives such as blocks, discs, chips, counters (if not using IWB)

Student: *Storybook 1;* copy of 8-Phonemic Awareness; 3 manipulatives such as blocks, discs, chips, counters

Part A: Phonemic and Phonological Awareness

3 minutes

IWB

Teacher Materials:
Phonemic Awareness

3 manipulatives such as blocks, discs, chips, counters

Student Materials:
Phonemic Awareness

3 manipulatives such as blocks, discs, chips, counters

Activity 1 Phoneme Blending for One-Syllable Words

Elicit responses. **Guide** as needed.
Let's put some sounds together and make words. I'm going to say a word very slowly so you can hear each sound. You'll need to listen carefully and say the sounds. Then we'll put the sounds together and say the word. Listen closely because the words are getting harder.

My turn. Listen. **/sss/ /www/ /ēēē /t/.**
Say the sounds. */sss/ /www/ /ēēē/ /t/.*
Again, say the sounds. */sss/ /www/ /ēēē/ /t/.*
Let's put it together. What word? *Sweet.*

(Continue the activity with the following words:
sweep [sss-www-ēēē-p], swim [sss-www-iii-mmm], swift [sss-www-iii-fff-t], swish [sss-www-iii-shshsh].)

Activity 2 Phoneme Segmentation

Show Phonemic Awareness. **Elicit** responses. **Guide** as needed.
Let's use our chips to show how many sounds there are in a word. For each sound in a word, we'll push one chip up to the arrow on the page. When we finish, we'll read the whole word.

Your turn. Say the sounds you hear in **rake,** and move a chip for each sound.
/rrr/ /āāā/ /k/.

Move your finger back to the dot. What word? *Rake.*
How many sounds are in the word **rake?** *Three.*
Correct. Now move your chips back to the bottom, and let's try another one.

(Continue the activity with the following words:
cake, take, make, bake.)

Part B: Vocabulary Development

Activity 1 Learn New Vocabulary Word

Elicit responses to questions. **Guide** as needed.
Today you'll learn a new vocabulary word. **Exhausted. Exhausted** means **tired.** What does **exhausted** mean? *Tired.*

Another word for **tired** is **exhausted.** What's another word for **tired?** *Exhausted.*

After finishing the marathon race, the runner was **tired.** He was **exhausted.**

What's another word for **tired?** *Exhausted.*

Discuss when students have been exhausted and how it feels to be exhausted.

Activity 2 Review Vocabulary Word

Elicit responses to questions. **Guide** as needed.
What does **suddenly** mean? *All at once.*
What's another word for **all at once?** *Suddenly.*

Review vocabulary words in appropriate context in *Storybook 1.*

12 minutes

IWB

Teacher Materials:
Storybook 1

Student Materials:
Storybook 1

Part C: Comprehension Strategies

Activity 1 Read with Prosody—A During-Reading Strategy

Direct students to Story 55, pages 139 and 140.

Dialogue is what characters say in a story. Narratives have lots of dialogue. Dialogue is marked in stories with quotations marks. This is the story "The Magic Pouch 5." The dialogue is marked with quotation marks. Each time a different character speaks, a new set of quotation marks begins. The parts with no quotation marks are for the narrator, or the one telling the story. Look at the story. Can you see where one character's dialogue ends and another character's begins? Can you see the parts without quotation marks for the narrator?

Select proficient readers to read parts with you. **Model** reading the story with expression several times until students are firm.

Listen to me read with two partners, taking turns on the dialogue. I will read the words for the elf. _____ will read the words for the girl. _____ will read the words of the narrator. We'll read the words so they sound interesting.

Model reading the elf's dialogue, the girl's dialogue, and narrator's part to the class with two students as your partners.

Group students in groups of three to read the story with expression, and **provide** guidance as needed.

Your turn to read the story the same way with two partners. Try to read with expression. Decide who will read which character's words and who will read the words of the narrator. Take turns and make the dialogue sound interesting.

Provide a reading center to display books being read so that students can enjoy them again during free time.

Part D: Fluency Building

5 minutes

Student Materials:
Storybook 1

Conduct after the lesson, using story of the day.

Activity 1 Partner Reading

It's time for partner reading.

Direct students to the story of the day. **Assign** student partners as Partner 1 and Partner 2. **Monitor** student reading. **Guide** as needed.

Lesson 57

Materials

Teacher: *Storybook 1;* 8-Phonemic Awareness; 3 manipulatives such as blocks, discs, chips, counters (if not using IWB)

Student: *Storybook 1;* copy of 8-Phonemic Awareness; 3 manipulatives such as blocks, discs, chips, counters

Part A: Phonemic and Phonological Awareness

10 minutes

IWB

Teacher Materials:
Phonemic Awareness

3 manipulatives such as blocks, discs, chips, counters

Student Materials:
Phonemic Awareness

3 manipulatives such as blocks, discs, chips, counters

Activity 1 Phoneme Blending for One-Syllable Words

Elicit responses. **Guide** as needed.
Let's put some sounds together and make words. I'm going to say a word very slowly so you can hear each sound. You'll need to listen carefully and say the sounds. Then we'll put the sounds together and say the word. Listen closely because the words are getting harder.

My turn. Listen. **/sss/ /lll/ /eee/ /d/.**
Say the sounds. */sss/ /lll/ /eee/ /d/.*
Again, say the sounds. */sss/ /lll/ /eee/ /d/.*
Let's put it together. What word? *Sled.*

My turn. Listen. **/sss/ /lll/ /iii/ /p/.**
Say the sounds. */sss/ /lll/ /iii/ /p/.*
Again, say the sounds. */sss/ /lll/ /iii/ /p/.*
Let's put it together. What word? *Slip.*

(Continue the activity with the following words:
slide [sss-lll-īīī-d], slow [sss-lll-ōōō], sleepy [sss-lll-ēēē-p-ēēē].)

Activity 2 Phoneme Segmentation

Show Phonemic Awareness. **Elicit** responses. **Guide** as needed.
Let's use our chips to show how many sounds there are in a word. For each sound in a word, we'll push one chip up to the arrow on the page. When we finish, we'll read the whole word.

Your turn. Say the sounds you hear in **sock,** and move a chip for each sound. */sss/ /ooo/ /k/.*

Move your finger back to the dot. What word? *Sock.*
How many sounds are in the word **sock?** *Three.*
Correct. Now move your chips back to the bottom, and let's try another one.

(Continue the activity with the following words:
lock, rock, dock, knock.)

Part B: Vocabulary Development

Activity 1 Learn New Vocabulary Word

Elicit responses to questions. **Guide** as needed.
Today you'll learn a new vocabulary word. **Remove. Remove** means **take off.** What does **remove** mean? *Take off.*

Another way to say **take off** is **remove.** What's another way to say **take off?** *Remove.*

Mom said to **take off** your shoes before coming in the house. Mom said to **remove** your shoes.

What's another word for **take off?** *Take off.*

Discuss things that students have to remove.

Activity 2 Review Vocabulary Word

Elicit responses to questions. **Guide** as needed.
What does **exhausted** mean? *Tired.*
What's another word for **tired?** *Exhausted.*

Review vocabulary words in appropriate context in *Storybook 1.*

Part C: Comprehension Strategies

Activity 1 Generate Questions—An After-Reading Strategy

Refer to Story 56, pages 141–143.

Elicit responses to questions. **Guide** as needed.
Asking questions is a strategy to use when you are reading stories. Why do you ask questions when you are reading? *To understand the story better.*

It takes practice to think of good questions. Let's practice asking questions some more.

Here is a sentence from the story. (Read first sentence from the second paragraph on page 141.) Help me make up a question. "What did the _____?" *Girl do.*

Yes! "What did the girl do?" Say the whole question with me. *"What did the girl do?"*

What is the answer to the question, "What did the girl do?" *Picked up the pouch.*

Here is another sentence from the story. (Read first sentence from the last paragraph on page 141.) Who can make up a question from that sentence? (Ideas: *"Who started down the mountain?" "What did the girl and the hound do?" "What did the girl and the hound start to do?"*)

It was smart to make a question instead of giving the answer to the question. What's the answer to the question you made up? (Student responses.)

Here is another sentence from the story. (Read last sentence from the first paragraph on page 142.) Who can make up a question about this information? (Ideas: *"Who ran to the house?" "Where did the girl run?" "Why did she run to her house?"*)

What is the answer to the question? (Student responses.)

You are getting good at asking questions.

Part D: Fluency Building

5 minutes

Student Materials:
Storybook 1

Conduct after the lesson, using story of the day.

Activity 1   Partner Reading

It's time for partner reading.
Direct students to the story of the day. **Assign** student partners as Partner 1 and Partner 2. **Monitor** student reading. **Guide** as needed.

Lesson 58

Materials

Teacher: Locate a copy of "Jack and the Beanstalk"; 8-Phonemic Awareness; 3 manipulatives such as blocks, discs, chips, counters (if not using IWB)

Student: Copy of 8-Phonemic Awareness; 3 manipulatives such as blocks, discs, chips, counters

---

Part A: Phonemic and Phonological Awareness

3 minutes

IWB

Teacher Materials:
Phonemic Awareness

3 manipulatives such as blocks, discs, chips, counters

Student Materials:
Phonemic Awareness

3 manipulatives such as blocks, discs, chips, counters

Activity 1 Phoneme Blending for One-Syllable Words

Elicit responses. **Guide** as needed.
Let's put some sounds together and make words. I'm going to say a word very slowly so you can hear each sound. You'll need to listen carefully and say the sounds. Then we'll put the sounds together and say the word. Listen closely because the words are getting harder.

My turn. Listen. **/p/ /lll/ /āāā/ /nnn/.**
Say the sounds. /p/ /lll/ /āāā/ /nnn/.
Again, say the sounds. /p/ /lll/ /āāā/ /nnn/.
Let's put it together. What word? *Plane.*

(Continue the activity with the following words:
plant [p-lll-aaa-nnn-t], please [p-lll-ēēē-zzz], plus [p-lll-uuu-sss], plum [p-lll-uuu-mmm].)

Activity 2 Phoneme Segmentation

Show Phonemic Awareness. **Elicit** responses. **Guide** as needed.
Let's use our chips to show how many sounds there are in a word. For each sound in a word, we'll push one chip up to the arrow on the page. When we finish, we'll read the whole word.

Your turn. Say the sounds you hear in **rain,** and move a chip for each sound. /rrr/ /āāā/ /nnn/.

Move your finger back to the dot. What word? *Rain.*
How many sounds are in the word **rain?** *Three.*
Correct. Now move your chips back to the bottom, and let's try another one.

(Continue the activity with the following words:
pain, chain, vane, cane.)

Part B: Vocabulary Development

Activity 1 | Learn New Vocabulary Word

Elicit responses to questions. **Guide** as needed.
Today you'll learn a new vocabulary word. **Wealthy. Wealthy** means **rich.**
What does **wealthy** mean? *Rich.*

Another word for **rich** is wealthy. What's another word for **rich?** *Wealthy.*

The famous author is **rich.** The famous author is **wealthy.**

What's another word for **rich?** *Wealthy.*

Discuss what it means to be wealthy.

Activity 2 | Review Vocabulary Word

Elicit responses to questions. **Guide** as needed.
What does **remove** mean? *Take off.*
What's another word for **take off?** *Remove.*

Review vocabulary words in appropriate context in *Storybook 1.*

Part C: Comprehension Strategies

Activity 1 | Prepare for a Text-to-Text Connection—A During-Reading Strategy

Today I'll read a story called "Jack and the Beanstalk." Listen carefully to the story, and look at the pictures. I want you to be able to tell me the parts of this narrative after I've read the story.

Discuss the story with students as you read story, asking questions to engage students during reading (e.g., who, what, when, where, why). **Elicit** responses to questions. **Guide** as needed.

Who is the main character in this story? *Jack.*

Who are the other characters in this story? (Idea: *The mother and the giant.*)

What is the setting? Where does the story take place? (Ideas: *Jack's house and the giant's house.*)

What events happened in the beginning of the story? (Idea: *Jack traded his cow for some beans.*)

What events happened in the middle of the story? (Ideas: *Jack's mother threw the beans out of the window. The beans were magic and grew up to the sky. Jack climbed the beanstalk and stole the goose that lays the golden eggs.*)

What events happened at the end of the story? (Ideas: *Jack escaped down the beanstalk and chopped down the beanstalk. His mother and he were wealthy.*)

Part D: Fluency Building

5 minutes

Student Materials:
Storybook 1

Conduct after the lesson, using story of the day.

Activity 1 Partner Reading

It's time for partner reading.
Direct students to the story of the day. **Assign** student partners as Partner 1 and Partner 2. **Monitor** student reading. **Guide** as needed.

Lesson 59

Materials

Teacher: *Storybook 1;* 8-Phonemic Awareness; 3 manipulatives such as blocks, discs, chips, counters (if not using IWB), 9-Text-to-Text Connection; locate a copy of "Jack in the Beanstalk"

Student: *Storybook 1;* copy of 8-Phonemic Awareness; 3 manipulatives such as blocks, discs, chips, counters

Part A: Phonemic and Phonological Awareness

3 minutes

IWB

Teacher Materials:
Phonemic Awareness

3 manipulatives such as blocks, discs, chips, counters

Student Materials:
Phonemic Awareness

3 manipulatives such as blocks, discs, chips, counters

Activity 1 Phoneme Blending for One-Syllable Words

Elicit responses. **Guide** as needed.
Let's put some sounds together and make words. I'm going to say a word very slowly so you can hear each sound. You'll need to listen carefully and say the sounds. Then we'll put the sounds together and say the word. Listen closely because the words are getting harder.

My turn. Listen. **/fff/ /lll/ /aaa/ /g/.**
Say the sounds. */fff/ /lll/ /aaa/ /g/.*
Again, say the sounds. */fff/ /lll/ /aaa/ /g/.*
Let's put it together. What word? *Flag.*

My turn. Listen. **/fff/ /lll/ /aaa/ /shshsh/.**
Say the sounds. */fff/ /lll/ /aaa/ /shshsh/.*
Again, say the sounds. */fff/ /lll/ /aaa/ /shshsh/.*
Let's put it together. What word? *Flash.*

(Continue the activity with the following words:
flip [fff-lll-iii-p], flop [fff-lll-ooo-p], fluff [fff-lll-uuu-fff].)

Activity 2 Phoneme Segmentation

Show Phonemic Awareness. **Elicit** responses. **Guide** as needed.
Let's use our chips to show how many sounds there are in a word. For each sound in a word, we'll push one chip up to the arrow on the page. When we finish, we'll read the whole word.

Your turn. Say the sounds you hear in **sun,** and move a chip for each sound. */sss/ /uuu/ /nnn/.*

Move your finger back to the dot. What word? *Sun.*
How many sounds are in the word **sun?** *Three.*
Correct. Now move your chips back to the bottom, and let's try another one.

(Continue the activity with the following words:
bun, fun, run, ton.)

Part B: Vocabulary Development

Student Materials:
Storybook 1

Activity 1 Learn New Vocabulary Word

Elicit responses to questions. **Guide** as needed.
Today you'll learn a new vocabulary word. **Site. Site** means **place.** What does **site** mean? *Place.*

Another word for **place** is **site.** What's another word for **place?** *Site.*

Daniel's family wanted to build a new house. They were looking for the perfect **place.** They were looking for the perfect **site** to build their new house.

What's another word for **place?** *Site.*

Discuss different sites in the community.

Activity 2 Review Vocabulary Word

Elicit responses to questions. **Guide** as needed.
What does **wealthy** mean? *Rich.*
What's another word for **rich?** *Wealthy.*

Review vocabulary words in appropriate context in *Storybook 1.*

Part C: Comprehension Strategies

Teacher Materials:
Text-to-Text Connection

Storybook 1

Copy of "Jack and the Beanstalk"

Student Materials:
Storybook 1

Activity 1 Text-to-Text—An After-Reading Strategy

Refer to *Storybook 1*, pages 128–149.

Display Text-to-Text Connection. **Refer** to "Jack and the Beanstalk."
We'll make a text-to-text connection today between "Jack and the Beanstalk" and "The Magic Pouch." Another way to make a text-to-text connection is to make a chart to compare the story elements. Let's think together and see if we can fill in all the parts of this chart.

Brainstorm with students to elicit story elements. **Complete** chart as students suggest ideas. **Guide** as needed.

Discuss similarities and differences between the elements as you complete chart.

Sample Chart for Text-To-Text Connection

	"Jack and the Beanstalk"	"The Magic Pouch"
Title of Story	"Jack and the Beanstalk"	"The Magic Pouch"
Main Characters	Jack and giant	the girl and the elf
Setting (Where)	Jack's house and giant's castle	the girl's house and the elf's house
Setting (When)	One day	Once upon a time
Beginning	Jack traded cow for beans.	Girl climbed the mountain.
Middle	Jack climbed the beanstalk.	Girl got pouch from elf.
End	Jack and his mother were rich from golden eggs.	Girl and her mother were rich from magic pouch.

When you make text-to-text connections, you are thinking hard and showing that you understand what you read.

Part D: Fluency Building

5 minutes

Student Materials:
Storybook 1

Conduct after the lesson, using story of the day.

Activity 1 Partner Reading

It's time for partner reading.
Direct students to the story of the day. **Assign** student partners as Partner 1 and Partner 2. **Monitor** student reading. **Guide** as needed.

Lesson 60

Materials

Teacher: *Storybook 1;* 8-Phonemic Awareness; 3 manipulatives such as blocks, discs, chips, counters (if not using IWB), 2-Vocabulary Acquisition and Use, 3-My Book Review

Student: *Storybook 1;* copy of 8-Phonemic Awareness; 3 manipulatives such as blocks, discs, chips, counters, Copy of 2-Vocabulary Acquisition and Use and 3-My Book Review

Part A: Phonemic and Phonological Awareness

3 minutes

IWB

Teacher Materials:
Phonemic Awareness

3 manipulatives such as blocks, discs, chips, counters

Student Materials:
Phonemic Awareness

3 manipulatives such as blocks, discs, chips, counters

Activity 1 Phoneme Blending for One-Syllable Words

Elicit responses. **Guide** as needed.

Let's put some sounds together and make words. I'm going to say a word very slowly so you can hear each sound. You'll need to listen carefully and say the sounds. Then we'll put the sounds together and say the word. Listen closely because the words are getting harder.

My turn. Listen. **/k/ /lll/ /aaa/ /sss/.**
Say the sounds. */k/ /lll/ /aaa/ /sss/.*
Again, say the sounds. */k/ /lll// /aaa/ /sss/.*
Let's put it together. What word? *Class.*

(Continue the activity with the following words:
clean [k-lll-ēēē-nnn], clip [k-lll-iii-p], clock [k-lll-ooo-k], cloth [k-lll-ooo-ththth].)

Activity 2 Phoneme Segmentation

Show Phonemic Awareness. **Elicit** responses. **Guide** as needed.

Let's use our chips to show how many sounds there are in a word. For each sound in a word, we'll push one chip up to the arrow on the page. When we finish, we'll read the whole word.

Your turn. Say the sounds you hear in **boat,** and move a chip for each sound.
/b/ /ōōō/ /t/.

Move your finger back to the dot. What word? *Boat.*
How many sounds are in the word **boat?** *Three.*
Correct. Now move your chips back to the bottom, and let's try another one.

(Continue the activity with the following words:
goat, coat, vote, tote.)

Part B: Vocabulary Development

Activity 1 Cumulative Vocabulary Review

Elicit responses to questions. **Guide** as needed.
Directions: Listen and tell me the correct vocabulary word for each question.

What's another word for **rich?** *Wealthy.*
What's another word for **bag?** *Pouch.*
What's another word for **take off?** *Remove.*
What's another word for **all at once?** *Suddenly.*
What's another word for **place?** *Site.*
What's another word for **clouds close to the ground?** *Fog.*
What's another word for **tired?** *Exhausted.*
What's another word for **almost straight up or down**? *Steep.*

Repeat difficult words as needed.

Review vocabulary words in appropriate context in *Storybook 1.*

Activity 2 Vocabulary Acquisition and Use

Display Vocabulary Acquisition and Use. **Have** students work with a neighbor to complete Vocabulary Acquisition and Use.
Today's vocabulary words are _____ and _____ [and _____ and _____].
Vocabulary words: **wealthy** and **rich; exhausted** and **tired**
Write the words on the lines provided. Then write the words in the boxes based on whether you think each word is less/smaller or more/larger than the other word. Below the boxes, write why you think word 1 is less/smaller and word 2 is more/larger than word 1.
Repeat for words 3 and 4. **Have** students share what they wrote. **Discuss** examples of how these words might be used.

Part C: Comprehension Strategies

Activity 1 Mental Imaging—A During-Reading Strategy

Refer to Story 59, pages 150–152.

Elicit responses to mental images. **Guide** as needed.
What do good readers do when they make mental images? Make pictures in their brains.

If you want to be a good reader, you need to practice making pictures in your brain when you read. This sentence says: (Read first sentence from the third paragraph on page 151.) Get a picture in your mind of that sentence. What picture do you see in your brain when you read that sentence? (Student response.)

How many bugs are there? (Student response.)

How big is the elephant? (Student response.)

Does the elephant look surprised? Sleepy? (Student response.)

Does the ground have grass or dirt? (Student response.)

When you make mental images as you read, you'll be better at understanding what you read

Activity 2 Activate Background Knowledge—A Before-Reading Strategy

Elicit responses to questions. **Guide** as needed.
We talked about schema. Schema is everything that you know in your brain. What do you call everything you know in your brain? *Schema.*

It is a good idea to think about what you know about a topic before you read a new story. Then you can connect what you know to the new information that you learn when you read.

Discuss background knowledge. **Guide** as needed.
Today the story is about a girl who has a pet goat. Open the file in your brain, and look in it to see what you know about goats. What is your schema for pets? (Student responses.)

What is your schema for goats? (Student responses.)

Do you know anyone who has a pet goat? (Student responses.)

Have you ever seen a goat? (Student responses.)

When you connect what you already know with the story you read Today you'll better understand today's story.

Activity 3 Develop Opinions—An After-Reading Strategy

Today we'll found out your opinion or how you feel about the stories you read. You will choose a book to read and then complete the My Book Review form. You'll need to tell if you like or don't like the book and why. You must give a reason for why you like or don't like the book. Finally, you can tell if you would recommend the book to others.

Have students read a narrative or expository trade book of their choice. **Have** students complete My Book Review form when they are finished reading their book. **Model** how to complete the My Book Review form. **Guide** students as needed. **Have** students share their book reviews with the class as time permits.

Part D: Fluency Building

5 minutes

Student Materials:
Storybook 1

Conduct after the lesson, using story of the day.

Activity 1 Partner Reading

It's time for partner reading.
Direct students to the story of the day. **Assign** student partners as Partner 1 and Partner 2. **Monitor** student reading. **Guide** as needed.

Lesson 61

Materials

Teacher: *Storybook 1;* 6-My Prediction Chart; 8-Phonemic Awareness; 3 manipulatives such as blocks, discs, chips, counters (if not using IWB)

Student: *Storybook 1;* copy of 8-Phonemic Awareness; 3 manipulatives such as blocks, discs, chips, counters

---

3 minutes

IWB

Teacher Materials:
Phonemic Awareness

3 manipulatives such as blocks, discs, chips, counters

Student Materials:
Phonemic Awareness

3 manipulatives such as blocks, discs, chips, counters

Part A: Phonemic and Phonological Awareness

Activity 1 Phoneme Blending for One-Syllable Words

Elicit responses. **Guide** as needed.
Let's put some sounds together and make words. I'm going to say a word very slowly so you can hear each sound. You'll need to listen carefully and say the sounds. Then we'll put the sounds together and say the word. Listen closely because the words are getting harder.

My turn. Listen. **/g/ /lll/ /aaa/ /d/.**
Say the sounds. */g/ /lll/ /aaa/ /d/.*
Again, say the sounds. */g/ /lll/ /aaa/ /d/.*
Let's put it together. What word? *Glad.*

My turn. Listen. **/g/ /lll/ /īī/ /d/.**
Say the sounds. */g/ /lll/ /īī/ /d/.*
Again, say the sounds. */g/ /lll/ /īī/ /d/.*
Let's put it together. What word? *Glide.*

(Continue the activity with the following words:
glow [g-lll-ōōō], globe [g-lll-ōōō-b], gloss [g-lll-ooo-sss].)

Activity 2 Phoneme Segmentation

Show Phonemic Awareness. **Elicit** responses. **Guide** as needed.
Let's use our chips to show how many sounds there are in a word. For each sound in a word, we'll push one chip up to the arrow on the page. When we finish, we'll read the whole word.

Your turn. Say the sounds you hear in **mash,** and move a chip for each sound. */mmm/ /aaa/ /shshsh/.*

Move your finger back to the dot. What word? *Mash.*
How many sounds are in the word **mash?** *Three.*
Correct. Now move your chips back to the bottom, and let's try another one.

(Continue the activity with the following words:
rash, cash, dash.)

5 minutes

Student Materials:
Storybook 1

Activity 1 Learn New Vocabulary Word

Elicit responses to questions. **Guide** as needed.
Today you'll learn a new vocabulary word. **Halt. Halt** means **stop.** What does **halt** mean? *Stop.*

Another word for **stop** is **halt.** What's another word for **stop?** *Halt.*

The policeman said, "**Stop**" to the man running down the road. The policeman told the man to **halt.**

What's another word for **stop?** *Halt.*

Discuss times students may need to halt.

Activity 2 Review Vocabulary Word

Elicit responses to questions. **Guide** as needed.
What does **site** mean? *Place.*
What's another word for **place?** *Site.*

Review vocabulary words in appropriate context in *Storybook 1.*

Part C: Comprehension Strategies

12 minutes

IWB

Teacher Materials:
Storybook 1

My Prediction Chart

Student Materials:
Storybook 1

Activity 1 Identify Setting in Narrative Text—An After-Reading Strategy

Refer to Story 60, pages 153 and 154.

Elicit responses to questions. **Guide** as needed.
To find out the setting, you have to figure out where the story happens and when the story happens. What is the setting? (Idea: *When and where a story happens.*)

When you want to find out where a story happens, you figure out in what place the story happens. Settings have a where. What do you try to find out when you figure out where a story happens? *The place.*

When you want to find out when a story happens, you have to figure out at what time the story happens. Settings have a when. What do you try to find out when you figure out the when in a story? *The time.*

What is the part of a narrative called that tells when and where? *The setting.*

Direct students to read the first three paragraphs of Story 60, page 153, to find the setting.

I want you to read "The Pet Goat" story on page 153 with a partner and try to find the setting of the story. Remember: You're looking for the where and the when in the story. Here's a hint. You'll find the setting somewhere in the first three paragraphs. Talk with your partner, and see if you can read and find the setting of the story. When you find it, write it by copying it out of the book. Then we will check to see if you found it. What are you looking for? *The setting.*

What parts are in a setting? (Idea: *When and where.*)

Debrief with students what they found for the setting. (First paragraph identifies "in her house" as where. Third paragraph indicates "one day" as when.)

Great job working together to find the setting.

Activity 2 Prediction—A Before-Reading Strategy

Refer to Story 61, pages 156–158.

Show My Prediction Chart. **Elicit** responses to questions. **Guide** as needed.
You're going to read the rest of the story about the goat. The story is called "The Goat Stops the Robber." What are you doing when you make predictions? (Idea: *Using clues to guess what will happen in the story.*)

Where do you get clues to make predictions? *From the title and the pictures.*

Discuss predictions with students.

Look at the story you're going to read, and make some predictions about what will happen in the story. Look at the title and the picture. See if there are clues to help you predict what might happen in this story.

Record two or three predictions.
I'll record your predictions. What do you predict will happen in this story? (Student response.)

What clue gives you that idea? (Student response.)

What else do you predict? (Student response.)

What gives a clue for that prediction? (Student response.)

Do you have any more predictions? (Student response.)

What clue makes you think that? (Student response.)

Remember: Making predictions helps you think about the story you will read and helps you be smart when you read.

Save recording of predictions for next lesson.

Provide a reading center to display books being read so that students can enjoy them again during free time.

Part D: Fluency Building

Conduct after the lesson, using story of the day.

Activity 1 Partner Reading

It's time for partner reading.

Direct students to the story of the day. **Assign** student partners as Partner 1 and Partner 2. **Monitor** student reading. **Guide** as needed.

Part A: Phonemic and Phonological Awareness

3 minutes

IWB

Teacher Materials:
Phonemic Awareness

3 manipulatives such as blocks, discs, chips, counters

Student Materials:
Phonemic Awareness

3 manipulatives such as blocks, discs, chips, counters

Activity 1 Phoneme Blending for One-Syllable Words

Elicit responses. **Guide** as needed.
Let's put some sounds together and make words. I'm going to say a word very slowly so you can hear each sound. You'll need to listen carefully and say the sounds. Then we'll put the sounds together and say the word. Listen closely because the words are getting harder.

My turn. Listen. /b/ **/lll/ /āāā/ /zzz/.**
Say the sounds. */b/ /lll/ /āāā/ /zzz/.*
Again, say the sounds. */b/ /lll/ /āāā/ /zzz/.*
Let's put it together. What word? *Blaze.*

(Continue the activity with the following words:
bleed [b-lll-ēēē-d], blind [b-lll-īīī-nnn-d], block [b-lll-ooo-k], blush [b-lll-uuu-shshsh].)

Activity 2 Phoneme Segmentation

Show Phonemic Awareness. **Elicit** responses. **Guide** as needed.
Let's use our chips to show how many sounds there are in a word. For each sound in a word, we'll push one chip up to the arrow on the page. When we finish, we'll read the whole word.

Your turn. Say the sounds you hear in **mine,** and move a chip for each sound. */mmm/ /īīī/ /nnn/.*

Move your finger back to the dot. What word? *Mine.*
How many sounds are in the word **mine?** *Three.*
Correct, now move your chips back to the bottom, and let's try another one.

(Continue the activity with the following words:
dine, fine, shine.)

Part B: Vocabulary Development

Activity 1 Learn New Vocabulary Word

Elicit responses to questions. **Guide** as needed.
Today you'll learn a new vocabulary word. **Enormous. Enormous** means **big.**
What does **enormous** mean? *Big.*

Another word for **big** is **enormous.** What's another word for **big?** *Enormous.*

Jane wanted a **big** kite. She wanted an **enormous** kite.

What's another word for **big?** *Enormous.*

Discuss things students think are enormous.

Activity 2 Review Vocabulary Word

Elicit responses to questions. **Guide** as needed.
What does **halt** mean? *Stop.*
What's another word for **stop?** *Halt.*

Review vocabulary words in appropriate context in *Storybook 1.*

Part C: Comprehension Strategies

12 minutes

IWB

Teacher Materials:
Storybook 1

My Prediction Chart

Student Materials:
Storybook 1

Activity 1 Confirm Predictions—An After-Reading Strategy

Refer to Story 61, pages 156–158.

Guide discussion based on what predictions were made in Lesson 61, based on recorded predictions. **Elicit** responses to questions. **Guide** as needed.
In the last lesson, you made some predictions about what would happen in the Pet Goat story. You made the predictions before you read the story. Making predictions helps you understand the story better. Now that you've read the story, let's check to see if your predictions were in the story. What will you do when you check to see if your predictions are correct? *Confirm predictions.*

What part in the story helps you confirm your predictions? (Student responses.)

Do all your predictions need to be correct? *No.*

Discuss value of making predictions with students.
Why not? (Idea: *Making predictions helps me understand the story even if the predictions are not correct, because I am thinking about confirming my predictions.*)

Activity 2 Identify Characters and Setting—An After-Reading Strategy

Direct student to Stories 60 and 61, pages 153–158.

In the last lesson, you told the setting for "The Pet Goat" story. Today I want you to work with your partner to find the main characters and any other characters in the story. Look at Stories 60 and 61 on pages 153–158. Copy the names of the main characters and any other characters in the story. What are you looking for when you try to find the characters? (Idea: *Who is in the story.*)

Debrief with students the main characters (the girl and the goat) and other characters (Dad).

Excellent working together to find the characters in the "The Pet Goat."

Part D: Fluency Building

5 minutes

Student Materials:
Storybook 1

Conduct after the lesson, using story of the day.

Activity 1 Partner Reading

It's time for partner reading.

Direct students to the story of the day. **Assign** student partners as Partner 1 and Partner 2. **Monitor** student reading. **Guide** as needed.

Lesson 63

Part A: Phonemic and Phonological Awareness

3 minutes

IWB

Teacher Materials:
Phonemic Awareness

3 manipulatives such as blocks, discs, chips, counters

Student Materials:
Phonemic Awareness

3 manipulatives such as blocks, discs, chips, counters

Activity 1 Phoneme Blending for One-Syllable Words

Elicit responses. **Guide** as needed.
Let's put some sounds together and make words. I'm going to say a word very slowly so you can hear each sound. You'll need to listen carefully and say the sounds. Then we'll put the sounds together and say the word. Listen closely because the words are getting harder.

My turn. Listen. **/fff/ /rrr/ /āāā/ /mmm/.**
Say the sounds. */fff/ /rrr/ /āāā/ /mmm/.*
Again, say the sounds. */fff/ /rrr/ /āāā/ /mmm/.*
Let's put it together. What word? *Frame.*

My turn. Listen. **/fff/ /rrr/ /eee/ /shshsh/.**
Say the sounds. */fff/ /rrr/ /eee/ /shshsh/.*
Again, say the sounds. */fff/ /rrr/ /eee/ /shshsh/.*
Let's put it together. What word? *Fresh.*

(Continue the activity with the following words:
free [fff-rrr-ēēē], fry [fff-rrr-īīī], frost [fff-rrr-ooo-sss-t].)

Activity 2 Phoneme Segmentation

Show Phonemic Awareness. **Elicit** responses. **Guide** as needed.
Let's use our chips to show how many sounds there are in a word. For each sound in a word, we'll push one chip up to the arrow on the page. When we finish, we'll read the whole word.

Your turn. Say the sounds you hear in **red,** and move a chip for each sound. */rrr/ /eee/ /d/.*

Move your finger back to the dot. What word? *Red.*
How many sounds are in the word **red?** *Three.*
Correct. Now move your chips back to the bottom, and let's try another one.

(Continue the activity with the following words:
shed, bed, fed.)

Part B: Vocabulary Development

Activity 1 Learn New Vocabulary Word

Elicit responses to questions. **Guide** as needed.
Today you'll learn a new vocabulary word. **Grasp. Grasp** means **hold on to.**
What does **grasp** mean? *Hold on to.*

Another word for **hold on to** is **grasp.** What's another word for **hold on to?**
Grasp.

Jane had to **hold on to** the kite string on the windy day. She had to **grasp** the
kite string when it was windy.

What's another word for **hold on to?** *Grasp.*

Discuss things students can grasp.

Activity 2 Review Vocabulary Word

Elicit responses to questions. **Guide** as needed.
What does **enormous** mean? *Big.*
What's another word for **big?** *Enormous.*

Review vocabulary words in appropriate context in *Storybook 1.*

Part C: Comprehension Strategies

Activity 1 Read with Prosody (Dialogue)—A During-Reading Strategy

Direct students to Story 62, pages 159 and 160.

Dialogue is what characters say in a story. Narratives have lots of dialogue.
How is dialogue marked in stories? (Idea: *With quotation marks.*)

This is the story "Jane Wanted to Fly, Fly, Fly." The dialogue is marked with
quotation marks. Each time a different character speaks, a new set of
quotation marks begins. The parts with no quotation marks are for
the narrator, or the one telling the story.

Select proficient readers to read parts with you. **Model** reading Jane's dialogue, Dad's
dialogue, and narrator's part to the class with two students as your partners.
Listen to me read with two partners, taking turns on the dialogue. I'll read the
words for Dad. _____ will read the words for Jane. _____ will read
the words for the narrator. We'll try to read the words so they sound interesting.

Model reading the story with expression several times until students are firm.

Your turn to read the story the same way with two partners. Try to read with expression. Decide who will read which character's words and who will read the words of the narrator. Take turns, and try to make the dialogue interesting.

Group students in groups of three to read the story with expression. **Provide** guidance as needed.

Part D: Fluency Building

5 minutes

Student Materials:
Storybook 1

Conduct after the lesson, using story of the day.

Activity 1 Partner Reading

It's time for partner reading.

Direct students to the story of the day. **Assign** student partners as Partner 1 and Partner 2. **Monitor** student reading. **Guide** as needed.

Lesson 64

Part A: Phonemic and Phonological Awareness

3 minutes

IWB

Teacher Materials:
Phonemic Awareness

3 manipulatives such as blocks, discs, chips, counters

Student Materials:
Phonemic Awareness

3 manipulatives such as blocks, discs, chips, counters

Activity 1 Phoneme Blending for One-Syllable Words

Elicit responses. **Guide** as needed.
Let's put some sounds together and make words. I'm going to say a word very slowly so you can hear each sound. You'll need to listen carefully and say the sounds. Then we'll put the sounds together and say the word. Listen closely because the words are getting harder.

My turn. Listen. **/d/ /rrr/ /eee/ /sss/.**
Say the sounds. */d/ /rrr/ /eee/ /sss/.*
Again, say the sounds. */d/ /rrr/ /eee/ /sss/.*
Let's put it together. What word? *Dress.*

(Continue the activity with the following words:
dream [d-rrr-ēēē-mmm], dry [d-rrr-īīī], drop [d-rrr-ooo-p], drum [d-rrr-uuu-mmm].)

Activity 2 Phoneme Segmentation

Show Phonemic Awareness. **Elicit** responses. **Guide** as needed.
Let's use our chips to show how many sounds there are in a word. For each sound in the word, we'll push one chip up to the arrow on the page. When we finish, we'll read the whole word.

Your turn. Say the sounds you hear in **mole,** and move a chip for each sound. */mmm/ /ōōō/ /lll/.*

Move your finger back to the dot. What word? *Mole.*
How many sounds are in the word **mole?** *Three.*
Correct. Now move your chips back to the bottom, and let's try another one.

(Continue the activity with the following words:
pole, roll, hole.)

Part B: Vocabulary Development

5 minutes

Student Materials:
Storybook 1

Activity 1 Learn New Vocabulary Word

Elicit responses to questions. **Guide** as needed.
Today you'll learn a new vocabulary word. **Proud. Proud** means **pleased with yourself.** What does **proud** mean? *Pleased with yourself.*

Another word for **pleased with yourself** is **proud.** What's another word for **pleased with yourself?** *Proud.*

Marie read 30 books over the summer. She was **pleased with herself.** She felt **proud** of her reading.

What's another word for **pleased with yourself?** *Proud.*

Discuss times when students have been proud of something.

Activity 2 Review Vocabulary Word

Elicit responses to questions. **Guide** as needed.
What does **grasp** mean? *Hold on to.*
What's another word for **hold on to?** *Grasp.*

Review vocabulary words in appropriate context in *Storybook 1.*

Part C: Comprehension Strategies

12 minutes

Teacher Materials:
Storybook 1

Student Materials:
Storybook 1

Activity 1 Mental Imaging—A During-Reading Strategy

Refer to Story 63, pages 161–163.

Elicit responses to questions. **Guide** as needed.
What do good readers do when they make mental images? *Make pictures in their brains.*

If you want to be a good reader, you need to practice making pictures in your brain when you read. When you make pictures in your brain, you want to think about what you "see" when you read a sentence.

Listen to me choose a sentence, read it, and then tell what I see.
Model think-aloud for finding a sentence in the story and telling what you see.

Sample Wording for Think-Aloud

(Read first sentence from second paragraph on page 161.) I see trees blowing, leaves falling off trees, and clouds moving fast in the sky.

Direct students to find a sentence that makes them have a picture in their brain. **Encourage** students to share their pictures with partner.

Now it's your turn. Choose a different sentence from Story 63, "Jane Goes Up, Up, Up." Read the sentence to your partner. Then get a picture in your mind of that sentence. What picture do you see in your brain when you read that sentence? Tell your partner what you see.

Direct partner to take a turn.

Now your partner should find a sentence. Read the sentence. Then tell the picture you see in your brain when you read the sentence.

Discuss sentence chosen and mental images developed.
Share with the class the sentence you chose, and tell the picture you saw in your brain.

When you make mental images as you read, you'll be better at understanding what you read

Part D: Fluency Building

5 minutes

Student Materials:
Storybook 1

Conduct after the lesson, using story of the day.

Activity 1 Partner Reading

It's time for partner reading.
Direct students to the story of the day. **Assign** student partners as Partner 1 and Partner 2. **Monitor** student reading. **Guide** as needed.

Materials

Teacher: *Storybook 1;* 8-Phonemic Awareness; 3 manipulatives such as blocks, discs, chips, counters (if not using IWB), 2-Vocabulary Acquisition and Use, Writing Prompts, 5-My Writing Checklist

Student: *Storybook 1;* copy of 8-Phonemic Awareness; 3 manipulatives such as blocks, discs, chips, counters, Copy of 2- Vocabulary Acquisition and Use and 3-My Writing Checklist; Lined Paper

Part A: Phonemic and Phonological Awareness

3 minutes

IWB

Teacher Materials:
Phonemic Awareness

3 manipulatives such as blocks, discs, chips, counters

Student Materials:
Phonemic Awareness

3 manipulatives such as blocks, discs, chips, counters

Activity 1 Phoneme Blending for One-Syllable Words

Elicit responses. **Guide** as needed.

Let's put some sounds together and make words. I'm going to say a word very slowly so you can hear each sound. You'll need to listen carefully and say the sounds. Then we'll put the sounds together and say the word. Listen closely because the words are getting harder.

My turn. Listen. **/t/ /rrr/ /āāā/ /nnn/.**
Say the sounds. */t/ /rrr/ /āāā/ /nnn/.*
Again, say the sounds. */t/ /rrr/ /āāā/ /nnn/.*
Let's put it together. What word? *Train.*

My turn. Listen. **/t/ /rrr/ /aaa/ /shshsh/.**
Say the sounds. */t/ /rrr/ /aaa/ /shshsh/.*
Again, say the sounds. */t/ /rrr/ /aaa/ /shshsh/.*
Let's put it together. What word? *Trash.*

(Continue the activity with the following words:
tree [t-rrr-ēēē], try [t-rrr-īīī], trust [t-rrr-uuu-sss-t].)

Activity 2 Phoneme Segmentation

Show Phonemic Awareness. **Elicit** responses. **Guide** as needed.

Let's use our chips to show how many sounds there are in a word. For each sound in the word, we'll push one chip up to the arrow on the page. When we finish, we'll read the whole word.

Your turn. Say the sounds you hear in **wig,** and move a chip for each sound.
/www/ /iii/ /g/.

Move your finger back to the dot. What word? *Wig.*
How many sounds are in the word **wig?** *Three.*
Correct. Now move your chips back to the bottom, and let's try another one.

(Continue the activity with the following words:
big, pig, dig.)

Part B: Vocabulary Development

IWB

Teacher Materials:
Vocabulary Acquisition and Use

Student Materials:
Storybook 1

Vocabulary Acquisition and Use

Activity 1 Cumulative Vocabulary Review

Elicit responses to questions. **Guide** as needed.
Directions: Listen and tell me the correct vocabulary word for each question.

What's another word for **big?** *Enormous.*
What's another word for **hold on to?** *Grasp.*
What's another word for **pleased with yourself?** *Proud.*
What's another word for **stop?** *Halt.*

Repeat difficult words as needed.

Review vocabulary words in appropriate context in *Storybook 1.*

Activity 2 Vocabulary Acquisition and Use

Display Vocabulary Acquisition and Use. **Have** students work with a neighbor to complete Vocabulary Acquisition and Use.
Today's vocabulary words are _____ and _____ [and _____ and _____].
Vocabulary words: **halt** and **stop; enormous** and **big**
Write the words on the lines provided. Then write the words in the boxes based on whether you think each word is less/smaller or more/larger than the other word. Below the boxes, write why you think word 1 is less/smaller and word 2 is more/larger than word 1.
Repeat for words 3 and 4. **Have** students share what they wrote. **Discuss** examples of how these words might be used.

Part C: Comprehension Strategies

IWB

Teacher Materials:
Storybook 1

Student Materials:
Storybook 1

Activity 1 Identify Problem in Narratives—A During-Reading Strategy

Elicit responses to questions. **Guide** as needed.
Another important part of all narratives is the **problem** in the story. The problem is what goes wrong in the story. The problem usually comes after the story tells you about the characters and the setting. What are the characters? (Idea: *Who is in the story.*)

What is the setting? (Idea: *When and where the story takes place.*)

The problem is the part in the story that goes wrong. What is the part called that tells what goes wrong? (Idea: *The problem.*)

The problem makes you want to read more of the story to find out what happens. Listen to me read the story. We will figure out the problem in the story.

Read Story 64, pages 164–166, with prosody.

Model think-aloud to identify the problem when you get to the last paragraph.

> ## Sample Wording for Think-Aloud
> This part tells the problem. The little cloud is being blown away from his parents. They can't hear him call them. I wonder what is going to happen to the little cloud. I want to keep reading to find out if this problem gets solved.

Activity 2   Sequencing—An After-Reading Strategy

Refer to Story 64, pages 164–166.

We're going to play the Put Events in Order game today. I'm going to tell you events that happened in the story. Since I get mixed up, I need you to help me put the events into the right order.

Read each sentence with a pause between sentences.
And that small cloud did grow.

The little cloud could not make rain.

That wind began to blow the little cloud far away.

Reread sentences again in the same order.

Elicit responses to questions. **Guide** as needed.
Which event happened first? (Idea: *The little cloud could not make rain.*)

What event happened next? (Idea: *And that small cloud did grow.*)

What event happened last? (Idea: *That wind began to blow the little cloud far away.*)

Good for you. You put the events in the right order.

Part D: Fluency Building

5 minutes

Student Materials:
Storybook 1

Conduct after the lesson, using story of the day.

Activity 1   Partner Reading

It's time for partner reading.
Direct students to the story of the day. **Assign** student partners as Partner 1 and Partner 2. **Monitor** student reading. **Guide** as needed.

10 minutes

IWB

Teacher Materials:
Writing Prompts

My Writing Checklist

Student Materials:
Lined Paper

My Writing Checklist

Activity 1 Write and Use Parts of Speech and Conventions

Time to write using a writing prompt based on the stories we've been reading.

Assign student partners. **Distribute** lined paper to students. **Display** writing prompts and have students choose one to write about or assign a writing prompt of your choice. **Review** parts of speech and punctuation as well as the writing checklist with students. **Tell** students to write one paragraph (minimum of four sentences per paragraph) on their own to answer the writing prompt. **Tell** them to use their writing checklist (first column labeled "Did I use them?") to ensure they include important parts of speech or punctuation in their writing. **Tell** students which parts of speech or punctuation to focus on, if you wish. **Model** what it means to answer a writing prompt and to use the writing checklist during and after the writing process, as needed. **Monitor** and guide students as needed. **Model** what it means to have a neighbor look over his or her neighbor's writing and to complete the writing checklist (second column labeled "Did my neighbor use them?"), as needed. **Have** students share what they wrote as time permits.

Writing Prompt 1	Writing Prompt 2	Writing Prompt 3
If you are good, the magic pouch is good to you. Tell me about some good things you could do.	Tell me how the fly and the elephant could have shared the fine spot in the sun.	What would it be like to have a pet goat?

Lesson 66

Materials

Teacher: *Storybook 1;* 8-Phonemic Awareness; 3 manipulatives such as blocks, discs, chips, counters (if not using IWB)

Student: *Storybook 1;* copy of 8-Phonemic Awareness; 3 manipulatives such as blocks, discs, chips, counters

Part A: Phonemic and Phonological Awareness

3 minutes

IWB

Teacher Materials:
Phonemic Awareness

3 manipulatives such as blocks, discs, chips, counters

Student Materials:
Phonemic Awareness

3 manipulatives such as blocks, discs, chips, counters

Activity 1 Phoneme Blending for One-Syllable Words

Elicit responses. **Guide** as needed.
Let's put some sounds together and make words. I'm going to say a word very slowly so you can hear each sound. You'll need to listen carefully and say the sounds. Then we'll put the sounds together and say the word. Listen closely because the words are getting harder.

My turn. Listen. **/b/ /rrr/ /āāā/ /nnn/.**
Say the sounds. */b/ /rrr/ /āāā/ /nnn/.*
Again, say the sounds. */b/ /rrr/ /āāā/ /nnn/.*
Let's put it together. What word? *Brain.*

(Continue the activity with the following words:
brick [b-rrr-iii-k], bride [b-rrr-īīī-d], broke [b-rrr-ōōō-k], brush [b-rrr-uuu-shshsh].)

Activity 2 Phoneme Segmentation

Show Phonemic Awareness. **Elicit** responses. **Guide** as needed.
Let's use our chips to show how many sounds there are in a word. For each sound in a word, we'll push one chip up to the arrow on the page. When we finish, we'll read the whole word.

Your turn. Say the sounds you hear in **same,** and move a chip for each sound. */sss/ /āāā/ mmm/.*

Move your finger back to the dot. What word? *Same.*
How many sounds are in the word **same?** *Three.*
Correct. Now move your chips back to the bottom, and let's try another one.

(Continue the activity with the following words:
game, came, tame.)

Part B: Vocabulary Development

Activity 1 Learn New Vocabulary Word

Elicit responses to questions. **Guide** as needed.
Today you'll learn a new vocabulary word. **Wade. Wade** means **walk through water.** What does **wade** mean? *Walk through water.*

Another word for **walk through water** is **wade.** What's another word for **walk through water?** *Wade.*

Jacob loved to **walk through water** as he looked for shells. His favorite thing was to **wade** in the ocean and look for shells.

What's another word for **walk through water?** *Wade.*

Discuss where students can wade.

Activity 2 Review Vocabulary Word

Elicit responses to questions. **Guide** as needed.
What does **proud** mean? *Pleased with yourself.*
What's another word for **pleased with yourself?** *Proud.*

Review vocabulary words in appropriate context in *Storybook 1.*

Part C: Comprehension Strategies

Activity 1 Identify the Problem in Narratives—An After-Reading Strategy

Elicit responses to questions. **Guide** as needed.
We learned that another important part of all narratives is the problem in the story. The problem is what goes wrong in the story. The problem usually comes after the story tells you about the characters and the setting.

What part tells who is in the story? *Characters.*

What part tells about when and where the story happens? *The setting.*

The problem is the part in the story that goes wrong. What is the part called that tells what goes wrong? *The problem.*

The problem makes you want to read more of the story to find out what happens.

Listen to me read the story. We will figure out the problem in the story.

Read Story 65, pages 167–169, with prosody.

Model think-aloud to identify the problem when you get to the fifth paragraph.

> ### Sample Wording for Think-Aloud
> This part tells the problem. The little cloud is being blown away from his parents. There is a forest fire, and the deer are trapped. I wonder what is going to happen to the deer and the little cloud. I want to keep reading to find out if this problem gets solved.

Activity 2 Reread (A Fix-Up Strategy)—A During-Reading Strategy

Elicit responses from questions. **Guide** as needed.
When you are reading, what should you be thinking as you read? (Idea: *Does this make sense.*)

If you are reading, and suddenly you realize that what you are reading does not make sense, what should you do? (Idea: *Reread the sentences until the story makes sense.*)

When you reread a sentence or a section that is confusing, you can usually understand the story. Remember to think about what you are reading, and reread if you get confused.

Part D: Fluency Building

5 minutes

Student Materials:
Storybook 1

Conduct after the lesson, using story of the day.

Activity 1 Partner Reading

It's time for partner reading.
Direct students to the story of the day. **Assign** student partners as Partner 1 and Partner 2. **Monitor** student reading. **Guide** as needed.

Materials

Teacher: 1-Narrative Story Map; *Storybook 1;* 8-Phonemic Awareness; 3 manipulatives such as blocks, discs, chips, counters (if not using IWB)

Student: *Storybook 1;* copy of 1-Narrative Story Map; copy of 8-Phonemic Awareness; 3 manipulatives such as blocks, discs, chips, counters

Part A: Phonemic and Phonological Awareness

3 minutes

IWB

Teacher Materials:
Phonemic Awareness

3 manipulatives such as blocks, discs, chips, counters

Student Materials:
Phonemic Awareness

3 manipulatives such as blocks, discs, chips, counters

Activity 1 Phoneme Blending for One-Syllable Words

Elicit responses. **Guide** as needed.
Let's put some sounds together and make words. I'm going to say a word very slowly so you can hear each sound. You'll need to listen carefully and say the sounds. Then we'll put the sounds together and say the word. Listen closely because the words are getting harder.

My turn. Listen. **/p/ /rrr/ /eee/ /sss/.**
Say the sounds. /p/ /rrr/ /eee/ /sss/.
Again, say the sounds. /p/ /rrr/ /eee/ /sss/.
Let's put it together. What word? *Press.*

My turn. Listen. **/p/ /rrr/ /īīī/ sss/.**
Say the sounds. /p/ /rrr/ /īīī/ /sss/.
Again, say the sounds. /p/ /rrr/ /īīī/ /sss/.
Let's put it together. What word? *Price.*

(Continue the activity with the following words:
pride [p-rrr-īīī-d], prince [p-rrr-iii-nnn-sss], print [p-rrr-iii-nnn-t].)

Activity 2 Phoneme Segmentation

Show Phonemic Awareness. **Elicit** responses. **Guide** as needed.
Let's use our chips to show how many sounds there are in a word. For each sound in a word, we'll push one chip up to the arrow on the page. When we finish, we'll read the whole word.

Your turn. Say the sounds you hear in **mop,** and move a chip for each sound. /mmm/ /ooo/ /p/.

Move your finger back to the dot. What word? *Mop.*
How many sounds are in the word **mop?** *Three.*
Correct. Now move your chips back to the bottom, and let's try another one.

(Continue the activity with the following words:
chop, shop, hop.)

Part B: Vocabulary Development

Student Materials:
Storybook 1

Activity 1 New Vocabulary Word

Elicit responses to questions. **Guide** as needed.
Today you'll learn a new vocabulary word. **Scare. Scare** means to **make afraid.** What does **scare** mean? *Make afraid.*

Another way to say **make afraid** is **scare.** What's another way to say **make afraid?** Scare.

Jess said he wanted to **make** his brother **afraid** during the Halloween party. Jess wanted to **scare** his brother during the Halloween party.

What's another word for **make afraid?** *Scare.*

Discuss things that might scare students.

Activity 2 Review Vocabulary Word

Elicit responses to questions. **Guide** as needed.
What does **wade** mean? *Walk through water.*
What's another word for **walk through water?** *Wade.*

Review vocabulary words in appropriate context in *Storybook 1.*

Part C: Comprehension Strategies

12 minutes

IWB

Teacher Materials:
Storybook 1

Narrative Story Map

Student Materials:
Storybook 1

Narrative Story Map

Activity 1 Narrative Story Map—An After-Reading Strategy

Refer to Stories 64–66, pages 164–172.

Show Narrative Story Map and touch each box as you introduce. **Provide** Narrative Story Map to each student.
Let's work together to fill in our Narrative Story Map about the "Little Cloud" story.

Touch the line for the title. This is a new place to fill in on your Story Map. These chapters had several titles, so we will just call the whole story "The Little Cloud." Write that on the line for the title.
Model writing the title on the map.

What will you draw for the main character? *The little cloud.* Draw that in the box for Characters.

This map has a new section. It has a place to fill in the setting.

Guide students as they draw pictures on their Narrative Story Maps.
What will you draw for where in the box for Setting? *The sky.*
What will you draw for when in the box for Setting? (Idea: *The story does not tell us. We can leave it blank or we can write one day.*)

What will you draw for events at the beginning? (Idea: *The little cloud was little and could not make thunder and rain.*)

What will you draw for events in the middle? (Ideas: *The wind blew the little cloud away from his mom and dad. There was a forest fire that trapped two deer. The little cloud was the only one who could help.*)

What will you draw at the end? (Idea: *The little cloud shook until he could make rain and save the two deer.*)

When you fill out a Narrative Story Map, you really show that you remember all about the story.

Save student copies of completed Narrative Story Map for Lesson 68.

Part D: Fluency Building

5 minutes

Student Materials:
Storybook 1

Conduct after the lesson, using story of the day.

Activity 1 Partner Reading

It's time for partner reading.

Direct students to the story of the day. **Assign** student partners as Partner 1 and Partner 2. **Monitor** student reading. **Guide** as needed.

Lesson 68

Materials

Teacher: *Storybook 1;* 1-Narrative Story Map (from Lesson 67); 8-Phonemic Awareness; 3 manipulatives such as blocks, discs, chips, counters (if not using IWB)

Student: *Storybook 1;* copy of 1-Narrative Story Map (from Lesson 67); copy of 8-Phonemic Awareness; 3 manipulatives such as blocks, discs, chips, counters

Part A: Phonemic and Phonological Awareness

3 minutes

IWB

Teacher Materials:
Phonemic Awareness

3 manipulatives such as blocks, discs, chips, counters

Student Materials:
Phonemic Awareness

3 manipulatives such as blocks, discs, chips, counters

Activity 1 Phoneme Blending for One-Syllable Words

Elicit responses. **Guide** as needed.
Let's put some sounds together and make words. I'm going to say a word very slowly so you can hear each sound. You'll need to listen carefully and say the sounds. Then we'll put the sounds together and say the word. Listen closely because the words are getting harder.

My turn. Listen. **/k/ /rrr/ /aaa/ /b/.**
Say the sounds. /k/ /rrr/ /aaa/ /b/.
Again, say the sounds. /k/ /rrr/ /aaa/ /b/.
Let's put it together. What word? *Crab.*

(Continue the activity with the following words:
cream [k-rrr-ēēē-mmm], crisp [k-rrr-iii-sss-p], cry [k-rrr-īīī], crust [k-rrr-uuu-sss-t].)

Activity 2 Phoneme Segmentation

Show Phonemic Awareness. **Elicit** responses. **Guide** as needed.
Let's use our chips to show how many sounds there are in a word. For each sound in a word, we'll push one chip up to the arrow on the page. When we finish, we'll read the whole word.

Your turn. Say the sounds you hear in **sight,** and move a chip for each sound. /sss/ /īīī/ /t/.

Move your finger back to the dot. What word? *Sight.*
How many sounds are in the word **sight?** *Three.*
Correct. Now move your chips back to the bottom, and let's try another one.

(Continue the activity with the following words:
night, fight, kite.)

Part B: Vocabulary Development

Activity 1 Learn New Vocabulary Word

Elicit responses to questions. **Guide** as needed.
Today you'll learn a new vocabulary word. **Count. Count** means **tell how many.** What does **count** mean? *Tell how many.*

Another word for **tell how many** is **count.** What's another word for **tell how many?** *Count.*

When you have a lot of pennies, you can **tell how many** you have in all. You can **count** your pennies.

What's another word for **tell how many?** *Count.*

Discuss things students can count.

Activity 2 Review Vocabulary Word

Elicit responses to questions. **Guide** as needed.
What does **scare** mean? *Make afraid.*
What's another word for **make afraid?** *Scare.*

Review vocabulary words in appropriate context in *Storybook 1.*

Part C: Comprehension Strategies

Activity 1 Narrative Story Map—A During-Reading Strategy

Teacher Materials:
Storybook 1

Narrative Story Map

Student Materials:
Storybook 1

Narrative Story Map

Provide Narrative Story maps completed in Lesson 67 to students.
You did a great job filling out your Narrative Story Maps in the last lesson. Today you will use your Narrative Story Map to retell the Little Cloud story. Start by telling the title. Then look at the picture clues in the different boxes of your map to help you retell the story. Tell the story to your partner. Then have your partner tell the story to you.

Monitor student partners as they retell the story from their Narrative Story Maps.

Activity 2 Activate Background Knowledge—A Before-Reading Strategy

Elicit responses to questions. **Guide** as needed.
We talked about schema. When you activate your schema, you check on what your brain knows about a topic. What do you call everything you know in your brain? *Schema.*

It's a good idea to think about what you know about a topic before you read a new story. Then you can connect what you know to the new information that you learn when you read.

Discuss background knowledge. **Guide** as needed.

Today the story is about a girl who likes to count. She walks by a railroad track on the way to school and begins an adventure.

Open the file in your brain, and look in it to see what your schema is about trains. Have you ever ridden on a train? (Student response.)

Do you know anyone who has been on a train? (Student response.)

What job do trains do? (Student response.)

What is your schema for railroad stations? (Student response.)

What is your schema for counting? (Student response.)

Where do you do counting? (Student response.)

Do you know anyone who is good at math and counting? (Student response.)

When you connect what you already know about trains and counting to the story you will read today, you will understand the story better.

Conduct after the lesson, using story of the day.

Part D: Fluency Building

5 minutes

Student Materials:
Storybook 1

Activity 1 Partner Reading

It's time for partner reading.

Direct students to the story of the day. **Assign** student partners as Partner 1 and Partner 2. **Monitor** student reading. **Guide** as needed.

Lesson 69

Materials

Teacher: *Storybook 1;* 8-Phonemic Awareness; 3 manipulatives such as blocks, discs, chips, counters (if not using IWB)

Student: *Storybook 1;* copy of 8-Phonemic Awareness; lined paper; 3 manipulatives such as blocks, discs, chips, counters

3 minutes

IWB

Teacher Materials:
Phonemic Awareness

3 manipulatives such as blocks, discs, chips, counters

Student Materials:
Phonemic Awareness

3 manipulatives such as blocks, discs, chips, counters

Part A: Phonemic and Phonological Awareness

Activity 1 Phoneme Blending for One-Syllable Words

Elicit responses. **Guide** as needed.
Let's put some sounds together and make words. I'm going to say a word very slowly so you can hear each sound. You'll need to listen carefully and say the sounds. Then we'll put the sounds together and say the word. Listen closely because the words are getting harder.

My turn. Listen. **/g/ /rrr/ /āāā/ /p/.**
Say the sounds. */g/ /rrr/ /āāā/ /p/.*
Again, say the sounds. */g/ /rrr/ /āāā/ /p/.*
Let's put it together. What word? *Grape.*

My turn. Listen. **/g/ /rrr/ /aaa/ /sss/.**
Say the sounds. */g/ /rrr/ /aaa/ /sss/.*
Again, say the sounds. */g/ /rrr/ /aaa/ /sss/.*
Let's put it together. What word? *Grass.*

(Continue the activity with the following words:
gray [g-rrr-āāā], green [g-rrr-ēēē-nnn], grow [g-rrr-ōōō].)

Activity 2 Phoneme Segmentation

Show Phonemic Awareness. **Elicit** responses. **Guide** as needed.
Let's use our chips to show how many sounds there are in a word. For each sound in a word, we'll push one chip up to the arrow on the page. When we finish, we'll read the whole word.

Your turn. Say the sounds you hear in **luck,** and move a chip for each sound. */lll/ /uuu/ /k/.*

Move your finger back to the dot. What word? *Luck.*
How many sounds are in the word **luck?** *Three.*
Correct. Now move your chips back to the bottom, and let's try another one.

(Continue the activity with the following words:
duck, tuck, shuck.)

Part B: Vocabulary Development

Activity 1 Learn New Vocabulary Word

Elicit responses to questions. **Guide** as needed.
Today you'll learn a new vocabulary word. **Missing. Missing** means **lost.**
What does **missing** mean? *Lost.*

Another word for **lost** is **missing.** What's another word for **lost?** *Missing.*

Payton's family was upset because their dog Spot was **lost.** Their dog Spot
was **missing,** so Payton's family was upset.

What's another word for **lost?** *Missing.*

Discuss when students have had something missing and how they felt about it.

Activity 2 Review Vocabulary Word

Elicit responses to questions. **Guide** as needed.
What does **count** mean? *Tell how many.*
What's another word for **tell how many?** *Count.*

Review vocabulary words in appropriate context in *Storybook 1.*

Part C: Comprehension Strategies

Activity 1 Identify the Problem—An After-Reading Strategy

Elicit responses to questions. **Guide** as needed.
An important part of all narratives is the problem in the story. The problem is
what goes wrong in the story. The problem usually comes after the story tells
you about the characters and the setting.
What part tells who is in the story? *Characters.*

What part tells about when and where the story happens? *The setting.*

The problem is the part in the story that tells what goes wrong. What is the
part called that tells what goes wrong? (Idea: *The problem.*)

The problem makes you want to read more of the story to find out what
happens.

Listen to me read the story. When you think you hear a problem, tell me to
stop reading.

Read Story 68, pages 176–178, with prosody.

Elicit identification of the problem when you get to the fifth paragraph.
Yes, the problem is that the TV sets are missing.

When I read the problem, it makes me want to read some more to find out what happens.

Activity 2 Identify the Characters and the Setting—An After-Reading Strategy

Direct students to Story 68, pages 176–178.

Provide lined paper to students. **Elicit** responses to questions. **Guide** as needed.
Today I want you to work by yourself to find the main characters and any other characters in the story. Look at Story 68. Copy the name of the main character and any other characters in the story. What are you looking for when you try to find the characters? (Idea: *Who is in the story.*)

Please write the name of the main character on your paper. Then write any other characters you find.

Now I want you to check the first three paragraphs of the story to find the setting. When you look for the setting, what will you look for? (Idea: *Where and when the story takes place.*)

Copy the words for the setting when you figure it out. Then we'll check to see if you found everything.

Discuss the answers. Main character is Sandy. Other characters are a man and a woman. The where for the setting is "on the way to school." The when for the setting is "one day."

Excellent job working hard to find the characters in the "Sandy Counted Everything".

Part D: Fluency Building

5 minutes

Student Materials:
Storybook 1

Conduct after the lesson, using story of the day.

Activity 1 Partner Reading

It's time for partner reading.
Direct students to the story of the day. **Assign** student partners as Partner 1 and Partner 2. **Monitor** student reading. **Guide** as needed.

Lesson 70

Part A: Phonemic and Phonological Awareness

3 minutes

IWB

Teacher Materials:
Phonemic Awareness

3 manipulatives such as blocks, discs, chips, counters

Student Materials:
Phonemic Awareness

3 manipulatives such as blocks, discs, chips, counters

Activity 1 Phoneme Blending for One-Syllable Words

Elicit responses. **Guide** as needed.
Let's put some sounds together and make words. I'm going to say a word very slowly so you can hear each sound. You'll need to listen carefully and say the sounds. Then we'll put the sounds together and say the word. Listen closely because the words are getting harder.

My turn. Listen. **/t/ /www/ /īīī/ /sss/.**
Say the sounds. /t/ /www/ /īīī/ /sss/.
Again, say the sounds. /t/ /www/ /īīī/ /sss/.
Let's put it together. What word? *Twice.*

(Continue the activity with the following words:
tweed [t-www-ēēē-d], twig [t-www-iii-g], twine [t-www-īīī-nnn], twist [t-www-iii-sss-t].)

Activity 2 Phoneme Segmentation

Show Phonemic Awareness. **Elicit** responses. **Guide** as needed.
Let's use our chips to show how many sounds there are in a word. For each sound in a word, we'll push one chip up to the arrow on the page. When we finish, we'll read the whole word.

Your turn. Say the sounds you hear in **time,** and move a chip for each sound. /t/ /īīī/ /mmm/.

Move your finger back to the dot. What word? *Time.*
How many sounds are in the word **time?** *Three.*
Correct. Now move your chips back to the bottom, and let's try another one.

(Continue the activity with the following words:
dime, lime, chime.)

5 minutes

IWB

Teacher Materials:
Vocabulary Acquisition
and Use

Student Materials:
Storybook 1

Vocabulary Acquisition
and Use

Part B: Vocabulary Development

Activity 1 Cumulative Vocabulary Review

Elicit responses to questions. **Guide** as needed.
Directions: Listen and tell me the correct vocabulary word for each question.

What's another word for **tell how many?** *Count.*
What's another word for **stop?** *Halt.*
What's another word for **make afraid?** *Scare.*
What's another word for **hold on to?** *Grasp.*
What's another word for **pleased with yourself?** *Proud.*
What's another word for **walk through water?** *Wade.*
What's another word for **big?** *Enormous.*
What's another word for **lost?** *Missing.*

Repeat difficult words as needed.

Review vocabulary words in appropriate context in *Storybook 1.*

Activity 2 Vocabulary Acquisition and Use

Display Vocabulary Acquisition and Use. **Have** students work with a neighbor to complete Vocabulary Acquisition and Use.
Today's vocabulary words are _____ and _____ [and _____ and _____].
Vocabulary words: **missing** and **lost; wade** and **walk**
Write the words on the lines provided. Then write the words in the boxes based on whether you think each word is less/smaller or more/larger than the other word. Below the boxes, write why you think word 1 is less/smaller and word 2 is more/larger than word 1.
Repeat for words 3 and 4. **Have** students share what they wrote. **Discuss** examples of how these words might be used.

12 minutes

IWB

Teacher Materials:
Storybook 1

My Book Review

Student Materials:
Storybook 1

My Book Review

Part C: Comprehension Strategies

Activity 1 Read with Prosody (Dialogue)—A During-Reading Strategy

Direct students to Story 69, pages 179–181.

Dialogue is what characters say in a story. Narratives have lots of dialogue. How is dialogue marked in stories? (Idea: *With quotation marks.*)

What is dialogue? (Idea: *The words characters say in the story.*)

Ask students to find the dialogue of different characters. **Monitor** groups as students review the stories.
This is the story "A Train Car Was Missing." I want you to find the dialogue for the characters. You will look for the words Sandy says, the words the two men say, the words the woman says, and the words for the narrator, which aren't in quotation marks.

Group students in groups of 5, and **provide** guidance as needed. **Monitor** groups as they practice dialogue.

Your turn to read the story the same way with five people. Try to read with expression. Decide who will read which character's words and who will read the words for the narrator. Take turns, and try to make the dialogue interesting.

Encourage students to perform the dialogue in front of the class, after practice.

Activity 2 Develop Opinions—An After-Reading Strategy

Today we'll found out your opinion or how you feel about the stories you read. You will choose a book to read and then complete the My Book Review form. You'll need to tell if you like or don't like the book and why. You must give a reason for why you like or don't like the book. Finally, you can tell if you would recommend the book to others.

Have students read a narrative or expository trade book of their choice. **Have** students complete My Book Review form when they are finished reading their book. **Model** how to complete the My Book Review form. **Guide** students as needed. **Have** students share their book reviews with the class as time permits.

Part D: Fluency Building

5 minutes

Student Materials:
Storybook 1

Conduct after the lesson, using story of the day.

Activity 1 Partner Reading

It's time for partner reading.

Direct students to the story of the day. **Assign** student partners as Partner 1 and Partner 2. **Monitor** student reading. **Guide** as needed.

Lesson 71

Materials

Teacher: *Storybook 1;* 8-Phonemic Awareness; 4 manipulatives such as blocks, discs, chips, counters (if not using IWB)

Student: *Storybook 1;* copy of 8-Phonemic Awareness; 4 manipulatives such as blocks, discs, chips, counters (note that one manipulative should have a letter printed on it – e.g., plastic disc with printed letter, preprinted letter tile, plastic letter)

Part A: Phonemic and Phonological Awareness

3 minutes

IWB

Teacher Materials:
Phonemic Awareness

4 manipulatives such as blocks, discs, chips, counters

Student Materials:
Phonemic Awareness

4 manipulatives such as blocks, discs, chips, counters

Activity 1   Phoneme Segmentation

Show Phonemic Awareness. **Elicit** responses. **Guide** as needed. **Add** more letters as students become proficient.

Let's use our chips to show the different sounds we hear in a word. Today we're going to use one chip that has the letter **s** on it. For each sound in the word, you'll push one chip up to the arrow on the page. You can use the letter **s** to show where the **/s/** sound is in the word. When we finish, we'll read the whole word.

Your turn. Say the sounds you hear in **sad.** */sss/ /aaa/ /d/.*
Your turn. Now say the sounds you hear in **sad,** and move a chip for each sound. Use the letter s for the /s/ sound. */sss/ /aaa/ /d/.*
Move your finger back to the dot. What word? *Sad.*
How many sounds are in the word **sad?** *Three.*
Correct. Now move your chips back to the bottom, and let's try another one.

(Continue the activity with the following words:
gas, ask, sun, bus, soft.)

Part B: Vocabulary Development

5 minutes

Student Materials:
Storybook 1

Activity 1   Learn New Vocabulary Word

Elicit responses to questions. **Guide** as needed.
Today you'll learn a new vocabulary word. **Hide. Hide** means **keep from being seen.** What does **hide** mean? *Keep from being seen.*

Another word for **keep from being seen** is **hide.** What's another word for **keep from being seen?** *Hide.*

The children wanted to play hide and seek during recess. Keisha wanted to **keep from being seen,** so she went to **hide** behind a really big tree. What's another word for **keep from being seen?** *Hide.*

Discuss places students can hide.

Activity 2 Review Vocabulary Word

Elicit responses to questions. **Guide** as needed.
What does **missing** mean? *Lost.*
What's another word for **lost?** *Missing.*

Review vocabulary words in appropriate context in *Storybook 1.*

Part C: Comprehension Strategies

12 minutes

Teacher Materials:
Storybook 1

Student Materials:
Storybook 1

Activity 1 Identify the Problem—An After-Reading Strategy

Elicit responses. **Guide** as needed.
You are learning how to figure out the problem in the story. What is the problem? (Idea: *What goes wrong in the story that makes you want to read to find out more.*)

The problem usually comes after the story tells you about the characters and the setting. What part tells who is in the story? *Characters.*

What part tells about when and where the story happens? *The setting.*

The problem is the part in the story that tells what goes wrong. What is the part called that tells what goes wrong? (Idea: *The problem.*)

The problem makes you want to read more of the story to find out what happens.

Listen to me read the story. When you think you hear a problem, tell me to stop reading.

Read Story 70, pages 182–184, with prosody.

Elicit problem identification when you get to the end of first paragraph.
The problem is that a train car is missing. I know that some TV sets are missing. I wonder if the missing TVs are in the missing train car. I need to read some more of the story to find out.

When I read the problem, it makes me want to read some more to find out what happens.

Activity 2 Summarize—An After-Reading Strategy

Read the first paragraph of Story 70, page 182.

After having read a part of a story, smart readers stop and tell themselves the story in their own words. You have been practicing retelling the story from a Narrative Story Map. So, you already have an idea how to do this.

I'll show you how I summarize the first paragraph of the story "Sandy Finds the Train Car." First I will read the paragraph to you, and then I will summarize it. **Model** think-aloud for summarizing the paragraph.

Sample Wording for Think-Aloud

Sandy was on her way home from school and noticed that there were only 99 cars. She was sure that before school there were 100. Sandy knows that one car is missing, because she is a good counter.

Putting part of the story in my own words helps me remember it and understand it. You'll be learning to put parts of stories in your own words too.

Provide a reading center to display books being read so that students can enjoy them again during free time.

Part D: Fluency Building

5 minutes

Student Materials:
Storybook 1

Conduct after the lesson, using story of the day.

Activity 1 Partner Reading

It's time for partner reading.
Direct students to the story of the day. **Assign** student partners as Partner 1 and Partner 2. **Monitor** student reading. **Guide** as needed.

Lesson 72

Materials

Teacher: *Storybook 1;* 8-Phonemic Awareness; 4 manipulatives such as blocks, discs, chips, counters (if not using IWB)

Student: *Storybook 1;* copy of 8-Phonemic Awareness; 4 manipulatives such as blocks, discs, chips, counters (note that one manipulative should have a letter printed on it – e.g., plastic disc with printed letter, preprinted letter tile, plastic letter)

Part A: Phonemic and Phonological Awareness

3 minutes

IWB

Teacher Materials:
Phonemic Awareness

4 manipulatives such as blocks, discs, chips, counters

Student Materials:
Phonemic Awareness

4 manipulatives such as blocks, discs, chips, counters

Activity 1 Phoneme Segmentation

Show Phonemic Awareness. **Elicit** responses. **Guide** as needed. **Add** more letters as students become proficient.

Let's use our chips to show the different sounds we hear in a word. Today we're going to use one chip that has the letter **m** on it. For each sound in the word, you'll push one chip up to the arrow on the page. You can use the letter **m** to show where the **/m/** sound is in the word. When we finish, we'll read the whole word.

Your turn. Say the sounds you hear in **mad.** */mmm/ /aaa/ /d/.*
Your turn. Now say the sounds you hear in **mad,** and move a chip for each sound. Use the letter **m** for the **/m/** sound. */mmm/ /aaa/ /d/.*
Move your finger back to the dot. What word? *Mad.*
How many sounds are in the word **mad?** *Three.*
Correct. Now move your chips back to the bottom, and let's try another one.

(Continue the activity with the following words:
gum, jam, mop, am, camp.)

Part B: Vocabulary Development

5 minutes

Student Materials:
Storybook 1

Activity 1 Learn New Vocabulary Word

Elicit responses to questions. **Guide** as needed.
Today you'll learn a new vocabulary word. **Escape. Escape** means **get away.**
What does **escape** mean? *Get away.*

Another word for **get away** is **escape.** What's another word for **get away?**
Escape.

The fly tried to **get away** from the spider's web. It wiggled and tried to **escape,** but the web was too sticky. The fly was caught.

What's another word for get away? *Escape.*

Discuss ways that people can escape something.

Activity 2 Review Vocabulary Word

Elicit responses to questions. **Guide** as needed.
What does **hide** mean? *Keep from being seen.*
What's another word for **keep from being seen?** *Hide.*

Review vocabulary words in appropriate context in *Storybook 1.*

Part C: Comprehension Strategies

12 minutes

Teacher Materials:
Storybook 1

Student Materials:
Storybook 1

Activity 1 Text-to-Self Connection—An After-Reading Strategy

Refer to Story 71, pages 185–187.

One way to understand stories better is to make text-to-self connections.
What do you do when you make text-to-self connections? (Idea: *Connect your own experiences with a story you read.*)

Read the last paragraph of the story to prepare for text-to-self connection.

Elicit responses to questions. **Discuss** connections that students make to the story. **Guide** as needed.
Does this part of the Sandy story make you think of any experience you have ever had? (Student response.)

Have you ever been so scared you couldn't talk? (Student response.)

Have you ever tried to think how to get out of a jam? (Student response.)

Have you ever been caught doing something you should not do? (Student response.)

How does your experience connect to this story? (Student response.)

Remember, when you connect something that has happened to you to something that happens in the story, you're making text-to-self connections. Thinking about your experiences when you read is a good strategy to help you understand what you read.

Activity 2 Set a Purpose for Reading—A Before-Reading Strategy

Reread last paragraph of Story 71, page 186.

You're smarter at reading when you think before you read about why you're reading the story. That is called setting a purpose for reading. Think about the last paragraph of the story that you just heard. Think about why you want to read the next part of a story.

Discuss the idea that the story ended with a cliff-hanger.
A cliff-hanger is a way the author gets you to read the next story.
Elicit reasons the students want to read the next story.

Part D: Fluency Building

5 minutes

Student Materials:
Storybook 1

Conduct after the lesson, using story of the day.

Activity 1 Partner Reading

It's time for partner reading.
Direct students to the story of the day. **Assign** student partners as Partner 1 and Partner 2. **Monitor** student reading. **Guide** as needed.

Lesson 73

Materials

Teacher: *Storybook 1;* 8-Phonemic Awareness; 4 manipulatives such as blocks, discs, chips, counters (if not using IWB)

Student: *Storybook 1;* copy of 8-Phonemic Awareness; 4 manipulatives such as blocks, discs, chips, counters (note that one manipulative should have a letter printed on it – e.g., plastic disc with printed letter, preprinted letter tile, plastic letter)

Part A: Phonemic and Phonological Awareness

3 minutes

IWB

Teacher Materials:
Phonemic Awareness

4 manipulatives such as blocks, discs, chips, counters

Student Materials:
Phonemic Awareness

4 manipulatives such as blocks, discs, chips, counters

Activity 1 Phoneme Segmentation

Show Phonemic Awareness. **Elicit** responses. **Guide** as needed.
Let's use our chips to show the different sounds we hear in a word. Today we're going to use one chip that has the letter **n** on it. For each sound in the word, you'll push one chip up to the arrow on the page. You can use the letter **n** to show where the **/n/** sound is in the word. When we finish, we'll read the whole word.

Your turn. Say the sounds you hear in **nut.** */nnn/ /uuu/ /t/.*
Your turn. Now say the sounds you hear in **nut,** and move a chip for each sound. Use the letter **n** for the **/n/** sound. */nnn/ /uuu/ /t/.*
Move your finger back to the dot. What word? *Nut.*
How many sounds are in the word **nut?** *Three.*
Correct. Now move your chips back to the bottom, and let's try another one.

(Continue the activity with the following words:
on, nest, can, in, no.)

Part B: Vocabulary Development

5 minutes

Student Materials:
Storybook 1

Activity 1 Learn New Vocabulary Word

Elicit responses to questions. **Guide** as needed.
Today you'll learn a new vocabulary word. **Explain. Explain** means **tell what happened.** What does **explain** mean? *Tell what happened.*

Another word for **tell what happened** is **explain.** What's another word for **tell what happened?** *Explain.*

Scott needed **to tell what happened** in the science experiment. He needed to **explain** the steps of the experiment.

What's another word for **tell what happened?** *Explain.*

Discuss ways that students can explain something.

Activity 2 Review Vocabulary Word

Elicit responses to questions. **Guide** as needed.
What does **escape** mean? *Get away.*
What's another word for **get away?** *Escape.*

Review vocabulary words in appropriate context in *Storybook 1.*

Part C: Comprehension Strategies

12 minutes

Teacher Materials:
Storybook 1

Student Materials:
Storybook 1

Activity 1 Read with Prosody (Dialogue)—A During-Reading Strategy

Direct students to Story 72, pages 188–190.

Dialogue is what characters say in a story. Narratives have lots of dialogue. How is dialogue marked in stories? (Idea: *With quotation marks.*)

What is dialogue? (Idea: *The words characters say in the story.*)

Ask students to find the dialogue of different characters. **Monitor** groups as students review the stories.
I want you to find the dialogue for the characters. You will look for the words Sandy says, the words the big man says, and the words for the narrator, which aren't in quotation marks.

Group students in groups of 3. **Provide** guidance as needed. **Monitor** groups as they review the story and practice dialogue.
Your turn to read the story the same way with three people. Try to read with expression. Decide who will read which character's words and who will read the words for the narrator. Take turns, and try to make the dialogue interesting.

Encourage students to perform the dialogue in front of the class, after practice.

Part D: Fluency Building

5 minutes

Student Materials:
Storybook 1

Conduct after the lesson, using story of the day.

Activity 1 Partner Reading

It's time for partner reading.
Direct students to the story of the day. **Assign** student partners as Partner 1 and Partner 2. **Monitor** student reading. **Guide** as needed.

Lesson 74

Materials

Teacher: *Storybook 1;* Expository text of choice about trains; 8-Phonemic Awareness; 4 manipulatives such as blocks, discs, chips, counters (if not using IWB)

Student: *Storybook 1;* copy of 8-Phonemic Awareness; 4 manipulatives such as blocks, discs, chips, counters (note that one manipulative should have a letter printed on it – e.g., plastic disc with printed letter, preprinted letter tile, plastic letter)

Part A: Phonemic and Phonological Awareness

3 minutes

IWB

Teacher Materials:
Phonemic Awareness

4 manipulatives such as blocks, discs, chips, counters

Student Materials:
Phonemic Awareness

4 manipulatives such as blocks, discs, chips, counters

Activity 1 Phoneme Segmentation

Show Phonemic Awareness. **Elicit** responses. **Guide** as needed.

Let's use our chips to show the different sounds we hear in a word. Today we're going to use one chip that has the letter **d** on it. For each sound in the word, you'll push one chip up to the arrow on the page. You can use the letter **d** to show where the **/d/** sound is in the word. When we finish, we'll read the whole word.

Your turn. Say the sounds you hear in **dog.** */d/ /ooo/ /g/.*
Your turn. Now say the sounds you hear in **dog,** and move a chip for each sound. Use the letter **d** for the **/d/** sound. */d/ /ooo/ /g/.*
Move your finger back to the dot. What word? *Dog.*
How many sounds are in the word **dog?** *Three.*
Correct. Now move your chips back to the bottom, and let's try another one.

(Continue the activity with the following words:
mud, desk, sad, lid, dip.)

Part B: Vocabulary Development

5 minutes

Student Materials:
Storybook 1

Activity 1 Learn New Vocabulary Word

Elicit responses to questions. **Guide** as needed.
Today you'll learn a new vocabulary word. **Unkind. Unkind** means **mean.**
What does **unkind** mean? *Mean.*

Another word for **unkind** is **mean.** What's another word for **unkind?** *Mean.*

The **mean** bully tried to take Isaiah's soccer ball. The bully was being **unkind.** Isaiah said, "Let's play together and share the ball." So the boys shared and had fun playing soccer.

Discuss Isaiah's solution to dealing with a mean bully.

What's another word for **mean?** *Unkind.*

Discuss what it means to be unkind and what students should do about it.

Elicit responses to questions. **Guide** as needed.
What does **explain** mean? *Tell what happened.*
What does **tell what happened** mean? *Explain.*

Review vocabulary words in appropriate context in *Storybook 1.*

Part C: Comprehension Strategies

12 minutes

Teacher Materials:
Expository text of choice about trains

Activity 1 Overview of Expository Text—A Before-Reading Strategy

Today you will hear a new kind of story. This text teaches you new information. It tells about things that are true. When you read this kind of story, you're getting ready to learn something new. We call this kind of story expository text. It is different than narrative text in lots of ways. Expository text does not have characters, setting, problems, beginning, middle, or end. Instead, expository text is organized around main ideas and topics. The expository text we'll read today is organized around the topic of trains. It will give you information that is true about trains. Another name for expository text is non-fiction. We read expository text to learn something new. Why will we read about trains today? (Idea: *To learn something new about trains.*)

Read expository text of choice about trains. **Note** features of expository text as you read, such as headings, captions, labels, lists, table of contents, photographs, and index.

Activity 2 What I Learned—An After-Reading Strategy

Think about and list information that was learned or known about trains.
After reading the expository text about trains, let's write down some of the things you learned about trains today.

Expository text like this story about trains is written to teach you new information. Why do you read expository text? *To learn new information.*

Part D: Fluency Building

5 minutes

Student Materials:
Storybook 1

Conduct after the lesson, using story of the day.

Activity 1 Partner Reading

It's time for partner reading.
Direct students to the story of the day. **Assign** student partners as Partner 1 and Partner 2. **Monitor** student reading. **Guide** as needed.

Lesson 75

Materials

Teacher: *Storybook 1;* 10-KWL Chart; 8-Phonemic Awareness; 4 manipulatives such as blocks, discs, chips, counters (if not using IWB), 2-Vocabulary Acquisition and Use, Writing Prompts, 5-My Writing Checklist

Student: *Storybook 1;* copy of 8-Phonemic Awareness; 4 manipulatives such as blocks, discs, chips, counters (note that one manipulative should have a letter printed on it – e.g., plastic disc with printed letter, preprinted letter tile, plastic letter), Copy of 2- Vocabulary Acquisition and Use and 3-My Writing Checklist; Lined Paper

Part A: Phonemic and Phonological Awareness

3 minutes

IWB

Teacher Materials:
Phonemic Awareness

4 manipulatives such as blocks, discs, chips, counters

Student Materials:
Phonemic Awareness

4 manipulatives such as blocks, discs, chips, counters

Activity 1 Phoneme Segmentation

Show Phonemic Awareness. **Elicit** responses. **Guide** as needed.

Let's use our chips to show the different sounds we hear in a word. Today we're going to use one chip that has the letter **t** on it. For each sound in the word, you'll push one chip up to the arrow on the page. When we finish, we'll read the whole word. You can use the letter **t** to show where the **/t/** sound is in the word. What sound are we listening for? /t/.

Your turn. Say the sounds you hear in **tap.** /t/ /aaa/ /p/.
Your turn. Now say the sounds you hear in **tap,** and move a chip for each sound. Use the letter **t** for the **/t/** sound. /t/ /aaa/ /p/.
Move your finger back to the dot. What word? *Tap.*
How many sounds are in the word **tap?** *Three.*
Correct. Now move your chips back to the bottom, and let's try another one.

(Continue the activity with the following words:
jet, nest, top, at, tub.)

Part B: Vocabulary Development

5 minutes

IWB

Teacher Materials:
Vocabulary Acquisition and Use

Student Materials:
Storybook 1

Vocabulary Acquisition and Use

Activity 1 Cumulative Vocabulary Review

Elicit responses to questions. **Guide** as needed.
Directions: Listen and tell me the correct vocabulary word for each question.

What's another word for **mean?** *Unkind.*
What's another word for **keep from being seen?** *Hide.*
What's another word for **get away?** *Escape.*
What's another word for **tell what happened?** *Explain.*

Repeat difficult words as needed.

Review vocabulary words in appropriate context in *Storybook 1.*

Activity 2 Vocabulary Acquisition and Use

Display Vocabulary Acquisition and Use. **Have** students work with a neighbor to complete Vocabulary Acquisition and Use.

Today's vocabulary words are _____ and _____ [and _____ and _____].

Vocabulary words: **explain** and **tell**; **unkind** and **mean**

Write the words on the lines provided. Then write the words in the boxes based on whether you think each word is less/smaller or more/larger than the other word. Below the boxes, write why you think word 1 is less/smaller and word 2 is more/larger than word 1.

Repeat for words 3 and 4. **Have** students share what they wrote. **Discuss** examples of how these words might be used.

Part C: Comprehension Strategies

12 minutes

IWB

Teacher Materials:
Storybook 1

KWL Chart

Student Materials:
Storybook 1

Activity 1 Introduce KWL Chart for Expository Text—A Before- and After-Reading Strategy

Show KWL Chart.

I want to show you a chart that you use when you are reading expository text. What is expository text? (Idea: *Stories that teach you new information.*)

Touch sections as you describe chart.

The KWL chart has three sections. The first section is a section that you fill out **before** reading your story. You list your schema, or what is already in your brain about the topic of your book.

The next section has a place to think of questions about the topic that you want to know. In that section, you think about questions you have and things you want to know. You fill this section out before you read.

The last section has a place to list what you learned about the topic from the book after you read. The list you made in the last lesson would go in this section of the chart. You fill in the last part of the chart after reading the book.

This chart is a great way to organize what you already know, what you want to know, and what you learned. When you make organized lists or fill out charts like this, it helps you remember what you learned about a topic from a book.

Let's practice by filling in the last section of the chart with information that we learned from the book about trains.

Elicit list of new information learned from expository book on trains and **write** on KWL Chart in the "What I Learned" section. **Guide** as needed.

We have learned that expository text is written to teach you new information, and the KWL chart is a great way to organize that information.

Part D: Fluency Building

Conduct after the lesson, using story of the day.

Activity 1 Partner Reading

It's time for partner reading.

Direct students to the story of the day. **Assign** student partners as Partner 1 and Partner 2. **Monitor** student reading. **Guide** as needed.

Part E: Writing/Language Arts

Activity 1 Write and Use Parts of Speech and Conventions

Time to write using a writing prompt based on the stories we've been reading.

Assign student partners. **Distribute** lined paper to students. **Display** writing prompts and have students choose one to write about or assign a writing prompt of your choice. **Review** parts of speech and punctuation as well as the writing checklist with students. **Tell** students to write one paragraph (minimum of four sentences per paragraph) on their own to answer the writing prompt. **Tell** them to use their writing checklist (first column labeled "Did I use them?") to ensure they include important parts of speech or punctuation in their writing. **Tell** students which parts of speech or punctuation to focus on, if you wish. **Model** what it means to answer a writing prompt and to use the writing checklist during and after the writing process, as needed. **Monitor** and guide students as needed. **Model** what it means to have a neighbor look over his or her neighbor's writing and to complete the writing checklist (second column labeled "Did my neighbor use them?"), as needed. **Have** students share what they wrote as time permits.

IWB

Teacher Materials:
Writing Prompts

My Writing Checklist

Student Materials:
Lined Paper

My Writing Checklist

10 minutes

Writing Prompt 1	Writing Prompt 2	Writing Prompt 3
Write a story like the one about the tall man and his dog. Be sure to repeat words like the dog did in your story.	Tell me about what things you like to count and why.	Have you ever found something for someone? Tell me about it.

Lesson 76

Materials

Teacher: 1-Narrative Story Map; *Storybook 1;* 8-Phonemic Awareness; 4 manipulatives such as blocks, discs, chips, counters (if not using IWB)

Student: *Storybook 1;* copy of 1-Narrative Story Map; copy of 8-Phonemic Awareness; 4 manipulatives such as blocks, discs, chips, counters (note that one manipulative should have a letter printed on it – e.g., plastic disc with printed letter, preprinted letter tile, plastic letter)

Part A: Phonemic and Phonological Awareness

3 minutes

IWB

Teacher Materials:
Phonemic Awareness

4 manipulatives such as blocks, discs, chips, counters

Student Materials:
Phonemic Awareness

4 manipulatives such as blocks, discs, chips, counters

Activity 1 Phoneme Segmentation

Show Phonemic Awareness. **Elicit** responses. **Guide** as needed.

Let's use our chips to show the different sounds we hear in a word. Today we're going to use one chip that has the letter **g** on it. For each sound in the word, you'll push one chip up to the arrow on the page. When we finish, we'll read the whole word. You can use the letter **g** to show where the **/g/** sound is in the word. What sound are we listening for? */g/.*

Your turn. Say the sounds you hear in **gum.** */g/ /uuu/ /mmm/.*
Your turn. Now say the sounds you hear in **gum,** and move a chip for each sound. Use the letter **g** for the **/g/** sound. */g/ /uuu/ /mmm/.*
Move your finger back to the dot. What word? *Gum.*
How many sounds are in the word **gum?** *Three.*
Correct. Now move your chips back to the bottom, and let's try another one.

(Continue the activity with the following words:
got, bug, pig, go, log.)

Part B: Vocabulary Development

5 minutes

Student Materials:
Storybook 1

Activity 1 Learn New Vocabulary Word

Elicit responses to questions. **Guide** as needed.

Today you'll learn a new vocabulary word. **Instructions. Instructions** are **directions.** What are **instructions?** *Directions.*

Another word for **directions** is **instructions.** What's another word for **directions?** *Instructions.*

Sam made things from kits. Once he made a car. He followed the **directions** in the kit, and the car he made was perfect. He used the **instructions** to build the car.

What's another word for **directions?** *Instructions.*

Discuss when students have used instructions.

Elicit responses to questions. **Guide** as needed.
What does **explain** mean? *Tell what happened.*
What's another word for **tell what happened?** *Explain.*

Review vocabulary words in appropriate context in *Storybook 1*.

Part C: Comprehension Strategies

12 minutes

IWB

Teacher Materials:
Storybook 1

Narrative Story Map

Student Materials:
Storybook 1

Narrative Story Map

Activity 1 Story Map—An After-Reading Strategy

Refer to Stories 68–75, pages 176–199.

Show Narrative Story Map. **Touch** each section, and **elicit** answers.
Let's work together to fill in our Narrative Story Map about the Sandy story.

Touch the line for the title. This is a new place to fill in on your Story Map. These chapters had several titles, so we will just call the whole story "The Sandy Story."

Model writing the title on the map.
Write that on the line for the title.

Assist students to draw and write information on their Narrative Story Maps.
What will you draw for the main character? *Sandy.*
Draw that in the box for Characters.

Who are other characters in the story? (Idea: *Big Bill, the cop, the woman, the crooks.*) We will not draw them in the box today.

This map has a new section. It has a place to fill in the setting. What will you draw for **where** in the box for Setting? *The train station.*

When does most of the Sandy story happen? (Idea: *Most of the story happens after school.*)

Model writing words in setting—when.
That is hard to draw, so it is easier to write the words—**after school.** Write that on the map.

What will you draw for events at the beginning? (Idea: *Sandy counted 100 cars. Then she found out a car with TV sets was missing.*)

What will you draw for events in the middle? (Ideas: *Sandy noticed the missing train car and found it in the shed. She told the cop. The cop came to the shed to check.*)

What will you draw at the end? (Idea: *Sandy helped the cops catch the crooks, and she got a TV.*)

When you fill out a Narrative Story Map, you really show that you remember all about the story.

Save student copies of completed Narrative Story Map for Lesson 77.

Provide a reading center to display books being read so that students can enjoy them again during free time.

Part D: Fluency Building

5 minutes

Student Materials:
Storybook 1

Conduct after the lesson, using story of the day.

Activity 1 Partner Reading

It's time for partner reading.
Direct students to the story of the day. **Assign** student partners as Partner 1 and Partner 2. **Monitor** student reading. **Guide** as needed.

Lesson 77

Materials

Teacher: *Storybook 1;* 8-Phonemic Awareness; 1-Narrative Story Map (from Lesson 76); 4 manipulatives such as blocks, discs, chips, counters (if not using IWB)

Student: *Storybook 1;* copy of 1-Narrative Story Map (from Lesson 76); copy of 8-Phonemic Awareness; 4 manipulatives such as blocks, discs, chips, counters (note that one manipulative should have a letter printed on it – e.g., plastic disc with printed letter, preprinted letter tile, plastic letter)

Part A: Phonemic and Phonological Awareness

3 minutes

IWB

Teacher Materials:
Phonemic Awareness

4 manipulatives such as blocks, discs, chips, counters

Student Materials:
Phonemic Awareness

4 manipulatives such as blocks, discs, chips, counters

Activity 1 Phoneme Segmentation

Show Phonemic Awareness. **Elicit** responses. **Guide** as needed.
Let's use our chips to show the different sounds we hear in a word. Today we're going to use one chip that has the letter **b** on it. For each sound in the word, you'll push one chip up to the arrow on the page. When we finish, we'll read the whole word. You can use the letter **b** to show where the **/b/** sound is in the word. What sound are we listening for? */b/.*

Your turn. Say the sounds you hear in **bad.** */b/ /aaa/ /d/.*
Your turn. Now say the sounds you hear in **bad,** and move a chip for each sound. Use the letter **b** for the **/b/** sound. */b/ /aaa/ /d/.*
Move your finger back to the dot. What word? *Bad.*
How many sounds are in the word **bad?** *Three.*
Correct. Now move your chips back to the bottom, and let's try another one.

(Continue the activity with the following words:
belt, tub, best, cab, web.)

Part B: Vocabulary Development

5 minutes

Student Materials:
Storybook 1

Activity 1 Learn New Vocabulary Word

Elicit responses to questions. **Guide** as needed.
Today you'll learn a new vocabulary word. **Grateful. Grateful** means **feeling of thanks.** What does **grateful** mean? *Feeling of thanks.*

Another way to say **feeling of thanks** is **grateful.** What's another way to say **feeling of thanks?** *Grateful.*

Dana was new at school and had no friends. She met Makyla, and they played together at every recess. That afternoon Dana had a **feeling of thanks** that Makyla had played with her. Dana was **grateful.**

What's another word for **feeling of thanks?** *Grateful.*

Discuss times when students feel grateful.

Activity 2   Review Vocabulary Word

Elicit responses to questions. **Guide** as needed.
What's another word for **instructions?** *Directions.*
What's another word for **directions?** *Instructions.*

Review vocabulary words in appropriate context in *Storybook 1.*

Part C: Comprehension Strategies

IWB

Teacher Materials:
Storybook 1

Narrative Story Map

Student Materials:
Storybook 1

Narrative Story Map

Activity 1   Retell—An After-Reading Strategy

Distribute to students Narrative Story Maps completed in Lesson 76.
You did a great job filling out your Narrative Story Maps in the last lesson. Today you will use your Narrative Story Map to retell the Sandy story. Start by telling the title. Then look at the picture clues in the different sections of your Narrative Story Map to help you retell the story. Tell the story to your partner. Then have your partner tell the story to you.

Monitor student partners as they retell the story from the Narrative Story Map.

Activity 2   Summarize—An After-Reading Strategy

After having read a part of a story, smart readers stop and tell themselves the story in their own words. You have been practicing retelling the story from a Narrative Story Map. So you already have an idea how to do this.

I will show you how I summarize the first paragraph of the story "Sam Gets a Kite Kit." First I will read the paragraph to you, and then I will summarize it. **Model** think-aloud for summarizing the paragraph.

Read the first paragraph of Story 76, page 200.

Sample Wording for Think-Aloud

I need to tell the main thing that the paragraph is about but not say all the words exactly like the story. I need to tell the main parts of the story. Let's see. Sam is a boy who likes to make things. He got a model car kit. His mom told him that he needed to follow the directions.

Notice that I told the story in my own words. I told the main thing that the paragraph was about, but I did not say all the words exactly like the story. I just told the main parts of the story. When I tell the main parts, I am summarizing.

Part D: Fluency Building

Conduct after the lesson, using story of the day.

Activity 1 **Partner Reading**

It's time for partner reading.

Direct students to the story of the day. **Assign** student partners as Partner 1 and Partner 2. **Monitor** student reading. **Guide** as needed.

Lesson 78

Part A: Phonemic and Phonological Awareness

3 minutes

IWB

Teacher Materials:
Phonemic Awareness

4 manipulatives such as blocks, discs, chips, counters

Student Materials:
Phonemic Awareness

4 manipulatives such as blocks, discs, chips, counters

Activity 1 Phoneme Segmentation

Show Phonemic Awareness. **Elicit** responses. **Guide** as needed.
Let's use our chips to show the different sounds we hear in a word. Today we're going to use one chip that has the letter **p** on it. For each sound in the word, you'll push one chip up to the arrow on the page. When we finish, we'll read the whole word. You can use the letter **p** to show where the **/p/** sound is in the word. What sound are we listening for? */p/.*

Your turn. Say the sounds you hear in **pan.** */p/ /aaa/ /nnn/.*
Your turn. Now say the sounds you hear in **pan,** and move a chip for each sound. Use the letter **p** for the **/p/** sound. */p/ /aaa/ /nnn/.*
Move your finger back to the dot. What word? *Pan.*
How many sounds are in the word **pan?** *Three.*
Correct. Now move your chips back to the bottom, and let's try another one.

(Continue the activity with the following words:
hop, pet, nap, stop, pot.)

Part B: Vocabulary Development

5 minutes

Student Materials:
Storybook 1

Activity 1 Learn New Vocabulary Word

Elicit responses to questions. **Guide** as needed.
Today you'll learn a new vocabulary word. **Assist. Assist** means **help.** What does **assist** mean? *Help.*

Another way to say **help** is **assist.** What's another way to say **help?** *Assist.*

One day Tyler went to the mall with his grandma. She had a sore arm, so when they reached the door, Tyler said, "Can I **help** you, Grandma?" He wanted to **assist** his grandma by opening the door for her.

What's another word for **help?** *Assist.*

Discuss ways students can assist others.

Activity 2 Review Vocabulary Word

Elicit responses to questions. **Guide** as needed.
What does **grateful** mean? *Feeling of thanks.*
What's another word for **feeling of thanks?** *Grateful.*

Review vocabulary words in appropriate context in *Storybook 1.*

Part C: Comprehension Strategies

12 minutes

Teacher Materials:
Storybook 1

Student Materials:
Storybook 1

Activity 1 Generate Questions—A During-Reading Strategy

Refer to Story 77, pages 204–206.

Elicit responses to questions. **Guide** as needed.
Asking questions is a strategy to use when you are reading stories. Why do you ask questions when you are reading? *To understand the story better.*

It takes practice to think of good questions. Let's practice asking questions some more.

Guide students to ask a question, not restate the information.
Here is a sentence from the story. (Read second sentence from story on page 201.) Who can make up a question from that sentence? (Ideas: *"What did he make from the kit?" "Who made a toy car?" "What did he use to make a toy car?"*)

It was smart to make a question instead of giving the answer to the question. What's the answer to the question you made up? (Student responses.)

Here is another sentence from the story. (Read second sentence from last paragraph on page 204.) Who can make up a question about that sentence? (Ideas: *"What was the kite made of?" "What did it look like?" "What looked like a small tent?"*)

It was smart to make a question instead of giving the answer to the question. What's the answer to the question you made up? (Student responses.)

Here is another sentence from the story. (Read first sentence from first paragraph on page 205.) Who can make up a question on this information? (Ideas: *"Who went to the park?" "Where did Sam and his mom go?" "Who went with Sam to the park?"*)

What is the answer to the question? (Student response.)

You are getting good at asking questions.

Part D: Fluency Building

5 minutes

Student Materials:
Storybook 1

Conduct after the lesson, using story of the day.

Activity 1 Partner Reading

It's time for partner reading.
Direct students to the story of the day. **Assign** student partners as Partner 1 and Partner 2. **Monitor** student reading. **Guide** as needed.

Lesson 79

Part A: Phonemic and Phonological Awareness

3 minutes

IWB

Teacher Materials:
Phonemic Awareness

4 manipulatives such as blocks, discs, chips, counters

Student Materials:
Phonemic Awareness

4 manipulatives such as blocks, discs, chips, counters

Activity 1 Phoneme Segmentation

Show Phonemic Awareness. **Elicit** responses. **Guide** as needed.
Let's use our chips to show the different sounds we hear in a word. Today we're going to use one chip that has the letter **a** on it. For each sound in the word, you'll push one chip up to the arrow on the page. When we finish, we'll read the whole word. You can use the letter **a** to show where the **/a/** sound is in the word. What sound are we listening for? */a/.*

Your turn. Say the sounds you hear in **at.** */aaa/ /t/.*
Your turn. Now say the sounds you hear in **at,** and move a chip for each sound. Use the letter **a** for the **/a/** sound. */aaa/ /t/.*

Move your finger back to the dot. What word? *At.*
How many sounds are in the word **at?** *Two.*
Correct. Now move your chips back to the bottom, and let's try another one.

(Continue the activity with the following words:
ask, mat, pan, sad, am.)

Part B: Vocabulary Development

5 minutes

Teacher Materials:
Storybook 1

Activity 1 Learn New Vocabulary Word

Elicit responses to questions. **Guide** as needed.
Today you'll learn a new vocabulary word. **Sly. Sly** means **sneaky.** What does **sly** mean? *Sneaky.*

Another way to say **sneaky** is **sly.** What's another way to say **sneaky?** *Sly.*

The cat tried to be **sneaky** by quietly following the mouse. The cat was being **sly** so the mouse wouldn't notice him.

What's another word for **sneaky?** *Sly.*

Discuss what it means to be sneaky and what times students might be sneaky.

Activity 2 Review Vocabulary Word

Elicit responses to questions. **Guide** as needed.
What does **assist** mean? *Help.*
What's another word for **help?** *Assist.*

Review vocabulary words in appropriate context in *Storybook 1.*

Part C: Comprehension Strategies

12 minutes

Teacher Materials:
Storybook 1

Student Materials:
Storybook 1

Activity 1 Activate Background Knowledge—A During-Reading Strategy

Elicit responses to questions. **Guide** as needed.
We talked about schema. When you activate your schema, you check on what your brain knows about a topic. What do you call everything you know in your brain? *Schema.*

When you figure out what you know, you activate your background knowledge. It is the same thing as checking your schema. Today you'll check your schema, or activate your background knowledge.

Why is it a good idea to think about what you know about a topic before you read a new story? (Idea: *Then you can connect what you know to the new information that you learn when you read.*)

Discuss background knowledge related to questions. **Guide** as needed.
Today the story is about a boy named Tim. He lives in a place where it snows during the winter. Open the file in your brain, and look in it to see what your schema is about winter. What is winter like where we live? (Student response.)

What do you know about snow? (Student response.)

What kinds of clothes do people wear in the winter? (Student response.)

What kinds of things do children do in the snow? (Student response.)

When you connect what you already know about winter to the story you'll read today, you'll understand the story better.

Activity 2 Identify the Problem—An After-Reading Strategy

Elicit responses to questions. **Guide** as needed.

You're learning how to figure out the problem in the story. What's the problem? (Idea: *What goes wrong in the story that makes you want to read to find out more.*)

Where in the story do you usually find the problem? (Idea: *The problem usually comes after the characters and the setting.*)

What part tells who is in the story? *Characters.*

What part tells about when and where the story happens? *The setting.*

The problem is the part in the story that tells what goes wrong. What is the part called that tells what goes wrong? *The problem.*

When you come to the problem, what do you usually want to do next? (Idea: *Read more to find out what happens next.*)

Listen to me read the story. When you think you hear a problem, tell me to stop reading.

Elicit identification of problem when you get to the end of third paragraph.

Read Story 79, page 210, with prosody.

What is the problem? (Idea: *Tim hid his hat, but now it is getting colder.*)

I know that Tim put his hat in a hole, but now snow is falling and it is getting colder. He needs his hat. I'll need to read more to find out what Sam does to solve this problem.

When I come to a problem in a story, usually it makes me want to read and find out how the problem is solved.

Part D: Fluency Building

5 minutes

Student Materials:
Storybook 1

Conduct after the lesson, using story of the day.

Activity 1 Partner Reading

It's time for partner reading.

Direct students to the story of the day. **Assign** student partners as Partner 1 and Partner 2. **Monitor** student reading. **Guide** as needed.

Lesson 80

Materials

Teacher: *Storybook 1*; chart with comprehension reading strategies from Lesson 40: Part C; 8-Phonemic Awareness; 4 manipulatives such as blocks, discs, chips, counters (if not using IWB), 2-Vocabulary Acquisition and Use, 3-My Book Review

Student: *Storybook 1*; copy of 8-Phonemic Awareness; 4 manipulatives such as blocks, discs, chips, counters (note that one manipulative should have a letter printed on it – e.g., plastic disc with printed letter, preprinted letter tile, plastic letter), Copy of 2-Vocabulary Acquisition and Use and 3-My Book Review

Part A: Phonemic and Phonological Awareness

3 minutes

IWB

Teacher Materials:
Phonemic Awareness

4 manipulatives such as blocks, discs, chips, counters

Student Materials:
Phonemic Awareness

4 manipulatives such as blocks, discs, chips, counters

Activity 1 Phoneme Segmentation

Show Phonemic Awareness. **Elicit** responses. **Guide** as needed.

Let's use our chips to show the different sounds we hear in a word. Today we're going to use one chip that has the letter **i** on it. For each sound in the word, you'll push one chip up to the arrow on the page. When we finish, we'll read the whole word. You can use the letter **i** to show where the **/i/** sound is in the word. What sound are we listening for? */i/.*

Your turn. Say the sounds you hear in **it.** */iii/ /t/.*
Your turn. Now say the sounds you hear in **it,** and move a chip for each sound. Use the letter **i** for the **/i/** sound. */iii/ /t/.*
Move your finger back to the dot. What word? *It*
How many sounds are in the word **it?** *Two.*
Correct. Now move your chips back to the bottom, and let's try another one.

(Continue the activity with the following words:
pig, lip, in, bit, dip.)

Part B: Vocabulary Development

5 minutes

IWB

Teacher Materials:
Vocabulary Acquisition and Use

Student Materials:
Storybook 1

Vocabulary Acquisition and Use

Activity 1 Cumulative Vocabulary Review

Elicit responses to questions. **Guide** as needed.
Directions: Listen and tell me the correct vocabulary word for each question.

What's another word for **sneaky?** *Sly.*
What's another word for **feeling of thanks?** *Grateful.*
What's another word for **tell what happened?** *Explain.*
What's another word for **get away?** *Escape.*
What's another word for **help?** *Assist.*
What's another word for **keep from being seen?** *Hide.*
What's another word for **mean?** *Unkind.*
What's another word for **directions?** *Instructions.*

Review difficult words

Review vocabulary words in appropriate context in *Storybook 1*.

Activity 2 Vocabulary Acquisition and Use

Display Vocabulary Acquisition and Use. **Have** students work with a neighbor to complete Vocabulary Acquisition and Use.

Today's vocabulary words are _____ and _____ [and _____ and _____].
Vocabulary words: **grateful** and **thankful; sly** and **sneaky**
Write the words on the lines provided. Then write the words in the boxes based on whether you think each word is less/smaller or more/larger than the other word. Below the boxes, write why you think word 1 is less/smaller and word 2 is more/larger than word 1.

Repeat for words 3 and 4. **Have** students share what they wrote. **Discuss** examples of how these words might be used.

Part C: Comprehension Strategies

12 minutes

IWB

Teacher Materials:
Storybook 1

Chart with comprehension strategies

My Book Review

Student Materials:
Storybook 1

My Book Review

Let's talk about things you do before, during, and after you read to help you understand narrative text better.

Record comprehension strategies on a chart, if desired (see chart developed in Lesson 40). If chart is made, you can reference it during later lessons to identify strategy being used. Chart can also be updated as lessons proceed.

Activity 1 Review—Before-Reading Strategies

Let's talk about things you do before you read to help you understand narrative text better.

Discuss strategies that students have been using before reading narratives. **Identify** examples of when the strategy was used.

What are some things to do before you read a new story? (Ideas: *Make predictions*—**Make Predictions**—*and think about how the story connects to what I already know*—**Activate Background Knowledge**—*or think about what I will try to learn*— **Set Purpose for Reading.**)

Activity 2 Review—During-Reading Strategies

Let's talk about things you do while you read to help you understand narrative text better.

Discuss strategies that students have been using during reading narratives. **Identify** examples of when the strategy was used.

What are some things you can do while you're reading to help you understand what you are reading? (Idea: *Ask questions*—**Generate Questions**—*reread*—**Fix-Up Strategy**—*tell the story in my own words*—**Summarize**—*and read while paying attention the ends of sentences or dialogue*—**Read with Prosody.**)

Activity 3 Review—After-Reading Strategies

Let's talk about things we do after we read to help us understand narrative text better.

Discuss strategies that students have been using after reading narratives. **Identify** examples of when the strategy was used.

What are some things you can do after you read a story to help you understand or remember the story? (Ideas: *Fill out a story map—***Identify Story Elements***—see if predictions were correct—***Confirming Predictions***—make text-to-self connections, make text-to-text connections, and retell the story.*)

Wow, you've learned a lot about things to do to help you understand the stories you read. When you understand what you read, you have good comprehension. Understanding what you read is really important.

Activity 4 Develop Opinions—An After-Reading Strategy

Today we'll found out your opinion or how you feel about the stories you read. You will choose a book to read and then complete the My Book Review form. You'll need to tell if you like or don't like the book and why. You must give a reason for why you like or don't like the book. Finally, you can tell if you would recommend the book to others.

Have students read a narrative or expository trade book of their choice. **Have** students complete My Book Review form when they are finished reading their book. **Model** how to complete the My Book Review form. **Guide** students as needed. **Have** students share their book reviews with the class as time permits.

Part D: Fluency Building

5 minutes

Student Materials:
Storybook 1

Conduct after the lesson, using story of the day.

Activity 1 Partner Reading

It's time for partner reading.
Direct students to the story of the day. **Assign** student partners as Partner 1 and Partner 2. **Monitor** student reading. **Guide** as needed.

Materials

Teacher: *Storybook 1*, Vocabulary Notebook

Student: *Storybook 1;* vocabulary notebook

5 minutes

Teacher Materials:
Vocabulary notebook

Student Materials:
Storybook 1

Vocabulary notebook

Part A: Vocabulary Development

Activity 1   Learn New Vocabulary Word

Elicit responses to questions. **Guide** as needed.
Today you'll learn a new vocabulary word. **Con. Con** means **trick.** What does **con** mean? *Trick.*

Another word for **trick** is **con.** What's another word for **trick?** *Con.*

The fox tried to **trick** the girl out of her ice-cream cone. He said his mouth was on fire. The girl was smart. She gave the fox water and ice instead of her ice-cream cone. The fox couldn't **con** this smart girl.

What's another word for **trick?** *Con.*
Discuss ways that someone might con someone else.

Show Vocabulary Notebook.
Today you'll start a vocabulary notebook. You'll keep track of new vocabulary words you learn in this program. I'll show you how to write your vocabulary word in your vocabulary notebook. Write **con** and what it means in your vocabulary notebook.

Model recording vocabulary word in vocabulary notebook. **Guide** as needed.

Review vocabulary words in appropriate context in *Storybook 1.*

Activity 2   Review Vocabulary Word

Elicit responses to questions. **Guide** as needed.
What does **sly** mean? *Sneaky.*
What's another word for **sneaky?** *Sly.*

Part B: Comprehension Strategies

Activity 1 **Read with Prosody (Dialogue)—A During-Reading Strategy**

Direct students to Story 80, pages 213–215.

Dialogue is what characters say in a story. Narratives have lots of dialogue.

How is dialogue marked in stories? (Idea: *With quotation marks.*)

What is dialogue? (Idea: *The words characters say in the story.*)

Ask students to find the dialogue of different characters.
This is the story "The Fox Wants a Cone." I want you to find the dialogue for the characters. You will look for the words the little girl says, the words the sly fox says, and the words for the narrator, which aren't in quotation marks.

Group students in groups of 3, and **provide** guidance as needed. **Monitor** groups as they review the story. **Monitor** groups as they practice dialogue.
Your turn to read the story with three people. Try to read with expression. Decide who will read which part. The colors will help you know when it's your turn. Take turns, and try to make the dialogue interesting.

Encourage students to perform the dialogue in front of the class, after practice.

Provide a reading center to display books being read so that students can enjoy them again during free time.

Part C: Fluency Building

Conduct after the lesson, using story of the day.

Activity 1 **Partner Reading**

It's time for partner reading.
Direct students to the story of the day. **Assign** student partners as Partner 1 and Partner 2. **Monitor** student reading. **Guide** as needed.

Lesson 82

Materials

Teacher: *Storybook 1;* 10-KWL Chart; expository text on topic of teacher choice
Student: *Storybook 1;* vocabulary notebook

Part A: Vocabulary Development

5 minutes

Student Materials:
Storybook 1

Vocabulary notebook

Activity 1 Learn New Vocabulary Word

Elicit responses to questions. **Guide** as needed.
Today you'll learn a new vocabulary word. **Lying. Lying** means **not telling the truth.** What does **lying** mean? *Not telling the truth.*

Another word for **not telling the truth** is **lying.** What's another word for **not telling the truth?** *Lying.*

The sly fox was **not telling the truth.** He did not give the ice cream man a dime for his cone. He was **lying.**

What's another word for **not telling the truth?** *Lying.*
Discuss why lying is not a good idea.

Write **lying** and what it means in your vocabulary notebook.
Direct students to write word in their vocabulary notebook. **Guide** as needed.

Activity 2 Review Vocabulary Word

Elicit responses to questions. **Guide** as needed.
What does **con** mean? *Trick.*
What's another word for **trick?** *Con.*

Review vocabulary words in appropriate context in *Storybook 1.*

Part B: Comprehension Strategies

12 minutes

IWB

Teacher Materials:
KWL Chart

Expository text

Activity 1 KWL Chart for Expository Text—A Before-Reading Strategy

Show KWL Chart. **Elicit** responses to questions. **Guide** as needed.
We will read a nonfiction or expository text on _____. Before we read this book, we will fill out the first two sections of the KWL Chart. The KWL Chart is helpful when we are reading expository text.

What is expository text? (Idea: *Stories that teach you new information.*)

Why will we read this book? (Idea: *To learn more about _____.*)

Elicit list of things to write in the What I Know column. **Guide** as needed.
The first section is the "What I Know," or the "K" section. You list your schema, or what is already in your brain about the topic of your book.
Let's think of some things you know about _____ and write them on the chart.

Elicit list of things to write in the What I Want to Know column. **Guide** as needed.
The next section is the "What I Want to Know," or the "W" section. In that section, you think about questions you have and things you want to know.
Let's think of some things you want to know about _____ and write them in this section.

The last section has a place to list what you learned about the topic from the book after you read. We'll fill out this section after we read the book.

This chart is a great way to organize what you already know, what you want to know, and what you learned. When you make organized lists or fill out charts like this, it helps you understand and remember what you learned about a topic from a book.

Save chart to complete in Lesson 83.

Part C: Fluency Building

5 minutes

Student Materials:
Storybook 1

Conduct after the lesson, using story of the day.

Activity 1 | Partner Reading

It's time for partner reading.
Direct students to the story of the day. **Assign** student partners as Partner 1 and Partner 2. **Monitor** student reading. **Guide** as needed.

Lesson 83

Materials

Teacher: *Storybook 1;* 10-KWL Chart (from Lesson 82); expository text on topic of teacher choice

Student: *Storybook 1;* vocabulary notebook

Part A: Vocabulary Development

5 minutes

Student Materials:
Storybook 1

Vocabulary notebook

Activity 1 Learn New Vocabulary Word

Elicit responses to questions. **Guide** as needed.
Today you'll learn a new vocabulary word. **Continue. Continue** means **go on.** What does **continue** mean? *Go on.*

Another word for **go on** is **continue.** What's another word for **go on?** *Continue.*

Sally said her story would **go on** for a long time. Her story would **continue.**

What's another word for go on? *Continue.*
Discuss stories students have read that continue.

Write **continue** and what it means in your vocabulary notebook.
Direct students to write word in their vocabulary notebook. **Guide** as needed.

Activity 2 Review Vocabulary Word

Elicit responses to questions. **Guide** as needed.
What does **lying** mean? *Not telling the truth.*
What's another word for **not telling the truth?** *Lying.*

Review vocabulary words in appropriate context in *Storybook 1.*

Part B: Comprehension Strategies

12 minutes

IWB

Teacher Materials:
KWL Chart

Expository text

Activity 1 Set a Purpose for Reading—A During-Reading Strategy

Elicit responses to questions. **Guide** as needed.
Today you will hear a book about _____. This text teaches you new information. It tells about things that are true. When you read this kind of story, you are getting ready to learn something new. We call this kind of book expository text. It is different than narrative text in lots of ways. Expository text does not have characters, setting, problems, beginning, middle, and end. Instead, expository text is organized around main ideas and topics. The expository text we will read today is organized around the topic of _____. It will give you information that is true about _____.

Another name for expository text is non-fiction text. We read expository text to learn something new.

Why will we read about _____ today? (Idea: *To learn something new about _____.*)

Read expository text of choice. **Note** features of expository text as you read, such as headings, captions, labels, lists, table of contents, photographs, and index.

Activity 2 KWL Chart—An After-Reading Strategy

Show KWL Chart from Lesson 82. **Complete** only the What I Learned column with suggestions from students.
We read _____ to learn something new. Now let's make a list of all the new things we learned.

This chart is a great way to organize what you already know, what you want to know, and what you learned. When you make organized lists or fill out charts like this, it helps you remember what you learned about a topic from a book.

Part C: Fluency Building

5 minutes

Student Materials:
Storybook 1

Conduct after the lesson, using story of the day.

Activity 1 Partner Reading

It's time for partner reading.
Direct students to the story of the day. **Assign** student partners as Partner 1 and Partner 2. **Monitor** student reading. **Guide** as needed.

Lesson 84

Materials

Teacher: *Storybook 1*

Student: *Storybooks 1;* vocabulary notebook

Part A: Vocabulary Development

5 minutes

Student Materials:
Storybook 1

Vocabulary notebook

Activity 1 Learn New Vocabulary Word

Elicit responses to questions. **Guide** as needed.
Today you'll learn a new vocabulary word. **Dim. Dim** means **not bright.**
What does **dim** mean? *Not bright.*

Another word for **not bright** is **dim.** What's another word for **not bright?** *Dim.*

When Don went down into the basement, it was **not bright.** Don said, "I can't see well. It's hard to see when it's **dim.**"

What's another word for **not bright?** *Dim.*
Discuss places that are dim.

Write **dim** and what it means in your vocabulary notebook.
Direct students to write word in their vocabulary notebook. **Guide** as needed.

Activity 2 Review Vocabulary Word

Elicit responses to questions. **Guide** as needed.
What does **continue** mean? *Go on.*
What's another word for **go on?** *Continue.*

Review vocabulary words in appropriate context in *Storybook 1.*

Part B: Comprehension Strategies

12 minutes

Teacher Materials:
Storybook 1

Student Materials:
Storybook 1

Activity 1 Summarize—An After-Reading Strategy

After you've read a part of a story, it is a smart strategy to stop and tell yourself the story in your own words. You have heard me summarize a paragraph before. I will show you again how I summarize the first paragraph of the story "Don Meets a Woman." First I'll read the paragraph to you, and then I'll summarize it.
Model think-aloud for summarizing a paragraph.

Read first paragraph of Story 83, page 222.

Sample Wording for Think-Aloud

Don heard a noise downstairs, so he went downstairs. There was a woman who asked him if he wanted to be a super man.

Notice that I told the story in my own words. I told the main thing that the paragraph was about, but I did not say all the words exactly like the story. I just told the main parts of the story. When I tell the main parts, I am summarizing.

Activity 2 Mental Imaging—A During-Reading Strategy

Refer to Story 83, pages 222–224.

Elicit response to question. **Guide** as needed.
What do good readers do when they make mental images? *Make pictures in their brains.*

If you want to be a good reader, you need to practice making pictures in your brain when you read. When you make pictures in your brain while you read, you "see" what the story is telling in words.

Listen to me choose some sentences, read them, and then tell what I see.
Model think-aloud for finding sentences in story and telling what you see.

Sample Wording for Think-Aloud

(Read second sentence from story on page 222.) I have a picture in my brain of stairs in my grandmother's house. They are steep and narrow. It is pretty dark downstairs. I see Don dropping his mop on the floor and rushing down those stairs.

Now it's your turn. Choose a different sentence from Story 83, "Don Meets a Woman." Read the sentence to your partner. Then get a picture in your mind of that sentence.
Guide student partners to find a sentence that makes them have a picture in their brain and share this with a partner.

What picture do you see in your brain when you read that sentence? (**Student response.**) Tell your partner what you see.

Now your partner should find a sentence. Read the sentence. Then tell the picture he or she sees in his or her brain.

Share with the class the sentence you chose and tell the picture you saw in your brain.
Discuss sentence chosen and mental images developed.

When you make mental images as you read, you will be better at understanding what you read.

Part C: Fluency Building

Conduct after the lesson, using story of the day.

Activity 1 Partner Reading

It's time for partner reading.

Direct students to the story of the day. **Assign** student partners as Partner 1 and Partner 2. **Monitor** student reading. **Guide** as needed.

Teacher: *Storybooks 1* and *2*; 1-Narrative Story Map, 2-Vocabulary Acquisition and Use, Writing Prompts, 5-My Writing Checklist

Student: *Storybooks 1* and *2*; copy of 1-Narrative Story Map, Copy of 2- Vocabulary Acquisition and Use and 5-My Writing Checklist; Lined Paper

Part A: Vocabulary Development

5 minutes

IWB

Teacher Materials:
Vocabulary Acquisition and Use

Student Materials:
Storybooks 1 and *2*

Vocabulary Acquisition and Use

Activity 1 Cumulative Vocabulary Review

Elicit responses to questions. **Guide** as needed.
Directions: Listen and tell me the correct vocabulary word for each question.

What's another word for **not bright?** *Dim.*
What's another word for **trick?** *Con.*
What's another word for **go on?** *Continue.*
What's another word for **not telling the truth?** *Lying.*

Repeat difficult words as needed.

Review vocabulary words in appropriate context in *Storybooks 1* and *2*.

Activity 2 Vocabulary Acquisition and Use

Display Vocabulary Acquisition and Use. **Have** students work with a neighbor to complete Vocabulary Acquisition and Use.
Today's vocabulary words are _____ and _____ [and _____ and _____].
Vocabulary words: **con** and **trick; continue** and **go**
Write the words on the lines provided. Then write the words in the boxes based on whether you think each word is less/smaller or more/larger than the other word. Below the boxes, write why you think word 1 is less/smaller and word 2 is more/larger than word 1.
Repeat for words 3 and 4. **Have** students share what they wrote. **Discuss** examples of how these words might be used.

12 minutes

IWB

Teacher Materials:
Storybooks 1 and *2*

Narrative Story Map

Student Materials:
Storybooks 1 and *2*

Narrative Story Map

Activity 1 Set Purpose for Reading—A Before-Reading Strategy

Elicit responses to questions. **Guide** as needed.

You get smart at reading when you think before you read about why you are reading the story. That is called setting a purpose for reading. Today as you read, you're going to try to find three story elements. The purpose for reading is to find the main character, the setting, and the problem.

Guide students as they skim Stories 82–84, pages 219–224 in *Storybook 1* and pages 1–3 in *Storybook 2*, to look for story elements.

Try to find the name of the main character in the story. Then look for where and when the story takes place. The last thing you'll look for is the problem.

When you look for the problem, what are you trying to find? (Idea: *What goes wrong in the story that makes you want to read more to find out what happens.*)

What three things will you look for in the story today? (Idea: *The main character, the setting, and the problem.*)

Activity 2 Identify Characters, Setting, and Problem—An After-Reading Strategy

Show Narrative Story Map.

Today our Narrative Story Map has a new section. You'll fill out the title, characters, setting, and problem on the Narrative Story Map. However, it is time to start writing the answers rather than drawing a picture.

Model writing the answers on Narrative Story Map. **Elicit** responses to questions. **Guide** as needed.

First, write "The Don Story" for the title. Copy what I write.

Next, who is the main character in the stories? *Don.* Touch the box for Characters. Write Don in the box for Characters. Who is another character in the story so far? *The woman.* Copy what I write.

Where does the story take place so far? *In the hat store.* Touch the box for the setting. Write these words in the box for setting.

When did the story take place? The story does not tell us. So we'll leave this part blank.

Now we need to figure out the problem. I'll show you how I try to figure out the problem in this story.

Model think-aloud for finding the problem in the story.

Sample Wording for Think-Aloud

(Read first sentence from story on page 219.) This sentence starts the story, and it tells me the problem right away. The story does not tell me about the characters or the setting first. It tells the problem first. Don hates his job.

Later Don says he wants to be a super man. Don wishes he was a super man. So now I think that he does not like his job, and he wants to be a super man. I think this is the problem; Don is not happy. He thinks being someone else will make him happy.

That makes me want to read more. I want to find out if he becomes a super man and if it makes him happy.

Touch the box for the problem. Write the problem.

Model writing, "Don hates his job, wants to become a super man" in Problem box.
Guide students to copy words.

Good for you. You're beginning to figure out hard story elements.

Part C: Fluency Building

5 minutes

Student Materials:
Storybook 2

Conduct after the lesson, using story of the day.

Activity 1 Partner Reading

It's time for partner reading.
Direct students to the story of the day. **Assign** student partners as Partner 1 and Partner 2. **Monitor** student reading. **Guide** as needed.

Part D: Writing/Language Arts

IWB

Teacher Materials:
Writing Prompts

My Writing Checklist

Student Materials:
Lined Paper

My Writing Checklist

Activity 1 Write and Use Parts of Speech and Conventions

Time to write using a writing prompt based on the stories we've been reading.

Assign student partners. **Distribute** lined paper to students. **Display** writing prompts and have students choose one to write about or assign a writing prompt of your choice. **Review** parts of speech and punctuation as well as the writing checklist with students. **Tell** students to write one paragraph (minimum of four sentences per paragraph) on their own to answer the writing prompt. **Tell** them to use their writing checklist (first column labeled "Did I use them?") to ensure they include important parts of speech or punctuation in their writing. **Tell** students which parts of speech or punctuation to focus on, if you wish. **Model** what it means to answer a writing prompt and to use the writing checklist during and after the writing process, as needed. **Monitor** and guide students as needed. **Model** what it means to have a neighbor look over his or her neighbor's writing and to complete the writing checklist (second column labeled "Did my neighbor use them?"), as needed. **Have** students share what they wrote as time permits.

Writing Prompt 1	Writing Prompt 2	Writing Prompt 3
Sam liked to make things. Tell me about something you like to make.	What is your favorite thing to wear? Why?	Why do you think it isn't nice to con someone out of something?

Materials

Teacher: *Storybook 2*

Student: *Storybook 2;* vocabulary notebook

Part A: Vocabulary Development

5 minutes

Student Materials:
Storybook 2

Vocabulary notebook

Activity 1 Learn New Vocabulary Word

Elicit responses to questions. **Guide** as needed.

Today you'll learn a new vocabulary word. **Heave. Heave** means **throw something heavy.** What does **heave** mean? *Throw something heavy.*

Another word for **throw something heavy** is **heave.** What's another word for **throw something heavy?** *Heave.*

Don picked up a bus and threw it. He showed that he could **throw something heavy.** He could **heave** a bus. Wow!

What's another word for **throw something heavy?** *Heave.*
Discuss examples of what students might heave.

Write **heave** and what it means in your vocabulary notebook.
Direct students to write word in their vocabulary notebook. **Guide** as needed.

Activity 2 Review Vocabulary Word

Elicit responses to questions. **Guide** as needed.
What does **dim** mean? *Not bright.*
What's another word for **not bright?** *Dim.*

Review vocabulary words in appropriate context in *Storybook 2.*

Part B: Comprehension Strategies

12 minutes

Teacher Materials:
Storybook 2

Student Materials:
Storybook 2

Activity 1 Generate Questions—A During-Reading Strategy

Refer to Story 85, pages 4–6.

Elicit response to questions. **Guide** as needed.
Asking questions is a strategy to use when you are reading stories. Why do you ask questions while you are reading? *To understand the story better.*

Guide students to ask questions about information with the question frame.
Elicit responses to questions. **Guide** as needed.

We will practice thinking up good questions. Here is something that happened in the story. Don was hopping around the store. Who can make up a question from that sentence that begins with "who?" (Idea: *"Who was hopping around the store?"*)

What's the answer? *Don.*

Who can ask a question that begins with "where?" (Idea: *"Where was Don hopping?"*) What's the answer? *The store.*

Who can make up a sentence that begins with "What?" (Idea: *"What was Don doing?"*) What's the answer? *Hopping around the store.*

Who can make up a question that begins with "why"? (Idea: *"Why is Don hopping around the store?"*) What's the answer? (Idea: *He is excited to be a super man.*)

Here is another part of the story. (Read first sentence from second paragraph on page 5.) Who can make up a question from that sentence that begins with "who?" (Idea: *"Who ran to the car?"*) What's the answer? *Don.*

Who can ask a question that begins with "where?" (Idea: *"Where was the car?"*) What's the answer? *Near the store.*

Who can make up a sentence that begins with "What?" (Idea: *"What was Don doing?"*) What's the answer? *Picking up the car.*

Who can make up a question that begins with "why?" (Idea: *"Why is Don picking up the car?"*) What's the answer? (Idea: *To show that he is a super man.*)

You are getting good at asking questions.

Provide a reading center to display books being read so that students can enjoy them again during free time.

Part C: Fluency Building

5 minutes

Student Materials:
Storybook 2

Conduct after the lesson, using story of the day.

Activity 1 **Partner Reading**

It's time for partner reading.
Direct students to the story of the day. **Assign** student partners as Partner 1 and Partner 2. **Monitor** student reading. **Guide** as needed.

Lesson 87

Materials

Teacher: *Storybook 2;* 6-My Prediction Chart

Student: *Storybook 2;* vocabulary notebook

Part A: Vocabulary Development

5 minutes

Student Materials:
Storybook 2

Vocabulary notebook

Activity 1 Learn New Vocabulary Word

Elicit responses to questions. **Guide** as needed.
Today you'll learn a new vocabulary word. **Hate. Hate** means **dislike very much.** What does **hate** mean? *Dislike very much.*

Another word for **dislike very much** is **hate.** What's another word for **dislike very much?** *Hate.*

Jane would **dislike very much** if a spider ran across her room. Jane would **hate** if a spider ran across her room.

What's another word for **dislike very much?** *Hate.*
Discuss things that students hate to do.

Write **hate** and what it means in your vocabulary notebook.
Direct students to write word in their vocabulary notebook. **Guide** as needed.

Activity 2 Review Vocabulary Word

Elicit responses to questions. **Guide** as needed.
What does **heave** mean? *Throw something heavy.*
What's another word for **throw something heavy?** *Heave.*

Review vocabulary words in appropriate context in *Storybook 2.*

Part B: Comprehension Strategies

12 minutes

IWB

Teacher Materials:
Storybook 2

My Prediction Chart

Student Materials:
Storybook 2

Activity 1 Prediction—A Before-Reading Strategy

Refer to Story 87, pages 10–12.

Show My Prediction Chart. **Elicit** responses to questions. **Guide** as needed.
You'll read the next story about Don. Good readers make predictions about what they'll read. Then they confirm their predictions while they read. That makes you think about what you are reading and be a smart reader.

What are you doing when you make predictions? (Idea: *Using clues to guess what will happen in the story.*)

Where do you get clues to make predictions? (Idea: *From the title and the pictures*.)

Look at the story you're going to read, and make some predictions about what will happen in the story. Look at the title and the picture. See if there are clues to help you predict what might happen in this story. I will record the predictions you make.

Discuss predictions with students. **Record** two or three predictions.

What do you predict will happen in this story? (Student response.)

What clue gives you that idea? (Student response.)

What else do you predict? (Student response.)

What gives a clue for that prediction? (Student response.)

Do you have any more predictions? (Student response.) What clue makes you think that? (Student response.)

Remember: Making predictions helps you think about the story you're reading. While you're reading the story, see if you can confirm your predictions.

Save predictions for Lesson 88.

Part C: Fluency Building

5 minutes

Student Materials:
Storybook 2

Conduct after the lesson, using story of the day.

Activity 1 Partner Reading

It's time for partner reading.
Direct students to the story of the day. **Assign** student partners as Partner 1 and Partner 2. **Monitor** student reading. **Guide** as needed.

Lesson 88

Materials

Teacher: 6-My Prediction Chart (from Lesson 87); *Storybook 2*

Student: *Storybook 2;* vocabulary notebook

Part A: Vocabulary Development

5 minutes

Student Materials:
Storybook 2
Vocabulary notebook

Activity 1 Learn New Vocabulary Word

Elicit responses to questions. **Guide** as needed.
Today you'll learn a new vocabulary word. **Pain. Pain** means **something that hurts.** What does **pain** mean? *Something that hurts.*

Another word for **something that hurts** is **pain.** What's another word for **something that hurts?** *Pain.*

Sybil said there was **something that hurts** in her leg. She started to limp. Sybil said there was **pain** in her leg.

This **pain** is spelled **p-a-i-n.** Spell **pain** that means **something that hurts.** *P-a-i-n.*

What's another word for **something that hurts?** *Pain.*
Discuss types of pain and things that cause pain.

Write **pain** and what it means in your vocabulary notebook.
Direct students to write word in their vocabulary notebook. **Guide** as needed.

Activity 2 Review Vocabulary Word

Elicit responses to questions. **Guide** as needed.
What does **hate** mean? *Dislike very much.*
What's another word for **dislike very much?** *Hate.*

Review vocabulary words in appropriate context in *Storybook 2.*

12 minutes

IWB

Teacher Materials:
Storybook 2

My Prediction Chart

Student Materials:
Storybook 2

Activity 1 Confirm Predictions—An After-Reading Strategy

Refer to Story 87, pages 10–12.

Show My Prediction Chart. **Elicit** responses to questions. **Guide** as needed.
In the last lesson, you made some predictions about what would happen in the Don story. You made the predictions before you read the story. Making predictions helps you understand the story better. Now that you've read the story, let's check to see if your predictions were in the story. What are you doing when you check to see if your predictions are correct? *Confirming predictions.*

Let's go over the predictions you made in the last lessons.

Discuss based on recorded predictions made in Lesson 87.

Was your prediction correct? (Student response.)

What part in the story helps you confirm your prediction? (Student response.)

Do all your predictions need to be correct? *No.*

Discuss value of making predictions with students.

Why not? (Idea: *Making predictions helps me understand the story even if they are not correct because I am thinking about confirming my predictio*ns.)

Activity 2 Text-to-Self Connections—An After-Reading Strategy

Refer to Story 87, pages 10–12.

Elicit response to question. **Guide** as needed.
One way to understand stories better is to make text-to-self connections. What do you do when you make text-to-self connections? (Idea: *Connect your own experiences with a story you read.*)

Read the first page of the story to prepare for text-to-self connection.
Discuss connections that students can make to the story. **Guide** as needed.
Does this part of the Don story make you think of any experience you have ever had? (Student response.)

Have you ever felt sad? Embarrassed? (Student response.)

Have you ever been mean to someone and then felt bad? (Student response.)

Have you ever had tears running down your cheeks? (Student response.)

Has anyone ever said "I hate you?" (Student response.)

How does your experience help you understand Don? (Student response.)

Remember, when you connect something that has happened to you to something that happens in the story, you're making text-to-self connections. Thinking about your experiences when you read is a good strategy to help you understand what you read.

Part C: Fluency Building

5 minutes

Student Materials:
Storybook 2

Conduct after the lesson, using story of the day.

Activity 1 Partner Reading

It's time for partner reading.

Direct students to the story of the day. **Assign** student partners as Partner 1 and Partner 2. **Monitor** student reading. **Guide** as needed.

Lesson 89

Materials

Teacher: *Storybook 2*

Student: *Storybook 2;* vocabulary notebook

Part A: Vocabulary Development

5 minutes

Student Materials:
Storybook 2

Vocabulary notebook

Activity 1 Learn New Vocabulary Word

Elicit responses to questions. **Guide** as needed.
Today you'll learn a new vocabulary word. **Useful. Useful** means **helpful.**
What does **useful** mean? *Helpful.*

Another word for **helpful** is **useful.** What's another word for **helpful?** *Useful.*

Students who pick up the trash, keep their desks clean, and keep the floor clean are very **helpful.** The custodian says, "These children are the most **useful** students in our school."

What's another word for **helpful?** *Useful.*
Discuss ways to be useful.

Write **useful** and what it means in your vocabulary notebook.
Direct students to write word in their vocabulary notebook. **Guide** as needed.

Activity 2 Review Vocabulary Word

Elicit responses to questions. **Guide** as needed.
What does **pain** mean? *Something that hurts.*
What's another word for **something that hurts?** *Pain.*

Review vocabulary words in appropriate context in *Storybook 2.*

Part B: Comprehension Strategies

12 minutes

Teacher Materials:
Storybook 2

Student Materials:
Storybook 2

Activity 1 Read with Prosody (Dialogue)—A During-Reading Strategy

Direct students to Story 88, pages 13–15.

Dialogue is what characters say in a story. Narratives have lots of dialogue.

How is dialogue marked in stories? (Idea: *With quotation marks.*)

What is dialogue? (Idea: *The words characters say in the story.*)

This is the story "Don Works Super Hard." I want you to find the dialogue for the characters. You will look for the words Don says, the words the super woman says, the words the small man says, and the words for the narrator, which aren't in quotation marks.

Ask students to find the dialogue of different characters. **Monitor** groups as students review the stories. **Group** students in groups of 4, and **provide** guidance as needed. **Monitor** groups as they review the story and practice dialogue.

Your turn to read the story with four people. Try to read with expression. Decide who will read which part. The quotation marks will help you know when it's your turn. Take turns, and try to make the dialogue interesting.

Encourage students to perform the dialogue in front of the class, after practice.

Part C: Fluency Building

5 minutes

Student Materials:
Storybook 2

Conduct after the lesson, using story of the day.

Activity 1 Partner Reading

It's time for partner reading.

Direct students to the story of the day. **Assign** student partners as Partner 1 and Partner 2. **Monitor** student reading. **Guide** as needed.

Lesson 90

Materials

Teacher: *Storybook 2*, 2-Vocabulary Acquisition and Use, 3-My Book Review

Student: *Storybook 2*, Copy of 2-Vocabulary Acquisition and Use and 3-My Book Review

Part A: Vocabulary Development

5 minutes

IWB

Teacher Materials:
Vocabulary Acquisition and Use

Student Materials:
Storybook 2

Vocabulary Acquisition and Use

Activity 1 Cumulative Vocabulary Review

Elicit responses to questions. **Guide** as needed.

Directions: Listen and tell me the correct vocabulary word for each question.

What's another word for **something that hurts?** *Pain.*
What's another word for **helpful?** *Useful.*
What's another word for **throw something heavy?** *Heave.*
What's another word for **dislike very much?** *Hate.*
What's another word for **not bright?** *Dim.*
What's another word for **trick?** *Con.*
What's another word for **go on?** *Continue.*
What's another word for **not telling the truth?** *Lying.*

Review difficult words.

Review vocabulary words in appropriate context in *Storybook 2*.

Activity 2 Vocabulary Acquisition and Use

Display Vocabulary Acquisition and Use. **Have** students work with a neighbor to complete Vocabulary Acquisition and Use.

Today's vocabulary words are _____ and _____ [and _____ and _____].

Vocabulary words: **heave** and **throw; useful** and **helpful**

Write the words on the lines provided. Then write the words in the boxes based on whether you think each word is less/smaller or more/larger than the other word. Below the boxes, write why you think word 1 is less/smaller and word 2 is more/larger than word 1.

Repeat for words 3 and 4. **Have** students share what they wrote. **Discuss** examples of how these words might be used.

12 minutes

IWB

Teacher Materials:
Storybook 2

My Book Review

Student Materials:
Storybook 2

My Book Review

Activity 1 Mental Imaging—A During-Reading Strategy

Refer to Story 89, pages 16–18.

Elicit responses to questions. **Guide** as needed.
What do you call it when you make pictures of what you are reading in your brain? *Mental imaging.*

When you make pictures in your brain while you read, you "see" what the story is telling in words. The words might also make you "feel" what the character is feeling. This is what I do when I read "feeling" words.

Model think-aloud for mental imaging of feelings.

Sample Wording for Think-Aloud

The end of the story says the man was happy. Happy is a feeling. I remember a time I was happy—the day I helped my mom clean the house. I was happy because I helped my mom and that made her happy. I remember the feeling.

Now it's your turn. Choose a sentence from Story 89, "Don Does Good Things." Read the sentence to your partner. Then get a picture in your mind of that sentence.
Guide student partners to find a sentence that makes them have a picture in their brain. **Encourage** them to share their pictures with partner.

What picture do you see in your brain when you read that sentence? (Student response.)

Does the sentence make you have any feelings? (Student response.) Tell your partner what you see or feel.

Now your partner should find a sentence, read the sentence, and then tell you the picture he or she sees in his or her brain or the feeling he or she feels.
Guide partner to take a turn.

Share with the class the sentence you chose and tell the picture you saw in your brain or the feelings you felt.

Discuss sentence chosen and mental images developed.

Activity 2 Summarize—An After-Reading Strategy

Refer to the Don Stories, Stories 82–89.

After you have read a story, it is smart strategy to stop and tell yourself the story in your own words. You have heard me summarize a paragraph before. I can also summarize a whole story. Listen!

Model think-aloud for summarizing the story.

Sample Wording for Think-Aloud

Don hates his job. Then a super woman helps him get super powers. She tells him that he must do good things. He does bad things and loses his super powers. He feels bad and starts to fix up all the things he destroyed. Then the woman gives him his super power back. He helps a small man with a sick baby. Then he decides to give his super powers to the man so that the man can take care of his baby. Don feels good because he helped someone else.

Notice that I told the story in my own words.

Elicit responses to questions. **Guide** as needed.
What did I do when I summarized the story? (Idea: *Told the story in your own words.*)

Activity 3 Develop Opinions—An After-Reading Strategy

Today we'll found out your opinion or how you feel about the stories you read. You will choose a book to read and then complete the My Book Review form. You'll need to tell if you like or don't like the book and why. You must give a reason for why you like or don't like the book. Finally, you can tell if you would recommend the book to others.

Have students read a narrative or expository trade book of their choice. **Have** students complete My Book Review form when they are finished reading their book. **Model** how to complete the My Book Review form. **Guide** students as needed. **Have** students share their book reviews with the class as time permits.

Part C: Fluency Building

Conduct after the lesson, using story of the day.

Activity 1 Partner Reading

It's time for partner reading.

Direct students to the story of the day. **Assign** student partners as Partner 1 and Partner 2. **Monitor** student reading. **Guide** as needed.

Lesson 91

Materials

Teacher: 1-Narrative Story Map; *Storybook 2*

Student: Copy of 1-Narrative Story Map; vocabulary notebook; *Storybook 2*

Part A: Vocabulary Development

5 minutes

Student Materials:
Storybook 2

Vocabulary notebook

Activity 1 Learn New Vocabulary Word

Elicit responses to questions. **Guide** as needed.
Today you'll learn a new vocabulary word. **Confused. Confused** means **mixed up.** What does **confused** mean? *Mixed up.*

Another word for **mixed up** is **confused.** What's another word for **mixed up?** *Confused.*

Rita was **mixed up** about how to do her homework. She was **confused.** She had to ask for help.

What's another word for **mixed up?** *Confused.*
Discuss times when students might be confused.

Write **confused** and what it means in your vocabulary notebook.
Direct students to write word in their vocabulary notebook. **Guide** as needed.

Activity 2 Review Vocabulary Word

Elicit responses to questions. **Guide** as needed.
What does **helpful** mean? *Useful.*
What's another word for **useful?** *Helpful.*

Review vocabulary words in appropriate context in *Storybook 2.*

12 minutes

IWB

Teacher Materials:
Storybook 2

Narrative Story Map

Student Materials:
Storybook 2

Narrative Story Map

Activity 1 **Set Purpose for Reading—A Before-Reading Strategy**

Elicit responses to questions. **Guide** as needed.
You get smart at reading when you think before you read about why you are reading the story. That's called setting a purpose for reading. Today as you read, you're going to try to find three story elements. The purpose for reading is to find the main character, the setting, and the problem.

Try to find the name of the main character in the story. Then look for where and when the story takes place. The last thing you'll look for is the problem.

When you look for the problem, what are you trying to find? (Idea: *What goes wrong in the story that makes you want to read more to find out what happens.*)

What three things will you look for in the story today? (Idea: *The main character, the setting, and the problem.*)

Guide students to skim Story 90, pages 19–21, and look for story elements.

Activity 2 **Identify Characters, Setting, and Problem—An After-Reading Strategy**

Show Narrative Story Map. **Elicit** responses to questions. **Guide** as needed.
Today our Narrative Story Map has a new section. Today you'll fill out the title, characters, setting, and problem on the Narrative Story Map. We'll write the answers rather than draw a picture. First, write "Sid Worked in a Seed Shop" for the title. Copy what I write.

Write answers on Narrative Story Map.
Next tell me the main character in the story. *Sid.* Write that in the box for Characters.

Who's another character in the story so far? *The boss.*

Where does the story take place so far? *In the seed shop.* Write these words in the setting box for where.

When did the story take place? (Idea: *One day.*) Write these words in the setting box for when.

Now we need to figure out the problem. I will show you how I try to figure out the problem in this story.
Model think-aloud for finding the problem in the story.

Touch the box for the problem. Write these words for the problem. **Model** writing "Sid did not do the right job" in Problem Box. **Guide** students to copy words.

Good for you. You're figuring out hard story elements.

Save Narrative Story Map for Lesson 95.

Part C: Fluency Building

5 minutes

Student Materials:
Storybook 2

Conduct after the lesson, using story of the day.

Activity 1 Partner Reading

It's time for partner reading.
Direct students to the story of the day. **Assign** student partners as Partner 1 and Partner 2. **Monitor** student reading. **Guide** as needed.

Materials

Teacher: *Storybook 2*

Student: Vocabulary notebook; *Storybook 2*

Part A: Vocabulary Development

5 minutes

Student Materials:
Storybook 2

Vocabulary notebook

Activity 1 Learn New Vocabulary Word

Elicit responses to questions. **Guide** as needed.
Today you'll learn a new vocabulary word. **Slope. Slope** means **hill.** What is **slope?** *Hill.*

Another word for **hill** is **slope.** What's another word for **hill?** *Slope.*

The boy and his dog start to climb up the **hill.** They start to climb up the **slope.**

What's another word for **hill?** *Slope.*
Discuss times when students have seen or been on a slope.

Write **slope** and what it means in your vocabulary notebook.
Direct students to write word in their vocabulary notebook. **Guide** as needed.

Activity 2 Review Vocabulary Word

Elicit responses to questions. **Guide** as needed.
What does **confused** mean? *Mixed up.*
What's another word for **mixed up?** *Confused.*

Review vocabulary words in appropriate context in *Storybook 2.*

Part B: Comprehension Strategies

Activity 1 Generate Questions—A During-Reading Strategy

Refer to Story 91, pages 22–24.

Elicit responses. **Guide** as needed.
Asking questions is a strategy to use when you are reading stories. Why do you ask questions when you are reading? *To understand the story better.*

We'll practice thinking up good questions. Here's a sentence from the story. (Read first sentence from story on page 22.)

Guide students to ask questions about information with the question frame.
Elicit answers to questions.
Who can make up a question from that sentence that begins with "who?" (Idea: *"Who did not read well?"*) What's the answer? *Sid.*

Who can make up a sentence that begins with "what?" (Idea: *"What did Sid do?"*) What's the answer? *Sid did not read well.*

Who can make up a question that begins with "why?" (Idea: *"Why does Sid not read well?"*) What's the answer? (Student response.)

Here's another sentence from the story. (Read third sentence from second paragraph on page 22.)

Who can make up a question from that sentence that begins with "who?" (Idea: *"Who did not read the words on the note?"*) What's the answer? *Sid.*

Who can make up a sentence that begins with "What?" (Idea: *"What was Sid trying to do?"*) What's the answer? *Read the words on the note.*

Who can make up a question that begins with "why?" (Idea: *"Why was Sid not reading the words?"*) What's the answer? (Student response.)

You're getting good at asking questions.

Part C: Fluency Building

Conduct after the lesson, using story of the day.

Activity 1 Partner Reading

It's time for partner reading.
Direct students to the story of the day. **Assign** student partners as Partner 1 and Partner 2. **Monitor** student reading. **Guide** as needed.

Materials

Teacher: 10-KWL Chart; expository text on topic of teacher choice; *Storybook 2*
Student: Vocabulary notebook; *Storybook 2*

---

5 minutes

Student Materials:
Storybook 2

Vocabulary notebook

Part A: Vocabulary Development

Activity 1 Learn New Vocabulary Word

Elicit responses to questions. **Guide** as needed.
Today you'll learn a new vocabulary word. **Pane. Pane** means **glass part of a window.** What does **pane** mean? *Glass part of a window.*

Another word for **glass part of a window** is **pane.** What's another word for **glass part of a window?** *Pane.*

The man saw that his windows were not clean. He wanted to clean the **glass part of a window** with a paper towel. He started to clean the **pane** with a paper towel.

This **pane** is spelled **p-a-n-e.** Spell **pane** that means **glass part of a window.** *P-a-n-e.*

What's another word for **glass part of a window?** *Pane.*
Discuss windows in buildings and the different panes windows have.

Write **pane** and what it means in your vocabulary notebook.
Direct students to write word in their vocabulary notebook. **Guide** as needed.

Activity 2 Review Vocabulary Word

Elicit responses to questions. **Guide** as needed.
What does **slope** mean? *Hill.*
What's another word for **hill?** *Slope.*

Review vocabulary words in appropriate context in *Storybook 2.*

12 minutes

IWB

Teacher Materials:
KWL Chart

Expository text

Activity 1 KWL Chart for Expository Text—A Before-Reading Strategy

Show KWL Chart. **Elicit** responses to questions. **Guide** as needed.
Here's a KWL chart that you can use when you are reading expository text.

What's expository text? (Idea: *Stories that teach you new information.*)

We'll read a nonfiction or expository text on _____. Before we read this book, we'll fill out the first two sections of the KWL Chart.

Why will we read this book? (Idea: *To learn more about _____.*)

Elicit list of things to write in the "What I Know" column.
The first section is the "What I Know" section. You list your schema, or what is already in your brain about the topic of your book. Let's think of some things you know about _____ and write them on the chart.

Elicit list of things to write in the "What I Want to Know" column.
The next section is the "What I Want to Know" section. In that section, you think about questions you have and things you want to know. Let's think of some things you want to know about _____ and write them in this section.

The last section has a place to list what you learned about the topic from the book after you read. We'll fill out this section after we read the book.

This chart is a great way to organize what you already know, what you want to know, and what you learned. When you make organized lists or fill out charts like this, it helps you remember what you learned about a topic from a book.

Save chart to complete in Lesson 94.

Part C: Fluency Building

5 minutes

Student Materials:
Storybook 2

Conduct after the lesson, using story of the day.

Activity 1 Partner Reading

It's time for partner reading.
Direct students to the story of the day. **Assign** student partners as Partner 1 and Partner 2. **Monitor** student reading. **Guide** as needed.

Materials

Teacher: 10-KWL Chart (from Lesson 93); expository book on topic of teacher choice; *Storybook 2*

Student: Vocabulary notebook; *Storybook 2*

⏱ **5 minutes**

Student Materials:
Storybook 2

Vocabulary notebook

Part A: Vocabulary Development

Activity 1 Learn New Vocabulary Word

Elicit responses to questions. **Guide** as needed.
Today you'll learn a new vocabulary word. **Week. Week** means **seven days.**
What does **week** mean? *Seven days.*

Another word for **seven days** is **week.** What's another word for **seven days?** *Week.*

The girl loved to eat popcorn. She ate it **seven days** in a row. She ate it for a **week.**

This **week** is spelled **w-e-e-k.** Spell **week** that means **seven days.** *W-e-e-k.*

What's another word for **seven days?** *Week.*
Discuss what students like to do during the week.

Write **week** and what it means in your vocabulary notebook.
Direct students to write word in their vocabulary notebook. **Guide** as needed.

Activity 2 Review Vocabulary Word

Elicit responses to questions. **Guide** as needed.
What does **glass part of a window** mean? *Pane.*
What's another word for **pane?** *Glass part of window.*

Review vocabulary words in appropriate context in *Storybook 2.*

12 minutes

IWB

Teacher Materials:
KWL Chart

Expository book

Activity 1 Set a Purpose for Reading—A Before-Reading Strategy

Elicit response to questions. **Guide** as needed.
Today you'll hear a book about _____. This text teaches you new information. It tells about things that are true. When you read this kind of story, you're getting ready to learn something new. We call this kind of book expository text.

How is expository text different from narrative text? (Idea: *Narrative text has characters, setting, a problem, and a beginning, middle, and end. Expository text is organized around main ideas and topics.*)

The expository text we'll read today is organized around the topic of _____. It will give you information that is true about _____. Another name for expository text is nonfiction. We read expository text to learn something new.

Why will we read about _____ today? (Idea: *To learn something new about _____.*)

Read expository text of choice. **Note** features of expository text as you read, such as headings, captions, labels, lists, table of contents, photographs, and index.

Activity 2 KWL Chart—An After-Reading Strategy

Show KWL Chart from Lesson 93. **Review** first two columns.
In the last lesson, we filled in two columns of our chart. Let's review what we wrote.

Elicit responses to fill in the "What I Learned" column.
Now we're ready to fill in the last column. We read _____ to learn something new about _____. Now let's make a list of all the new things we learned. What did we learn? (**Student responses.**)

This chart is a great way to organize what you already know, what you want to know, and what you learned. When you make organized lists or fill out charts like this, it helps you remember what you learned about a topic from a book.

Part C: Fluency Building

5 minutes

Student Materials:
Storybook 2

Conduct after the lesson, using story of the day.

Activity 1 Partner Reading

It's time for partner reading.
Direct students to the story of the day. **Assign** student partners as Partner 1 and Partner 2. **Monitor** student reading. **Guide** as needed.

Lesson 95

Part A: Vocabulary Development

5 minutes

IWB

Teacher Materials:
Vocabulary Acquisition and Use

Student Materials:
Storybooks 2

Vocabulary notebook

Vocabulary Acquisition and Use

Activity 1 Vocabulary Notebook Review

Today you'll learn to study from your vocabulary notebook. Studying your words and what they mean will help you know your words even better. You'll look at the four words we studied this week. Watch as I study **confused.** **Write** confused on board, and model think-aloud for studying the word and its meaning.

Sample Wording for Think-Aloud

Confused means **mixed up.** First I cover what the word means with my hand. I cover **mixed up** with my hand like this. Then I think of what it means. Confused means . . . **mixed up.** I remove my hand, and I check to see if I'm right. I am. Now I cover the word with my hand. I cover **confused** and read what it means—**mixed up.** The word that means **mixed up** is **confused.** I remove my hand, and I check to see if I'm right. I am. Now I read both the word and its meaning. I say, **confused** means **mixed up.** I am finished studying this word.

You'll study each word this way to learn your vocabulary words at a high level.

Guide students through confused, slope, pane, and week.

Activity 2 Cumulative Vocabulary Review

Elicit responses to questions. **Guide** as needed.
Directions: Listen and tell me the correct vocabulary word for each question.

What's another word for **hill?** *Slope.*
What's another word for **seven days?** *Week.*
What's another word for **mixed up?** *Confused.*
What's another word for **glass part of a window?** *Pane.*

Repeat difficult words as needed.

Review vocabulary words in appropriate context in *Storybook 2.*

Activity 3 | Vocabulary Acquisition and Use

Display Vocabulary Acquisition and Use. **Have** students work with a neighbor to complete Vocabulary Acquisition and Use.

Today's vocabulary words are _____ and _____ [and _____ and _____].
Vocabulary words: **slope** and **hill; confused** and **baffled**
Write the words on the lines provided. Then write the words in the boxes based on whether you think each word is less/smaller or more/larger than the other word. Below the boxes, write why you think word 1 is less/smaller and word 2 is more/larger than word 1.

Repeat for words 3 and 4. **Have** students share what they wrote. **Discuss** examples of how these words might be used.

Part B: Comprehension Strategies

Activity 1 | Story Map—An After-Reading Strategy

12 minutes

IWB

Teacher Materials:
Narrative Story Map

Storybook 2

Student Materials:
Narrative Story Map

Storybook 2

Refer to Stories 90–94, pages 19–32.

Return Narrative Story Maps to students. **Elicit** responses. **Guide** as needed.
Today you'll finish the Narrative Story Maps you started in Lesson 91. You've already filled in the sections of the map for the Characters, Setting, and Problem for the Sid story. Let's review.

Look at what you wrote on your map to tell the answers. Who is the main character? *Sid.*

Where did the story take place? *In the seed shop.*

When did the story take place? *One day.*

What is the problem in the story? *Sid did not do the right job.*

Now it's time for you to complete the Narrative Story Map.

Model writing student-generated ideas in Beginning, Middle, and End boxes of Narrative Story Map so that students can copy.
What should you write for the Beginning box? (Idea: *Sid did not read the notes the right way.*)

What should you write for the Middle box? (Idea: *Sid made lots of mistakes in the Seed Shop.*)

What should you write for the End box? (Idea: *The boss taught Sid to read; when he read the notes the right way, he did the jobs the right way.*)

Now it's time to use your Narrative Story Map to retell the Sid story to the class.
Encourage students to retell the Sid story by referring to their Narrative Story Maps.

Part C: Fluency Building

5 minutes

Student Materials:
Storybook 2

Conduct after the lesson, using story of the day.

Activity 1 | Partner Reading

It's time for partner reading.

Direct students to the story of the day. **Assign** student partners as Partner 1 and Partner 2. **Monitor** student reading. **Guide** as needed.

Part D: Writing/Language Arts

10 minutes

IWB

Teacher Materials:
Writing Prompts

My Writing Checklist

Student Materials:
Lined Paper

My Writing Checklist

Activity 1 | Write and Use Parts of Speech and Conventions

Time to write using a writing prompt based on the stories we've been reading.

Assign student partners. **Distribute** lined paper to students. **Display** writing prompts and have students choose one to write about or assign a writing prompt of your choice. **Review** parts of speech and punctuation as well as the writing checklist with students. **Tell** students to write one paragraph (minimum of four sentences per paragraph) on their own to answer the writing prompt. **Tell** them to use their writing checklist (first column labeled "Did I use them?") to ensure they include important parts of speech or punctuation in their writing. **Tell** students which parts of speech or punctuation to focus on, if you wish. **Model** what it means to answer a writing prompt and to use the writing checklist during and after the writing process, as needed. **Monitor** and guide students as needed. **Model** what it means to have a neighbor look over his or her neighbor's writing and to complete the writing checklist (second column labeled "Did my neighbor use them?"), as needed. **Have** students share what they wrote as time permits.

Writing Prompt 1	Writing Prompt 2	Writing Prompt 3
Tell me about what kind of job you'd like to have.	Tell me one super thing you could do for somebody else.	Why do you think it is important to learn how to read?

Lesson 96

Part A: Vocabulary Development

5 minutes

Student Materials:
Storybook 2

Vocabulary notebook

Activity 1 Learn New Vocabulary Word

Elicit responses to questions. **Guide** as needed.

Today you'll learn a new vocabulary word. **Smart. Smart** means **quick at learning.** What does **smart** mean? *Quick at learning.*

Another word for **quick at learning** is **smart.** What's another word for **quick at learning?** *Smart.*

The student was **quick at learning.** She was **smart.**

What's another word for **quick at learning?** *Smart.*
Discuss ways students can be smart.

Write **smart** and what it means in your vocabulary notebook.
Direct students to write word in their vocabulary notebook. **Guide** as needed.

Activity 2 Review Vocabulary Word

Elicit responses to questions. **Guide** as needed.
What does **week** mean? *Seven days.*
What's another word for **seven days?** *Week.*

Review vocabulary words in appropriate context in *Storybook 2.*

Part B: Comprehension Strategies

12 minutes

Teacher Materials:
Storybook 2

Student Materials:
Storybook 2

Activity 1 Set a Purpose—A Before-Reading Strategy

Elicit responses to questions. **Guide** as needed.
You get smart at reading when you think before you read about why you're reading the story. That's called setting a purpose for reading.

What's it called when you think about why you are reading before you read? *Setting a purpose for reading.*

Today you're going to read the first paragraph on page 35 so that you can summarize it.
What are you doing when you summarize? (Idea: *Tell the main ideas of a story in your own words.*)

Activity 2 Summarize—An After-Reading Strategy

Guide students to read the first paragraph on page 35 (second page of story) in Story 95.

Elicit responses to questions. **Guide** as needed.
We'll work together to summarize the paragraph. First you need to read the paragraph. Think hard about what you're reading because then we'll close the book and retell the main parts of the paragraph.

I'll tell the first sentence of our summary. Dan was a great teacher.

You tell the next important idea of the paragraph in your own words.
(Idea: *He helped them read and spell hard words.*)

Fantastic! Telling the paragraph in your own words is hard, but you're getting smart.

Provide a reading center to display books being read so that students can enjoy them again during free time.

Part C: Fluency Building

5 minutes

Student Materials:
Storybook 2

Conduct after the lesson, using story of the day.

Activity 1 Partner Reading

It's time for partner reading.
Direct students to the story of the day. **Assign** student partners as Partner 1 and Partner 2. **Monitor** student reading. **Guide** as needed.

Lesson 97

Materials

Teacher: 1-Narrative Story Map; *Storybook 2*

Student: Copy of 1-Narrative Story Map; *Storybook 2;* vocabulary notebook

5 minutes

Student Materials:
Storybook 2

Vocabulary notebook

Part A: Vocabulary Development

Activity 1 Learn New Vocabulary Word

Elicit responses to questions. **Guide** as needed.

Today you'll learn a new vocabulary word. **Trade. Trade** means **give something to get something.** What does **trade** mean? *Give something to get something.*

Another word for **give something to get something** is **trade.** What's another way to say **give something to get something?** *Trade.*

Rico offers to **give something to get something** when he asks his mom if he can **trade** doing dishes for a new baseball card.

What's another word for **give something to get something?** *Trade.*
Discuss what it means to trade. **Ask** students if they have ever traded anything.

Write **trade** and what it means in your vocabulary notebook.
Direct students to write word in their vocabulary notebook. **Guide** as needed.

Activity 2 Review Vocabulary Word

Elicit responses to questions. **Guide** as needed.
What does **smart** mean? *Quick at learning.*
What's another word for **quick at learning?** *Smart.*

Review vocabulary words in appropriate context in *Storybook 2.*

Part B: Comprehension Strategies

IWB

Teacher Materials:
Storybook 2

Narrative Story Map

Student Materials:
Storybook 2

Narrative Story Map

Activity 1 Set Purpose for Reading—A Before-Reading Strategy

Elicit responses to questions. **Guide** as needed.
It's a good idea to set a purpose for reading before you read.

Why do you set a purpose for reading? (Idea: *So you know what to think about as you read.*)

Today as you read, you're going to try to find three story elements.

The purpose for reading is to find the main character, the setting, and the problem.

Try to find the name of the main character in the story. Then look for where and when the story takes place. The last thing you'll look for is the problem.

When you look for the problem, what are you trying to find? (Idea: *What goes wrong in the story that makes you want to read more to find out what happens.*)

What three things will you look for in the story today? (Idea: *The main character, the setting, and the problem.*)

Guide students to skim the first page of Stories 95 and 96, pages 34–37, and look for story elements.

Activity 2 Identify Characters, Setting, and Problem—An After-Reading Strategy

Show Narrative Story Map. **Elicit** responses to questions. **Guide** as needed.
Today you'll fill out the title, characters, setting, and problem on the Narrative Story Map. Find the title on page 34, and copy it onto your Narrative Story Map.

Allow students to copy words from *Storybook 2*, rather than model answer on Narrative Story Map.

Next, tell me the main characters in the story. *Ann and Dan.* Write that in the box for Characters.

Who are other characters in the story so far? *The teacher, the students.*

Where does the story take place so far? *At school.*
Copy these words from the book in the part for where.

When did the story take place? *One day.*
Copy those words from the book in the part for when.

Now we need to figure out the problem. Look carefully, and see if you can figure out a problem in the story.

What are some suggestions you see for the problem in the story? (Idea: *The teacher does not want a dog in school.*)

Choose the best suggestion. **Model** writing problem on Narrative Story Map. **Guide** students to copy words.
Touch the box for the problem. Write these words for the problem.

Good for you. You're figuring out hard story elements.

Save Narrative Story Map for Lesson 98.

Part C: Fluency Building

5 minutes

Student Materials:
Storybook 2

Conduct after the lesson, using story of the day.

Activity 1 Partner Reading

It's time for partner reading.
Direct students to the story of the day. **Assign** student partners as Partner 1 and Partner 2. **Monitor** student reading. **Guide** as needed.

Lesson 98

Materials

Teacher: 1-Narrative Story Map (from Lesson 97); *Storybook 2*

Student: Copy of 1-Narrative Story Map (from Lesson 97); vocabulary notebook; *Storybook 2*

Part A: Vocabulary Development

5 minutes

Student Materials:
Storybook 2

Vocabulary notebook

Activity 1 Learn New Vocabulary Word

Elicit responses to questions. **Guide** as needed.

Today you'll learn a new vocabulary word. **Tame. Tame** means **gentle.** What does **tame** mean? *Gentle.*

Another word for **gentle** is **tame.** What's another word for **gentle?** *Tame.*

Sally's horse was very **gentle.** It was **tame.** Everyone in the neighborhood could ride it.

What's another word for **gentle?** *Tame.*

Discuss what it means to be tame and animals that are tame.

Write **tame** and what it means in your vocabulary notebook.

Direct students to write word in their vocabulary notebook. **Guide** as needed.

Activity 2 Review Vocabulary Word

Elicit responses to questions. **Guide** as needed.

What does **trade** mean? *Give something to get something.*

What's another word for **give something to get something?** *Trade.*

Review vocabulary words in appropriate context in *Storybook 2.*

12 minutes

IWB

Teacher Materials:
Storybook 2

Narrative Story Map

Student Materials:
Storybook 2

Narrative Story Map

Part B: Comprehension Strategies

Activity 1 Story Map—An After-Reading Strategy

Refer to Stories 95 and 96, pages 34–37.

Return Narrative Story Maps to students. **Elicit** responses. **Guide** as needed.
Today you'll finish the Narrative Story Maps you started in Lesson 97. You've already filled in the sections of the map for the Characters, Setting, and Problem for the Dan story. Let's review. Look at what you wrote on your map to tell the answers.

Who are the main characters? *Ann and Dan.*

Where did the story take place? *In school.*

When did the story take place? *One day.*

What is the problem in the story? (Idea: *The teacher did not want a dog in school.*)

Now it's time for you to complete the Narrative Story Map.

Model writing student generated ideas in Beginning, Middle, and End section of visual for Narrative Story Map so that students can copy.
What should you write for the Beginning box? (Idea: *Ann took Dan to school, but the teacher did not want him there.*)

What should you write for the Middle box? (Idea: *The teacher left, so Dan taught the kids.*)

What should you write for the End box? (Idea: *The teacher let Dan stay as a teacher helper.*)

Time to use your Story Map to retell the Dan story to the class.
Encourage students to retell the Dan story by referring to their Narrative Story Maps.

Part C: Fluency Building

Conduct after the lesson, using story of the day.

Activity 1 Partner Reading

It's time for partner reading.
Direct students to the story of the day. **Assign** student partners as Partner 1 and Partner 2. **Monitor** student reading. **Guide** as needed.

Lesson 99

Part A: Vocabulary Development

5 minutes

Student Materials:

Storybook 2

Vocabulary notebook

Activity 1 Learn New Vocabulary Word

Elicit responses to questions. **Guide** as needed.

Today you'll learn a new vocabulary word. **Gust. Gust** means **big blast of wind.** What does **gust** mean? *Big blast of wind.*

Another word for **big blast of wind** is **gust.** What's another word for **big blast of wind?** *Gust.*

Ava got very wet when she was outside in the rain. Then a **big blast of wind** came along. A **gust** came along. It blew Ava's umbrella away!

What's another word for **big blast of wind?** *Gust.*

Discuss things that can gust.

Write **gust** and what it means in your vocabulary notebook.

Direct students to write word in their vocabulary notebook. **Guide** as needed.

Activity 2 Review Vocabulary Word

Elicit responses to questions. **Guide** as needed.

What does **tame** mean? *Gentle.*

What's another word for **gentle?** *Tame.*

Review vocabulary words in appropriate context in *Storybook 2.*

12 minutes

IWB

Teacher Materials:
Storybook 2

Compare and Contrast
Venn Diagram

Student Materials:
Storybook 2

Activity 1 Compare/Contrast Characters—An After-Reading Strategy

Refer to Story 98, pages 41–43.

Show Compare and Contrast Venn Diagram. **Elicit** responses to questions. **Guide** as needed.

Today we'll compare the two characters in the story with each other. Characters in stories are interesting because they are not the same. They are different from each other.

Who are the characters in "Spot Meets a Tall Girl?" (Idea: *Spot and the tall girl.*)

In the middle of our diagram, we'll write how the characters are the same. You can get information from the story or the picture. Let's think about some ways that they are the same. If the characteristics are the same, your sentence can begin by saying, "They both . . ." (Ideas: *They are both nice; they are taking walks; they both talk; they both go to the mall; they both met a pig.*)

Model think-aloud for contrasting characters. **Substitute** your own words for idea presented, if you wish.

Sample Wording for Think-Aloud

Now we'll tell about how the two characters are different. This part is a little harder. On one side of the diagram, we will write **Spot.** On the other side, we will write **tall girl.** Now we'll think about how they are different. But this is tricky because we have to tell how they are different about the same characteristic. One way they're different is that Spot is a dog, but the tall girl is a girl. The wrong way to contrast these characters would be to say that Spot is a dog, but the tall girl has a skirt, because we are not talking about the same characteristic. We could say that Spot has spots, but the tall girl has clothes. Spot is deaf, but the tall girl can hear. Spot talks in a normal voice, but the girl shouts.

Now we'll write how Spot and the girl are different, using our ideas but making sure that we are talking about the same characteristic.

Elicit responses, and **write** information on diagram. **Guide** as needed.

Student Materials:
Storybook 2

Conduct after the lesson, using story of the day.

Activity 1 Partner Reading

It's time for partner reading.

Direct students to the story of the day. **Assign** student partners as Partner 1 and Partner 2. **Monitor** student reading. **Guide** as needed.

Lesson 100

Part A: Vocabulary Development

5 minutes

IWB

Teacher Materials:
Vocabulary Acquisition and Use

Student Materials:
Storybook 2

Vocabulary Notebook

Vocabulary Acquisition and Use

Activity 1 Vocabulary Notebook Review

Today you'll study from your vocabulary notebook. Studying your words and what they mean will help you know your words even better. You'll study the eight words we studied this week.

Model how to study <u>smart</u>.

Guide students as they study <u>confused</u>, <u>slope</u>, <u>pane</u>, <u>week</u>, <u>smart</u>, <u>trade</u>, <u>tame</u>, and <u>gust</u>.

Activity 2 Cumulative Vocabulary Review

Elicit responses to questions. **Guide** as needed.
Directions: Listen and tell me the correct vocabulary word for each question.

What's another word for **give something to get something?** *Trade.*
What's another word for **quick at learning?** *Smart.*
What's another word for **mixed up?** *Confused.*
What's another word for **hill?** *Slope.*
What's another word for **big blast of wind?** *Gust.*
What's another word for **glass part of a window?** *Pane.*
What's another word for **seven days?** *Week.*
What's another word for **gentle?** *Tame.*

Repeat difficult words as needed.

Review vocabulary words in appropriate context in *Storybook 2.*

Activity 3 Vocabulary Acquisition and Use

Display Vocabulary Acquisition and Use. **Have** students work with a neighbor to complete Vocabulary Acquisition and Use.
Today's vocabulary words are _____ and _____ [and _____ and _____].
Vocabulary words: **tame** and **gentle; smart** and **intelligent**
Write the words on the lines provided. Then write the words in the boxes based on whether you think each word is less/smaller or more/larger than the other word. Below the boxes, write why you think word 1 is less/smaller and word 2 is more/larger than word 1.
Repeat for words 3 and 4. **Have** students share what they wrote. **Discuss** examples of how these words might be used.

Part B: Comprehension Strategies

IWB

Teacher Materials:
Storybook 2

My Book Review

Student Materials:
Storybook 2

My Book Review

Activity 1   Set a Purpose—A Before-Reading Strategy

Elicit responses to questions. **Guide** as needed.
You get smart at reading when you think before you read about why you are reading the story. That is called setting a purpose for reading.

What's it called when you think about why you are reading before you read? *Setting a purpose.*

Today you are going to read the first paragraph on page 44 so that you can summarize it. What are you doing when you summarize? (Idea: *Tell the main ideas of a story in your own words.*)

Activity 2   Summarize—An After-Reading Strategy

Guide students to read the first paragraph on page 44, Story 99.

Elicit responses to questions. **Guide** as needed.
First you need to read the paragraph. Think hard about what you are reading because then we will close the book and retell the main parts of the paragraph.

I'll tell the first sentence of our summary. Spot and a tall girl met a crying pig. You tell the next important idea of the paragraph in your own words. (Idea: *The pig was crying because the wind blew his wig away.*)

Fantastic! Telling the story in your own words is hard, but you are getting smart.

Activity 3   Develop Opinions—An After-Reading Strategy

Today we'll found out your opinion or how you feel about the stories you read. You will choose a book to read and then complete the My Book Review form. You'll need to tell if you like or don't like the book and why. You must give a reason for why you like or don't like the book. Finally, you can tell if you would recommend the book to others.

Have students read a narrative or expository trade book of their choice. **Have** students complete My Book Review form when they are finished reading their book. **Model** how to complete the My Book Review form. **Guide** students as needed. **Have** students share their book reviews with the class as time permits.

Part C: Fluency Building

5 minutes

Student Materials:
Storybook 2

Conduct after the lesson, using story of the day.

Activity 1   Partner Reading

It's time for partner reading.
Direct students to the story of the day. **Assign** student partners as Partner 1 and Partner 2. **Monitor** student reading. **Guide** as needed.

Lesson 101

Materials

Teacher: *Storybook 2;* electronic resource: http://www.childrensbooksonline.org/The_Ugly_Duckling/index.htm; alternate resource: locate copy of "The Ugly Duckling"

Student: Vocabulary notebook; *Storybook 2*

Part A: Vocabulary Development

5 minutes

Student Materials:
Storybook 2

Activity 1 Learn New Vocabulary Word

Elicit responses to questions. **Guide** as needed.
Today you'll learn a new vocabulary word. **Duckling. Duckling** means **baby duck.** What does **duckling** mean? *Baby duck.*

Another word for **baby duck** is **duckling.** What's another word for **baby duck?** *Duckling.*

Susanna went to the lake. She saw a **baby duck** swimming with its mom. She saw a **duckling** swimming in the lake.

What's another word for **baby duck?** *Duckling.*
Discuss ducks and ducklings with students.

Write **duckling** and what it means in your vocabulary notebook.
Direct students to write word in their vocabulary notebook. **Guide** as needed.

Activity 2 Review Vocabulary Word

Elicit responses to questions. **Guide** as needed.
What does **gust** mean? *Big blast of wind.*
What's another word for **big blast of wind?** *Gust.*

Review vocabulary words in appropriate context in *Storybook 2.*

Part B: Comprehension Strategies

12 minutes

Teacher Materials:
The Ugly Duckling

Activity 1 Teach Genre: Fable—A Before-Reading Strategy

Locate Web site and download file, or **read** alternate version of fable.
"The Ugly Duckling" is a fable that was written a long time ago. Since then, many people have taken this story and written it in their own words. Fables are usually short to read. They're written to tell a story that is fun but also teaches a lesson. A lesson learned from a story is a moral. You learned that in Lesson 21. More than one hundred years ago, a man named Hans Christian Andersen wrote a version of "The Ugly Duckling." That book is so old that it might be hard to find on a library shelf. But there is a Web site on the Internet

that has pictures of each page of the story. Let's look at the Web site and see what this folktale looked like more than one hundred years ago.

Read or **scan** different version of story. **Discuss** the differences between the two stories. Remember: Fables are stories that are written to tell stories that are not only fun to read but also teach you a lesson. A lesson learned from a story is called what? *A moral.*

Provide a reading center to display books being read so that students can enjoy them again during free time.

Part C: Fluency Building

5 minutes

Student Materials:
Storybook 2

Conduct after the lesson, using story of the day.

Activity 1 Partner Reading

It's time for partner reading.
Direct students to the story of the day. **Assign** student partners as Partner 1 and Partner 2. **Monitor** student reading. **Guide** as needed.

Lesson 102

Materials

Teacher: *Storybook 2*

Student: *Storybook 2*; Vocabulary notebook

Part A: Vocabulary Development

5 minutes

Student Materials:
Storybook 2

Vocabulary notebook

Activity 1 Learn New Vocabulary Word

Elicit responses to questions. **Guide** as needed.

Today you'll learn a new vocabulary word. **Homeless. Homeless** means **without a home.** What does **homeless** mean? *Without a home.*

Another word for **without a home** is **homeless.** What's another word for **without a home?** *Homeless.*

Some people live in different types of homes. Other people live **without a home.** These people are **homeless.**

What's another word for **without a home?** *Homeless.*
Discuss what it means to be homeless.

Write **homeless** and what it means in your vocabulary notebook.
Direct students to write word in their vocabulary notebook. **Guide** as needed.

Activity 2 Review Vocabulary Word

Elicit responses to questions. **Guide** as needed.
What does **duckling** mean? *Baby duck.*
What's another word for **baby duck?** *Duckling.*

Review vocabulary words in appropriate context in *Storybook 2.*

Part B: Comprehension Strategies

12 minutes

Teacher Materials:
Storybook 2

Student Materials:
Storybook 2

Activity 1 Determine Moral—An After-Reading Strategy

Refer to Story 100, pages 47–49.

Remember, fables are stories that are not only fun to read but also teach a lesson. Remember, a lesson learned from a story is called what? *A moral.*

Reread Story 100 aloud, with prosody.

To figure out the moral this story is trying to teach, I need to think about the events of the story and how the story ends. Then I need to think about what the story was trying to teach me—the lesson I'm supposed to learn. I'll show you how I think about "The Ugly Duckling" to figure out what the story is trying the teach me. I'll summarize the story and think about what I can learn from the story.

Model think-aloud for finding moral of the story. **Substitute** your own words for finding the moral of the story, if you wish.

Sample Wording for Think-Aloud

At the beginning, a mother duck found a big egg that wasn't hers, and she put it in her nest to hatch. When the egg hatched, the new duckling did not look the same as her other ducklings because it was so big. The other ducklings made fun of the big duckling. I think that was mean. The big duckling grew up sad and lonely. When all the ducklings grew up, they discovered that the ugly duckling had turned into a beautiful swan. They had made a big mistake to make fun of the ugly duckling when he was small. That makes me think that there is a lesson to learn from this story. I think that this fable is trying to teach that you should not be mean to someone who looks different from you. The moral of this story is that you should not be mean to someone who looks different from you. That is the lesson learned from the story.

What was the moral of "The Ugly Duckling?" (Idea: *You should not be mean to someone who looks different from you.*)

Discuss application of moral to students' lives.

Part C: Fluency Building

5 minutes

Student Materials:
Storybook 2

Conduct after the lesson, using story of the day.

Activity 1 Partner Reading

It's time for partner reading.
Direct students to the story of the day. **Assign** student partners as Partner 1 and Partner 2. **Monitor** student reading. **Guide** as needed.

Lesson 103

Teacher: *Storybooks 1* and *2*; 9-Text-to-Text Connection
Student: *Storybooks 1* and *2*; vocabulary notebook

Part A: Vocabulary Development

5 minutes

Student Materials:
Storybook 2

Vocabulary notebook

Activity 1 Learn New Vocabulary Word

Elicit responses to questions. **Guide** as needed.
Today you'll learn a new vocabulary word. **Heap. Heap** means **pile.** What does **heap** mean? *Pile.*

Another word for **pile** is **heap.** What's another word for **pile?** *Heap.*

Rachelle's room was a mess. Her parents told her to clean up her **heap** of toys. Her parents said to clean her **pile** of toys.

What's another word for **pile?** *Heap.*
Discuss what things might be in a heap.

Write **heap** and what it means in your vocabulary notebook.
Direct students to write word in their vocabulary notebook. **Guide** as needed.

Activity 2 Review Vocabulary Word

Elicit responses to questions. **Guide** as needed.
What does **homeless** mean? *Without a home.*
What's another word for **without a home?** *Homeless.*

Review vocabulary words in appropriate context in *Storybook 2.*

12 minutes

IWB

Teacher Materials:
Storybooks 1 and *2*

Text-to-Text Connection

Student Materials:
Storybooks 1 and *2*

Activity 1 **Text-to-Text Connection—An After-Reading Strategy**

Refer to Stories 101 and 102, pages 50–53, *Storybook 2*.
You read "The Kitten Needs a Home" and "The Kitten's New Home." If you wanted to make a text-to-text connection, what story can you think of to connect to the kitten stories?

Remind students of the "Bug and the Ball" Stories 34–38, pages 80–96, *Storybook 1*.

Elicit responses to questions.

You can make text-to-text connections by telling how the stories are the same and different in a Venn Diagram. We call that compare and contrast. You can also make text-to-text connections by comparing story elements on a chart. Let's compare the stories on a chart of story elements today.
Prepare chart for story elements. **Brainstorm** with students to **elicit** story elements. **Complete** chart as students suggest ideas. Ideas filled in chart are only suggestions. **Discuss** likenesses and differences between elements as you complete chart.
Guide as needed.

Sample Story-Elements Chart		
Title of story	Kitten Story	Bug and the Ball Story
Main Characters	Little Kitten	The bug and the girl
Setting (Where)	Changes until kitten finds a home on the farm	Changes until the bug finds a home in a ball
Setting (When)	Story does not tell	Story does not tell
Beginning	Kitten could not find a home	The bug could not find a home
Middle	Girl finds kitten	The bug helped the girl with a bet
End	Kitten gets to live on a farm with the girl	The bug got to live in the ball

Part C: Fluency Building

Conduct after the lesson, using story of the day.

Activity 1 Partner Reading

It's time for partner reading.

Direct students to the story of the day. **Assign** student partners as Partner 1 and Partner 2. **Monitor** student reading. **Guide** as needed.

Materials

Teacher: 10-KWL Chart; expository text on topic of teacher choice; *Storybook 2*
Student: Vocabulary notebook; *Storybook 2*

Part A: Vocabulary Development

5 minutes

Student Materials:
Storybook 2

Vocabulary notebook

Activity 1 Learn New Vocabulary Word

Elicit responses to questions. **Guide** as needed.
Today you'll learn a new vocabulary word. **Sob. Sob** means **cry.** What does **sob** mean? *Cry.*

Another word for **cry** is **sob.** What's another word for **cry?** *Sob.*

Jack began to **cry** when his mother left for work. He began to **sob.**

What's another word for **cry?** *Sob.*
Discuss times when someone might sob.

Write **sob** and what it means in your vocabulary notebook.
Direct students to write word in their vocabulary notebook. **Guide** as needed.

Activity 2 Review Vocabulary Word

Elicit responses to questions. **Guide** as needed.
What does **heap** mean? *Pile.*
What's another word for **pile?** *Heap.*

Review vocabulary words in appropriate context in *Storybook 2.*

Part B: Comprehension Strategies

12 minutes

IWB

Teacher Materials:
KWL Chart

Expository text

Activity 1 KWL Chart for Expository Text—A Before-Reading Strategy

Show KWL Chart. **Elicit** responses to questions. **Guide** as needed.
Here's a KWL chart that you can use when you're reading expository text.

What is expository text? (Idea: *Stories that teach you new information.*)

Why do you use a KWL chart? (Idea: *To help organize and remember information.*)

What do you fill in the "K" section? (Idea: *You list your schema, or what is already in your brain about the topic of your book. The "K" stands for know.*)

What do you fill in the "W" section? (Idea: *Questions you have and things you want to know. The "W" stands for want.*)

What do you fill in the "L" section? (Idea: *What you learned about the topic from the book after you read. The "L" stands for learned.*)

We will read a nonfiction or expository text on _____ . Before we read this book, we will fill out the first two sections of the KWL Chart. Why will we read this book? (Idea: *To learn more about _____.*)

Elicit list of things to write in the "What I Know" column. **Guide** as needed.
Let's think of some things you know about _____ and write them on the chart in the "K" section.

Elicit list of things to write in the "What I Want to Know" column.
Let's think of some things you want to know about _____ and write them in the "W" section.

The last section has a place to list what you learned about the topic from the book after you read. We'll fill out this section after we read the book.

When you make organized lists or fill out charts like this, it helps you remember what you learned about a topic from a book.

Save chart to complete in Lesson 105.

Part C: Fluency Building

5 minutes

Student Materials:
Storybook 2

Conduct after the lesson, using story of the day.

Activity 1 Partner Reading

It's time for partner reading.
Direct students to the story of the day. **Assign** student partners as Partner 1 and Partner 2. **Monitor** student reading. **Guide** as needed.

Lesson 104 **307**

Lesson 105

Materials

Teacher: 10-KWL Chart (from Lesson 104); expository book on topic of teacher choice; *Storybook 2,* 2-Vocabulary Acquisition and Use, Writing Prompts, 5-My Writing Checklist

Student: Vocabulary notebook; *Storybook 2,* Copy of 2-Vocabulary Acquisition and Use and 5-My Writing Checklist; Lined Paper

Part A: Vocabulary Development

5 minutes

IWB

Teacher Materials:
Vocabulary Acquisition and Use

Student Materials:
Storybooks 2

Vocabulary notebook

Vocabulary Acquisition and Use

Activity 1 Vocabulary Notebook Review

Today, you'll study from your vocabulary notebook. Studying your words and what they mean will help you know your words even better. You'll study the four words we studied this week.

Guide students as they study duckling, homeless, heap, and sob.

Activity 2 Cumulative Vocabulary Review

Elicit responses to questions. **Guide** as needed.
Directions: Listen and tell me the correct vocabulary word for each question.

What's another word for **without a home?** *Homeless.*
What's another word for **cry?** *Sob.*
What's another word for **baby duck?** *Duckling.*
What's another word for **pile?** *Heap.*

Repeat difficult words as needed.

Review vocabulary words in appropriate context in *Storybook 2.*

Activity 3 Vocabulary Acquisition and Use

Display Vocabulary Acquisition and Use. **Have** students work with a neighbor to complete Vocabulary Acquisition and Use.
Today's vocabulary words are _____ and _____ [and _____ and _____].
Vocabulary words: **sob** and **cry; heap** and **pile**
Write the words on the lines provided. Then write the words in the boxes based on whether you think each word is less/smaller or more/larger than the other word. Below the boxes, write why you think word 1 is less/smaller and word 2 is more/larger than word 1.
Repeat for words 3 and 4. **Have** students share what they wrote. **Discuss** examples of how these words might be used.

Part B: Comprehension Strategies

Activity 1 Set a Purpose for Reading—A Before-Reading Strategy

Elicit responses to questions. **Guide** as needed.
Today you'll hear a book about _____ . When you read this kind of story, you're getting ready to learn something new. We call this kind of book expository text.

How is expository text different from narrative text? (Idea: *Narrative text has characters, setting, a problem, and a beginning, middle and end. Expository text is organized around main ideas and topics.*)

The expository text we'll read today is organized around the topic of _____ . It will give you information that is true about _____ . Another name for expository text is non-fiction. We read expository text to learn something new.

Why will we read about _____ today? (Idea: *To learn something new about _____ .*)
Read expository text of choice. **Note** features of expository text as you read, such as headings, captions, labels, lists, table of contents, photographs, and index.

Activity 2 KWL Chart—An After-Reading Strategy

Show KWL Chart from Lesson 104. **Review** first two columns.
In the last lesson, we filled in two columns of our chart.

Elicit responses to fill in the "What I Learned" column.
Now we are ready to fill in the last column. We read _____ to learn something new about _____ . Now let's make a list of all the new things we learned.

This chart is a great way to organize what you already know, what you want to know, and what you learned.

What is the name of the chart that helps you organize information from an expository text? *A KWL chart.*

Part C: Fluency Building

Conduct after the lesson, using story of the day.

Activity 1 Partner Reading

It's time for partner reading.
Direct students to the story of the day. **Assign** student partners as Partner 1 and Partner 2. **Monitor** student reading. **Guide** as needed.

10 minutes

IWB

Teacher Materials:
Writing Prompts

My Writing Checklist

Student Materials:
Lined Paper

My Writing Checklist

Activity 1 Write and Use Parts of Speech and Conventions

Time to write using a writing prompt based on the stories we've been reading.

Assign student partners. **Distribute** lined paper to students. **Display** writing prompts and have students choose one to write about or assign a writing prompt of your choice. **Review** parts of speech and punctuation as well as the writing checklist with students. **Tell** students to write one paragraph (minimum of four sentences per paragraph) on their own to answer the writing prompt. **Tell** them to use their writing checklist (first column labeled "Did I use them?") to ensure they include important parts of speech or punctuation in their writing. **Tell** students which parts of speech or punctuation to focus on, if you wish. **Model** what it means to answer a writing prompt and to use the writing checklist during and after the writing process, as needed. **Monitor** and guide students as needed. **Model** what it means to have a neighbor look over his or her neighbor's writing and to complete the writing checklist (second column labeled "Did my neighbor use them?"), as needed. **Have** students share what they wrote as time permits.

Writing Prompt 1	Writing Prompt 2	Writing Prompt 3
Tell me what you like to eat on a hot summer day.	Would a kitten make a good pet? Why or why not?	Would Boo be a good friend to have? Why?

Lesson 106

Part A: Vocabulary Development

5 minutes

Student Materials:
Storybook 2

Vocabulary notebook

Activity 1 Learn New Vocabulary Word

Elicit responses to questions. **Guide** as needed.
Today you'll learn a new vocabulary word. **Rod. Rod** means a **long, thin pole.** What does **rod** mean? *Long, thin pole.*

Another word for a **long, thin pole** is **rod.** What's another word for a **long, thin pole?** *Rod.*

Ashleigh and Baxter were using a **long, thin pole** to knock apples from the tree. They were using a **rod** to reach the apples.

What's another word for a **long, thin pole?** *Rod.*
Discuss different uses for a rod.

Write **rod** and what it means in your vocabulary notebook.
Direct students to write word in their vocabulary notebook. **Guide** as needed.

Activity 2 Review Vocabulary Word

Elicit responses to questions. **Guide** as needed.
What does **sob** mean? *Cry.*
What's another word for **cry?** *Sob.*

Review vocabulary words in appropriate context in *Storybook 2.*

Part B: Comprehension Strategies

12 minutes

Teacher Materials:
Storybook 2

Student Materials:
Storybook 2

Activity 1 Act Out the Story—An After-Reading Strategy

Refer to Stories 103 and 104, pages 54–59.

Putting on a play is a great way to help you remember what you read. Today you can put on a play. But first we have to make some decisions.

Elicit responses to questions, and **choose** students to play parts in the play.

What's the setting of the Boo story? (Idea: *Big old house.*)

Where will the house be in our classroom? (Student response.)

Who's the main character in the story? *Boo.*

Who will play the Boo part? (Student response.)

Who are other characters in the story? (Idea: *Five ghosts, farmer and horses, child, big green frog.*)

Who will play those parts? (Student response.)

I'll tell the story. Sometimes I will tell you to say a part. You can move around to act out the story as I tell the story. Here we go.

Position actors appropriately. **Side-coach** by **retelling** the story and **prompting** students to move or say dialogue as appropriate. **Substitute** your retelling and prompting of the play, if you wish.

Sample Wording for Play

Boo was a ghost who was nice. (Prompt Boo to smile and look nice.) He lived with five mean ghosts. (Prompt 5 ghosts to look mean.) Every day, the five mean ghosts tried to think of mean things to do. They would hide and scare children. (Prompt ghosts to scare child by yelling, "Ooooow.") Sometimes they would scare the farmer and his horses by jumping out and yelling, "Ooooow." (Prompt ghosts to scare the farmer and horses by saying, "Ooooow.") But Boo was not mean. (Prompt Boo to smile and say, "I don't like to scare children or farmers.") Boo tried to ride the horses, but they were scared of him. (Prompt Boo to act like he is going to ride the horse, but the horse should run away.) Boo wanted to play games with children, but they were scared of him. (Prompt Boo to try to play with child, but child should run away.) People were afraid of Boo, but the five mean ghosts were not afraid. They did not like him. (Prompt five mean ghosts to say, "You are not a good ghost because you are not mean.") Then the five mean ghosts made Boo leave the house. (Prompt mean ghosts to tell Boo to leave house and Boo to leave.) Boo picked up his books and walked down the road. (Prompt Boo to leave the house with a pile of books in his hands.) Suddenly, Boo heard crying. He saw a big green frog. (Prompt the frog to say, "Are you really a ghost?" Prompt Boo to say, "Yes, are you really a talking frog?" The frog should say, "No, I am a king, but a monster cast a spell on me and turned me into a frog.) Boo wanted to help the frog. (Prompt Boo to ask if he can help.) The frog said, "No one can help me now." (Prompt frog to say words and look very sad.)

Oh, my. We can't act out any more until we read the rest of the story.
Remind actors to take a bow. **Remind** the audience to <u>applaud</u> (a previous vocabulary word).

Part C: Fluency Building

5 minutes

Student Materials:
Storybook 2

Conduct after the lesson, using story of the day.

Activity 1 Partner Reading

It's time for partner reading.
Direct students to the story of the day. **Assign** student partners as Partner 1 and Partner 2. **Monitor** student reading. **Guide** as needed.

Materials

Teacher: *Storybook 2*

Student: Vocabulary notebook; *Storybook 2*

Part A: Vocabulary Development

5 minutes

Student Materials:
Storybook 2

Vocabulary notebook

Activity 1 Learn New Vocabulary Word

Elicit responses to questions. **Guide** as needed.
Today you'll learn a new vocabulary word. **Glide. Glide** means **float.** What does **glide** mean? *Float.*

Another word for **float** is **glide.** What's another word for **float?** *Glide.*

Boo and the other ghosts **float** to the castle to stop the monster. They **glide** through the air without making a sound.

What's another word for **float?** *Glide.*
Discuss things that can glide.

Write **glide** and what it means in your vocabulary notebook.
Direct students to write word in their vocabulary notebook. **Guide** as needed.

Activity 2 Review Vocabulary Word

Elicit responses to questions. **Guide** as needed.
What does **rod** mean? *Long, thin pole.*
What's another word for **long, thin pole?** *Rod.*

Review vocabulary words in appropriate context in *Storybook 2.*

Part B: Comprehension Strategies

12 minutes

Teacher Materials:
Storybook 2

Student Materials:
Storybook 2

Activity 1 Generate Questions—A During-Reading Strategy

Refer to Story 106, pages 63–65.

Elicit responses to questions. **Guide** as needed.
Asking questions is a strategy to use when you are reading stories. Why do you ask questions when you are reading? *To understand the story better.*

We'll practice thinking up good questions.

Here is a sentence from the story. (Read first sentence on page 63.)

Guide students to ask questions about information with the question frame.
Who can make up a question from that sentence that begins with "who?"
(Idea: *"Who was inside the castle?"*)
What's the answer? *Boo.*

Who can make up a sentence that begins with "where?" (Idea: *"Where was Boo?"*) What's the answer? *Inside the castle.*

Who can make up a question that begins with "why?" (Idea: *"Why is Boo in the castle?"*) What's the answer? (Student response.)

Here are some sentences from the story. (Read first two sentences in second paragraph on page 64.)
Who can use those sentences to make up a question that begins with "who"?
(Idea: *"Who got out of there?"*)
What's the answer? *Boo.*
Who can make up a sentence that begins with "where?" (Idea: *"Where was Boo when he got scared?"*)
What's the answer? *In the castle.*

Guide students to ask questions about information with the question frame.
Elicit responses to questions. Guide as needed.
Who can make up a sentence that begins with "what?" (Idea: *"What did Boo do when he got far from the castle?"*) What's the answer? (Idea: *Stopped and looked at himself.*)

Who can make up a question that begins with "why?" (Idea: *"Why did Boo get far from the castle?"*) What's the answer? (Idea: *He was scared.*)

You're getting good at asking questions.

Part C: Fluency Building

5 minutes

Student Materials:
Storybook 2

Conduct after the lesson, using story of the day.

Activity 1 Partner Reading

It's time for partner reading.
Direct students to the story of the day. **Assign** student partners as Partner 1 and Partner 2. **Monitor** student reading. **Guide** as needed.

Lesson 108

Materials

Teacher: *Storybook 2*

Student: *Storybook 2;* vocabulary notebook

Part A: Vocabulary Development

5 minutes

Student Materials:
Storybook 2

Vocabulary notebook

Activity 1 Learn New Vocabulary Word

Elicit responses to questions. **Guide** as needed.
Today you'll learn a new vocabulary word. **Plan. Plan** means **idea made ahead of time.** What does **plan** mean? *Idea made ahead of time.*

Another word for **idea made ahead of time** is **plan.** What's another word for **idea made ahead of time?** *Plan.*

Jason wanted to make money over the summer. He asked his grandma for some help. Together, they had an **idea made ahead of time.** With his grandma's help, Jason had a **plan.**

What's another word for **idea made ahead of time?** *Plan.*
Discuss times when students might make a plan.

Write **plan** and what it means in your vocabulary notebook.
Direct students to write word in their vocabulary notebook. **Guide** as needed.

Activity 2 Review Vocabulary Word

Elicit responses to questions. **Guide** as needed.
What does **glide** mean? *Float.*
What's another word for **float?** *Glide.*

Review vocabulary words in appropriate context in *Storybook 2.*

Part B: Comprehension Strategies

12 minutes

Teacher Materials:
Storybook 2

Student Materials:
Storybook 2

Activity 1 Set a Purpose—A Before-Reading Strategy

Elicit responses. **Guide** as needed.
You get smart at reading when you think before you read about why you are reading the story. That is called setting a purpose for reading.

What's it called when you think about why you are reading before you read? *Setting a purpose.*

Today you are going to read the first paragraph on page 66 so that you can summarize it.

What are you doing when you summarize? (Idea: *Telling the main ideas of a story in your own words.*)

Activity 2 Summarize—An After-Reading Strategy

We'll work together to summarize the paragraph. First you need to read the paragraph. Think hard about what you are reading, because then we'll close the book and retell the main parts of the paragraph.

Guide students to read the first paragraph on page 66 in Story 107.

Elicit responses to questions. **Guide** as needed.
I'll tell the first sentence of our summary. Boo had a plan to get rid of the monster. You tell the next important idea of the paragraph in your own words. (Idea: *He went back to the ghost's house.*)

Fantastic! Telling the paragraph in your own words is hard, but you're getting smart.

Part C: Fluency Building

5 minutes

Student Materials:
Storybook 2

Conduct after the lesson, using story of the day.

Activity 1 Partner Reading

It's time for partner reading.
Direct students to the story of the day. **Assign** student partners as Partner 1 and Partner 2. **Monitor** student reading. **Guide** as needed.

Lesson 109

Materials

Teacher: Chart with comprehension reading strategies from Lesson 40: Part C; *Storybook 2*

Student: Vocabulary notebook; *Storybook 2*

Part A: Vocabulary Development

10 minutes

Student Materials:
Storybook 2
Vocabulary notebook

Activity 1 Learn New Vocabulary Word

Elicit responses to questions. **Guide** as needed.
Today you'll learn a new vocabulary word. **Ram. Ram** means **run into something hard.** What does **ram** mean? *Run into something hard.*

Another word for **run into something hard** is **ram.** What's another word for **run into something hard?** *Ram.*

Shiloh likes to play chase in the backyard with her dog Bingo. Sometimes Bingo will **run into something hard** like the trash can. He will **ram** the trash can and tip it over.

What's another word for **run into something hard?** *Ram.*
Discuss what things students can ram.

Write **ram** and what it means in your vocabulary notebook.
Direct students to write word in their vocabulary notebook. **Guide** as needed.

Activity 2 Review Vocabulary Word

Elicit responses to questions. **Guide** as needed.
What does **plan** mean? *Idea made ahead of time.*
What's another word for **idea made ahead of time?** *Plan.*

Review vocabulary words in appropriate context in *Storybook 2.*

Part B: Comprehension Strategies

12 minutes

Teacher Materials:
Chart with comprehension strategies

Activity 1 Review Strategies for Monitoring Comprehension—A During-Reading Strategy

Reference comprehension-strategies chart developed in Lesson 40.

Elicit "reread" as strategy. **Guide** as needed.
Whenever you read, you should always be talking to yourself in your brain about whether what you're reading makes sense. When you're reading and you suddenly realize that what you're reading does not make sense, what is the first thing you should think to do? (Idea: *Say to myself, "That part did not*

---

318   *Lesson 109*

make sense to me. I was not thinking when I read it. If I stop and reread it, I might understand it better.")

Elicit words for "read with prosody."
Sometimes, you were not paying attention to the end marks or the dialogue in the story. Reading the story the right way will help you understand the story. So, another thing to do when reading does not make sense is to make sure that you are reading sentences the right way.

What's another way to make sure you understand what you're reading? (Idea: *Pay attention to the end marks or dialogue and read the right way.*)

Elicit "retell" and "summarize" strategies. **Guide** as needed.
When I am reading and it does not make sense, another thing I can do is to stop and retell myself the all the things that happened before it did not make sense. Summarizing the story is another way to retell the story in your own words. That may help you understand the story better.

What is a third thing I can do if the story does not make sense? (Idea: *Retell or summarize the story.*)

Elicit "mental imaging" strategy. **Guide** as needed.
You have also learned to make pictures in your mind when you are reading words.

What do you call it when you make pictures in your mind? *Mental imaging.*

Think of a time you used mental imaging. What did you do? (Student response.)

Great ideas for helping make sure you always understand what you read.

Part C: Fluency Building

5 minutes

Student Materials:
Storybook 2

Conduct after the lesson, using story of the day.

Activity 1 **Partner Reading**

It's time for partner reading.
Direct students to the story of the day. **Assign** student partners as Partner 1 and Partner 2. **Monitor** student reading. **Guide** as needed.

Lesson 110

Materials

Teacher: *Storybook 2;* 6-My Prediction Chart, 2-Vocabulary Acquisition and Use, 3-My Book Review

Student: *Storybook 2;* vocabulary notebook, Copy of 2-Vocabulary Acquisition and Use and 3-My Book Review

Part A: Vocabulary Development

5 minutes

IWB

Teacher Materials:
Vocabulary Acquisition and Use

Student Materials:
Storybook 2

Vocabulary Notebook

Vocabulary Acquisition and Use

Activity 1 Vocabulary Notebook Review

Today, you'll study from your vocabulary notebook. Studying your words and what they mean will help you know your words even better. You'll study the eight words we studied this week.
Guide students as they study <u>duckling</u>, <u>homeless</u>, <u>heap</u>, <u>sob</u>, <u>rod</u>, <u>glide</u>, <u>plan</u>, and <u>ram</u>.

Activity 2 Cumulative Vocabulary Review

Elicit responses to questions. **Guide** as needed.
Directions: Listen and tell me the correct vocabulary word for each question.

What's another word for **pile?** *Heap.*
What's another word for **baby duck?** *Duckling.*
What's another word for **without a home?** *Homeless.*
What's another word for **idea made ahead of time?** *Plan.*
What's another word for **run into something hard?** *Ram.*
What's another word for **cry?** *Sob.*
What's another word for **long, thin pole?** *Rod.*
What's another word for **float?** *Glide.*

Repeat difficult words as needed.

Review vocabulary words in appropriate context in *Storybook 2*.

Activity 3 Vocabulary Acquisition and Use

Display Vocabulary Acquisition and Use. **Have** students work with a neighbor to complete Vocabulary Acquisition and Use.
Today's vocabulary words are ＿＿＿ and ＿＿＿ [and ＿＿＿ and ＿＿＿].
Vocabulary words: **glide** and **float; ram** and **hit**
Write the words on the lines provided. Then write the words in the boxes based on whether you think each word is less/smaller or more/larger than the other word. Below the boxes, write why you think word 1 is less/smaller and word 2 is more/larger than word 1.
Repeat for words 3 and 4. **Have** students share what they wrote. **Discuss** examples of how these words might be used.

12 minutes

IWB

Teacher Materials:
Storybook 2

My Prediction Chart

My Book Review

Student Materials:
Storybook 2

My Book Review

Activity 1 | Prediction—A Before-Reading Strategy

Refer to Story 110, pages 75–77.

Show My Prediction Chart. **Elicit** responses to questions. **Guide** as needed.
You'll read the next story about Boo. Good readers make predictions about what they'll read. Then they confirm their predictions while they read. That makes you think about what you are reading so that you are a smart reader.

What are you doing when you make predictions? (Idea: *Using clues to guess what will happen in the story.*)

Where do you get clues to make predictions? *From the title and the pictures.*

Look at the story you're going to read, and make some predictions about what will happen in the story. Look at the title and the picture. See if there are clues to help you predict what might happen in this story. I'll record the predictions you make.

Discuss predictions with students. **Record** two or three predictions.
What do you predict will happen in this story? (Student response.)

What clue gives you that idea? (Student response.)

What else do you predict? (Student response.)

What gives a clue for that prediction? (Student response.)

Do you have any more predictions? (Student responses.)
What clue makes you think that? (Student response.)

Remember: Making predictions helps you think about the story you're reading. While you are reading the story, see if you can confirm your predictions.

Save predictions for Lesson 111.

Activity 2 Develop Opinions—An After-Reading Strategy

Today we'll found out your opinion or how you feel about the stories you read. You will choose a book to read and then complete the My Book Review form. You'll need to tell if you like or don't like the book and why. You must give a reason for why you like or don't like the book. Finally, you can tell if you would recommend the book to others.

Have students read a narrative or expository trade book of their choice. **Have** students complete My Book Review form when they are finished reading their book. **Model** how to complete the My Book Review form. **Guide** students as needed. **Have** students share their book reviews with the class as time permits.

Part C: Fluency Building

5 minutes

Student Materials:
Storybook 2

Conduct after the lesson, using story of the day.

Activity 1 Partner Reading

It's time for partner reading.
Direct students to the story of the day. **Assign** student partners as Partner 1 and Partner 2. **Monitor** student reading. **Guide** as needed.

Materials

Teacher: *Storybook 2;* 6-My Prediction Chart (from Lesson 110)

Student: *Storybook 2;* vocabulary notebook

Part A: Vocabulary Development

5 minutes

Student Materials:
Storybook 2

Vocabulary notebook

Activity 1 Learn New Vocabulary Word

Elicit responses to questions. **Guide** as needed.
Today you'll learn a new vocabulary word. **Appear. Appear** means **come into sight.** What does **appear** mean? *Come into sight.*

Another word for **come into sight** is **appear.** What's another word for **come into sight?** *Appear.*

We wait by the woods until the deer **come into sight.** We wait there until they **appear.**

What's another word for **come into sight?** *Appear.*
Discuss things that can appear and then disappear.

Write **appear** and what it means in your vocabulary notebook.
Direct students to write word in their vocabulary notebook. **Guide** as needed.

Activity 2 Review Vocabulary Word

Elicit responses to questions. **Guide** as needed.
What does **ram** mean? *Run into something hard.*
What's another word for **run into something hard?** *Ram.*

Review vocabulary words in appropriate context in *Storybook 2.*

Part B: Comprehension Strategies

12 minutes

IWB

Teacher Materials:
Storybook 2

My Prediction Chart

Student Materials:
Storybook 2

Activity 1 Confirm Predictions—An After-Reading Strategy

Refer to Story 110, pages 75–77.

Guide discussion based on recorded predictions made in Lesson 110. **Elicit** responses to questions. **Guide** as needed.
In the last lesson, you made some predictions about what would happen in the Boo story. You made the predictions before you read the story.

Why do you make predictions? (Idea: *Making predictions helps you understand the story better.*)

Now that you've read the story, let's check to see if your predictions were in the story. That's called confirming predictions.

What are you doing when you check to see if your predictions are correct? *Confirming predictions.*

Let's go over the predictions you made in the last lessons.

Was your prediction correct? (Student response.)

What part in the story helps you confirm your prediction? (Student response.)

Do all your predictions need to be correct? *No.*

Discuss value of making predictions with students.
Why is making predictions a good "before reading" strategy? (Idea: *As you read, your brain has to think about confirming the prediction.*)

Activity 2 Summarize—An After-Reading Strategy

Guide students to read the first four paragraphs on page 75, Story 110.

Elicit responses to questions. **Guide** as needed.
We'll work together to summarize the paragraph. First, you need to read the paragraphs. Think hard about what you're reading, because then we'll close the book and retell the main parts of the paragraphs in our own words.

I'll tell the first sentence of our summary. The ghosts found out they had to read to make the magic rod work.

You tell the next important idea of the paragraph in your own words. (Idea: *Boo got the rod and said he would try to read the words.*)

Fantastic! Summarizing in your own words is hard, but you're getting the hang of it.

Provide a reading center to display books being read so that students can enjoy them again during free time.

Part C: Fluency Building

5 minutes

Student Materials:
Storybook 2

Conduct after the lesson, using story of the day.

Activity 1 Partner Reading

It's time for partner reading.
Direct students to the story of the day. **Assign** student partners as Partner 1 and Partner 2. **Monitor** student reading. **Guide** as needed.

Lesson 112

Materials

Teacher: *Storybook 2*

Student: Vocabulary notebook; *Storybook 2*

Part A: Vocabulary Development

5 minutes

Student Materials:
Storybook 2

Vocabulary notebook

Activity 1 Learn New Vocabulary Word

Elicit responses to questions. **Guide** as needed.

Today you'll learn a new vocabulary word. **Puff. Puff** means **small amount.** What does **puff** mean? *Small amount.*

Another word for **small amount** is **puff.** What's another word for **small amount?** *Puff.*

When a genie comes out of a bottle, there is a **small amount** of smoke. There is a **puff** of smoke that comes out of the bottle.

What's another word for **small amount?** *Puff.*
Discuss what there might be a puff of.

Write **puff** and what it means in your vocabulary notebook.
Direct students to write word in their vocabulary notebook. **Guide** as needed.

Activity 2 Review Vocabulary Word

Elicit responses to questions. **Guide** as needed.
What does **appear** mean? *Come into sight.*
What's another word for **come into sight?** *Appear.*

Review vocabulary words in appropriate context in *Storybook 2.*

Part B: Comprehension Strategies

12 minutes

Teacher Materials:
Storybook 2

Student Materials:
Storybook 2

Activity 1 Put on a Play—A During-Reading Strategy

Refer to Stories 105–111, pages 60–80.

Today you can finish the play you started a few days ago. You have finished the Boo stories, so now you know the end of the story. First, we have to make some decisions.

Elicit responses to questions and choose students to play parts in the play.
What is the setting of the Boo story now? *The castle.*

Where will that be in our classroom? (Student response.)

Who is the main character in the story? *Boo.*

Who will play the part of Boo? (Student response.)

Who are the other characters in the story? (Idea: *Five mean ghosts, the monster, and the big green frog.*)

Who will play those parts? (Student response.)

I'll tell the story. Sometimes I'll tell you to say a part. You can move around to act out the story as I tell the story. Here we go.

Position actors appropriately. **Side-coach** by **retelling** the story and **prompting** students to move or say dialogue as appropriate. **Substitute** your words for retelling and prompting of the play, if you wish.

Sample Wording for Play

Boo wanted to help the big green frog who was really a king. (Prompt Boo to say something appropriate.) The frog told him there was a monster at his castle. (Prompt the frog to tell Boo what to do.) Boo went to the castle to try to get rid of the monster. (Prompt the monster to yell at Boo.) Boo thought it was the meanest-looking monster he had ever seen. The monster had a gold rod. (Prompt the monster to tell Boo he can cast spells with his rod.) Boo tried to scare the monster. (Prompt Boo to make a scary noise.) But Boo was still very small, and he didn't look mean. The monster cast a spell. (Prompt monster to say funny words.) Suddenly, Boo had a fish tail and a fin. Boo was scared, so he left the castle in a hurry. (Prompt Boo to leave.) Boo thought a long time and made a plan to get the gold rod from the monster. Boo went to the ghosts' house. (Prompt Boo to say the words that trick the ghosts into helping him scare the monster.) The five ghosts jumped up and went with Boo to the castle. (Prompt the ghosts and Boo to go to the castle.) All the ghosts worked together to scare the monster, who ran away. (Prompt the ghosts to scare the monster away.) Then the biggest ghost picked up the gold rod and turned himself into a red flower. (Prompt biggest ghost to drop gold rod and pose as a flower.) The next ghost grabbed the rod and turned himself into a leaf. (Prompt next ghost to drop rod and pose as a leaf.) The next ghost picked up the rod. (Prompt the next ghost to say he sees words on the rod. Prompt the other ghosts to tell him to read the words.) The ghost gave the rod to Boo because he could read. (Prompt Boo to turn the ghosts into nice ghosts and to make his tail and fins go away.) Then Boo went to the frog and turned him into a king. (Prompt the king to invite Boo to live with him.) Now, things are good in the land. The people have a good king. All the ghosts are good. And Boo lived with the king for many years.

Remind actors to take a bow. **Remind** the audience to <u>applaud</u> (a previous vocabulary word).

Part C: Fluency Building

Conduct after the lesson, using story of the day.

Activity 1 | Partner Reading

It's time for partner reading.

Direct students to the story of the day. **Assign** student partners as Partner 1 and Partner 2. **Monitor** student reading. **Guide** as needed.

Lesson 113

Materials

Teacher: Chart with comprehension reading strategies from Lesson 40: Part C; *Storybook 2*

Student: Vocabulary notebook; *Storybook 2*

Part A: Vocabulary Development

5 minutes

Student Materials:
Storybook 2

Vocabulary notebook

Activity 1 Learn New Vocabulary Word

Elicit responses to questions. **Guide** as needed.
Today you'll learn a new vocabulary word. **Test. Test** means **questions to find out what you know.** What does **test** mean? *Questions to find out what you know.*

Another word for **questions to find out what you know** is **test.** What's another word for **questions to find out what you know?** *Test.*

The teacher asked you some **questions to find out what you know** about animals. The teacher gave you a **test.**

What's another word for **questions to find out what you know?** *Test.*
Discuss tests and why students have them.

Write **test** and what it means in your vocabulary notebook.
Direct students to write word in their vocabulary notebook. **Guide** as needed.

Activity 2 Review Vocabulary Word

Elicit responses to questions. **Guide** as needed.
What does **puff** mean? *Small amount.*
What's another word for **small amount?** *Puff.*

Review vocabulary words in appropriate context in *Storybook 2.*

Part B: Comprehension Strategies

12 minutes

Teacher Materials:
Chart with comprehension strategies

Activity 1 Review Before-Reading Strategies—A Before-Reading Strategy

Reference comprehension-strategies chart developed in Lesson 40. **Elicit** responses to questions. **Guide** as needed.
Before you read, there are some strategies you can use to help you understand what you read. Setting a purpose for reading is one great way to get ready to understand what you read.

What's it called when you think about why you're reading before you read? *Setting a purpose.*

Think of a time when you set a purpose for reading. What did you do? (Student response.)

Making predictions is another great strategy when you're getting ready to read.

What do you do when you make predictions? (Idea: *Look at the title and the picture for clues to what the story is about, and then tell what I think will happen.*)

Think of a time when you made a prediction. What did you do? (Student response.)

Activating background knowledge is a third strategy to use before reading. What do you do when you activate your schema? (Idea: *Think of everything I know about a topic.*)

Why is it a good idea to think about what you know about a topic before you read a new story? (Idea: *Then you can connect what you know to the new information that you learn when you read.*)

Think of a time when you activated your schema. What did you do? (Student response.)

These are great ideas to help make sure you think about what you're going to read before you read.

Part C: Fluency Building

5 minutes

Student Materials:
Storybook 2

Conduct after the lesson, using story of the day.

Activity 1 Partner Reading

It's time for partner reading.
Direct students to the story of the day. **Assign** student partners as Partner 1 and Partner 2. **Monitor** student reading. **Guide** as needed.

Lesson 114

Materials

Teacher: 10-KWL Chart; expository text on topic of teacher choice; *Storybook 2*

Student: Vocabulary review; *Storybook 2*

Part A: Vocabulary Development

5 minutes

Student Materials:
Storybook 2

Vocabulary notebook

Activity 1 — Learn New Vocabulary Word

Elicit responses to questions. **Guide** as needed.

Today you'll learn a new vocabulary word. **Disappear. Disappear** means **go out of sight.** What does **disappear** mean? *Go out of sight.*

Another word for **go out of sight** is **disappear.** What's another word for **go out of sight?** *Disappear.*

Sydney watched the balloon **go out of sight** as it floated away in the wind. "The balloon will soon **disappear,"** she thought to herself.

What's another word for **go out of sight?** *Disappear.*
Discuss things that appear and then disappear.

Write **disappear** and what it means in your vocabulary notebook.
Direct students to write word in their vocabulary notebook. **Guide** as needed.

Activity 2 — Review Vocabulary Word

Elicit responses to questions. **Guide** as needed.
What does **test** mean? *Questions to find out what you know.*
What's another word for **questions to find out what you know?** *Test.*

Review vocabulary words in appropriate context in *Storybook 2.*

Part B: Comprehension Strategies

12 minutes

IWB

Teacher Materials:
KWL Chart

Expository text

Activity 1 — KWL Chart for Expository Text—A Before-Reading Strategy

Show KWL Chart. **Elicit** responses to questions. **Guide** as needed.

Here is a KWL chart that you can use when you are reading expository text.

What kind of text teaches you new information? (Idea: *To help organize and remember information.*)

Why do you use a KWL chart? (Idea: *To help organize and remember information.*)

What do you write in the "K" section? (Idea: *You list your schema, or what is already in your brain about the topic of your book.*)

What do you write in the "W" section? (Idea: *Questions you have and things you want to know.*)

What do you write in the "L" section? (Idea: *What you learned about the topic from the book after you read.*)

We'll read a nonfiction or expository text on _____. Before we read this book, we'll fill out the first two sections of the KWL Chart. Why will we read this book? (Idea: *To learn more about _____.*)

Elicit list of things to write in the "What I Know" column. **Guide** as needed.
Let's think of some things you know about _____ and write them on the chart in the "K" section.

Elicit list of things to write in the "What I Want to Know" column.
Let's think of some things you want to know about _____ and write them on the chart in the "W" section.

The last section has a place to list what you learned about the topic from the book after you read. We'll fill out this section after we read the book.

When you make organized lists or fill out charts like this, it helps you remember what you learned about a topic from a book.

Save chart to complete in Lesson 115.

Part C: Fluency Building

5 minutes

Student Materials:
Storybook 2

Conduct after the lesson, using story of the day.

Activity 1 Partner Reading

It's time for partner reading.
Direct students to the story of the day. **Assign** student partners as Partner 1 and Partner 2. **Monitor** student reading. **Guide** as needed.

Lesson 115

Materials

Teacher: 10-KWL Chart (from Lesson 114); expository book on a topic of teacher choice; *Storybook 2*, 2-Vocabulary Acquisition and Use, Writing Prompts, 5-My Writing Checklist

Student: Vocabulary review; *Storybook 2*, Copy of 2-Vocabulary Acquisition and Use and 5-My Writing Checklist; Lined Paper

Part A: Vocabulary Development

5 minutes

IWB

Teacher Materials:
Vocabulary Acquisition and Use

Student Materials:
Storybooks 2

Vocabulary notebook

Vocabulary Acquisition and Use

Activity 1 Vocabulary Notebook Review

Today you'll study from your vocabulary notebook. Studying your words and what they mean will help you know your words even better. You'll study the four words we studied this week.

Guide students as they study <u>appear</u>, <u>puff</u>, <u>test</u>, and <u>disappear</u>.

Activity 2 Cumulative Vocabulary Review

Elicit responses to questions. **Guide** as needed.
Directions: Listen and tell me the correct vocabulary word for each question.

What's another word for **small amount?** *Puff*.
What's another word for **come into sight?** *Appear*.
What's another word for **go out of sight?** *Disappear*.
What's another word for **questions to find out what you know?** *Test*.

Repeat difficult words as needed.

Review vocabulary words in appropriate context in *Storybook 2*.

Activity 3 Vocabulary Acquisition and Use

Display Vocabulary Acquisition and Use. **Have** students work with a neighbor to complete Vocabulary Acquisition and Use.
Today's vocabulary words are _____ and _____ [and _____ and _____].
Vocabulary words: **yelled** and **screamed; smiling** and **grinning**
Write the words on the lines provided. Then write the words in the boxes based on whether you think each word is less/smaller or more/larger than the other word. Below the boxes, write why you think word 1 is less/smaller and word 2 is more/larger than word 1.
Repeat for words 3 and 4. **Have** students share what they wrote. **Discuss** examples of how these words might be used.

12 minutes

IWB

Teacher Materials:
KWL Chart

Expository text

Activity 1 Set a Purpose for Reading—A Before-Reading Strategy

Today you'll hear a book about _____. When you read this kind of story, you're getting ready to learn something new.

What do you call this kind of text? *Expository text.*

How is expository text organized? (Idea: *Around topics or ideas.*)

What kinds of things do you find in expository text? (Idea: *Headings, captions, labels, lists, table of contents, photographs, and index.*)

The expository text we'll read today is organized around the topic of _____. It will give you information that is true about _____.

Why will we read about _____ today? (Idea: *To learn something new about _____.*)

Read expository text of choice. **Note** features of expository text as you read, such as headings, captions, labels, lists, table of contents, photographs, and index.

Activity 2 KWL Chart—An After-Reading Strategy

Show KWL Chart from Lesson 114. **Review** first two columns.
In the last lesson, we filled in two columns of our chart.

Elicit responses to fill in the "What I Learned" column.
Now we're ready to fill in the last column. We read _____ to learn something new about _____. Now let's make a list of all the new things we learned.

This chart is a great way to organize what you already know, what you want to know, and what you learned.

What is the name of the chart that helps you organize information from an expository text? *A KWL chart.*

Provide a reading center to display books being read so that students can enjoy them again during free time.

Part C: Fluency Building

Conduct after the lesson, using story of the day.

Activity 1 | Partner Reading

It's time for partner reading.

Direct students to the story of the day. **Assign** student partners as Partner 1 and Partner 2. **Monitor** student reading. **Guide** as needed.

Part D: Writing/Language Arts

10 minutes

IWB

Teacher Materials:
Writing Prompts

My Writing Checklist

Student Materials:
Lined Paper

My Writing Checklist

Activity 1 | Write and Use Parts of Speech and Conventions

Time to write using a writing prompt based on the stories we've been reading.

Assign student partners. **Distribute** lined paper to students. **Display** writing prompts and have students choose one to write about or assign a writing prompt of your choice. **Review** parts of speech and punctuation as well as the writing checklist with students. **Tell** students to write one paragraph (minimum of four sentences per paragraph) on their own to answer the writing prompt. **Tell** them to use their writing checklist (first column labeled "Did I use them?") to ensure they include important parts of speech or punctuation in their writing. **Tell** students which parts of speech or punctuation to focus on, if you wish. **Model** what it means to answer a writing prompt and to use the writing checklist during and after the writing process, as needed. **Monitor** and guide students as needed. **Model** what it means to have a neighbor look over his or her neighbor's writing and to complete the writing checklist (second column labeled "Did my neighbor use them?"), as needed. **Have** students share what they wrote as time permits.

Writing Prompt 1	Writing Prompt 2	Writing Prompt 3
Tell me about a plan that you developed that worked.	If someone is mean or sad, what might you do to make him or her happy again?	If you could make one wish of a genie, what would that wish be?

Lesson 116

Materials

Teacher: Chart paper or IWB; sticky notes; *Storybook 2*

Student: *Storybook 2;* vocabulary notebook

Part A: Vocabulary Development

5 minutes

Student Materials:
Storybook 2

Vocabulary notebook

Activity 1 Learn New Vocabulary Word

Elicit responses to questions. **Guide** as needed.
Today you'll learn a new vocabulary word. **Serve. Serve** means **give something that someone wants.** What does **serve** mean? *Give something that someone wants.*

Another word for **give something that someone wants** is **serve.** What's another word for **give something that someone wants?** *Serve.*

I need to **give something** to my little brother **that he wants.** I need to **serve** a sandwich and chips to my little brother, because he asked me to make him lunch.

What's another word for **give something that someone wants?** *Serve.*
Discuss what you can serve and who can serve you.

Write **serve** and what it means in your vocabulary notebook.
Direct students to write word in their vocabulary notebook. **Guide** as needed.

Activity 2 Review Vocabulary Word

Elicit responses to questions. **Guide** as needed.
What does **disappear** mean? *Go out of sight.*
What's another word for **go out of sight?** *Disappear.*

Review vocabulary words in appropriate context in *Storybook 2.*

12 minutes

Teacher Materials:
Storybook 2

Chart paper/IWB

Sticky notes

Student Materials:
Storybook 2

Activity 1 Generate Questions—A During-Reading Strategy

Refer to Story 115, pages 90–92.

Asking questions is a strategy to use when you are reading stories.

Why do you ask questions when you're reading? *To understand the story better.*

Draw chart on paper/IWB for posting sentence and question notes. **Elicit** responses to questions. **Guide** as needed.
You have practiced asking questions for a long time. Today you're going to work with a partner to find a sentence in the story and think up some questions about that sentence. You'll write your sentence on a sticky note. Then you'll write questions on other sticky notes. When you and your partner are finished, you can bring me your notes, and we'll post them on our chart.

Post a sticky note with sentences on one side of the chart and the sticky notes with the questions on the other side of the chart across from the sentence.

Sample Chart for Questions	
Sentences	**Questions**

Discuss sentences chosen and questions generated. **Share** with class examples of good questions. **Choose** some of the questions generated. **Elicit** responses to these questions.

Part C: Fluency Building

5 minutes

Student Materials:
Storybook 2

Conduct after the lesson, using story of the day.

Activity 1 Partner Reading

It's time for partner reading.
Direct students to the story of the day. **Assign** student partners as Partner 1 and Partner 2. **Monitor** student reading. **Guide** as needed.

Lesson 117

Materials

Teacher: Chart with comprehension reading strategies from Lesson 40: Part C; *Storybook 2*

Student: Vocabulary notebook; *Storybook 2*

Part A: Vocabulary Development

5 minutes

Student Materials:
Storybook 2
Vocabulary notebook

Activity 1   Learn New Vocabulary Word

Elicit responses to questions. **Guide** as needed.
Today you'll learn a new vocabulary word. **Promptly. Promptly** means **quickly.** What does **promptly** mean? *Quickly.*

Another word for **quickly** is **promptly.** What's another word for **quickly?** *Promptly.*

Juan had to go to class **quickly** so he would not be late. He made it to class **promptly.**

What's another word for **quickly?** *Promptly.*
Discuss times when you have to make it to places promptly.

Write **promptly** and what it means in your vocabulary notebook.
Direct students to write word in their vocabulary notebook. **Guide** as needed.

Activity 2   Review Vocabulary Word

Elicit responses to questions. **Guide** as needed.
What does **serve** mean? *Give something that someone wants.*
What's another word for **give something that someone wants?** *Serve.*

Review vocabulary words in appropriate context in *Storybook 2.*

Part B: Comprehension Strategies

12 minutes

Teacher Materials:
Chart with comprehension strategies

Activity 1   Review After-Reading Strategies—An After-Reading Strategy

Reference comprehension-strategies chart developed in Lesson 40. **Elicit** responses to questions. **Guide** as needed.
Let's talk about things we do after we read to help us understand narrative text better. One thing you've done after reading to help you make sure you understand what you read is to fill out a Narrative Story Map.

What are you thinking about when you fill out a Narrative Story Map? (Idea: *Story elements like characters, setting, problem, beginning, middle, and end.*)

Think of a time when you filled out a Narrative Story Map. What did you do? (Student response.)

After filling out a Story Map, you retold the story. What do you do when you retell the story? (Idea: *Tell the story in my own words.*)

What is another word for "tell the story in your own words?" (Idea: *Summarize.*)

What do you do when you summarize? (Idea: *Tell the story in my own words.*)

Another thing you've done after reading is confirm predictions. What do you do when you confirm predictions? (Idea: *Check to see if what I thought was going to happen did.*)

Think of a time when you've confirmed a prediction. What did you do? Student response.

Sometimes you make text-to-text connections. What do you do when you make text-to-text connections? (Idea: *Tell how two stories are the same and different.*)

Think of a time you made a text-to-text connection. What did you do? (Student response.)

You have also made text-to-self connections. What do you do when you make text-to-self connections? (Idea: *Think about how the story connects to my experience.*)

Think of a time you made a text-to-self connection. What did you do? (Student response.)

You have used another chart to organize your thinking when you read expository text. Who knows the name of the chart? *KWL Chart.*

Think of a time you used a KWL Chart. What did you do? (Student response.)

You have reviewed lots of great things to do after reading to help make sure you understand what you read. Congratulations!

Part C: Fluency Building

5 minutes

Student Materials:
Storybook 2

Conduct after the lesson, using story of the day.

Activity 1 Partner Reading

It's time for partner reading.
Direct students to the story of the day. **Assign** student partners as Partner 1 and Partner 2. **Monitor** student reading. **Guide** as needed.

Lesson 118

Materials

Teacher: *Storybook 2*

Student: *Storybook 2*; vocabulary notebook

Part A: Vocabulary Development

5 minutes

Student Materials:
Storybook 2

Vocabulary notebook

Activity 1 Learn New Vocabulary Word

Elicit responses to questions. **Guide** as needed.
Today you'll learn a new vocabulary word. **Wise. Wise** means **very smart.**
What does **wise** mean? *Very smart.*

Another word for **very smart** is **wise.** What's another word for **very smart?** *Wise.*

Cameron wanted to learn about dinosaurs, so he talked with a **very smart** woman who worked at the museum. This woman was **wise** about dinosaurs.

What's another word for **very smart?** *Wise.*
Discuss what makes someone wise.

Write **wise** and what it means in your vocabulary notebook.
Direct students to write word in their vocabulary notebook. **Guide** as needed.

Activity 2 Review Vocabulary Word

Elicit responses to questions. **Guide** as needed.
What does **promptly** mean? *Quickly.*
What's another word for **quickly?** *Promptly.*

Review vocabulary words in appropriate context in *Storybook 2*.

Part B: Comprehension Strategies

12 minutes

Teacher Materials:
Storybook 2

Student Materials:
Storybook 2

Activity 1 Set a Purpose—A Before-Reading Strategy

Elicit responses. **Guide** as needed.
You get smart at reading when you think before you read about why you are reading the story. That is called setting a purpose for reading.

What's it called when you think about why you are reading before you read? *Setting a purpose.*

Today you're going to read the first paragraph on page 96 so that you can summarize it.

What do you do when you summarize? (Idea: *Tell the main ideas of a story in your own words.*)

Activity 2 Summarize—An After-Reading Strategy

Guide students to read the first paragraph on page 96 in Story 117.

Elicit responses to questions. **Guide** as needed.
We'll work together to summarize the paragraph. First you need to read the paragraph. Think hard about what you are reading because then we'll close the book and retell the main parts of the paragraph.

I'll tell the first sentence of our summary. Carla and Ott were in the forest, and Ott failed to get Carla a hot dog.

You tell the next important idea of the paragraph in your own words. (Idea: *Carla asked Ott if he could call for help.*)

Nice job summarizing the paragraph.

Part C: Fluency Building

5 minutes

Student Materials:
Storybook 2

Conduct after the lesson, using story of the day.

Activity 1 Partner Reading

It's time for partner reading.
Direct students to the story of the day. **Assign** student partners as Partner 1 and Partner 2. **Monitor** student reading. **Guide** as needed.

Lesson 119

Materials

Teacher: *Storybook 2*

Student: *Storybook 2*; vocabulary notebook

Part A: Vocabulary Development

5 minutes

Student Materials:
Storybook 2

Vocabulary notebook

Activity 1 Learn New Vocabulary Word

Elicit responses to questions. **Guide** as needed.
Today you'll learn a new vocabulary word. **Toss. Toss** means **throw.**
What does **toss** mean? *Throw.*

Another word for **throw** is **toss.** What's another word for **throw?** *Toss.*

At recess the kids like to **throw** the ball to each other. They **toss** the ball
back and forth until recess is over.

What's another word for **throw?** *Toss.*
Discuss things you can toss.

Write **toss** and what it means in your vocabulary notebook.
Direct students to write word in their vocabulary notebook. **Guide** as needed.

Activity 2 Review Vocabulary Word

Elicit responses to questions. **Guide** as needed.
What does **wise** mean? *Very smart.*
What's another word for **very smart?** *Wise.*

Review vocabulary words in appropriate context in *Storybook 2.*

12 minutes

Teacher Materials:
Storybook 2

Student Materials:
Storybook 2

Activity 1 Text-to-Self Connections—An After-Reading Strategy

Refer to Story 118, pages 99–101.

One way to understand stories better is to make text-to-self connections. What do you do when you make text-to-self connections? (Idea: *Connect your own experiences with a story you read.*)

Read the first page of the story to prepare for text-to-self connection. **Elicit** responses to questions.

Discuss personal experience connections that students can make to the story. **Guide** as needed.

Does this part of the Carla and Ott story make you think of any experience you've ever had? (Student response.)

Have you ever felt sad? Embarrassed? (Student response.)

Have you ever made a mistake and then felt bad? (Student response.)

Have you ever had tears running down your cheeks? (Student response.)

Have you ever told a lie? (Student response.)

How does your experience help you understand Ott? (Student response.)

Remember: When you connect something that has happened to you to something that happens in the story, you're making text-to-self connections. Thinking about your experiences when you read is a good strategy to help you understand what you read.

Activity 2 —An After-Reading Strategy

Refer to Story 118, pages 99–101.

Elicit responses to questions. **Guide** as needed.
What do you call it when you make pictures of what you are reading in your brain? *Mental imaging.*

When you make pictures in your brain while you read, you "see" what the story is telling in words. The words might also make you "feel" what the character is feeling.

Choose a sentence from Story 118, "Ott Disappears." Read the sentence to your partner. Then get a picture in your mind of that sentence.
Guide student partners to find a sentence that makes them have a picture in their brain. **Encourage** them to share their pictures with partner.

What picture do you see in your brain when you read that sentence? (Student response.)

Does the sentence make you have any feelings? (Student response.) Tell your partner what you see or feel.

Now your partner should find a sentence, read the sentence, and then tell you the picture he or she sees in his or her brain or the feeling he or she feels.

Share with the class the sentence you chose, and tell the picture you saw in your brain or the feelings you felt.

Part C: Fluency Building

5 minutes

Student Materials:
Storybook 2

Conduct after the lesson, using story of the day.

Activity 1 Partner Reading

It's time for partner reading.

Direct students to the story of the day. **Assign** student partners as Partner 1 and Partner 2. **Monitor** student reading. **Guide** as needed.

Lesson 120

Materials

Teacher: Chart with comprehension reading strategies from Lesson 40: Part C; *Storybook 2*, 2-Vocabulary Acquisition and Use, 3-My Book Review

Student: Vocabulary notebook; *Storybook 2*, Copy of 2-Vocabulary Acquisition and Use and 3-My Book Review

Part A: Vocabulary Development

5 minutes

IWB

Teacher Materials:
Vocabulary Acquisition and Use

Student Materials:
Storybook 2

Vocabulary Notebook

Vocabulary Acquisition and Use

Activity 1 Vocabulary Notebook Review

Today you'll study from your vocabulary notebook. Studying your words and what they mean will help you know your words even better. You'll study the eight words we studied this week.

Guide students as they study <u>appear</u>, <u>puff</u>, <u>test</u>, <u>disappear</u>, <u>serve</u>, <u>promptly</u>, <u>wise</u>, and <u>toss</u>.

Activity 2 Cumulative Vocabulary Review

Elicit responses to questions. **Guide** as needed.
Directions: Listen and tell me the correct vocabulary word for each question.

What's another word for **come into sight?** *Appear.*
What's another word for **throw?** *Toss.*
What's another word for **quickly?** *Promptly.*
What's another word for **small amount?** *Puff.*
What's another word for **very smart?** *Wise.*
What's another word for **give something that someone wants?** *Serve.*
What's another word for **go out of sight?** *Disappear.*
What's another word for **questions to find out what you know?** *Test.*

Repeat difficult words as needed.

Review vocabulary words in appropriate context in *Storybook 2*.

Activity 3 Vocabulary Acquisition and Use

Display Vocabulary Acquisition and Use. **Have** students work with a neighbor to complete Vocabulary Acquisition and Use.
Today's vocabulary words are _____ and _____ [and _____ and _____].
Vocabulary words: **wise** and **smart; toss** and **throw**
Write the words on the lines provided. Then write the words in the boxes based on whether you think each word is less/smaller or more/larger than the other word. Below the boxes, write why you think word 1 is less/smaller and word 2 is more/larger than word 1.
Repeat for words 3 and 4. **Have** students share what they wrote. **Discuss** examples of how these words might be used.

12 minutes

Teacher Materials:
Storybook 2

My Book Review

Chart with comprehension strategies

Student Materials:
Storybook 2

My Book Review

Let's talk about things you've learned to do before, during, and after you read to help you understand narrative text better.

Record comprehension strategies on a chart, if desired (see chart developed in Lesson 40). If chart is made, you can reference it during later lessons to identify strategy being used. Chart can also be updated as lessons proceed.

Activity 1 Review—Before-Reading Strategies

Let's talk about things you do before you read to help you understand narrative text better.

Discuss strategies that students have been using before reading narratives. **Identify** examples of when the strategy was used.
What are some things to do before you read a new story? (Ideas: *Make predictions*—**Make Predictions**—*and think about how the story connects to what I already know*—**Activate Background Knowledge**—*or think about what I will try to learn*—**Set Purpose for Reading**—*fill out the "K" and "W" section of KWL Chart for expository text.*)

Activity 2 Review—During-Reading Strategies

Let's talk about things you do while you read to help you understand narrative textbetter.

Discuss strategies that students have been using during reading narratives. **Identify** examples of when the strategy was used.
What are some things you can do while you're reading to help you understand what you are reading? (Idea: *Ask questions*—**Generate Questions**—*reread*—**Fix-Up Strategy**—*tell the story in my own words*—**Summarize**—*read while paying attention the ends of sentences or dialogue*—**Read with Prosody**—*and make pictures in my mind of the story*—**Mental Imaging.**)

Activity 3 Review—After-Reading Strategies

Let's talk about things we do after we read to help us understand narrative text better.

Discuss strategies that students have been using after reading narratives. **Identify** examples of when the strategy was used.
What are some things you can do after you read a story to help you understand or remember the story? (Ideas: *Fill out a story map*—**Identify Story Elements**—*see if predictions were correct*—**Confirming Predictions**—*make text-to-self connections; make text-to-text connections; retell the story; tell main points of story in own words*—**Summarize**—*and fill out the "L" section of KWL Chart.*)

Wow, you've learned a lot about things to do to help you understand the stories you read. When you understand what you read, you have good comprehension. Understanding what you read is really important.

Activity 4 Develop Opinions—An After-Reading Strategy

Today we'll found out your opinion or how you feel about the stories you read. You will choose a book to read and then complete the My Book Review form. You'll need to tell if you like or don't like the book and why. You must give a reason for why you like or don't like the book. Finally, you can tell if you would recommend the book to others.

Have students read a narrative or expository trade book of their choice. **Have** students complete My Book Review form when they are finished reading their book. **Model** how to complete the My Book Review form. **Guide** students as needed. **Have** students share their book reviews with the class as time permits.

Part C: Fluency Building

5 minutes

Student Materials:
Storybook 2

Conduct after the lesson, using story of the day.

Activity 1 Partner Reading

It's time for partner reading.

Direct students to the story of the day. **Assign** student partners as Partner 1 and Partner 2. **Monitor** student reading. **Guide** as needed.

Lesson 121

Materials

Teacher: *Storybook 2*

Student: *Storybook 2;* sticky notes; vocabulary notebook

Part A: Vocabulary Development

5 minutes

Student Materials:
Storybook 2

Vocabulary notebook

Activity 1 | Learn New Vocabulary Word

Elicit responses to questions. **Guide** as needed.
Today you'll learn a new vocabulary word. **Remember. Remember** means **keep in mind.** What does **remember** mean? *Keep in mind.*

Another word for **keep in mind** is **remember.** What's another word for **keep in mind?** *Remember.*

When I hear a new word, I **keep it in mind.** I **remember** the new word.

What's another word for **keep in mind?** *Remember.*
Discuss things students try to remember.

Write **remember** and what it means in your vocabulary notebook.
Direct students to write word in their vocabulary notebook. **Guide** as needed.

Activity 2 | Review Vocabulary Word

Elicit responses to questions. **Guide** as needed.
What does **toss** mean? *Throw.*
What's another word for **throw?** *Toss.*

Review vocabulary words in appropriate context in *Storybook 2.*

Part B: Comprehension Strategies

12 minutes

Teacher Materials:
Storybook 2

Student Materials:
Storybook 2

Sticky notes

Activity 1 | Set a Purpose to Read—A Before-Reading Strategy

Elicit responses to questions. **Guide** as needed.
What's it called when you figure out why you're reading before you read? (Idea: *Setting a purpose.*)

Today your purpose while you read is to make mental images. As you read, you'll try to "see" or "feel" the words in the story.

Activity 2 Mental Imaging—A During-Reading Strategy

Elicit responses to questions. **Guide** as needed.
What do you call it when you make pictures of what you're reading in your brain? *Mental imaging.*

When you make pictures in your brain while you read, you "see" what the story is telling in words. The words might also make you "feel" what the character is feeling.

Guide students to read Story 120, pages 105 and 106, and to record mental images on sticky notes.

Read the story, and mark the sentence with a sticky note when you have a mental image. Draw a quick sketch on the sticky note to remind you what your mental image was. Stick it in your book next to the sentence that that gave you the mental image. When you're finished, we'll share our mental images with the class.

Discuss sentence chosen and mental images developed. **Guide** as needed.
Share with the class the sentence you chose, and tell the picture you saw in your brain or the feelings you felt.

Part C: Fluency Building

5 minutes

Student Materials:
Storybook 2

Conduct after the lesson, using story of the day.

Activity 1 Partner Reading

It's time for partner reading.
Direct students to the story of the day. **Assign** student partners as Partner 1 and Partner 2. **Monitor** student reading. **Guide** as needed.

Lesson 122

Part A: Vocabulary Development

5 minutes

Student Materials:
Storybook 2

Vocabulary notebook

Activity 1 Learn New Vocabulary Word

Elicit responses to questions. **Guide** as needed.
Today you'll learn a new vocabulary word. **Human. Human** means **man, woman, or child.** What does **human** mean? *Man, woman, or child.*

Another word for **man, woman, or child** is **human.** What's another word for **man, woman, or child?** *Human.*

In the story about Ott and Carla, the kids in genie school didn't think that a **man, woman, or child** could do the simplest of tricks. They didn't think a **human** was smart.

What's another word for **man, woman, or child?** *Human.*
Discuss what it means to be a human.

Write **human** and what it means in your vocabulary notebook.
Direct students to write word in their vocabulary notebook. **Guide** as needed.

Activity 2 Review Vocabulary Word

Elicit responses to questions. **Guide** as needed.
What does **remember** mean? *Keep in mind.*
What's another word for **keep in mind?** *Remember.*

Review vocabulary words in appropriate context in *Storybook 2.*

Part B: Comprehension Strategies

Teacher Materials:
Storybook 2

Chart paper/IWB

Student Materials:
Storybook 2

Sticky notes

Activity 1 Generate Questions—A During-Reading Strategy

Refer to Story 121, pages 107–109.

Asking questions is a strategy to use when you're reading stories.

Why do you ask questions when you're reading? *To understand the story better.*

Draw chart (on paper or IWB) for posting sentence and question notes. **Elicit** responses to questions. **Guide** as needed.
You have practiced asking questions for a long time. Today you're going to work to find a sentence in the story and think up some questions about that sentence by yourself. You'll write your sentence on a sticky note. Then you'll write questions on other sticky notes. When you're finished, you can bring me your notes and we'll post them on our chart.

Post a sticky note with sentences on one side of the chart and the sticky notes with the questions on the other side of the chart, across from the sentence.

Sample Chart for Questions	
Sentences	**Questions**
☐	☐ ☐ ☐

Discuss sentences chosen and questions generated. **Share** examples of good questions.

Choose some of the questions generated, and **elicit** responses.
Answer the questions. (Sample response.)

Part C: Fluency Building

Conduct after the lesson, using story of the day.

Activity 1 Partner Reading

It's time for partner reading.
Direct students to the story of the day. **Assign** student partners as Partner 1 and Partner 2. **Monitor** student reading. **Guide** as needed.

Lesson 123

Materials

Teacher: *Storybook 2*

Student: *Storybook 2*; vocabulary notebook

Part A: Vocabulary Development

5 minutes

Student Materials:
Storybook 2

Vocabulary notebook

Activity 1 Learn New Vocabulary Word

Elicit responses to questions. **Guide** as needed.
Today you'll learn a new vocabulary word. **Instant. Instant** means **short time.** What does **instant** mean? *Short time.*

Another word for **short time** is **instant.** What's another word for **short time?** *Instant.*

The genie appeared in a **short time.** The genie appeared in an **instant.**

What's another word for **short time?** *Instant.*
Discuss things that could be done in an instant.

Write **instant** and what it means in your vocabulary notebook.
Direct students to write word in their vocabulary notebook. **Guide** as needed.

Activity 2 Review Vocabulary Word

Elicit responses to questions. **Guide** as needed.
What does **human** mean? *Man, woman, or child.*
What's another word for **man, woman, or child?** *Human.*

Review vocabulary words in appropriate context in *Storybook 2.*

Part B: Comprehension Strategies

12 minutes

Teacher Materials:
Storybook 2

Student Materials:
Storybook 2

Activity 1 Set a Purpose—A Before-Reading Strategy

Elicit responses to questions. **Guide** as needed.
You get smart at reading when you think before you read about why you're reading the story. That's called setting a purpose for reading.

What's it called when you think about why you're reading before you read?
Setting a purpose.

Today you're going to read the first paragraph on page 110 so that you can summarize it.

What do you do when you summarize? (Idea: *Tell the main ideas of a story in your own words.*)

Activity 2 Summarize—An After-Reading Strategy

Guide students to read the first paragraph on page 110 in Story 122.

First you need to read the paragraph. Think hard about what you're reading because then you'll close the book and work with a partner to retell the main parts of the paragraph. When you think you can retell the main ideas, write your words down so you can remember your ideas. Then you and your partner can share the words of your summary with us.

Elicit responses for summaries and **discuss** fix-ups. **Guide** as needed.

Summarizing paragraphs is very hard work. It takes lots of practice. Keep trying until you know how to do it.

Part C: Fluency Building

5 minutes

Student Materials:
Storybook 2

Conduct after the lesson, using story of the day.

Activity 1 Partner Reading

It's time for partner reading.

Direct students to the story of the day. **Assign** student partners as Partner 1 and Partner 2. **Monitor** student reading. **Guide** as needed.

Lesson 124

Materials

Teacher: *Storybook 2*

Student: *Storybook 2;* vocabulary notebook

Part A: Vocabulary Development

5 minutes

Student Materials:
Storybook 2

Vocabulary notebook

Activity 1 Learn New Vocabulary Word

Elicit responses to questions. **Guide** as needed.
Today you'll learn a new vocabulary word. **Vow. Vow** means **promise.**
What does **vow** mean? *Promise.*

Another word for **promise** is **vow.** What's another word for **promise?** *Vow.*

When the big day came, Carla needed to make a **promise** to become a genie.
She realized that she didn't want to be a genie, so she didn't take the **vow.**

What's another word for **promise?** *Vow.*
Discuss what a vow is and when a vow might be made.

Write **vow** and what it means in your vocabulary notebook.
Direct students to write word in their vocabulary notebook. **Guide** as needed.

Activity 2 Review Vocabulary Word

Elicit responses to questions. **Guide** as needed.
What does **instant** mean? *Short time.*
What's another word for **short time?** *Instant.*

Review vocabulary words in appropriate context in *Storybook 2.*

Part B: Comprehension Strategies

12 minutes

Teacher Materials:
Storybook 2

Student Materials:
Storybook 2

Activity 1 Read with Prosody (Dialogue)—A During-Reading Strategy

Direct students to Story 123, pages 113–115.

Elicit responses to questions. **Guide** as needed.
Dialogue is what characters say in a story. Narratives have lots of dialogue.
How is dialogue marked in stories? (Idea: *With quotation marks.*)

What is dialogue? (Idea: *The words characters say in the story.*)

Lesson 124 **353**

This is the story "Carla Goes to Genie School." I want you to find the dialogue for the characters. You will look for the words Carla says, the words the old genie says, and the words for the narrator that aren't in quotation marks.

Group students into groups of 3, and **provide** guidance as needed while they find the dialogue. **Monitor** groups as they review the story and practice dialogue. **Encourage** students to perform the dialogue in front of the class, after practice. Your turn to read the story with three people. Try to read with expression. Decide who will read which part. The quotation marks will help you know when it is your turn. Take turns, and try to make the dialogue interesting.

Part C: Fluency Building

5 minutes

Student Materials:
Storybook 2

Conduct after the lesson, using story of the day.

Activity 1 **Partner Reading**

It's time for partner reading.
Direct students to the story of the day. **Assign** student partners as Partner 1 and Partner 2. **Monitor** student reading. **Guide** as needed.

Lesson 125

Part A: Vocabulary Development

5 minutes

IWB

Teacher Materials:
Vocabulary Acquisition and Use

Student Materials:
Storybook 2

Vocabulary notebook

Vocabulary Acquisition and Use

Activity 1 Vocabulary Notebook Review

Today you'll study from your vocabulary notebook. Studying your words and what they mean will help you know your words even better. You'll study the four words we studied this week.

Guide students as they study remember, human, instant, and vow.

Activity 2 Cumulative Vocabulary Review

Elicit responses to questions. **Guide** as needed.
Directions: Listen and tell me the correct vocabulary word for each question.

What's another word for **short time?** *Instant.*
What's another word for **keep in mind?** *Remember.*
What's another word for **man, woman, or child?** *Human.*
What's another word for **vow?** *Promise.*

Repeat difficult words as needed.

Review vocabulary words in appropriate context in *Storybook 2*.

Activity 3 Vocabulary Acquisition and Use

Display Vocabulary Acquisition and Use. **Have** students work with a neighbor to complete Vocabulary Acquisition and Use.
Today's vocabulary words are _____ and _____ [and _____ and _____].
Vocabulary words: **folded** and **crossed; bad** and **terrible**
Write the words on the lines provided. Then write the words in the boxes based on whether you think each word is less/smaller or more/larger than the other word. Below the boxes, write why you think word 1 is less/smaller and word 2 is more/larger than word 1.
Repeat for words 3 and 4. **Have** students share what they wrote. **Discuss** examples of how these words might be used.

Part B: Comprehension Strategies

Activity 1 Set a Purpose for Reading—A Before-Reading Strategy

Elicit responses to questions. **Guide** as needed.
Today we'll read this book about _____.

What kind of text do you think it is? (Idea: *Expository text.*)

Why do you think it is expository text? (Sample response.)

How will this book be organized? (Idea: *It will tell all about the topic of _____.*)

Why will you read it? (Idea: *To learn about _____.*)

Activity 2 Identify Features of Expository Text—An After-Reading Strategy

As we read this book, we'll make a list of the things we notice about the way this book is organized that is different from narrative stories.

When you notice something, put your hand up and we'll put it on our list.

Read expository text to students, noting the features of expository text, such as headings, captions, labels, lists, table of contents, photographs, diagrams, and index.

List features as you come to them, and note that all these features should be read so you learn all the text is trying to teach.

Call attention to the idea that expository text does not have to be read in order.

Tell me what you've learned about how expository text is organized.
Review features on list.

  Provide a reading center to display books being read so that students can enjoy them again during free time.

Part C: Fluency Building

  Conduct after the lesson, using story of the day.

Activity 1 Partner Reading

It's time for partner reading.
Direct students to the story of the day. **Assign** student partners as Partner 1 and Partner 2. **Monitor** student reading. **Guide** as needed.

10 minutes

IWB

Teacher Materials:
Writing Prompts

My Writing Checklist

Student Materials:
Lined Paper

My Writing Checklist

Activity 1 Write and Use Parts of Speech and Conventions

Time to write using a writing prompt based on the stories we've been reading.

Assign student partners. **Distribute** lined paper to students. **Display** writing prompts and have students choose one to write about or assign a writing prompt of your choice. **Review** parts of speech and punctuation as well as the writing checklist with students. **Tell** students to write one paragraph (minimum of four sentences per paragraph) on their own to answer the writing prompt. **Tell** them to use their writing checklist (first column labeled "Did I use them?") to ensure they include important parts of speech or punctuation in their writing. **Tell** students which parts of speech or punctuation to focus on, if you wish. **Model** what it means to answer a writing prompt and to use the writing checklist during and after the writing process, as needed. **Monitor** and guide students as needed. **Model** what it means to have a neighbor look over his or her neighbor's writing and to complete the writing checklist (second column labeled "Did my neighbor use them?"), as needed. **Have** students share what they wrote as time permits.

Writing Prompt 1	*Writing Prompt 2*	*Writing Prompt 3*
If you could go to genie school, what would you like to learn to do?	How can you become the best student in a class?	Would you want to be a genie? Why or why not?

Materials

Teacher: Examples of expository text and narrative story; 7-Compare and Contrast Venn Diagram; *Storybook 2*

Student: Vocabulary notebook; *Storybook 2*

Part A: Vocabulary Development

⏱ **5 minutes**

Student Materials:
Storybook 2

Vocabulary notebook

Activity 1 Learn New Vocabulary Word

Elicit responses to questions. **Guide** as needed.
Today you'll learn a new vocabulary word. **Alaska. Alaska is the largest state in the United States.** What is **Alaska?** *The largest state in the United States.*

The largest state in the United States is **Alaska.** What's the **largest state in the United States?** *Alaska.*

Show location of Alaska with globe or map.
The largest state in the United States is popular to visit, especially the places you can see glaciers. **Alaska** is a popular place to visit.

What's **the largest state in the United States?** *Alaska.*
Discuss facts about Alaska.

Write **Alaska** and what it is in your vocabulary notebook.
Direct students to write word in their vocabulary notebook. **Guide** as needed.

Activity 2 Review Vocabulary Word

Elicit responses to questions. **Guide** as needed.
What does **vow** mean? *Promise.*
What's another word for **promise?** *Vow.*

Review vocabulary words in appropriate context in *Storybook 2.*

IWB

Part B: Comprehension Strategies

Activity 1 Compare Features between Expository/Narrative—An After-Reading Strategy

Show Compare and Contrast Venn Diagram.
Let's compare how narrative stories are different from expository text.
To compare things, you'll need to tell how they are the same and how they are different. A Venn diagram is a great way to organize the information.

Let's write your ideas on the Compare and Contrast Venn Diagram.

Elicit responses for things that are the same for the center of the diagram: title, illustrations, you learn things, fun to read.

Elicit responses for things that narratives have for one side of the chart: beginning, middle, end, setting, characters, problem, events, read from front to back in order.

Elicit responses for things that expository text has for the other side of the diagram: table of contents, photographs, captions, labels, diagrams, information, index, headings, ideas, read in any order.

You can set a purpose for reading books when you know how they're organized. You know you'll read for fun or to learn something new.

Provide a reading center to display books being read so that students can enjoy them again during free time.

Part C: Fluency Building

Conduct after the lesson, using story of the day.

Activity 1 Partner Reading

It's time for partner reading.
Direct students to the story of the day. **Assign** student partners as Partner 1 and Partner 2. **Monitor** student reading. **Guide** as needed.

Materials

Teacher: 1-Narrative Story Map; *Storybook 2*

Student: Copy of 1-Narrative Story Map; *Storybook 2*; vocabulary notebook

Part A: Vocabulary Development

5 minutes

Student Materials:
Storybook 2

Vocabulary notebook

Activity 1 Learn New Vocabulary Word

Elicit responses to questions. **Guide** as needed.

Today you'll learn a new vocabulary word. **Vane. A vane is a tool to show which way the wind blows.** What does **vane** mean? *Tool to show which way the wind blows.*

Another word for a **tool to show which way the wind blows is vane.** What's another way to say a **tool to show which way the wind blows?** *Vane.*

The farmer has a **tool to show which way the wind blows.** He puts this tool on top of his barn. It's called a weather **vane.**

This **vane** is spelled **v-a-n-e.** Spell the **vane** that means a **tool to show which way the wind blows.** *V-a-n-e.*

What's another word for a **tool to show which way the wind blows?** *Vane.*
Discuss weather vanes and why they are needed.

Write **vane** and what it means in your vocabulary notebook.
Direct students to write word in their vocabulary notebook. **Guide** as needed.

Activity 2 Review Vocabulary Word

Elicit responses to questions. **Guide** as needed.
What is **Alaska?** *The largest state in the United States.*
What's **the largest state in the United States?** *Alaska.*

Review vocabulary words in appropriate context in *Storybook 2*.

12 minutes

IWB

Teacher Materials:
Storybook 2

Narrative Story Map

Student Materials:
Storybook 2

Narrative Story Map

Activity 1 | Set a Purpose for Reading—A Before-Reading Strategy

Elicit responses to questions. **Guide** as needed.
Why do you set a purpose for reading? (Idea: *So you know what to think about as you read.*)

Today as you read, you're going to try to find three story elements so you can fill out part of a Narrative Story Map.

The purpose for reading is to find the main character, the setting, and the problem. Try to find the name of the main character in the story. Then look for where and when the story takes place. The last thing you'll look for is the problem.

When you look for the problem, what are you trying to find? (Idea: *What goes wrong in the story that makes you want to read more.*)

What three things will you look for in the story today? (Idea: *The main character, the setting, and the problem.*)

Guide students to skim Story 126, pages 122–124, and look for story elements.

Activity 2 | Identify Characters, Setting, and Problem—An After-Reading Strategy

Show Narrative Story Map. **Give** students Narrative Story Map.
Today you'll fill out the title, characters, setting, and problem on the Narrative Story Map.

Allow students to copy words from *Storybook 2*, rather than model answer on Narrative Story Map.

Find the title on page 126, and copy it on to your Narrative Story Map.

Next, find the main characters in the story, and write that in the box for Characters.

Figure out where this story takes place, and copy these words from the book in the part for where.

This story does not tell when, so skip that part on your Narrative Story Map.

Now we need to figure out the problem. Look carefully, and see if you can figure out a problem in the story.

Elicit suggestions for the problem in the story. (Idea: *The school needs to train more genies.*)

Choose the best suggestion. **Model** writing on Narrative Story Map only for Problem. **Guide** students to copy words.

Touch the box for the Problem. Write these words for the problem.

Good for you. You're figuring out hard story elements.

Part C: Fluency Building

5 minutes

Student Materials:
Storybook 2

Conduct after the lesson, using story of the day.

Activity 1 Partner Reading

It's time for partner reading.

Direct students to the story of the day. **Assign** student partners as Partner 1 and Partner 2. **Monitor** student reading. **Guide** as needed.

Lesson 128

Materials

Teacher: *Storybook 2;* 7-Compare and Contrast Venn Diagram
Student: *Storybook 2;* vocabulary notebook

Part A: Vocabulary Development

5 minutes

Student Materials:
Storybook 2

Vocabulary notebook

Activity 1 Learn New Vocabulary Word

Elicit responses to questions. **Guide** as needed.
Today you'll learn a new vocabulary word. **Trunk.** A **trunk** is a **large suitcase.** What does **trunk** mean? *Large suitcase.*

What's another word for a **large suitcase?** *Trunk.*

Kim wanted to move to a new house on the other side of town. She got a **large suitcase** and put all her clothes, stuffed animals, and toys inside. Kim filled the **trunk** and moved to the other side of town.

What's another word for **large suitcase?** *Trunk.*
Discuss when you might use a trunk.

Write **trunk** and what it means in your vocabulary notebook.
Direct students to write word in their vocabulary notebook. **Guide** as needed.

Activity 2 Review Vocabulary Word

Elicit responses to questions. **Guide** as needed.
What does **vane** mean? *Tool to show which way the wind blows.*
What's another word for a **tool to show which way the wind blows?** *Vane.*

Review vocabulary words in appropriate context in *Storybook 2.*

12 minutes

IWB

Teacher Materials:
Storybook 2

Compare and Contrast
Venn Diagram

Student Materials:
Storybook 2

Activity 1 Text-to-Text Connection—An After-Reading Strategy

Refer to Story 127, pages 125–127.

You read "The Van and the Vane." If you wanted to make a text-to-text connection, what story can you think of to connect to this story? (Sample response.)

Remind students of the "Sid" stories, Stories 90–94, pages 19–33. **Guide** as needed.

Show Compare and Contrast Venn Diagram. **Elicit** responses to questions.
You can make text-to-text connections by telling how the stories are the same and different on a Compare and Contrast Venn Diagram.

Brainstorm with students to elicit how stories are the same and different.
Complete Compare and Contrast Venn Diagram as students suggest ideas. **Guide** as needed. (Ideas: *Both main characters cannot read or spell well; not reading well makes problems. Sid worked at a job; tried to read notes; made mistakes. Kim is at home; she is trying to move; she orders the wrong things.*)
Discuss likenesses and differences as you complete chart.

Making text-to-text connections helps you understand your reading.

Part C: Fluency Building

5 minutes

Student Materials:
Storybook 2

Conduct after the lesson, using story of the day.

Activity 1 Partner Reading

It's time for partner reading.
Direct students to the story of the day. **Assign** student partners as Partner 1 and Partner 2. **Monitor** student reading. **Guide** as needed.

Lesson
129

Materials
Teacher: 10-KWL Chart; expository book of teacher choice; *Storybook 2*
Student: Copy of 10-KWL Chart; vocabulary notebook; *Storybook 2*

Part A: Vocabulary Development

5 minutes

Student Materials:
Storybook 2

Vocabulary notebook

Activity 1 Learn New Vocabulary Word

Elicit responses to questions. **Guide** as needed.
Today you'll learn a new vocabulary word. **Service. Service** is **work done for someone.** What does **service** mean? *Work done for someone.*

Another word for **work done for someone** is **service.** What's another word for **work done for someone?** *Service.*

When kids **do work for someone,** they do a **service.** When kids mow the lawn for a friend, they do a **service.** When kids wash the car for their grandpa, they do a **service.**

What's another word for **work done for someone?** *Service.*
Discuss service work students can do.

Write **service** and what it means in your vocabulary notebook.
Direct students to write word in their vocabulary notebook. **Guide** as needed.

Activity 2 Review Vocabulary Word

Elicit responses to questions. **Guide** as needed.
What does a **trunk** mean? *Large suitcase.*
What's another word for **large suitcase?** *Trunk.*

Review vocabulary words in appropriate context in *Storybook 2.*

12 minutes

IWB

Teacher Materials:
KWL Chart

Expository book

Student Materials:
KWL Chart

Activity 1 KWL Chart for Expository Text—A Before-Reading Strategy

Show KWL Chart. **Give** students KWL Chart. **Elicit** responses to questions. **Guide** as needed.
Here is a KWL chart that you can use when you are reading expository text.

Why do you use a KWL chart? (Idea: *To help organize and remember information.*)

What do you write in the "K" section? (Idea: *You list your schema, or what is already in your brain about the topic of your book.*)

What do you write in the "W" section? (Idea: *Questions you have and things you want to know.*)

What do you write in the "L" section? (Idea: *What you learned about the topic from the book **after** you read.*)

We'll read a nonfiction or expository text on _____. Before we read this book, you'll fill out the first two sections of the KWL Chart.

Elicit list of things to write in the "What I Know" column and model writing for students to copy. **Guide** as needed.
Let's think of some things you know about _____ and write them on the chart in the "K" section. Great ideas. Copy them on your chart.

Elicit list of things to write in the "What I Want to Know" column, and model writing for students to copy. **Guide** as needed.
Let's think of some things you want to know about _____ and write them on the chart in the "W" section. Great ideas. Copy them on your chart.

 The last section has a place to list what you learned about the topic from the book after you read. We'll fill out this section after we read the book.

Why do you fill out a chart like this? (Idea: *It helps you remember what you learned about a topic from a book.*)

Save chart to complete in Lesson 130.

Part C: Fluency Building

Student Materials:
Storybook 2

Conduct after the lesson, using story of the day.

Activity 1 **Partner Reading**

It's time for partner reading.

Direct students to the story of the day. **Assign** student partners as Partner 1 and Partner 2. **Monitor** student reading. **Guide** as needed.

Lesson 130

Materials

Teacher: 10-KWL Chart (from Lesson 129); expository text of teacher choice; *Storybook 2*, 2-Vocabulary Acquisition and Use, 3-My Book Review

Student: Copy of 10-KWL Chart from (Lesson 129); vocabulary notebook; *Storybook 2*, Copy of 2-Vocabulary Acquisition and Use and 3-My Book Review

---

🕐 **5 minutes**

IWB

Teacher Materials:
Vocabulary Acquisition and Use

Student Materials:
Storybook 2

Vocabulary Notebook

Vocabulary Acquisition and Use

Part A: Vocabulary Development

Activity 1 Vocabulary Notebook Review

Today you'll study from your vocabulary notebook. Studying your words and what they mean will help you know your words even better. You'll study the eight words we studied this week.

Guide students as they study <u>remember</u>, <u>human</u>, <u>instant</u>, <u>vow</u>, <u>Alaska</u>, <u>vane</u>, <u>trunk</u>, and <u>service</u>.

Activity 2 Cumulative Vocabulary Review

Elicit responses to questions. **Guide** as needed.
Directions: Listen and tell me the correct vocabulary word for each question.

What's another word for **the largest state in the United States?** *Alaska.*
What's another word for **short time?** *Instant.*
What's another word for **promise?** *Vow.*
What's another word for **large suitcase?** *Trunk.*
What's another word for **work done for someone?** *Service.*
What's another word for a **tool to show which way the wind blows?** *Vane.*
What's another word for a **man, woman, or child?** *Human.*
What's another word for **keep in mind?** *Remember.*

Repeat difficult words as needed.

📖 **Review** vocabulary words in appropriate context in *Storybook 2*.

Activity 3 Vocabulary Acquisition and Use

Display Vocabulary Acquisition and Use. **Have** students work with a neighbor to complete Vocabulary Acquisition and Use.
Today's vocabulary words are _____ and _____ [and _____ and _____].
Vocabulary words: **biggest** and **largest; tossed** and **pitched**
Write the words on the lines provided. Then write the words in the boxes based on whether you think each word is less/smaller or more/larger than the other word. Below the boxes, write why you think word 1 is less/smaller and word 2 is more/larger than word 1.
Repeat for words 3 and 4. **Have** students share what they wrote. **Discuss** examples of how these words might be used.

Part B: Comprehension Strategies

IWB

Teacher Materials:
Expository Text

KWL Chart

My Book Review

Student Materials:
KWL Chart

My Book Review

Activity 1 Set a Purpose for Reading—A Before-Reading Strategy

Elicit responses to questions. **Guide** as needed.
Today you'll hear a book about _____ . What's your purpose for listening to this book? (Idea: *Learn something new.*)

What do you call this kind of text? *Expository text.*

How is expository text organized? (Idea: *Around topics or ideas.*)

What kinds of things do you find in expository text? (Idea: *Headings, captions, labels, lists, table of contents, photographs, and index.*)

The expository text we'll read today is organized around the topic of _____ . It will give you information that is true about _____ .

Read expository text of choice. **Note** features of expository text as you read, such as headings, captions, labels, lists, table of contents, photographs, index, and diagrams.

Activity 2 KWL Chart—An After-Reading Strategy

Show KWL Chart from Lesson 129. **Review** first two columns.
In the last lesson, we filled in two columns of our chart.

Now we're ready to fill in the last column. We read _____ to learn something new about _____ . Now let's make a list of all the new things we learned.

Elicit responses to fill in the "What I Learned" column, and model writing so that students can copy.
Great ideas. Copy them on your chart. What's the name of the chart that helps you organize information from an expository text? *A KWL chart.*

Provide a reading center to display books being read so that students can enjoy them again during free time.

Activity 3 Develop Opinions—An After-Reading Strategy

Today we'll found out your opinion or how you feel about the stories you read. You will choose a book to read and then complete the My Book Review form. You'll need to tell if you like or don't like the book and why. You must give a reason for why you like or don't like the book. Finally, you can tell if you would recommend the book to others.

Have students read a narrative or expository trade book of their choice. **Have** students complete My Book Review form when they are finished reading their book. **Model** how to complete the My Book Review form. **Guide** students as needed. **Have** students share their book reviews with the class as time permits.

Part C: Fluency Building

Conduct after the lesson, using story of the day.

Activity 1 Partner Reading

It's time for partner reading.

Direct students to the story of the day. **Assign** student partners as Partner 1 and Partner 2. **Monitor** student reading. **Guide** as needed.

Lesson 131

Materials

Teacher: Chart paper/IWB; *Storybook 2*

Student: *Storybook 2*; sticky notes; vocabulary notebook

Part A: Vocabulary Development

5 minutes

Student Materials:
Storybook 2

Vocabulary notebook

Activity 1 Learn New Vocabulary Word

Elicit responses to questions. **Guide** as needed.

Today you'll learn a new vocabulary word. **Experiment. Experiment** means a **test to learn something new.** What does **experiment** mean? *Test to learn something new.*

Another word for **test to learn something new** is **experiment.** What's another word for a **test to learn something new?** *Experiment.*

The students wanted to know if a plant could grow in water, so they decided to do a **test to learn something new.** They did an **experiment.**

What's another word for a **test to learn something new?** *Experiment.*
Discuss why scientists do experiments.

Write **experiment** and what it means in your vocabulary notebook.
Direct students to write word in their vocabulary notebook. **Guide** as needed.

Activity 2 Review Vocabulary Word

Elicit responses to questions. **Guide** as needed.
What does **service** mean? *Work done for someone.*
What's another word for **work done for someone?** *Service.*

Review vocabulary words in appropriate context in *Storybook 2*.

Part B: Comprehension Strategies

Teacher Materials:
Storybook 2

Chart/IWB

Student Materials:
Storybook 2

Sticky notes

Activity 1 **Generate Questions—A During-Reading Strategy**

Refer to Story 130, pages 135–137.

Asking questions is a strategy to use when you are reading stories.

Why do you ask questions when you are reading? *To understand the story better.*

Draw chart/IWB for posting sentence and question notes. **Elicit** responses to questions. **Guide** as needed.

Today you are going to work to find a sentence in the story and think up some questions about that sentence by yourself. You'll write your sentence on a sticky note. Then you'll write questions on other sticky notes. When you're finished, you can bring me your notes, and we'll post them on our chart.

Post a sticky note with sentences on one side of the chart and the sticky notes with the questions on the other side of the chart across from the sentence.

Sample Chart for Questions		
Sentences	**Questions**	
☐	☐ ☐ ☐	

Discuss sentences chosen and questions generated. **Share** with class examples of good questions. **Choose** some of the questions generated, and **elicit** responses. **Guide** as needed.
Answer the questions. (Sample responses.)

Part C: Fluency Building

Conduct after the lesson, using story of the day.

Activity 1 **Partner Reading**

It's time for partner reading.
Direct students to the story of the day. **Assign** student partners as Partner 1 and Partner 2. **Monitor** student reading. **Guide** as needed.

Lesson 132

Materials

Teacher: Locate online version of "The Crow and the Pitcher"; 7-Compare and Contrast Venn Diagram; *Storybook 2*

Student: *Storybook 2*; vocabulary notebook

Part A: Vocabulary Development

10 minutes

Student Materials:
Storybook 2

Vocabulary notebook

Activity 1 Learn New Vocabulary Word

Elicit responses to questions. **Guide** as needed.
Today you'll learn a new vocabulary word. **Handsome. Handsome** means **looks good.** What does **handsome** mean? *Looks good.*

Another word for **looks good** is **handsome.** What's another word for **looks good?** *Handsome.*

Jarissa says her brother **looks good** for his first date. She says her brother looks **handsome** for his first date.

What's another word for **looks good?** *Handsome.*
Discuss what it means to be handsome.

Write **handsome** and what it means in your vocabulary notebook.
Direct students to write word in their vocabulary notebook. **Guide** as needed.

Activity 2 Review Vocabulary Word

Elicit responses to questions. **Guide** as needed.
What does **experiment** mean? *Test to learn something new.*

What's another word for **test to learn something new?** *Experiment.*

Review vocabulary words in appropriate context in *Storybook 2.*

Part B: Comprehension Strategies

IWB

Teacher Materials:
"The Crow and the Pitcher"

Compare and Contrast Venn Diagram

Storybook 2

Student Materials:
Storybook 2

Activity 1 **Text-to-Text Connection—An After-Reading Strategy**

Refer to Story 131, pages 138–140.

Show Compare and Contrast Venn Diagram.
"The Crow and the Pitcher" is a fable that was written a long, long time ago by a Greek man named Aesop. Aesop wrote more than 600 fables. Since then, many people have taken this story and written it in their own words. "Ellen the Eagle" is one of those versions, so the two stories are similar. You can compare and contrast the two fables on a Compare and Contrast Venn Diagram.

Read "The Crow and the Pitcher" to students for text-to-text connection. **Discuss** the comparisons between the two stories. **Fill** the chart with student-generated responses. (Ideas: *Both fill something with stones; both are thirsty; both get drinks; both solve a problem; both stories teach a moral. Ellen: character is an eagle; she fills a deep hole. The crow: character is a crow; she fills a pitcher.*)

Remember, fables are stories that are not only fun to read but also teach a lesson. A lesson learned from a story is called a moral.

What do you think the moral these stories are trying to teach? (Sample response.)

Discuss the moral and its application to students' lives

Part C: Fluency Building

Conduct after the lesson, using story of the day.

Activity 1 **Partner Reading**

It's time for partner reading.
Direct students to the story of the day. **Assign** student partners as Partner 1 and Partner 2. **Monitor** student reading. **Guide** as needed.

Lesson 133

Materials

Teacher: Locate online version of "The Fox and the Crow"; 7-Compare and Contrast Venn Diagram; *Storybook 2*

Student: *Storybook 2*; vocabulary notebook

Part A: Vocabulary Development

5 minutes

Student Materials:
Storybook 2

Vocabulary notebook

Activity 1 Learn New Vocabulary Word

Elicit responses to questions. **Guide** as needed.
Today you'll learn a new vocabulary word. **Reptile. A reptile** is an **animal like a snake or turtle.** What is a **reptile?** *An animal like a snake or turtle.*

Another word for **animal like a snake or turtle** is **reptile.** What's another word for **animal like a snake or turtle?** *Reptile.*

A snake and a turtle are animals. They have the same temperature as the air around them. They hatch from eggs and have scaly skin. An **animal like a snake or turtle** is a **reptile.**

What's another word for **animal like a snake or turtle?** *Reptile.*
Discuss what other animals are reptiles.

Write **reptile** and what it means in your vocabulary notebook.
Direct students to write word in their vocabulary notebook. **Guide** as needed.

Activity 2 Review Vocabulary Word

Elicit responses to questions. **Guide** as needed.
What does **handsome** mean? *Looks good.*
What's another word for **looks good?** *Handsome.*

Review vocabulary words in appropriate context in *Storybook 2*.

12 minutes

IWB

Teacher Materials:
"The Fox and the Crow"

Compare and Contrast
Venn Diagram

Storybook 2

Student Materials:
Storybook 2

Activity 1 Text-to-Text Connection—An After-Reading Strategy

Refer to Story 132, pages 141–144.

Show Compare and Contrast Venn Diagram.
"The Fox and the Crow" is another fable that was written by Aesop. Who remembers how many fables Aesop wrote? (Idea: *More than 600 fables.*)

Since then, many people have taken this story and written it in their own words. "Carl Tricks the Crow" is one of those versions, so the two stories are similar. You can compare and contrast the two fables on a Compare and Contrast Venn Diagram.

Read "The Fox and the Crow" to students for text-to-text connection. **Discuss** the comparisons between the two stories. **Fill** the chart with student generated responses. (Ideas: *Both trick a crow; both want to eat what the crow has; both got something to eat; both stories teach a moral. Carl shares food. The fox: character is a fox; story is short; fox eats food himself.*)

What are fables? (Idea: *Stories written to be fun to read but also to teach a lesson.*)

What is another name for the lesson learned from a story or fable? *The moral.*

What do you think the moral is that these stories are trying to teach? (Sample response.)

Discuss the moral and its application to students' lives.
The moral of the story is that you need to be careful of what people want from you when they suddenly start saying nice things to you.

5 minutes

Student Materials:
Storybook 2

Conduct after the lesson, using story of the day.

Activity 1 Partner Reading

It's time for partner reading.
Direct students to the story of the day. **Assign** student partners as Partner 1 and Partner 2. **Monitor** student reading. **Guide** as needed.

Lesson 134

Part A: Vocabulary Development

5 minutes

Student Materials:
Storybook 2

Vocabulary notebook

Activity 1 Learn New Vocabulary Word

Elicit responses to questions. **Guide** as needed.
Today you'll learn a new vocabulary word. **Amphibian.** An **amphibian** is **an animal that lives in water and on land.**

Another word for **animal that lives in water and on land** is **amphibian.** What's another word for **animal that lives in water and on land?** *Amphibian.*

A frog is an **animal that lives in water and on land.** A frog is an **amphibian.**

What's another word for **animal that lives in water and on land?** *Amphibian.*
Discuss what other animals are amphibians.

Write **amphibian** and what it means in your vocabulary notebook.
Direct students to write word in their vocabulary notebook. **Guide** as needed.

Activity 2 Review Vocabulary Word

Elicit responses to questions. **Guide** as needed.
What is a **reptile?** *An animal like a snake or a turtle.*
What's another word for **an animal like a snake or turtle?** *Reptile.*

Review vocabulary words in appropriate context in *Storybook 2.*

12 minutes

IWB

Teacher Materials:
Storybook 2

Narrative Story Map

Student Materials:
Storybook 2

Narrative Story Map

Activity 1 Set a Purpose for Reading—A Before-Reading Strategy

Elicit responses to questions. **Guide** as needed.
Why do you set a purpose for reading? (Idea: *So you know what to think about as you read.*)

Today as you read, you're going to try to find three story elements so you can fill out part of a Narrative Story Map.

The purpose for reading is to find the main character, the setting, and the problem. Try to find the name of the main character in the story. Then look for where and when the story takes place. The last thing you'll look for is the problem.

When you look for the problem, what are you trying to find? (Idea: *What goes wrong in the story that makes you want to read more.*)

What three things will you look for in the story today? (Idea: *The main character, the setting and the problem.*)

Guide students to skim Story 133, pages 145–147, and look for story elements.

Activity 2 Identify Characters, Setting, and Problem—An After-Reading Strategy

Show Narrative Story Map. **Give** students Narrative Story Map
Today you'll fill out the title, characters, setting, and problem on the Narrative Story Map.

Allow students to copy words from *Storybook 2*, rather than model answer on Narrative Story Map.

Find the title of the story on page 145, and copy it onto the line for the title.

Next, find the main characters in the story, and write that in the box for Characters.

Figure out where this story takes place, and copy these words from the book in the part for where.

This story does not tell when, so skip that part on your Narrative Story Map.

Now we need to figure out the problem. Look carefully, and see if you can figure out a problem in the story.
Elicit suggestions for the problem in the story. **Choose** the best student-generated suggestion. (Idea: *The frog was mean to the turtle so the turtle felt worthless.*)

Touch the box for the problem. Write these words for the problem.
Model writing on Narrative Story Map only for problem. **Guide** students to copy words.

Good for you. You're thinking hard, and finding the story elements by yourself.
Save Narrative Story Map for Lesson 138.

Part C: Fluency Building

5 minutes

Student Materials:
Storybook 2

Conduct after the lesson, using story of the day.

Activity 1 Partner Reading

It's time for partner reading.
Direct students to the story of the day. **Assign** student partners as Partner 1 and Partner 2. **Monitor** student reading. **Guide** as needed.

Lesson 135

Materials

Teacher: *Storybook 2*, 2-Vocabulary Acquisition and Use, Writing Prompts, 5-My Writing Checklist

Student: *Storybook 2;* vocabulary notebook, Copy of 2- Vocabulary Acquisition and Use and 5-My Writing Checklist; Lined Paper

Part A: Vocabulary Development

5 minutes

IWB

Teacher Materials:
Vocabulary Acquisition and Use

Student Materials:
Storybook 2

Vocabulary notebook

Vocabulary Acquisition and Use

Activity 1 Vocabulary Notebook Review

Today you'll study from your vocabulary notebook. Studying your words and what they mean will help you know your words even better. You'll study the four words we studied this week.

Guide students as they study <u>experiment</u>, <u>handsome</u>, <u>reptile</u>, and <u>amphibian</u>.

Activity 2 Cumulative Vocabulary Review

Elicit responses to questions. **Guide** as needed.
Directions: Listen and tell me the correct vocabulary word for each question.

What's another word for **looks good?** *Handsome.*
What's another word for **test to learn something new?** *Experiment.*
What's another word for **animal like a snake or turtle?** *Reptile.*
What's another word for **animal that lives in water and on land?** *Amphibian.*

Repeat difficult words as needed.

Review vocabulary words in appropriate context in *Storybook 2.*

Activity 3 Vocabulary Acquisition and Use

Display Vocabulary Acquisition and Use. **Have** students work with a neighbor to complete Vocabulary Acquisition and Use.
Today's vocabulary words are _____ and _____ [and _____ and _____].
Vocabulary words: **handsome** and **gorgeous; want** and **desire**
Write the words on the lines provided. Then write the words in the boxes based on whether you think each word is less/smaller or more/larger than the other word. Below the boxes, write why you think word 1 is less/smaller and word 2 is more/larger than word 1.
Repeat for words 3 and 4. **Have** students share what they wrote. **Discuss** examples of how these words might be used.

12 minutes

Teacher Materials:
Storybook 2

Student Materials:
Storybook 2

Activity 1 Set a Purpose for Reading—A Before-Reading Strategy

Elicit responses to questions. **Guide** as needed.
What should you do before reading a book? (Idea: *Set a purpose for reading so I know why I am reading.*)

Today you're going to read the first paragraph on page 110 so that you can summarize it.

What do you do when you summarize? (Idea: *Tell the main ideas of a story in your own words.*)

Activity 2 Summarize—An After-Reading Strategy

Guide students to read the first paragraph on page 110 in Story 122.

Elicit responses for summaries and **discuss** fix-ups. **Guide** as needed.
First you need to read the paragraph. Think hard about what you're reading because then you'll close the book and work with a partner to retell the main parts of the paragraph. When you think you can retell the main ideas, write your words down so you can remember your ideas. Then you and your partner can share the words of your summary with us.

Summarizing paragraphs is hard work. Keep doing a good job.

Part C: Fluency Building

5 minutes

Student Materials:
Storybook 2

Conduct after the lesson, using story of the day.

Activity 1 Partner Reading

It's time for partner reading.
Direct students to the story of the day. **Assign** student partners as Partner 1 and Partner 2. **Monitor** student reading. **Guide** as needed.

10 minutes

IWB

Teacher Materials:
Writing Prompts

My Writing Checklist

Student Materials:
Lined Paper

My Writing Checklist

Activity 1 Write and Use Parts of Speech and Conventions

Time to write using a writing prompt based on the stories we've been reading.

Assign student partners. **Distribute** lined paper to students. **Display** writing prompts and have students choose one to write about or assign a writing prompt of your choice. **Review** parts of speech and punctuation as well as the writing checklist with students. **Tell** students to write one paragraph (minimum of four sentences per paragraph) on their own to answer the writing prompt. **Tell** them to use their writing checklist (first column labeled "Did I use them?") to ensure they include important parts of speech or punctuation in their writing. **Tell** students which parts of speech or punctuation to focus on, if you wish. **Model** what it means to answer a writing prompt and to use the writing checklist during and after the writing process, as needed. **Monitor** and guide students as needed. **Model** what it means to have a neighbor look over his or her neighbor's writing and to complete the writing checklist (second column labeled "Did my neighbor use them?"), as needed. **Have** students share what they wrote as time permits.

Writing Prompt 1	*Writing Prompt 2*	*Writing Prompt 3*
What does it mean to be a good teacher?	Is spelling important? Why or why not?	Describe a time when you were very thirsty. What were you doing and what did you drink?

Materials

Teacher: *Storybook 2*

Student: Vocabulary notebook; *Storybook 2*

Part A: Vocabulary Development

5 minutes

Student Materials:
Storybook 2

Vocabulary notebook

Activity 1 Learn New Vocabulary Word

Elicit responses to questions. **Guide** as needed.
Today you'll learn a new vocabulary word. **Toadstool. A toadstool** is a **wild mushroom.** What's another word for a **toadstool?** *Wild mushroom.*

Another word for a **wild mushroom** is a **toadstool.** What's another word for a **wild mushroom?** *Toadstool.*

One day José noticed a **wild mushroom** growing in the woods behind his house. He told his mom about it, and she said, "Oh that's a **toadstool."**

What's another word for **wild mushroom?** *Toadstool.*
Discuss toadstools and why students must never touch or eat them.

Write **toadstool** and what it means in your vocabulary notebook.
Direct students to write word in their vocabulary notebook. **Guide** as needed.

Activity 2 Review Vocabulary Word

Elicit responses to questions. **Guide** as needed.
What is an **amphibian?** *An animal that lives in water and on land.*
What's another word for **an animal that lives in water and on land?**
An amphibian.

Review vocabulary words in appropriate context in *Storybook 2.*

Part B: Comprehension Strategies

12 minutes

Teacher Materials:
Storybook 2

Student Materials:
Storybook 2

Activity 1 Set a Purpose for Reading—A Before-Reading Strategy

Elicit the strategy that students would like to use before reading. If they want to Activate Background Knowledge, allow them to discuss their schema for topics in the story. If they want to Set a Purpose, let them decide what purpose they will use.
Before you read the story, you've learned some strategies to use to help you understand what you read. What strategy would be best for reading Story 135, "Flame the Snake is a Sneak"? (Sample response.)

Activity 2 Choose a Strategy—A During-Reading Strategy

Elicit strategies student would like to apply during reading. Possible choices are Mental imaging; Reading with Prosody; Generating Questions; or Summarizing. **Allow** students to follow procedures learned for strategy.

You learned some strategies to use during reading to help you understand what you read. What strategy would you like to use? (Sample response.)

Activity 3 Choose a Strategy—An After-Reading Strategy

Elicit strategy students would like to apply after reading. Possible choices are Identify Story Elements; Retell the Story; Summarize the Story; and Text-to-Self Connections. **Allow** students to follow procedures learned for strategy.

Last, you have learned some strategies to use after you read to help you understand what you read. What strategy would you like to use?

Smart choosing strategies to use when you read that help you have good comprehension.

Part C: Fluency Building

5 minutes

Student Materials:
Storybook 2

Conduct after the lesson, using story of the day.

Activity 1 Partner Reading

It's time for partner reading.

Direct students to the story of the day. **Assign** student partners as Partner 1 and Partner 2. **Monitor** student reading. **Guide** as needed.

Lesson 137

Materials

Teacher: *Storybook 2*

Student: *Storybook 2;* vocabulary notebook

Part A: Vocabulary Development

5 minutes

Student Materials:
Storybook 2

Vocabulary notebook

Activity 1 Learn New Vocabulary Word

Elicit responses to questions. **Guide** as needed.

Today you'll learn a new vocabulary word. **Cooperate. Cooperate** means **get along.** What does **cooperate** mean? *Get along.*

Another word for **get along** is **cooperate.** What's another word for **get along?** *Cooperate.*

When you play on a soccer team, it's important to **get along.** You should **cooperate** with your teammates.

What's another word for **get along?** *Cooperate.*

Discuss why it is important to cooperate with others and under what circumstances students should cooperate.

Write **cooperate** and what it means in your vocabulary notebook.

Direct students to write word in their vocabulary notebook. **Guide** as needed.

Activity 2 Review Vocabulary Word

Elicit responses to questions. **Guide** as needed.

What does **toadstool** mean? *Wild mushroom.*

What's another word for **wild mushroom?** *Toadstool.*

Review vocabulary words in appropriate context in *Storybook 2.*

Part B: Comprehension Strategies

12 minutes

Teacher Materials:
Storybook 2

Student Materials:
Storybook 2

Activity 1 Read with Prosody—A During-Reading Strategy

Guide students to read Story 136, pages 155 and 156, with prosody.

You have learned a lot about reading stories the right way. You know how to read questions. You know how to read and pay attention to the punctuation. You even know about dialogue. Today you'll practice reading the whole story yourself with expression. Read the whole story to your partner. Your partner will be listening for you to read with expression. Make your voice really interesting. Read the dialogue with different voices. Make sure your voice goes up at the end of the questions. And take a small breath between sentences. It should be fun to listen to you read the whole story. Reread a sentence if you make a little mistake.

Monitor partner reading. **Guide** partners to take a turn reading with prosody. Now let your partner do the same thing while you listen to the story. This should be fun.

Part C: Fluency Building

5 minutes

Student Materials:
Storybook 2

Conduct after the lesson, using story of the day.

Activity 1 | Partner Reading

It's time for partner reading.
Direct students to the story of the day. **Assign** student partners as Partner 1 and Partner 2. **Monitor** student reading. **Guide** as needed.

Materials

Teacher: 1-Narrative Story Map from Lesson 134; *Storybook 2*

Student: Copy of 1-Narrative Story Map from Lesson 134; *Storybook 2;* vocabulary notebook

---

Part A: Vocabulary Development

5 minutes

Student Materials:
Storybook 2

Vocabulary notebook

Activity 1 Learn New Vocabulary Word

Elicit responses to questions. **Guide** as needed.
Today you'll learn a new vocabulary word. **Bored. Bored** means **tired of.**
What does **bored** mean? *Tired of.*

Another word for **tired of** is **bored.** What's another word for **tired of?** *Bored.*

The boy went to the hills to watch his sheep. He watched and watched, and soon he was **tired of** watching the sheep. He felt **bored.**

What's another word for **tired of?** *Bored.*
Discuss things that make you bored.

Write **bored** and what it means in your vocabulary notebook.
Direct students to write word in their vocabulary notebook. **Guide** as needed.

Activity 2 Review Vocabulary Word

Elicit responses to questions. **Guide** as needed.
What does **cooperate** mean? *Get along.*
What's another word for **get along?** *Cooperate.*

Review vocabulary words in appropriate context in *Storybook 2.*

12 minutes

IWB

Teacher Materials:
Storybook 2

Narrative Story Map

Student Materials:
Storybook 2

Narrative Story Map

Activity 1 **Story Map—An After-Reading Strategy**

Refer to Stories 133–137, pages 145–160.

Show Narrative Story Map started in Lesson 134 to students. **Elicit** responses to questions. **Guide** as needed.

Today you'll finish the Narrative Story Maps you started in Lesson 134. You have already filled in the sections of the map for the Characters, Setting, and Problem for the Turtle story. Let's review.

Look at what you wrote on your map to tell the answers.

Who are the main characters? *The turtle, the frog, and the snake.*

Where did the story take place? *At a pond.*

When did the story take place? *Once.*

What's the problem in the story? (Idea: *The frog was mean to the turtle.*)

Now it's time for you to complete the Narrative Story Map.

Model writing student-generated ideas in Beginning, Middle, and End boxes of Narrative Story Map so that students can copy.

What should you write for the Beginning box? (Idea: *The frog made the turtle feel bad. But soon a snake wanted to eat the frog.*)

What should you write for the Middle box? (Idea: *The turtle protected the frog from the snake.*)

What should you write for the End? (Idea: *The snake, the turtle, and the frog decided to get along.*)

Time to use your Narrative Story Map to retell the Turtle story to the class.

Encourage students to retell the Turtle story by referring to their Narrative Story Maps.

Part C: Fluency Building

5 minutes

Student Materials:
Storybook 2

Conduct after the lesson, using story of the day.

Activity 1 **Partner Reading**

It's time for partner reading.

Direct students to the story of the day. **Assign** student partners as Partner 1 and Partner 2. **Monitor** student reading. **Guide** as needed.

Lesson 139

Materials

Teacher: Locate online version of "The Boy Who Yelled 'Wolf'"; chart paper;
9-Text-to-Text Connection; *Storybook 2*

Student: *Storybook 2;* vocabulary notebook

Part A: Vocabulary Development

5 minutes

Student Materials:
Storybook 2

Vocabulary notebook

Activity 1 Learn New Vocabulary Word

Elicit responses to questions. **Guide** as needed.
Today you'll learn a new vocabulary word. **Few. Few** means **not many.**
What does **few** mean? *Not many.*

Another word for **not many** is **few.** What's another word for **not many?** *Few.*

"**Not many** people like to eat snails," said the cook. "**Few** people like to eat snails."

What's another word for **not many?** *Few.*
Discuss what it means to have few of something.

Write **few** and what in means in your vocabulary notebook.
Direct students to write word in their vocabulary notebook. **Guide** as needed.

Activity 2 Review Vocabulary Word

Elicit responses to questions. **Guide** as needed.
What does **bored** mean? *Tired of.*
What's another word for **tired of?** *Bored.*

Review vocabulary words in appropriate context in *Storybook 2.*

12 minutes

IWB

Teacher Materials:
"The Boy Who Yelled 'Wolf'"

Text-to-Text Connection

Storybook 2

Student Materials:
Storybook 2

Activity 1 Text-to-Text Connection—An After-Reading Strategy

Refer to Story 138, pages 161–163.

Elicit responses to question. **Guide** as needed.
"The Boy Who Yelled 'Wolf'" is another fable that was written by Aesop. Who remembers how many fables Aesop wrote? (Idea: *More than 600 fables.*)

Since then, many people have taken this story and written it in their own words. "The Boy Who Cried Wolf" is one of those versions, so the two stories are similar. You can compare the two stories on a Text-to-Text Connection Chart.

Show Text-to-Text Connection. **Read** "The Boy Who Yelled 'Wolf'" to students for text-to-text connection. **Brainstorm** with students to elicit story elements. **Complete** chart as students suggest ideas. Ideas filled in chart are only suggestions. **Discuss** the comparisons between the two stories. **Guide** as needed.

Text-to-Text Connection		
Title of Story	The Boy Who Yelled "Wolf"	The Boy Who Cried Wolf
Main Characters	The boy	The shepherd boy
Setting (Where)	Side of a mountain	Outside village
Setting (When)	Once	Once
Problem	Played a trick	Played a joke
Beginning	Cried "wolf," and people ran to help	Cried "wolf," and people ran to help
Middle	Cried "wolf" again, and people ran to help	Cried "wolf" again, and people ran to help
Ending	The wolf came and ate some sheep.	The wolf came and ate all the sheep.

What are fables? (Idea: *Stories written to be fun to read but also to teach a lesson.*)

What's another name for the lesson you learn from a story or fable? *The moral.*

The moral of the story is that people who lie will not be believed, even when they are telling the truth.

Discuss the moral and its application to students' lives.

Part C: Fluency Building

5 minutes

Student Materials:
Storybook 2

Conduct after the lesson, using story of the day.

Activity 1 Partner Reading

It's time for partner reading.

Direct students to the story of the day. **Assign** student partners as Partner 1 and Partner 2. **Monitor** student reading. **Guide** as needed.

Lesson 140

Materials

Teacher: Chart paper/IWB; *Storybook 2*, 2-Vocabulary Acquisition and Use, 3-My Book Review

Student: *Storybook 2;* vocabulary notebook, Copy of 2-Vocabulary Acquisition and Use and 3-My Book Review

Part A: Vocabulary Development

5 minutes

IWB

Teacher Materials:
Vocabulary Acquisition and Use

Student Materials:
Storybook 2

Vocabulary Notebook

Vocabulary Acquisition and Use

Activity 1 Vocabulary Notebook Review

Today you'll study from your vocabulary notebook. Studying your words and what they mean will help you know your words even better. You'll study the eight words we studied this week.

Guide students as they study <u>experiment</u>, <u>handsome</u>, <u>reptile</u>, <u>amphibian</u>, <u>toadstool</u>, <u>cooperate</u>, <u>bored</u>, and <u>few</u>.

Activity 2 Review Vocabulary Words

Elicit responses to questions. **Guide** as needed.
Directions: Listen and tell me the correct vocabulary word for each question.

What's another word for **get along?** *Cooperate.*
What's another word for **tired of?** *Bored.*
What's another word for **looks good?** *Handsome.*
What's another word for a **test to learn something new?** *Experiment.*
What's another word for **animal like a snake or turtle?** *Reptile.*
What's another word for **animal that lives in water and on land?** *Amphibian.*
What's another word for **not many?** *Few.*
What's another word for a **wild mushroom?** *Toadstool.*

Repeat difficult words as needed.

Review vocabulary words in appropriate context in *Storybook 2*.

Activity 3 Vocabulary Acquisition and Use

Display Vocabulary Acquisition and Use. **Have** students work with a neighbor to complete Vocabulary Acquisition and Use.
Today's vocabulary words are _____ and _____ [and _____ and _____].
Vocabulary words: **bored** and **tired; fast** and **quick**
Write the words on the lines provided. Then write the words in the boxes based on whether you think each word is less/smaller or more/larger than the other word. Below the boxes, write why you think word 1 is less/smaller and word 2 is more/larger than word 1.
Repeat for words 3 and 4. **Have** students share what they wrote. **Discuss** examples of how these words might be used.

12 minutes

IWB

Teacher Materials:
Storybook 2

Chart paper/IWB

My Book Review

Student Materials:
Storybook 2

My Book Review

Activity 1 Set a Purpose for Reading—A Before-Reading Strategy

Have students Story 139, pages 165–167.

Today the purpose of reading the story is to find out how the rabbit and the turtle are different from each other. Read Story 139, and think about what the two characters are like. Then you will tell how the characters are different.

Activity 2 Contrast the Characters—An After-Reading Strategy

Elicit ideas from students to fill in chart/IWB. Answers filled in the chart are only suggestions.

Sample Chart for Contrasting Characters		
The Rabbit		**The Turtle**
Ran fast	but	Walked slowly
Bragged	but	Did not brag
Fastest in the woods	but	Slowest in the woods
Laughed at turtle	but	Did not laugh at rabbit
Thought he would win	but	Did not think he would win
Took a nap	but	Kept going
Lost race	but	Won race

Characters in stories are different from each other. That makes stories interesting.

Activity 3 Develop Opinions—An After-Reading Strategy

Today we'll found out your opinion or how you feel about the stories you read. You will choose a book to read and then complete the My Book Review form. You'll need to tell if you like or don't like the book and why. You must give a reason for why you like or don't like the book. Finally, you can tell if you would recommend the book to others.

Have students read a narrative or expository trade book of their choice. **Have** students complete My Book Review form when they are finished reading their book. **Model** how to complete the My Book Review form. **Guide** students as needed. **Have** students share their book reviews with the class as time permits.

Part C: Fluency Building

Conduct after the lesson, using story of the day.

Activity 1 Partner Reading

It's time for partner reading.

Direct students to the story of the day. **Assign** student partners as Partner 1 and Partner 2. **Monitor** student reading. **Guide** as needed.

Lesson 141

Materials

Teacher: *Storybook 2*

Student: *Storybook 2;* vocabulary notebook

Part A: Vocabulary Development

5 minutes

Student Materials:
Storybook 2
Vocabulary notebook

Activity 1 Learn New Vocabulary Word

Elicit responses to questions. **Guide** as needed.
Today you'll learn a new vocabulary word. **Thorn.** Thorn means the **sharp part of a plant.** What does **thorn** mean? *Sharp part of a plant.*

Another word for **sharp part of a plant** is **thorn.** What's another word for the **sharp part of a plant?** *Thorn.*

Eva wanted to take some roses to her friend. She cut the stems but got pricked by **the sharp part of a plant.** It was the **thorn** that pricked her finger.

What's another word for **the sharp part of a plant?** *Thorn.*
Discuss that some plants have thorns.

Write **thorn** and what it means in your vocabulary notebook.
Direct students to write word in their vocabulary notebook. **Guide** as needed.

Activity 2 Review Vocabulary Word

Elicit responses to questions. **Guide** as needed.
What does **few** mean? *Not many.*
What's another word for **not many?** *Few.*

Review vocabulary words in appropriate context in *Storybook 2.*

Part B: Comprehension Strategies

12 minutes

Teacher Materials:
Storybook 2

Student Materials:
Storybook 2

Activity 1 Set a Purpose for Reading—A Before-Reading Strategy

Elicit responses to questions. **Guide** as needed.
What should you do before reading? (Idea: *Think about why I am reading or set a purpose for reading.*)

Today you're going to read the first paragraph on page 168 so that you can summarize it.

What do you do when you summarize? (Idea: *Tell the main ideas of a story in Your own words.*)

Lesson 141   **395**

Activity 2 Summarize—An After-Reading Strategy

Guide students to read the first paragraph in Story 140, page 168.

Elicit responses for summaries and **discuss** fix-ups. **Guide** as needed.
First you need to read the paragraph. Think hard about what you're reading because then you'll close the book and work with a partner to retell the main parts of the paragraph. When you think you can retell the main ideas, write your words down so you can remember your ideas.
Then you and your partner can share the words of your summary with us.

Summarizing paragraphs is hard work. The more you practice, the better you'll get at doing it.

Activity 3 Activate Background Knowledge—An After-Reading Strategy

Refer to Story 141, pages 172–175.

Elicit responses to questions. **Guide** as needed.
We talked about schema.

What is schema? (Idea: *Everything you know in your brain about a topic.*)

When you figure out what you know, you activate your schema. Today you'll activate your schema.

Why is it a good idea to think about what you know about a topic before you read a new story? (Idea: *Then you can connect what you know to the new information that you learn when you read.*)

Today the story is a fable. Since the story is a fable, what will you find at the end of the story? (Idea: *A moral; lesson.*)

Discuss background knowledge related to questions. **Guide** as needed.
This fable has a lion in it. What is your schema for lions? (Student response.)

This story also has a mouse in it. What is your schema for mice? (Student response.)

What is your schema for how mice and lions get along? (Student response.)

When you connect what you already know to the story you'll read today, you'll understand the story better. Be sure to look for the moral at the end of the story.

Part C: Fluency Building

5 minutes

Student Materials:
Storybook 2

Conduct after the lesson, using story of the day.

Activity 1 Partner Reading

It's time for partner reading.
Direct students to the story of the day. **Assign** student partners as Partner 1 and Partner 2. **Monitor** student reading. **Guide** as needed.

Lesson 142

Materials

Teacher: *Storybook 2;* 9-Text-to-Text Connection; digital version of "The Lion and the Mouse" from www.umass.edu/aesop/fables.php; alternate print version of "The Lion and the Mouse"; globe or world map

Student: *Storybook 2;* vocabulary notebook

Part A: Vocabulary Development

5 minutes

Teacher Materials:
Globe or world map

Student Materials:
Storybook 2

Vocabulary notebook

Activity 1 Learn New Vocabulary Word

Elicit responses to questions. **Guide** as needed.

Today you'll learn a new vocabulary word. **Japan. Japan** is **an island country.** What is **Japan?** *An island country.*

Another word for **an island country** is **Japan.** What's another word for **an island country?** *Japan.*

Conner and his family flew to **an island country** to visit his grandparents. They flew to **Japan.**

Display globe and world map, and **discuss** where Japan is located.

What's another word for **an island country?** *Japan.*

Write **Japan** and what it means in your vocabulary notebook.

Direct students to write word in their vocabulary notebook. **Guide** as needed.

Activity 2 Review Vocabulary Word

Elicit responses to questions. **Guide** as needed.

What does **thorn** mean? *The sharp part of a plant.*

What's another word for **sharp part of a plant?** *Thorn.*

Review vocabulary words in appropriate context in *Storybook 2.*

12 minutes

IWB

Teacher Materials:
Storybook 2

Text-to-Text Connection

"The Lion and the Mouse"

Student Materials:
Storybook 2

Activity 1 Text-to-Text Connection—An After-Reading Strategy

Refer to Story 141, pages 172–175.

Show Text-to-Text Connection.

"The Lion and the Mouse" is another fable that was written by Aesop. Many people have taken this story and written it in their own words. You can find versions of this story on the internet. There are also versions in print. Read a couple; then you can compare the stories on a Story-Elements Chart.

Read another version of "The Lion and the Mouse" to students for text-to-text connection. **Brainstorm** with students to **elicit** story elements. **Complete** chart as students suggest ideas. Ideas filled in chart are only suggestions. **Discuss** the comparisons between the two stories, noting that the differences are minor. **Guide** as needed.

Text-to-Text Connection		
Title of Story	"The Lion and the Mouse"	"The Lion and the Mouse"
Main Characters	The lion and the mouse	The lion and the mouse
Setting (Where)	The jungle	Does not tell
Setting (When)	Once	Once
Problem	Mouse wants to be friends with lion.	Mouse bothered lion.
Beginning	Lion laughed when mouse wanted to be his friend.	Mouse ran across lion's paw, so lion wanted to eat him.
Middle	Lion got a thorn in his paw.	Hunters tied up lion.
Ending	The mouse got the thorn out.	The mouse chewed the ropes so that the lion could escape.

What are fables? (Idea: *Stories written to be fun to read but also to teach a lesson.*)

What's another name for the lesson that fables try to teach? *Moral.*

What do you think the moral of this fable is? (Idea: *The moral of the story is that even little friends can be valuable.*)

Discuss the moral and its application to students' lives.

Part C: Fluency Building

5 minutes

Student Materials:
Storybook 2

Conduct after the lesson, using story of the day.

Activity 1 Partner Reading

It's time for partner reading.

Direct students to the story of the day. **Assign** student partners as Partner 1 and Partner 2. **Monitor** student reading. **Guide** as needed.

Lesson 143

Materials

Teacher: 1-Narrative Story Map; *Storybook 2*

Student: Copy of 1-Narrative Story Map; *Storybook 2;* vocabulary notebook

---

Part A: Vocabulary Development

5 minutes

Student Materials:
Storybook 2
Vocabulary notebook

Activity 1 Learn New Vocabulary Word

Elicit responses to questions. **Guide** as needed.
Today you'll learn a new vocabulary word. **Deck. Deck** means **ship's floor.**
What does **deck** mean? *Ship's floor.*

Another word for **ship's floor** is **deck.** What's another word for **ship's floor?**
Deck.

The man saw an enormous dog on the **ship's floor.** He felt afraid of that dog
on the **deck.**

What's another word for **ship's floor?** *Deck.*
Discuss where students might see ships with a deck.

Write **deck** and what it means in your vocabulary notebook.
Direct students to write word in their vocabulary notebook. **Guide** as needed.

Activity 2 Review Vocabulary Word

Elicit responses to questions. **Guide** as needed.
What is **Japan?** *An island country.*
What's another word for **an island country?** *Japan.*

Review vocabulary words in appropriate context in *Storybook 2.*

Part B: Comprehension Strategies

IWB

Teacher Materials:
Storybook 2

Narrative Story Map

Student Materials:
Storybook 2

Narrative Story Map

Activity 1 **Set a Purpose for Reading—A Before-Reading Strategy**

Elicit responses to questions. **Guide** as needed.
Why do you set a purpose for reading? (Idea: *So you know what to think about as you read.*)

Guide students to skim Story 142, pages 176–178, and look for Narrative Story Map elements.

Today as you read, you're going to get ready to fill out a Narrative Story Map.

What is your purpose for reading the story? (Idea: *To get ready to fill out the Narrative Story Map.*)

Activity 2 **Story Map—An After-Reading Strategy**

Show Narrative Story Map.
Today you'll work with a partner to fill out the Narrative Story Map for "Casey the Rabbit."
Allow students to attempt to fill out all the parts of the Narrative Story Map with a partner. **Assure** students that if they get stuck, you'll work together with them tomorrow to find and finish the answers.

Good for you. You're thinking hard and finding the story elements by yourself.

Save Narrative Story Maps to debrief in Lesson 144.

Part C: Fluency Building

Conduct after the lesson using the story of the day.

Activity 1 **Partner Reading**

It's time for partner reading.
Direct students to the story of the day. **Assign** student partners as Partner 1 and Partner 2. **Monitor** student reading. **Guide** as needed.

Lesson 144

Part A: Vocabulary Development

5 minutes

Student Materials:
Storybook 2
Vocabulary notebook

Activity 1 Learn New Vocabulary Word

Elicit responses to questions. **Guide** as needed.
Today you'll learn a new vocabulary word. **Sink. Sink** means **go to the bottom of water.** What does **sink** mean? *Go to the bottom of water.*

Another word for **go to the bottom of water** is **sink.** What's another word for **go to the bottom of water?** *Sink.*

If Mia throws that rock into the lake, the rock will **go to the bottom of the water.** The rock is so heavy it will **sink.**

What's another word for **go to the bottom of water?** *Sink.*
Discuss things that sink in water.

Write **sink** and what it means in your vocabulary notebook.
Direct students to write word in their vocabulary notebook. **Guide** as needed.

Activity 2 Review Vocabulary Word

Elicit responses to questions. **Guide** as needed.
What does **deck** mean? *Ship's floor.*
What's another word for **ship's floor?** *Deck.*

Review vocabulary words in appropriate context in *Storybook 2.*

12 minutes

IWB

Teacher Materials:
Storybook 2

Narrative Story Map

Student Materials:
Storybook 2

Narrative Story Map

Activity 1 **Review Narrative Story Map—An After-Reading Strategy**

Write answers on Narrative Story Map as students answer questions. **Elicit** responses to questions. **Guide** as needed.
We'll look at your Narrative Story Maps from the last lesson. Tell me how you filled out your map.

Encourage student partners to fill in any blanks on their maps by copying.
What did you write on the line for the title? *"Casey the Rabbit."*

Who are the main characters in the story? *Casey and the fox.*

What did you write in the Setting box for where? *In the woods.*

What did you write in the Setting box for when? *One day.*

What did you write in the box for the problem? (Student response.)

Elicit several suggestions for the problem, beginning, middle, and ending and write the best student generated response in the box.
What did you write for the beginning? (Student response.)

What did you write for the middle? (Student response.)

What did you write for the end? (Student response.)

Did you like this story? Why? (Student response.)

Great job filling out a Narrative Story Map with a partner.

5 minutes

Student Materials:
Storybook 2

Part C: Fluency Building

Conduct after the lesson, using story of the day.

Activity 1 **Partner Reading**

It's time for partner reading.
Direct students to the story of the day. **Assign** student partners as Partner 1 and Partner 2. **Monitor** student reading. **Guide** as needed.

Lesson 145

Materials

Teacher: 10-KWL Chart; expository book of teacher choice; *Storybook 2,* 2-Vocabulary Acquisition and Use, Writing Prompts, 5-My Writing Checklist

Student: Copy of 10-KWL Chart; vocabulary notebook; *Storybook 2,* Copy of 2-Vocabulary Acquisition and Use and 5-My Writing Checklist; Lined Paper

Part A: Vocabulary Development

5 minutes

IWB

Teacher Materials:
Vocabulary Acquisition and Use

Student Materials:
Storybook 2

Vocabulary notebook

Vocabulary Acquisition and Use

Activity 1 Vocabulary Notebook Review

Today you'll study from your vocabulary notebook. Studying your words and what they mean will help you know your words even better. You'll study the four words we studied this week.

Guide students as they study <u>thorn</u>, <u>Japan</u>, <u>deck</u>, and <u>sink</u>.

Activity 2 Cumulative Vocabulary Review

Elicit responses to questions. **Guide** as needed.
Directions: Listen and tell me the correct vocabulary word for each question.

What's another word for **ship's floor?** *Deck.*
What's another word for **an island country?** *Japan.*
What's another word for **go to the bottom of water?** *Sink.*
What's another word for the **sharp part of a plant?** *Thorn.*

Repeat difficult words as needed.

Review vocabulary words in appropriate context in *Storybook 2.*

Activity 3 Vocabulary Acquisition and Use

Display Vocabulary Acquisition and Use. **Have** students work with a neighbor to complete Vocabulary Acquisition and Use.
Today's vocabulary words are _____ and _____ [and _____ and _____].
Vocabulary words: **sink** and **drop; roared** and **screamed**
Write the words on the lines provided. Then write the words in the boxes based on whether you think each word is less/smaller or more/larger than the other word. Below the boxes, write why you think word 1 is less/smaller and word 2 is more/larger than word 1.
Repeat for words 3 and 4. **Have** students share what they wrote. **Discuss** examples of how these words might be used.

12 minutes

IWB

Teacher Materials:
KWL Chart

Expository book

Student Materials:
KWL Chart

Activity 1 KWL Chart for Expository Text—A Before-Reading Strategy

Show visual of KWL Chart. **Elicit** answers from students. **Guide** as needed.
Here's a KWL chart that you can use when you're reading expository text.

Why do you use a KWL chart? (Idea: *To help organize and remember information.*)

We'll read a nonfiction or expository text on _____.

Why will we read this book about _____ ? (Idea: *To learn more about _____.*)

Before we read this book, you will fill out the first two sections of the KWL Chart.

Allow students a few minutes to write. **Elicit** ideas and write them on the chart for students to copy, as needed. **Guide** as needed.
Let's think of some things you know about _____ and write them on the chart in the "K" section.

Let's think of some things you want to know about _____ and write them on the chart in the "W" section.

The last section has a place to list what you learned about the topic from the book after you read. We'll fill out this section after we read the book.

Why do you fill out a chart like this? (Idea: *It helps you remember what you learned about a topic from a book.*)

Save chart to complete in Lesson 146.

Part C: Fluency Building

5 minutes

Student Materials:
Storybook

Conduct after the lesson, using story of the day.

Activity 1 Partner Reading

It's time for partner reading.
Direct students to the story of the day. **Assign** student partners as Partner 1 and Partner 2. **Monitor** student reading. **Guide** as needed.

10 minutes

Teacher Materials:
Writing Prompts

My Writing Checklist

Student Materials:
Lined Paper

My Writing Checklist

Activity 1 Write and Use Parts of Speech and Conventions

Time to write using a writing prompt based on the stories we've been reading.

Assign student partners. **Distribute** lined paper to students. **Display** writing prompts and have students choose one to write about or assign a writing prompt of your choice. **Review** parts of speech and punctuation as well as the writing checklist with students. **Tell** students to write one paragraph (minimum of four sentences per paragraph) on their own to answer the writing prompt. **Tell** them to use their writing checklist (first column labeled "Did I use them?") to ensure they include important parts of speech or punctuation in their writing. **Tell** students which parts of speech or punctuation to focus on, if you wish. **Model** what it means to answer a writing prompt and to use the writing checklist during and after the writing process, as needed. **Monitor** and guide students as needed. **Model** what it means to have a neighbor look over his or her neighbor's writing and to complete the writing checklist (second column labeled "Did my neighbor use them?"), as needed. **Have** students share what they wrote as time permits.

Writing Prompt 1	Writing Prompt 2	Writing Prompt 3
Should you ever yell wolf when there isn't a wolf? Why or why not?	What does "it takes more than speed to win a race" mean to you?	If a prince were once a tramp, how would it help him be a better prince?

Lesson 146

Part A: Vocabulary Development

5 minutes

Student Materials:
Storybook 2

Vocabulary notebook

Activity 1 Learn New Vocabulary Word

Elicit responses to questions. **Guide** as needed.

Today you'll learn a new vocabulary word. **Famished. Famished** means **hungry.** What does **famished** mean? *Hungry.*

Another word for **famished** is **hungry.** What's another word for **famished?** *Hungry.*

The stray dog was **famished** when he wandered into our backyard. He was **hungry.**

What's another word for **hungry?** *Famished.*

Discuss when someone or something might be famished.

Write **famished** and what it means in your vocabulary notebook.

Direct students to write word in their vocabulary notebook. **Guide** as needed.

Activity 2 Review Vocabulary Word

Elicit responses to questions. **Guide** as needed.

What does **sink** mean? *Go to the bottom of water.*

What's another word for **go the bottom of water?** *Sink.*

Review vocabulary words in appropriate context in *Storybook 2.*

12 minutes

Teacher Materials:
KWL Chart

Expository book

Student Materials:

KWL Chart

Activity 1 Set a Purpose for Reading—A Before-Reading Strategy

Today you'll hear a book about _____. What's your purpose for listening to this book? (Idea: *Learn something new.*)

What do you call this kind of text? *Expository text.*

How is expository text organized? (Idea: *Around topics or ideas.*)

What kinds of things do you find in expository text? (Idea: *Headings, captions, labels, lists, table of contents, photographs, and index.*)

The expository text we'll read today is organized around the topic of _____. It will give you information that is true about _____.
Read expository text of choice. **Note** features of expository text as you read, such as headings, captions, labels, lists, table of contents, photographs, index, and diagrams.

Activity 2 KWL Chart—An After-Reading Strategy

Show KWL Chart from Lesson 145. **Review** first two columns.
In the last lesson, we filled in two columns of our chart.

Now we're ready to fill in the last column.

Allow students time to fill in last section of chart independently. **Elicit** responses to fill in the "What I Learned" column, and **model** writing so students can copy.
We read _____ to learn something new about _____. Now let's make a list of all the new things we learned.

What is the name of the chart that helps you organize information from an expository text? *A KWL chart.*

Provide a reading center to display books being read so that students can enjoy them again during free time.

Part C: Fluency Building

5 minutes

Student Materials:
Storybook 2

Conduct after the lesson, using story of the day.

Activity 1 Partner Reading

It's time for partner reading.
Direct students to the story of the day. **Assign** student partners as Partner 1 and Partner 2. **Monitor** student reading. **Guide** as needed.

Lesson 147

Materials

Teacher: *Storybook 2*

Student: *Storybook 2;* sticky notes; vocabulary notebook

Part A: Vocabulary Development

5 minutes

Student Materials:
Storybook 2

Vocabulary notebook

Activity 1 Learn New Vocabulary Word

Elicit responses to questions. **Guide** as needed.
Today you'll learn a new vocabulary word. **Peevish. Peevish** means **cranky.**
What does **peevish** mean? *Cranky.*

Another word for **cranky** is **peevish.** What's another word for **cranky?**
Peevish.

Michael was **cranky** when he lost his best baseball mitt. His mom said he was
peevish because he was so mad at himself for losing his mitt.

What's another word for **cranky?** *Peevish.*
Discuss when students have felt peevish.

Write **peevish** and what it means in your vocabulary notebook.
Direct students to write word in their vocabulary notebook. **Guide** as needed.

Activity 2 Review Vocabulary Word

Elicit responses to questions. **Guide** as needed.
What does **famished** mean? *Hungry.*
What's another word for **hungry?** *Famished.*

Review vocabulary words in appropriate context in *Storybook 2.*

Part B: Comprehension Strategies

12 minutes

Teacher Materials:
Storybook 2

Student Materials:
Storybook 2

Sticky notes

Activity 1 Set a Purpose for Reading—A Before-Reading Strategy

Elicit responses to questions. **Guide** as needed.
What's it called when you figure out why you're reading before you read?
(Idea: *Setting a purpose.*)

Today your purpose while you read is to make mental images. As you read,
you'll try to "see" or "feel" the words in the story.

Mental Imaging—A During-Reading Strategy

Elicit responses to questions. **Guide** as needed.
What do you call it when you make pictures of what you are reading in your brain? *Mental imaging.*

When you make pictures in your brain while you read, you "see" what the story is telling in words. The words might also make you "feel" what the character is feeling.

Guide students to read Story 146, pages 190–192, and to record mental images on sticky notes.
Read the story, and mark the sentence with a sticky note when you have a mental image. Draw a quick sketch or write some words on the sticky note to remind you what your mental image was. Stick it in your book next to the sentence that that gave you the mental image. When you're finished, we'll share our mental images with the class.

Discuss sentence chosen and mental images developed.
Share with the class the sentence you chose, and tell the picture you saw in your brain or the feelings you felt.

Part C: Fluency Building

5 minutes

Student Materials:
Storybook 2

Conduct after the lesson, using story of the day.

Activity 1 **Partner Reading**

It's time for partner reading.
Direct students to the story of the day. **Assign** student partners as Partner 1 and Partner 2. **Monitor** student reading. **Guide** as needed.

Lesson 148

Materials

Teacher: *Storybook 2*

Student: *Storybook 2;* sticky notes; vocabulary notebook

Part A: Vocabulary Development

5 minutes

Student Materials:
Storybook 2

Vocabulary notebook

Activity 1 Learn New Vocabulary Word

Elicit responses to questions. **Guide** as needed.
Today you'll learn a new vocabulary word. **Rid. Rid** means **do away with.**
What does **rid** mean? *Do away with.*

Another word for **do away with** is **rid.** What's another word for **do away with?** *Rid.*

The teacher asked Ashley to **do away with** all the trash in her desk. The teacher said Ashley should get **rid** of the trash.

What's another word for **do away with?** *Rid.*
Discuss things students get rid of.

Write **rid** and what it means in your vocabulary notebook.
Direct students to write word in their vocabulary notebook. **Guide** as needed.

Activity 2 Review Vocabulary Word

Elicit responses to questions. **Guide** as needed.
What does **peevish** mean? *Cranky.*
What's another word for **cranky?** *Peevish.*

Review vocabulary words in appropriate context in *Storybook 2.*

Part B: Comprehension Strategies

12 minutes

Teacher Materials:
Storybook 2

Student Materials:
Storybook 2

Sticky notes

Activity 1 Text-to-Self Connections—An After-Reading Strategy

Refer to Story 147, pages 193–195.

One way to understand stories better is to make text-to-self connections.

What do you do when you make text-to-self connections? (Idea: *Connect your own experiences with a story you read.*)

Read the story, and find a place in the story to make a text-to-self connection. Mark the place with your sticky note. Think about your experience and how it connects to this part of the story. Share your connection with the class. **Read** the story to think of a text-to-self connection. **Elicit** responses, and **discuss** connections that students can make to the story. **Guide** as needed.

Remember: When you connect something that has happened to you to something that happens in the story, you're making text-to-self connections. Thinking about your experiences when you read is a good strategy to help you understand what you read.

Part C: Fluency Building

5 minutes

Student Materials:
Storybook 2

Conduct after the lesson, using story of the day.

Activity 1 Partner Reading

It's time for partner reading.
Direct students to the story of the day. **Assign** student partners as Partner 1 and Partner 2. **Monitor** student reading. **Guide** as needed.

Lesson 149

Materials

Teacher: Narrative trade book of teacher choice; 1-Narrative Story Map; *Storybook 2*
Student: Copy of 1-Narrative Story Map; vocabulary notebook; *Storybook 2*

Part A: Vocabulary Development

5 minutes

Student Materials:
Storybook 2
Vocabulary notebook

Activity 1 Learn New Vocabulary Word

Elicit responses to questions. **Guide** as needed.
Today you'll learn a new vocabulary word. **Stroll. Stroll** means **walk.**
What does **stroll** mean? *Walk.*

Another word for **walk** is **stroll.** What's another word for **walk?** *Stroll.*

Dad took the baby for a **stroll** in the park. They got good exercise on their **walk.**

What's another word for **walk?** *Stroll.*
Discuss when students might stroll.

Write **stroll** and what it means in your vocabulary notebook.
Direct students to write word in their vocabulary notebook. **Guide** as needed.

Activity 2 Review Vocabulary Word

Elicit responses to questions. **Guide** as needed.
What does **rid** mean? *Do away with.*
What's another word for **do away with?** *Rid.*

Review vocabulary words in appropriate context in *Storybook 2.*

Part B: Comprehension Strategies

Teacher Materials:
Narrative trade book

Narrative Story Map

Student Materials:
Narrative Story Map

Activity 1 Set a Purpose for Reading—A Before-Reading Strategy

Elicit responses to questions. **Guide** as needed.
Why do you set a purpose for reading? (Idea: *So you know what to think about as you read*.)

Today as you read, you're going to get ready to fill out a Narrative Story Map.

What is your purpose for reading the story? (Idea: *To get ready to fill out the Narrative Story Map.*)

Read narrative trade book of choice to students. **Discuss** story elements as you read the book to prepare students to fill out Narrative Story Map about the trade book.

Activity 2 Story Map—An After-Reading Strategy

Show Narrative Story Map.
Today you'll work with a partner to fill out the Narrative Story Map for
_____ .

Allow students to attempt to fill out all parts of the Narrative Story Map with a partner. **Assure** students that if they get stuck, you'll work together with them tomorrow to find and finish the answers.

Good for you. You're thinking hard and finding the story elements by yourself.
Save Narrative Story Maps to debrief in Lesson 144.

Provide a reading center to display books being read so that students can enjoy them again during free time.

Part C: Fluency Building

Conduct after the lesson, using story of the day.

Activity 1 Partner Reading

It's time for partner reading.

Direct students to the story of the day. **Assign** student partners as Partner 1 and Partner 2. **Monitor** student reading. **Guide** as needed.

Lesson 150

Part A: Vocabulary Development

5 minutes

IWB

Teacher Materials:
Vocabulary Acquisition and Use

Student Materials:
Storybook 2

Vocabulary Notebook

Vocabulary Acquisition and Use

Activity 1 Vocabulary Notebook Review

Today you'll study from your vocabulary notebook. Studying your words and what they mean will help you know your words even better. You'll study the eight words we studied this week.
Guide students as they study <u>thorn</u>, <u>Japan</u>, <u>deck</u>, <u>sink</u>, <u>famished</u>, <u>peevish</u>, <u>rid</u>, and <u>stroll</u>.

Activity 2 Cumulative Vocabulary Review

Elicit responses to questions. **Guide** as needed.
Directions: Listen and tell me the correct vocabulary word for each question.

What's another word for **do away with?** *Rid.*
What's another word for **walk?** *Stroll.*
What's another word for **hungry?** *Famished.*
What's another word for the **sharp part of a plant?** *Thorn.*
What's another word for **an island country?** *Japan.*
What's another word for **cranky?** *Peevish.*
What's another word for **ship's floor?** *Deck.*
What's another word for **go to the bottom of water?** *Sink.*

Repeat difficult words as needed.

Review vocabulary words in appropriate context in *Storybook 2*.

Activity 3 Vocabulary Acquisition and Use

Display Vocabulary Acquisition and Use. **Have** students work with a neighbor to complete Vocabulary Acquisition and Use.
Today's vocabulary words are _____ and _____ [and _____ and _____].
Vocabulary words: **famished** and **hungry; stroll** and **walk**
Write the words on the lines provided. Then write the words in the boxes based on whether you think each word is less/smaller or more/larger than the other word. Below the boxes, write why you think word 1 is less/smaller and word 2 is more/larger than word 1.
Repeat for words 3 and 4. **Have** students share what they wrote. **Discuss** examples of how these words might be used.

12 minutes

IWB

Teacher Materials:
Narrative Story Map

Narrative trade book

My Book Review

Student Materials:
Narrative Story Map

My Book Review

Activity 1 Review Narrative Story Map—An After-Reading Strategy

Write answers on Narrative Story Map as students answer questions.
We'll look at your Narrative Story Maps from the last lesson. Tell me how you filled out your map.

Encourage student partners to fill in any blanks on their maps by copying.
What did you write on the line for the title? (Student response.)

Who are the main characters in the story? (Student response.)

What did you write in the Setting box for where? (Student response.)

What did you write in the Setting box for when? (Student response.)

What did you write in the box for the problem? (Student responses.)

Elicit several suggestions for the problem, beginning, middle, and end, and write the best student-generated response in the box.
What did you write for the beginning? (Student responses.)

What did you write for the middle? (Student responses.)

What did you write for the end? (Student responses.)

Did you like this story? Why? (Student responses.)

Great job filling out a Narrative Story Map with a partner.

Provide a reading center to display books being read so that students can enjoy them again during free time.

Activity 2 Develop Opinions—An After-Reading Strategy

Today we'll found out your opinion or how you feel about the stories you read. You will choose a book to read and then complete the My Book Review form. You'll need to tell if you like or don't like the book and why. You must give a reason for why you like or don't like the book. Finally, you can tell if you would recommend the book to others.

Have students read a narrative or expository trade book of their choice. **Have** students complete My Book Review form when they are finished reading their book. **Model** how to complete the My Book Review form. **Guide** students as needed. **Have** students share their book reviews with the class as time permits.

Part C: Fluency Building

Conduct after the lesson, using the story of the day.

Activity 1 Partner Reading

It's time for partner reading.

Direct students to the story of the day. **Assign** student partners as Partner 1 and Partner 2. **Monitor** student reading. **Guide** as needed.

Lesson 151

Materials

Teacher: *Storybook 2*

Student: *Storybook 2;* vocabulary notebook

Part A: Vocabulary Development

5 minutes

Student Materials:
Storybook 2

Vocabulary notebook

Activity 1 Learn New Vocabulary Word

Elicit responses to questions. **Guide** as needed.
Today you'll learn a new vocabulary word. **Reply. Reply** means **answer.**
What does **reply** mean? *Answer.*

Another word for **answer** is **reply.** What's another word for **answer?** *Reply.*

The teacher asked for an **answer** to the math problem. Jamal was quick to **reply,** "Eight."

What's another word for **answer?** *Reply.*
Discuss times when students reply.

Write **reply** and what it means in your vocabulary notebook.
Direct students to write word in their vocabulary notebook. **Guide** as needed.

Activity 2 Review Vocabulary Word

Elicit responses to questions. **Guide** as needed.
What does **stroll** mean? *Walk.*
What's another word for **walk?** *Stroll.*

Review vocabulary words in appropriate context in *Storybook 2.*

Part B: Comprehension Strategies

Activity 1 Read with Prosody—A During-Reading Strategy

Guide students to read choice of Stories 146–149, pages 190–202, with prosody.

Each student should read only one story. **Monitor** partner reading.

You have learned a lot about reading stories the right way. You know how to read questions. You know how to read and pay attention to the punctuation. You even know about dialogue. Today you'll practice reading the whole story yourself with expression. Read the whole story to your partner. Your partner will be listening for you to read with expression. Make your voice really interesting. Read the dialogue with different voices. Make sure your voice goes up at the ends of the questions. Take a small breath between sentences. It should be fun to listen to you read the whole story. Reread a sentence if you make a little mistake.

Now let your partner do the same thing while you listen to the story. This should be fun.

Guide partners to read a different story with prosody.

Part C: Fluency Building

Conduct after the lesson, using story of the day.

Activity 1 Partner Reading

It's time for partner reading.

Direct students to the story of the day. **Assign** student partners as Partner 1 and Partner 2. **Monitor** student reading. **Guide** as needed.

Lesson 152

Part A: Vocabulary Development

5 minutes

Student Materials:
Storybook 2

Vocabulary notebook

Activity 1 Learn New Vocabulary Word

Elicit responses to questions. **Guide** as needed.
Today you'll learn a new vocabulary word. **Memorize. Memorize** means **remember.** What does **memorize mean?** *Remember.*

Another word for **remember** is **memorize.** What's another word for **remember?** *Memorize.*

I want to **remember** the math facts, so I will **memorize** the facts this year.

What's another word for **remember?** *Memorize.*
Discuss things students want or need to memorize.

Write **memorize** and what it means in your vocabulary notebook.
Direct students to write word in their vocabulary notebook. **Guide** as needed.

Activity 2 Review Vocabulary Word

Elicit responses to questions. **Guide** as needed.
What does **reply** mean? *Answer.*
What's another word for **answer?** *Reply.*

Review vocabulary words in appropriate context in *Storybook 2.*

Part B: Comprehension Strategies

12 minutes

Teacher Materials:
Chart/IWB

Student Materials:
Narrative books

Sticky notes

Activity 1 Generate Questions—A During-Reading Strategy

Refer to narrative stories chosen by students.
Asking questions is a strategy to use when you are reading stories.

Why do you ask questions when you're reading? *To understand the story better.*

Draw chart/IWB for posting sentence and question notes. **Elicit** responses to questions.
Guide as needed.

You get to choose a narrative story to read yourself. You're going to work to find a sentence in the story and think up some questions about that sentence by yourself. You'll write the title of the book and your sentence on a sticky note. Then you'll write questions on other sticky notes. When you're finished, you can bring me your notes, and we'll post them on our chart.

Post a sticky note with sentences on one side of the chart and the sticky notes with the questions on the other side of the chart across from the sentence. **Discuss** sentences chosen and questions generated. **Share** with class examples of good questions.

Sample Chart for Questions	
Sentences	**Questions**
☐	☐ ☐ ☐

Choose some of the questions generated, and **elicit** responses from the student who read the book.

Answer the questions. (Student responses.)
Save student-choice narrative books for further activities in the next lesson.

Part C: Fluency Building

5 minutes

Student Materials:
Storybook 2

Conduct after the lesson, using story of the day.

Activity 1 Partner Reading

It's time for partner reading.
Direct students to the story of the day. **Assign** student partners as Partner 1 and Partner 2. **Monitor** student reading. **Guide** as needed.

Lesson 153

Part A: Vocabulary Development

5 minutes

Student Materials:
Storybook 2

Vocabulary notebook

Activity 1 Learn New Vocabulary Word

Elicit responses to questions. **Guide** as needed.
Today you'll learn a new vocabulary word. **Repeat. Repeat** means **say or do again.** What does **repeat** mean? *Say or do again.*

Another word for **say or do again** is **repeat.** What's another word for **say or do again?** *Repeat.*

When Hannah wants to remember something important, she will **say it again.** She will **repeat it** until she remembers.

What's another word for **say or do again?** *Repeat.*
Discuss things students repeat to learn.

Write **repeat** and what it means in your vocabulary notebook.
Direct students to write word in their vocabulary notebook. **Guide** as needed.

Activity 2 Review Vocabulary Word

Elicit responses to questions. **Guide** as needed.
What does **memorize** mean? *Remember.*
What's another word for **remember?** *Memorize.*

Review vocabulary words in appropriate context in *Storybook 2.*

Part B: Comprehension Strategies

12 minutes

Student Materials:
Narrative books

Sticky notes

Activity 1 Text-to-Self Connections—An After-Reading Strategy

Refer to narrative trade books chosen by students in Lesson 152.
One way to understand stories better is to make text-to-self connections.

What do you do when you make text-to-self connections? (Idea: *Connect your own experiences with a story you read.*)

Read the story, and find a place in the story to make a text-to-self connection. Mark the place with your sticky note. Think about your experience and how it connects to this part of the story. Share your connection with the class.

Read the story to think of a text-to-self connection. **Elicit** responses, and **discuss** connections that students can make to the story. **Guide** as needed.

Remember: When you connect something that has happened to you to something that happens in the story, you are making text-to-self connections. Thinking about your experiences when you read is a good strategy to help you understand what you read.

Part C: Fluency Building

5 minutes

Student Materials:
Storybook 2

Conduct after the lesson, using story of the day.

Activity 1 Partner Reading

It's time for partner reading.

Direct students to the story of the day. **Assign** student partners as Partner 1 and Partner 2. **Monitor** student reading. **Guide** as needed.

Lesson 154

Materials

Teacher: 10-KWL Chart; *Storybook 2*

Student: Expository texts of student choice; copy of 10-KWL Chart; vocabulary notebook; *Storybook 2*

Part A: Vocabulary Development

5 minutes

Student Materials:
Storybook 2
Vocabulary notebook

Activity 1 Learn New Vocabulary Word

Elicit responses to questions. **Guide** as needed.

Today you'll learn a new vocabulary word. **Reflection. Reflection** means **image of yourself.** What does **reflection** mean? *Image of yourself.*

Another word for **image of yourself** is **reflection.** What's another word for **image of yourself?** *Reflection.*

Jean ran to the lake to see an **image of herself** in the water. She looked at her **reflection** and saw that there was mud on her cheek.

What's another word for **image of yourself?** *Reflection.*
Discuss what you use to see your reflection.

Write **reflection** and what it means in your vocabulary notebook.
Direct students to write word in their vocabulary notebook. **Guide** as needed.

Activity 2 Review Vocabulary Word

Elicit responses to questions. **Guide** as needed.
What does **repeat** mean? *Say or do it again.*
What's another word for **say or do it again?** *Repeat.*

Review vocabulary words in appropriate context in *Storybook 2.*

Part B: Comprehension Strategies

12 minutes

Teacher Materials:
KWL Chart

Student Materials:
Expository texts

KWL Chart

Activity 1 KWL Chart for Expository Text—A Before-Reading Strategy

Refer to expository texts of student choice. **Show** KWL Chart. **Elicit** responses to questions. **Guide** as needed.
Here's a KWL chart that you can use when you are reading expository text.

Why do you use a KWL chart? (Idea: *To help organize and remember information.*)

You and your partner will choose a book to read that is expository text. Before you read this book, you'll fill out the first two sections of the KWL Chart.

Allow students a few minutes to write. Then **elicit** ideas. **Guide** as needed.
Think of some things you know about your topic, and write them on the chart in the "K" section.

Think of some things you want to know about your topic, and write them on the chart in the "W" section.

The last section has a place to list what you learned about the topic from the book after you read it. You'll fill out this section after you read the book with your partner.

Why do you fill out a chart like this? (Idea: *It helps you remember what you learned about a topic.*)

Save charts and books to complete in Lesson 155.

Part C: Fluency Building

5 minutes

Student Materials:
Storybook 2

Conduct after the lesson, using story of the day.

Activity 1 Partner Reading

It's time for partner reading.
Direct students to the story of the day. **Assign** student partners as Partner 1 and Partner 2. **Monitor** student reading. **Guide** as needed.

Lesson 155

Materials

Teacher: 10-KWL Chart (from Lesson 154); *Storybook 2*, 2-Vocabulary Acquisition and Use, Writing Prompts, 5-My Writing Checklist

Student: Expository books of student choice; copy of 10-KWL Chart (from Lesson 154); vocabulary notebook; *Storybook 2*, Copy of 2- Vocabulary Acquisition and Use and 5-My Writing Checklist; Lined Papers

Part A: Vocabulary Development

5 minutes

IWB

Teacher Materials:
Vocabulary Acquisition and Use

Student Materials:
Storybook 2

Vocabulary notebook

Vocabulary Acquisition and Use

Activity 1 | Vocabulary Notebook Review

Today, you'll study from your vocabulary notebook. Studying your words and what they mean will help you know your words even better. You'll study the four words we studied this week.

Guide students as they study <u>reply</u>, <u>memorize</u>, <u>repeat</u>, and <u>reflection</u>.

Activity 2 | Cumulative Vocabulary Review

Elicit responses to questions. **Guide** as needed.
Directions: Listen and tell me the correct vocabulary word for each question.

What's another word for **image of yourself?** *Reflection.*
What's another word for **say or do again?** *Repeat.*
What's another word for **answer?** *Reply.*
What's another word for **remember?** *Memorize.*

Repeat difficult words as needed.

Review vocabulary words in appropriate context in *Storybook 2*.

Activity 3 | Vocabulary Acquisition and Use

Display Vocabulary Acquisition and Use. **Have** students work with a neighbor to complete Vocabulary Acquisition and Use.
Today's vocabulary words are _____ and _____ [and _____ and _____].
Vocabulary words: **reply** and **answer; memorize** and **remember**
Write the words on the lines provided. Then write the words in the boxes based on whether you think each word is less/smaller or more/larger than the other word. Below the boxes, write why you think word 1 is less/smaller and word 2 is more/larger than word 1.
Repeat for words 3 and 4. **Have** students share what they wrote. **Discuss** examples of how these words might be used.

12 minutes

Teacher Materials:
KWL Chart

Student Materials:
Expository texts

KWL Chart

Activity 1 Set a Purpose for Reading—A Before-Reading Strategy

Elicit responses to questions. **Guide** as needed.
Today you'll read a book you have chosen with your partner. What's your purpose for reading this book? (Idea: *Learn something new.*)

What do you call this kind of text? *Expository text.*

How is expository text organized? (Idea: *Around topics or ideas.*)

What kinds of things do you find in expository text? (Idea: *Headings, captions, labels, lists, table of contents, photographs, and index.*)

Activity 2 KWL Chart—An After-Reading Strategy

Show KWL Chart from Lesson 154. **Guide** students to review their first two columns of the chart.
In the last lesson, you filled in two columns of your chart. Look over what you wrote to help you think about what you and your partner wanted to learn from this book.
Guide students to read expository text of choice with a partner.

Now you're ready to fill in the last column. Work with your partner to write the new things you learned from this book.
Allow students time to fill in last section of chart independently. Then **elicit** responses to fill in the "What I Learned" column, and model writing so students can copy.

Way to work hard to learn something new. You'll have a chance to share what you learned in the next lesson.

Part C: Fluency Building

5 minutes

Student Materials:
Storybook 2

Conduct after the lesson, using story of the day.

Activity 1 Partner Reading

It's time for partner reading.
Direct students to the story of the day. **Assign** student partners as Partner 1 and Partner 2. **Monitor** student reading. **Guide** as needed.

Part D: Writing/Language Arts

IWB

Teacher Materials:
Writing Prompts

My Writing Checklist

Student Materials:
Lined Paper

My Writing Checklist

Activity 1 Write and Use Parts of Speech and Conventions

Time to write using a writing prompt based on the stories we've been reading.

Assign student partners. **Distribute** lined paper to students. **Display** writing prompts and have students choose one to write about or assign a writing prompt of your choice. **Review** parts of speech and punctuation as well as the writing checklist with students. **Tell** students to write one paragraph (minimum of four sentences per paragraph) on their own to answer the writing prompt. **Tell** them to use their writing checklist (first column labeled "Did I use them?") to ensure they include important parts of speech or punctuation in their writing. **Tell** students which parts of speech or punctuation to focus on, if you wish. **Model** what it means to answer a writing prompt and to use the writing checklist during and after the writing process, as needed. **Monitor** and guide students as needed. **Model** what it means to have a neighbor look over his or her neighbor's writing and to complete the writing checklist (second column labeled "Did my neighbor use them?"), as needed. **Have** students share what they wrote as time permits.

Writing Prompt 1	*Writing Prompt 2*	*Writing Prompt 3*
Would you like to have a funny green animal with big hands and red feet as a pet? Why or why not?	Have you ever had a strange dream? Tell me about it.	What would you do if you woke up and were covered in red stripes and had white hair?

Lesson 156

Materials

Teacher: *Storybook 2*

Student: Expository book from Lessons 154 and 155; KWL Chart (from Lesson 155); vocabulary notebook; *Storybook 2*

Part A: Vocabulary Development

5 minutes

Student Materials:
Storybook 2
Vocabulary notebook

Activity 1 — Learn New Vocabulary Word

Elicit responses to questions. **Guide** as needed.
Today you'll learn a new vocabulary word. **Howl. Howl** means **a long, loud cry.** What does **howl** mean? *Long, loud cry.*

Another word for **long, loud cry** is **howl.** What's another word for **long, loud cry?** *Howl.*

The hound dog gave a **long, loud cry.** She gave a **howl.**

What's another word for **long, loud cry?** *Howl.*
Discuss animals that howl.

Write **howl** and what it means in your vocabulary notebook.
Direct students to write word in their vocabulary notebook. **Guide** as needed.

Activity 2 — Review Vocabulary Word

Elicit responses to questions. **Guide** as needed.
What does **reflection** mean? *Image of yourself.*
What's another word for **image of yourself?** *Reflection.*

Review vocabulary words in appropriate context in *Storybook 2*.

Part B: Comprehension Strategies

12 minutes

Student Materials:
Expository book
KWL Chart

Activity 1 — Sharing—An After-Reading Strategy

Allow student partners to share their books and their learning.
You will share your expository book and your KWL Chart with the class.

Tell us what you and your partner wanted to learn, and then tell us the new information you learned.

Then show us your favorite page from your book, and tell us why it is your favorite.

End by telling us if you recommend that we read your book and, if so, why.

Provide a reading center to display books being read so that students can enjoy them again during free time.

Part C: Fluency Building

5 minutes

Student Materials:
Storybook 2

Conduct after the lesson, using story of the day.

Activity 1 Partner Reading

It's time for partner reading.

Direct students to the story of the day. **Assign** student partners as Partner 1 and Partner 2. **Monitor** student reading. **Guide** as needed.

Lesson 157

Part A: Vocabulary Development

5 minutes

Student Materials:
Storybook 2
Vocabulary notebook

Activity 1 Learn New Vocabulary Word

Elicit responses to questions. **Guide** as needed.
Today you'll learn a new vocabulary word. **Chuckle. Chuckle** means **laugh.**
What does **chuckle** mean? *Laugh.*

Another word for **laugh** is **chuckle.** What's another word for **laugh?** *Chuckle.*

Mom will **laugh** when she hears my funny riddle. She will **chuckle** at my riddle.

What's another word for **laugh?** *Chuckle.*
Discuss what makes you chuckle.

Write **chuckle** and what it means in your vocabulary notebook.
Direct students to write word in their vocabulary notebook. **Guide** as needed.

Activity 2 Review Vocabulary Word

Elicit responses to questions. **Guide** as needed.
What does **howl** mean? *Long, loud cry.*
What's another word for **long, loud cry?** *Howl.*

Review vocabulary words in appropriate context in *Storybook 2.*

Part B: Comprehension Strategies

Teacher Materials:
Chart with comprehension strategies

Student Materials:
Narrative trade book

Activity 1 Set a Purpose for Reading—A Before-Reading Strategy

Reference comprehension-strategies chart developed in Lesson 40. **Elicit** responses to questions. **Guide** as needed.
You have learned some strategies to use before you read to help you understand what you read.

Elicit strategies that students know and would like to use before reading. If they want to Activate Background Knowledge, allow them to discuss their schema for topics in the story. If they want to Set a Purpose, let them decide what purpose they will use. If they want to Predict what will happen in the story based on the title and the pictures, allow them to do so. **Guide** as needed.
Tell me some strategies that you know how to use before you read a book. (Student responses.)

What strategy would be best to use before reading the book you chose? (Student responses.)

Tell your partner what strategy you will use. Use your strategy before you read. Then read your book.

After you read, tell your partner if the strategy you used helped you understand your book and, if so, how it helped you.

Save your book for the next lesson.

You are smart for choosing strategies to use before you read that help you have good comprehension.

Part C: Fluency Building

Student Materials:
Storybook 2

Conduct after the lesson, using story of the day.

Activity 1 Partner Reading

It's time for partner reading.
Direct students to the story of the day. **Assign** student partners as Partner 1 and Partner 2. **Monitor** student reading. **Guide** as needed.

Lesson 158

Materials

Teacher: Chart with comprehension reading strategies from Lesson 40: Part C; *Storybook 2*

Student: Narrative trade book of student choice from Lesson 157; vocabulary notebook; *Storybook 2*

Part A: Vocabulary Development

5 minutes

Student Materials:
Storybook 2
Vocabulary notebook

Activity 1 Learn New Vocabulary Word

Elicit responses to questions. **Guide** as needed.
Today you'll learn a new vocabulary word. **Stare. Stare** means **look at for a long time.** What does **stare** mean? *Look at for a long time.*

Another word for **look at for a long time** is **stare.** What's another word for **look at for a long time?** *Stare.*

Max and Alex liked to **look at** each other **for a long time**. They would **stare** at each other until one looked away.

What's another word for **look at for a long time?** *Stare.*
Discuss things you might stare at.

Write **stare** and what it means in your vocabulary notebook.
Direct students to write word in their vocabulary notebook. **Guide** as needed.

Activity 2 Review Vocabulary Word

Elicit responses to questions. **Guide** as needed.
What does **chuckle** mean? *Laugh.*
What's another word for **laugh?** *Chuckle.*

Review vocabulary words in appropriate context in *Storybook 2.*

Part B: Comprehension Strategies

12 minutes

Teacher Materials:
Chart with comprehension strategies

Student Materials:
Narrative trade book

Activity 1 Choose a Strategy—A During-Reading Strategy

Reference comprehension-strategies chart developed in Lesson 40. **Elicit** responses to questions. **Guide** as needed.
You have learned some strategies to use while you read to help you understand what you read.

Elicit the strategies that students know and would like to use during reading.
Possible choices are Mental Imaging; Reading with Prosody; Generating Questions; Summarizing; and Rereading.

Tell me some strategies that you know how to use while you are reading a book. (Student response.)

What strategy would be best to use while reading the book you chose? (Student response.)

Allow students to follow procedures learned for strategy. **Guide** as needed.
Tell your partner what strategy you will use. Use your strategy while you read your book.

After you read, tell your partner if the strategy you used helped you understand your book and, if so, how it helped you.

Save your book for the next lesson.

You are smart for choosing strategies to use while you read so you have good comprehension.

Part C: Fluency Building

5 minutes

Student Materials:
Storybook 2

Conduct after the lesson, using story of the day.

Activity 1 **Partner Reading**

It's time for partner reading.
Direct students to the story of the day. **Assign** student partners as Partner 1 and Partner 2. **Monitor** student reading. **Guide** as needed.

Lesson 159

Materials

Teacher: Chart with comprehension reading strategies from Lesson 40: Part C; *Storybook 2*

Student: Narrative book of student choice from Lessons 157 and 158; vocabulary notebook; *Storybook 2*

Part A: Vocabulary Development

5 minutes

Student Materials:
Storybook 2
Vocabulary notebook

Activity 1 Learn New Vocabulary Word

Elicit responses to questions. **Guide** as needed.
Today you'll learn a new vocabulary word. **SOS. SOS** means **a call for help.** What does **SOS** mean? *A call for help.*

Another word for **a call for help** is **SOS.** What's another word for **call for help?** *SOS.*

Jean wanted to leave so she gave a **call for help.** It was an **SOS.**

What's another word for **a call for help?** *SOS.*
Discuss times when people need to use SOS.

Write **SOS** and what it means in your vocabulary notebook.
Direct students to write word in their vocabulary notebook. **Guide** as needed.

Activity 2 Review Vocabulary Word

Elicit responses to questions. **Guide** as needed.
What does **stare** mean? *Look at for a long time.*
What's another word for **look at for a long time?** *Stare.*

Review vocabulary words in appropriate context in *Storybook 2.*

Part B: Comprehension Strategies

12 minutes

Teacher Materials:
Chart with comprehension strategies

Student Materials:
Narrative book

Activity 1 Choose a Strategy—An After-Reading Strategy

Reference comprehension-strategies chart developed in Lesson 40. **Elicit** responses to questions. **Guide** as needed.
You have learned some strategies to use after you read to help you understand what you read.

Elicit the strategies that students know and would like to use after reading. Possible choices are Identify Story Elements; Retell the story; Summarize the story; Text-to-Self connections; Text-to-Text connection; and Confirm Predictions. **Guide** as needed.
Tell me some strategies that you know how to use after you read a book. (Student response.)

What strategy would be best to use after reading the book you chose? (Student response.)

Allow students time to follow procedures for strategy chosen.
Tell your partner what strategy you will use. Use your strategy to show that you read your book.

Tell your partner if the strategy you used helped you understand your book and, if so, how it helped you.

You are smart for choosing strategies to use after you read so you have good comprehension.

Part C: Fluency Building

5 minutes

Student Materials:
Storybook 2

Conduct after the lesson, using story of the day.

Activity 1 Partner Reading

It's time for partner reading.
Direct students to the story of the day. **Assign** student partners as Partner 1 and Partner 2. **Monitor** student reading. **Guide** as needed.

Materials

Teacher: Chart with comprehension reading strategies from Lesson 40: Part C; *Storybook 2*

Student: Vocabulary notebook; *Storybook 2*

Part A: Vocabulary Development

5 minutes

IWB

Teacher Materials:
Vocabulary Acquisition and Use

Student Materials:
Storybook 2

Vocabulary Notebook

Vocabulary Acquisition and Use

Activity 1 Vocabulary Notebook Review

Today, you'll study from your vocabulary notebook. Studying your words and what they mean will help you know your words even better. You'll study the eight words we studied this week.

Guide students as they study <u>reply</u>, <u>memorize</u>, <u>repeat</u>, <u>reflection</u>, <u>howl</u>, <u>chuckle</u>, <u>stare</u>, and <u>SOS</u>.

Activity 2 Cumulative Vocabulary Review

Elicit responses to questions. **Guide** as needed.
Directions: Listen and tell me the correct vocabulary word for each question.

What's another word for **image of yourself?** *Reflection.*
What's another word for **say again?** *Repeat.*
What's another word for **answer?** *Reply.*
What's another word for **laugh?** *Chuckle.*
What's another word for **remember?** *Memorize.*
What's another word for **long, loud cry?** *Howl.*
What's another word for **look at for a long time?** *Stare.*
What's another word for **a call for help?** *SOS.*

Repeat difficult words as needed.

Review vocabulary words in appropriate context in *Storybook 2.*

Activity 3 Vocabulary Acquisition and Use

Display Vocabulary Acquisition and Use. **Have** students work with a neighbor to complete Vocabulary Acquisition and Use.
Today's vocabulary words are _____ and _____ [and _____ and _____].
Vocabulary words: **chuckle** and **laugh; howl** and **cry**
Write the words on the lines provided. Then write the words in the boxes based on whether you think each word is less/smaller or more/larger than the other word. Below the boxes, write why you think word 1 is less/smaller and word 2 is more/larger than word 1.
Repeat for words 3 and 4. **Have** students share what they wrote. **Discuss** examples of how these words might be used.

12 minutes

IWB

Teacher Materials:
Chart with comprehension strategies

My Book Review

Student Materials:
My Book Review

Reference comprehension-strategies chart developed in Lesson 40. **Elicit** responses to questions. **Guide** as needed.

Let's talk about things you have learned to do before, during, and after you read to help you understand narrative text better.

Activity 1 Review—Before-Reading Strategies

Let's talk about things you do before you read to help you understand narrative text better.

Discuss strategies that students have been using before reading narratives. **Identify** examples of when the strategy was used. **Guide** as needed.

What are some things to do before you read a new story? (Ideas: *Make predictions*—**Make Predictions**—*think about how the story connects to what I already know*—**Activate Background Knowledge**—*think about what I will try to learn*—**Set a Purpose for Reading**—*fill out the "K" and "W" section of KWL Chart for expository text.*)

Activity 2 Review—During-Reading Strategies

Let's talk about things you do while you read to help you understand narrative text better.

Discuss strategies that students have been using during reading narratives. **Identify** examples of when the strategy was used. **Guide** as needed.

What are some things you can do while you are reading to help you understand what you are reading? (Idea: *Ask questions*—**Generate Questions**—*reread*—**Fix-Up Strategy**—*tell the story in my own words*—**Summarize**—*read while paying attention to the ends of sentences or dialogue*—**Read with Prosody**—*make pictures in my mind of the story*—**Mental Imaging.**)

Activity 3 Review—After-Reading Strategies

Let's talk about things you do after you read to help you understand narrative text better.

Discuss strategies that students have been using after reading narratives. **Identify** examples of when the strategy was used. **Guide** as needed.

What are some things you can do after you read a story to help you understand or remember the story? (Ideas: *Fill out a story map*—**Identify Story Elements**—*see if predictions were correct*—**Confirming Predictions**—*make text-to-self connections; make text-to-text connections; tell the story in your own words*—**Retell**—*tell main points of story in own words*—**Summarize**—*and fill out the "L" section of KWL Chart.*)

Wow, you've learned a lot of things to do to help you understand the stories you read. When you understand what you read, you have good comprehension, which makes reading lots of fun.

Activity 4 Develop Opinions—An After-Reading Strategy

Today we'll found out your opinion or how you feel about the stories you read. You will choose a book to read and then complete the My Book Review form. You'll need to tell if you like or don't like the book and why. You must give a reason for why you like or don't like the book. Finally, you can tell if you would recommend the book to others.

Have students read a narrative or expository trade book of their choice. **Have** students complete My Book Review form when they are finished reading their book. **Model** how to complete the My Book Review form. **Guide** students as needed. **Have** students share their book reviews with the class as time permits.

Part C: Fluency Building

5 minutes

Student Materials:
Storybook 2

Conduct after the lesson, using story of the day.

Activity 1 Partner Reading

It's time for partner reading.

Direct students to the story of the day. **Assign** student partners as Partner 1 and Partner 2. **Monitor** student reading. **Guide** as needed.

Appendix A

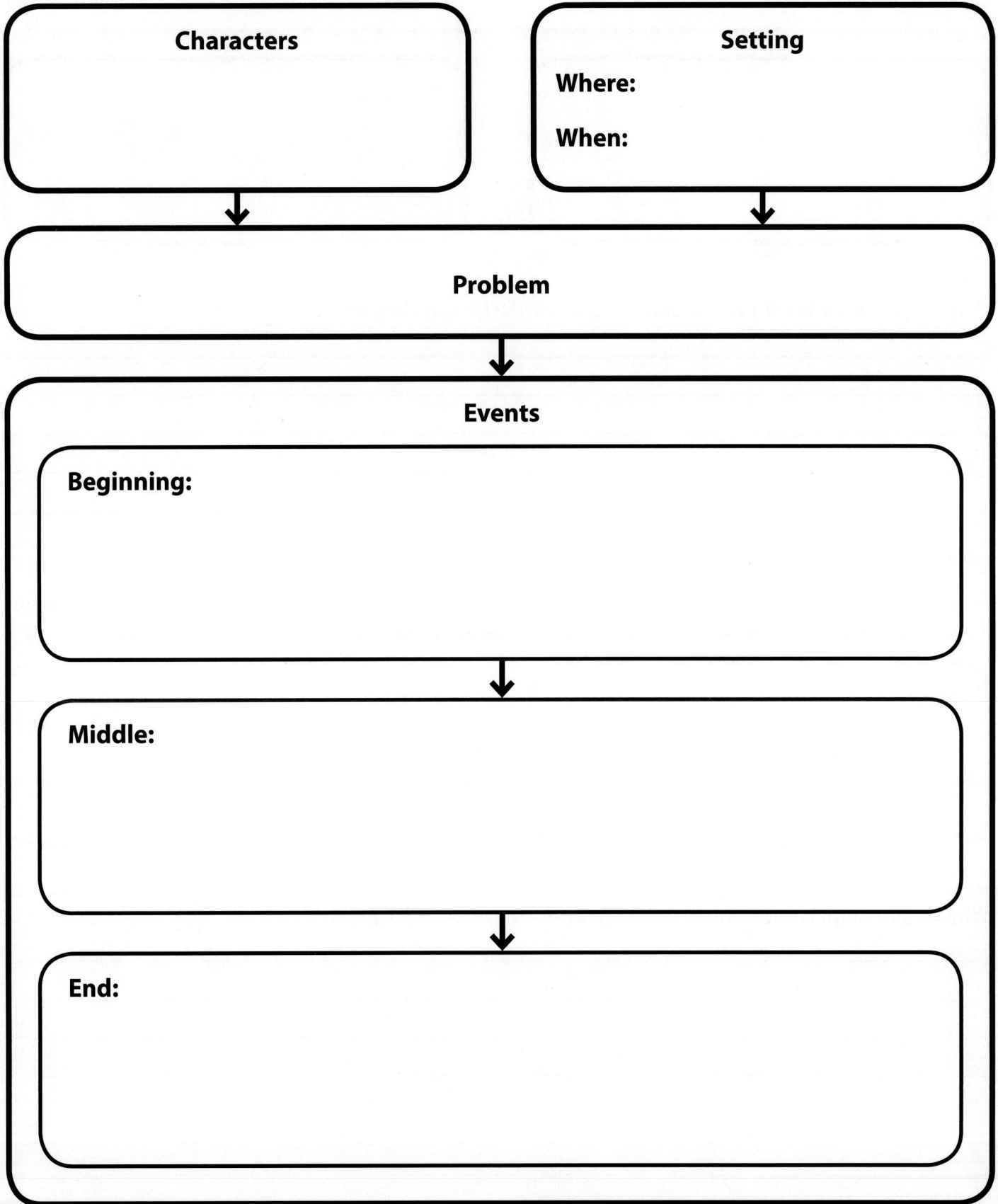

Name _____   Date _____

1: Narrative Story Map

Title: _____

Characters	Setting
	Where:
	When:

↓   ↓

Problem

↓

Events

Beginning:

↓

Middle:

↓

End:

Name _____   Date _____

2: Vocabulary Acquisition and Use

Words: _____   _____

Less/Smaller   **More/Larger**

←————————————————————————————————————→

Word 1:

Word 2:

Why do you think Word 1 is less/smaller and Word 2 is more/larger?

_____

_____

_____

_____

Words: _____   _____

Less/Smaller   **More/Larger**

←————————————————————————————————————→

Word 3:

Word 4:

Why do you think Word 3 is less/smaller and Word 4 is more/larger?

_____

_____

_____

Name _____   Date _____

3: My Book Review

Title of Book: _____

My opinion of this book is (circle one):

I like it   I do not like it

...because _____

_____ .

My reasons for this opinion are:

1. _____

_____ .

2. _____

_____ .

I think you (circle one)

should read this book   should not read this book

Name _____   Date _____

4: Semantic Web

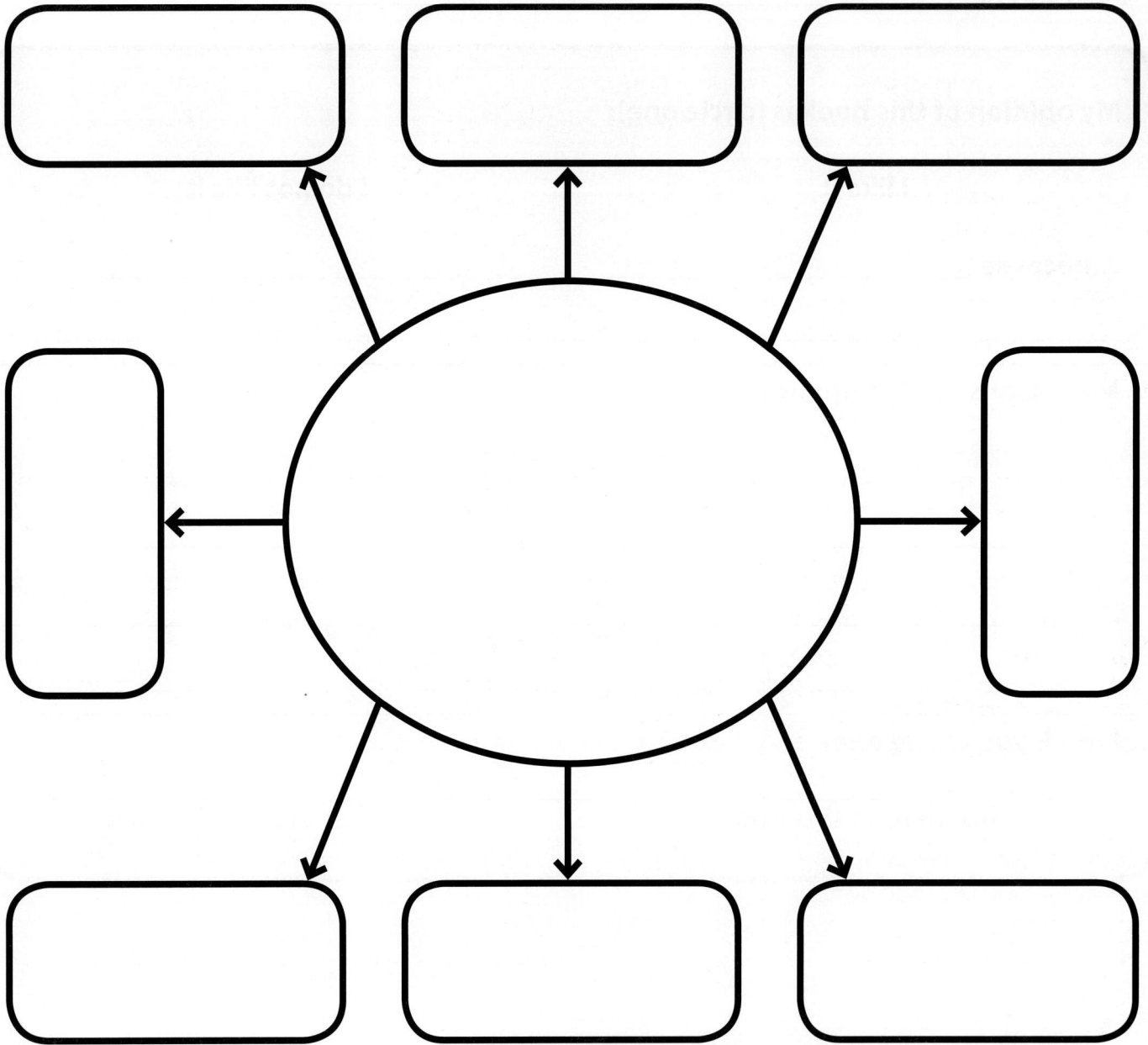

Name _____   Date _____

5: My Writing Chart
Level 1

My Neighbor's Name _____

Parts to include:	Did I use them? (circle one)		Did my neighbor use them? (circle one)	
1. **Nouns (person, place, thing, names, ownership)**	Yes	No	Yes	No
2. **Pronouns (he, she, him, her, I, me, my, they, them, their, anyone, everything)**	Yes	No	Yes	No
3. **Conjunctions (and, but, or, so, because)**	Yes	No	Yes	No
4. **Determiners (a, an, the)**	Yes	No	Yes	No
5. **Prepositions (in, on, over, under, during, beyond, toward)**	Yes	No	Yes	No
6. **Commas (dates, separate words in a series)**	Yes	No	Yes	No

Name _____   Date _____

6: My Prediction Chart

Book Title:

↓

I Predict That:

↓

Was My Prediction Correct?

Yes   No

Name _____   Date _____

7: Compare-Contrast Venn Diagram

_____   _____

Story Title   **Story Title**

Same

8: Phonemic Awareness

→

_____

9: Text-to-Text Connection

Title of Story		
Main Characters		
Setting (Where)		
Setting (When)		
Beginning		
Middle		
End		

Name _____   Date _____

10: KWL Chart

What I know	What I want to know	What I learned

Test	Tips for Teachers	Home Connections
Reading Hard Words Test (Lesson 4) **Approaching Mastery**	• See guidelines noted for Tasks 4 and 5 on pages 18 and 20 in *Presentation Book A*. Refer also to *Teacher's Guide* for remediation details. • Partner with "at mastery" student and review hard words. • Reteach difficult words using "good-bye" list: Write difficult words on board; place check mark for each day completed correctly; after 3 consecutive days completed correctly, say "good-bye" to word. • Conduct "see-say-write": Student sees word, says word, and writes word until firm. • Conduct "cover-copy-compare": Student sees word, covers word, writes word, uncovers model word, compares to word written, and corrects spelling if incorrect.	• Provide word flash cards for children to take home for additional practice. • Encourage children to share their take-home sheets with their families. • Encourage adult at home to conduct "see-say-write" activity for each word. • Encourage adult at home to conduct "cover-copy-compare" activity for each word. • Have adult at home access SRA's Home Connection Activities listed at *www.sraonline.com* • Direct Instruction • *Reading Mastery Signature Edition* • Activities
At Mastery	• See guidelines noted for Tasks 4 and 5 on pages 18 and 20 in *Presentation Book A*. • Have student "be the teacher": Partner with "approaching mastery" or ELL student and review words. • Direct student to reading and writing center in classroom to reinforce literacy and writing skills (e.g., audio books, worksheets, books, computer, writing paper).	
ELL	• See "Tips for Teachers" for "approaching mastery" and "at mastery" students. • Describe and model mouth formations for difficult sounds and words, then guide student while practicing with mirror. • Show realia or other visuals of objects (e.g., farm, yard) and concepts (e.g., don't, do). • Use gestures (e.g., clap) to demonstrate action word. • Use primary language equivalents when available and then ask student to say words in English.	• See "Home Connections" for "approaching mastery" and "at mastery" students. • Provide recording for use with word flash cards to take home for additional practice; encourage children to practice with a mirror at home, as needed. • Encourage adult at home to help children identify realia and other visuals of objects and concepts at home. • Encourage adult at home to help children practice using primary language equivalents and English words when possible.
Test		
Individual Checkout (Lesson 5) **Approaching Mastery**	• See guidelines for students who do not read within error or time limit for Lesson 5 on page 28 in *Presentation Book A*. • Partner with "at mastery" student and have him or her model reading story; have student read story. • Reteach difficult words using "good-bye" list. • Review finger placement and tracking for sentence reading. • Have adult model reading story; have student read story until firm.	• Provide word flash cards for children to take home for additional practice. • Have adult at home model reading story; have children listen and track during story reading; have children read story; have adult at home review difficult words following story reading.

Test	Tips for Teachers	Home Connections
	• Use paired reading: Good reader reads until student signals for his or her turn to read. • Develop recording of story read by good reader (e.g., at mastery student, adult); have student listen to recording and whisper read.	
At Mastery	• See guidelines for students who read within error and time limit for Lesson 5 on page 28 in *Presentation Book A*. • Partner with "approaching mastery" or ELL student and model reading story; have student read story. • Have student record self reading story as model for "approaching mastery" or ELL student. • Direct student to reading and writing center in classroom to reinforce literacy and writing skills.	
ELL	• See "Tips for Teachers" for "approaching mastery" and "at mastery" students. • Describe and model mouth formations for difficult sounds and words, then guide student while practicing with mirror. • Use sentence strips to practice reading sentences in story. • Show student how to recognize punctuation (e.g., question marks, quotation marks) when reading with prosody using a model think-aloud (e.g., I see a sentence that ends with a question mark. I need to raise my tone of voice to show that this sentence asks a question; I see quotation marks, that means that somebody is talking, so I can change my voice to sound like the person talking). • Show realia or other visuals illustrating meaning of difficult words and sentences in story. • Use primary language equivalents when available and then ask student to say words and sentences in English.	• See "Home Connections" for "approaching mastery" and "at mastery" students. • Provide recording to use with sentence strips and word flash cards for additional practice; encourage children to practice with a mirror at home, as needed. • Provide recording of story; have children listen and track during story reading; then children read aloud with recording while tracking; then children read aloud and track independently; have adult at home review difficult words following independent story reading. • Encourage adult at home to help children tell a similar story using primary language equivalents. • Encourage adult at home to help children identify realia and other visuals illustrating meaning of the sentences in story.

Test

Test	Tips for Teachers	Home Connections

Reading Hard Words Test (Lesson 9)
 	
Approaching Mastery
	• See guidelines noted for Task 4 on page 45 in *Presentation Book A*. Refer also to *Teacher's Guide* for remediation details.
	• Partner with "at mastery" student and review hard words.
	• Reteach difficult words using "good-bye" list.
	• Conduct "see-say-write" until firm.
	• Conduct "cover-copy-compare" until firm.
		• Provide word flash cards for children to take home for additional practice.
		• Encourage children to share their take-home sheets with their families.
		• Encourage adult at home to conduct "see-say-write" activity for each word.
		• Encourage adult at home to conduct "cover-copy-compare" activity for each word.
		• Have adult at home access SRA's Home Connection Activities listed at *www.sraonline.com*
		• Direct Instruction
		  • *Reading Mastery Signature Edition*
		    • Activities

Test	Tips for Teachers	Home Connections
At Mastery	• See guidelines noted for Task 4 on page 45 in *Presentation Book A.* • Have student "be the teacher": Partner with "approaching mastery" or ELL student and review words. • Direct student to reading and writing center in classroom to reinforce literacy and writing skills.	
ELL	• See "Tips for Teachers" for "approaching mastery" and "at mastery" students. • Describe and model mouth formations for difficult sounds and words, then guide student while practicing with mirror. • Show realia or other visuals of objects and concepts. • Use primary language equivalents when available and then ask student to say words in English.	• See "Home Connections" for "approaching mastery" and "at mastery" students. • Provide recording for use with word flash cards to take home for additional practice; encourage children to practice with a mirror at home, as needed. • Encourage adult at home to help children identify realia and other visuals of objects and concepts at home. • Encourage adult at home to help children practice using primary language equivalents and English words when possible.

Test		
Individual Checkout (Lesson 10) **Approaching Mastery**	• See guidelines for students who do not read within error or time limit for Lesson 10 on page 52 in *Presentation Book A.* • Partner with "at mastery" student and have him or her model reading story; have student read story. • Reteach difficult words using "good-bye" list. • Review finger placement and tracking for sentence reading. • Have adult model reading story; have student read story until firm. • Use paired reading. • Develop recording of story read by good reader; have student listen to recording and whisper read.	• Provide word flash cards for children to take home for additional practice. • Have adult at home model reading story; have children listen and track during story reading; have children read story; have adult at home review difficult words following story reading.
At Mastery	• See guidelines for students who read within error and time limit for Lesson 10 on page 52 in *Presentation Book A.* • Partner with "approaching mastery" or ELL student and model reading story; have student read story. • Have student record self reading story as model for "approaching mastery" or ELL student. • Direct student to reading and writing center in classroom to reinforce literacy and writing skills.	

Test	Tips for Teachers	Home Connections
ELL	• See "Tips for Teachers" for "approaching mastery" and "at mastery" students. • Describe and model mouth formations for difficult sounds and words, then guide student while practicing with mirror. • Use sentence strips to practice reading sentences in story. • Show student how to recognize punctuation when reading with prosody. • Show realia or other visuals illustrating meaning of difficult words and sentences in story. • Use primary language equivalents when available and then ask student to say words and sentences in English.	• See "Home Connections" for "approaching mastery" and "at mastery" students. • Provide recording to use with sentence strips and word flash cards for additional practice; encourage children to practice with a mirror at home, as needed. • Provide recording of story; have children listen and track during story reading; then children read aloud with recording while tracking; then children read aloud and track independently; have adult at home review difficult words following independent story reading. • Encourage adult at home to help children tell a similar story using primary language equivalents. • Encourage adult at home to help children identify realia and other visuals illustrating meaning of the sentences in story.

Reading Hard Words Test (Lesson 13)
 	
Approaching Mastery
	• See guidelines noted for Task 4 on page 70 in *Presentation Book A*. Refer also to *Teacher's Guide* for remediation details.
	• Partner with "at mastery" student and review hard words.
	• Reteach difficult words using "good-bye" list.
	• Conduct "see-say-write" until firm.
	• Conduct "cover-copy-compare" until firm.
		• Provide word flash cards for children to take home for additional practice.
		• Encourage children to share their take-home sheets with their families.
		• Encourage adult at home to conduct "see-say-write" activity for each word.
		• Encourage adult at home to conduct "cover-copy-compare" activity for each word.
		• Have adult at home access SRA's Home Connection Activities listed at *www.sraonline.com*
		  • Direct Instruction
		    • *Reading Mastery Signature Edition*
		      • Activities

At Mastery	• See guidelines noted for Task 4 on page 70 in *Presentation Book A*. • Have student "be the teacher": Partner with "approaching mastery" or ELL student and review words. • Direct student to reading and writing center in classroom to reinforce literacy and writing skills.	
ELL	• See "Tips for Teachers" for "approaching mastery" and "at mastery" students. • Describe and model mouth formations for difficult sounds and words, then guide student while practicing with mirror. • Show realia or other visuals of objects and concepts. • Use pantomime (e.g., swim) and gestures to demonstrate action words. • Use primary language equivalents when available and then ask student to say words in English.	• See "Home Connections" for "approaching mastery" and "at mastery" students. • Provide recording for use with word flash cards to take home for additional practice; encourage children to practice with a mirror at home, as needed. • Encourage adult at home to help children identify realia and other visuals of objects and concepts at home. • Encourage adult at home to help children practice using primary language equivalents and English words when possible.

Test	Tips for Teachers	Home Connections
Individual Checkout (Lesson 15) **Approaching Mastery**	• See guidelines for students who do not read within error or time limit for Lesson 15 on page 83 in *Presentation Book A*. • Partner with "at mastery" student and have him or her model reading story; have student read story. • Reteach difficult words using "good-bye" list. • Review finger placement and tracking for sentence reading. • Have adult model reading story; have student read story until firm. • Use paired reading. • Develop recording of story read by good reader; have student listen to recording and whisper read.	• Provide word flash cards for children to take home for additional practice. • Have adult at home model reading story; have children listen and track during story reading; have children read story; have adult at home review difficult words following story reading.
At Mastery	• See guidelines for students who read within error and time limit for Lesson 15 on page 83 in *Presentation Book A*. • Partner with "approaching mastery" or ELL student and model reading story; have student read story. • Have student record self reading story as model for "approaching mastery" or ELL student. • Direct student to reading and writing center in classroom to reinforce literacy and writing skills.	
ELL	• See "Tips for Teachers" for "approaching mastery" and "at mastery" students. • Describe and model mouth formations for difficult sounds and words, then guide student while practicing with mirror. • Use sentence strips to practice reading sentences in story. • Show student how to recognize punctuation when reading with prosody. • Show realia or other visuals illustrating meaning of difficult words and sentences in story. • Use primary language equivalents when available and then ask student to say words and sentences in English.	• See "Home Connections" for "approaching mastery" and "at mastery" students. • Provide recording to use with sentence strips and word flash cards for additional practice; encourage children to practice with a mirror at home, as needed. • Provide recording of story; have children listen and track during story reading; then children read aloud with recording while tracking; then children read aloud and track independently; have adult at home review difficult words following independent story reading. • Encourage adult at home to help children tell a similar story using primary language equivalents. • Encourage adult at home to help children identify realia and other visuals illustrating meaning of the sentences in story.
Test		

Group Accuracy Test (Lesson 20)
 	
Approaching Mastery
	• See guidelines noted for Task 11 on page 109 in *Presentation Book A*.
	• Partner with "at mastery" student and review hard words.
	• Partner with "at mastery" student and have him or her model reading title and first three sentences; have student repeat.
	• Have adult model reading title and first three sentences; have student repeat until firm.
		• Provide word flash cards for children to take home for additional practice.
		• Encourage children to share their take-home sheets with their families.
		• Have adult at home review title and first three sentences of story.
		• Have adult at home access SRA's Home Connection Activities listed at *www.sraonline.com*
		  • Direct Instruction
		    • *Reading Mastery Signature Edition*
		      • Activities

Test	Tips for Teachers	Home Connections
At Mastery	• See guidelines noted for Task 11 on page 109 in *Presentation Book A*. • Partner with "approaching mastery" or ELL student and review hard words. • Partner with "approaching mastery" or ELL student and model reading title and first three sentences; have student repeat. • Direct student to reading and writing center in classroom to reinforce literacy and writing skills.	
ELL	• See "Tips for Teachers" for "approaching mastery" and "at mastery" students. • Describe and model mouth formations for difficult sounds and words, then guide student while practicing with mirror. • Use sentence strips to practice reading sentences in story. • Show student how to recognize punctuation when reading with prosody. • Show realia or other visuals illustrating meaning of difficult words and sentences in story. • Use primary language equivalents when available and then ask student to say words and sentences in English.	• See "Home Connections" for "approaching mastery" and "at mastery" students. • Provide recording to use with sentence strips and word flash cards for additional practice; encourage children to practice with a mirror at home, as needed. • Provide recording of story; have children listen and track during story reading; then children read aloud with recording while tracking; then children read aloud and track independently; have adult at home review difficult words following independent story reading. • Encourage adult at home to help children tell a similar story using primary language equivalents. • Encourage adult at home to help children identify realia and other visuals illustrating meaning of the sentences in story.

Test

Test	Tips for Teachers	Home Connections
Individual Checkout (Lesson 20) **Approaching Mastery**	• See guidelines for students who do not read within error or time limit for Lesson 20 on page 111 in *Presentation Book A*. • Partner with "at mastery" student and have him or her model reading story; have student read story. • Reteach difficult words using "good-bye" list. • Review finger placement and tracking for sentence reading. • Have adult model reading story; have student read story until firm. • Use paired reading. • Develop recording of story read by good reader; have student listen to recording and whisper read.	• Provide word flash cards for children to take home for additional practice. • Have adult at home model reading story; have children listen and track during story reading; have children read story; have adult at home review difficult words following story reading.
At Mastery	• See guidelines for students who read within error and time limit for Lesson 20 on page 111 in *Presentation Book A*. • Partner with "approaching mastery" or ELL student and model reading story; have student read story. • Have student record self reading story as model for "approaching mastery" or ELL student. • Direct student to reading and writing center in classroom to reinforce literacy and writing skills.	

Test	Tips for Teachers	Home Connections
ELL	• See "Tips for Teachers" for "approaching mastery" and "at mastery" students. • Describe and model mouth formations for difficult sounds and words, then guide student while practicing with mirror. • Use sentence strips to practice reading sentences in story. • Show student how to recognize punctuation when reading with prosody. • Show realia or other visuals illustrating meaning of difficult words and sentences in story. • Use primary language equivalents when available and then ask student to say words and sentences in English.	• See "Home Connections" for "approaching mastery" and "at mastery" students. • Provide recording to use with sentence strips and word flash cards for additional practice; encourage children to practice with a mirror at home, as needed. • Provide recording of story; have children listen and track during story reading; then children read aloud with recording while tracking; then children read aloud and track independently; have adult at home review difficult words following independent story reading. • Encourage adult at home to help children tell a similar story using primary language equivalents. • Encourage adult at home to help children identify realia and other visuals illustrating meaning of the sentences in story.

Test

Test	Tips for Teachers	Home Connections

Assessment (after Lesson 20)
 	
Approaching Mastery
	• See "Remedial Exercises and Retesting the Students" guidelines on pages 54 and 55 in *Curriculum-Based Assessment and Fluency Teacher Handbook.*
	• Partner with "at mastery" student and review various activities.
	• Reteach difficult words using "good-bye" list.
	• Conduct "see-say-write" until firm.
	• Practice circling responses and "reading activities to yourself."
		• Provide word flash cards for children to take home for additional practice.
		• Encourage children to share their take-home sheets with their families.
		• Encourage adult at home to conduct "see-say-write" activity for each difficult word.
		• Have adult at home access SRA's Home Connection Activities listed at *www.sraonline.com*
		  • Direct Instruction
		    • *Reading Mastery Signature Edition*
		      • Activities

At Mastery	• Have student "be the teacher": Partner with "approaching mastery" or ELL student and review various activities. • Direct student to reading and writing center in classroom to reinforce literacy and writing skills.	
ELL	• See "Tips for Teachers" for "approaching mastery" and "at mastery" students. • Describe and model mouth formations for difficult sounds and words, then guide student while practicing with mirror. • Show realia or other visuals of objects or concepts to illustrate meaning of sentences. • Use primary language equivalents when available and then ask student to say words and sentences in English.	• See "Home Connections" for "approaching mastery" and "at mastery" students. • Provide recording for use with word flash cards and sentence strips to take home for additional practice; encourage children to practice with a mirror at home, as needed. • Encourage adult at home to help children identify realia and other visuals of objects or concepts to illustrate meaning of sentences at home. • Encourage adult at home to help children tell a similar story using primary language equivalents. • Encourage adult at home to help children practice using primary language equivalents and English words and sentences when possible.

Test	Tips for Teachers	Home Connections
Individual Checkout (Lesson 25) **Approaching Mastery**	• See guidelines for students who do not read within error or time limit for Lesson 25 on page 141 in *Presentation Book A*. • Partner with "at mastery" student and have him or her model reading story; have student read story. • Reteach difficult words using "good-bye" list. • Review finger placement and tracking for sentence reading. • Have adult model reading story; have student read story until firm. • Use paired reading. • Develop recording of story read by good reader; have student listen to recording and whisper read.	• Provide word flash cards for children to take home for additional practice. • Have adult at home model reading story; have children listen and track during story reading; have children read story; have adult at home review difficult words following story reading.
At Mastery	• See guidelines for students who read within error and time limit for Lesson 25 on page 141 in *Presentation Book A*. • Partner with "approaching mastery" or ELL student and model reading story; have student read story. • Have student record self reading story as model for "approaching mastery" or ELL student. • Direct student to reading and writing center in classroom to reinforce literacy and writing skills.	
ELL	• See "Tips for Teachers" for "approaching mastery" and "at mastery" students. • Describe and model mouth formations for difficult sounds and words, then guide student while practicing with mirror. • Use sentence strips to practice reading sentences in story. • Show student how to recognize punctuation when reading with prosody. • Show realia or other visuals illustrating meaning of difficult words and sentences in story. • Use primary language equivalents when available and then ask student to say words and sentences in English.	• See "Home Connections" for "approaching mastery" and "at mastery" students. • Provide recording to use with sentence strips and word flash cards for additional practice; encourage children to practice with a mirror at home, as needed. • Provide recording of story; have children listen and track during story reading; then children read aloud with recording while tracking; then children read aloud and track independently; have adult at home review difficult words following independent story reading. • Encourage adult at home to help children tell a similar story using primary language equivalents. • Encourage adult at home to help children identify realia and other visuals illustrating meaning of the sentences in story.
Test		
Group Accuracy Test (Lesson 26) **Approaching Mastery**	• See guidelines noted for Task 12 on page 145 in *Presentation Book A*. • Partner with "at mastery" student and review hard words. • Partner with "at mastery" student and have him or her model reading title and first three sentences; have student repeat.	• Provide word flash cards for children to take home for additional practice. • Encourage children to share their take-home sheets with their families. • Have adult at home review title and first three sentences of story.

Test	Tips for Teachers	Home Connections

	• Have adult model reading title and first three sentences; have student repeat until firm.	• Have adult at home access SRA's Home Connection Activities listed at *www.sraonline.com*
		  • Direct Instruction
		    • *Reading Mastery Signature Edition*
		      • Activities

At Mastery	• See guidelines noted for Task 12 on page 145 in *Presentation Book A*. • Partner with "approaching mastery" or ELL student and review hard words. • Partner with "approaching mastery" or ELL student and model reading title and first three sentences; have student repeat. • Direct student to reading and writing center in classroom to reinforce literacy and writing skills.	
ELL	• See "Tips for Teachers" for "approaching mastery" and "at mastery" students. • Describe and model mouth formations for difficult sounds and words, then guide student while practicing with mirror. • Use sentence strips to practice reading sentences in story. • Show student how to recognize punctuation when reading with prosody. • Show realia or other visuals illustrating meaning of difficult words and sentences in story. • Use primary language equivalents when available and then ask student to say words and sentences in English.	• See "Home Connections" for "approaching mastery" and "at mastery" students. • Provide recording to use with sentence strips and word flash cards for additional practice; encourage children to practice with a mirror at home, as needed. • Provide recording of story; have children listen and track during story reading; then children read aloud with recording while tracking; then children read aloud and track independently; have adult at home review difficult words following independent story reading. • Encourage adult at home to help children tell a similar story using primary language equivalents. • Encourage adult at home to help children identify realia and other visuals illustrating meaning of the sentences in story.

Test

Test	Tips for Teachers	Home Connections
Individual Checkout (Lesson 30) **Approaching Mastery**	• See guidelines for students who do not read within error or time limit for Lesson 30 on page 171 in *Presentation Book A*. • Partner with "at mastery" student and have him or her model reading story; have student read story. • Reteach difficult words using "good-bye" list. • Review finger placement and tracking for sentence reading. • Have adult model reading story; have student read story until firm. • Use paired reading. • Develop recording of story read by good reader; have student listen to recording and whisper read.	• Provide word flash cards for children to take home for additional practice. • Have adult at home model reading story; have children listen and track during story reading; have children read story; have adult at home review difficult words following story reading.

Test	Tips for Teachers	Home Connections
At Mastery	• See guidelines for students who read within error and time limit for Lesson 30 on page 171 in *Presentation Book A*. • Partner with "approaching mastery" or ELL student and model reading story; have student read story. • Have student record self reading story as model for "approaching mastery" or ELL student. • Direct student to reading and writing center in classroom to reinforce literacy and writing skills.	
ELL	• See "Tips for Teachers" for "approaching mastery" and "at mastery" students. • Describe and model mouth formations for difficult sounds and words, then guide student while practicing with mirror. • Use sentence strips to practice reading sentences in story. • Show student how to recognize punctuation when reading with prosody. • Show realia or other visuals illustrating meaning of difficult words and sentences in story. • Use primary language equivalents when available and then ask student to say words and sentences in English.	• See "Home Connections" for "approaching mastery" and "at mastery" students. • Provide recording to use with sentence strips and word flash cards for additional practice; encourage children to practice with a mirror at home, as needed. • Provide recording of story; have children listen and track during story reading; then children read aloud with recording while tracking; then children read aloud and track independently; have adult at home review difficult words following independent story reading. • Encourage adult at home to help children tell a similar story using primary language equivalents. • Encourage adult at home to help children identify realia and other visuals illustrating meaning of the sentences in story.

Test

Test	Tips for Teachers	Home Connections
Individual Checkout (Lesson 35) **Approaching Mastery**	• See guidelines for students who do not read within error or time limit for Lesson 35 on page 200 in *Presentation Book A*. • Partner with "at mastery" student and have him or her model reading story; have student read story. • Reteach difficult words using "good-bye" list. • Review finger placement and tracking for sentence reading. • Have adult model reading story; have student read story until firm. • Use paired reading. • Develop recording of story read by good reader; have student listen to recording and whisper read.	• Provide word flash cards for children to take home for additional practice. • Have adult at home model reading story; have children listen and track during story reading; have children read story; have adult at home review difficult words following story reading.
At Mastery	• See guidelines for students who read within error and time limit for Lesson 35 on page 200 in *Presentation Book A*. • Partner with "approaching mastery" or ELL student and model reading story; have student read story.	

Test	Tips for Teachers	Home Connections
	• Have student record self reading story as model for "approaching mastery" or ELL student. • Direct student to reading and writing center in classroom to reinforce literacy and writing skills.	
ELL	• See "Tips for Teachers" for "approaching mastery" and "at mastery" students. • Describe and model mouth formations for difficult sounds and words, then guide student while practicing with mirror. • Use sentence strips to practice reading sentences in story. • Show student how to recognize punctuation when reading with prosody. • Show realia or other visuals illustrating meaning of difficult words and sentences in story. • Use primary language equivalents when available and then ask student to say words and sentences in English.	• See "Home Connections" for "approaching mastery" and "at mastery" students. • Provide recording to use with sentence strips and word flash cards for additional practice; encourage children to practice with a mirror at home, as needed. • Provide recording of story; have children listen and track during story reading; then children read aloud with recording while tracking; then children read aloud and track independently; have adult at home review difficult words following independent story reading. • Encourage adult at home to help children tell a similar story using primary language equivalents. • Encourage adult at home to help children identify realia and other visuals illustrating meaning of the sentences in story.

Test

Test	Tips for Teachers	Home Connections
Group Accuracy Test (Lesson 36) **Approaching Mastery**	• See guidelines noted for Task 20 on page 205 in *Presentation Book A.* • Partner with "at mastery" student and review hard words. • Partner with "at mastery" student and have him or her model reading title and first three sentences; have student repeat. • Have adult model reading title and first three sentences; have student repeat until firm.	• Provide word flash cards for children to take home for additional practice. • Encourage children to share their take-home sheets with their families. • Have adult at home review title and first three sentences of story. • Have adult at home access SRA's Home Connection Activities listed at *www.sraonline.com* • Direct Instruction • *Reading Mastery Signature Edition* • Activities
At Mastery	• See guidelines noted for Task 20 on page 205 in *Presentation Book A.* • Partner with "approaching mastery" or ELL student and review hard words. • Partner with "approaching mastery" or ELL student and model reading title and first three sentences; have student repeat. • Direct student to reading and writing center in classroom to reinforce literacy and writing skills.	
ELL	• See "Tips for Teachers" for "approaching mastery" and "at mastery" students. • Describe and model mouth formations for difficult sounds and words, then guide student while practicing with mirror.	• See "Home Connections" for "approaching mastery" and "at mastery" students. • Provide recording to use with sentence strips and word flash cards for additional practice; encourage children to practice with a mirror at home, as needed.

Test	Tips for Teachers	Home Connections
	• Use sentence strips to practice reading sentences in story. • Show student how to recognize punctuation when reading with prosody. • Show realia or other visuals illustrating meaning of difficult words and sentences in story. • Use primary language equivalents when available and then ask student to say words and sentences in English.	• Provide recording of story; have children listen and track during story reading; then children read aloud with recording while tracking; then children read aloud and track independently; have adult at home review difficult words following independent story reading. • Encourage adult at home to help children tell a similar story using primary language equivalents. • Encourage adult at home to help children identify realia and other visuals illustrating meaning of the sentences in story.
Test		
Individual Checkout (Lesson 40) **Approaching Mastery**	• See guidelines for students who do not read within error or time limit for Lesson 40 on page 234 in *Presentation Book A*. • Partner with "at mastery" student and have him or her model reading story; have student read story. • Reteach difficult words using "good-bye" list. • Review finger placement and tracking for sentence reading. • Have adult model reading story; have student read story until firm. • Use paired reading. • Develop recording of story read by good reader; have student listen to recording and whisper read.	• Provide word flash cards for children to take home for additional practice. • Have adult at home model reading story; have children listen and track during story reading; have children read story; have adult at home review difficult words following story reading.
At Mastery	• See guidelines for students who read within error and time limit for Lesson 40 on page 234 in *Presentation Book A*. • Partner with "approaching mastery" or ELL student and model reading story; have student read story. • Have student record self reading story as model for "approaching mastery" or ELL student. • Direct student to reading and writing center in classroom to reinforce literacy and writing skills.	
ELL	• See "Tips for Teachers" for "approaching mastery" and "at mastery" students. • Describe and model mouth formations for difficult sounds and words, then guide student while practicing with mirror. • Use sentence strips to practice reading sentences in story. • Show student how to recognize punctuation when reading with prosody. • Show realia or other visuals illustrating meaning of difficult words and sentences in story.	• See "Home Connections" for "approaching mastery" and "at mastery" students. • Provide recording to use with sentence strips and word flash cards for additional practice; encourage children to practice with a mirror at home, as needed. • Provide recording of story; have children listen and track during story reading; then children read aloud with recording while tracking; then children read aloud and track independently; have adult at home review difficult words following independent story reading.

Test	Tips for Teachers	Home Connections
Test	• Use primary language equivalents when available and then ask student to say words and sentences in English.	• Encourage adult at home to help children tell a similar story using primary language equivalents. • Encourage adult at home to help children identify realia and other visuals illustrating meaning of the sentences in story.

Assessment (after Lesson 40)
 	
Approaching Mastery
	• See "Remedial Exercises and Retesting the Students" guidelines on page 8 in *Curriculum-Based Assessment and Fluency Teacher Handbook*.
	• Partner with "at mastery" student and review various activities.
	• Reteach difficult words using "good-bye" list.
	• Conduct "see-say-write" until firm.
	• Practice circling responses and "reading activities to yourself."
		• Provide word flash cards for children to take home for additional practice.
		• Encourage children to share their take-home sheets with their families.
		• Encourage adult at home to conduct "see-say-write" activity for each difficult word.
		• Have adult at home access SRA's Home Connection Activities listed at *www.sraonline.com*
		  • Direct Instruction
		    • *Reading Mastery Signature Edition*
		      • Activities

At Mastery	• Have student "be the teacher": Partner with "approaching mastery" or ELL student and review various activities. • Direct student to reading and writing center in classroom to reinforce literacy and writing skills.	
ELL **Test**	• See "Tips for Teachers" for "approaching mastery" and "at mastery" students. • Describe and model mouth formations for difficult sounds and words, then guide student while practicing with mirror. • Show realia or other visuals of objects or concepts to illustrate meaning of sentences. • Use primary language equivalents when available and then ask student to say words and sentences in English.	• See "Home Connections" for "approaching mastery" and "at mastery" students. • Provide recording for use with word flash cards and sentence strips to take home for additional practice; encourage children to practice with a mirror at home, as needed. • Encourage adult at home to help children identify realia and other visuals of objects or concepts to illustrate meaning of sentences at home. • Encourage adult at home to help children tell a similar story using primary language equivalents. • Encourage adult at home to help children practice using primary language equivalents and English words and sentences when possible.
Individual Checkout (Lesson 45) **Approaching Mastery**	• See guidelines for students who do not read within error or time limit for Lesson 45 on page 262 in *Presentation Book A*. • Partner with "at mastery" student and have him or her model reading story; have student read story. • Reteach difficult words using "good-bye" list. • Review finger placement and tracking for sentence reading. • Have adult model reading story; have student read story until firm. • Use paired reading. • Develop recording of story read by good reader; have student listen to recording and whisper read.	• Provide word flash cards for children to take home for additional practice. • Have adult at home model reading story; have children listen and track during story reading; have children read story; have adult at home review difficult words following story reading.

Test	Tips for Teachers	Home Connections
At Mastery	• See guidelines for students who read within error and time limit for Lesson 45 on page 262 in *Presentation Book A*. • Partner with "approaching mastery" or ELL student and model reading story; have student read story. • Have student record self reading story as model for "approaching mastery" or ELL student. • Direct student to reading and writing center in classroom to reinforce literacy and writing skills.	
ELL	• See "Tips for Teachers" for "approaching mastery" and "at mastery" students. • Describe and model mouth formations for difficult sounds and words, then guide student while practicing with mirror. • Use sentence strips to practice reading sentences in story. • Show student how to recognize punctuation when reading with prosody. • Show realia or other visuals illustrating meaning of difficult words and sentences in story. • Use primary language equivalents when available and then ask student to say words and sentences in English.	• See "Home Connections" for "approaching mastery" and "at mastery" students. • Provide recording to use with sentence strips and word flash cards for additional practice; encourage children to practice with a mirror at home, as needed. • Provide recording of story; have children listen and track during story reading; then children read aloud with recording while tracking; then children read aloud and track independently; have adult at home review difficult words following independent story reading. • Encourage adult at home to help children tell a similar story using primary language equivalents. • Encourage adult at home to help children identify realia and other visuals illustrating meaning of the sentences in story.

Test

Test	Tips for Teachers	Home Connections
Individual Checkout (Lesson 50) **Approaching Mastery**	• See guidelines for students who do not read within error or time limit for Lesson 50 on page 12 in *Presentation Book B*. • Partner with "at mastery" student and have him or her model reading story; have student read story. • Reteach difficult words using "good-bye" list. • Review finger placement and tracking for sentence reading. • Have adult model reading story; have student read story until firm. • Use paired reading. • Develop recording of story read by good reader; have student listen to recording and whisper read.	• Provide word flash cards for children to take home for additional practice. • Have adult at home model reading story; have children listen and track during story reading; have children read story; have adult at home review difficult words following story reading. • Have children read story to a pet, stuffed animal, or sibling for extra practice.
At Mastery	• See guidelines for students who read within error and time limit for Lesson 50 on page 12 in *Presentation Book B*. • Partner with "approaching mastery" or ELL student and model reading story; have student read story. • Have student record self reading story as model for "approaching mastery" or ELL student. • Direct student to reading and writing center in classroom to reinforce literacy and writing skills.	

Test	Tips for Teachers	Home Connections
ELL	• See "Tips for Teachers" for "approaching mastery" and "at mastery" students. • Describe and model mouth formations for difficult sounds and words, then guide student while practicing with mirror. • Use sentence strips to practice reading sentences in story. • Show student how to recognize punctuation when reading with prosody. • Show realia or other visuals illustrating meaning of difficult words and sentences in story. • Use primary language equivalents when available and then ask student to say words and sentences in English.	• See "Home Connections" for "approaching mastery" and "at mastery" students. • Provide recording to use with sentence strips and word flash cards for additional practice; encourage children to practice with a mirror at home, as needed. • Provide recording of story; have children listen and track during story reading; then children read aloud with recording while tracking; then children read aloud and track independently; have adult at home review difficult words following independent story reading. • Encourage adult at home to help children tell a similar story using primary language equivalents. • Encourage adult at home to help children identify realia and other visuals illustrating meaning of the sentences in story.
Test **Individual Checkout** (Lesson 55) **Approaching Mastery**	• See guidelines for students who do not read within error or time limit for Lesson 55 on page 40 in *Presentation Book B*. • Partner with "at mastery" student and have him or her model reading story; have student read story. • Reteach difficult words using "good-bye" list. • Review finger placement and tracking for sentence reading. • Have adult model reading story; have student read story until firm. • Use paired reading. • Develop recording of story read by good reader; have student listen to recording and whisper read.	• Provide word flash cards for children to take home for additional practice. • Have adult at home model reading story; have children listen and track during story reading; have children read story; have adult at home review difficult words following story reading. • Have children read story to a pet, stuffed animal, or sibling for extra practice.
At Mastery	• See guidelines for students who read within error and time limit for Lesson 55 on page 40 in *Presentation Book B*. • Partner with "approaching mastery" or ELL student and model reading story; have student read story. • Have student record self reading story as model for "approaching mastery" or ELL student. • Direct student to reading and writing center in classroom to reinforce literacy and writing skills.	
ELL	• See "Tips for Teachers" for "approaching mastery" and "at mastery" students. • Describe and model mouth formations for difficult sounds and words, then guide student while practicing with mirror. • Use sentence strips to practice reading sentences in story.	• See "Home Connections" for "approaching mastery" and "at mastery" students. • Provide recording to use with sentence strips and word flash cards for additional practice; encourage children to practice with a mirror at home, as needed.

Test	Tips for Teachers	Home Connections
	• Show student how to recognize punctuation when reading with prosody. • Show realia or other visuals illustrating meaning of difficult words and sentences in story. • Discuss sound word and how its meaning is shared by other cultures (e.g., "owwwww"), if appropriate. • Use primary language equivalents when available and then ask student to say words and sentences in English.	• Provide recording of story; have children listen and track during story reading; then children read aloud with recording while tracking; then children read aloud and track independently; have adult at home review difficult words following independent story reading. • Encourage adult at home to help children tell a similar story using primary language equivalents. • Encourage adult at home to help children identify realia and other visuals illustrating meaning of the sentences in story.
Test		
Individual Checkout (Lesson 60) **Approaching Mastery**	• See guidelines for students who do not read within error or time limit for Lesson 60 on page 67 in *Presentation Book B.* • Partner with "at mastery" student and have him or her model reading story; have student read story. • Reteach difficult words using "good-bye" list. • Review finger placement and tracking for sentence reading. • Have adult model reading story; have student read story until firm. • Use paired reading. • Develop recording of story read by good reader; have student listen to recording and whisper read.	• Provide word flash cards for children to take home for additional practice. • Have adult at home model reading story; have children listen and track during story reading; have children read story; have adult at home review difficult words following story reading. • Have children read story to a pet, stuffed animal, or sibling for extra practice.
At Mastery	• See guidelines for students who read within error and time limit for Lesson 60 on page 67 in *Presentation Book B.* • Partner with "approaching mastery" or ELL student and model reading story; have student read story. • Have student record self reading story as model for "approaching mastery" or ELL student. • Direct student to reading and writing center in classroom to reinforce literacy and writing skills.	
ELL	• See "Tips for Teachers" for "approaching mastery" and "at mastery" students. • Describe and model mouth formations for difficult sounds and words, then guide student while practicing with mirror. • Use sentence strips to practice reading sentences in story. • Show student how to recognize punctuation when reading with prosody. • Show realia or other visuals illustrating meaning of difficult words and sentences in story. • Use primary language equivalents when available and then ask student to say words and sentences in English.	• See "Home Connections" for "approaching mastery" and "at mastery" students. • Provide recording to use with sentence strips and word flash cards for additional practice; encourage children to practice with a mirror at home, as needed. • Provide recording of story; have children listen and track during story reading; then children read aloud with recording while tracking; then children read aloud and track independently; have adult at home review difficult words following independent story reading. • Encourage adult at home to help children tell a similar story using primary language equivalents. • Encourage adult at home to help children identify realia and other visuals illustrating meaning of the sentences in story.

Test	Tips for Teachers	Home Connections
Assessment (after Lesson 60) **Approaching Mastery**	• See "Remedial Exercises and Retesting the Students" guidelines on pages 10 and 11 in *Curriculum-Based Assessment and Fluency Teacher Handbook*. • Partner with "at mastery" student and review various activities. • Reteach difficult words using "good-bye" list. • Conduct "see-say-write" until firm. • Practice circling responses and "reading activities to yourself."	• Provide word flash cards for children to take home for additional practice. • Encourage children to share their take-home sheets with their families. • Encourage adult at home to conduct "see-say-write" activity for each difficult word. • Have adult at home access SRA's Home Connection Activities listed at *www.sraonline.com* • Direct Instruction • *Reading Mastery Signature Edition* • Activities
At Mastery	• Have student "be the teacher": Partner with "approaching mastery" or ELL student and review various activities. • Direct student to reading and writing center in classroom to reinforce literacy and writing skills.	
ELL	• See "Tips for Teachers" for "approaching mastery" and "at mastery" students. • Describe and model mouth formations for difficult sounds and words, then guide student while practicing with mirror. • Show realia or other visuals of objects or concepts to illustrate meaning of sentences. • Model rereading strategy to improve comprehension by using think-aloud (e.g., I'm reading that the elf gave a little girl a magic pouch. That sounds pretty important, I better remember about the magic pouch). • Model story retelling by using think-aloud (e.g., I remember the first thing that happened was the elf gave a little girl a magic bag that would be good to her if she was good and bad to her if she was bad; the next thing that happened was the girl said she had been good, so she would see if the bag would be good to her; the last thing that happened was that she found gold). • Use primary language equivalents when available and then ask student to say words and sentences in English.	• See "Home Connections" for "approaching mastery" and "at mastery" students. • Provide recording for use with word flash cards and sentence strips to take home for additional practice; encourage children to practice with a mirror at home, as needed. • Encourage adult at home to help children identify realia and other visuals of objects or concepts to illustrate meaning of sentences at home. • Encourage adult at home to help children tell a similar story using primary language equivalents. • Encourage adult at home to help children retell the beginning, middle, and end of story in their primary language and in English.

Test

Test	Tips for Teachers	Home Connections
Individual Checkout (Lesson 65) **Approaching Mastery**	• See guidelines for students who do not read within error or time limit for Lesson 65 on page 96 in *Presentation Book B*. • Partner with "at mastery" student and have him or her model reading story; have student read story. • Reteach difficult words using "good-bye" list. • Review finger placement and tracking for sentence reading. • Have adult model reading story; have student read story until firm. • Use paired reading. • Develop recording of story read by good reader; have student listen to recording and whisper read.	• Provide word flash cards for children to take home for additional practice. • Have adult at home model reading story; have children listen and track during story reading; have children read story; have adult at home review difficult words following story reading. • Have children read story to a pet, stuffed animal, or sibling for extra practice.

Test	Tips for Teachers	Home Connections
At Mastery	• See guidelines for students who read within error and time limit for Lesson 65 on page 96 in *Presentation Book B*. • Partner with "approaching mastery" or ELL student and model reading story; have student read story. • Have student record self reading story as model for "approaching mastery" or ELL student. • Direct student to reading and writing center in classroom to reinforce literacy and writing skills.	
ELL	• See "Tips for Teachers" for "approaching mastery" and "at mastery" students. • Describe and model mouth formations for difficult sounds and words, then guide student while practicing with mirror. • Use sentence strips to practice reading sentences in story. • Show student how to recognize punctuation when reading with prosody. • Show realia or other visuals illustrating meaning of difficult words and sentences in story. • Use primary language equivalents when available and then ask student to say words and sentences in English.	• See "Home Connections" for "approaching mastery" and "at mastery" students. • Provide recording to use with sentence strips and word flash cards for additional practice; encourage children to practice with a mirror at home, as needed. • Provide recording of story; have children listen and track during story reading; then children read aloud with recording while tracking; then children read aloud and track independently; have adult at home review difficult words following independent story reading. • Encourage adult at home to help children tell a similar story using primary language equivalents. • Encourage adult at home to help children identify realia and other visuals illustrating meaning of the sentences in story.

Test

Test	Tips for Teachers	Home Connections
Individual Checkout (Lesson 70) **Approaching Mastery**	• See guidelines for students who do not read within error or time limit for Lesson 70 on page 122 in *Presentation Book B*. • Partner with "at mastery" student and have him or her model reading story; have student read story. • Reteach difficult words using "good-bye" list. • Review finger placement and tracking for sentence reading. • Have adult model reading story; have student read story until firm. • Use paired reading. • Develop recording of story read by good reader; have student listen to recording and whisper read.	• Provide word flash cards for children to take home for additional practice. • Have adult at home model reading story; have children listen and track during story reading; have children read story; have adult at home review difficult words following story reading. • Have children read story to a pet, stuffed animal, or sibling for extra practice.
At Mastery	• See guidelines for students who read within error and time limit for Lesson 70 on page 122 in *Presentation Book B*. • Partner with "approaching mastery" or ELL student and model reading story; have student read story. • Have student record self reading story as model for "approaching mastery" or ELL student. • Direct student to reading and writing center in classroom to reinforce literacy and writing skills.	

Test	Tips for Teachers	Home Connections
ELL	• See "Tips for Teachers" for "approaching mastery" and "at mastery" students. • Describe and model mouth formations for difficult sounds and words, then guide student while practicing with mirror. • Use sentence strips to practice reading sentences in story. • Show student how to recognize punctuation when reading with prosody. • Show realia or other visuals illustrating meaning of difficult words and sentences in story. • Use primary language equivalents when available and then ask student to say words and sentences in English.	• See "Home Connections" for "approaching mastery" and "at mastery" students. • Provide recording to use with sentence strips and word flash cards for additional practice; encourage children to practice with a mirror at home, as needed. • Provide recording of story; have children listen and track during story reading; then children read aloud with recording while tracking; then children read aloud and track independently; have adult at home review difficult words following independent story reading. • Encourage adult at home to help children tell a similar story using primary language equivalents. • Encourage adult at home to help children identify realia and other visuals illustrating meaning of the sentences in story.

Test

Test	Tips for Teachers	Home Connections
Individual Checkout (Lesson 75) **Approaching Mastery**	• See guidelines for students who do not read within error or time limit for Lesson 75 on page 146 in *Presentation Book B*. • Partner with "at mastery" student and have him or her model reading story; have student read story. • Reteach difficult words using "good-bye" list. • Review finger placement and tracking for sentence reading. • Have adult model reading story; have student read story until firm. • Use paired reading. • Develop recording of story read by good reader; have student listen to recording and whisper read.	• Provide word flash cards for children to take home for additional practice. • Have adult at home model reading story; have children listen and track during story reading; have children read story; have adult at home review difficult words following story reading. • Have children read story to a pet, stuffed animal, or sibling for extra practice.
At Mastery	• See guidelines for students who read within error and time limit for Lesson 75 on page 146 in *Presentation Book B*. • Partner with "approaching mastery" or ELL student and model reading story; have student read story. • Have student record self reading story as model for "approaching mastery" or ELL student. • Direct student to reading and writing center in classroom to reinforce literacy and writing skills.	
ELL	• See "Tips for Teachers" for "approaching mastery" and "at mastery" students. • Describe and model mouth formations for difficult sounds and words, then guide student while practicing with mirror. • Use sentence strips to practice reading sentences in story.	• See "Home Connections" for "approaching mastery" and "at mastery" students. • Provide recording to use with sentence strips and word flash cards for additional practice; encourage children to practice with a mirror at home, as needed.

Test	Tips for Teachers	Home Connections
Test	• Show student how to recognize punctuation when reading with prosody. • Show realia or other visuals illustrating meaning of difficult words and sentences in story. • Use primary language equivalents when available and then ask student to say words and sentences in English.	• Provide recording of story; have children listen and track during story reading; then children read aloud with recording while tracking; then children read aloud and track independently; have adult at home review difficult words following independent story reading. • Encourage adult at home to help children tell a similar story using primary language equivalents. • Encourage adult at home to help children identify realia and other visuals illustrating meaning of the sentences in story.
Individual Checkout (Lesson 80) **Approaching Mastery**	• See guidelines for students who do not read within error or time limit for Lesson 80 on page 171 in *Presentation Book B*. • Partner with "at mastery" student and have him or her model reading story; have student read story. • Reteach difficult words using "good-bye" list. • Review finger placement and tracking for sentence reading. • Have adult model reading story; have student read story until firm. • Use paired reading. • Develop recording of story read by good reader; have student listen to recording and whisper read.	• Provide word flash cards for children to take home for additional practice. • Have adult at home model reading story; have children listen and track during story reading; have children read story; have adult at home review difficult words following story reading. • Have children read story to a pet, stuffed animal, or sibling for extra practice.
At Mastery	• See guidelines for students who read within error and time limit for Lesson 80 on page 171 in *Presentation Book B*. • Partner with "approaching mastery" or ELL student and model reading story; have student read story. • Have student record self reading story as model for "approaching mastery" or ELL student. • Direct student to reading and writing center in classroom to reinforce literacy and writing skills.	
ELL	• See "Tips for Teachers" for "approaching mastery" and "at mastery" students. • Describe and model mouth formations for difficult sounds and words, then guide student while practicing with mirror. • Use sentence strips to practice reading sentences in story. • Show student how to recognize punctuation when reading with prosody. • Show realia or other visuals illustrating meaning of difficult words and sentences in story. • Use primary language equivalents when available and then ask student to say words and sentences in English.	• See "Home Connections" for "approaching mastery" and "at mastery" students. • Provide recording to use with sentence strips and word flash cards for additional practice; encourage children to practice with a mirror at home, as needed. • Provide recording of story; have children listen and track during story reading; then children read aloud with recording while tracking; then children read aloud and track independently; have adult at home review difficult words following independent story reading. • Encourage adult at home to help children tell a similar story using primary language equivalents. • Encourage adult at home to help children identify realia and other visuals illustrating meaning of the sentences in story.

Test	Tips for Teachers	Home Connections

Assessment (after Lesson 80)	• See "Remedial Exercises and Retesting the Students" guidelines on pages 13 and 14 in *Curriculum-Based Assessment and Fluency Teacher Handbook*.	• Provide word flash cards for children to take home for additional practice.
		• Encourage children to share their take-home sheets with their families.
		• Encourage adult at home to conduct "see-say-write" activity for each difficult word.
		• Have adult at home access SRA's Home Connection Activities listed at *www.sraonline.com*
		  • Direct Instruction
		    • *Reading Mastery Signature Edition*
		      • Activities

Approaching Mastery	• Partner with "at mastery" student and review various activities. • Reteach difficult words using "good-bye" list. • Conduct "see-say-write" until firm. • Practice circling responses and "reading activities to yourself."	
At Mastery	• Have student "be the teacher": Partner with "approaching mastery" or ELL student and review various activities. • Direct student to reading and writing center in classroom to reinforce literacy and writing skills.	
ELL	• See "Tips for Teachers" for "approaching mastery" and "at mastery" students. • Describe and model mouth formations for difficult sounds and words, then guide student while practicing with mirror. • Show realia or other visuals of objects or concepts to illustrate meaning of sentences. • Model rereading strategy to improve comprehension by using think-aloud. • Model story retelling by using think-aloud. • Use primary language equivalents when available and then ask student to say words and sentences in English.	• See "Home Connections" for "approaching mastery" and "at mastery" students. • Provide recording for use with word flash cards and sentence strips to take home for additional practice; encourage children to practice with a mirror at home, as needed. • Encourage adult at home to help children identify realia and other visuals of objects or concepts to illustrate meaning of sentences at home. • Encourage adult at home to help children tell a similar story using primary language equivalents. • Encourage adult at home to help children retell the beginning, middle, and end of story in their primary language and in English.

Test

Test	Tips for Teachers	Home Connections
Individual Checkout (Lesson 85)	• See guidelines for students who do not read within error or time limit for Lesson 85 on page 199 in *Presentation Book B*.	• Provide word flash cards for children to take home for additional practice. • Have adult at home model reading story; have children listen and track during story reading; have children read story; have adult at home review difficult words following story reading. • Have children read story to a pet, stuffed animal, or sibling for extra practice.
Approaching Mastery	• Partner with "at mastery" student and have him or her model reading story; have student read story. • Reteach difficult words using "good-bye" list. • Review finger placement and tracking for sentence reading. • Have adult model reading story; have student read story until firm. • Use paired reading. • Develop recording of story read by good reader; have student listen to recording and whisper read.	
At Mastery	• See guidelines for students who read within error and time limit for Lesson 85 on page 199 in *Presentation Book B*. • Partner with "approaching mastery" or ELL student and model reading story; have student read story.	

Test	Tips for Teachers	Home Connections
	• Have student record self reading story as model for "approaching mastery" or ELL student. • Direct student to reading and writing center in classroom to reinforce literacy and writing skills.	
ELL **Test**	• See "Tips for Teachers" for "approaching mastery" and "at mastery" students. • Describe and model mouth formations for difficult sounds and words, then guide student while practicing with mirror. • Use sentence strips to practice reading sentences in story. • Show student how to recognize punctuation when reading with prosody. • Show realia or other visuals illustrating meaning of difficult words and sentences in story. • Use primary language equivalents when available and then ask student to say words and sentences in English.	• See "Home Connections" for "approaching mastery" and "at mastery" students. • Provide recording to use with sentence strips and word flash cards for additional practice; encourage children to practice with a mirror at home, as needed. • Provide recording of story; have children listen and track during story reading; then children read aloud with recording while tracking; then children read aloud and track independently; have adult at home review difficult words following independent story reading. • Encourage adult at home to help children tell a similar story using primary language equivalents. • Encourage adult at home to help children identify realia and other visuals illustrating meaning of the sentences in story.
Individual Checkout (Lesson 90) **Approaching Mastery**	• See guidelines for students who do not read within error or time limit for Lesson 90 on page 225 in *Presentation Book B*. • Partner with "at mastery" student and have him or her model reading story; have student read story. • Reteach difficult words using "good-bye" list. • Review finger placement and tracking for sentence reading. • Have adult model reading story; have student read story until firm. • Use paired reading. • Develop recording of story read by good reader; have student listen to recording and whisper read.	• Provide word flash cards for children to take home for additional practice. • Have adult at home model reading story; have children listen and track during story reading; have children read story; have adult at home review difficult words following story reading. • Have children read story to a pet, stuffed animal, or sibling for extra practice.
At Mastery	• See guidelines for students who read within error and time limit for Lesson 90 on page 225 in *Presentation Book B*. • Partner with "approaching mastery" or ELL student and model reading story; have student read story. • Have student record self reading story as model for "approaching mastery" or ELL student. • Direct student to reading and writing center in classroom to reinforce literacy and writing skills.	

Test	Tips for Teachers	Home Connections
ELL	• See "Tips for Teachers" for "approaching mastery" and "at mastery" students. • Describe and model mouth formations for difficult sounds and words, then guide student while practicing with mirror. • Use sentence strips to practice reading sentences in story. • Show student how to recognize punctuation and when reading with prosody. • Show realia or other visuals illustrating meaning of difficult words and sentences in story. • Use primary language equivalents when available and then ask student to say words and sentences in English.	• See "Home Connections" for "approaching mastery" and "at mastery" students. • Provide recording to use with sentence strips and word flash cards for additional practice; encourage children to practice with a mirror at home, as needed. • Provide recording of story; have children listen and track during story reading; then children read aloud with recording while tracking; then children read aloud and track independently; have adult at home review difficult words following independent story reading. • Encourage adult at home to help children tell a similar story using primary language equivalents. • Encourage adult at home to help children identify realia and other visuals illustrating meaning of the sentences in story.

Test

Test	Tips for Teachers	Home Connections
Individual Checkout (Lesson 95) **Approaching Mastery**	• See guidelines for students who do not read within error or time limit for Lesson 95 on page 250 in *Presentation Book B.* • Partner with "at mastery" student and have him or her model reading story; have student read story. • Reteach difficult words using "good-bye" list. • Review finger placement and tracking for sentence reading. • Have adult model reading story; have student read story until firm. • Use paired reading. • Develop recording of story read by good reader; have student listen to recording and whisper read.	• Provide word flash cards for children to take home for additional practice. • Have adult at home model reading story; have children listen and track during story reading; have children read story; have adult at home review difficult words following story reading. • Have children read story to a pet, stuffed animal, or sibling for extra practice.
At Mastery	• See guidelines for students who read within error and time limit for Lesson 95 on page 250 in *Presentation Book B.* • Partner with "approaching mastery" or ELL student and model reading story; have student read story. • Have student record self reading story as model for "approaching mastery" or ELL student. • Direct student to reading and writing center in classroom to reinforce literacy and writing skills.	
ELL	• See "Tips for Teachers" for "approaching mastery" and "at mastery" students. • Describe and model mouth formations for difficult sounds and words, then guide student while practicing with mirror. • Use sentence strips to practice reading sentences in story.	• See "Home Connections" for "approaching mastery" and "at mastery" students. • Provide recording to use with sentence strips and word flash cards for additional practice; encourage children to practice with a mirror at home, as needed.

Test	Tips for Teachers	Home Connections
Test	• Show student how to recognize punctuation when reading with prosody. • Show realia or other visuals illustrating meaning of difficult words and sentences in story. • Use primary language equivalents when available and then ask student to say words and sentences in English.	• Provide recording of story; have children listen and track during story reading; then children read aloud with recording while tracking; then children read aloud and track independently; have adult at home review difficult words following independent story reading. • Encourage adult at home to help children tell a similar story using primary language equivalents. • Encourage adult at home to help children identify realia and other visuals illustrating meaning of the sentences in story.
Individual Checkout (Lesson 100) **Approaching Mastery**	• See guidelines for students who do not read within error or time limit for Lesson 100 on page 271 in *Presentation Book B*. • Partner with "at mastery" student and have him or her model reading story; have student read story. • Reteach difficult words using "good-bye" list. • Review finger placement and tracking for sentence reading. • Have adult model reading story; have student read story until firm. • Use paired reading. • Develop recording of story read by good reader; have student listen to recording and whisper read.	• Provide word flash cards for children to take home for additional practice. • Have adult at home model reading story; have children listen and track during story reading; have children read story; have adult at home review difficult words following story reading. • Have children read story to a pet, stuffed animal, or sibling for extra practice.
At Mastery	• See guidelines for students who read within error and time limit for Lesson 100 on page 271 in *Presentation Book B*. • Partner with "approaching mastery" or ELL student and model reading story; have student read story. • Have student record self reading story as model for "approaching mastery" or ELL student. • Direct student to reading and writing center in classroom to reinforce literacy and writing skills.	
ELL	• See "Tips for Teachers" for "approaching mastery" and "at mastery" students. • Describe and model mouth formations for difficult sounds and words, then guide student while practicing with mirror. • Use sentence strips to practice reading sentences in story. • Show student how to recognize punctuation when reading with prosody. • Show realia or other visuals illustrating meaning of difficult words and sentences in story. • Use primary language equivalents when available and then ask student to say words and sentences in English.	• See "Home Connections" for "approaching mastery" and "at mastery" students. • Provide recording to use with sentence strips and word flash cards for additional practice; encourage children to practice with a mirror at home, as needed. • Provide recording of story; have children listen and track during story reading; then children read aloud with recording while tracking; then children read aloud and track independently; have adult at home review difficult words following independent story reading. • Encourage adult at home to help children tell a similar story using primary language equivalents. • Encourage adult at home to help children identify realia and other visuals illustrating meaning of the sentences in story.

Test	Tips for Teachers	Home Connections
Assessment (after Lesson 100) **Approaching Mastery**	• See "Remedial Exercises and Retesting the Students" guidelines on pages 16 and 17 in *Curriculum-Based Assessment and Fluency Teacher Handbook*. • Partner with "at mastery" student and review various activities. • Reteach difficult words using "good-bye" list. • Conduct "see-say-write" until firm. • Practice circling responses and "reading activities to yourself."	• Provide word flash cards for children to take home for additional practice. • Encourage children to share their take-home sheets with their families. • Encourage adult at home to conduct "see-say-write" activity for each difficult word. • Have adult at home access SRA's Home Connection Activities listed at *www.sraonline.com* • Direct Instruction • *Reading Mastery Signature Edition* • Activities
At Mastery	• Have student "be the teacher": Partner with "approaching mastery" or ELL student and review various activities. • Direct student to reading and writing center in classroom to reinforce literacy and writing skills.	
ELL	• See "Tips for Teachers" for "approaching mastery" and "at mastery" students. • Describe and model mouth formations for difficult sounds and words, then guide student while practicing with mirror. • Show realia or other visuals of objects or concepts to illustrate meaning of sentences. • Model rereading strategy to improve comprehension by using think-aloud. • Model story retelling by using think-aloud. • Model making predictions to improve comprehension by using think-aloud (e.g., I'm reading that Sid keeps reading his boss's notes the wrong way. I can predict that he will tap a cup near the door instead of recording a cup near the door like the note said). • Use primary language equivalents when available and then ask student to say words and sentences in English.	• See "Home Connections" for "approaching mastery" and "at mastery" students. • Provide recording for use with word flash cards and sentence strips to take home for additional practice; encourage children to practice with a mirror at home, as needed. • Encourage adult at home to help children identify realia and other visuals of objects or concepts to illustrate meaning of sentences at home. • Encourage adult at home to help children tell a similar story using primary language equivalents. • Encourage adult at home to help children retell the beginning, middle, and end of story in their primary language and in English. • Encourage adult at home to help children make predictions in everyday life.

Test

Test	Tips for Teachers	Home Connections
Individual Checkout (Lesson 105) **Approaching Mastery**	• See guidelines for students who do not read within error or time limit for Lesson 105 on page 4 in *Presentation Book C*. • Partner with "at mastery" student and have him or her model reading story; have student read story. • Reteach difficult words using "good-bye" list. • Review finger placement and tracking for sentence reading. • Have adult model reading story; have student read story until firm. • Use paired reading. • Develop recording of story read by good reader; have student listen to recording and whisper read.	• Provide word flash cards for children to take home for additional practice. • Have adult at home model reading story; have children listen and track during story reading; have children read story; have adult at home review difficult words following story reading. • Have children read story to a pet, stuffed animal, or sibling for extra practice.

Test	Tips for Teachers	Home Connections
At Mastery	• See guidelines for students who read within error and time limit for Lesson 105 on page 4 in *Presentation Book C*. • Partner with "approaching mastery" or ELL student and model reading story; have student read story. • Have student record self reading story as model for "approaching mastery" or ELL student. • Direct student to reading and writing center in classroom to reinforce literacy and writing skills.	
ELL	• See "Tips for Teachers" for "approaching mastery" and "at mastery" students. • Describe and model mouth formations for difficult sounds and words, then guide student while practicing with mirror. • Use sentence strips to practice reading sentences in story. • Show student how to recognize punctuation when reading with prosody. • Show realia or other visuals illustrating meaning of difficult words and sentences in story. • Use primary language equivalents when available and then ask student to say words and sentences in English.	• See "Home Connections" for "approaching mastery" and "at mastery" students. • Provide recording to use with sentence strips and word flash cards for additional practice; encourage children to practice with a mirror at home, as needed. • Provide recording of story; have children listen and track during story reading; then children read aloud with recording while tracking; then children read aloud and track independently; have adult at home review difficult words following independent story reading. • Encourage adult at home to help children tell a similar story using primary language equivalents. • Encourage adult at home to help children identify realia and other visuals illustrating meaning of the sentences in story.

Test

Test	Tips for Teachers	Home Connections
Individual Checkout (Lesson 110) **Approaching Mastery**	• See guidelines for students who do not read within error or time limit for Lesson 110 on page 24 in *Presentation Book C*. • Partner with "at mastery" student and have him or her model reading story; have student read story. • Reteach difficult words using "good-bye" list. • Review finger placement and tracking for sentence reading. • Have adult model reading story; have student read story until firm. • Use paired reading. • Develop recording of story read by good reader; have student listen to recording and whisper read.	• Provide word flash cards for children to take home for additional practice. • Have adult at home model reading story; have children listen and track during story reading; have children read story; have adult at home review difficult words following story reading. • Have children read story to a pet, stuffed animal, or sibling for extra practice.
At Mastery	• See guidelines for students who read within error and time limit for Lesson 110 on page 24 in *Presentation Book C*. • Partner with "approaching mastery" or ELL student and model reading story; have student read story. • Have student record self reading story as model for "approaching mastery" or ELL student. • Direct student to reading and writing center in classroom to reinforce literacy and writing skills.	

Test	Tips for Teachers	Home Connections
ELL	• See "Tips for Teachers" for "approaching mastery" and "at mastery" students. • Describe and model mouth formations for difficult sounds and words, then guide student while practicing with mirror. • Use sentence strips to practice reading sentences in story. • Show student how to recognize punctuation when reading with prosody. • Show realia or other visuals illustrating meaning of difficult words and sentences in story. • Use primary language equivalents when available and then ask student to say words and sentences in English.	• See "Home Connections" for "approaching mastery" and "at mastery" students. • Provide recording to use with sentence strips and word flash cards for additional practice; encourage children to practice with a mirror at home, as needed. • Provide recording of story; have children listen and track during story reading; then children read aloud with recording while tracking; then children read aloud and track independently; have adult at home review difficult words following independent story reading. • Encourage adult at home to help children tell a similar story using primary language equivalents. • Encourage adult at home to help children identify realia and other visuals illustrating meaning of the sentences in story.

Test

Test	Tips for Teachers	Home Connections
Individual Checkout (Lesson 115) **Approaching Mastery**	• See guidelines for students who do not read within error or time limit for Lesson 115 on page 44 in *Presentation Book C*. • Partner with "at mastery" student and have him or her model reading story; have student read story. • Reteach difficult words using "good-bye" list. • Review finger placement and tracking for sentence reading. • Have adult model reading story; have student read story until firm. • Use paired reading. • Develop recording of story read by good reader; have student listen to recording and whisper read.	• Provide word flash cards for children to take home for additional practice. • Have adult at home model reading story; have children listen and track during story reading; have children read story; have adult at home review difficult words following story reading. • Have children read story to a pet, stuffed animal, or sibling for extra practice.
At Mastery	• See guidelines for students who read within error and time limit for Lesson 115 on page 44 in *Presentation Book C*. • Partner with "approaching mastery" or ELL student and model reading story; have student read story. • Have student record self reading story as model for "approaching mastery" or ELL student. • Direct student to reading and writing center in classroom to reinforce literacy and writing skills.	
ELL	• See "Tips for Teachers" for "approaching mastery" and "at mastery" students. • Describe and model mouth formations for difficult sounds and words, then guide student while practicing with mirror. • Use sentence strips to practice reading sentences in story.	• See "Home Connections" for "approaching mastery" and "at mastery" students. • Provide recording to use with sentence strips and word flash cards for additional practice; encourage children to practice with a mirror at home, as needed.

Test	Tips for Teachers	Home Connections
Test	• Show student how to recognize punctuation when reading with prosody. • Show realia or other visuals illustrating meaning of difficult words and sentences in story. • Use primary language equivalents when available and then ask student to say words and sentences in English.	• Provide recording of story; have children listen and track during story reading; then children read aloud with recording while tracking; then children read aloud and track independently; have adult at home review difficult words following independent story reading. • Encourage adult at home to help children tell a similar story using primary language equivalents. • Encourage adult at home to help children identify realia and other visuals illustrating meaning of the sentences in story.
Individual Checkout (Lesson 120) **Approaching Mastery**	• See guidelines for students who do not read within error or time limit for Lesson 120 on page 64 in *Presentation Book C*. • Partner with "at mastery" student and have him or her model reading story; have student read story. • Reteach difficult words using "good-bye" list. • Review finger placement and tracking for sentence reading. • Have adult model reading story; have student read story until firm. • Use paired reading. • Develop recording of story read by good reader; have student listen to recording and whisper read.	• Provide word flash cards for children to take home for additional practice. • Have adult at home model reading story; have children listen and track during story reading; have children read story; have adult at home review difficult words following story reading. • Have children read story to a pet, stuffed animal, or sibling for extra practice.
At Mastery	• See guidelines for students who read within error and time limit for Lesson 120 on page 64 in *Presentation Book C*. • Partner with "approaching mastery" or ELL student and model reading story; have student read story. • Have student record self reading story as model for "approaching mastery" or ELL student. • Direct student to reading and writing center in classroom to reinforce literacy and writing skills.	
ELL	• See "Tips for Teachers" for "approaching mastery" and "at mastery" students. • Describe and model mouth formations for difficult sounds and words, then guide student while practicing with mirror. • Use sentence strips to practice reading sentences in story. • Show student how to recognize punctuation when reading with prosody. • Show realia or other visuals illustrating meaning of difficult words and sentences in story. • Use primary language equivalents when available and then ask student to say words and sentences in English.	• See "Home Connections" for "approaching mastery" and "at mastery" students. • Provide recording to use with sentence strips and word flash cards for additional practice; encourage children to practice with a mirror at home, as needed. • Provide recording of story; have children listen and track during story reading; then children read aloud with recording while tracking; then children read aloud and track independently; have adult at home review difficult words following independent story reading. • Encourage adult at home to help children tell a similar story using primary language equivalents. • Encourage adult at home to help children identify realia and other visuals illustrating meaning of the sentences in story.

Test	Tips for Teachers	Home Connections

Assessment (after Lesson 120)
 	
Approaching Mastery
	• See "Remedial Exercises and Retesting the Students" guidelines on pages 19 and 20 in *Curriculum-Based Assessment and Fluency Teacher Handbook*.
	• Partner with "at mastery" student and review various activities.
	• Reteach difficult words using "good-bye" list.
	• Conduct "see-say-write" until firm.
	• Practice circling responses and "reading activities to yourself."
		• Provide word flash cards for children to take home for additional practice.
		• Encourage children to share their take-home sheets with their families.
		• Encourage adult at home to conduct "see-say-write" activity for each difficult word.
		• Have adult at home access SRA's Home Connection Activities listed at *www.sraonline.com*
		 • Direct Instruction
		  • *Reading Mastery Signature Edition*
		   • Activities

At Mastery	• Have student "be the teacher": Partner with "approaching mastery" or ELL student and review various activities. • Direct student to reading and writing center in classroom to reinforce literacy and writing skills.	
ELL	• See "Tips for Teachers" for "approaching mastery" and "at mastery" students. • Describe and model mouth formations for difficult sounds and words, then guide student while practicing with mirror. • Show realia or other visuals of objects or concepts to illustrate meaning of sentences. • Model rereading strategy to improve comprehension by using think-aloud. • Model story retelling by using think-aloud. • Model making predictions to improve comprehension by using think-aloud. • Use primary language equivalents when available and then ask student to say words and sentences in English.	• See "Home Connections" for "approaching mastery" and "at mastery" students. • Provide recording for use with word flash cards and sentence strips to take home for additional practice; encourage children to practice with a mirror at home, as needed. • Encourage adult at home to help children identify realia and other visuals of objects or concepts to illustrate meaning of sentences at home. • Encourage adult at home to help children tell a similar story using primary language equivalents. • Encourage adult at home to help children retell the beginning, middle, and end of story in their primary language and in English. • Encourage adult at home to help children make predictions in everyday life.
Test		
Individual Checkout (Lesson 125) **Approaching Mastery**	• See guidelines for students who do not read within error or time limit for Lesson 125 on page 88 in *Presentation Book C*. • Partner with "at mastery" student and have him or her model reading story; have student read story. • Reteach difficult words using "good-bye" list. • Review finger placement and tracking for sentence reading. • Have adult model reading story; have student read story until firm. • Use paired reading. • Develop recording of story read by good reader; have student listen to recording and whisper read.	• Provide word flash cards for children to take home for additional practice. • Have adult at home model reading story; have children listen and track during story reading; have children read story; have adult at home review difficult words following story reading. • Have children read story to a pet, stuffed animal, or sibling for extra practice.

Test	Tips for Teachers	Home Connections
At Mastery	• See guidelines for students who read within error and time limit for Lesson 125 on page 88 in *Presentation Book C*. • Partner with "approaching mastery" or ELL student and model reading story; have student read story. • Have student record self reading story as model for "approaching mastery" or ELL student. • Direct student to reading and writing center in classroom to reinforce literacy and writing skills.	
ELL	• See "Tips for Teachers" for "approaching mastery" and "at mastery" students. • Describe and model mouth formations for difficult sounds and words, then guide student while practicing with mirror. • Use sentence strips to practice reading sentences in story. • Show student how to recognize punctuation when reading with prosody. • Show realia or other visuals illustrating meaning of difficult words and sentences in story. • Use primary language equivalents when available and then ask student to say words and sentences in English.	• See "Home Connections" for "approaching mastery" and "at mastery" students. • Provide recording to use with sentence strips and word flash cards for additional practice; encourage children to practice with a mirror at home, as needed. • Provide recording of story; have children listen and track during story reading; then children read aloud with recording while tracking; then children read aloud and track independently; have adult at home review difficult words following independent story reading. • Encourage adult at home to help children tell a similar story using primary language equivalents. • Encourage adult at home to help children identify realia and other visuals illustrating meaning of the sentences in story.

Test

	Tips for Teachers	Home Connections
Individual Checkout (Lesson 130) **Approaching Mastery**	• See guidelines for students who do not read within error or time limit for Lesson 130 on page 112 in *Presentation Book C*. • Partner with "at mastery" student and have him or her model reading story; have student read story. • Reteach difficult words using "good-bye" list. • Review finger placement and tracking for sentence reading. • Have adult model reading story; have student read story until firm. • Use paired reading. • Develop recording of story read by good reader; have student listen to recording and whisper read.	• Provide word flash cards for children to take home for additional practice. • Have adult at home model reading story; have children listen and track during story reading; have children read story; have adult at home review difficult words following story reading. • Have children read story to a pet, stuffed animal, or sibling for extra practice.
At Mastery	• See guidelines for students who read within error and time limit for Lesson 130 on page 112 in *Presentation Book C*. • Partner with "approaching mastery" or ELL student and model reading story; have student read story. • Have student record self reading story as model for "approaching mastery" or ELL student. • Direct student to reading and writing center in classroom to reinforce literacy and writing skills.	

Test	Tips for Teachers	Home Connections
ELL	• See "Tips for Teachers" for "approaching mastery" and "at mastery" students. • Describe and model mouth formations for difficult sounds and words, then guide student while practicing with mirror. • Use sentence strips to practice reading sentences in story. • Show student how to recognize punctuation when reading with prosody. • Show realia or other visuals illustrating meaning of difficult words and sentences in story. • Use primary language equivalents when available and then ask student to say words and sentences in English.	• See "Home Connections" for "approaching mastery" and "at mastery" students. • Provide recording to use with sentence strips and word flash cards for additional practice; encourage children to practice with a mirror at home, as needed. • Provide recording of story; have children listen and track during story reading; then children read aloud with recording while tracking; then children read aloud and track independently; have adult at home review difficult words following independent story reading. • Encourage adult at home to help children tell a similar story using primary language equivalents. • Encourage adult at home to help children identify realia and other visuals illustrating meaning of the sentences in story.
Test		
Individual Checkout (Lesson 135) **Approaching Mastery**	• See guidelines for students who do not read within error or time limit for Lesson 135 on page 133 in *Presentation Book C*. • Partner with "at mastery" student and have him or her model reading story; have student read story. • Reteach difficult words using "good-bye" list. • Review finger placement and tracking for sentence reading. • Have adult model reading story; have student read story until firm. • Use paired reading. • Develop recording of story read by good reader; have student listen to recording and whisper read.	• Provide word flash cards for children to take home for additional practice. • Have adult at home model reading story; have children listen and track during story reading; have children read story; have adult at home review difficult words following story reading. • Have children read story to a pet, stuffed animal, or sibling for extra practice.
At Mastery	• See guidelines for students who read within error and time limit for Lesson 135 on page 133 in *Presentation Book C*. • Partner with "approaching mastery" or ELL student and model reading story; have student read story. • Have student record self reading story as model for "approaching mastery" or ELL student. • Direct student to reading and writing center in classroom to reinforce literacy and writing skills.	
ELL	• See "Tips for Teachers" for "approaching mastery" and "at mastery" students. • Describe and model mouth formations for difficult sounds and words, then guide student while practicing with mirror. • Use sentence strips to practice reading sentences in story.	• See "Home Connections" for "approaching mastery" and "at mastery" students. • Provide recording to use with sentence strips and word flash cards for additional practice; encourage children to practice with a mirror at home, as needed.

Test	Tips for Teachers	Home Connections
Test	• Show student how to recognize punctuation when reading with prosody. • Show realia or other visuals illustrating meaning of difficult words and sentences in story. • Use primary language equivalents when available and then ask student to say words and sentences in English.	• Provide recording of story; have children listen and track during story reading; then children read aloud with recording while tracking; then children read aloud and track independently; have adult at home review difficult words following independent story reading. • Encourage adult at home to help children tell a similar story using primary language equivalents. • Encourage adult at home to help children identify realia and other visuals illustrating meaning of the sentences in story.
Individual Checkout (Lesson 140) **Approaching Mastery**	• See guidelines for students who do not read within error or time limit for Lesson 140 on page 153 in *Presentation Book C*. • Partner with "at mastery" student and have him or her model reading story; have student read story. • Reteach difficult words using "good-bye" list. • Review finger placement and tracking for sentence reading. • Have adult model reading story; have student read story until firm. • Use paired reading. • Develop recording of story read by good reader; have student listen to recording and whisper read.	• Provide word flash cards for children to take home for additional practice. • Have adult at home model reading story; have children listen and track during story reading; have children read story; have adult at home review difficult words following story reading. • Have children read story to a pet, stuffed animal, or sibling for extra practice.
At Mastery	• See guidelines for students who read within error and time limit for Lesson 140 on page 153 in *Presentation Book C*. • Partner with "approaching mastery" or ELL student and model reading story; have student read story. • Have student record self reading story as model for "approaching mastery" or ELL student. • Direct student to reading and writing center in classroom to reinforce literacy and writing skills.	
ELL	• See "Tips for Teachers" for "approaching mastery" and "at mastery" students. • Describe and model mouth formations for difficult sounds and words, then guide student while practicing with mirror. • Use sentence strips to practice reading sentences in story. • Show student how to recognize punctuation when reading with prosody. • Show realia or other visuals illustrating meaning of difficult words and sentences in story. • Use primary language equivalents when available and then ask student to say words and sentences in English.	• See "Home Connections" for "approaching mastery" and "at mastery" students. • Provide recording to use with sentence strips and word flash cards for additional practice; encourage children to practice with a mirror at home, as needed. • Provide recording of story; have children listen and track during story reading; then children read aloud with recording while tracking; then children read aloud and track independently; have adult at home review difficult words following independent story reading. • Encourage adult at home to help children tell a similar story using primary language equivalents. • Encourage adult at home to help children identify realia and other visuals illustrating meaning of the sentences in story.

Test	Tips for Teachers	Home Connections

Assessment (after Lesson 140) **Approaching Mastery**	• See "Remedial Exercises and Retesting the Students" guidelines on pages 22 and 23 in *Curriculum-Based Assessment and Fluency Teacher Handbook.*
	• Partner with "at mastery" student and review various activities.
	• Reteach difficult words using "good-bye" list.
	• Conduct "see-say-write" until firm.
	• Practice circling responses and "reading activities to yourself."
		• Provide word flash cards for children to take home for additional practice.
		• Encourage children to share their take-home sheets with their families.
		• Encourage adult at home to conduct "see-say-write" activity for each difficult word.
		• Have adult at home access SRA's Home Connection Activities listed at *www.sraonline.com*
		  • Direct Instruction
		    • *Reading Mastery Signature Edition*
		      • Activities

At Mastery	• Have student "be the teacher": Partner with "approaching mastery" or ELL student and review various activities. • Direct student to reading and writing center in classroom to reinforce literacy and writing skills.	
ELL	• See "Tips for Teachers" for "approaching mastery" and "at mastery" students. • Describe and model mouth formations for difficult sounds and words, then guide student while practicing with mirror. • Show realia or other visuals of objects or concepts to illustrate meaning of sentences. • Model rereading strategy to improve comprehension by using think-aloud. • Model story retelling by using think-aloud. • Model making predictions to improve comprehension by using think-aloud. • Use primary language equivalents when available and then ask student to say words and sentences in English.	• See "Home Connections" for "approaching mastery" and "at mastery" students. • Provide recording for use with word flash cards and sentence strips to take home for additional practice; encourage children to practice with a mirror at home, as needed. • Encourage adult at home to help children identify realia and other visuals of objects or concepts to illustrate meaning of sentences at home. • Encourage adult at home to help children tell a similar story using primary language equivalents. • Encourage adult at home to help children retell the beginning, middle, and end of story in their primary language and in English. • Encourage adult at home to help children make predictions in everyday life.
Test		
Individual Checkout (Lesson 145) **Approaching Mastery**	• See guidelines for students who do not read within error or time limit for Lesson 145 on page 173 in *Presentation Book C.* • Partner with "at mastery" student and have him or her model reading story; have student read story. • Reteach difficult words using "good-bye" list. • Review finger placement and tracking for sentence reading. • Have adult model reading story; have student read story until firm. • Use paired reading. • Develop recording of story read by good reader; have student listen to recording and whisper read.	• Provide word flash cards for children to take home for additional practice. • Have adult at home model reading story; have children listen and track during story reading; have children read story; have adult at home review difficult words following story reading. • Have children read story to a pet, stuffed animal, or sibling for extra practice.

Test	Tips for Teachers	Home Connections
At Mastery	• See guidelines for students who read within error and time limit for Lesson 145 on page 173 in *Presentation Book C*. • Partner with "approaching mastery" or ELL student and model reading story; have student read story. • Have student record self reading story as model for "approaching mastery" or ELL student. • Direct student to reading and writing center in classroom to reinforce literacy and writing skills.	
ELL	• See "Tips for Teachers" for "approaching mastery" and "at mastery" students. • Describe and model mouth formations for difficult sounds and words, then guide student while practicing with mirror. • Use sentence strips to practice reading sentences in story. • Show student how to recognize punctuation when reading with prosody. • Show realia or other visuals illustrating meaning of difficult words and sentences in story. • Use primary language equivalents when available and then ask student to say words and sentences in English.	• See "Home Connections" for "approaching mastery" and "at mastery" students. • Provide recording to use with sentence strips and word flash cards for additional practice; encourage children to practice with a mirror at home, as needed. • Provide recording of story; have children listen and track during story reading; then children read aloud with recording while tracking; then children read aloud and track independently; have adult at home review difficult words following independent story reading. • Encourage adult at home to help children tell a similar story using primary language equivalents. • Encourage adult at home to help children identify realia and other visuals illustrating meaning of the sentences in story.

Test

Test	Tips for Teachers	Home Connections
Individual Checkout (Lesson 150) **Approaching Mastery**	• See guidelines for students who do not read within error or time limit for Lesson 150 on page 194 in *Presentation Book C*. • Partner with "at mastery" student and have him or her model reading story; have student read story. • Reteach difficult words using "good-bye" list. • Review finger placement and tracking for sentence reading. • Have adult model reading story; have student read story until firm. • Use paired reading. • Develop recording of story read by good reader; have student listen to recording and whisper read.	• Provide word flash cards for children to take home for additional practice. • Have adult at home model reading story; have children listen and track during story reading; have children read story; have adult at home review difficult words following story reading. • Have children read story to a pet, stuffed animal, or sibling for extra practice.
At Mastery	• See guidelines for students who read within error and time limit for Lesson 150 on page 194 in *Presentation Book C*. • Partner with "approaching mastery" or ELL student and model reading story; have student read story. • Have student record self reading story as model for "approaching mastery" or ELL student. • Direct student to reading and writing center in classroom to reinforce literacy and writing skills.	

Test	Tips for Teachers	Home Connections
ELL	• See "Tips for Teachers" for "approaching mastery" and "at mastery" students. • Describe and model mouth formations for difficult sounds and words, then guide student while practicing with mirror. • Use sentence strips to practice reading sentences in story. • Show student how to recognize punctuation when reading with prosody. • Show realia or other visuals illustrating meaning of difficult words and sentences in story. • Use primary language equivalents when available and then ask student to say words and sentences in English.	• See "Home Connections" for "approaching mastery" and "at mastery" students. • Provide recording to use with sentence strips and word flash cards for additional practice; encourage children to practice with a mirror at home, as needed. • Provide recording of story; have children listen and track during story reading; then children read aloud with recording while tracking; then children read aloud and track independently; have adult at home review difficult words following independent story reading. • Encourage adult at home to help children tell a similar story using primary language equivalents. • Encourage adult at home to help children identify realia and other visuals illustrating meaning of the sentences in story.

Test

Test	Tips for Teachers	Home Connections
Individual Checkout (Lesson 155) **Approaching Mastery**	• See guidelines for students who do not read within error or time limit for Lesson 155 on page 214 in *Presentation Book C.* • Partner with "at mastery" student and have him or her model reading story; have student read story. • Reteach difficult words using "good-bye" list. • Review finger placement and tracking for sentence reading. • Have adult model reading story; have student read story until firm. • Use paired reading. • Develop recording of story read by good reader; have student listen to recording and whisper read.	• Provide word flash cards for children to take home for additional practice. • Have adult at home model reading story; have children listen and track during story reading; have children read story; have adult at home review difficult words following story reading. • Have children read story to a pet, stuffed animal, or sibling for extra practice.
At Mastery	• See guidelines for students who read within error and time limit for Lesson 155 on page 214 in *Presentation Book C.* • Partner with "approaching mastery" or ELL student and model reading story; have student read story. • Have student record self reading story as model for "approaching mastery" or ELL student. • Direct student to reading and writing center in classroom to reinforce literacy and writing skills.	
ELL	• See "Tips for Teachers" for "approaching mastery" and "at mastery" students. • Describe and model mouth formations for difficult sounds and words, then guide student while practicing with mirror. • Use sentence strips to practice reading sentences in story.	• See "Home Connections" for "approaching mastery" and "at mastery" students. • Provide recording to use with sentence strips and word flash cards for additional practice; encourage children to practice with a mirror at home, as needed.

Test	Tips for Teachers	Home Connections
Test	• Show student how to recognize punctuation when reading with prosody. • Show realia or other visuals illustrating meaning of difficult words and sentences in story. • Use primary language equivalents when available and then ask student to say words and sentences in English.	• Provide recording of story; have children listen and track during story reading; then children read aloud with recording while tracking; then children read aloud and track independently; have adult at home review difficult words following independent story reading. • Encourage adult at home to help children tell a similar story using primary language equivalents. • Encourage adult at home to help children identify realia and other visuals illustrating meaning of the sentences in story.
Individual Checkout (Lesson 160) **Approaching Mastery**	• See guidelines for students who do not read within error or time limit for Lesson 160 on page 235 in *Presentation Book C*. • Partner with "at mastery" student and have him or her model reading story; have student read story. • Reteach difficult words using "good-bye" list. • Review finger placement and tracking for sentence reading. • Have adult model reading story; have student read story until firm. • Use paired reading. • Develop recording of story read by good reader; have student listen to recording and whisper read.	• Provide word flash cards for children to take home for additional practice. • Have adult at home model reading story; have children listen and track during story reading; have children read story; have adult at home review difficult words following story reading. • Have children read story to a pet, stuffed animal, or sibling for extra practice.
At Mastery	• See guidelines for students who read within error and time limit for Lesson 160 on page 235 in *Presentation Book C*. • Partner with "approaching mastery" or ELL student and model reading story; have student read story. • Have student record self reading story as model for "approaching mastery" or ELL student. • Direct student to reading and writing center in classroom to reinforce literacy and writing skills.	
ELL	• See "Tips for Teachers" for "approaching mastery" and "at mastery" students. • Describe and model mouth formations for difficult sounds and words, then guide student while practicing with mirror. • Use sentence strips to practice reading sentences in story. • Show student how to recognize punctuation when reading with prosody. • Show realia or other visuals illustrating meaning of difficult words and sentences in story. • Use primary language equivalents when available and then ask student to say words and sentences in English.	• See "Home Connections" for "approaching mastery" and "at mastery" students. • Provide recording to use with sentence strips and word flash cards for additional practice; encourage children to practice with a mirror at home, as needed. • Provide recording of story; have children listen and track during story reading; then children read aloud with recording while tracking; then children read aloud and track independently; have adult at home review difficult words following independent story reading. • Encourage adult at home to help children tell a similar story using primary language equivalents. • Encourage adult at home to help children identify realia and other visuals illustrating meaning of the sentences in story.

Test	Tips for Teachers	Home Connections

Assessment (after Lesson 160) **Approaching Mastery**	• See "Remedial Exercises and Retesting the Students" guidelines on pages 25 and 26 in *Curriculum-Based Assessment and Fluency Teacher Handbook.*
	• Partner with "at mastery" student and review various activities.
	• Reteach difficult words using "good-bye" list.
	• Conduct "see-say-write" until firm.
	• Practice circling responses and "reading activities to yourself."
		• Provide word flash cards for children to take home for additional practice.
		• Encourage children to share their take-home sheets with their families.
		• Encourage adult at home to conduct "see-say-write" activity for each difficult word.
		• Have adult at home access SRA's Home Connection Activities listed at *www.sraonline.com*
		 • Direct Instruction
		  • *Reading Mastery Signature Edition*
		   • Activities

At Mastery	• Have student "be the teacher": Partner with "approaching mastery" or ELL student and review various activities. • Direct student to reading and writing center in classroom to reinforce literacy and writing skills.	
ELL	• See "Tips for Teachers" for "approaching mastery" and "at mastery" students. • Describe and model mouth formations for difficult sounds and words, then guide student while practicing with mirror. • Show realia or other visuals of objects or concepts to illustrate meaning of sentences. • Model rereading strategy to improve comprehension by using think-aloud. • Model story retelling by using think-aloud. • Model making predictions to improve comprehension by using think-aloud. • Use primary language equivalents when available and then ask student to say words and sentences in English.	• See "Home Connections" for "approaching mastery" and "at mastery" students. • Provide recording for use with word flash cards and sentence strips to take home for additional practice; encourage children to practice with a mirror at home, as needed. • Encourage adult at home to help children identify realia and other visuals of objects or concepts to illustrate meaning of sentences at home. • Encourage adult at home to help children tell a similar story using primary language equivalents. • Encourage adult at home to help children retell the beginning, middle, and end of story in their primary language and in English. • Encourage adult at home to help children make predictions in everyday life.

Appendix C

Levels of Support for Students with Intellectual Disabilities

The following table presents helpful tips to help ensure maximum access for students with intellectual disabilities. These suggestions use foundational skills that are clearly linked to the **Reading Mastery** content to aid such students in achieving academic success. These suggestions are provided at three levels of support (from least to most) to allow all learners the opportunity to access learning at the highest possible in program materials.

Levels of Support for Students with Intellectual Disabilities *Reading Mastery Signature Edition* **Grade 1**
***Level 1 (less support needed):* The student will**
<ul><li>locate printed words on a page.</li><li>identify where to begin reading (top to bottom, left to right).</li><li>name fifteen or more upper/lower case letters and produce their sounds.</li><li>identify, blend, and segment syllables in words.</li><li>recognize and produce words that rhyme.</li><li>identify initial sounds in one-syllable words.</li><li>identify and blend phonemes in selected VC and CVC words.</li><li>produce the most common sounds associated with ten or more letters.</li><li>blend sounds to decode VC and CVC words.</li><li>read two or more words.</li><li>use new vocabulary that is taught directly and relate it to prior knowledge.</li><li>listen to, make predictions about, and discuss stories.</li><li>identify and describe persons/objects/actions/settings in familiar stories.</li><li>identify similarities and differences between characters in read-aloud stories.</li><li>identify important story details (e.g., who, what, when).</li><li>use strategies to repair comprehension.</li><li>identify main events of read-aloud stories.</li><li>select and listen to a variety of fiction and nonfiction materials.</li></ul>

Level 2 (more support needed): The student will

- hold books correctly, turning pages one at a time.
- name five or more letters and say whether they are capitals or not.
- identify words that rhyme.
- segment auditory sentences into words.
- identify whether words or sounds are the same or different.
- identify own first name in print along with its initial sound.
- use new vocabulary that is taught directly.
- listen to and interact with stories.
- identify pictures of persons/objects/actions/settings in familiar stories.
- use pictures to identify meaning of unknown words.
- identify familiar characters/objects/settings pictured in read-aloud stories.
- imitate rhythm and rhyming words in read-aloud stories.
- select and listen to a variety of fiction and nonfiction materials.

Level 3 (most support needed): The student will

- respond to a familiar person reading a book aloud.
- attend to print by touching/looking/listening.
- recognize if a book is upside down or backwards.
- respond to the book cover or illustrations of a familiar story.
- imitate sounds or rhythm.
- respond to spoken words in familiar stories.
- request continuation of a familiar story when it is interrupted.
- respond to new vocabulary that is taught directly.
- match familiar objects to tasks in routines.
- respond to events in familiar read-aloud stories.
- seek assistance to clarify meaning of pictures and activities with prompting.
- attend to read-aloud fiction and nonfiction materials.

Appendix D

Professional Development
Fluency Building and Reading Level Determination

What is Fluency Building?

Fluency is the ability to read text quickly, accurately, and with expression (Armbruster et al., 2003; Hasbrouck, 2006; NICHD, 2000). It goes beyond automaticity and fast, effortless reading to include prosody or reading with expression as a critical aspect. Students who know how to read fluently read text smoothly with few, if any, decoding errors; they also read with proper expression, placing vocal emphasis and inflection where needed in the text (e.g., dialogue, punctuation, key words).

Why Fluency Building?

Fluency building is critical because "it provides a bridge between word recognition and comprehension. Because fluent readers do not have to concentrate on decoding the words, they can focus their attention on what the text means. They can make connections among the ideas in the text and between the text and their background knowledge" (Armbruster et al., 2003, p. 22).

However, Hasbrouck (2006) notes "fluency is necessary, but not sufficient, for understanding the meaning of text. When children read too slowly or haltingly, the text devolves into a broken string of words and/or phrases; it's a struggle just to remember what's been read, much less extract its meaning" (p. 24). Thus, reading programs should focus not only on building fluency but also on building vocabulary and text comprehension strategies to ensure that students read with understanding. *Core Lesson Connections* includes fluency practice as well as vocabulary and comprehension strategies as key aspects of the reading program.

Is Fluency Building Included in Core Lesson Connections?

Yes. Each lesson of *Core Lesson Connections* (starting at Lesson 1) includes **Part C: Fluency Building**. After each *Reading Mastery Signature Edition* program lesson, you will have students reread the story of the day with a partner. This rereading is done orally; repeated oral reading has been shown to substantially improve reading fluency and overall reading achievement (Armbruster et al., 2003; Hasbrouck, 2006; NICHD, 2000). Oral reading with a partner is a key part of *Core Lesson Connections* and takes no more than 5 minutes of instructional time, with long-lasting results. The fluency-building activities in *Core Lesson Connections* are further extensions of the individual fluency checkouts already found in the *Reading Mastery Signature Edition* program.

Conduct after the lesson, using the story of the day.	**Part C: Fluency Building**
Direct students to story of day. **Assign** student partners as Partner 1 and Partner 2. **Read** or **explain** Activity 1. **Monitor** partner reading. **Guide** as needed.	**Activity 1 Partner Reading** It's time for partner reading.

What are Accurate Descriptions of Independent, Instructional, and Frustrational Reading Levels for Individual Students?

"Fluency develops as a result of many opportunities to practice reading with a high degree of success. Therefore, your students should practice orally rereading text that is reasonably easy for them" (Armbruster et al., 2003, p. 27). Students can encounter three types of text (Katz, Polkoff, & Gurvitz, 2005; Osborn, Lehr, & Hiebert, 2003):

- Independent level text (relatively easy for the reader, with no more than approximately 1 in 20 words difficult for the reader; 95% success or higher; with 90% comprehension).
- Instructional level text (challenging but manageable text for the reader, with no more than approximately 1 in 10 words difficult for the reader; 90% to 94% success; with 75% comprehension).
- Frustrational level text (problematic text for the reader, with more than 1 in 10 words difficult for the reader; less than 90% success; with 50% comprehension).

Most researchers advocate the use of text containing words students know or can decode easily (e.g., Allington, 2002; Armbruster et al., 2003; Hasbrouck, 2006). You can determine if a story or text is appropriate for students to read independently using the following steps:

1. Select a 50–100 word passage from a book that the student has not read previously.

2. Have the student read the passage aloud. Make sure you start at the beginning of a paragraph and avoid paragraphs with lots of dialogue. Count substitutions, mispronunciations, omissions, reversals, and hesitations (of more than 3 seconds) as errors; insertions, self corrects, and repetitions do not count as errors.

3. Subtract the number of errors the student made from the total number of words—this will yield the number of correct words read by the student; divide the number of correct words read by the student by the total number of words in the passage and multiply by 100.

Example: passage length = 50 words; student makes 3 errors yielding 47 correct words read; divide 47 correct words by 50 total words equaling .94; multiply .94 by 100 to get 94%.

4. Compare the student's calculated accuracy level to the reading level percentages (i.e., 95% or higher = independent level; 90%–94% = instructional; below 90% = frustrational); in the above example, the student would be at an instructional reading level (94% falls in the 90% to 94% range).

5. Develop 5-8 comprehension questions (at least one "who, what, where, why, and inference-type" question). Ask these comprehension questions after the student reads the passage.

6. Subtract the number of questions answered incorrectly from the total number of questions; divide the number of correctly answered questions by the total number of questions and multiply by 100.

Example: number of questions = 6; student answers 1 incorrectly yielding 5 correctly answered questions; divide 5 correctly answered questions by 6 total questions yielding .83; multiply .83 by 100 to get 83%.

7. Compare the student's calculated percentage correct to the comprehension levels (i.e., 90% = independent; 75% = instructional; 50% = frustrational); in the above example, the student would be at an instructional level (83% is above 75% and less than 90%).

How Can You Tell If Students Are Working At The Appropriate Instructional Level in Reading Mastery Signature Edition?

The *Reading Mastery Signature Edition* program is designed with student success in mind.

- Only a small amount of new learning (10%–15% of the total lesson) occurs in each lesson.
- New concepts and skills are presented in two or three consecutive lessons to provide students with enough exposure to new material to use it in other applications.
- The majority of each lesson firms and reviews material and skills presented earlier in the program.

The small-step design of the program promises successful learning for students who are placed appropriately. Four criteria help you determine if students are working at the appropriate instructional level during lessons (Engelmann,1999).

1. Each time a task is presented, the group either responds correctly (all students respond correctly and in unison) or incorrectly (some students give the wrong response, no response, or do not respond in unison). Students should be at least 70% correct on information that is being introduced for the first time. If students are much below 70%, they will find it difficult to learn the skills being presented. If they are only at 50%, they are at chance levels and are probably guessing.

2. Students should be at least 90% correct on parts of the lesson that deal with skills and information taught earlier in the program (assuming previous skill mastery). For example, when students read a passage, they should read at least 90% of the words correctly on the first reading because virtually all of the words should be familiar. If students are consistently below the 90% correct level, the amount of new learning is too great.

3. At the end of a lesson, all students should be "virtually 100% firm on all tasks and activities" (p. 6). For example, on the second reading of the passage, students should read with close to 100% accuracy.

4. Students should be at least 85% correct on independent work.

To determine student-reading level, you should complete the reading checkout and words correct per minute (WCPM) calculation as scripted.

You can compare your student's WCPM to the 2005 Hasbrouck and Tindal Oral Reading Fluency Data Chart (see *How do You Help Readers who Struggle with Fluency?* below) to establish who is in need of additional fluency practice.

How Can You Help Students Select Appropriate Material to Read for Personal Pleasure?

Independent reading is the key to success as a life-long reader (Katz et al., 2005). Scaffolded independent reading should be done daily in the classroom; up to 30 minutes of independent reading time is advocated. Scaffolded independent reading involves opportunities for pleasurable, student-selected reading.

To accomplish this scaffolded independent reading, students should be taught a good way to self-select books that are "just right" for their independent reading level. The "Five Finger Rule" or "Goldilocks Method" helps students determine if books are "too easy."

Goldilocks Method

Level	Ask Yourself:
Too Easy	• Have you read it many times? • Do you understand the story very well? • Do you know almost every word? • Can you read it smoothly?
Too Hard	• Are there more than 5 words on the page you don't know? • Are you confused about what is happening in most of this book? • When you read, does it sound choppy?
Just Right	• Is the book new to you? • Do you understand a lot of the book? • Are there just a few words on a page that you don't know? • When you read, are some places smooth and some places choppy?

Routman (2003).

Students may ask themselves these questions or use the steps below to choose an independent-level book:

1. Choose a book

2. Open it anywhere

3. Make a fist

4. Read the page and hold up one finger for every unknown word or mistake you come across

5. Determine book level: 0–1 mistakes = too easy; 2–3 mistakes = just right; 4 or more mistakes = too hard.

How Should a Fluency Building Lesson Be Conducted?

You should assign student partners for the fluency building activity. To ensure success, students should be matched as closely as possible both in terms of their reading levels and their fluency rates. Given the emphasis on placement testing and flexible skill grouping in the *Reading Mastery Signature Edition* program, this matching should be relatively easy to accomplish.

Next, you should introduce and teach students how to conduct fluency practice properly in the classroom; this training should be conducted over 1 week. Even after training, you should carefully monitor student pairs during fluency practice activities. The following table presents an overview of what should be taught and how to teach it. If students struggle with fluency goals even after partner reading, they can be encouraged to repeat fluency practice two or more times with their partners (Note: Armbruster et al., 2003 report up to four repeated reads of the same passage may be needed to build fluency). However, if students continue to struggle, fluency intervention may be needed (see "How do you Help Readers Who Struggle with Fluency" below).

What to Teach	How to Teach It
Importance of fluency	• Discuss why fluent reading is important.
Fluency partnership behavior	• Discuss how to treat others (e.g., no arguing, be positive). • Set rules/expectations.
Fluency practice procedure	• Model and practice how/where to sit (across from one another in desks or at table; side by side in desks or at table). • Model and practice set up (one student gets own textbook, one student has copy of textbook story on which to record errors/last word read). • Model and practice what errors are (unknown/incorrect words). • Model and practice partner reading procedure (teacher times all students for 1 minute; recording partners underline unknown/incorrect words and draw slash after last word read when timer sounds; following timing, recording partners go over errors and follow standard error correct procedure [i.e., "That word is brother. What word?"]; recording partners record last word read, number of errors, calculate CWPM [correct words per minute], and graph partners' data; student roles are reversed and same procedure is followed).

How do You Help Readers who Struggle with Fluency?

Hasbrouck and Tindal (2006) completed an extensive study of oral reading fluency. They recommended using the 2005 Hasbrouck and Tindal Oral Reading Fluency Data Chart (at end of section) to establish who is in need of additional fluency practice beyond that accomplished by partner reading in the classroom. Students scoring below the 50th percentile using an average of two unpracticed readings from grade-level materials need a regimented fluency-building intervention. Additionally, teachers can use the chart to establish long-range goals for students or "aim lines" that can appear on graphs as a visual aid for students.

Students scoring at the frustrational reading level may be an indication of the following:

- A failure to achieve 70% correct on new information, 90% on skills taught earlier in the program, and virtually 100% on all tasks/activities by the end of a lesson—further training on the program may be warranted.
- Program placement that is too high—re-administer placement test to ensure appropriate program placement.
- Double-dosing or completing a lesson a second time to ensure skill mastery—once students are above the 90% accuracy level, they can participate more successfully in fluency building activities; fluency building should occur on independent level text although some researchers advocate the use of independent or instructional level text—see Osborn et al., 2003 for details).

Several research-validated strategies can be used to improve fluency.

Problem	Fluency Strategy	How to Do It
Reading without prosody	Teacher modeling of prosody (echo reading)	Teacher reads story with prosody; approaching-mastery student tracks as teacher models prosody; teacher provides guided practice on reading with prosody; sentences or paragraphs can be alternated between teacher and student.
	Tape-assisted modeling of prosody	Approaching-mastery student listens to tape of story read with prosody; student whisper reads and tracks as tape is played a second time.
	Tutoring	At-mastery student paired with approaching-mastery student; at-mastery student reads, modeling prosody; at-mastery student provides guided practice on reading with prosody.

Problem	Fluency Strategy	How to Do It
Failure to meet individual rate and accuracy checkout goals or score below 50% percentile on Hasbrouck and Tindal (2006) fluency data chart	Choral reading	Teacher models reading at appropriate pace; approaching-mastery students then read along with teacher at appropriate pace.
	Student-adult reading	Adult reads story first, modeling appropriate pace (and prosody); approaching-mastery student reads same story with adult providing assistance as needed.
	Tape-assisted reading	Approaching-mastery student listens to tape of story read at appropriate pace; student whisper reads and tracks as tape is played a second time.
	Paired or tandem reading	At-mastery student is paired with an approaching-mastery student; at-mastery student reads along with approaching-mastery student at appropriate pace noting, "whenever you want to read alone, just tap the back of my hand"); at-mastery student fades him/herself from reading as approaching-mastery student reads more and more of story.
	Cloze reading	Teacher models reading at appropriate pace; once or twice every few sentences, teacher omits important words and approaching-mastery students read words aloud in choral fashion.

Problem	Fluency Strategy	How to Do It
Errors occur on particular words.	Error word drill.	At end of fluency building session, teacher records all "error" words on whiteboard or index cards; approaching-mastery student reviews cards 3-4 times with teacher.
	Reading racetrack.	Teacher records troublesome words on "track segments" forming a racetrack; approaching-mastery student points to words on racetrack and reads them for 1 minute, circling the track as many times as possible (Falk, Band, & McLaughlin, 2003).
	Good-bye list.	Teacher writes troublesome words on board; teacher practices words on daily basis; teacher has approaching-mastery students say "good-bye" to words that are stated correctly 3 sessions in a row.

Hasbrouck & Tindal Oral Reading Fluency Data

Jan Hasbrouck and Gerald Tindal completed an extensive study of oral reading fluency in 2004. The results of their study are published in a technical report entitled "Oral Reading Fluency: 90 Years of Measurement," which is available on the University of Oregon's Web site, brt.uoregon.edu/tech_reports.htm and in THE READING TEACHER volume 59, 2006.

This table shows the oral reading fluency rates of students in grades 1 through 8 as determined by Hasbrouck and Tindal's data.

You can use the information in this table to draw conclusions and make decisions about the oral reading fluency of your students. **Students scoring below the 50th percentile using the average score of two unpracticed readings from grade-level materials need a fluency-building program.** In addition, teachers can use the table to set the long-term fluency goals for their struggling readers.

Average weekly improvement is the average words per week growth you can expect from a student. It was calculated by subtracting the fall score from the spring score and dividing the difference by 32, the typical number of weeks between the fall and spring assessments. For grade 1, since there is no fall assessment, the average weekly improvement was calculated by subtracting the winter score from the spring score and dividing the difference by 16, the typical number of weeks between the winter and spring assessments.

Grade	Percentile	Fall WCPM*	Winter WCPM*	Spring WCPM*	Avg. Weekly Improvement**
1	90		81	111	1.9
	75		47	82	2.2
	50		23	53	1.9
	25		12	28	1.0
	10		6	15	0.6
2	90	106	125	142	1.1
	75	79	100	117	1.2
	50	51	72	89	1.2
	25	25	42	61	1.1
	10	11	18	31	0.6
3	90	128	146	162	1.1
	75	99	120	137	1.2
	50	71	92	107	1.1
	25	44	62	78	1.1
	10	21	36	48	0.8
4	90	145	166	180	1.1
	75	119	139	152	1.0
	50	94	112	123	0.9
	25	68	87	98	0.9
	10	45	61	72	0.8
5	90	166	182	194	0.9
	75	139	156	168	0.9
	50	110	127	139	0.9
	25	85	99	109	0.8
	10	61	74	83	0.7
6	90	177	195	204	0.8
	75	153	167	177	0.8
	50	127	140	150	0.7
	25	98	111	122	0.8
	10	68	82	93	0.8
7	90	180	192	202	0.7
	75	156	165	177	0.7
	50	128	136	150	0.7
	25	102	109	123	0.7
	10	79	88	98	0.6
8	90	185	199	199	0.4
	75	161	173	177	0.5
	50	133	146	151	0.6
	25	106	115	124	0.6
	10	77	84	97	0.6

*WCPM = Words Correct per Minute

**Average Words per Week Growth

Oral Reading Fluency Data Chart from Oral Reading Fluency: 90 Years of Measurement

Fluent	Level 4	Reads primarily in larger, meaningful phrase groups. Although some regressions, repetitions, and deviations from text may be present, these do not appear to detract from the overall structure of the story. Preservation of the author's syntax is consistent. Some or most of the story is read with expressive interpretation.
	Level 3	Reads primarily in three- or four-word phrase groups. Some small groupings may be present. However, the majority of phrasing seems appropriate and preserves the syntax of the author. Little or no expressive interpretation is present.
Nonfluent	Level 2	Reads primarily in two-word phrases with some three- or four-word groupings. Some word-by-word reading may be present. Word groupings may seem awkward and unrelated to larger context of sentence or passage.
	Level 1	Reads primarily word-by-word. Occasional two-word or three-word phrases may occur—but these are infrequent and/or they do not preserve meaningful syntax.

National Center for Education Statistics, U.S. Department of Education

References

Allington, R. L. (2002). What I've learned about effective reading instruction from a decade of studying exemplary elementary classroom teachers. *Phi Delta Kappan*, 83, 740-747.

Armbruster, B., Lehr, F., & Osborn, J. (2003). *Put reading first: The research building blocks of reading instruction: Grades K-3* (2nd ed.). Washington, DC: Center for the Improvement of Early Reading Achievement, National Institute for Literacy, U.S. Department of Education.

Carnine, D. W., Silbert, J., Kame'enui, E. J., & Tarver, S. G. (2004). *Direct Instruction reading* (4th ed.). Upper Saddle River, NJ: Pearson Education.

Engelmann, S. (1999, July). *Student-program alignment and teaching to mastery*. Paper presented at the 25th National Direct Instruction Conference, Eugene, OR.

Falk, M., Band, M., & McLaughlin, T. F. (2003). The effects of reading racetracks and flashcards on sight word vocabulary of three third grade students with a specific learning disability: A further replication and analysis. *International Journal of Special Education*, 18(2), 57-61.

Hasbrouck, J. (2006). Drop everything and read—but how?: For students who are not yet fluent, silent reading is not the best use of classroom time. *American Educator*, 30(2), 22-27, 30-31, 46-47.

Hasbrouck, J., & Tindal, G. A. (2006). ORF norms: A valuable assessment tool for reading teachers. *The Reading Teacher*, 59, 636-644.

Katz, C. A., Polkoff, L., & Gurvitz, D. (2005, January). "Shhh...I'm reading:" Scaffolded independent-level reading. *School Talk*. Urbana, IL: National Council of Teachers of English.

National Institute of Child Health and Human Development [NICHD]. (2000). *Report of the National Reading Panel. Teaching children to read: An evidence-based assessment of the scientific research literature on reading and its implications for reading instruction: Reports of the subgroups* (NIH Publication NO. 00-4754). Washington, DC: U.S. Government Printing Office.

Osborn, J., Lehr, F., & Hiebert, E. (2003). *A focus on fluency*. Honolulu, HI: Pacific Resources for Education and Learning.

Routman, R. (2003). *Reading essentials: The specifics you need to teach reading well*. Portsmouth, NH: Heineman.

Vaughn, S., & Linan-Thompson, S. (2004). *Research-based methods of reading instruction: Grades K-3*. Alexandria, VA: ASCD.

Appendix E

Fluency/Paired Reading Guidelines

Lesson 1

Part C: Fluency Building

Conduct after lesson, using story of day.

Activity 1 Partner Reading

Direct students to story of day.

The more time you spend reading, the better your reading skills will be. You're going to learn to read with a partner to help improve your reading skills. When you partner read, you'll take turns reading with your partner. You'll do this every day using the story we just read during reading group.

Before you learn how to do partner reading, it's important to learn how to **act** as a partner. While you're **listening** to your partner read, you should sit quietly and listen very carefully for errors. You should follow along with your finger so you don't lose your place. You should also be very positive, saying things like "good job" or "nice reading." You should treat your partner the way you'd like to be treated.

Discuss partner behavior, adding points not mentioned by students.

What kinds of things should you be doing as your partner is reading? (Ideas: *Follow along in story by tracking with finger; listen for errors; listen carefully; sit quietly; be positive.*)

Why is it important to do these things? (Student responses.)

When you're **reading** to your partner, you should read with expression so you're interesting to listen to. You should also read loud enough so your partner can hear you. Finally, when your partner helps you with troublesome words, make the correction and go on. You shouldn't argue. You should be positive—your partner is trying to help you become an even better reader.

What kinds of things should you do as you're reading the story to your partner? (Ideas: *Read with expression; read loudly enough; accept corrections without arguing; be positive.*)

Being a good partner is an important responsibility. I know you can do it!

As your partner is reading, you also need to know how to correct errors. First, let's talk about what errors are.

Discuss errors one could make during reading: mispronunciations, substitutions, omissions, reversals, skipping line(s); give examples.

Write error correction steps on the board.

Second, let's review the steps to correcting an error. Here they are:

Discuss each step.

Step 1: Stop your partner and tell your partner what he/she did.

Step 2: Tell partner what it should be.

Step 3: Have your partner say it correctly.

Step 4: Have your partner start over at the beginning of the sentence.

Model think-aloud for partner reading. **Call** on student to serve as sample "partner." **Model** error correction steps for each error. **Model** praise. **Guide** student volunteer as necessary as he/she serves as partner.

Now, watch as I show you how to partner read.

Sample Wording for Think-Aloud

(Student's name) and I are going to show you how to do partner reading. (Student's name) will read today's story and make three or four different kinds of errors. I'll listen to him/her read and correct the errors I hear. Follow along in your story as (Student's name) reads. Here we go.

1. Stop. You said _____.
2. The word is _____.
3. What word?
4. Start over at the beginning of the sentence.

Super job reading this story.

Now (Student's name) and I are going to switch roles. I'll read the story and (Student's name) will listen to me read. I'll make a few errors so we can practice our error correction steps. Here we go.

We'll practice this more later.

Part C: Fluency Building

Conduct after lesson, using story of day.

Activity 1 Partner Reading

Direct students to story of day.

In the last lesson, you learned that when you partner read, you take turns reading with your partner. You'll do this every day using the story we just read during reading group.

Discuss with students.

You learned how to act during partner reading. How should the person who is **listening** act? (Student responses.)

How should the person who is **reading** act? (Student responses.)

Write error correction steps on the board.

As your partner is reading, you also need to know how to correct errors. Give me some examples of what errors are. (Student responses.)

Discuss each step. **Point** to each step on board as you read them together.

What are the steps to correcting an error?

Step 1: Stop your partner, and tell your partner what he/she did.

Step 2: Tell partner what it should be.

Step 3: Have your partner say it correctly.

Step 4: Have your partner start over at the beginning of the sentence.

Now, watch as I show you how to partner read once again.

Model partner reading. **Call** on student to serve as sample "partner." **Model** error correction steps for each error. **Model** praise. **Guide** student volunteer as necessary as he/she serves as partner.

We'll practice this more later.

Part C: Fluency Building

Conduct after lesson, using story of day.

Activity 1 Partner Reading

Direct students to story of day. **Elicit** responses to questions. **Guide** as needed.

What is partner reading? (Idea: *Taking turns reading with a partner.*)

What story do you read? (Idea: *The story from today's lesson.*)

You learned how to act during partner reading. How should the person who is **listening** act? (Student responses.)

How should the person who is **reading** act? (Student responses.)

As your partner is reading, you also need to correct errors. Give me some examples of errors. (Student responses.)

Write error correction steps on the board. **Point** to each step on board as you read them together. **Discuss** each step.

What are the steps to correcting an error?

Step 1: Stop your partner, and tell your partner what he/she did.

Step 2: Tell partner what it should be.

Step 3: Have your partner say it correctly.

Step 4: Have your partner start over at the beginning of the sentence.

Assign student partners as Partner 1 and Partner 2. **Monitor** partner reading. **Guide** as needed.

Now, you'll practice partner reading with another student. Partner 1 will read and Partner 2 will listen. Partner 1, remember to make a couple of errors to allow your partner a chance to practice using the error correction steps.

Reverse roles. Now Partner 2 will read and Partner 1 will listen. Partner 2, remember to make a couple of errors to allow your partner a chance to practice using the error correction steps.

Discuss with students.

Let's talk about how this went. What questions do you have?

We'll practice this more later.

Lessons 7–9

Part C: Fluency Building

Conduct after lesson, using story of day.

Activity 1 Partner Reading

Direct students to story of day. **Assign** student partners as Partner 1 and Partner 2. **Monitor** partner reading. **Guide** as needed.

Partner 1 will read to Partner 2. When you're done, reverse roles. Partner 2 will then read to Partner 1. Remember to be positive and treat your partner as you would like to be treated.

Discuss with students.

Let's talk about how this went. What questions do you have?

Lessons 10 to end of program

Part C: Fluency Building

Conduct after lesson, using story of day.

Activity 1 Partner Reading

Direct students to story of day. **Assign** student partners as Partner 1 and Partner 2. **Monitor** partner reading. **Guide** as needed.

It's time for partner reading.

Appendix F

Strand Component	Lessons 1-5	Lessons 6-10	Lessons 11-15	Lessons 16-20
Core Lesson Connections	**Phonemic Awareness** – 1:a; 2:a; 3:a; 4:a; 5:a **Vocabulary Development** – 1:b; 2:b; 3:b; 4:b; 5:b **Comprehension** – 1:c; 2:c; 3:c; 4:c; 5:c **Fluency** – 2:d; 3:d; 4:d; 5:d	**Phonemic Awareness** – 6:a; 7:a; 8:a; 9:a; 10:a **Vocabulary Development** – 6:b; 7:b; 8:b; 9:b; 10:b **Comprehension** – 6:c; 7:c; 8:c; 9:c; 10:c **Fluency** – 6:d; 7:d; 8:d; 9:d; 10:d	**Phonemic Awareness** – 11:a; 12:a; 13:a; 14:a; 15:a **Vocabulary Development** – 11:b; 12:b; 13:b; 14:b; 15:b **Comprehension** – 11:c; 12:c; 13:c; 14:c; 15:c **Fluency** – 11:d; 12:d; 13:d; 14:d; 15:d **Writing** – 15:e	**Phonemic Awareness** – 16:a; 17:a; 18:a; 19:a; 20:a **Vocabulary Development** – 16:b; 17:b; 18:b; 19:b; 20:b **Comprehension** – 16:c; 17:c; 18:c; 19:c; 20:c **Fluency** – 16:d; 17:d; 18:d; 19:d; 20:d
Reading Strand *Reading Mastery*	**Presentation Book A** **Phonemic Awareness** – 1:16; 2:18; 3:6; 4:6 **Letter / Sound Correspondence** – 1:1; 1:4; 1:5; 1:7; 1:8; 1:15; 1:16; 2:1; 2:7; 2:8; 2:9; 2:10; 2:11; 2:17; 2:18; 3:1; 3:7; 3:11; 4:1; 4:7; 4:11; 5:1; 5:18 **Phonics and Word Recognition** – 1:2-12; 1:14; 1:16; 2:2-6; 2:8-14; 2:16; 2:18; 3:2; 3:4; 3:5; 3:6; 3:8; 4:2; 4:4; 4:5; 4:6; 4:8; 5:2-11; 5:13-15; 5:17; 5:18 **Fluency** – 1:2; 1:3; 1:5; 1:6; 1:7; 1:8; 1:9; 1:12; 2:2; 2:3; 2:4; 2:5; 2:6; 2:8; 2:9; 2:10; 2:11; 2:14; 3:5; 4:5; 5:2-10; 5:15 **Comprehension** – 1:12; 1:13; 1:14; 1:16; 2:14; 2:15; 2:16; 2:18; 3:3; 3:6; 3:10; 4:3; 4:6; 4:10; 5:12; 5:15; 5:16; 5:17; 5:18 **Spelling** – 1:1-5; 2:1-3; 3:1-3; 4:1-5; 5:1-3	**Presentation Book A** **Letter / Sound Correspondence** – 6:1; 6:19; 6:20; 7:1; 7:5; 7:6; 7:7; 7:18; 7:19; 7:20; 8:1; 8:7-9; 9:1; 9:7-9 10:1; 10:8; 10:17 **Phonics and Word Recognition** – 6:2-10; 6:12; 6:14; 6:16; 6:18; 6:20; 7:2-10; 7:12-14; 7:16; 7:18; 7:20; 8:2; 8:4; 8:5; 8:7; 8:9; 9:2; 9:4; 9:5; 9:7; 9:9; 10:2-13; 10:15; 10:16 **Fluency** – 6:2-10; 6:14; 7:2-10; 7:14; 8:4; 9:4; 10:2-10; 10:13 **Comprehension** – 6:11; 6:14; 6:15; 6:16; 6:18; 7:11; 7:14; 7:15; 7:16; 7:18; 8:3; 8:7; 9:3; 9:7; 10:13-17 **Spelling** – 6:1-3; 7:1-2; 8:1-2; 9:1-3; 10:1-3	**Presentation Book A** **Letter / Sound Correspondence** – 11: 1; 11:4; 11:5; 11:6; 12:1; 12:4; 12:6; 12:17; 12:18; 12:23; 12:24; 13:1; 13:9; 13:10; 14:1; 14:18; 14:19; 15:1; 15:16 **Phonics and Word Recognition** – 11:2-16; 11:18; 11:19; 11:21; 11:22; 12:2-14; 12:16; 12:17; 12:19; 12:20; 13:4; 13:5; 14:2-14; 15:2-14 **Fluency** – 11:2; 11:3; 11:5-13; 11:16; 11:25; 12:2-11; 12:14; 12:17; 13:4; 13:10; 14:2-10; 14:14; 14:18; 15:2-10; 15:14; 15:16 **Comprehension** – 11:16; 11:17; 11:22; 11:24; 11:27; 12:14; 12:15; 12:16; 12:19; 12:20; 12:22; 12:25; 13:3; 13:5; 13:7; 13:8; 14:11; 14:14; 14:15; 14:17; 14:20; 14:21; 15:11; 15:14; 15:15; 15:16 **Spelling** – 11:1-4; 12:1-5; 13:1-4; 14:1-4; 15:1-5	**Presentation Book A** **Letter / Sound Correspondence** – 16:1; 16:17; 16:18; 17:1; 17:18; 17:19; 18:1; 18:9; 18:10; 19:1; 19:18; 19:20; 20:1; 20:16 **Phonics and Word Recognition** – 16:2-9; 16:11-13; 17:2-10; 17:12-14; 18:2; 18:4; 18:5; 19:2-8; 19:10-12; 19:14; 20:3-9; 20:11-13; 20:15 **Fluency** – 16:2-9; 16:13; 16:17; 17:2-10; 17:14; 17:18; 18:4; 18:9; 19:2-8; 19:12; 19:18; 20:2-9; 20:13; 20:16 **Comprehension** – 16:10; 16:13; 16:14; 16:16; 16:19; 16:20; 17:11; 17:14; 17:15; 17:17; 17:20; 17:21; 18:3; 18:5; 18:7; 18:8; 19: 9; 19:12; 19:13; 19:14; 19:16; 19:17; 19:19; 20:10; 20:12-16 **Spelling** – 16:1-4; 17:1-5; 18:1-5; 19:1-5; 20:1-5
Language Arts Strand *Reading Mastery*	**Vocabulary** *Classification* – 1:1; 1:3; 1:4; 1:8; 2:1; 2:4; 2:10; 3:1; 3:4; 3:10; 4:1; 4:4; 5:2; 5:10 *Opposites* – 1:2, 2:5; 3:5; 4:5; 5:5	**Vocabulary** *Classification* – 6:1; 6:5; 7:5; 7:9; 8:5; 8:9; 9:2; 10:2 *Opposites* – 6:6; 9:4; 10:3 *Same/Different* – 8:4; 9:6; 10:5 *Absurdity* – 9:7 *Common Information* – 7:3	**Vocabulary** *Classification* – 11:2; 11:9; 12:2; 13:2; 14:8 *Opposites* – 11:4; 12:4; 13:3 *Same/Different* – 11:6; 12:6; 13:5; 14:4; 15:5 *Absurdity* – 13:4 *True/False* – 14:5; 15:2	**Vocabulary** *Opposites* – 17:7; 18:3; 19:3; 20:4 *Same/Different* – 16:3; 17:6 *Materials* – 16:4; 16:5; 17:4; 17:5; 18:2; 19:2; 20:2 *True/False* – 16:6; 17:9 *Absurdity* – 17:3

Strand Component	Lessons 1-5	Lessons 6-10	Lessons 11-15	Lessons 16-20
Language Arts Strand *Reading Mastery* (continued)	**Listening**/Speaking/Viewing *Story Telling* – 1:5; 2:7; 3:7; 4:7; 5:7 *Story Details* – 1:6; 2:8; 3:8; 4:8; 5:8 *Following Directions* – 1:7; 2:9; 3:9; 4:9; 4:10; 5:9 *Actions* – 5:1 **Grammar, Usage, and Mechanics** – 2:2; 3:2; 4:2; 5:3 **Calendar Facts** – 2:3; 2:6; 3:3; 3:6; 4:3; 4:6; 5:4; 5:6	**Listening/Speaking/Viewing** *Story Telling* – 6:8; 7:7 *Story Details* – 6:9 *Story Review* – 8:7; 9:9; 10:7 *Sequencing* – 8:8; 9:10 *Following Directions* – 7:8; 8:10; 9:10; 9:11; 10:8; 10:9 *Actions* – 8:1; 9:1; 10:1 **Grammar, Usage, and Mechanics** – 6:2; 6:4; 7:1; 7:2; 8:2; 9:3 **Calendar Facts** – 6:3; 6:7; 7:1; 7:2; 8:2; 9:3	**Listening/Speaking/Viewing** *Story Telling* – 12:8; 15:7 *Story Details* – 12:9; 15:8 *Sequencing* – 11:8; 13:8; 14:3 14:7; 15:6 *Following Directions* – 11:10; 12:10; 12:11; 14:9 *Actions* – 11:1; 12:1; 13:1; 14:1; 15:1 **Grammar, Usage, and Mechanics** – 11:3; 12:3; 14:6 **Calendar Facts** – 11:5; 11:7; 12:5; 12:7; 13:6; 13:7; 14:2; 15:3; 15:4	**Listening/Speaking/Viewing** *Sequencing* – 16:2; 16:9; 17:8; 17:11; 18:7; 18:8; 19:5; 19:8; 20:8 *Following Directions* – 16:10; 16:11; 17:13; 17:14; 18:10; 20:10 *Actions* – 16:1; 17:1; 18:1; 19:1; 20:1 *Extrapolation* – 17:12 **Grammar, Usage, and Mechanics** – 17:2; 18:4; 18:5; 18:9; 19:4; 20:3; 20:6 **Calendar Facts** – 16:7; 16:8; 17:10; 18:6; 19:6; 19:7; 20:5; 20:7 **Inquiry** – 20:9
Literature Strand *Reading Mastery*	*One Little Kitten* – 5 Sequence of Events Picture Details		*The Carrot Seed* – 15 Sequence of Events Picture Details	*Who Took the Farmer's Hat?* – 20 Sequence of Events Picture Details
Formal Assessment	**Individual Reading Checkout** – 5:19	**Individual Reading Checkout** – 10:18	**Individual Reading Checkout** – 15:17	**Individual Reading Checkout** – 20:17 **Reading Assessment** – 20

Strand Component	Lessons 21-25	Lessons 26-30	Lessons 31-35	Lessons 36-40
Core Lesson Connections	**Phonemic Awareness** – 21:a; 22:a; 23:a; 24:a; 25:a **Vocabulary Development** – 21:b; 22:b; 23:b; 24:b; 25:b **Comprehension** – 21:c; 22:c; 23:c; 24:c; 25:c **Fluency** – 21:d; 22:d; 23:d; 24:d; 25:d **Writing** – 25:e	**Phonemic Awareness** – 26:a; 27:a; 28:a; 29:a; 30:a **Vocabulary Development** – 26:b; 27:b; 28:b; 29:b; 30:b **Comprehension** – 26:c; 27:c; 28:c; 29:c; 30:c **Fluency** – 26:d; 27:d; 28:d; 29:d; 30:d	**Phonemic Awareness** – 31:a; 32:a; 33:a; 34:a; 35:a **Vocabulary Development** – 31:b; 32:b; 33:b; 34:b; 35:b **Comprehension** – 31:c; 32:c; 33:c; 34:c; 35:c **Fluency** – 31:d; 32:d; 33:d; 34:d; 35:d **Writing** – 35:e	**Phonemic Awareness** – 36:a; 37:a; 38:a; 39:a; 40:a **Vocabulary Development** – 36:b; 37:b; 38:b; 39:b; 40:b **Comprehension** – 36:c; 37:c; 38:c; 39:c; 40:c **Fluency** – 36:d; 37:d; 38:d; 39:d; 40:d
Reading Strand *Reading Mastery*	**Presentation Book A** **Letter / Sound Correspondence** – 21:1; 21:8; 21:20; 21:22; 22:1; 22:19; 22:21; 23:1; 23:21; 23:23; 24:1; 24:5; 24:17; 24:19; 25:1; 25:7; 25:20 **Phonics and Word Recognition** – 21:2-10; 21:12-14; 22:2-9; 22:11-13; 23:2-10; 23:13-15; 24:2-7; 24:9-11; 25:2-14; 25:16-18 **Fluency** – 21:2-10; 21:14; 21:21; 22:2-9; 22:13; 22:19; 23:2-11; 23:15; 23:21; 24:2-7; 24:11; 24:17; 25:2-14; 25:18; 25:20	**Presentation Book A** **Letter / Sound Correspondence** – 26:1; 26:19; 27:1; 27:13; 27:23; 28:1; 28:6; 28:7; 28:19; 29:1; 29:10; 29:21; 30:1; 30:7; 30:11; 30:20 **Phonics and Word Recognition** – 26: 2-10; 26:12-14; 27:2-14; 27: 16-18; 28:2-10; 28:12-14; 29: 2-12; 29:14-16; 30:2-14; 16-18 **Fluency** – 26:2-10; 26:14; 26:19; 27:2-14; 27:18; 27:23; 28:2-10; 28:14; 28:19; 29:2-12; 29:16; 29:21; 30:2-10; 30:12-14; 30:18; 30:20	**Presentation Book A** **Letter / Sound Correspondence** – 31:1; 31:7-10; 31:21; 32:1; 32:9; 33:1; 33:8; 33:9; 33:22; 34:1; 34:2; 34:14; 34:15; 34:17; 34:29; 35:1; 35:2; 35:13-16; 35:26 **Phonics and Word Recognition** – 31:2-6; 31:8-12; 31:14-16; 32:2; 32:4; 32:6; 33:2-7; 33:9-12; 33:14-16; 34:3-19; 34:21-23; 35:3-20; 35:22-24 **Fluency** – 31:2-6; 31:8-12; 31:16; 32:2; 32:4; 32:6; 33:2-7; 33:9-12; 33:16; 34:3-19; 34:23; 35:3-20; 35:24	**Presentation Book A** **Letter / Sound Correspondence** – 36:1, 36:2, 36:12, 36:16, 36:28; 37:1; 37:15-17; 37:28; 38:1; 38:13; 38:14; 38:25; 39:1; 39:12; 39:26; 40:1; 40:2; 40:13; 40:15; 40:23 **Phonics and Word Recognition** – 36:3-18; 36:20-22; 37:2-18; 37:20-22; 38:2-15; 38:17-19; 39:3-16; 39:18-20; 40:3-20; 40:22 **Fluency** – 36:3-18, 36:22, 36:28; 37:2-18, 37:22, 37:28; 38:2-15; 38:19; 38:25; 39:3-16; 39:20; 39:26; 40:3-17; 40:20; 40:23

Strand Component	Lessons 21-25	Lessons 26-30	Lessons 31-35	Lessons 36-40
Reading Strand *Reading Mastery* (continued)	**Comprehension –** 21:11; 21:13-15; 21:17-19; 21:21; 22:10; 22:12-14; 22:16-18; 22:20; 23:12; 23:14; 23:15; 23:18-20; 23:22; 24:8; 24:10-12; 24:14-16; 24:18; 25:15; 25:17-20 **Spelling –** 21:1-5; 22:1-4; 23:1-5; 24:1-7; 25:1-7	**Comprehension –** 26:11; 26:13-15; 26:17; 26:18; 26:20; 27:15; 27:17-19; 27:21; 27:22; 27:24; 28:11; 28:13-15; 28:17; 28:18; 28:20; 29:13; 29:16; 29:17; 29:19; 29:20; 29:22; 30:15; 30:17; 30:18; 30:20 **Spelling –** 26:1-6; 27:1-6; 28:1-5; 29:1-6; 30:1-5	**Comprehension –** 31:13; 31:15-17; 31:19; 31:20; 31:22; 32:3; 32:5; 32:8; 32:10; 33:13; 33:16; 33:17; 33:19-21; 34:20; 34:23; 34:24; 34:26-28; 35:21; 35:24-26 **Spelling –** 31:1-5; 32:1-6; 33:1-7; 34:1-4; 35:1-5	**Comprehension –** 36:19; 36:22; 36:23; 36:25-27; 37:19; 37:22; 37:23; 37:25-27; 38:16; 38:19; 38:20; 38:22-24; 39:17; 39:20; 39:21; 39:23-25; 40:20-23 **Spelling –** 36:1-3; 37:1-3; 38:1-3; 39:1-4; 40:1-5
Language Arts Strand *Reading Mastery*	**Vocabulary** *Classification –* 21:6; 22:3; 23:5; 24:3; 25:5 *Opposites –* 21:5; 22:7; 23:3; 24:4; 25:4 *Materials –* 21:4; 22:6; 24:1; 24:6 *Absurdity –* 21:2; 23:4 **Listening/Speaking/ Viewing** *Sequencing –* 23:8; 24:7 *Following Directions –* 21:12; 22:9; 22:11; 23:10; 25:8; 25:10 *Actions –* 21:1; 22:1; 23:1 *Story Telling –* 21:9; 21:10; 22:8; 25:7 **Grammar, Usage, and Mechanics –** 21:3; 21:7; 22:2; 22:5; 23:2; 24:5; 25:2; 25:3 **Calendar Facts –** 21:8; 22:4; 23:6; 23:7; 24:2; 25:6 **Inquiry –** 21:11; 22:10; 23:9; 25:1; 25:9	**Vocabulary** *Classification –* 26:5; 28:5; 29:3; 29:10; 30:5 *Opposites –* 26:6; 27:6; 28:4; 29:4; 30:3 *Materials –* 30:2 **Listening/Speaking/ Viewing** *Sequencing –* 26:7; 27:8; 29:5; 29:8 *Following Directions –* 26:9; 27:10; 30:9 *Actions –* 27:1; 28:1; 29:1; 30:1 *Story Telling –* 28:7 *Story Recall –* 30:7 **Grammar, Usage, and Mechanics –** 26:1; 27:2; 27:4; 28:2; 28:8; 29:6 **Calendar Facts –** 26:2; 26:3; 27:3; 27:7; 28:3; 28:6; 29:2; 29:7; 30:5 **Inquiry –** 26:4; 26:8; 27:5; 27:9; 29:8; 30:6 30:8	**Vocabulary** *Classification –* 31:1; 31:5; 32:1; 32:2; 33:1; 33:4; 34:1; 34:2; 35:4 *Opposites –* 31:2 *Materials –* 35:5 **Listening/Speaking/ Viewing** *Sequencing –* 32:7 *Following Directions –* 31:9; 32:9; 34:7 *Actions –* 34:5; 35:1 *Story Telling –* 33:6 *Story Recall –* 31:6; 31:7; 33:7; 34:6; 35:6 **Grammar, Usage, and Mechanics** *Who, When, What, Why, Where, How –* 31:4; 32:4; 33:2; 34:4; 35:3 *From/To –* 32:8; 34:7; 35: 7 **Calendar Facts –** 31:3; 32:3; 32:5; 33:5; 34:3; 35;2 **Inquiry –** 31:8; 32:6; 33:3; 35:8	**Vocabulary** *Classification –* 36:1; 36:4; 38:1; 38:11; 39:1; 40:1; 40:7 *Opposites –* 37:5; 39:3; 40:4 *Materials –* 36:5; 38:10; 39:8 *Only –* 38:3; 38:5; 39:2; 40:2 **Listening/Speaking/ Viewing** *Sequencing –* 36:8; 37:8; 39:5 *Actions –* 37:1 *Story Telling –* 38:8 *Story Recall –* 38:9 *Putting on a Play –* 39:6; 40:9 **Grammar, Usage, and Mechanics** *Who, When, What, Why, Where, How –* 36:2; 36:6; 37:3; 37:6; 38:2; 40:3; 40:5 *From/To –* 36:9; 37;2; 39:7; 40:8 **Calendar Facts –** 36:3; 36:7; 37:4; 37:7; 38:4; 38:7; 39:4; 40:6 **Inquiry –** 36:10; 38:6
Literature Strand *Reading Mastery*	*A Kiss for Little Bear –* 25 Sequence of Events Picture Details	*Molly's Bracelet –* 30 Sequence of Events Picture Details	*There Stood Our Dog –* 35 Sequence of Events Picture Details	*Fat Cat Tompkin –* 40 Sequence of Events Picture Details
Formal Assessment	**Individual Reading Checkout –** 25:21	**Individual Reading Checkout –** 30:21	**Individual Reading Checkout –** 35:27	**Individual Reading Checkout –** 40:24 **Reading Assessment –** 40

Strand Component	Lessons 41-45	Lessons 46-50	Lessons 51-55	Lessons 56-60
Core Lesson Connections	**Phonemic Awareness** – 41:a; 42:a; 43:a; 44:a; 45:a **Vocabulary Development** – 41:b; 42:b; 43:b; 44:b; 45:b **Comprehension –** 41:c; 42:c; 43:c; 44:c; 45:c **Fluency –** 41:d; 42:d; 43:d; 44:d; 45:d **Writing –** 45:e	**Phonemic Awareness** – 46:a; 47:a; 48:a; 49:a; 50:a **Vocabulary Development** – 46:b; 47:b; 48:b; 49:b; 50:b **Comprehension –** 46:c; 47:c; 48:c; 49:c; 50:c **Fluency –** 46:d; 47:d; 48:d; 49:d; 50:d	**Phonemic Awareness** – 51:a; 52:a; 53:a; 54:a; 55:a **Vocabulary Development** – 51:b; 52:b; 53:b; 54:b; 55:b **Comprehension –** 51:c; 52:c; 53:c; 54:c; 55:c **Fluency –** 51:d; 52:d; 53:d; 54:d; 55:d **Writing –** 55:e	**Phonemic Awareness** – 56:a; 57:a; 58:a; 59:a; 60:a **Vocabulary Development** – 56:b; 57:b; 58:b; 59:b; 60:b **Comprehension –** 56:c; 57:c; 58:c; 59:c; 60:c **Fluency –** 56:d; 57:d; 58:d; 59:d; 60:d

Strand Component	Lessons 41-45	Lessons 46-50	Lessons 51-55	Lessons 56-60
Reading Strand *Reading Mastery*	**Presentation Book A** **Letter / Sound Correspondence** – 41:1; 41:12; 41:13; 41:24; 42:1; 42:2; 42:7; 42:9; 42:18; 43:1; 43:8; 43:9; 43:18; 44:1; 44:2; 44:11; 44:12; 44:21; 45:1; 45:2; 45:4; 45:5-10; 45:19 **Phonics and Word Recognition** – 41:3-17; 42:3-12; 43:2-12; 44:3-15; 45:4; 45:5; 45:7-17 **Fluency** – 41:3-14; 41:17; 41:24; 42:3-9; 42:12; 42:18; 43:2-9; 43:12; 43:18; 44:3-12; 44:15; 44:21; 45:3-5; 45:7-14; 45:17; 45:19 **Comprehension** – 41:17; 41:18; 41:21-23; 42:12; 42:13; 42:15-17; 43:12; 43:13; 43:15-17; 44:15; 44:16; 44:18-20; 45:17-19 **Spelling** – 41:1-3; 42:1-3; 43:1-3; 44:1-4; 45:1-4	**Presentation Books A and B** **Letter / Sound Correspondence** – 46:1; 46:2; 46:9-13; 46:23; 47:1; 48:1; 48:2; 48:11-13; 48:23; 49:1; 49:2; 49:9-13; 50:1; 50:13; 50:14 **Phonics and Word Recognition** – 46:3-10; 46:12-17; 47:2; 47:4; 47:6; 48:3-17; 49:3-16; 50:2-18 **Fluency** – 46:3-10; 46:12-14; 46:17; 46:23; 47:2; 47:4; 47:6; 48:3-14; 48:17; 48:23; 49:3-13; 49:16; 50:2-15; 50:18 **Comprehension** – 46:17; 46:18; 46:20-22; 47:3; 47:5; 47:7-9; 47:11; 48:15-17; 48:19-22; 49:15:19; 49:19-22; 50:18-20 **Spelling** – 46:1-3; 47:1-3; 48:1-3; 49:1-3; 50:1-4	**Presentation Book B** **Letter / Sound Correspondence** – 51:1; 51:12; 51:13; 52:1; 52:2; 52:12; 52:14; 53:9; 53:10; 54:1 **Phonics and Word Recognition** – 51:2-17; 52:3-17; 53:1-13; 54:2-14; 55:1-14 **Fluency** – 51:2-14; 51:17; 52:3-14; 52:17; 53:1-10; 53:13; 54:3-11; 54:14; 55:1-11; 55:14 **Comprehension** – 51:17; 51:18; 51:20-23; 52:16-18; 52:20-23; 53:12-14; 53:16-19; 54:13-15; 54:17-20; 55:13-16 **Spelling** – 51:1-5; 52:1-5; 53:1-5; 54:1-5; 55:1-3	**Presentation Book B** **Letter / Sound Correspondence** – 56:17; 57:2; 57:7; 59:2-4; 60:1-3 **Phonics and Word Recognition** – 56:1-20; 57:1; 57:3-16; 58:1-13; 59:1-15; 60:1-18 **Fluency** – 56:1-17; 56:20; 57:1; 57:3-13; 57:16; 58:1-10; 58:13; 59:1-12; 59:15; 60:1-15; 60:18 **Comprehension** – 56:20; 56:21; 56:23-26; 57:15-17; 57:19-22; 58:12-14; 58:16-19; 59:15; 59:16; 59:18-20; 60:18-20 **Spelling** – 56:1-4; 57:1-5; 58:1-4; 59:1-4; 60:1-5
Language Arts Strand *Reading Mastery*	**Vocabulary** *Classification* – 41:4; 41:9; 42:3; 43:6; 43:9; 44:2; 45:5; 45:10 *Definitions* – 41:1; 42:2; 43:2 *Can/Do* – 41:3; 42:6; 42:7; 44:5; 45:2; 45:6 *True/False* – 42:8; 43:4; 44:6; 45:7 **Listening/Speaking/ Viewing** *Actions* – 42:1; 43:1; 44:1; 45:1 *Story Telling* – 43:7; 44:7; 45:8 *Story Recall* – 41:8; 43:8; 44:8; 45:9 *Putting on a Play* – 39:6; 40:9 *Following Directions* – 41:10; 44:10; 45:11 **Grammar, Usage, and Mechanics** *Who, When, What, Why, Where, How* – 45:3 *From/To* – 41:2; 42:5; 43:10; 44:4; 44:9 *Verb Tense* – 43:5 **Calendar Facts** – 41:5; 42:4; 43:3; 44:3; 45:4 **Data Collection** – 42:9	**Vocabulary** *Classification* – 46:3; 47:3; 48:7; 48:12; 49:2; 50:2; 50:7 *Can/Do* – 46:4; 47:7; 47:8; 48:5; 48:6; 49:5; 50:3 *True/False* – 49:7 *Opposites* – 46:6; 50:6 *Materials* – 47:13; 48:13; 49:6; 50:5; 50:11 *Description* – 47:4; 48:8; 49:4; 50:4 *Absurdity* – 47:6 *Analogies* – 49:11; 50:10 **Listening/Speaking/ Viewing** *Actions* – 47:1; 48:1; 49:1; 50:1 *Story Telling* – 49:9 *Story Recall* – 47:10; 47:11; 49:10 *Following Directions* – 49:12 *Sequencing* – 46:8; 48:11 **Grammar, Usage, and Mechanics** *Who, When, What, Why, Where, How* – 46:5; 47:5; 48:9 *From/To* – 47:12; 48:2 *Verb Tense* – 46:1; 48:3 **Calendar Facts** – 46:2; 47:2; 48:4; 49:3 **Data Collection** – 50:9 **Map Reading** – 46:7; 47;9; 48:10; 49:8; 50:8	**Vocabulary** *Classification* – 52:2; 52:8; 53:5; 55:2 *Can/Do* – 52:4; 53:2; 54:3; 55:1 *True/False* – 53:4 *Opposites* – 55:4 *Materials* – 51:3; 51:4; 53:3; 54:2; 54:6; 55:3 *Description* – 51:2; 52:3 *Analogies* – 52:9 **Listening/Speaking/ Viewing** *Actions* – 51:1; 52:1; 53:1; 54:1 *Story Telling* – 54:5 *Story Recall* – 52:7; 54:6 **Grammar, Usage, and Mechanics** *Verb Tense* – 51:6 **Sentence Construction** – 51:8; 53:8; 55:3 **Calendar Facts** – 51:5; 52:56; 53:6; 54:4; 55:5 **Map Reading** – 51:7; 52:6; 53:7; 54:7	**Vocabulary** *Classification* – 57:7; 60:2 *Can/Do* – 56:1; 57:5; 58:1; 59:1 *True/False* – 56:4; 57:2 *Opposites* – 56:2; 57:3; 58:3; 59:7; 60:4 *Materials* – 56:5; 57:6 *Description* – 57:1; 58:2; 58:5; 59:5; 60:1; 60:3 *Analogies* – 57:8 *Extrapolation* – 57:7 *Statements* – 59:4 **Listening/Speaking/ Viewing** *Actions* – 59:3 *Story Telling* – 58:6; 59:8 *Story Recall* – 56:7 **Grammar, Usage, and Mechanics** *Verb Tense* – 59:2 **Calendar Facts** – 56:3; 56:6; 57:4; 58:4; 58:7; 59:6; 59:9; 60:5; 60:6; 60:8 **Map Reading** – 56:8; 58:8

Strand Component	Lessons 41-45	Lessons 46-50	Lessons 51-55	Lessons 56-60
Literature Strand *Reading Mastery*	*In the Forest* – 45 Sequence of Events Picture Details	*The Perfects* – 50 Sequence of Events Picture Details	*One Little Kitten* – 55 New vocabulary with traditional orthography	
Formal Assessment	**Individual Reading Checkout** – 45:20	**Individual Reading Checkout** – 50:21	**Individual Reading Checkout** – 55:17	**Individual Reading Checkout** – 60:21 **Reading Assessment** – 60

Strand Component	Lessons 61-65	Lessons 66-70	Lessons 71-75	Lessons 76-80
Core Lesson Connections	**Phonemic Awareness** – 61:a; 62:a; 63:a; 64:a; 65:a **Vocabulary Development** – 61:b; 62:b; 63:b; 64:b; 65:b **Comprehension** – 61:c; 62:c; 63:c; 64:c; 65:c **Fluency** – 61:d; 62:d; 63:d; 64:d; 65:d **Writing** – 65:e	**Phonemic Awareness** – 66:a; 67:a; 68:a; 69:a; 70:a **Vocabulary Development** – 66:b; 67:b; 68:b; 69:b; 70:b **Comprehension** – 66:c; 67:c; 68:c; 69:c; 70:c **Fluency** – 66:d; 67:d; 68:d; 69:d; 70:d	**Phonemic Awareness** – 71:a; 72:a; 73:a; 74:a; 75:a **Vocabulary Development** – 71:b; 72:b; 73:b; 74:b; 75:b **Comprehension** – 71:c; 72:c; 73:c; 74:c; 75:c **Fluency** – 71:d; 72:d; 73:d; 74:d; 75:d **Writing** – 75:e	**Phonemic Awareness** – 76:a; 77:a; 78:a; 79:a; 80:a **Vocabulary Development** – 76:b; 77:b; 78:b; 79:b; 80:b **Comprehension** – 76:c; 77:c; 78:c; 79:c; 80:c **Fluency** – 76:d; 77:d; 78:d; 79:d; 80:d
Reading Strand *Reading Mastery*	**Presentation Book B** **Letter / Sound Correspondence** – 61:9; 61:10; 62:1; 62:9; 62:10; 62:11; 63:1; 63:8; 63:9; 64:1; 64:6; 64:7; 64:10; 65:1; 65:11; 65:15; 65:16 **Phonics and Word Recognition** – 61:1-18; 62:2-17; 63:2-18; 64:2-17; 65:2-19 **Fluency** – 61:1-15; 61:18; 62:2-14; 62:17; 63:2-15; 63:18; 64:2-14; 64:17; 65:2-16; 65:19 **Comprehension** – 61:18; 61:19; 61:20; 61:21; 61:23; 61:24; 62:17; 62:18; 62:19; 62:21-23; 63:18; 63:19; 63:21-24; 64:17; 64:18; 64:20-23; 65:19; 65:20; 65:21 **Spelling** – 61:1-5; 62:1-5; 63:1-6; 64:1-4; 65:1-3	**Presentation Book B** **Letter / Sound Correspondence** – 66:1; 66:3; 66:4; 66:5; 67:11; 68:3; 68:9; 69:7; 69:8 **Phonics and Word Recognition** – 66:2-20; 67:1-15; 68:1-12; 69:1-15; 70:1-11 **Fluency** – 66:2-17; 66:20; 67:1-12; 67:15; 68:1-9; 68:12; 69:1-12; 69:15; 70:1-8; 70:11 **Comprehension** – 66:20; 66:21; 66:23-26; 67:15; 67:16; 67:18-21; 68:12; 68:13; 68:15-18; 69:14-16; 69:18-21; 70:11-13 **Spelling** – 66:1-4; 67:1-5; 68:1-5; 69:1-5; 70:1-5	**Presentation Book B** **Letter / Sound Correspondence** – 72:1; 73:1; 73:6; 73:7; 74:1; 74:6; 74:7 **Phonics and Word Recognition** – 71:1-11; 72:1-12; 73:1-10; 74:1-13; 75:1-10 **Fluency** – 71:1-8; 71:11; 72:1-9; 72: 12; 73:1-7; 73:10; 74:1-10; 74:13; 75:1-7; 75:10 **Comprehension** – 71:11; 71:12; 71:14-17; 72:12; 72:13; 72:15-18; 73:10-12; 74:13; 74:14; 74:16; 75:10-12 **Spelling** – 71:1-4; 72:1-4; 73:1-4; 74:1-3; 75:1-3	**Presentation Book B** **Letter / Sound Correspondence** – 76:2; 76:3; 77:1; 77:7; 78:8; 78:9; 80:6; 80:7; 80:8; 80:9 **Phonics and Word Recognition** – 76:1-9; 77:1-12; 78:1-14; 79:1-13; 80:1-15 **Fluency** – 76:1-6; 76:9; 77:1-9; 77:12; 78:1-11; 78:14; 79:1-10; 79:13; 80:1-12; 80:15 **Comprehension** – 76:9; 76:10; 76:12-15; 77:12; 77:13; 77:15-18; 78:14; 78:15; 78:17-20; 79:13; 79:14; 79:16-19; 80:15-17 **Spelling** – 76:1-3; 77:1-4; 78:1-5; 79:1-5; 80:1-4
Language Arts Strand *Reading Mastery*	**Vocabulary** *Classification* – 61:7; 63:7; 64:1; 65:4 *Who, When, What, Why, Where, How* – 61:3; 62:3 *Can/Do* – 62:1 *True/False* – 61:2 *Opposites* – 61:4; 62:4; 63:4; 64:2; 65:1 *Materials* – 65:10 *Description* – 61:1; 62:2; 63:3; 64:3; 64:4; 65:3 *Analogies* – 61:8; 62:9; 65:6 *Statements* – 63:2; 65:2	**Vocabulary** *Classification* – 67:8; 70:7 *Can/Do* – 68:2; 69:2 *Opposites* – 66:3; 67:1; 68:1; 68:3; 69:4; 70:3 *Description* – 66:1; 67:2; 69:5 *Analogies* – 66:2; 67:5; 68:5; 68:9; 69:6; 70:1; 70:8 *Statements* – 67:4; 70:2	**Vocabulary** *Classification* – 71:5; 72:8; 73:5; 74:8; 75:2; 75:8 *Who, When, What, Why, Where, How* – 72:5; 74:6 *Can/Do* – 72:6; 73:4; 74:5 *True/False* – 74:2; 75:3 *Opposites* – 72:2 *Description* – 71:3; 71:4; 72:4; 73:1; 75:5 *Analogies* – 71:1; 72:1; 73:2; 74:1; 75:1 *Materials* – 71:8; 72:9; 74:9	**Vocabulary** *Classification* – 76:9; 79:7; 80:8 *Who, When, What, Why, Where, How* – 76:2 *Can/Do* – 78:1 *True/False* – 76:1; 77:8; 78:6 *Description* – 76:4; 77:7; 78:7; 79:3; 80:2 *Analogies* – 76:5; 76:10; 77:4; 78:3; 79:1; 80:1; 80:9 *Materials* – 776:6; 77:1; 79:5; 80:5 *Same/Different* – 77:5; 78:5; 79:6

Strand Component	Lessons 61-65	Lessons 66-70	Lessons 71-75	Lessons 76-80
Language Arts Strand *Reading Mastery* (continued)	**Listening/Speaking/Viewing** *Actions* – 63:1 *Story Telling* – 65:7 *Story Recall* – 62:7 *Story Completion* – 62:6; 63:6 *Following Directions* – 63:8 **Grammar, Usage, and Mechanics** *Sentence Construction* – 61:6; 64:6 **Calendar Facts** – 61:5; 62:5; 63:5; 64:5; 65:5; 65:8 **Map Reading** – 62:8; 65:9	**Listening/Speaking/Viewing** *Actions* – 69:1; 70:5 *Story Telling* – 66:5 *Story Details* – 69:8 *Sequencing* – 67:6 *Putting on a Play* – 67:7; 69:7 *Extrapolation* – 70:6 **Calendar Facts** – 66:4; 66:6; 67:3; 68:4; 68:6; 68:7; 69:3; 70:4	**Listening/Speaking/Viewing** *Actions* – 74:4 *Sequencing* – 71:6 *Extrapolation* – 72:7 *Following Directions* – 75:9 **Grammar, Usage, and Mechanics** *Sentence Construction* – 73:6; 74:7; 75:7 **Calendar Facts** – 71:2; 72:3; 73:3; 74:3; 75:4; 75:6 **Map Reading** – 71:7	*Absurdity* – 76:7; 79:8; 80:6 *Synonyms* – 77:2; 77:6; 78:4; 79:4; 80:4 **Listening/Speaking/Viewing** *Story Recall* – 77:11; 79:9; 79:11 *Story Completion* – 77:9 Putting on a Play: 77:10; 79:10 Grammar, Usage, and Mechanics Sentence Construction: 76:8; 78:8 Calendar Facts 76:3; 77:1; 79:5; 80:5
Literature Strand *Reading Mastery*	*The Carrot Seed* – 65 New vocabulary with traditional orthography	*Who Took the Farmer's Hat?* – 70 New vocabulary with traditional orthography	*A Kiss for Little Bear* – 75 New vocabulary with traditional orthography	*Molly's Bracelet* – 80 New vocabulary with traditional orthography
Formal Assessment	Individual Reading Checkout – 65:22	Individual Reading Checkout – 70:14	Individual Reading Checkout – 75:13	Individual Reading Checkout – 80:18 Reading Assessment– 80

Strand Component	Lessons 81-85	Lessons 86-90	Lessons 91-95	Lessons 96-100
Core Lesson Connections	**Vocabulary Development** – 81:a; 82:a; 83:a; 84:a; 85:a **Comprehension** – 81:b; 82:b; 83:b; 84:b; 85:b **Fluency** – 81:c; 82:c; 83:c; 84:c; 85:c **Writing/Language Arts** – 85:d	**Vocabulary Development** – 86:a; 87:a; 88:a; 89:a; 90:a **Comprehension** – 86:b; 87:b; 88:b; 89:b; 90:b **Fluency** – 86:c; 87:c; 88:c; 89:c; 90:c	**Vocabulary Development** – 91:a; 92:a; 93:a; 94:a; 95:a **Comprehension** – 91:b; 92:b; 93:b; 94:b; 95:b **Fluency** – 91:c; 92:c; 93:c; 94:c; 95:c **Writing/Language Arts** – 95:d	**Vocabulary Development** – 96:a; 97:a; 98:a; 99:a; 100:a **Comprehension** – 96:b; 97:b; 98:b; 99:b; 100:b **Fluency** – 96:c; 97:c; 98:c; 99:c; 100:c
Reading Strand *Reading Mastery*	**Presentation Book B** **Print Awareness** – 81:6; 83:1; 83:2; 84:1; 84:2; 85:1-4 **Letter / Sound Correspondence** – 81:4; 82:2; 83:4; 84:3; 85:5 **Phonics and Word Recognition** – 81:2-8; 81:10; 81:11; 82:2-8; 82:10; 82:11; 83:4-9; 83:11; 83:12; 84:3-8; 84:10; 85:5-9; 85:11 **Fluency** – 81:2-7; 81:11; 82:2-7; 82:11; 83:4-8; 83:12; 84:3-7; 85:5-8 **Comprehension** – 81:9; 81:11-13; 82:9; 82:12-14; 83:10; 83:12-14; 84:9-12; 85:10-13 **Spelling** – 81:1-4; 82:1-4; 83:1-4; 84:1-4; 85:1-4	**Presentation Book B** **Print Awareness** – 86:1; 86:2; 87:1; 88:1; 89:1; 89:2; 90:1 **Letter / Sound Correspondence** – 87:4; 88:4; 89:7; 90:6 **Phonics and Word Recognition** – 86:3-7; 86:9; 87:2-6; 87:8; 88:2-6; 88:8; 89:3-8; 89:10; 90:2-7; 90:9 **Fluency** – 86:3-6; 87:2-5; 88:2-5; 89:3-7; 90:2-6 **Comprehension** – 86:8; 86:9-11; 87:7; 87:8-10; 88:7; 88:1-10; 89:9; 89:10-12; 90:8; 90:9-11 **Spelling** – 86:1-4; 87:1-4; 88:1-4; 89:1-4; 90:1-4	**Presentation Book B** **Print Awareness** – 91:1; 91:2; 92:1; 93:1; 94:1 **Letter / Sound Correspondence** – 91:7; 92:6; 93:5; 94:3; 95:2; 95:3 **Phonics and Word Recognition** – 91:3-8; 91:10; 92:2-7; 92:9; 93:2-6; 93:8; 94:2-7; 94:9; 95:1-5 **Fluency** – 91:3-7; 92:2-6; 93:2-5; 94:2-6; 95:1-4 **Comprehension** – 91:9-12; 92:8-11; 93:7-10; 94:8-11; 95:5-8 **Spelling** – 91:1-4; 92:1-4; 93:1-4; 94:1-4; 95:1-3	**Presentation Book B** **Letter / Sound Correspondence** – 97:2; 98:2; 98:3; 99:2 **Phonics and Word Recognition** – 96:1-5; 97:1-5; 98:1-6; 99:1-5; 100:1-5 **Fluency** – 96:1-4; 97:1-4; 98:1-5; 99:1-4; 100:1-4 **Comprehension** – 96:5-8; 97:5-8; 98:6-9; 99:5-8; 100:5-7 **Spelling** – 96:1-3; 97:1-3; 98:1-3; 99:1-3; 100:1-3

Strand Component	Lessons 81-85	Lessons 86-90	Lessons 91-95	Lessons 96-100
Language Arts Strand *Reading Mastery*	**Vocabulary** *Classification* – 81:9; 82:7; 83:9; 84:7; 85:9 *Who, When, What, Why, Where, How* – 85:5; 85:7 *Can/Do* – 81:5; 83:6 *Description* – 81:1; 81:7; 82:4; 85:2 *Analogies* – 81:2; 81:10; 82:1; 82:5; 83:1; 83:10; 84:3 *Absurdity* – 81:3; 85:8 *Synonyms* – 81:6; 83:5; 84:4; 85:1 **Listening/Speaking/ Viewing** *Story Recall* – 82:6 *Sequencing* – 85:10 *Inquiry* – 83:2; 85:6 **Grammar, Usage, and Mechanics** *Sentence Writing* – 81:8; 83:8; 84:5 **Calendar Facts** – 81:4; 82:2; 83:3; 83:7; 84:1; 84:2; 85:3 **Map Reading** – 82:3; 83:4; 84:6; 85:4	**Vocabulary** *Classification* – 86:10; 88:2; 88:7; 89:1; 89:10; 90:8 *Who, When, What, Why, Where, How* – 86:8; 89:5 *Can/Do* – 86:3 *Description* – 86:7; 87:2; 88:4; 89:2; 90:2 *Analogies* – 86:1; 87:1; 88:1; 89:9; 90:4 *Absurdity* – 89:7 *Materials* – 86:11; 89:6 *Synonyms* – 86:4; 87:5; 88:5; 89:3; 90:1 *Synonyms/Opposites* – 86:5 **Listening/Speaking/ Viewing** *Inquiry* – 86:6; 87:4; 90:3 **Grammar, Usage, and Mechanics** *Sentence Writing* – 86:9; 87:6; 88:6; 89:8; 90:6 **Calendar Facts** – 86:2; 87:3; 88:3; 89:4; 90:4; 90:5 **Map Reading** – 90:7 **Data Collection** – 87:7	**Vocabulary** *Classification* – 93:8: 95:7 *Who, When, What, Why, Where, How* – 991:5; 92:1; 94:5; 95:4 *Description* – 91:2; 92:4; 93:3; 93:5; 94:1; 95:2 *Analogies* – 91:4; 93:1; 93:4; 94:4; 95:1 *Statements* – 95:3 *Materials* – 95:8 *Synonyms* – 91:1; 91:3; 92:5; 94:2 *Synonyms/Opposites* – 95:5 **Listening/Speaking/ Viewing** *Inquiry* – 91:7; 92:2; 92:7; 94:3 **Grammar, Usage, and Mechanics** *Sentence Writing* – 91:7; 92:6; 93:6; 94:7 *If/Then Application* – 94:6; 95:6 *Verb Tense* – 98:5 **Calendar Facts** – 91:6; 92:3; 93:2 **Map Reading** – 93:7	**Vocabulary** *Classification* – 97:7 *Who, When, What, Why, Where, How* – 99:6 *Description* – 96:2; 96:6; 97:3; 98:6; 99:1; 100:3 *Analogies* – 96:1; 97:5; 98:4; 98:9; 99:4; 100:2 *Statements* – 96:4; 98:2 *Absurdity* – 97:2; 100:5 *Opposites* – 98:3; 100:1 *Synonyms* – 97:1; 99:2; 100:4 *Synonyms/Opposites* – 96:3; 97:4; 98:1 **Listening/Speaking/ Viewing** *Inquiry* – 96:5; 97:6; 99:5 *Extrapolation* – 96:8 **Grammar, Usage, and Mechanics** *Sentence Writing* – 96:7; 98:7; 99:8; 100:7 *If/Then Application* – 99:7; 100:6 *Verb Tense* – 98:5 **Calendar Facts** – 99:3 **Map Reading** – 98:8
Literature Strand *Reading Mastery*	*There Stood Our Dog* – 85 New vocabulary with traditional orthography	*Fat Cat Tompkin* – 90 New vocabulary with traditional orthography	*In the Forest* – 95 New vocabulary with traditional orthography	*The Perfects* – 100 New vocabulary with traditional orthography
Formal Assessment	**Individual Reading Checkout** – 85:14	**Individual Reading Checkout** – 90:12	**Individual Reading Checkout** – 95:9	**Individual Reading Checkout** – 100:8 **Reading Assessment** – 100

Strand Component	Lessons 101-105	Lessons 106-110	Lessons 111-115	Lessons 116-120
Core Lesson Connections	**Vocabulary** **Development** – 101:a; 102:a; 103:a; 104:a; 105:a **Comprehension** – 101:b; 102:b; 103:b; 104:b; 105:b **Fluency** – 101:c; 102:c; 103:c; 104:c; 105:c **Writing/Language Arts** – 105:d	**Vocabulary** **Development** – 106:a; 107:a; 108:a; 109:a; 110:a **Comprehension** – 106:b; 107:b; 108:b; 109:b; 110:b **Fluency** – 106:c; 107:c; 108:c; 109:c; 110:c	**Vocabulary** **Development** – 111:a; 112:a; 113:a; 114:a; 115:a **Comprehension** – 111:b; 112:b; 113:b; 114:b; 115:b **Fluency** – 111:c; 112:c; 113:c; 114:c; 115:c **Writing/Language Arts** – 115:d	**Vocabulary** **Development** – 116:a; 117:a; 118:a; 119:a; 120:a **Comprehension** – 116:b; 117:b; 118:b; 119:b; 120:b **Fluency** – 116:c; 117:c; 118:c; 119:c; 120:c

Strand Component	Lessons 101-105	Lessons 106-110	Lessons 111-115	Lessons 116-120
Reading Strand *Reading Mastery*	**Presentation Books B and C** **Letter / Sound Correspondence** – 101:2; 102:2; 103:2; 104:3; 105:3 **Phonics and Word Recognition** – 101:1-5; 102:1-5; 103:1-5; 104:1-6; 105:1-5 **Fluency** – 101:1-4; 102:1-4; 103:1-4; 104:1-5; 105:1-4 **Comprehension** – 101:5-8; 102:5-7; 103:5-7; 104:6-7; 105:5-7 **Spelling** – 101:1-3; 102:1-3; 103:1-3; 104:1-3; 105:1-3	**Presentation Book C** **Letter / Sound Correspondence** – 107:2; 108:2; 109:2; 110:2 **Phonics and Word Recognition** – 106:1-5; 107:1-5; 108:1-5; 109:1-5; 110:1-5 **Fluency** – 106:1-4; 107:1-4; 108:1-4; 109:1-4; 110:1-4 **Comprehension** – 106:5-7; 107:5-7; 108:5-7; 109:5-7; 110:5-7 **Spelling** – 106:1-3; 107:1-3; 108:1-3; 109:1-3; 110:1-3	**Presentation Book C** **Letter / Sound Correspondence** – 111:2; 112:2; 114:2; 114:3; 115:2 Phonics **and Word Recognition** – 111:1-5; 112:1-5; 113:1-5; 114:1-5; 115:1-5 **Fluency** – 111:1-4; 112:1-4; 113:1-4; 114:1-4; 115:1-4 **Comprehension** – 111:5-7; 112:5-7; 113:5-7; 114:5-7; 115:5-7 **Spelling** – 111:1-3; 112:1-3; 113:1-3; 114:1-3; 115:1-3	**Presentation Book C** **Letter / Sound Correspondence** – 116:2; 117:2; 118:2; 119:2 **Phonics and Word Recognition** – 116:1-5; 117:1-5; 118:1-5; 119:1-6; 120:1-5 **Fluency** – 116:1-4; 117:1-4; 118:1-4; 119:1-5; 120:1-4 **Comprehension** – 116:5-7; 117:5-7; 118:5-7; 119:6-8; 120:5-7 **Spelling** – 116:1-3; 117:1-3; 118:1-3; 119:1-3; 120:1-3
Language Arts Strand *Reading Mastery*	**Vocabulary** *Classification* – 101:9; 102:7; 103:3; 103:8; 104:5; 104:8; 105:3 *Who, When, What, Why, Where, How* – 104:4 *Description* – 101:4; 103:4; 105:4 *Analogies* – 102:1; 103:1; 103:7; 104:2; 105:1 *Statements* – 105:2 *Absurdity* – 101:6 *Opposites* – 101:2; 102:2; 103:2; 104:3 *Materials* – 102:4 *Synonyms* – 101:1; 101:5; 102:3; 103:5; 105:5 **Listening/Speaking/ Viewing** *Inquiry* – 105:7 **Grammar, Usage, and Mechanics** *Sentence Writing* – 101:7; 102:6; 103:6; 104:6; 105:6 *Verb Tense* – 101:3; 102:5 **Map Reading** – 101:8; 102:8; 104:1; 104:7	**Vocabulary** *Classification* – 107:1; 107:8;108:8; 110:7 *Description* – 106:3; 107:2; 108:3; 109:5; 110:4 *Analogies* – 106:1; 106:7; 107:7; 108:1; 109:1; 110:5 *Absurdity* – 108:4; 110:2 *Opposites* – 106:2; 107:3; 108:5; 109:2 *Materials* – 106:8; 108:2 *Synonyms* – 110:1 *Synonyms/Opposites* – 106:4; 107:5 **Listening/Speaking/ Viewing** *Inquiry* – 107:4; 109:4 **Grammar, Usage, and Mechanics** *Sentence Writing* – 106:6; 107:6; 108:6; 109:7 *Sentence Construction* – 110:6 *Verb Tense* – 109:3; 110:3 *If/Then Application* – 109:6 **Calendar Facts** – 106:5 **Map Reading** – 108:7; 110:8	**Vocabulary** *Classification* – 111:7; 112:8 *Who, When, What, Why, Where, How* – 112:2 *Description* – 112:3; 112:5; 114:3; 115:4 *Analogies* – 111:8; 113:8 *Absurdity* – 111:5; 115:2 *Opposites* – 111:4; 112:8; 113:1; 113:3; 113:8; 115:1 *Materials* – 114:2 *Statements* – 114:4 *Synonyms* – 111:1; 111:2; 112:1; 113:5; 114:1; 115:3 **Listening/Speaking/ Viewing** *Inquiry* – 113:4 *Actions* – 113:2 *Story Recall* – 115:6 *Story Completion* – 115:5 **Grammar, Usage, and Mechanics** *Sentence Writing* – 111:6; 112:6; 113:6; 114:7 *Verb Tense* – 112:4 *If/Then Application* – 114:6 **Calendar Facts** – 111:3; 114:5	**Vocabulary** *Classification* – 116:7; 117:7; 119:8 *Who, When, What, Why, Where, How* – 120:1 *Description* – 116:3; 117:3; 118:4; 119:4; 119:5; 120:5 *Analogies* – 119:9 *Absurdity* – 120:2 *Opposites* – 116:2; 116:8; 117:4; 119:1; 120:4 *Statements* – 118:2 *Synonyms* – 116:4; 116:5; 117:2; 118:3; 119:3 **Listening/Speaking/ Viewing** *Inquiry* – 118:1; 120:7 *Extrapolation* – 118:6 **Grammar, Usage, and Mechanics** *Sentence Writing* – 116:6; 117:6; 118:7; 119:7 *Sequence Sentence Writing* – 120:6 *Verb Tense* – 119:2 *If/Then Application* – 116:1; 117:1; 118:5; 119:6 *ContrActions* – 120:3 **Calendar Facts** – 117:5 **Map Reading** – 117:8
Literature Strand *Reading Mastery*	*Our Little Kitten* – 105 Fluency		*The Carrot Seed* – 115 Fluency	*Who Took the Farmer's Hat?* – 120 Fluency
Formal Assessment	**Individual Reading Checkout** – 105:8	**Individual Reading Checkout** – 110:8	**Individual Reading Checkout** – 115:8	**Individual Reading Checkout** – 120:8 **Reading Assessment** – 120

Strand Component	Lessons 121-125	Lessons 126-130	Lessons 131-135	Lessons 136-140
Core Lesson Connections	**Vocabulary Development** – 121:a; 122:a; 123:a; 124:a; 125:a **Comprehension** – 121:b; 122:b; 123:b; 124:b; 125:b **Fluency** – 121:c; 122:c; 123:c; 124:c; 125:c **Writing/Language Arts** – 125:d	**Vocabulary Development** – 126:a; 127:a; 128:a; 129:a; 130:a **Comprehension** – 126:b; 127:b; 128:b; 129:b; 130:b **Fluency** – 126:c; 127:c; 128:c; 129:c; 130:c	**Vocabulary Development** – 131:a; 132:a; 133:a; 134:a; 135:a **Comprehension** – 131:b; 132:b; 133:b; 134:b; 135:b **Fluency** – 131:c; 132:c; 133:c; 134:c; 135:c **Writing/Language Arts** – 135:d	**Vocabulary Development** – 136:a; 137:a; 138:a; 139:a; 140:a **Comprehension** – 136:b; 137:b; 138:b; 139:b; 140:b **Fluency** – 136:c; 137:c; 138:c; 139:c; 140:c
Reading Strand *Reading Mastery*	**Presentation Book C** **Letter / Sound Correspondence** – 123:3; 124:2; 124:4; 125:2 **Phonics and Word Recognition** – 121:1-7; 122:1-6; 123:1-6; 124:1-6; 125:1-5 **Fluency** – 121:1-6; 122:1-5; 123:1-5; 124:1-5; 125:1-4 **Comprehension** – 121:7-10; 122:6-9; 123:6-9; 124:6-9; 125:5-8 **Spelling** – 121:1-3; 122:1-3; 123:1-3; 124:1-3; 125:1-3	**Presentation Book C** **Letter / Sound Correspondence** – 126:2; 127:4; 128:2; 129:2 **Phonics and Word Recognition** – 126:1-6; 127:1-6; 128:1-6; 129:1-6; 130:1-5 **Fluency** – 126:1-5; 127:1-5; 128:1-5; 129:1-5; 130:1-4 **Comprehension** – 126:6-8; 127:6-8; 128:6-8; 129:6-8; 130:5-7 **Spelling** – 126:1-3; 127:1-3; 128:1-3; 129:1-3; 130:1-3	**Presentation Book C** **Letter / Sound Correspondence** – 131:2; 132:2; 135:2 **Phonics and Word Recognition** – 131:1-5; 132:1-6; 133:1-5; 134:1-5; 135:1-4 **Fluency** – 131:1-4; 132:1-5; 133:1-4; 134:1-4; 135:1-3 **Comprehension** – 131:5-7; 132:6-9; 133:5-8; 134:5-8; 135:4-7 **Spelling** – 131:1-3; 132:1-3; 133:1-3; 134:1-3; 135:1-3	**Presentation Book C** **Letter / Sound Correspondence** – 136:2; 137:2; 138:2; 139:2; 140:2 **Phonics and Word Recognition** – 136:1-5; 137:1-5; 138:1-5; 139:1-5; 140:1-5 **Fluency** – 136:1-4; 137:1-4; 138:1-4; 139:1-4; 140:1-4 **Comprehension** – 136:5-8; 137:5-7; 138:5-7; 139:5-7; 140:5-7 **Spelling** – 136:1-3; 137:1-3; 138:1-3; 139:1-3; 140:1-3
Language Arts Strand *Reading Mastery*	**Vocabulary** *Classification* – 122:7; 124:6; 125:7 *Description* – 123:2; 124:3; 125:2 *Analogies* – 121:7; 124:7 *Absurdity* – 125:4 *Opposites* – 121:3; 121:6; 122:4; 123:5; 125:3; 125:6 *Statements* – 122:3; 125:1 *Synonyms* – 123:3 *Synonyms/Opposites* – 122:1 **Listening/Speaking/ Viewing** *Inquiry* – 121:2 **Grammar, Usage, and Mechanics** *Sentence Writing* – 121:5; 122:6; 124:5 *Sequence Sentence Writing* – 125:5 *Sentence Construction* – 123:6 *Verb Tense* – 121:1; 122:2; 123:1; 124:2 *ContrActions* – 121:4; 122:5; 123:4; 124:1 **Calendar Facts** – 124:4 **Map Reading** – 122:8 **Correcting Work** – 123:7	**Vocabulary** *Classification* – 129:8 *Who, When, What, Why, Where, How* – 127:4 *Description* – 126:3; 126:4; 127:2; 128:2; 129:4; 130:5 *Analogies* – 129:7 *Absurdity* – 127:5; 128:4; 129:2 *Opposites* – 126:6; 128:7; 130:4 *Statements* – 128:5; 129:1 *Synonyms/Opposites* – 129:3 **Listening/Speaking/ Viewing** *Inquiry* – 127:3 *Actions* – 126:2; 130:2 *Story Recall* – 127:7 *Story Completion* – 127:6 **Grammar, Usage, and Mechanics** *Sentence Writing* – 126:5; 128:6; 129:6 *Verb Tense* – 128:1; 130:3 *ContrActions* – 126:1; 127:1; 128:3; 129:5; 130:1 **Map Reading** – 126:6; 128:8 **Writing Stories About Characters** – 130:6	**Vocabulary** *Classification* – 132:7; 133:7; 135:6 *Who, When, What, Why, Where, How* – 133:1 *Description* – 131:4; 132:4; 132:5; 133:5 *Analogies* – 132:8; 134:6 *Absurdity* – 133:2 *Opposites* – 132:1; 133:4; 134:3; 134:5; 135:4 *Statements* – 131:2; 135:3 *Synonyms* – 131:3; 132:3 *Synonyms/Opposites* – 135:1 **Listening/Speaking/ Viewing** *Inquiry* – 131:1; 134:2 *Story Telling* – 131:6 **Grammar, Usage, and Mechanics** *Verb Tense* – 132:2; 134:1; 135:2 *ContrActions* – 133:3; 134:4; 135:5 *If/Then Application* – 131:5; 132:6 **Map Reading** – 133:6; 135:7 **Writing Dialog** – 131:7 **Revising** – 131:8	
Literature Strand *Reading Mastery*	*A Kiss for Little Bear* – 125 Fluency	*Molly's Bracelet* – 130 Fluency	*There Stood Our Dog* – 135 Fluency	

Strand Component	Lessons 121-125	Lessons 126-130	Lessons 131-135	Lessons 136-140
Formal Assessment	Individual Reading Checkout – 125:9	Individual Reading Checkout – 130:8	Individual Reading Checkout – 135:8	Reading Assessment – 140

Strand Component	Lessons 141-145	Lessons 146-150	Lessons 151-155	Lessons 156-160
Core Lesson Connections	**Vocabulary Development** – 141:a; 142:a; 143:a; 144:a; 145:a **Comprehension** – 141:b; 142:b; 143:b; 144:b; 145:b **Fluency** – 141:c; 142:c; 143:c; 144:c; 145:c **Writing/Language Arts** – 145:d	**Vocabulary Development** – 146:a; 147:a; 148:a; 149:a; 150:a **Comprehension** – 146:b; 147:b; 148:b; 149:b; 150:b **Fluency** – 146:c; 147:c; 148:c; 149:c; 150:c	**Vocabulary Development** – 151:a; 152:a; 153:a; 154:a; 155:a **Comprehension** – 151:b; 152:b; 153:b; 154:b; 155:b **Fluency** – 151:c; 152:c; 153:c; 154:c; 155:c **Writing/Language Arts** – 155:d	**Vocabulary Development** – 156:a; 157:a; 158:a; 159:a; 160:a **Comprehension** – 156:b; 157:b; 158:b; 159:b; 160:b **Fluency** – 156:c; 157:c; 158:c; 159:c; 160:c
Reading Strand *Reading Mastery*	**Presentation Book C** **Letter / Sound Correspondence** – 142:2; 143:2; 144:2 **Phonics and Word Recognition** – 141:1-5; 142:1-5; 143:1-5; 144:1-5; 145:1-5 **Fluency** – 141:1-4; 142:1-4; 143:1-4; 144:1-4; 145:1-4 **Comprehension** – 141:5-7; 142:5-8; 143:5-8; 144:5-7; 145:5; 145:6; 145:8 **Spelling** – 141:1-3; 142:1-3; 143:1-3; 144:1-3; 145:1-3	**Presentation Book C** **Letter / Sound Correspondence** – 146:2; 147:2; 148:2; 149:2 **Phonics and Word Recognition** – 146:1-5; 147:1-3; 147:5; 148:1-3; 148:5; 149:1-3; 149:5; 150:1-4; 150:6 **Fluency** – 146:1-4; 147:1-3; 148:1-3; 149:1-3; 150:1-4 **Comprehension** – 146:5; 146:6; 146:8; 147:4-7; 148:4-8; 149:4-8; 150:5-7; 150:10 **Spelling** – 146:1-3; 147:1-3; 148:1-3; 149:1-3; 150:1-3	**Presentation Book C** **Letter / Sound Correspondence** – 151:2; 154:3; 155:2 **Phonics and Word Recognition** – 151:1-4; 151:6; 152:1-4; 152:6; 153:1-4; 153:6; 154:1-3; 154:5; 155:1-4; 155:6 **Fluency** – 151:1-4; 152:1-4; 153:1-4; 154:1-3; 155:1-4 **Comprehension** – 151:5-7; 151:9; 152:5-7; 152:9; 153:5-7; 153:9; 154:4-5; 154:8; 155:5-8 **Spelling** – 151:1-3; 152:1-3; 153:1-3; 154:1-3; 155:1-3	**Presentation Book C** **Letter / Sound Correspondence** – 157:4; 159:2; 160:2 **Phonics and Word Recognition** – 156:1-4; 156:6; 157:1-4; 157:6; 158:1-4; 158:6; 159:1-3; 159:5; 160:1-4; 160:6 **Fluency** – 156:1-4; 157:1-4; 158:1-4; 159:1-3; 160:1-4 **Comprehension** – 156:5-7; 156:9; 157:5-7; 157:9; 158:5-7; 158:9; 159:4-6; 159:8; 160:5-7; 160:9 **Spelling** – 156:1-3; 157:1-3; 158:1-3; 159:1-3; 160:1; 160:2
Language Arts Strand *Reading Mastery*	**Vocabulary** *Classification* – 137:5; 138:6; 140:1 *Description* – 136:2; 137:3; 138:2; 139;3; 139:4 *Analogies* – 137:6; 140:2 *Absurdity* – 138:4 *Opposites* – 136:5; 138:3; 138:5; 139:5 *Statements* – 138:1 *Synonyms* – 136:3 **Listening/Speaking/Viewing** *Story Telling* – 136:6 *Actions* – 139:2 **Grammar, Usage, and Mechanics** *Verb Tense* – 136:1; 137:2 *ContrActions* – 136:4; 137:1; 139:1 **Map Reading** – 139:6 **Revising** – 136:7 **Calendar Facts** – 137:4	**Vocabulary** *Classification* – 143:7; 145:3 *Who, When, What, Why, Where, How* – 141:4 *Description* – 141:2; 143:4; 144:5 *Analogies* – 143:6; 145:6 *Absurdity* – 141:5; 142:4; 143:2 *Opposites* – 142:6; 144:4; 144:6; 145:5 *Statements* – 142:5; 143:1 *Synonyms* – 145:4 *Synonyms/Opposites* – 143:3 **Listening/Speaking/Viewing** *Story Details* – 141:7 *Actions* – 144:2 *Inquiry* – 141:3 *Putting on a Play* – 141:6		

F12

Strand Component	Lessons 141-145	Lessons 146-150	Lessons 151-155	Lessons 156-160
Language Arts Strand *Reading Mastery* (continued)		**Grammar, Usage, and Mechanics** *Verb Tense* – 142:1; 144:3 *ContrActions* – 141:1; 142:3; 143:5; 144:7; 145:1 **Map Reading** – 142:7; 144:7 **Calendar Facts** – 145:2		
Literature Strand *Reading Mastery*	*Fat Cat Tompkin* – 140 Fluency	*In the Forest* – 145 Fluency	*The Perfects* – 150 Fluency	
Formal Assessment	**Individual Reading Checkout** – 140:8 **Reading Benchmark Test** – 140	**Individual Reading Checkout** – 145:9 **Individual Reading Checkout** – 150:11	**Individual Reading Checkout** – 155:9	**Individual Reading Checkout** – 160:10 **Reading Assessment** – 160

Appendix G

SRA Reading Mastery
Signature Edition

English Language Arts Standards

CCSS COMMON CORE STATE STANDARDS ALIGNMENT

GRADE 1

GRADE 1 STANDARDS		PAGE REFERENCES
	**Reading Standards for Literature: Key Ideas and Details**	
RL.1.1	Ask and answer questions about key details in a text.	**Reading Presentation Book A:** (Lesson.Exercise) 1.12, 2.14, 5.15, 6.14, 7.14, 10.13, 11.16, 12.14, 14.14, 15.14, 16.13, 17.14, 19.11, 19.12, 20.12, 20.13, 21.13, 21.14, 22.12, 22.13, 23.14, 23.15, 24.10, 24.11, 25.17, 25.18, 26.13, 26.14, 27.17, 27.18, 28.13, 28.14, 29.16, 29.17, 30.17, 30.18, 31.15, 31.16, 33.15, 33.16, 34.23, 35.24, 36.22, 37.22, 38.19, 39.20, 40.20, 42.12, 43.12, 44.15, 45.17, 46.17, 47.7, 48.12; Planning page 234b **Reading Presentation Book B:** (Lesson.Exercise) 49.15, 49.16, 50.18, 51.17, 52.16, 52.17, 53.12, 53.13, 54.14, 55.13, 55.14, 56.20, 57.16, 58.12, 58.13, 59.15, 60.18, 62.17, 63.18, 64.17, 65.19, 66.20, 67.15, 68.12, 69.14, 69.15, 70.11, 71.11, 62.12, 73.10, 74.14, 75.10, 76.9, 77.12, 78.14, 79.13, 80.15, 81.11, 82.11, 83.12, 84.15, 85.11, 86.9, 87.8, 88.8, 89.10, 90.9, 91.10, 92.9, 93.8, 94.9, 95.5, 96.5, 97.5, 98.6, 99.5, 100.5, 101.5, 102.5, 103.5, 104.6 **Reading Presentation Book C:** (Lesson.Exercise) 105.5, 106.5, 107.5, 108.5, 109.5, 110.5, 111.5, 112.5, 113.5, 114.5, 115.5, 116.5, 117.5, 118.5, 119.6, 120.5, 121.7, 122.6, 123.6, 124.6, 125.5, 126.6, 127.5, 128.6, 129.6, 130.5, 131.5, 132.6, 133.5, 134.5, 135.4, 136.5, 137.5, 138.5, 139.5, 140.5, 141.5, 142.5, 143.5, 144.5, 145.5, 146.5, 147.5, 149.5, 149.5, 150.6, 151.6, 152.6, 153.6, 154.5, 155.6, 156.6, 157.6, 158.6, 159.6, 160.6 **Storybook 1:** Lessons 1–83 **Storybook 2:** Lessons 84–160 **Language Presentation Book A:** (Lesson.Exercise) 1.6, 2.8, 3.8, 4.8, 5.8, 6.9, 7.7, 8.8, 9.10, 11.8, 12.9, 13.8, 14.7, 15.8, 16.9, 17.11, 18.8, 19.8, 20.8, 21.10, 22.9, 23.8, 24.7, 25.8, 26.7, 27.8, 28.8, 29.8, 31.7, 32.7, 33.7, 35.6, 36.8, 37.8, 38.9, 30.5, 41.8, 44.8, 45.8, 46.8, 48.11, 54.6 **Language Presentation Book B:** (Lesson.Exercise) 62.7, 67.6, 69.8, 71.6, 77.11, 79.11, 85.10 **Core Lesson Connections:** (Lesson.Part.Activity) 6.C.2, 7.C.2, 8.C.2, 9.C.2, 10.C.2, 11.C.3, 12.C.3, 13.C.2, 15.C.2, 17.C.1, 18.C.1, 19.C.3, 20.C., 21.C.2, 24.C.2, 25.C.1, 26.C.1, 28.C.1, 31.C.2, 32.C.2, 33.C.3, 34.C.2, 34.C.3, 35.C.1, 36.C.1, 37.C.1, 38.C.1, 38.C.2, 39.C.2, 42.C.2, 43.C.2, 44.C.1, 44.C.2, 45.C.1, 46.C.1, 46.C.2, 47.C.2, 49.C.2, 52.C.1, 53.C.1, 55.C.1, 57.C.1, 58.C.1, 59.C.1, 61.C.1, 61.C.2, 65.C.1, 65.C.2, 68.C.2, 69.C.1, 69.C.2, 71.C.1, 72.C.1, 76.C.1, 78.C.1, 79.C.2, 85.B.2, 86.B.1, 88.B.2, 91.B.2, 92.B.1, 95.B.1, 97.B.2, 98.B.1, 99.B.1, 103.B.1, 106.B.1, 107.B.1, 112.B.1, 116.B.1, 119.B.1, 122.B.1, 123.B.2, 131.B.1, 138.B.1, 139.B.1, 140.B.1, 142.B.1, 144.B.1, 152.B.1, 153.B.1 **Literature Guide:** Lessons 5, 15, 20, 25, 30, 35, 40, 45, 50 **Read Aloud Library:** (Week.Day) 1.1, 1.2, 2.1, 2.2, 3.1, 3.2, 4.1, 4.2, 5.1, 5.2, 6.1, 6.2, 7.1, .2, 8.1, 8.2, 9.1, 9.2, 10.1, 10.2, 11.1, 11.2, 12.1, 12.2, 13.1, 13.2, 14.1, 14.2, 15.1, 15.2, 26.1, 26.2, 27.1, 27.2, 28.1, 28.2, 29.1, 29.2, 30.1, 30.2
RL.1.2	Retell stories, including key details, and demonstrate understanding of their central message or lesson.	**Core Lesson Connections:** (Lesson.Part.Activity) 17.C.1, 18.C.1, 41.C.2, 43.C.2, 44.C.2, 45.C.1, 48.C.1, 49.C.2, 53.C.2, 65.C.2, 68.C.2, 71.C.2, 77.C.1, 77.C.2, 84.B.1, 90.B.2, 96.B.2, 100.B.1, 106.B.1, 108.B.2, 111.B.2, 112.B.1, 118.B.2, 135.B.1, 141.B.2 **Literature Collection/Guide:** Lessons 5, 15, 20, 25, 30, 35, 40, 45, 50 **Read Aloud Library:** (Week.Day) 1.3, 1.5, 2.3, 2.5, 3.3, 3.5, 4.5, 5.5, 6.5, 7.5, 8.5, 9.5, 10.5, 11.3, 11.5, 12.3, 12.5, 13.5, 14.3, 14.5, 15.3, 15.5

GRADE 1 STANDARDS		PAGE REFERENCES
RL.1.3	Describe characters, settings, and major events in a story, using key details.	**Reading Presentation Book A:** (Lesson.Exercise) 1.12, 2.14, 5.15, 6.14, 7.14, 10.13, 11.16, 12.14, 14.14, 15.14, 16.13, 17.14, 19.11, 19.12, 20.12, 20.13, 21.13, 21.14, 22.12, 22.13, 23.14, 23.15, 24.10, 24.11, 25.17, 25.18, 26.13, 26.14, 27.17, 27.18, 28.13, 28.14, 29.16, 29.17, 30.17, 30.18, 31.15, 31.16, 33.15, 33.16, 34.23, 35.24, 36.22, 37.22, 38.19, 39.20, 40.20, 42.12, 43.12, 44.15, 45.17, 46.17, 47.7, 48.12; Planning page 111b **Reading Presentation Book B:** (Lesson.Exercise) 49.15, 49.16, 50.18, 51.17, 52.16, 52.17, 53.12, 53.13, 54.14, 55.13, 55.14, 56.20, 57.16, 58.12, 58.13, 59.15, 60.18, 62.17, 63.18, 64.17, 65.19, 66.20, 67.15, 68.12, 69.14, 69.15, 70.11, 71.11, 62.12, 73.10, 74.14, 75.10, 76.9, 77.12, 78.14, 79.13, 80.15, 81.11, 82.11, 83.12, 84.15, 85.11, 86.9, 87.8, 88.8, 89.10, 90.9, 91.10, 92.9, 93.8, 94.9, 95.5, 96.5, 97.5, 98.6, 99.5, 100.5, 101.5, 102.5, 103.5, 104.6 **Reading Presentation Book C:** (Lesson.Exercise) 105.5, 106.5, 107.5, 108.5, 109.5, 110.5, 111.5, 112.5, 113.5, 114.5, 115.5, 116.5, 117.5, 118.5, 119.6, 120.5, 121.7, 122.6, 123.6, 124.6, 125.5, 126.6, 127.5, 128.6, 129.6, 130.5, 131.5, 132.6, 133.5, 134.5, 135.4, 136.5, 137.5, 138.5, 139.5, 140.5, 141.5, 142.5, 143.5, 144.5, 145.5, 146.5, 147.5, 149.5, 149.5, 150.6, 151.6, 152.6, 153.6, 154.5, 155.6, 156.6, 157.6, 158.6, 159.6, 160.6; Planning page 64b **Storybook 1:** Lessons 1–83 **Storybook 2:** Lessons 84–160 **Core Lesson Connections:** (Lesson.Part.Activity) 2.C.2, 3.C.3, 4.C.2, 5.C.2, 6.C.1, 7.C.2, 8.C.2, 9.C.2, 10.C.2, 11.C.1–3, 12.C.1–3, 13.C.2, 15.C.1, 15.C.2, 17.C.1, 18.C.1, 19.C.3, 21.C.2, 28.C.1, 33.C.3, 34.C.1, 36.C.2, 46.C.1, 47.C.2, 52.C.1, 61.C.1, 62.C.2, 66.C.1, 69.C.2, 76.C.1, 85.B.2, 91.B.2, 97.B.2, 98.B.1, 99.B.1, 127.B.2, 134.B.2, 138.B.1, 140.B.2, 144.B.1, 150.B.1 **Literature Collection/Guide:** Lessons 5, 15, 20, 25, 30, 35, 40, 45, 50 **Read Aloud Library:** (Week.Day) 1.2, 1.3, 2.2, 2.3, 3.2, 3.3, 4.2, 4.3, 5.2, 5.3, 6.2, 6.3, 7.2, 7.3, 8.2, 8.3, 9.2, 9.3, 10.2, 1.3, 11.2, 11.3, 12.2, 12.3, 13.2, 13.3, 14.2, 15.2
Reading Standards for Literature: Craft and Structure		
RL.1.4	Identify words and phrases in stories or poems that suggest feelings or appeal to the senses.	**Core Lesson Connections:** (Lesson.Part.Activity) 41.C.1, 42.C.1, 43.C.1, 49.C.1, 54.C.1, 60.C.1, 64.C.1, 84.B.2, 90.B.1, 121.B.2, 147.B.2 **Literature Collection/Guide:** Lessons 5, 15, 20, 25, 30, 35, 40, 45, 50 **Read Aloud Library:** (Week.Day) 1.3, 1.4, 2.3, 2.4, 3.3, 3.4, 4.3, 5.3, 6.3, 7.3, 8.3, 9.3, 10.3, 11.3, 12.3, 13.3, 14.3, 15.4, 26.3, 27.3, 28.3, 29.3, 30.3
RL.1.5	Explain major differences between books that tell stories and books that give information, drawing on a wide reading of a range of text types.	**Core Lesson Connections:** (Lesson.Part.Activity) 1.C.2, 3.C.1, 4.C.1, 5.C.1, 9.C.1, 10.C.1, 11.C.1, 14.C.1, 19.C.1, 33.C.1, 52.C.1, 56.C.1, 65.C.1, 74.C.1, 75.C.1, 83.B.1, 85.B.1, 91.B.1, 94.B.1, 96.B.1, 97.B.1, 100.B.1, 101.B.1, 105.B.1, 108.B.1, 115.B.1, 118.B.1, 121.B.1, 123.B.1, 125.B.2, 126.B.1, 127.B.1, 130.B.1, 134.B.1, 135.B.1, 136.B.1, 140.B.1, 141.B.1, 141.B.3, 143.B.1, 145.B.1, 147.B.1, 149.B.1, 157.B.1 **Literature Collection/Guide:** Lessons 5, 15, 20, 25, 30, 35, 40, 45, 50 **Read Aloud Library:** (Week.Day) 1.4, 2.4, 3.4, 4.4, 5.4, 6.4, 7.4, 8.4, 9.4, 10.4, 11.4, 12.4, 13.4, 14.3, 14.4, 15.3, 15.4, 16.1, 16.4, 17.1, 17.4, 18.1, 18.4, 19.1, 19.4, 20.1, 20.4, 21.1, 21.4, 22.1, 22.4, 23.1, 23.4, 24.1, 24.4, 25.1, 25.4, 26.1, 26.4, 27.1, 27.4, 28.1, 28.4, 29.1, 29.4, 30.1, 30.4
RL.1.6	Identify who is telling the story at various points in a text.	**Read Aloud Library:** (Week.Day) 4.4, 5.4, 6.4, 7.4, 11.4, 12.4, 13.4, 29.2

GRADE 1 STANDARDS		PAGE REFERENCES
Reading Standards for Literature: Integration of Knowledge and Ideas		
RL.1.7	Use illustrations and details in a story to describe its characters, setting, or events.	**Reading Presentation Book A:** (Lesson.Exercise) 1.13, 2.15, 5.15, 6.15, 7.15, 10.14, 11.17, 12.15, 14.15, 15.15, 16.14, 17.15, 19.13, 20.14, 21.15, 22.14, 23.16, 24.12, 25.19, 26.15, 27.19, 28.15, 29.17, 30.19, 31.17, 33.17, 34.24, 35.25, 36.23, 37.23, 38.20, 39.21, 40.21, 41.18, 42.13, 43.13, 44.16, 45.18, 46.18, 48.18 **Reading Presentation Book B:** (Lesson.Exercise) 49.17, 50.19, 51.18, 52.18, 53.13, 54.15, 55.15, 56.21, 57.17, 58.14, 59.16, 60.19, 61.19, 62.18, 63.19, 64.18, 65.20, 66.21, 67.16, 68.13, 69.16, 70.12, 71.12, 72.13, 73.11, 74.14, 75.11, 76.10, 77.13, 78.15, 79.14, 80.16, 81.12, 82.12, 83.13, 84.11, 85.12, 85.10, 87.9, 88.9, 89.11, 90.10, 91.11, 92.10, 93.9, 94.10, 95.6, 96.6, 97.6, 98.7, 99.6, 100.6, 101.6, 102.6, 103.6, 104.7 **Reading Presentation Book C:** (Lesson.Exercise) 105.6, 106.6, 107.6, 108.6, 109.6, 110.6, 111.6, 112.6, 113.6, 114.6, 115.6, 116.6, 117.6, 118.6, 119.7, 120.6, 121.8, 122.7, 123.7, 124.7, 125.6, 126.7, 127.7, 128.7, 129.7, 130.6, 131.6, 132.7, 133.6, 134.6, 135.5, 136.6, 137.6, 138.6, 139.6, 140.6, 141.6, 142.6, 143.6, 144.6, 145.6, 146.6, 147.6, 148.6, 149.6, 150.7, 151.7, 152.7, 153.7, 154.6, 155.7, 155.7, 156.7, 158.7, 159.7, 160.7 **Storybook 1:** Lessons 1–83 **Storybook 2:** Lessons 84–160 **Language Presentation Book A:** (Lesson.Exercise) 17.12, 57.7 **Language Presentation Book B:** (Lesson.Exercise) 70.6, 72.7, 96.8, 118.6, 130.6 **Language Workbook:** (Lesson.Exercise) 17, 57, 70, 72, 96, 118, 130 **Core Lesson Connections:** (Lesson.Part.Activity) 36.C.2, 85.B.2, 99.B.1, 106.B.1, 112.B.1 **Literature Collection/Guide:** Lessons 5, 15, 20, 25, 30, 35, 40, 45, 50 **Read Aloud Library:** (Week.Day) 1.1, 2.1, 3.1, 4.1, 5.1, 6.1, 7.1, 8.1, 9.1, 10.1, 11.1, 12.1, 12.1, 13.1, 14.1, 15.1, 26.1, 27.1, 28.1, 29.1, 30.1
RL.1.8	*(Not applicable to literature)*	
RL.1.9	Compare and contrast the adventures and experiences of characters in stories.	**Core Lesson Connections:** (Lesson.Part.Activity) 22.C.1, 23.C.2, 29.C.1, 58.C.1, 59.C.1, 99.B.1, 101.B.1, 103.B.1, 116.B.1, 122.B.1, 126.B.1, 128.B.1, 132.B.1, 133.B.1, 139.B.1, 140.B.1, 142.B.1 **Read Aloud Library:** (Week.Day) 6.3, 7.3, 8.3, 10.3

GRADE 1 STANDARDS		PAGE REFERENCES
Reading Standards for Literature: Range of Reading and Level of Text Complexity		
RL.1.10	With prompting and support, read prose and poetry of appropriate complexity for grade 1.	**Reading Presentation Book A:** (Lesson.Exercise) 1.10–12, 2.12–14, 5.13–15, 6.12–14, 7.12–14, 10.11–13, 11.14–16, 12.12–14, 14.12–14, 15.12–14, 16.11–13, 17.12–14, 19.10–12, 20.11–13, 21.12–14, 22.11–13, 23.13–15, 24.9–11, 25.16–18, 26.12–14, 27.16–18, 28.12–14, 29.14–16, 30.16–18, 31.14–16, 33.14–16, 34.21–23, 35.22–24, 36.20–22, 37.20–22, 38.17–19, 39.18–20, 40.18–20, 41.15–17, 42.10–12, 43.10–12, 44.13–15, 45.15–17, 46.15–17, 48.15–17 **Reading Presentation Book B:** (Lesson.Exercise) 49.14–16, 50.16–18, 51.15–17, 52.15–17, 53.11–13, 54.12–14, 55.12–14, 56.18–20, 57.14–16, 58.11–13, 59.13–15, 60.16–18, 61.16–18, 62.15–17, 63.16–18, 64.15–17, 65.17–19, 66.18–20, 67.13–15, 68.10–12, 69.13–15, 70.9–11, 71.9–11, 72.10–12, 73.8–10, 74.11–13, 75.8–10, 76.7–9, 77.10–12, 78.12–14, 79.11–13, 80.13–15, 81.10, 81.11, 82.10, 82.11, 83.11, 83.12, 84.10, 85.11, 86.9, 87.8, 88.8, 89.10, 90.9, 91.10, 92.9, 93.8, 94.9, 95.5, 96.5, 97.5, 98.5, 98.6, 99.5, 100.5, 101.5, 102.5, 103.5, 104.5, 104.6 **Reading Presentation Book C:** (Lesson.Exercise) 105.5, 106.5, 107.5, 108.5, 109.5, 110.5, 111.5, 112.5, 113.5, 114.5, 115.5, 116.5, 117.5, 118.5, 119.6, 120.5, 121.7, 122.6, 123.6, 124.6, 125.5, 126.6, 127.6, 128.6, 129.6, 130.5, 131.5, 132.6, 133.5, 134.5, 135.4, 136.5, 137.5, 138.5, 139.5, 140.5, 141.5, 142.5, 143.5, 144.5, 145.5, 146.5, 147.5, 148.5, 149.5, 150.5, 151.6, 152.6, 153.6, 154.5, 155.6, 156.6, 157.6, 158.6, 159.6, 160.6 **Storybook 1:** Lessons 1–83 **Storybook 2:** Lessons 84–160 **Core Lesson Connections:** (Lesson.Part.Activity) 1.C.2, 2.C.1, 3.C.2, 4.C.1, 5.C.1, 6.C.2, 7.C.1, 8.C.1, 9.C.1, 1 0.C.1, 11.C.2, 12.C.2, 13.C.1, 14.C.2, 15.C.1, 16.C.1, 19.C.2, 20.C.1, 21.C.2, 23.C.1, 24.C.1, 25.C.1, 26.C.1, 27.C.1, 30.C.1, 31.C.1, 33.C.2, 34.C.1, 36.C.1, 37.C.1, 38.C.1, 39.C.2, 41.C.1, 42.C.1, 43.C.1, 44.C.1, 46.C.1, 50.C.1, 51.C.1, 52.C.2, 53.C.1, 54.C.1, 55.C.1, 56.C.1, 57.C.1, 59.C.1, 60.C.1, 61.C.1, 62.C.1, 63.C.1, 64.C.1, 65.C.1, 66.C.1, 67.C.1, 69.C.1, 70.C.1, 71.C.1, 72.C.1, 73.C.1, 77.C.2, 78.C.1, 79.C.3, 81.B.1, 84.B.1, 88.B.1, 89.B.1, 90.B.1, 91.B.1, 95.B.1, 96.B.2, 97.B.1, 98.B.1, 99.B.1, 100.B.1, 101.B.1, 102.B.1, 103.B.1, 107.B.1, 108.B.2, 111.B.1, 119.B.1, 121.B.2, 124.B.1, 127.B.1, 128.B.1, 131.B.1, 132.B.1, 134.B.2, 137.B.1, 138.B.1, 139.B.1, 140.B.1, 141.B.1, 142.B.1, 143.B.1, 146.B.2, 149.B.1, 151.B.1, 152.B.1, 153.B.1 **Decodable Stories** **Independent Readers** **Literature Collection/Guide:** Lessons 5, 15, 20, 25, 30, 35, 40, 45, 50 **Read Aloud Library:** (Week.Day) 1.1, 1.2, 2.1, 2.2, 3.1, 3.2, 4.1, 4.2, 5.1, 5.2, 6.1, 6.2, 7.1, 7.2, 8.1, 8.2, 9.1, 9.2, 10.1, 10.2, 11.1, 11.2, 12.1, 12.2, 13.1, 13.2, 14.1, 14.2, 15.1, 15.2, 26.1, 26.2, 27.1, 27.2, 28.1, 28.2, 29.1, 29.2, 30.1, 30.2
Reading Standards for Informational Text: Key Ideas and Details		
RI.1.1	Ask and answer questions about key details in a text.	**Core Lesson Connections:** (Lesson.Part.Activity) 74.C.1, 74.C.2, 75.C.1, 82.B.1, 83.B.1, 83.B.2, 93.B.1, 94.B.1, 94.B.2, 104.B.1, 105.B.1, 105.B.2, 114.B.1, 115.B.1, 115.B.2, 117.B.1, 120.B.1, 125.B.1, 125.B.2, 126.B.1, 129.B.1, 130.B.1, 145.B.1, 146.B.1, 146.B.2, 154.B.1, 155.B.1, 155.B.2, 156.B.1, 160.B.1 **Read Aloud Library:** (Week.Day) 14.4, 15.3, 16.1–5, 17.1–5, 18.1–5, 19.1–5, 20.1–5, 21.1–5, 22.1–5, 23.1–5, 24.1–5, 25.1–5
RI.1.2	Identify the main topic and retell key details of a text.	**Core Lesson Connections:** (Lesson.Part.Activity) 83.B.2, 94.B.2, 105.B.2, 115.B.2, 130.B.2, 146.B.2, 154.B.2 **Read Aloud Library:** (Week.Day) 16.3, 17.3, 18.3, 19.3, 20.3, 21.5, 22.5, 23.5, 24.5, 25.5

	GRADE 1 STANDARDS	PAGE REFERENCES
RI.1.3	Describe the connection between two individuals, events, ideas, or pieces of information in a text.	**Core Lesson Connections:** (Lesson.Part.Activity) 75.C.1, 82.B.1, 93.B.1, 103.B.1, 104.B.1, 126.B.1, 128.B.1, 129.B.1, 132.B.1, 133.B.1, 139.B.1, 140.B.1, 142.B.1, 145.B.1, 154.B.1 **Read Aloud Library:** (Week.Day) 16.1, 16.5, 17.1, 17.5, 18.1, 18.5, 19.1, 19.5, 20.1, 20.5, 21.1, 21.5, 22.1, 22.5, 23.1, 23.5, 24.1, 24.5, 25.1, 25.5
	Reading Standards for Informational Text: Craft and Structure	
RI.1.4	Ask and answer questions to help determine or clarify the meaning of words and phrases in a text.	**Read Aloud Library:** (Week.Day) 16.1–5, 17. 1–5, 18.1–5, 19.1–5, 20.1–5, 21.1–5, 22.1–5, 23.1–5, 24.1–5, 25.1–5
RI.1.5	Know and use various text features (e.g., headings, tables of contents, glossaries, electronic menus, icons) to locate key facts or information in a text.	**Core Lesson Connections:** (Lesson.Part.Activity) 74.C.1, 83.B.1, 94.B.1, 105.B.1, 115.B.1, 125.B.1, 126.B.1, 130.B.1, 146.B.1 **Read Aloud Library:** (Week.Day) 16.3, 17.3, 18.3, 19.3, 20.3, 23.3, 25.3
RI.1.6	Distinguish between information provided by pictures or other illustrations and information provided by the words in a text.	**Read Aloud Library:** Lessons 16.1, 17.1, 18.1, 19.1, 20.1, 21.1, 22.1, 23.1, 24.1, 25.1
	Reading Standards for Informational Text: Integration of Knowledge and Ideas	
RI.1.7	Use the illustrations and details in a text to describe its key ideas.	**Core Lesson Connections:** (Lesson.Part.Activity) 83.B.2, 94.B.2, 105.B.2, 130.B.2, 146.B.2, 154.B.2 **Read Aloud Library:** (Week.Day) 14.4, 15.3, 16.1, 17.1, 18.1, 19.1, 2 0.1, 21.1, 22.1, 23.1, 24.1, 25.1
RI.1.8	Identify the reasons an author gives to support points in a text.	**Core Lesson Connections:** (Lesson.Part.Activity) 83.B.2, 94.B.2, 105.B.2, 130.B.2, 146.B.2, 154.B.2 **Read Aloud Library:** (Week.Day) 16.3, 16.4, 17.3, 17.4, 18.3, 18.4, 19.3, 19.4, 20.3, 20.4, 21.3, 21.4, 22.3, 22.4, 23.3, 23.4, 24.3, 24.4, 25.3, 25.4
RI.1.9	Identify basic similarities in and differences between two texts on the same topic (e.g., in illustrations, descriptions, or procedures).	**Read Aloud Library:** (Week.Day) 19.3
	Reading Standards for Informational Text: Range of Reading and Level of Text Complexity	
RI.1.10	With prompting and support, read informational texts appropriately complex for grade 1.	**Core Lesson Connections:** (Lesson.Part.Activity) 74.C.1, 83.B.1, 94.B.1, 105.B.1, 115.B.1, 125.B.1, 130.B.1, 145.B.1, 146.B.1, 154.B.1, 156.B.1 **Read Aloud Library:** (Week.Day) 14.4, 15.3, 16.1–5, 17.1–5, 18.1–5, 19.1–5, 20.1–5, 21.1–5, 22.1–5, 23.1–5, 24.1–5, 25.1–5
	Reading Standards for Foundational Skills: Print Concepts	
RF.1.1	Demonstrate understanding of the organization and basic features of print.	

GRADE 1 STANDARDS		PAGE REFERENCES
RF.1.1a	Recognize the distinguishing features of a sentence (e.g., first word, capitalization, ending punctuation).	**Language Presentation Book A:** (Lesson.Exercise) 51.8, 53.8, 55.6 **Language Presentation Book B:** (Lesson.Exercise) 61.6, 64.6, 73.6, 74.7, 75.7, 76.8, 78.8, 80.7, 81.8, 83.8, 84.5, 86.9, 87.6, 88.6, 89.8, 90.6, 91.7, 92.6, 93.6, 94.7, 96.7, 98.7, 99.8, 100.7, 101.7, 102.6, 103.6, 104.6, 105.6, 106.6, 107.6, 108.6, 109.7, 110.6, 111.6, 112.6, 113.6, 114.7, 116.6, 117.6, 118.7, 119.7, 120.6, 121.5, 122.6, 123.6, 124.5, 125.5, 126.5, 128.6, 129.6 **Language Workbook:** Lessons 51, 53, 55, 61, 64, 73, 74, 75, 76, 78, 80, 81, 83, 84, 86, 87, 88, 89, 90, 91, 92, 93, 94, 96, 98, 99, 100, 101, 102, 103, 104, 105, 106, 107, 108, 109, 110, 111, 112, 113, 114, 116, 117, 118, 119, 120, 121, 122, 123, 124, 125, 126, 128, 129 **Student Practice CD**
Reading Standards for Foundational Skills: Phonological Awareness		
RF.1.2	Demonstrate understanding of spoken words, syllables, and sounds (phonemes).	
RF.1.2a	Distinguish long from short vowel sounds in spoken single-syllable words.	**Reading Presentation Book A:** (Lesson.Exercise) 40.8, 40.9, 41.3, 41.4, 42.3, 42.4, 43.2, 43.3, 44.3, 44.4, 45.11, 45.12, 46.3, 46.4, 48.3, 48.5 **Reading Presentation Book B:** (Lesson.Exercise) 49.3–5, 50.2–4, 51.2–4, 52.2–4, 53.2–4, 54.5–8, 55.5–8, 56.6–9, 57.3–5, 57.9–13, 58.2–5, 58.7, 58.8, 59.5–9, 59.12, 60.4–7, 60.10–13, 61.5–8, 61.11–13, 62.5–7, 62.12, 63.2–4, 64.2, 65.2–4, 66.2, 66.15, 67.3, 68.5, 69.15, 70.1–3, 71.1, 72.8, 73.2, 74.7, 76.4, 76.6, 77.8, 78.1, 79.4, 80.3, 81.7, 82.7, 84.5, 88.3, 89.4, 90.3, 92.4, 94.6 **Seatwork Blackline Master Book:** Lessons 21, 26, 61, 65, 71, 75, 81, 85, 105, 129, 145 **Student Practice CD**

GRADE 1 STANDARDS		PAGE REFERENCES
RF.1.2b	Orally produce single-syllable words by blending sounds (phonemes), including consonant blends.	**Reading Presentation Book A:** (Lesson.Exercise) 1.2–9, 2.2–11, 3.4, 3.5, 4.4, 4.5, 5.2–10, 6.2–9, 7.2–9, 8.4, 9.4, 10.2–10, 11.2–13, 12.2–11, 13.4, 14.2–9, 15.2–9, 16.2–8, 17.2–9, 18.4, 19.2–7, 20.2–8, 21.2–9, 22.2–8, 23.2–10, 24.2–6, 25.2–13, 26.2–9, 27.2–13, 28.2–9, 29.2–11, 30.2–13, 31.2–11, 32.6, 33.2–11, 34.3–18, 35.3–19, 36.3–17, 37.2–17, 38.2–14, 39.2–15, 30.3–17, 41.2–14, 42.3–9, 43.2–9, 44.3–13, 45.3–14, 46.3–14, 37.6, 48.3–14 **Reading Presentation Book B:** (Lesson.Exercise) 49.3–13, 50.2–15, 51.2–14, 52.2–14, 53.1–10, 54.2–11, 55.1–11, 56.1–17, 57.1–13, 58.1–10, 59.1–12, 60.1–15, 61.1–15, 62.2–14, 63.2–15, 64.2–14, 65.2–16, 66.2–17, 67.1–12, 68.1–9, 69.1–12, 70.1–8, 71.1–8, 72.1–9, 73.1–7, 74.1–10, 75.1–7, 76.1–6, 77.1–9, 78.1–11, 79.1–10, 80.1–12, 81.2–7, 82.1–7, 83.3–8, 84.3–7, 85.5–8, 86.3–6, 87.2–5, 88.2–5, 89.3–7, 90.2–6, 91.2–7, 92.2–6, 93.2–5, 94.2–6, 95.1–4, 96.1–4, 97.1–4, 98.1–5, 99.1–4, 100.1–4, 101.1–4, 102.1–4, 103.1–4, 104.1–5 **Reading Presentation Book C:** (Lesson.Exercise) 105.1–4, 106.1–4, 107.1–4, 108.1–4, 109.1–4, 110.1–4, 111.1–4, 112.1–14, 113.1–14, 114.1–4, 115.1–14, 116.1–14, 117.1–4, 118.1–5, 119.1–5, 120.1–4, 121.1–6, 122.1–5, 123.1–5, 124.1–5, 125.1–4, 126.1–5, 127.1–5, 128.1–5, 129.1–5, 130.1–4, 131.1–4, 132.1–5, 133.1–4, 134.1–4, 135.1–3, 136.1–4, 137.1–4, 138.1–4, 139.1–4, 140.1–4, 141.1–4, 142.1–4, 143.1–4, 144.1–4, 145.1–4, 146.1–4, 147.1–3, 148.1–3, 149.1–3, 150.1–4, 151.1–4, 152.1–4, 153.1–4, 154.1–3, 155.1–4, 156.1–4, 157.1–4, 158.1–4, 159.1–4, 160.1–4 **Storybook 1:** Lessons 1–83 **Storybook 2:** Lessons 84–160 **Core Lesson Connections:** (Lesson.Part.Activity) 1.A.1, 2.A.1, 3.A.1, 4.A.1, 5.A.1, 6.A.1, 7.A.1, 8.A.1, 9.A.1, 10.A.1, 11.A.1, 11.A.2, 12.A.1, 12.A.2, 13.A.1, 13.A.2, 14.A.1, 14.A.2, 15.A.1, 15.A.2, 16.A.1, 16.A.2, 17.A.1, 17.A.2, 18.A.1, 18.A.2, 19.A.1, 19.A.2, 20.A.1, 20.A.2, 21.A.1, 21.A.2, 22.A.1, 22.A.2, 23.A.1, 23.A.2, 24.A.1, 24.A.2, 25.A.1, 25.A.2, 26.A.1, 26.A.2, 27.A.1, 27.A.2, 28.A.1, 28.A.2, 29.A.1, 29.A.2, 30.A.1, 30.A.2, 31.A.1, 31.A.2, 32.A.1, 32.A.2, 33.A.1, 33.A.2, 34.A.1, 34.A.2, 35.A.1, 35.A.2, 36.A.1, 36.A.2, 37.A.1, 37.A.2, 38.A.1, 38.A.2, 39.A.1, 39.A.2, 40.A.1, 40.A.2, 41.A.1, 41.A.2, 42.A.1, 42.A.2, 43.A.1, 43.A.2, 44.A.1, 44.A.2, 45.A.1, 45.A.2, 46.A.1, 46.A.2, 47.A.1, 47.A.2, 48.A.1, 48.A.2, 49.A.1, 49.A.2, 50.A.1, 50.A.2, 51.A.1, 51.A.2, 52.A.1, 52.A.2, 53.A.1, 53.A.2, 54.A.1, 54.A.2, 55.A.1, 55.A.2, 56.A.1, 56.A.2, 57.A.1, 57.A.2, 58.A.1, 58.A.2, 59.A.1, 59.A.2, 60.A.1, 60.A.2, 61.A.1, 61.A.2, 62.A.1, 62.A.2, 63.A.1, 63.A.2, 64.A.1, 64.A.2, 65.A.1, 65.A.2, 66.A.1, 66.A.2, 67.A.1, 67.A.2, 68.A.1, 68.A.2, 69.A.1, 69.A.2, 70.A.1, 70.A.2, 71.A.1, 72.A.1, 73.A.1, 74.A.1, 75.A.1, 76.A.1, 77.A.1, 78.A.1, 79.A.1, 80.A.1 **Spelling Presentation Book:** Lessons 1–160 **Seatwork Blackline Master Book:** Lessons 1, 4, 6, 9, 11, 14, 16, 19, 21, 24, 26, 29, 31, 34, 36, 39, 41, 44, 46, 49, 53, 57, 58, 61, 65, 71, 75, 81, 85, 89, 101, 105, 113, 117, 125, 129, 137, 145
RF.1.2c	Isolate and pronounce initial, medial vowel, and final sounds (phonemes) in spoken single-syllable words.	**Core Lesson Connections:** (Lesson.Part.Activity) 11.A.2, 12.A.2, 13.A.2, 14.A.2, 15.A.2, 16A.2, 17.A.2, 18.A.2, 19.A.2, 20.A.2, 21.A.2, 22.A.2, 23.A.2, 24.A.2, 25.A.2, 26.A.2, 27.A.2, 28.A.2, 29.A.2, 30.A.2, 31.A.2, 32.A.2, 33.A.2, 34.A.2, 35.A.2, 36.A.2, 37.A.2, 38.A.2, 39.A.2, 40.A.2, 41.A.2, 42.A.2, 43.A.2, 44.A.2, 45.A.2, 46.A.2, 47.A.2, 48.A.2, 49.A.2, 50.A.2, 51.A.2, 52.A.2, 53.A.2, 54.A.2, 55.A.2, 56.A.2, 57.A.2, 58.A.2, 59.A.2, 60.A.2, 61.A.2, 62.A.2, 63.A.2, 64.A.2, 65.A.2, 66.A.2, 67.A.2, 68.A.2, 69.A.2, 70.A.2, 71.A.1, 72.A.1, 73.A.1, 74.A.1, 75.A.1, 76.A.1, 77.A.1, 78,.A.1, 79.A.1, 80.A.1 **Seatwork Blackline Master Book:** Lessons 1, 6, 11, 16, 21, 26, 31, 36, 41, 89 **Student Practice CD**

GRADE 1 STANDARDS		PAGE REFERENCES
RF.1.2d	Segment spoken single-syllable words into their complete sequence of individual sounds (phonemes).	**Core Lesson Connections:** (Lesson.Part.Activity) 1.A.1, 2.A.1, 3.A.1, 4.A.1, 5.A.1, 6.A.1, 7.A.1, 8.A.1, 9.A.1, 10.A.1, 11.A.1, 11.A.2, 12.A.1, 12.A.2, 13.A.1, 13.A.2, 14.A.1, 14.A.2, 15.A.1, 15.A.2, 16.A.1, 16.A.2, 17.A.1, 17.A.2, 18.A.1, 18.A.2, 19.A.1, 19.A.2, 20.A.1, 20.A.2, 21.A.1, 21.A.2, 22.A.1, 22.A.2, 23.A.1, 23.A.2, 24.A.1, 24.A.2, 25.A.1, 25.A.2, 26.A.1, 26.A.2, 27.A.1, 27.A.2, 28.A.1, 28.A.2, 29.A.1, 29.A.2, 30.A.1, 30.A.2, 31.A.1, 31.A.2, 32.A.1, 32.A.2, 33.A.1, 33.A.2, 34.A.1, 34.A.2, 35.A.1, 35.A.2, 36.A.1, 36.A.2, 37.A.1, 37.A.2, 38.A.1, 38.A.2, 39.A.1, 39.A.2, 40.A.1, 40.A.2, 41.A.1, 41.A.2, 42.A.1, 42.A.2, 43.A.1, 43.A.2, 44.A.1, 44.A.2, 45.A.1, 45.A.2, 46.A.1, 46.A.2, 47.A.1, 47.A.2, 48.A.1, 48.A.2, 49.A.1, 49.A.2, 50.A.1, 50.A.2, 51.A.1, 51.A.2, 52.A.1, 52.A.2, 53.A.1, 53.A.2, 54.A.1, 54.A.2, 55.A.1, 55.A.2, 56.A.1, 56.A.2, 57.A.1, 57.A.2, 58.A.1, 58.A.2, 59.A.1, 59.A.2, 60.A.1, 60.A.2, 61.A.1, 61.A.2, 62.A.1, 62.A.2, 63.A.1, 63.A.2, 64.A.1, 64.A.2, 65.A.1, 65.A.2, 66.A.1, 66.A.2, 67.A.1, 67.A.2, 68.A.1, 68.A.2, 69.A.1, 69.A.2, 70.A.1, 70.A.2, 71.A.1, 72.A.1, 73.A.1, 74.A.1, 75.A.1, 76.A.1, 77.A.1, 78.A.1, 79.A.1, 80.A.1 **Spelling Presentation Book:** Lessons 1.2–5, 2.2, 2.3, 3.2, 3.3, 4.2,–5, 5.2, 5.3, 6.2, 6.3, 7.2, 8.2, 9.2, 9.3, 10.2, 10.3, 11.3, 11.4, 12.2, 12.3, 12.5, 13.3, 13.4, 14.3, 14.4, 15.3–5, 16.3, 17.2–4, 18.3, 18.4, 19.3, 19.4, 20.3, 20.4, 21.2, 21.3, 22.2, 23.3, 24.3–5, 25.3–5, 26.3, 26.4, 27.3, 27.4, 28.3, 29.3, 29.4, 30.3, 30.4, 31.3, 31.4, 32.3, 32.4, 33.3–5, 34.2, 35.2, 35.3, 36.1, 37.1, 38.1, 39.1, 39.2, 40.1–3, 41.1, 42.1, 43.1, 44.1, 44.2, 45.1, 45.2, 46.1, 47.1, 48.1, 49.1, 50.2, 51.2, 51.3, 52.2, 52.3, 53.2, 53.3, 54.2, 54.3, 55.1, 56.2, 57.2, 57.3, 58.1, 59.2, 60.2, 60.3, 61.2, 61.3, 62.2, 62.3, 63.–4, 64.2, 65.1, 66.2, 67.2, 67.3, 68.2, 68.3, 69.2, 69.3, 70.2, 70.3, 71.2, 72.2, 73.2, 74.1, 75.1, 76.1, 77.2, 78.2, 78.3, 79.2, 79.3, 80.2, 80.3, 81.2, 81.3, 82.2, 83.2, 84.2, 85.1, 86.3, 91.2, 92.1, 92.2, 93.1, 93.2, 94.1, 96.1, 98.1, 106.1, 110.1, 113.1, 115.2, 120.2, 123.2, 124.1, 125.1, 129.1, 135.2, 138.1, 143.2, 146.2, 150.1, 151.1, 154.1, 57.1 **Student Practice CD**
Reading Standards for Foundational Skills: Phonics and Word Recognition		
RF.1.3	Know and apply grade-level phonics and word analysis skills in decoding words.	
RF.1.3a	Know the spelling-sound correspondences for common consonant digraphs (two letters that represent one sound).	**Reading Presentation Book B:** (Lesson.Exercise) 67.11, 68.9, 69.11, 69.12, 72.1, 73.1, 74.1, 74.2, 75.4, 75.6, 76.2, 77.1, 78.8 **Spelling Presentation Book:** Lessons 11.2, 12.4, 12.5, 13.2, 13.3, 14.2, 14.3, 15.2, 15.3, 16.2, 17.4, 23.2, 24.2, 24.3, 25.2, 25.3, 26.2, 26.3, 27.2, 27.3, 28.2, 29.2, 30.2, 56.1, 57.1, 58.1, 59.1, 60.1, 60.2, 61.1, 61.2, 62.1, 62.2, 63.1, 63.2, 77.1, 78.1, 78.2, 79.1, 79.2, 80.1, 80.2, 81.2, 82.1, 83.1, 84.1, 86.3, 91.1, 103.1, 110.2 **Student Practice CD**

GRADE 1 STANDARDS		PAGE REFERENCES
RF.1.3b	Decode regularly spelled one-syllable words.	**Reading Presentation Book A:** (Lesson.Exercise) 1.2–9, 2.–11, 3.2–5, 4.2–5, 5.2–10, 6.2–9, 7.2–9, 8.2–4, 9.2–4, 10.2–10, 11.2–13, 12.2–11, 13.2–4, 14.2–9, 15.2–9, 16.2–8, 17.2–9, 18.2–4, 19.2–7, 20.2–8, 21.2–9, 22.2–8, 23.2–10, 24.2–6, 25.2–13, 26.2–9, 27.2–13, 28.2–9, 29.2–11, 30.2–13, 31.2–11, 32.6, 33.2–11, 34.2–18, 35.3–19, 36.3–17, 37.2–17, 38.2–14, 39.2–15, 40.2–10, 41.3–14, 42.3–9, 43.2–9, 44.3–12, 45.3–14, 46.3–14, 47.6, 48.3–14
		Reading Presentation Book B: (Lesson.Exercise) 49.3–13, 50.2–15, 51.2–14, 52.3–14, 53.1–10, 54.2–11, 55.1–11, 56.1–17, 57.3–13, 58.1–10, 59.1–12, 60.1–15, 61.1–15, 62.2–14, 63.2–15, 64.2–14, 65.2–16, 66.2–17, 67.1–12, 68.1–9, 69.1–12, 70.1–8, 71.1–8, 72.1–9, 73..1–7, 74.1–10, 75.1–7, 76.1–6, 77.1–9, 78.1–11, 79.1–10, 80.1–12, 81.1–7, 82.1–7, 83.3–8, 84.3–7, 85.5–8, 86.3–6, 87.2–5, 88.2–5, 89.3–7, 90.2–6, 91.3–7, 92.2–6, 93.2–5, 94.2–6, 95.1–4, 96.1–4, 97.1–4, 98.1–5, 99.1–4, 100.1–4, 101.1–4, 102.1–4, 103.1–4, 104.1–5
		Reading Presentation Book C: (Lesson.Exercise) 105.1–4, 106.1–4, 107.1–4, 08.1–4, 109.1–4, 110.1–4, 111.1–4, 112.1–4, 113.1–14, 114.1–14, 115.1–4, 116.1–4, 117.1–4, 118.1–4, 119.1–4, 120.1–4, 121.1–5, 122.1–5, 123.1–5, 124.1–5, 125.1–4, 126.1–5, 127.1–5, 128.1–5, 129.1–5, 130.1–4, 131.1–4, 132.1–5, 133.1–4, 134.1–4, 135.1–3, 136.1–4, 137.1–4, 138.1–4, 139.1–4, 140.1–4, 141.1–4, 142.1–4, 143.1–4, 144.1–14, 145.1–4, 146.1–4, 147.1–3, 148.1–3, 149.1–3, 150.1–4, 151.1–4, 152.1–4, 153.1–4, 154.1–4, 155.1–4, 156.1–4, 157.1–4, 159.1–4, 160.1–4
		Storybook 1: Lessons 1–83
		Storybook 2: Lessons 84–160
		Core Lesson Connections: (Lesson.Part.Activity) 1.B.1, 2.B.1, 2.B.2, 3.B.1,3.B.2, 4.B.1, 4.B.2, 5.B.1, 6.B.1, 6.B.2, 7.B.1, 7.B.2, 8.B.1, 8.B.2, 9.B.1, 9.B.2, 10.B.1, 11.B.1, 11.B.2, 12.B.1, 12.B.2, 13.B.1, 13.B.2, 14.B.1, 14.B.2, 15.B.1, 16.B.1, 16.B.2, 17.B.1, 17.B.2, 18.B.1, 18.B.2, 19.B.1, 19.B.2, 20.B.1, 21.B.1, 21.B.2, 22.B.1, 22.B.2, 23.B.1, 23.B.2, 24.B.1, 24.B.2, 25.B.1, 26.B.1, 26.B.2, 27.B.1, 27.B.2, 28.B.1, 28.B.2, 29.B.1, 29.B.2, 30.B.1, 31.B.1, 31.B.2, 32.B.1, 32.B.2, 33.B.1, 33.B.2, 34.B.1, 34.B.2, 35.B.1, 36.B,1, 36.B.2, 37.B.1, 37.B.2, 38.B.1, 38.B.2, 39.B.1, 39.B.2, 40.B.1, 41.B.1, 41.B.2, 42.B.1, 42.B.2, 43.B.1, 43.B.2, 44.B.1, 44.B.2, 45.B.1, 46.B.1, 46.B.2, 47.B.1, 47.B.2, 48.B.1, 48.B.2, 49.B.1, 49.B.2, 50.B.1, 51.B.1, 51.B.2, 52.B.1, 52.B.2, 53.B.1, 53.B.1, 54.B.1, 54.B.2, 55.B.1, 56.B.1, 56.B.2, 57.B.1, 57.B.2, 58.B.1, 58.B.2, 59.B.1, 59.B.2, 60.B.1, 61.B.1, 61.B.2, 62.B.1, 62.B.2, 63.B.1, 63.B.2, 64.B.1, 64.B.2, 65.B.1, 66.B.1, 66.B.2, 67.B.1, 67.B.2, 68.B.1, 68.B.2, 69.B.1, 69.B.1, 70.B.1, 71.B.1, 71.B.2, 72.B.1, 72.B.2, 73.B.1, 73.B.2, 74.B.1, 74.B.2, 75.B.1, 76.B.1, 76.B.2, 77.B.1, 77.B.2, 78.B.1, 78.B.1, 79.B.1, 79.B.2, 80.B.1, 81.A.1, 81.A.2, 82.A.1, 82.A.2, 83.A.1, 83.A.2, 84.A.1, 84.A.2, 85.A.1, 86.A.1, 86.A.2, 87.A.1, 87.A.2, 88.A.1, 88.A.2, 89.A.1, 89.A.2, 90.A.1, 91.A.1, 91.A.2, 92.A.1, 92.A.2, 93.A.1, 93.A.2, 94.A.1, 94.A.2, 95.A.1, 96.A.1, 96.A.2, 97.A.1, 97.A.2, 98.A.1, 98.A.2, 99.A.1, 99.A.2, 100.A.1, 101.A.1, 101.A.2, 102.A.1, 102.A,2, 103.A.1, 103.A.2, 104.A.1, 104.A.2, 105.A.1, 106.A.1, 106.A.2, 107.A.1, 107.A.2, 108.A,1, 109.A,1, 109.A.2, 110.A.1, 111.A.1, 111.A.2, 112.A.1, 112.A.2, 113.A.1, 113.A.2, 114.A.1, 114.A.2, 115.A.1, 116.A.1, 116.A.2, 117.A.1, 117.A.2, 118.A.1, 118.A.2, 119.A.1, 119.A.2, 120.A.1, 121.A.1, 121.A.2, 122.A.1, 122.A.2, 123.A,1, 123.A.2, 124.A.1, 124.A.2, 125.A.1, 126.A.1, 126.A.2, 127.A.1, 127.A.2, 128.A.1, 128.A.2, 129.A.1, 129.A.2, 130.A.1, 131.A.1, 131.A.2, 132.A.1, 132.A.2, 133.A.1, 133.A.2, 134.A.1, 134.A.2, 135.A.1, 136.A.1, 136.A.2, 137.A.1, 137.A.2, 138.A.1, 138.A.2, 139.A.1, 139.A.2, 140.A.1, 141.A.1, 141.A.2, 142.A.1, 143.A.1, 143.A.2, 144.A.1, 144.A.2, 145.A.1, 146.A.1, 146.A.2, 147.A.1, 147.A.2, 148.A.1, 148.A.2, 149.A.1, 149.A.2, 150.A.1, 151.A.1, 151.A.2, 152.A.1, 152.A.2, 153.A.1, 153.A.2, 154.A.1, 154.A.2, 155.A.1, 156.A.1, 156.A.2, 157.A.1, 157.A.2, 158.A.1, 158.A.2, 159.A.1, 159.A.2, 160.A.1
		Seatwork Blackline Master Book: Lessons 1, 4, 6, 9, 11, 14, 16, 19, 21, 24, 26, 29, 31, 34, 36, 39, 41, 44, 45, 49, 53, 57, 58, 61, 65, 71, 75, 81, 85, 89, 101, 105, 113, 117, 125, 129, 137, 145
		Student Practice CD

GRADE 1 STANDARDS		PAGE REFERENCES
RF.1.3c	Know final -e and common vowel team conventions for representing long vowel sounds.	**Reading Presentation Book A:** Planning pages vb, 111b, 234b **Reading Presentation Book B:** Planning pages 67b, 171b, 271b **Reading Presentation Book C:** Planning pages 64b, 153b **Language Presentation Book A:** (Lesson.Exercise) 58.7, 59.9, 60.8 **Language Presentation Book B:** (Lesson.Exercise) 61.6, 65.8, 66.6, 68.7, 69.8 **Language Workbook:** Lessons 58, 59, 60, 61, 65, 66, 68, 69 **Spelling Teacher Presentation Book:** Lessons 141.1, 142.1, 143.1 **Seatwork Blackline Master Book:** Lessons 61, 65, 71, 75, 81, 85, 105, 129
RF.1.3d	Use knowledge that every syllable must have a vowel sound to determine the number of syllables in a printed word.	**Reading Presentation Book A:** (Lesson.Exercise) 36.6–8, 37.3, 37.4, 38.4–7, 39.13, 39.14, 41.8–10, 44.7, 44.8, 45.13, 45.14, 48.7, 48.8 **Reading Presentation Book B:** (Lesson.Exercise) 50.7–9, 51.10, 53.2–4, 54.3, 54.4, 55.10, 56.15, 56.16, 58.9, 58.10, 60.8, 60.9, 61.14, 62.13, 63.12–14, 65.6–8, 66.10–12, 67.10, 67.12, 68.1, 68.2, 68.4, 69.2–4, 70.5, 70.6, 71.2–4, 72.6, 72.7, 74.8, 74.9 **Student Practice CD**
RF.1.3e	Decode two-syllable words following basic patterns by breaking the words into syllables.	**Reading Presentation Book A:** (Lesson.Exercise) 1.4–8, 7.5–7, 31.7–11, 33.8–11, 34.15–18, 35.14–19, 36.16, 36.17, 38.12, 38.14 **Reading Presentation Book B:** (Lesson.Exercise) 67.11, 68.9, 72.1, 73.1, 74.1 **Core Lesson Connections:** (Lesson.Part.Activity) 1.A.1, 2.A.1, 3.A.1, 4.A.1, 5.A.1, 6.A.1, 7.A.1, 8.A.1, 9.A.1, 10.A.1, 11.A.1, 11.A.2, 12.A.1, 12.A.2, 13.A.1, 13.A.2, 14.A.1, 14.A.2, 15.A.1, 15.A.2, 16.A.1, 16.A.2, 17.A.1, 17.A.2, 18.A.1, 18.A.2, 19.A.1, 19.A.2, 20.A.1, 20.A.2, 21.A.1, 21.A.2, 22.A.1, 22.A.2, 23.A.1, 23.A.2, 24.A.1, 24.A.2, 25.A.1, 25.A.2, 26.A.1, 26.A.2, 27.A.1, 27.A.2, 28.A.1, 28.A.2, 29.A.1, 29.A.2, 30.A.1, 30.A.2, 31.A.1, 31.A.2, 32.A.1, 32.A.2, 33.A.1, 33.A.2, 34.A.1, 34.A.2, 35.A.1, 35.A.2, 36.A.1, 36.A.2, 37.A.1, 37.A.2, 38.A.1, 38.A.2, 39.A.1, 39.A.2, 40.A.1, 40.A.2, 41.A.1, 41.A.2, 42.A.1, 42.A.2, 43.A.1, 43.A.2, 44.A.1, 44.A.2, 45.A.1, 45.A.2, 46.A.1, 46.A.2, 47.A.1, 47.A.2, 48.A.1, 48.A.2, 49.A.1, 49.A.2, 50.A.1, 50.A.2, 51.A.1, 51.A.2, 52.A.1, 52.A.2, 53.A.1, 53.A.2, 54.A.1, 54.A.2, 55.A.1, 55.A.2, 56.A.1, 56.A.2, 57.A.1, 57.A.2, 58.A.1, 58.A.2, 59.A.1, 59.A.2, 60.A.1, 60.A.2, 61.A.1, 61.A.2, 62.A.1, 62.A.2, 63.A.1, 63.A.2, 64.A.1, 64.A.2, 65.A.1, 65.A.2, 66.A.1, 66.A.2, 67.A.1, 67.A.2, 68.A.1, 68.A.2, 69.A.1, 69.A.2, 70.A.1, 70.A.2, 71.A.1, 72.A.1, 73.A.1, 74.A.1, 75.A.1, 76.A.1, 77.A.1, 78.A.1, 79.A.1, 80.A.1 **Student Practice CD**

GRADE 1 STANDARDS		PAGE REFERENCES
RF.1.3f	Read words with inflectional endings.	**Reading Presentation Book A:** (Lesson.Exercise) 5.4, 5.5, 6.9, 7.8, 10.3, 10.10, 11.5, 11.9, 11.13, 12.2–4, 12.6, 12.7, 12.10, 12.11, 13.3, 14.4, 14.7, 17.7, 18.3, 19.3–7, 20.2, 20.6, 21.2, 21.5, 22.5, 22.7, 23.3, 23.7, 24.2, 24.3, 24.5, 25.3, 25.7–10, 25.13, 26.2, 26.5, 26.6, 26.9, 27.3, 27.11, 28.5, 28.6, 31.5, 33.7, 34.1, 34.3, 35.7, 35.8, 35.11, 36.1, 36.3, 37.2, 37.6, 36.10, 38.2, 38.3, 38.12, 39.7, 40.2, 40.7, 41.5, 41.6, 42.5, 42.6, 43.5–7, 44.6, 45.3, 45.5, 46.6–8, 48.9 **Reading Presentation Book B:** (Lesson.Exercise) 49.7, 49.12, 50.10, 51.14, 52.7, 52.8, 52.10, 52.11, 53.5, 54.3, 54.4, 55.1, 55.2, 55.9, 55.11, 56.1–3, 56.12, 57.8, 58.1, 58.9, 60.9, 60.15, 61.1, 61.3, 61.10, 61.14, 61.15, 62.9, 62.13, 63.5, 63.9–14, 64.5, 64.7, 64.9, 64.13, 65.5, 65.12, 65.13, 65.15, 66.8, 66.16, 67.7, 67.9, 67.10, 68.3, 68.6, 68.7, 69.5, 69.6, 70.4, 71.6–8, 72.4, 72.5, 72.7, 72.9, 73.13, 74.4, 74.5, 75.4, 75.5, 76.2–5, 77.15, 78.6, 78.8, 78.10, 79.5–7, 80.7, 80.10, 80.12, 81.5, 81.6, 82.3–5, 83.6, 84.6, 85.5, 85.6, 85.8, 86.6, 87.5, 88.3, 88.5, 89.3, 89.4, 89.6, 89.7, 90.3, 90.6, 91.6, 91.7, 92.4, 92.5, 93.4, 93.5, 94.4, 94.6, 95.3, 95.4, 96.2, 97.3, 98.3, 98.5, 99.3, 100.2, 100.4, 101.2, 102.4, 103.2, 104.1–3, 104.5 **Reading Presentation Book C:** (Lesson.Exercise) 105.3, 105.4, 106.2–4, 108.2, 108.3, 109.2, 109.4, 110.3, 111.2, 111.4, 112.4, 113.1, 113.2, 113.4, 114.2, 114.4, 115.2–4, 116.1, 116.2, 117.1–4, 118.2, 119.1, 1191.2, 119.4, 120.2, 120.4, 121.3, 122.1, 122.3, 122.5, 123.2, 123.4, 123.5, 124.1, 24.2, 124.4, 125.3, 125.4, 126.2, 126.3, 127.2, 127.4, 127.5, 128.2, 128.4, 129.2, 130.1, 130.2, 130.4, 131.3, 132.3, 133.4, 134.1, 134.2, 134.4, 135.2, 136.2, 136.3, 138.2, 138.4, 139.3, 140.3, 140.4, 141.2, 141.3, 142.4, 143.2, 143.3, 144.2–4, 145.2, 145.4, 147/2. 148.3, 149.1–3, 150.4, 151.2–4, 152.1, 152.4, 153.2–4, 154.2, 155.2, 155.3, 156.4, 157.2, 158.2, 158.4, 159.2, 160.2, 160.4 **Spelling Teacher Presentation Book:** Lessons 126.2, 127.1, 137.2, 138.2, 139.2, 147.2, 148.2, 149.2, 151.2, 153.2, 154.2, 158.2, 159.2 **Student Practice CD**
RF.1.3g	Recognize and read grade-appropriate irregularly spelled words.	**Reading Presentation Book A:** (Lesson.Exercise) 1.2–9, 2.2–11, 3.4, 3.5, 4.4, 4.5, 5.2–10, 6.2–9, 7.2–9, 8.4, 9.4, 10.2–10, 11.2–13, 12.2–11, 13.4, 14.2–9, 15.2–9, 16.2–8, 17.2–9, 18.4, 19.2–7, 20.2–8, 21.2–9, 22.2–8, 23.2–10, 24.2–6, 25.2–13, 26.2–9, 27.2–13, 28.2–9, 29.2–11, 30.2–13, 31.2–11, 32.6, 33.2–11, 34.3–18, 35.3–19, 36.3–17, 37.2–17, 38.2–14, 39.2–15, 30.3–17, 41.2–14, 42.3–9, 43.2–9, 44.3–13, 45.3–14, 46.3–14, 37.6, 48.3–14 **Reading Presentation Book B:** (Lesson.Exercise) 49.3–13, 50.2–15, 51.2–14, 52.2–14, 53.1–10, 54.2–11, 55.1–11, 56.1–17, 57.1–13, 58.1–10, 59.1–12, 60.1–15, 61.1–15, 62.2–14, 63.2–15, 64.2–14, 65.2–16, 66.2–17, 67.1–12, 68.1–9, 69.1–12, 70.1–8, 71.1–8, 72.1–9, 73.1–7, 74.1–10, 75.1–7, 76.1–6, 77.1–9, 78.1–11, 79.1–10, 80.1–12, 81.2–7, 82.1–7, 83.3–8, 84.3–7, 85.5–8, 86.3–6, 87.2–5, 88.2–5, 89.3–7, 90.2–6, 91.2–7, 92.2–6, 93.2–5, 94.2–6, 95.1–4, 96.1–4, 97.1–4, 98.1–5, 99.1–4, 100.1–4, 101.1–4, 102.1–4, 103.1–4, 104.1–5 **Reading Presentation Book C:** (Lesson.Exercise) 105.1–4, 106.1–4, 107.1–4, 108.1–4, 109.1–4, 110.1–4, 111.1–4, 112.1–14, 113.1–14, 114.1–4, 115.1–14, 116.1–14, 117.1–4, 118.1–5, 119.1–5, 120.1–4, 121.1–6, 122.1–5, 123.1–5, 124.1–5, 125.1–4, 126.1–5, 127.1–5, 128.1–5, 129.1–5, 130.1–4, 131.1–4, 132.1–5, 133.1–4, 134.1–4, 135.1–3, 136.1–4, 137.1–4, 138.1–4, 139.1–4, 140.1–4, 141.1–4, 142.1–4, 143.1–4, 144.1–4, 145.1–4, 146.1–4, 147.1–3, 148.1–3, 149.1–3, 150.1–4, 151.1–4, 152.1–4, 153.1–4, 154.1–3, 155.1–4, 156.1–4, 157.1–4, 158.1–4, 159.1–4, 160.1–4 **Student Practice CD**
Reading Standards for Foundational Skills: Fluency		
RF.1.4	Read with sufficient accuracy and fluency to support comprehension.	

GRADE 1 STANDARDS		PAGE REFERENCES
RF.1.4a	Read grade-level text with purpose and understanding.	**Reading Presentation Book A:** (Lesson.Exercise) 1.10–12, 2.12–14, 5.13–15, 6.12–14, 7.12–14, 10.11–13, 11.14–16, 12.12–14, 14.12–14, 15.12–14, 16.11–13, 17.12–14, 19.10–12, 20.11–13, 21.12–14, 22.11–13, 23.13–15, 24.9–11, 25.16–18, 26.12–14, 27.16–18, 28.12–14, 29.14–16, 30.16–18, 31.14–16, 33.14–16, 34.21–23, 35.22–24, 36.20–22, 37.20–22, 38.17–19, 39.18–20, 40.18–20, 41.15–17, 42.10–12, 43.10–12, 44.13–15, 45.15–17, 46.15–17, 48.15–17 **Reading Presentation Book B:** (Lesson.Exercise) 49.14–16, 50.16–18, 51.15–17, 52.15–17, 53.11–13, 54.12–14, 55.12–14, 56.18–20, 57.14–16, 58.11–13, 59.13–15, 60.16–18, 61.16–18, 62.15–17, 63.16–18, 64.15–17, 65.17–19, 66.18–20, 67.13–15, 68.10–12, 69.13–15, 70.9–11, 71.9–11, 72.10–12, 73.8–10, 74.11–13, 75.8–10, 76.7–9, 77.10–12, 78.12–14, 79.11–13, 80.13–15, 81.10, 81.11, 82.10, 82.11, 83.11, 83.12, 84.10, 85.11, 86.9, 87.8, 88.8, 89.10, 90.9, 91.10, 92.9, 93.8, 94.9, 95.5, 96.5, 97.5, 98.5, 98.6, 99.5, 100.5, 101.5, 102.5, 103.5, 104.5, 104.6 **Reading Presentation Book C:** (Lesson.Exercise) 105.5, 106.5, 107.5, 108.5, 109.5, 110.5, 111.5, 112.5, 113.5, 114.5, 115.5, 116.5, 117.5, 118.5, 119.6, 120.5, 121.7, 122.6, 123.6, 124.6, 125.5, 126.6, 127.6, 128.6, 129.6, 130.5, 131.5, 132.6, 133.5, 134.5, 135.4, 136.5, 137.5, 138.5, 139.5, 140.5, 141.5, 142.5, 143.5, 144.5, 145.5, 146.5, 147.5, 148.5, 149.5, 150.5, 151.6, 152.6, 153.6, 154.5, 155.6, 156.6, 157.6, 158.6, 159.6, 160.6 **Storybook 1:** Lessons 1–83 **Storybook 2:** Lessons 84–160 **Core Lesson Connections:** (Lesson.Part.Activity) 1.C.2, 2.C.1, 3.C.2, 4.C.1, 5.C.1, 6.C.2, 7.C.1, 8.C.1, 9.C.1, 1 0.C.1, 11.C.2, 12.C.2, 13.C.1, 14.C.2, 15.C.1, 16.C.1, 19.C.2, 20.C.1, 21.C.2, 23.C.1, 24.C.1, 25.C.1, 26.C.1, 27.C.1, 30.C.1, 31.C.1, 33.C.2, 34.C.1, 36.C.1, 37.C.1, 38.C.1, 39.C.2, 41.C.1, 42.C.1, 43.C.1, 44.C.1, 46.C.1, 50.C.1, 51.C.1, 52.C.2, 53.C.1, 54.C.1, 55.C.1, 56.C.1, 57.C.1, 59.C.1, 60.C.1, 61.C.1, 62.C.1, 63.C.1, 64.C.1, 65.C.1, 66.C.1, 67.C.1, 69.C.1, 70.C.1, 71.C.1, 72.C.1, 73.C.1, 77.C.2, 78.C.1, 79.C.3, 81.B.1, 84.B.1, 88.B.1, 89.B.1, 90.B.1, 91.B.1, 95.B.1, 96.B.2, 97.B.1, 98.B.1, 99.B.1, 100.B.1, 101.B.1, 102.B.1, 103.B.1, 107.B.1, 108.B.2, 111.B.1, 119.B.1, 121.B.2, 124.B.1, 127.B.1, 128.B.1, 131.B.1, 132.B.1, 134.B.2, 137.B.1, 138.B.1, 139.B.1, 140.B.1, 141.B.1, 142.B.1, 143.B.1, 146.B.2, 149.B.1, 151.B.1, 152.B.1, 153.B.1 **Decodable Stories** **Independent Readers** **Literature Collection/Guide:** Lessons 5, 15, 20, 25, 30, 35, 40, 45, 50 **Read Aloud Library:** (Week.Day) 1.1, 1.2, 2.1, 2.2, 3.1, 3.2, 4.1, 4.2, 5.1, 5.2, 6.1, 6.2, 7.1, 7.2, 8.1, 8.2, 9.1, 9.2, 10.1, 10.2, 11.1, 11.2, 12.1, 12.2, 13.1, 13.2, 14.1, 14.2, 15.1, 15.2, 16.1, 16.2, 17.1, 17.2, 18.1, 18.2, 19.1, 19.2, 20.1, 20.2, 21.1, 21.2, 22.1, 22.2, 23.1, 23.2, 24.1, 24.2, 25.1, 25.2, 26.1, 26.2, 27.1, 27.2, 28.1, 28.2, 29.1, 29.2, 30.1, 30.2

GRADE 1 STANDARDS		PAGE REFERENCES
RF.1.4b	Read grade-level text orally with accuracy, appropriate rate, and expression.	**Reading Presentation Book A:** (Lesson.Exercise) 1.10–12, 2.12–14, 5.13–15, 6.12–14, 7.12–14, 10.11–13, 11.14–16, 12.12–14, 14.12–14, 15.12–14, 16.11–13, 17.12–14, 19.10–12, 20.11–13, 21.12–14, 22.11–13, 23.13–15, 24.9–11, 25.16–18, 26.12–14, 27.16–18, 28.12–14, 29.14–16, 30.16–18, 31.14–16, 33.14–16, 34.21–23, 35.22–24, 36.20–22, 37.20–22, 38.17–19, 39.18–20, 40.18–20, 41.15–17, 42.10–12, 43.10–12, 44.13–15, 45.15–17, 46.15–17, 48.15–17 **Reading Presentation Book B:** (Lesson.Exercise) 49.14–16, 50.16–18, 51.15–17, 52.15–17, 53.11–13, 54.12–14, 55.12–14, 56.18–20, 57.14–16, 58.11–13, 59.13–15, 60.16–18, 61.16–18, 62.15–17, 63.16–18, 64.15–17, 65.17–19, 66.18–20, 67.13–15, 68.10–12, 69.13–15, 70.9–11, 71.9–11, 72.10–12, 73.8–10, 74.11–13, 75.8–10, 76.7–9, 77.10–12, 78.12–14, 79.11–13, 80.13–15, 81.10, 81.11, 82.10, 82.11, 83.11, 83.12, 84.10, 85.11, 86.9, 87.8, 88.8, 89.10, 90.9, 91.10, 92.9, 93.8, 94.9, 95.5, 96.5, 97.5, 98.5, 98.6, 99.5, 100.5, 101.5, 102.5, 103.5, 104.5, 104.6 **Reading Presentation Book C:** (Lesson.Exercise) 105.5, 106.5, 107.5, 108.5, 109.5, 110.5, 111.5, 112.5, 113.5, 114.5, 115.5, 116.5, 117.5, 118.5, 119.6, 120.5, 121.7, 122.6, 123.6, 124.6, 125.5, 126.6, 127.6, 128.6, 129.6, 130.5, 131.5, 132.6, 133.5, 134.5, 135.4, 136.5, 137.5, 138.5, 139.5, 140.5, 141.5, 142.5, 143.5, 144.5, 145.5, 146.5, 147.5, 148.5, 149.5, 150.5, 151.6, 152.6, 153.6, 154.5, 155.6, 156.6, 157.6, 158.6, 159.6, 160.6 **Storybook 1:** Lessons 1–83 **Storybook 2:** Lessons 84–160 **Core Lesson Connections:** (Lesson.Part.Activity) 1.C.2, 2.C.1, 3.C.2, 4.C.1, 5.C.1, 6.C.2, 7.C.1, 8.C.1, 9.C.1, 1 0.C.1, 11.C.2, 12.C.2, 13.C.1, 14.C.2, 15.C.1, 16.C.1, 19.C.2, 20.C.1, 21.C.2, 23.C.1, 24.C.1, 25.C.1, 26.C.1, 27.C.1, 30.C.1, 31.C.1, 33.C.2, 34.C.1, 36.C.1, 37.C.1, 38.C.1, 39.C.2, 41.C.1, 42.C.1, 43.C.1, 44.C.1, 46.C.1, 50.C.1, 51.C.1, 52.C.2, 53.C.1, 54.C.1, 55.C.1, 56.C.1, 57.C.1, 59.C.1, 60.C.1, 61.C.1, 62.C.1, 63.C.1, 64.C.1, 65.C.1, 66.C.1, 67.C.1, 69.C.1, 70.C.1, 71.C.1, 72.C.1, 73.C.1, 77.C.2, 78.C.1, 79.C.3, 81.B.1, 84.B.1, 88.B.1, 89.B.1, 90.B.1, 91.B.1, 95.B.1, 96.B.2, 97.B.1, 98.B.1, 99.B.1, 100.B.1, 101.B.1, 102.B.1, 103.B.1, 107.B.1, 108.B.2, 111.B.1, 119.B.1, 121.B.2, 124.B.1, 127.B.1, 128.B.1, 131.B.1, 132.B.1, 134.B.2, 137.B.1, 138.B.1, 139.B.1, 140.B.1, 141.B.1, 142.B.1, 143.B.1, 146.B.2, 149.B.1, 151.B.1, 152.B.1, 153.B.1 **Decodable Stories** **Independent Readers** **Literature Collection/Guide:** Lessons 5, 15, 20, 25, 30, 35, 40, 45, 50 **Read Aloud Library:** (Week.Day) 1.1, 1.2, 2.1, 2.2, 3.1, 3.2, 4.1, 4.2, 5.1, 5.2, 6.1, 6.2, 7.1, 7.2, 8.1, 8.2, 9.1, 9.2, 10.1, 10.2, 11.1, 11.2, 12.1, 12.2, 13.1, 13.2, 14.1, 14.2, 15.1, 15.2, 16.1, 16.2, 17.1, 17.2, 18.1, 18.2, 19.1, 19.2, 20.1, 20.2, 21.1, 21.2, 22.1, 22.2, 23.1, 23.2, 24.1, 24.2, 25.1, 25.2, 26.1, 26.2, 27.1, 27.2, 28.1, 28.2, 29.1, 29.2, 30.1, 30.2

GRADE 1 STANDARDS		PAGE REFERENCES
RF.1.4c	Use context to confirm or self-correct word recognition and understanding, rereading as necessary.	**Reading Presentation Book A:** (Lesson.Exercise) 1.10–12, 2.12–14, 5.13–15, 6.12–14, 7.12–14, 10.11–13, 11.14–16, 12.12–14, 14.12–14, 15.12–14, 16.11–13, 17.12–14, 19.10–12, 20.11–13, 21.12–14, 22.11–13, 23.13–15, 24.9–11, 25.16–18, 26.12–14, 27.16–18, 28.12–14, 29.14–16, 30.16–18, 31.14–16, 33.14–16, 34.21–23, 35.22–24, 36.20–22, 37.20–22, 38.17–19, 39.18–20, 40.18–20, 41.15–17, 42.10–12, 43.10–12, 44.13–15, 45.15–17, 46.15–17, 48.15–17 **Reading Presentation Book B:** (Lesson.Exercise) 49.14–16, 50.16–18, 51.15–17, 52.15–17, 53.11–13, 54.12–14, 55.12–14, 56.18–20, 57.14–16, 58.11–13, 59.13–15, 60.16–18, 61.16–18, 62.15–17, 63.16–18, 64.15–17, 65.17–19, 66.18–20, 67.13–15, 68.10–12, 69.13–15, 70.9–11, 71.9–11, 72.10–12, 73.8–10, 74.11–13, 75.8–10, 76.7–9, 77.10–12, 78.12–14, 79.11–13, 80.13–15, 81.10, 81.11, 82.10, 82.11, 83.11, 83.12, 84.10, 85.11, 86.9, 87.8, 88.8, 89.10, 90.9, 91.10, 92.9, 93.8, 94.9, 95.5, 96.5, 97.5, 98.5, 98.6, 99.5, 100.5, 101.5, 102.5, 103.5, 104.5, 104.6 **Reading Presentation Book C:** (Lesson.Exercise) 105.5, 106.5, 107.5, 108.5, 109.5, 110.5, 111.5, 112.5, 113.5, 114.5, 115.5, 116.5, 117.5, 118.5, 119.6, 120.5, 121.7, 122.6, 123.6, 124.6, 125.5, 126.6, 127.6, 128.6, 129.6, 130.5, 131.5, 132.6, 133.5, 134.5, 135.4, 136.5, 137.5, 138.5, 139.5, 140.5, 141.5, 142.5, 143.5, 144.5, 145.5, 146.5, 147.5, 148.5, 149.5, 150.5, 151.6, 152.6, 153.6, 154.5, 155.6, 156.6, 157.6, 158.6, 159.6, 160.6 **Storybook 1:** Lessons 1–83 **Storybook 2:** Lessons 84–160 **Core Lesson Connections:** (Lesson.Part.Activity) 1.C.2, 2.C.1, 3.C.2, 4.C.1, 5.C.1, 6.C.2, 7.C.1, 8.C.1, 9.C.1, 1 0.C.1, 11.C.2, 12.C.2, 13.C.1, 14.C.2, 15.C.1, 16.C.1, 19.C.2, 20.C.1, 21.C.2, 23.C.1, 24.C.1, 25.C.1, 26.C.1, 27.C.1, 30.C.1, 31.C.1, 33.C.2, 34.C.1, 36.C.1, 37.C.1, 38.C.1, 39.C.2, 41.C.1, 42.C.1, 43.C.1, 44.C.1, 46.C.1, 50.C.1, 51.C.1, 52.C.2, 53.C.1, 54.C.1, 55.C.1, 56.C.1, 57.C.1, 59.C.1, 60.C.1, 61.C.1, 62.C.1, 63.C.1, 64.C.1, 65.C.1, 66.C.1, 67.C.1, 69.C.1, 70.C.1, 71.C.1, 72.C.1, 73.C.1, 77.C.2, 78.C.1, 79.C.3, 81.B.1, 84.B.1, 88.B.1, 89.B.1, 90.B.1, 91.B.1, 95.B.1, 96.B.2, 97.B.1, 98.B.1, 99.B.1, 100.B.1, 101.B.1, 102.B.1, 103.B.1, 107.B.1, 108.B.2, 111.B.1, 119.B.1, 121.B.2, 124.B.1, 127.B.1, 128.B.1, 131.B.1, 132.B.1, 134.B.2, 137.B.1, 138.B.1, 139.B.1, 140.B.1, 141.B.1, 142.B.1, 143.B.1, 146.B.2, 149.B.1, 151.B.1, 152.B.1, 153.B.1 **Decodable Stories** **Independent Readers** **Literature Collection/Guide:** Lessons 5, 15, 20, 25, 30, 35, 40, 45, 50 **Read Aloud Library:** (Week.Day) 1.1, 1.2, 2.1, 2.2, 3.1, 3.2, 4.1, 4.2, 5.1, 5.2, 6.1, 6.2, 7.1, 7.2, 8.1, 8.2, 9.1, 9.2, 10.1, 10.2, 11.1, 11.2, 12.1, 12.2, 13.1, 13.2, 14.1, 14.2, 15.1, 15.2, 16.1, 16.2, 17.1, 17.2, 18.1, 18.2, 19.1, 19.2, 20.1, 20.2, 21.1, 21.2, 22.1, 22.2, 23.1, 23.2, 24.1, 24.2, 25.1, 25.2, 26.1, 26.2, 27.1, 27.2, 28.1, 28.2, 29.1, 29.2, 30.1, 30.2

Writing Standards: Text Types and Purposes

W.1.1	Write opinion pieces in which they introduce the topic or name the book they are writing about, state an opinion, supply a reason for the opinion, and provide some sense of closure.	**Core Lesson Connections:** (Lesson.Part.Activity) 10.C.3, 20.C.4, 30.C.2, 40.C.4, 50.C.3, 60.C.3, 70.C.2, 80.C.4, 90.B.3, 100.B.3, 110.B.2, 120.B.4, 130.B.3, 140.B.3, 150.B.2, 160.B.4
W.1.2	Write informative/explanatory texts in which they name a topic, supply some facts about the topic, and provide some sense of closure.	**Reading Presentation Book C:** Planning page 153b **Core Lesson Connections:** (Lesson.Part.Activity) 74.C.2, 83.B.2, 94.B.2, 105.B.2, 115.B.2, 130.B.2, 146.B.2, 155.B.2 **Read Aloud Library:** (Week.Day) 14.3, 16.2, 16.3, 17.2, 17.3, 18.2, 18.3, 19.2, 19.3, 20.2, 20.3

GRADE 1 STANDARDS		PAGE REFERENCES
W.1.3	Write narratives in which they recount two or more appropriately sequenced events, include some details regarding what happened, use temporal words to signal event order, and provide some sense of closure.	**Reading Presentation Book A:** Planning page 234b **Reading Presentation Book B:** Planning page 271b **Read Aloud Library:** (Week.Day) 7.4, 11.3, 12.3, 15.3
Writing Standards: Production and Distribution of Writing		
W.1.4	*(Begins in Grade 3)*	
W.1.5	With guidance and support from adults, focus on a topic, respond to questions and suggestions from peers, and add details to strengthen writing as needed.	**Reading Presentation Book A:** Planning page 234b **Reading Presentation Book B:** Planning page 277b **Read Aloud Library:** (Week.Day) 4.3, 5.3, 6.3, 7.3, 7.4, 8.3, 9.3, 10.3, 11.3, 12.3, 13.3, 14.3, 15.3, 16.5, 17.5, 18.5, 19.5, 20.5, 21.5, 22.5, 23.5, 24.5, 25.5, 26.4, 26.5, 27.4, 27.5, 28.4, 28.5, 29.4, 29.5, 30.4, 30.5
W.1.6	With guidance and support from adults, use a variety of digital tools to produce and publish writing, including in collaboration with peers.	**Student Practice CD**
Writing Standards: Research to Build and Present Knowledge		
W.1.7	Participate in shared research and writing projects (e.g., explore a number of "how-to" books on a given topic and use them to write a sequence of instructions).	**Read Aloud Library:** (Week.Day) 16.3, 16.4, 17.3, 17.4, 18.3, 18.4, 19.3, 19.4, 20.3, 20.4, 21.3, 21.4, 22.3, 22.4, 23.3, 23.4, 24.3, 24.4, 25.3, 25.4
W.1.8	With guidance and support from adults, recall information from experiences or gather information from provided sources to answer a question.	**Read Aloud Library:** (Week.Day) 16.3, 16.4, 17.3, 17.4, 18.3, 18.4, 19.3, 19.4, 20.3, 20.4, 21.3, 21.4, 22.3, 22.4, 23.3, 23.4, 24.3, 24.4, 25.3, 25.4
W.1.9	*(Begins in Grade 4)*	
Writing Standards: Range of Writing		
W.1.10	*(Begins in Grade 3)*	
Speaking & Listening Standards: Comprehension and Collaboration		
SL.1.1	Participate in collaborative conversations with diverse partners about *grade 1 topics and texts* with peers and adults in small and larger groups.	

GRADE 1 STANDARDS		PAGE REFERENCES
SL.1.1a	Follow agreed-upon rules for discussions (e.g., listening to others with care, speaking one at a time about the topics and texts under discussion).	**Reading Presentation Book A:** Planning pages vb, 111b, 234b **Reading Presentation Book B:** Planning pages 67b, 171b, 277b **Reading Presentation Book C:** Planning pages 64b, 153b **Read Aloud Library:** (Week.Day) 1.2, 2.2, 3.2, 4.2, 5.2, 6.2, 7.2, 8.2, 9.2, 10.2, 11.2, 12.2, 13.2, 14.2, 15.2, 16.2, 17.2, 18.2, 19.2, 20.2, 21.2, 22.2, 23.2, 24.2, 25.2, 26.2, 27.2, 28.2, 29.2, 30.2
SL.1.1b	Build on others' talk in conversations by responding to the comments of others through multiple exchanges.	**Reading Presentation Book A:** (Lesson.Exercise) 1.10–13, 2.12–15, 5.13–16, 6.12–15, 7.12–15, 10.11–14, 11.14–17, 12.12–15, 14.12–15, 15.12–15, 16.11–14, 17.12–15, 19.10–13, 20.11–14, 21.12–14, 22.11–14, 23.13–16, 24.9–12, 25.16–19, 26.12–15, 27.16–19, 28.12–15, 29.14–17, 30.16–19, 31.14–17, 33.14–17, 34.21–24, 35.22–25, 36.20–23, 37.20–23, 38.17–20, 39.18–21, 40.18–21, 41.15–18, 42.10–13, 43.10–13, 44.13–16, 45.16–18, 46.15–18, 48.15–18; Planning pages vb, 111b, 234b **Reading Presentation Book B:** (Lesson.Exercise) 49.14–17, 50.16–19, 51.15–18, 52.15–18, 53.11–14, 54.12–15, 55.12–15, 56.18–21, 57.14–17, 58.11–14, 59.13–16, 60.16–19, 61.16–19, 62.15–18, 63.16–19, 64.15–18, 65.17–20, 66.18–21, 67.13–16, 68.10–13, 69.13–16, 70.9–12, 71.9–12, 72.10–13, 73.8–11, 74.11–14, 75.8–11, 76.7–10, 77.10–13, 78.12–15, 79.11–14, 80.13–16, 781.10–12, 82.10–12, 83.11–13, 84.10, 84.11, 85.11, 85.12, 86.9, 86.10, 87.8, 87.8, 88.8, 88.9, 89.10, 89.11, 90.9, 90.10, 91.10, 91.11, 92.9, 92.10, 93.8, 93.9, 94.9, 94.10, 95.5, 95.6, 96.5, 96.6, 97.5, 97.6, 98.6, 98.7, 99.5, 99.6, 100.5, 100.6, 101.5, 101.6, 102.5, 102.6, 103.5, 103.6, 104.6, 104.7; Planning pages 67b, 171b, 277b **Reading Presentation Book C:** (Lesson.Exercise) 105.5, 105.6, 106.5, 106.6, 107.5, 107.6, 108.5, 108.6, 109.5, 109.6, 110.5, 110.6, 111.5, 111.6, 112.5, 112.6, 113.5, 113.6, 114.5, 114.6, 115.5, 115.6, 116.5, 116.6, 117.5, 117.6, 118.5, 118.6, 119.6, 119.7, 120.5, 120.6, 121.7, 121.8, 122.6, 122.7, 123.6, 123.7, 124.6, 124.7, 125.5, 125.6, 126.6, 126.7, 127.6, 127.7, 128.6, 128.7, 129.6, 129.7, 130.5, 130.6, 131.5, 131.6, 132.6, 132.7, 133.5, 133.6, 134.5, 134.6, 135.4, 135.5, 1366.5, 136.6, 137.5, 137.6, 138.5, 138.6, 139.5, 139.6, 140.5, 140.6, 141.5, 141.6, 142.5, 142.6, 143.5, 143.6, 144.5, 144.6, 145.5, 145.6, 146.5, 146.6, 147.5, 147.6, 148.5, 148.6, 149.5, 149.6, 150.6, 150.7, 151.6, 151.7, 152.6, 152.7, 153.6, 153.7, 154.5, 154.6, 155.6, 155.7, 156.6, 156.7, 157.6, 157.7, 58.6, 158.7, 159.6, 159.7, 160.6, 160.7; Planning pages 64b, 153b **Language Presentation Book A:** (Lesson.Exercise) 1.5, 2.7, 3.7, 4.7, 5.7, 6.8, 8.7, 9.9, 10.7, 12.8, 15.7, 21.9, 22.8, 25.7, 28.7, 30.7, 31.6, 33.6, 34.6, 38.8, 41.7, 42.9, 43.7, 44.7, 45.8, 47.10, 49.9, 52.7, 54.5, 56.7, 58.6, 59.8, 60.6 **Language Presentation Book B:** (Lesson.Exercise) 62.6, 63.6, 65.7, 66.5, 68.6, 77.9, 79.9, 82.6 **Literature Collection/Guide:** Lessons 5, 15, 20, 25, 30, 35, 40, 45, 50 **Read Aloud Library:** (Week.Day) 1.1, 1.2, 1.5, 2.1, 2.2, 2.5, 3.1, 3.2, 3.5, 4.1, 4.2, 4.5, 5.1, 5.2, 5.5, 6.1, 6.2, 6.5, 7.1, 7.2, 7.5, 8.1, 8.2, 8.5, 9.1, 9.2, 9.5, 10.1, 10.2, 10.5, 11.1, 11.2, 11.5, 12.1, 12.2, 12.5, 13.1, 13.2, 13.5, 14.1, 14.2, 14.5, 15.1, 15.2, 15.5, 16.1, 16.2, 16.4, 16.5, 17.1, 17.2, 17.4, 17.5, 18.1, 18.2, 18.4, 18.5, 19.1, 19.2, 19.4, 19.5, 20.1, 20.2, 20.4, 20.5, 21.1, 21.2, 21.4, 21.5, 22.1, 22.2, 22.4, 22.5, 23.1, 23.2, 23.4, 23.5, 24.1, 24.2, 24.4, 24.5, 25.1, 25.2, 25.4, 25.5, 26.1, 26.2, 26.5, 27.,1, 27.2, 27.5, 28.1, 28.2, 28.5, 29.1, 29.2, 29.5, 30.1, 30.2, 30.5

GRADE 1 STANDARDS		PAGE REFERENCES
SL.1.1c	Ask questions to clear up any confusion about the topics and texts under discussion.	**Reading Presentation Book A:** Planning page vb **Reading Presentation Book B:** Planning page 271b **Language Presentation Book A:** (Lesson.Exercise) 7.7, 8.8, 9.10, 11.8, 13.8, 14.7, 16.9, 17.8, 17.11, 18.7, 18.8, 19.5, 19.8, 20.8, 21.7, 21.9, 21.11, 23.8, 24.7, 26.7, 27.8, 29.5, 29.8, 32.7, 35.3, 36.8, 37.8, 39.5, 46.8, 48.11 **Language Presentation Book B:** (Lesson.Exercise) 67.6, 71.6, 74.6, 76.2, 85.10 **Language Workbook:** (Lesson.Exercise) 7, 8, 9, 11, 13, 14, 16, 17, 18, 19, 20, 21, 23, 24, 26, 27, 29, 32, 36, 37, 46, 48, 67, 71, 74, 85 **Core Lesson Connections:** (Lesson.Part.Activity) 24.C.2, 25.C.1, 26.C.1, 32.C.2, 34.C.2, 35.C.1, 36.C.1, 37.C.1, 38.C.1, 40.C.2, 44.C.1, 55.C.1, 57.C.1, 78.C.1, 80.C.2, 82.B.1, 86.B.1, 92.B.1, 93.B.1, 107.B.1, 114.B.1, 116.B.1, 120.B.2, 122.B.1, 129.B.2, 131.B.1, 145.B.1, 152.B.1, 154.B.1, 160.B.2 **Read Aloud Library:** (Week.Day) 1.1, 2.1, 3.1, 4.1, 5.1, 6.1, 7.1, 8.1, 9.1, 10.1, 11.1, 12.1, 13.1, 14.1, 15.1, 16.1, 17.1, 18.1, 19.1, 20.1, 21.1, 22.1, 23.1, 24.1, 25.1, 26.1, 27.1, 28.1, 29.1, 30.1
SL.1.2	Ask and answer questions about key details in a text read aloud or information presented orally or through other media.	**Reading Presentation Book A:** (Lesson.Exercise) 1.12, 2.14, 5.15, 6.14, 7.14, 10.13, 11.16, 12.14, 14.14, 15.14, 16.13, 17.14, 19.11, 19.12, 20.12, 20.13, 21.13, 21.14, 22.12, 22.13, 23.14, 23.15, 24.10, 24.11, 25.17, 25.18, 26.13, 26.14, 27.17, 27.18, 28.13, 28.14, 29.16, 29.17, 30.17, 30.18, 31.15, 31.16, 33.15, 33.16, 34.23, 35.24, 36.22, 37.22, 38.19, 39.20, 40.20, 42.12, 43.12, 44.15, 45.17, 46.17, 47.7, 48.12; Planning page 234b **Reading Presentation Book B:** (Lesson.Exercise) 49.15, 49.16, 50.18, 51.17, 52.16, 52.17, 53.12, 53.13, 54.14, 55.13, 55.14, 56.20, 57.16, 58.12, 58.13, 59.15, 60.18, 62.17, 63.18, 64.17, 65.19, 66.20, 67.15, 68.12, 69.14, 69.15, 70.11, 71.11, 62.12, 73.10, 74.14, 75.10, 76.9, 77.12, 78.14, 79.13, 80.15, 81.11, 82.11, 83.12, 84.15, 85.11, 86.9, 87.8, 88.8, 89.10, 90.9, 91.10, 92.9, 93.8, 94.9, 95.5, 96.5, 97.5, 98.6, 99.5, 100.5, 101.5, 102.5, 103.5, 104.6 **Reading Presentation Book C:** (Lesson.Exercise) 105.5, 106.5, 107.5, 108.5, 109.5, 110.5, 111.5, 112.5, 113.5, 114.5, 115.5, 116.5, 117.5, 118.5, 119.6, 120.5, 121.7, 122.6, 123.6, 124.6, 125.5, 126.6, 127.5, 128.6, 129.6, 130.5, 131.5, 132.6, 133.5, 134.5, 135.4, 136.5, 137.5, 138.5, 139.5, 140.5, 141.5, 142.5, 143.5, 144.5, 145.5, 146.5, 147.5, 149.5, 149.5, 150.6, 151.6, 152.6, 153.6, 154.5, 155.6, 156.6, 157.6, 158.6, 159.6, 160.6 **Storybook 1:** Lessons 1–83 **Storybook 2:** Lessons 84–160 **Language Presentation Book A:** (Lesson.Exercise) 1.6, 2.8, 3.8, 4.8, 5.8, 6.9, 7.7, 8.8, 9.10, 11.8, 12.9, 13.8, 14.7, 15.8, 16.9, 17.11, 18.8, 19.8, 20.8, 21.10, 22.9, 23.8, 24.7, 25.8, 26.7, 27.8, 28.8, 29.8, 31.7, 32.7, 33.7, 35.6, 36.8, 37.8, 38.9, 30.5, 41.8, 44.8, 45.8, 46.8, 48.11, 54.6 **Language Presentation Book B:** (Lesson.Exercise) 62.7, 67.6, 69.8, 71.6, 77.11, 79.11, 85.10 **Core Lesson Connections:** (Lesson.Part.Activity) 6.C.2, 7.C.2, 8.C.2, 9.C.2, 10.C.2, 11.C.3, 12.C.3, 13.C.2, 15.C.2, 17.C.1, 18.C.1, 19.C.3, 20.C., 21.C.2, 24.C.2, 25.C.1, 26.C.1, 28.C.1, 31.C.2, 32.C.2, 33.C.3, 34.C.2, 34.C.3, 35.C.1, 36.C.1, 37.C.1, 38.C.1, 38.C.2, 39.C.2, 42.C.2, 43.C.2, 44.C.1, 44.C.2, 45.C.1, 46.C.1, 46.C.2, 47.C.2, 49.C.2, 52.C.1, 53.C.1, 55.C.1, 57.C.1, 58.C.1, 59.C.1, 61.C.1, 61.C.2, 65.C.1, 65.C.2, 68.C.2, 69.C.1, 69.C.2, 71.C.1, 72.C.1, 76.C.1, 78.C.1, 79.C.2, 85.B.2, 86.B.1, 88.B.2, 91.B.2, 92.B.1, 95.B.1, 97.B.2, 98.B.1, 99.B.1, 103.B.1, 106.B.1, 107.B.1, 112.B.1, 116.B.1, 119.B.1, 122.B.1, 123.B.2, 131.B.1, 138.B.1, 139.B.1, 140.B.1, 142.B.1, 144.B.1, 152.B.1, 153.B.1 **Literature Guide:** Lessons 5, 15, 20, 25, 30, 35, 40, 45, 50 **Read Aloud Library:** (Week.Day) 1.1, 1.2, 2.1, 2.2, 3.1, 3.2, 4.1, 4.2, 5.1, 5.2, 6.1, 6.2, 7.1, .2, 8.1, 8.2, 9.1, 9.2, 10.1, 10.2, 11.1, 11.2, 12.1, 12.2, 13.1, 13.2, 14.1, 14.2, 15.1, 15.2, 26.1, 26.2, 27.1, 27.2, 28.1, 28.2, 29.1, 29.2, 30.1, 30.2

GRADE 1 STANDARDS		PAGE REFERENCES
SL.1.3	Ask and answer questions about what a speaker says in order to gather additional information or clarify something that is not understood.	**Read Aloud Library:** (Week.Day) 1.1, 1.2, 2.1, 2.2, 3.1, 3.2, 4.1, 4.2, 5.1, 5.2, 6.1, 6.2, 7.1, 7.2, 8.1, 8.2, 9.1, 9.2, 10.1, 10.2, 11.1, 11.2, 12.1, 12.2, 13.1, 13.2, 14.1, 14.2, 15.1, 15.2, 16.1, 16.2, 17.1, 17.2, 18.1, 18.2, 19.1, 19.2, 20.1, 20.2, 21.1, 21.2, 22.1, 22.2, 23.1, 23.2, 24.1, 24.2, 25.1, 25.2, 26.1, 26.2, 27.1, 27.2, 28.1, 28.2, 29.1, 29.2, 30.1, 30.2
Speaking & Listening Standards: Presentation of Knowledge and Ideas		
SL.1.4	Describe people, places, things, and events with relevant details, expressing ideas and feelings clearly.	**Read Aloud Library:** (Week.Day) 26.4, 26.5, 27.3, 27.4, 27.5, 28.4, 28.5, 29.4, 29.5, 30.3, 30.5
SL.1.5	Add drawings or other visual displays to descriptions when appropriate to clarify ideas, thoughts, and feelings.	**Read Aloud Library:** (Week.Day) 16.3, 16.4, 17.3, 17.4, 18.3, 18.4, 19.3, 19.4, 20.3, 20.4, 21.3, 21.4, 22.3, 22.4, 23.3, 23.4, 24.3, 24.4, 25.3, 25.4
SL.1.6	Produce complete sentences when appropriate to task and situation.	**Reading Presentation Book B:** Planning page 271b **Reading Presentation Book C:** Planning pages 64b, 153b **Language Presentation Book A:** (Lesson.Exercise) 39.6, 40.9, 60.7 **Language Presentation Book B:** (Lesson.Exercise) 62.6, 63.6, 67.7, 69.7, 75.9, 75.10, 79.9, 79.10, 130.6 **Read Aloud Library:** (Week.Day) 26.5, 27.5, 28.5, 29.5, 30.5
Language Standards: Conventions of Standard English		
L.1.1	Demonstrate command of the conventions of standard English grammar and usage when writing or speaking.	
L.1.1a	Print all upper- and lowercase letters.	**Reading Presentation Book A:** Planning pages vb, 234b **Reading Presentation Book B:** Planning page 271b **Language Presentation Book A:** (Lesson.Exercise) 51.8, 53.8, 55.6, 58.7, 59.9, 60.8 **Language Presentation Book B:** (Lesson.Exercise) 61.6, 64.6, 65.8, 66.6, 68.7, 73.6, 74.7, 75.7, 76.6, 77.8, 80.7, 81.8, 83.8, 84.5, 86.9, 87.6, 88.6, 89.8, 90.6, 91.7, 92.6, 93.6, 94.7, 96.7, 98.7, 99.8, 100.7, 101.7, 102.6, 103.6, 104.6, 105.6, 106.6, 107.6, 108.6, 109.7, 110.6, 111.6, 112.6, 113.6, 114.7, 115.6, 116.6, 117.6, 118.7, 119.7, 120.6, 121.56, 122.6, 123.6, 124.5, 125.5, 126.5, 127.5, 128.6, 129.6, 130.6 **Language Workbook:** (Lesson.Exercise) 51, 53, 55, 58, 59, 60, 61, 64, 65, 66, 68, 73, 74, 75, 76, 77, 80, 81, 83, 84, 86, 87, 88, 89, 90, 91, 92, 93, 94, 96, 98–130 **Seatwork Blackline Master Book:** Lessons 2, 4, 8, 9, 12, 14, 18, 19, 20, 22, 24, 28, 29, 32, 34, 38, 39, 42, 44, 49, 53, 55, 57, 60, 61, 62, 65, 71, 74, 75, 81, 83, 85, 91, 105, 113, 129, 145 **Spelling Teacher Presentation Book:** Lessons 1–160 **Read Aloud Library:** (Week.Day) 16.5, 17.5, 18.5, 19.5, 20.5, 21.5, 22.5, 23.5, 24.5, 25.5, 26.5, 27.5, 28.5, 29.5, 30.5
L.1.1b	Use common, proper, and possessive nouns.	**Core Lesson Connections:** (Lesson.Part.Activity) 15.E.1, 25.E.1, 35.E.1, 45.E.1, 55.E.1, 65.E.1, 75.E.1, 85.D.1, 95.D.1, 105.D.1, 115.D.1, 125.D.1, 135.D.1, 145.D.1, 155.D.1

	GRADE 1 STANDARDS	PAGE REFERENCES
L.1.1c	Use singular and plural nouns with matching verbs in basic sentences (e.g., He hops; We hop).	**Reading Presentation Book B:** Planning page 271b **Reading Presentation Book C:** Planning pages 64b, 153b **Language Presentation Book A:** (Lesson.Exercise) 39.6, 40.9, 60.7 **Language Presentation Book B:** (Lesson.Exercise) 62.6, 63.6, 67.7, 69.7, 75.9, 75.10, 79.9, 79.10, 130.6 **Seatwork Blackline Master Book:** Lessons 55, 63, 74, 83, 91 **Read Aloud Library:** (Week.Day) 26.5, 27.5, 28.5, 29.5, 30.5
L.1.1d	Use personal, possessive, and indefinite pronouns (e.g., I, me, my; they, them, their, anyone, everything).	**Core Lesson Connections:** (Lesson.Part.Activity) 15.E.1, 25.E.1, 35.E.1, 45.E.1, 55.E.1, 65.E.1, 75.E.1, 85.D.1, 95.D.1, 105.D.1, 115.D.1, 125.D.1, 135.D.1, 145.D.1, 155.D.1
L.1.1e	Use verbs to convey a sense of past, present, and future (e.g., Yesterday I walked home; Today I walk home; Tomorrow I will walk home).	**Language Presentation Book A:** (Lesson.Exercise) 43.5, 48.3, 51.6, 59.2 **Language Presentation Book B:** (Lesson.Exercise) 98.5, 101.3, 102.5, 109.3, 110.3, 112.4, 119.2, 121.1, 122.2, 123.1, 124.2, 128.1, 130.3
L.1.1f	Use frequently occurring adjectives.	**Read Aloud Library:** (Week.Day) 9.3, 15.3
L.1.1g	Use frequently occurring conjunctions (e.g., *and, but, or, so, because*).	**Core Lesson Connections:** (Lesson.Part.Activity) 15.E.1, 25.E.1, 35.E.1, 45.E.1, 55.E.1, 65.E.1, 75.E.1, 85.D.1, 95.D.1, 105.D.1, 115.D.1, 125.D.1, 135.D.1, 145.D.1, 155.D.1
L.1.1h	Use determiners (e.g., articles, demonstratives).	**Core Lesson Connections:** (Lesson.Part.Activity) 15.E.1, 25.E.1, 35.E.1, 45.E.1, 55.E.1, 65.E.1, 75.E.1, 85.D.1, 95.D.1, 105.D.1, 115.D.1, 125.D.1, 135.D.1, 145.D.1, 155.D.1
L.1.1i	Use frequently occurring prepositions (e.g., *during, beyond, toward*).	**Core Lesson Connections:** (Lesson.Part.Activity) 15.E.1, 25.E.1, 35.E.1, 45.E.1, 55.E.1, 65.E.1, 75.E.1, 85.D.1, 95.D.1, 105.D.1, 115.D.1, 125.D.1, 135.D.1, 145.D.1, 155.D.1
L.1.1j	Produce and expand complete simple and compound declarative, interrogative, imperative, and exclamatory sentences in response to prompts.	**Reading Presentation Book A:** Planning page vb **Reading Presentation Book B:** Planning page 277b **Reading Presentation Book C:** Planning page 153b **Language Presentation Book A:** (Lesson.Exercise) 51.8, 53.8, 55.6 **Language Presentation Book B:** (Lesson.Exercise) 61.6, 64.6, 72.6, 74.7, 75.7, 76.8, 78.8, 80.7, 81.8, 83.8, 84.5, 86.9, 87.6, 88.6, 89.8, 90.6, 91.7, 92.6, 93.6, 94.7, 95.7, 96.7, 98.7, 99.8, 100.7, 101.7, 102.6, 103.6, 104.6, 105.6, 106.6, 07.6, 108.6, 109.7, 110.6, 111.6, 112.6, 113.6, 114.7, 115.6, 116.6, 117.6, 118.7, 119.7, 120.6, 121.5, 122.6, 123.6, 124.5, 125.5, 126.5, 127.7, 128.6, 129.6, 130.6 **Language Workbook:** (Lesson.Exercise) 51, 53, 55, 61, 64, 72, 74, 75, 76, 78, 80, 81, 83, 84, 86, 87, 88, 89, 90, 91, 92, 93, 94, 95, 96, 98–130 **Seatwork Blackline Master Book:** Lessons 2, 12, 22, 32, 42, 55, 63, 74, 83, 91 **Read Aloud Library:** (Week.Day) 1.3, 2.3, 3.3, 4.3, 5.3, 9.3, 11.3, 12.3, 13.3, 14.3, 15.3, 16.5, 17.5, 18.5, 19.5, 20.5, 21.5, 22.5, 23.5, 24.5, 25.5, 26.5, 27.5, 28.5, 29.5, 30.5
L.1.2	Demonstrate command of the conventions of standard English capitalization, punctuation, and spelling when writing.	
L.1.2a	Capitalize dates and names of people.	**Language Presentation Book B:** (Lesson.Exercise) 80.7, 81.8, 83.8, 84.5, 86.9, 87.6, 88.6, 89.8, 90.6, 91.7, 92.6, 93.6, 94.7, 96.7, 98.7, 99.8, 100.7, 101.7, 102.6, 103.6, 104.6, 105.6, 106.6, 107.6, 108.6, 109.7, 110.6, 111.6, 112.6, 113.6, 114.7, 115.6, 116.6, 117.6, 118.7, 119.7, 120.6, 121.5, 122.6, 123.6, 124.5, 125.5, 126.5, 127.6, 128.6, 129.6, 130.6

GRADE 1 STANDARDS		PAGE REFERENCES
L.1.2b	Use end punctuation for sentences.	**Language Presentation Book B:** (Lesson.Exercise) 80.7, 81.8, 83.8, 84.5, 86.9, 87.6, 88.6, 89.8, 90.6, 91.7, 92.6, 93.6, 94.7, 96.7, 98.7, 99.8, 100.7, 101.7, 102.6, 103.6, 104.6, 105.6, 106.6, 107.6, 108.6, 109.7, 110.6, 111.6, 112.6, 113.6, 114.7, 115.6, 116.6, 117.6, 118.7, 119.7, 120.6, 121.5, 122.6, 123.6, 124.5, 125.5, 126.5, 127.6, 128.6, 129.6, 130.6 **Spelling Teacher Presentation Book:** (Lesson.Exercise) 21.5, 22.4, 23.5, 24.7, 25.7, 26.6, 27.6, 28.5, 29.6, 30.5, 31.5, 332.6, 33.7, 34.4, 35.5, 36.3, 37.3, 38.3, 39.4, 40.5, 41.2, 42.3, 43.3, 44.4, 45.4, 46.3, 47.3, 48.3, 49.3, 50.4, 51.5, 52.5, 53.5, 54.5, 55.3, 56.4, 57.5, 58.4, 59.4, 60.5, 61.5, 62.5, 63.6, 64.4, 65.3, 66.4, 67.5, 68.5, 69.5, 70.5, 71.4, 72.4, 73.4, 74.3, 75.3, 76.3, 77.4, 78.5, 79.5, 80.4, 81.4, 82.4, 83.4, 84.4, 85.4, 86.4, 87.4, 88.4, 89.4, 90.4, 91.4, 92.4, 93.4, 94.4, 102.2, 112.3, 113.3, 115.3, 116.3, 119.3, 120.4, 126.3, 127.3, 130.3, 131.3, 135.3, 137.1, 137.3, 139.3, 140.3, 141.3, 142.3, 144.3, 146.3, 139.3, 151.3, 152.3, 153.3, 157.3, 158.3, 160.2
L.1.2c	Use commas in dates and to separate single words in a series.	**Core Lesson Connections:** (Lesson.Part.Activity) 15.E.1, 25.E.1, 35.E.1, 45.E.1, 55.E.1, 65.E.1, 75.E.1, 85.D.1, 95.D.1, 105.D.1, 115.D.1, 125.D.1, 135.D.1, 145.D.1, 155.D.1
L.1.2d	Use conventional spelling for words with common spelling patterns and for frequently occurring irregular words.	**Reading Presentation Book A:** Planning pages vb, 234b **Reading Presentation Book B:** Planning page 271b **Spelling Teacher Presentation Book:** Lessons 1–160 **Read Aloud Library:** (Week.Day) 16.5, 17.5, 18.5, 19.5, 20.5, 21.5, 22.5, 23.5, 24.5, 25.5, 26.5, 27.5, 28.5, 29.5, 30.5
L.1.2e	Spell untaught words phonetically, drawing on phonemic awareness and spelling conventions.	**Reading Presentation Book A:** Planning pages vb, 234b **Reading Presentation Book B:** Planning page 271b **Spelling Teacher Presentation Book:** Lessons 1–160 **Read Aloud Library:** (Week.Day) 16.5, 17.5, 18.5, 19.5, 20.5, 21.5, 22.5, 23.5, 24.5, 25.5, 26.5, 27.5, 28.5, 29.5, 30.5
Language Standards: Knowledge of Language		
L.1.3	*(Begins in Grade 2)*	
Language Standards: Vocabulary Acquisition and Use		
L.1.4	Determine or clarify the meaning of unknown and multiple-meaning words and phrases based on *grade 1 reading and content*, choosing flexibly from an array of strategies.	

GRADE 1 STANDARDS		PAGE REFERENCES
L.1.4a	Use sentence-level context as a clue to the meaning of a word or phrase.	**Language Presentation Book A:** (Lesson.Exercise) 49.11, 50.10, 52.10, 57.9 **Language Presentation Book B:** (Lesson.Exercise) 61.8, 62.9, 65.6, 66.2, 67.5, 68.5, 68.9, 69.6, 70.1, 70.8, 71.1, 72.1, 73.2, 74.1, 75.1, 76.5, 76,10, 77.4, 78.3, 79.1, 80.1, 80.9, 81.2, 81.10, 82.1, 82.15, 83.1, 83.10, 84.3, 86.1, 87.1, 88.1, 88.5, 89.9, 90.4, 91.4, 93.1, 93.4, 94.4, 95.1, 96.1, 97.5, 98.1, 98.3, 98.9, 99.4, 100.2, 101.1, 102.1, 103.1, 103.7, 104.2, 105.1, 106.1, 106.7, 107.7, 108.1, 109.1, 110.5, 111.6, 113.7, 119.9, 121.7, 124.7, 129.7 **Language Workbook:** (Lesson.Exercise) 49, 50, 52, 57, 61, 62, 68, 70, 76, 80, 81, 83, 89, 98, 103, 106, 107, 111, 113, 119, 121, 124, 129 **Core Lesson Connections:** (Lesson.Part.Activity) 1.B.1, 2.B.1, 2.B.2, 3.B.1,3.B.2, 4.B.1, 4.B.2, 5.B.1, 6.B.1, 6.B.2, 7.B.1, 7.B.2, 8.B.1, 8.B.2, 9.B.1, 9.B.2, 10.B.1, 11.B.1, 11.B.2, 12.B.1, 12.B.2, 13.B.1, 13.B.2, 14.B.1, 14.B.2, 15.B.1, 16.B.1, 16.B.2, 17.B.1, 17.B.2, 18.B.1, 18.B.2, 19.B.1, 19.B.2, 20.B.1, 21.B.1, 21.B.2, 22.B.1, 22.B.2, 23.B.1, 23.B.2, 24.B.1, 24.B.2, 25.B.1, 26.B.1, 26.B.2, 27.B.1, 27.B.2, 28.B.1, 28.B.2, 29.B.1, 29.B.2, 30.B.1, 31.B.1, 31.B.2, 32.B.1, 32.B.2, 33.B.1, 33.B.2, 34.B.1, 34.B.2, 35.B.1, 36.B,1, 36.B.2, 37.B.1, 37.B.2, 38.B.1, 38.B.2, 39.B.1, 39.B.2, 40.B.1, 41.B.1, 41.B.2, 42.B.1, 42.B.2, 43.B.1, 43.B.2, 44.B.1, 44.B.2, 45.B.1, 46.B.1, 46.B.2, 47.B.1, 47.B.2, 48.B.1, 48.B.2, 49.B.1, 49.B.2, 50.B.1, 51.B.1, 51.B.2, 52.B.1, 52.B.2, 53.B.1, 53.B.1, 54.B.1, 54.B.2, 55.B.1, 56.B.1, 56.B.2, 57.B.1, 57.B.2, 58.B.1, 58.B.2, 59.B.1, 59.B.2, 60.B.1, 61.B.1, 61.B.2, 62.B.1, 62.B.2, 63.B.1, 63.B.2, 64.B.1, 64.B.2, 65.B.1, 66.B.1, 66.B.2, 67.B.1, 67.B.2, 68.B.1, 68.B.2, 69.B.1, 69.B.1, 70.B.1, 71.B.1, 71.B.2, 72.B.1, 72.B.2, 73.B.1, 73.B.2, 74.B.1, 74.B.2, 75.B.1, 76.B.1, 76.B.2, 77.B.1, 77.B.2, 78.B.1, 78.B.1, 79.B.1, 79.B.2, 80.B.1, 81.A.1, 81.A.2, 82.A.1, 82.A.2, 83.A.1, 83.A.2, 84.A.1, 84.A.2, 85.A.1, 86.A.1, 86.A.2, 87.A.1, 87.A.2, 88.A.1, 88.A.2, 89.A.1, 89.A.2, 90.A.1, 91.A.1, 91.A.2, 92.A.1, 92.A.2, 93.A.1, 93.A.2, 94.A.1, 94.A.2, 95.A.1, 96.A.1, 96.A.2, 97.A.1, 97.A.2, 98.A.1, 98.A.2, 99.A.1, 99.A.2, 100.A.1, 101.A.1, 101.A.2, 102.A.1, 102.A,2, 103.A.1, 103.A.2, 104.A.1, 104.A.2, 105.A.1, 106.A.1, 106.A.2, 107.A.1, 107.A.2, 108.A,1, 109.A,1, 109.A.2, 110.A.1, 111.A.1, 111.A.2, 112.A.1, 112.A.2, 113.A.1, 113.A.2, 114.A.1, 114.A.2, 115.A.1, 116.A.1, 116.A.2, 117.A.1, 117.A.2, 118.A.1, 118.A.2, 119.A.1, 119.A.2, 120.A.1, 121.A.1, 121.A.2, 122.A.1, 122.A.2, 123.A,1, 123.A.2, 124.A.1, 124.A.2, 125.A.1, 126.A.1, 126.A.2, 127.A.1, 127.A.2, 128.A.1, 128.A.2, 129.A.1, 129.A.2, 130.A.1, 131.A.1, 131.A.2, 132.A.1, 132.A.2, 133.A.1, 133.A.2, 134.A.1, 134.A.2, 135.A.1, 136.A.1, 136.A.2, 137.A.1, 137.A.2, 138.A.1, 138.A.2, 139.A.1, 139.A.2, 140.A.1, 141.A.1, 141.A.2, 142.A.1, 143.A.1, 143.A.2, 144.A.1, 144.A.2, 145.A.1, 146.A.1, 146.A.2, 147.A.1, 147.A.2, 148.A.1, 148.A.2, 149.A.1, 149.A.2, 150.A.1, 151.A.1, 151.A.2, 152.A.1, 152.A.2, 153.A.1, 153.A.2, 154.A.1, 154.A.2, 155.A.1, 156.A.1, 156.A.2, 157.A.1, 157.A.2, 158.A.1, 158.A.2, 159.A.1, 159.A.2, 160.A.1 **Read Aloud Library:** (Week.Day) 1.1–5, 2.1–5, 3.1–5, 4.1–5, 5.1–5, 6.1–5, 7.1–5, 8.1–5, 9.1–5, 10.1–5, 11.1–5, 12.1–5, 13.1–5, 14.1–5, 15.1–5, 16.1–5, 17.1–5, 18.1–5, 19.1–5, 20.1–5, 21.1–5, 22.1–5, 23.1–5, 24.1–5, 25.1–5, 26.1–5, 27.1–5, 28.1–5, 29.1–5, 30.1–5
L.1.4b	Use frequently occurring affixes as a clue to the meaning of a word.	**Core Lesson Connections:** (Lesson.Part.Activity) 41.B.1, 42.B.2, 74.B.1, 75.B.1, 89.A.1, 90.A.1 **Spelling Teacher Presentation Book:** Lessons 126.1, 127.1, 137.2, 138.2, 139.2, 147.2, 148.1, 149.2

GRADE 1 STANDARDS		PAGE REFERENCES
L.1.4c	Identify frequently occurring root words (e.g., *look*) and their inflectional forms (e.g., *looks, looked, looking*).	**Reading Presentation Book A:** (Lesson.Exercise) 5.4, 5.5, 6.9, 7.8, 10.3, 10.10, 11.5, 11.9, 11.13, 12.2–4, 12.6, 12.7, 12.10, 12.11, 13.3, 14.4, 14.7, 17.7, 18.3, 19.3–7, 20.2, 20.6, 21.2, 21.5, 22.5, 22.7, 23.3, 23.7, 24.2, 24.3, 24.5, 25.3, 25.7–10, 25.13, 26.2, 26.5, 26.6, 26.9, 27.3, 27.11, 28.5, 28.6, 31.5, 33.7, 34.1, 34.3, 35.7, 35.8, 35.11, 36.1, 36.3, 37.2, 37.6, 36.10, 38.2, 38.3, 38.12, 39.7, 40.2, 40.7, 41.5, 41.6, 42.5, 42.6, 43.5–7, 44.6, 45.3, 45.5, 46.6–8, 48.9 **Reading Presentation Book B:** (Lesson.Exercise) 49.7, 49.12, 50.10, 51.14, 52.7, 52.8, 52.10, 52.11, 53.5, 54.3, 54.4, 55.1, 55.2, 55.9, 55.11, 56.1–3, 56.12, 57.8, 58.1, 58.9, 60.9, 60.15, 61.1, 61.3, 61.10, 61.14, 61.15, 62.9, 62.13, 63.5, 63.9–14, 64.5, 64.7, 64.9, 64.13, 65.5, 65.12, 65.13, 65.15, 66.8, 66.16, 67.7, 67.9, 67.10, 68.3, 68.6, 68.7, 69.5, 69.6, 70.4, 71.6–8, 72.4, 72.5, 72.7, 72.9, 73.13, 74.4, 74.5, 75.4, 75.5, 76.2–5, 77.15, 78.6, 78.8, 78.10, 79.5–7, 80.7, 80.10, 80.12, 81.5, 81.6, 82.3–5, 83.6, 84.6, 85.5, 85.6, 85.8, 86.6, 87.5, 88.3, 88.5, 89.3, 89.4, 89.6, 89.7, 90.3, 90.6, 91.6, 91.7, 92.4, 92.5, 93.4, 93.5, 94.4, 94.6, 95.3, 95.4, 96.2, 97.3, 98.3, 98.5, 99.3, 100.2, 100.4, 101.2, 102.4, 103.2, 104.1–3, 104.5 **Reading Presentation Book C:** (Lesson.Exercise) 105.3, 105.4, 106.2–4, 108.2, 108.3, 109.2, 109.4, 110.3, 111.2, 111.4, 112.4, 113.1, 113.2, 113.4, 114.2, 114.4, 115.2–4, 116.1, 116.2, 117.1–4, 118.2, 119.1, 1191.2, 119.4, 120.2, 120.4, 121.3, 122.1, 122.3, 122.5, 123.2, 123.4, 123.5, 124.1, 24.2, 124.4, 125.3, 125.4, 126.2, 126.3, 127.2, 127.4, 127.5, 128.2, 128.4, 129.2, 130.1, 130.2, 130.4, 131.3, 132.3, 133.4, 134.1, 134.2, 134.4, 135.2, 136.2, 136.3, 138.2, 138.4, 139.3, 140.3, 140.4, 141.2, 141.3, 142.4, 143.2, 143.3, 144.2–4, 145.2, 145.4, 147/2. 148.3, 149.1–3, 150.4, 151.2–4, 152.1, 152.4, 153.2–4, 154.2, 155.2, 155.3, 156.4, 157.2, 158.2, 158.4, 159.2, 160.2, 160.4 **Spelling Teacher Presentation Book:** Lessons 126.2, 127.1, 137.2, 138.2, 139.2, 147.2, 148.2, 149.2
L.1.5	With guidance and support from adults, demonstrate understanding of figurative language, word relationships and nuances in word meanings.	
L.1.5a	Sort words into categories (e.g., colors, clothing) to gain a sense of the concepts the categories represent.	**Language Presentation Book A:** (Lesson.Exercise) 1.1, 1.3, 1.4, 1.8, 2.1, 2.4, 2.10, 3.1, 3.4, 3.10, 4.1, 4.4, 5.2, 5.10, 6.1, 6.5, 7.9, 8.5, 8.9, 9.2, 10.2, 11.2, 11.9, 12.2, 13.2, 13.10, 14.8, 21.6, 22.3, 23.5, 24.3, 25.5, 26.5, 28.5, 28.10, 29.3, 29.10, 30.5, 31.1, 31.5, 32.1, 32.3, 32.5, 33.1, 33.4, 34.1, 34.2, 35.4, 36.1, 36.4, 38.1, 38.4, 39.1, 40.1, 41.4, 41.9, 42.3, 43.6, 43.9, 44.2, 45.5, 45.10, 46.3, 47.3, 48.7, 48.12, 49.2, 50.2, 52.2, 52.9, 53.5, 55.2, 57.8, 60.2 **Language Presentation Book B:** (Lesson.Exercise) 61.7, 63.7, 64.1, 65.4, 70.7, 71.5, 72.8, 73.5, 74.8, 75.2, 75.8, 76.9, 79.7, 80.8, 81.9, 92.7, 83.9, 84.7, 85.9, 86.10, 88.2, 88.7, 89.1, 89.10, 90.8, 93.9, 95.7, 97.7, 101.9, 102.7, 103.3, 103.8, 104.5, 104.8, 105.3, 107.1, 107.8, 108.8, 110.7, 111.7, 112.8, 116.7, 117.7, 119.8, 122.7, 124.6, 125.7, 129.8 **Language Workbook:** (Lesson.Exercise) 1, 2, 3, 5, 7, 8, 11, 13, 14, 28, 29, 38, 41, 43, 45, 48, 52, 57, 61, 63, 70, 72, 74, 75, 76, 80, 81, 82, 83, 84, 85, 86, 88, 89, 90, 93, 95, 97, 101, 1012, 103, 104, 107, 108, 110, 111, 112, 116, 117, 119, 122, 124, 125, 129 **Read Aloud Library:** (Week.Day) 16.5, 17.5, 18.5, 19.5, 20.5

GRADE 1 STANDARDS		PAGE REFERENCES
L.1.5b	Define words by category and by one or more key attributes (e.g., a *duck* is a bird that swims; a *tiger* is a large cat with stripes).	**Language Presentation Book A:** (Lesson.Exercise) 1.1, 1.3, 1.4, 1.8, 2.1, 2.4, 2.10, 3.1, 3.4, 3.10, 4.1, 4.4, 5.2, 5.10, 6.1, 6.5, 7.9, 8.5, 8.9, 9.2, 10.2, 11.2, 11.9, 12.2, 13.2, 13.10, 14.8, 21.6, 22.3, 23.5, 24.3, 25.5, 26.5, 28.5, 28.10, 29.3, 29.10, 30.5, 31.1, 31.5, 32.1, 32.3, 32.5, 33.1, 33.4, 34.1, 34.2, 35.4, 36.1, 36.4, 38.1, 38.4, 39.1, 40.1, 41.4, 41.9, 42.3, 43.6, 43.9, 44.2, 45.5, 45.10, 46.3, 47.3, 48.7, 48.12, 49.2, 50.2, 52.2, 52.9, 53.5, 55.2, 57.8, 60.2 **Language Presentation Book B:** (Lesson.Exercise) 61.7, 63.7, 64.1, 65.4, 70.7, 71.5, 72.8, 73.5, 74.8, 75.2, 75.8, 76.9, 79.7, 80.8, 81.9, 92.7, 83.9, 84.7, 85.9, 86.10, 88.2, 88.7, 89.1, 89.10, 90.8, 93.9, 95.7, 97.7, 101.9, 102.7, 103.3, 103.8, 104.5, 104.8, 105.3, 107.1, 107.8, 108.8, 110.7, 111.7, 112.8, 116.7, 117.7, 119.8, 122.7, 124.6, 125.7, 129.8 **Language Workbook:** (Lesson.Exercise) 1, 2, 3, 5, 7, 8, 11, 13, 14, 28, 29, 38, 41, 43, 45, 48, 52, 57, 61, 63, 70, 72, 74, 75, 76, 80, 81, 82, 83, 84, 85, 86, 88, 89, 90, 93, 95, 97, 101, 1012, 103, 104, 107, 108, 110, 111, 112, 116, 117, 119, 122, 124, 125, 129 **Read Aloud Library:** (Week.Day) 16.5, 17.5, 18.5, 19.5, 20.5
L.1.5c	Identify real-life connections between words and their use (e.g., note places at home that are *cozy*).	**Language Presentation Book A:** (Lesson.Exercise) 1.1, 1.3, 1.4, 1.8, 2.1, 2.4, 2.10, 3.1, 3.4, 3.10, 4.1, 4.4, 5.2, 5.10, 6.1, 6.5, 7.9, 8.5, 8.9, 9.2, 10.2, 11.2, 11.9, 12.2, 13.2, 13.10, 14.8, 21.6, 22.3, 23.5, 24.3, 25.5, 26.5, 28.5, 28.10, 29.3, 29.10, 30.5, 31.1, 31.5, 32.1, 32.3, 32.5, 33.1, 33.4, 34.1, 34.2, 35.4, 36.1, 36.4, 38.1, 38.4, 39.1, 40.1, 41.4, 41.9, 42.3, 43.6, 43.9, 44.2, 45.5, 45.10, 46.3, 47.3, 48.7, 48.12, 49.2, 50.2, 52.2, 52.9, 53.5, 55.2, 57.8, 60.2 **Language Presentation Book B:** (Lesson.Exercise) 61.7, 63.7, 64.1, 65.4, 70.7, 71.5, 72.8, 73.5, 74.8, 75.2, 75.8, 76.9, 79.7, 80.8, 81.9, 92.7, 83.9, 84.7, 85.9, 86.10, 88.2, 88.7, 89.1, 89.10, 90.8, 93.9, 95.7, 97.7, 101.9, 102.7, 103.3, 103.8, 104.5, 104.8, 105.3, 107.1, 107.8, 108.8, 110.7, 111.7, 112.8, 116.7, 117.7, 119.8, 122.7, 124.6, 125.7, 129.8 **Language Workbook:** (Lesson.Exercise) 1, 2, 3, 5, 7, 8, 11, 13, 14, 28, 29, 38, 41, 43, 45, 48, 52, 57, 61, 63, 70, 72, 74, 75, 76, 80, 81, 82, 83, 84, 85, 86, 88, 89, 90, 93, 95, 97, 101, 1012, 103, 104, 107, 108, 110, 111, 112, 116, 117, 119, 122, 124, 125, 129 **Read Aloud Library:** (Week.Day) 16.5, 17.5, 18.5, 19.5, 20.5
L.1.5d	Distinguish shades of meaning among verbs differing in manner (e.g., *look, peek, glance, stare, glare, scowl*) and adjectives differing in intensity (e.g., large, gigantic) by defining or choosing them or by acting out the meanings.	**Core Lesson Connections:** (Lesson.Part.Activity) 5.B.2, 10.B.2, 15.B.2, 20.B.2, 25.B.2, 30.B.2, 35.B.2, 40.B.2, 45.B.2, 50.B.2, 55.B.2, 60.B.2, 65.B.2, 70.B.2, 75.B.2, 80.B.2, 85.A.2, 90.A.2, 95.A.3, 100.A.3, 105.A.3, 110.A.3, 115.A.3, 120.A.3, 125.A.3, 130.A.3, 135.A.3, 140.A.3, 145.A.3, 150.A.3, 155.A.3, 160.A.3

GRADE 1 STANDARDS		PAGE REFERENCES
L.1.6	Use words and phrases acquired through conversations, reading and being read to, and responding to texts, including using frequently occurring conjunctions to signal simple relationships (e.g., *because*).	**Reading Presentation Book A:** (Lesson.Exercise) 1.2–9, 2.–11, 3.2–5, 4.2–5, 5.2–10, 6.2–9, 7.2–9, 8.2–4, 9.2–4, 10.2–10, 11.2–13, 12.2–11, 13.2–4, 14.2–9, 15.2–9, 16.2–8, 17.2–9, 18.2–4, 19.2–7, 20.2–8, 21.2–9, 22.2–8, 23.2–10, 24.2–6, 25.2–13, 26.2–9, 27.2–13, 28.2–9, 29.2–11, 30.2–13, 31.2–11, 32.6, 33.2–11, 34.2–18, 35.3–19, 36.3–17, 37.2–17, 38.2–14, 39.2–15, 40.2–10, 41.3–14, 42.3–9, 43.2–9, 44.3–12, 45.3–14, 46.3–14, 47.6, 48.3–14 **Reading Presentation Book B:** (Lesson.Exercise) 49.3–13, 50.2–15, 51.2–14, 52.3–14, 53.1–10, 54.2–11, 55.1–11, 56.1–17, 57.3–13, 58.1–10, 59.1–12, 60.1–15, 61.1–15, 62.2–14, 63.2–15, 64.2–14, 65.2–16, 66.2–17, 67.1–12, 68.1–9, 69.1–12, 70.1–8, 71.1–8, 72.1–9, 73..1–7, 74.1–10, 75.1–7, 76.1–6, 77.1–9, 78.1–11, 79.1–10, 80.1–12, 81.1–7, 82.1–7, 83.3–8, 84.3–7, 85.5–8, 86.3–6, 87.2–5, 88.2–5, 89.3–7, 90.2–6, 91.3–7, 92.2–6, 93.2–5, 94.2–6, 95.1–4, 96.1–4, 97.1–4, 98.1–5, 99.1–4, 100.1–4, 101.1–4, 102.1–4, 103.1–4, 104.1–5 **Reading Presentation Book C:** (Lesson.Exercise) 105.1–4, 106.1–4, 107.1–4, 08.1–4, 109.1–4, 110.1–4, 111.1–4, 112.1–4, 113.1–14, 114.1–14, 115.1–4, 116.1–4, 117.1–4, 118.1–4, 119.1–4, 120.1–4, 121.1–5, 122.1–5, 123.1–5, 124.1–5, 125.1–4, 126.1–5, 127.1–5, 128.1–5, 129.1–5, 130.1–4, 131.1–4, 132.1–5, 133.1–4, 134.1–4, 135.1–3, 136.1–4, 137.1–4, 138.1–4, 139.1–4, 140.1–4, 141.1–4, 142.1–4, 143.1–4, 144.1–14, 145.1–4, 146.1–4, 147.1–3, 148.1–3, 149.1–3, 150.1–4, 151.1–4, 152.1–4, 153.1–4, 154.1–4, 155.1–4, 156.1–4, 157.1–4, 159.1–4, 160.1–4 **Language Presentation Book A:** (Lesson.Exercise) 1.1, 1.4, 1.8, 2.1, 2.4, 2.5, 2.10, 3.1, 3.4, 3.5, 3.10, 4.1, 4.4, 4.5, 5.2, 5.5, 5.10, 6.1, 6.5, 6.6, 7.5, 7.9, 8.5, 8.9, , 9.2, 9.4, 10.2, 10.3, 11.2, 11.4, 11.9, 12.2, 12.4, 13.2, 13.3, 13.10, 14.8, 16.4, 16.5, 17.4, 17.5, 17.7, 18.2, 18.3, 19.2, 19.3, 20.2, 20.4, 21.4, 21.5, 22.3, 22.6, 22.7, 23.3, 23.5, 24.1, 24.3, 24.4, 25.1, 25.4, 25.5, 26.4–6, 27.5, 27.6, 28.4, 28.5, 28.10, 29.3, 29.4, 29.10, 30.2, 30.3, 30.5, 30.6, 30.8, 31.1, 31.2, 31.5, 31.8, 32.1, 32.2, 32.5, 32.6, 33.1, 33.3, 33.4, 34.1, 34.2, 35.4, 35.5, 35.8, 36.1, 36.4, 36.5, 36.10, 37.5, 38.1, 38.6, 38.11, 39.1, 3 9.3, 39.8, 40.1, 40.4, 40.7, 41.1, 41.4, 41.9, 42.2, 42.3, 43.2, 43.6, 43.9, 44.2, 45.5, 45.10, 46.3, 46.6, 47.3, 47.4, 47.13, 48.7, 48.8, 48.12, 48.13, 49.2, 49.4, 49.6, 49.11, 50.2, 50.4–6, 50.1, 50.11, 51.2–4, 52.2, 52.3, 52.9, 52.10, 53.3, 53.5, 54.2, 54.8, 55.2–4, 56.2, 56.5, 57.1, 57.3, 57.6, 57.8, 57.9, 58.2, 58.3, 58.4, 59.5, 59.7, 60.1–4 **Language Presentation Book B:** (Lesson.Exercise) 61.1, 61.4, 61.7, 61.8, 62.2, 62.4, 62.9, 63.3, 63.4, 63.7, 64.1–4, 65.1, 65.3, 65.4, 65.6, 65.9, 66.1–3, 67.1, 67.2, 68.1, 68.3, 68.5, 68.8, 68.9, 69.4–6, 70.1, 70.3, 70.7, 70.8, 71.1, 71.3–5, 71.8, 72.1, 72.2, 72.4, 72.8, 72.9, 73.1, 73.2, 73.5, 74.1, 74.8, 74.9, 75.1, 75.2, 75.5, 75.8, 76.4–6, 76.9, 76.10, 77.1, 77.2, 77.4, 77.6, 77.7, 78.3, 78.4, 78.7, 79.1, 79.3–5, 79.7, 80.1, 80.2, 80.4, 80.5, 80.8, 80.9, 81.1, 81.2, 81.6, 81.7, 18.9, 81.10, 82.1, 82.4, 82.5, 8.7, 83.1, 83.5, 83.9, 83.10, 84.3, 84.4, 84.7, 85.1, 85.2, 85.9, 86.1, 86.4, 86.5, 86.7, 86.10, 86.11, 87.1, 87.2, 87.5, 88.1, 88.2, 88.4, 88.7, 89.1–3, 89.6, 89.9, 89.10, 90.1, 90.2, 90.4, 90.8, 91.1–4, 92.4, 92.5, 93.1, 93.3–5, 93.8, 94.1, 94.2, 94.4, 95.1, 95.2, 95.5, 95.7, 95.8, 96.1–3, 96.6, 97.1, 97.3–5, 97.7, 98.1, 98.3, 98.4, 98.6, 98.9, 99.1, 99.2, 99.4, 100.1–4, 101.1, 101.2, 101.4, 101.5, 101.9, 102.1–4, 103.1–5, 103.7, 103.8, 104.2, 104.3, 104.5, 104.8, 105.1, 105.3–5, 106.1–6, 104.7, 106.8, 107.1–3, 107.5, 107.7, 107.8, 108.1–3, 108.5, 108.8, 109.1, 109.2, 109.5, 110.1, 110.4, 110.5, 110.7, 111.1, 111.2, 111.4, 111.7, 111.8, 112.1, 112.3, 112.5, 112.7, 112.8, 113.1, 113.3, 113.5, 113.7, 113.8, 114.1–3, 115.1, 115.3, 115.4, 116.2–5, 116.7, 116.8, 117.2–4, 117.7, 118.3, 118.4, 119.1, 119.3–5, 119.8, 119.9, 120.4, 120.5, 121.3, 121.6, 121.7, 122.1, 122.4, 122.7, 123.2, 123.3, 123.5, 124.3, 124.6, 124.7, 125.2, 125.3, 125.6, 125.7, 126.3, 126.4, 126.6, 127.2, 128.2, 128.7, 129.3, 129.4, 129.7, 129.8, 130.1, 130.4, 130.5

GRADE 1 STANDARDS	PAGE REFERENCES
	Language Workbook: (Lesson.Exercise) 1, 2, 3, 5, 7, 8, 11, 12, 14, 28, 29, 30, 31, 35, 36, 38, 39, 40, 41, 43, 45, 47, 48, 49, 50, 52, 54, 57, 61, 62, 63, 65, 68, 70, 71, 72, 74, 75, 76, 77, 79, 80, 81, 82, 83, 84, 85, 86, 88, 89, 90, 92, 95, 97, 99, 101, 103, 104, 106, 107, 108, 110, 111, 112, 113, 116, 117, 119, 121, 122, 124, 125, 126, 128, 129
	Core Lesson Connections: (Lesson.Part.Activity) 1.B.1, 2.B.1, 2.B.2, 3.B.1, 3.B.2, 4.B.1, 4.B.2, 5.B.1, 6.B.1, 6.B.2, 7.B.1, 7.B.2, 8.B.1, 8.B.2, 9.B.1, 9.B.2, 10.B.1, 11.B.1, 11.B.2, 12.B.1, 12.B.2, 13.B.1, 13.B.2, 14.B.1, 14.B.2, 15.B.1, 16.B.1, 16.B.2, 17.B.1, 17.B.2, 18.B.1, 18.B.2, 19.B.1, 19.B.2, 20.B.1, 21.B.1, 21.B.2, 22.B.1, 22.B.2, 23.B.1, 23.B.2, 24.B.1, 24.B.2, 25.B.1, 26.B.1, 26.B.2, 27.B.1, 27.B.2, 28.B.1, 28.B.2, 29.B.1, 29.B.2, 30.B.1, 31.B.1, 31.B.2, 32.B.1, 32.B.2, 33.B.1, 33.B.2, 34.B.1, 34.B.2, 35.B.1, 36.B.1, 36.B.2, 37.B.1, 37.B.2, 38.B.1, 38.B.2, 39.B.1, 39.B.2, 40.B.1, 41.B.1, 41.B.2, 42.B.1, 42.B.2, 43.B.1, 43.B.2, 44.B.1, 44.B.2, 45.B.1, 46.B.1, 46.B.2, 47.B.1, 47.B.2, 48.B.1, 48.B.2, 49.B.1, 49.B.2, 50.B.1, 51.B.1, 51.B.2, 52.B.1, 52.B.2, 53.B.1, 53.B.1, 54.B.1, 54.B.2, 55.B.1, 56.B.1, 56.B.2, 57.B.1, 57.B.2, 58.B.1, 58.B.2, 59.B.1, 59.B.2, 60.B.1, 61.B.1, 61.B.2, 62.B.1, 62.B.2, 63.B.1, 63.B.2, 64.B.1, 64.B.2, 65.B.1, 66.B.1, 66.B.2, 67.B.1, 67.B.2, 68.B.1, 68.B.2, 69.B.1, 69.B.1, 70.B.1, 71.B.1, 71.B.2, 72.B.1, 72.B.2, 73.B.1, 73.B.2, 74.B.1, 74.B.2, 75.B.1, 76.B.1, 76.B.2, 77.B.1, 77.B.2, 78.B.1, 78.B.1, 79.B.1, 79.B.2, 80.B.1, 81.A.1, 81.A.2, 82.A.1, 82.A.2, 83.A.1, 83.A.2, 84.A.1, 84.A.2, 85.B.1, 86.A.1, 86.A.2, 87.A.1, 87.A.2, 88.A.1, 88.A.2, 89.A.1, 89.A.2, 90.A.1, 91.A.1, 91.A.2, 92.A.1, 92.A.2, 93.A.1, 93.A.2, 94.A.1, 94.A.2, 95.A.1, 96.A.1, 96.A.2, 97.A.1, 97.A.2, 98.A.1, 98.A.2, 99.A.1, 99.A.2, 100.A.1, 101.A.1, 101.A.2, 102.A.1, 102.A,2, 103.A.1, 103.A.2, 104.A.1, 104.A.2, 105.A.1, 106.A.1, 106.A.2, 107.A.1, 107.A.2, 108.A,1, 109.A,1, 109.A.2, 110.A.1, 111.A.1, 111.A.2, 112.A.1, 112.A.2, 113.A.1, 113.A.2, 114.A.1, 114.A.2, 115.A.1, 116.A.1, 116.A.2, 117.A.1, 117.A.2, 118.A.1, 118.A.2, 119.A.1, 119.A.2, 120.A.1, 121.A.1, 121.A.2, 122.A.1, 122.A.2, 123.A,1, 123.A.2, 124.A.1, 124.A.2, 125.A.1, 126.A.1, 126.A.2, 127.A.1, 127.A.2, 128.A.1, 128.A.2, 129.A.1, 129.A.2, 130.A.1, 131.A.1, 131.A.2, 132.A.1, 132.A.2, 133.A.1, 133.A.2, 134.A.1, 134.A.2, 135.A.1, 136.A.1, 136.A.2, 137.A.1, 137.A.2, 138.A.1, 138.A.2, 139.A.1, 139.A.2, 140.A.1, 141.A.1, 141.A.2, 142.A.1, 143.A.1, 143.A.2, 144.A.1, 144.A.2, 145.A.1, 146.A.1, 146.A.2, 147.A.1, 147.A.2, 148.A.1, 148.A.2, 149.A.1, 149.A.2, 150.A.1, 151.A.1, 151.A.2, 152.A.1, 152.A.2, 153.A.1, 153.A.2, 154.A.1, 154.A.2, 155.A.1, 156.A.1, 156.A.2, 157.A.1, 157.AB.2, 158.A.1, 158.A.2, 159.A.1, 159.A.2, 160.A.1 **Student Practice CD** **Literature Collection/Guide:** Lessons 5, 15, 20, 25, 30, 35, 40, 45, 50 **Read Aloud Library:** (Week.Day) 1.1–5, 2.1–5, 3.1–5, 4.1–5, 5.1–5, 6.1–5, 7.1–5, 8.1–5, 9.1–5, 10.1–5, 11.1–5, 12.1–5, 13.1–5, 14.1–5, 15.1–5, 16.1–5, 17.1–5, 18.1–5, 19.1–5, 20.1–5, 21.1–5, 22.1–5, 23.1–5, 24.1–5, 25.1–5, 26.1–5, 27.1–5, 28.1–5, 29.1–5, 30.1–5

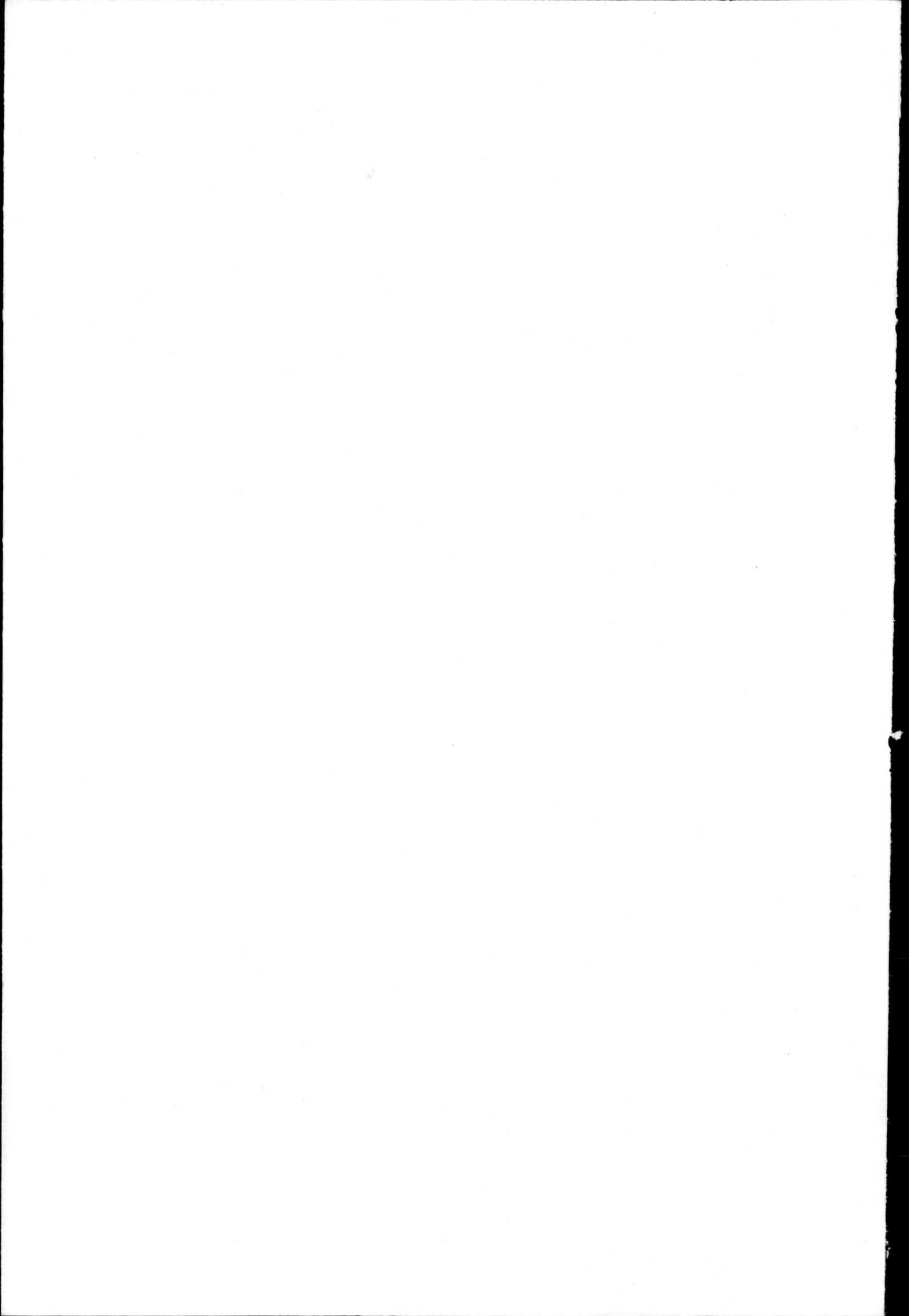